ART IN IRELAND SINCE 1910

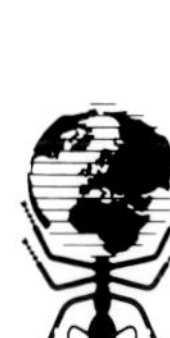

Art in Ireland
since 1910

FIONNA BARBER

REAKTION BOOKS

Art in Ireland: Political Chronology, 1900–2010

1912   April: Third Home Rule Bill approved by the British Parliament. Home Rule planned for 1914.

1913   January: Formation of the Ulster Volunteer Force opposed to Home Rule.

1916   24 April: The Easter Rising begins: the Irish Republican Brotherhood and other organizations launch an attack on British rule in Ireland. Patrick Pearse issues the Proclamation of the Irish Republic on the steps of the General Post Office, Dublin. Five days later, the republicans surrender and most of the leaders are subsequently executed.

1919   21 January: Irish War of Independence begins.

1920   December: Government of Ireland Act allows for Partition of Ireland. Partition is supported by a majority of Unionists in the six counties that would become Northern Ireland, and opposed by nationalists who remain in the minority.

1921   6 December: End of the War of Independence with the signing of the Anglo-Irish Treaty and formation of the Irish Free State.

1922   June: Irish Civil War begins.
        22 August: Death of Michael Collins in an ambush at Béal na mBláth.

1923   Civil War ends.

1937   29 December: Constitution of Ireland. The Irish Free State now becomes Eire.

1948   December: Ireland leaves the Commonwealth and becomes a fully independent nation with the signing of the Republic of Ireland Act.

1955   14 December: Ireland joins the United Nations.

1967   January: Northern Ireland Civil Rights Association (NICRA) is formed.

1968   Civil Rights protest marches in Northern Ireland.

1969   August: British troops deployed on the streets of Northern Ireland.

1971	*August 9:* Introduction of internment in Northern Ireland. The majority of internees are derived from the nationalist community and held in Long Kesh prison, subsequently renamed The Maze.
1972	*30 January:* British soldiers open fire on a peaceful march organized by NICRA in Derry to protest against internment. Fourteen people are killed in what becomes known as 'Bloody Sunday'. The subsequent upsurge in violence leads to the suspension of Northern Ireland's parliament and the introduction of Direct Rule from Westminster.
1973	*1 January:* The Republic of Ireland joins the European Community.
1974	IRA military campaign extends to bombings in mainland Britain, including Birmingham and Woolwich.
1981	The failure of both 'blanket protest' and 'no wash protest' by republicans in The Maze prison leads to the beginnings of the hunger strikes, led by Bobby Sands. In addition to Sands, a further nine republican prisoners die as a result.
1985	*15 November:* Britain and Ireland sign the Anglo-Irish Agreement, although it is never fully implemented.
1988	*October:* The British government introduces the Broadcasting Ban, mainly directed towards republican organizations.
1990	*3 December:* Mary Robinson becomes the first female president of Ireland.
1993	*15 December:* The Downing Street Declaration is a significant move towards powersharing between Unionists and nationalists in Northern Ireland.
1994	*August:* IRA ceasefire, followed one month later by loyalist paramilitaries also laying down weapons.
1995	Ireland's 'Celtic Tiger' period begins: a massive upsurge in economic prosperity.
1998	*April:* Belfast / Good Friday Agreement is signed, agreeing powersharing between the main political parties in Northern Ireland.
2006	*October:* The demolition of The Maze prison begins, six years after its closure.
2007	The financial downturn signals the end of Irish economic prosperity.

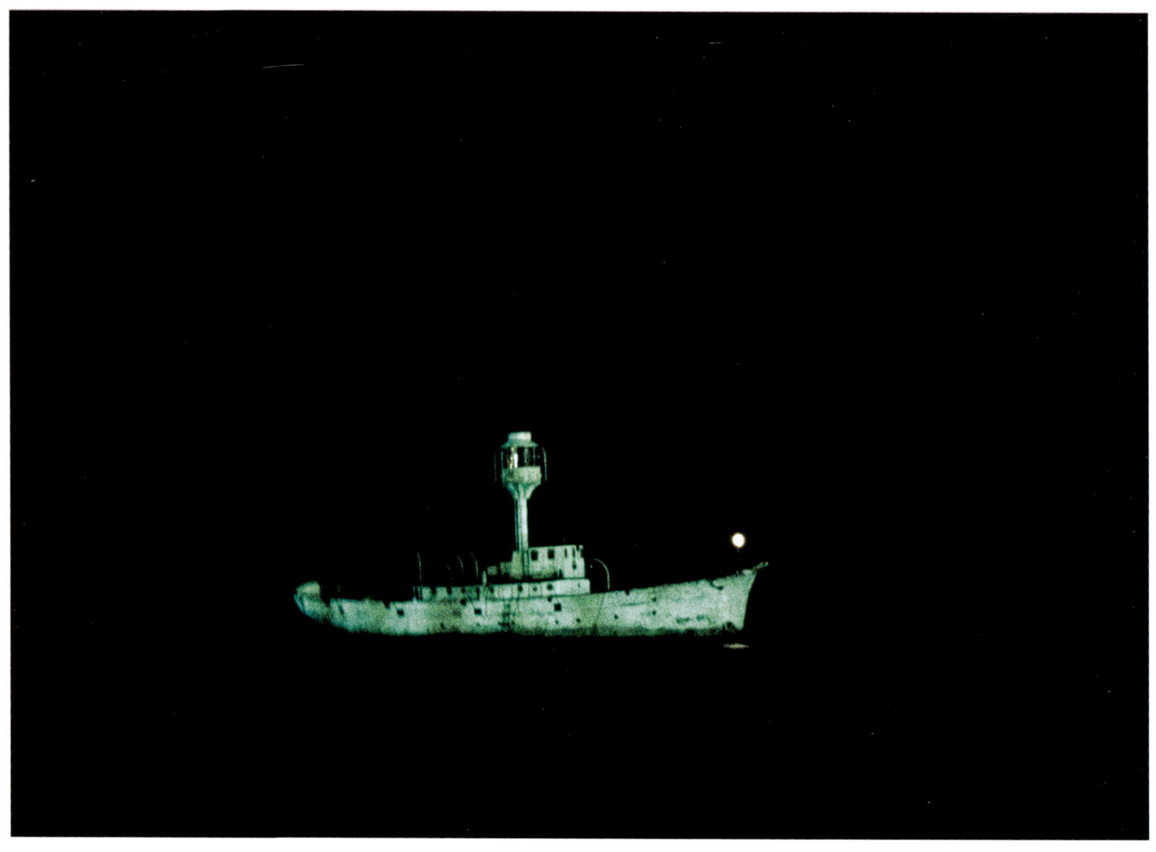

1 Dorothy Cross, *Ghost Ship* (Nissan Art Project), 1999, photograph.

INTRODUCTION
THE *GHOST SHIP*, NATION AND MODERNITY

Over a period of three weeks in February 1999, the coastal waters off Dún Laoghaire, just south of Dublin, were haunted by a mysterious nocturnal vision that glowed and faded repeatedly over a period of several hours. This was the *Ghost Ship*, a project by the artist Dorothy Cross that won the Nissan Art Prize that year, awarded jointly with the Irish Museum of Modern Art (IMMA). Possibly the artist's best-known work, the origins of the *Ghost Ship* lay in the memories of her childhood in County Cork, when her father used to take her out in the family's boat to visit the men on a lightship moored off the coast above a perilous reef. Later, she discovered that the decommissioned vessel that would be the basis for her project was in fact the same one that they used to visit, tethered securely to the Daunt Rock beneath. The old ship – named *Albatross* – was rescued from its dry dock, coated in phosphorescent paint and towed out to Scotsman's Bay where, every night for three weeks, it lit up the waters in an uncanny semblance of its former role.

Yet the fascination of the *Ghost Ship* goes far beyond its striking presence on the video footage that Cross recorded every night, or indeed the work's role in restaging her own nostalgia. The *Ghost Ship* appeared not just on the eve of the millennium, but at the close of a century during which Ireland became an independent, modern nation. This involved numerous changes unprecedented in Ireland's history, including a shift away from ideas of the land and the sea as dominating a sense of Irish identity and towards an increasing concern with the urban and the modern. As Dorothy Cross observed in relation to the project, 'The role of the sea has now diminished for Irish people and the view is inward towards the cities.'[1] Yet the dilapidated, peeling exterior of the old vessel, emphasized by its luminescence, suggests a distance from modernity's emphasis on technological achievement, implying that this too has become part of the past.

This book examines the ability of art, like the *Ghost Ship*, to absorb and engage with wider social forces and processes of cultural change in Ireland, from the early years of the twentieth century to the aftermath of the millennium. It is the first book to cover this period in its entirety. As might be expected, the nature of Irish art practice changed considerably over this period, and in forms that engaged with the often contradictory forces at work in the emergent nation. During the struggles for Irish independence in the early part of the century and its aftermath in the formation of the Irish Free State, a major preoccupation in the work of many artists like Paul Henry or Charles Lamb was the visualization of a distinctive Irish nation through the predominance of images of rugged landscape and sea, mainly focused around the western coastline. Yet even at this point there were divergent efforts towards identifying the types of visual language best suited to articulating the changing conditions of Irish modernity such as Mainie Jellett's brave attempts to introduce a form of abstraction that owed much to a sense of European modernism extending beyond Ireland's isolationist nationalism in the 1920s and 1930s. By the end of the twentieth century, however, an increasing diversification of art practice in Ireland – as elsewhere – emerged and developed within a context of a range of very different social and political forces. These included not just the conflict in the North and its eventual resolution, but the increasing recognition of both the role of women and the significance of large-scale emigration as two of the factors that contributed to the unravelling of entrenched concepts of Irish identity. Both art practice and the sense of Ireland as a nation were to a large extent unrecognizable in terms that would have been current a hundred years previously.

The writing of Irish art history

All historians, including art historians, select and give order to their material according to a set of priorities. My interest here in the forces of nation and modernity as the definitive factors shaping Irish art in the period covered by this book to some extent echoes and builds on the preoccupations of previous writers, but with some fundamental differences.

Published in 1991, S. B. Kennedy's *Irish Art and Modernism, 1880–1950* introduced a much needed rigour and systematic approach to the study of Irish art between 1910 and 1950. Its scholarship, however, is ultimately reliant on definitions of quality based on formalist principles rather than the attempt to situate art practice in relation to the changing nature of the society within which it has been produced.[2] Kennedy, who was then curator of twentieth-century art at the Ulster Museum in Belfast, acknowledged the contradictions of modernism and national identity in Ireland. But it is clear that, for him, modernism was the more progressive term. As 'the art of a rapidly changing world which saw many of the social characteristics of the preceeding [sic] age disappear', for Kennedy it remained 'surprising' that modernism was not more readily adopted in post-revolutionary Ireland.[3] The aesthetic and emancipatory possibilities of modernism were formulated elsewhere in the metropolitan centres of mainland Europe and filtered outward to peripheral regions such as Ireland: the work of Irish artists is thus evaluated in terms of the extent to which they responded to these innovatory practices.

A very different account is provided by Dorothy Walker's *Modern Art in Ireland* (1997), and not just because its focus is later, on the period between the Second World War to the 1990s. *Modern Art in Ireland* did to some degree acknowledge the relationship of art to the wider forces of modernization in Irish culture, although in comparison with Kennedy, Walker made little attempt at an academic impartiality. Both a collector and an independent curator until her death in 2002, her writing bore the traces of her friendships and alliances with many of the artists she discussed. Yet Walker's account of art in Ireland was continually underpinned by a meta-narrative of essential Irish experience, allowing her to read, for example, Seán Scully's abstract grid paintings of the 1970s as 'direct descendants of Celtic interlacing, layered linearity in a dynamic large-scale version of Early Christian graphic art'.[4] Although her aim was to create a distinctive position for Irish art, one problem is that Irish artists are instead pathologized, bound only to express a repetitive set of formal strategies within their work.[5] Walker's reading of twentieth-century art practice in terms of its intuitive homologies with the distant past was also a model of identity drawing on powerful emotional resonances of nationhood that were themselves subject to question by the time of the book's publication.

By comparison, what I am suggesting here is the need for a more dynamic sense of how the forces of nation and modernity have shaped art in twentieth-century Ireland. In a similar vein, James Elkins also criticized the weakness of Irish art history in comparison with the flourishing international awareness in Irish art criticism. In his essay 'The State of Irish Art History' (2003), Elkins was critical of a tendency in common with other 'smaller first-world countries' to 'practice a kind of art history that is in general . . . methodologically, chronologically, and geographically unadventurous'.[6] Yet, as he also observed, art history's neglect as a subject within Irish higher education also contributed to a lack of recognition of the value of critical approaches.

The situation began to change in the years after Elkins was writing, with increased opportunities for study and an expanding debate around the relationship of Irish art history with art criticism and visual culture, or indeed Irish Studies, another important frame of reference.[7] Irish Studies initially developed as an academic subject in support of a perceived tradition of Irish writing. In the late 1980s more critical tendencies began to emerge, focused around the publication of David Cairns and Shaun Richards's *Writing Ireland: Colonialism, Nationalism and Culture*.[8] The recognition in *Writing Ireland* of Irish culture as situated within a framework of struggles around colonialism developed in the context of the more radical tendencies within British academicism, yet Cairns and Richards's book also echoed some of the concerns of the ongoing project of Field Day, taking shape in the very different

circumstances of political strife in Northern Ireland.[9] Founded in 1980 as a theatre company in Derry by the actor Stephen Rae and playwright Brian Friel, Field Day also initiated a publishing project that increasingly began to situate Irish culture in relation to a wider awareness of postcolonialism. The radicalization of Irish Studies began to extend to the analysis of visual culture in, for example, critical essays by Luke Gibbons incorporating the deconstruction of a variety of visual forms including painting, film and photography within a more inclusive cultural analysis.[10] This was reinforced by the emergence of a critically informed engagement with contemporary art practice in the journal *Circa*. However, the inherent conservatism of Irish art history at the time meant that the discipline itself remained largely impervious to these moves to open up the frame of debate.

In these circumstances it is perhaps unsurprising that a more critical take on Irish art history might begin to emerge within academic frameworks elsewhere. In Britain the emergence of the 'New Art History' in the 1980s had attempted to politicize the subject through the incorporation of Marxist and feminist methodologies that sought to challenge the existing focus on connoisseurship and iconographical attribution, subsequently augmented by a focus on issues of race and postcolonialism.[11] This was an important context for the development of Fintan Cullen's reading of Irish art history, initially published in 1997 as *Visual Politics: The Representation of Ireland, 1750 to 1930*, although he also explicitly acknowledged the post-Field Day radicalization of Irish studies.[12] Cullen's *Visual Politics* represented a paradigmatic shift from earlier canonical accounts of Irish art, such as Anne Crookshank and the Knight of Glin's *The Painters of Ireland, c. 1660–1920*.[13] It also helped to lay the groundwork for other critically positioned accounts of the history of Irish art, such as this one.

Nation and modernity

The concept of nation is one of the most powerful means of identity formation in modern Western culture. As Benedict Anderson suggests, it represents an 'imagined political community', sustained through a deep sense of belonging that goes beyond rationality to draw on a sense of deep emotional and intuitive connection. Nation involves both spatial and temporal dimensions as a basis for a sense of community: spatial in its reference to a territory where members of a community feel that they belong, and temporal in that this sense of belonging is ratified by past experience – this is a place where your ancestors lived.[14] This goes beyond history and into the realms of the mythical as a means of strengthening the bonds within the imagined community in the present. As Seamus Deane points out, it is a tendency of nationalism to provide an ideological impetus in claiming an 'Edenic moment', the sense of a utopian past where the political contradictions of the present are displaced in favour of mythological narratives of conflict and resolution.[15] In Ireland, this is a tendency associated with the late nineteenth- and early twentieth-century Cultural Revival's fascination with the deep past represented by the story-cycles surrounding such mythical figures as the hero Cuchulainn, which helped to provide a cultural counterpart to the role of political nationalism in the struggles around independence. Yet the re-imagining of the Celtic past also played an important role in later twentieth-century Irish art practice, helping to embody in visual form ideas and feelings about belonging and identity.

In Irish painting, as elsewhere, the representation of the land – particularly the western seaboard – becomes a place where the deep emotional pull of the nation has been staged in visual form.[16] The symbolic role played by the land is also reinforced by the nation's personification as female; the figure of Mother Ireland played an important role in signifying resistance in the face of colonial oppression.[17] One of the concerns of this book is to examine how shifting and evolving forms of art practice also register changes in the visual construction of the nation. This includes the points also where the nation is present in a work's meaning even when it appears not to be visible in its iconography; abstraction and modernism can be regarded as providing a more deeply embedded set of relationships between painted surface, the viewer's response and cultural experience than are at first apparent.

The meanings of nation, then, are far from static, but subject to change in relation to the wider network of social, cultural, economic and political forces brought into being within modernity itself.[18] Processes of modernity have also been experienced differently in areas that are not just geographically peripheral to centres of power, but are themselves subject to jurisdiction from the centre through colonial rule. In an Irish context the development of modernity was one that took place over roughly the same time period as in continental Europe, but on very different terms, beginning with the inception of British domination and the destruction of the old Gaelic civilization in the sixteenth and seventeenth centuries. The massive political, legal and social changes ushered in at this point created a set of conditions subsequently modified by the United Irishmen's radical appropriation of the principles of the European Enlightenment or the cataclysmic effects of the Famine in the late 1840s that decimated a rapidly expanding population under British rule. The ways that this history can be interpreted also inform how Irish art can be understood. One view is to suggest that the experience of modernity at the periphery is shaped by processes and decisions made elsewhere. In S. B. Kennedy's writing, for example, the work of artists has been evaluated according to the extent to which they have interpreted or rejected the utopian promises of continental modernism. Yet an alternative reading might suggest that these are moments giving rise to a distinctive experience of modernity fundamentally different from that lived out within centres of cultural and political power.[19] It is this sense of a clash of experience as a founding moment of an alienated identity that gives rise to a range of cultural forms, including art practice. The early emergence of distinctive artistic identities was also problematized and mediated by Ireland's colonial status. One example is the Cork-born painter James Barry, whose career as a painter in late eighteenth-century London was characterized by repeated challenges to the authority of both the Royal Academy, where he was Professor of Painting, and the British state itself.[20]

Like other eighteenth-century Irish artists, Barry had to leave his homeland to pursue a career as a painter; in colonial Ireland neither patronage nor prestige were forthcoming. The necessity of this move anticipated journeys made by numerous other Irish artists throughout the nineteenth and twentieth centuries. As a result of the Famine (1845–9), approximately one million people were driven by poverty and starvation to emigrate to either Britain or the New World; this enforced mobility has been a recurring feature of the experience of modernity at the peripheries. However, as Edward Said pointed out, the category of the artist who leaves their homeland voluntarily is different from migration due to war and other catastrophe.[21] For an émigré artist like Louis le Brocquy, a major figure in the development of Irish modernism, the move to London enabled him to participate in a relative cosmopolitanism unavailable within the conservative Dublin of the 1940s. His subsequent relocation to the South of France also facilitated an engagement with European modernism similar to

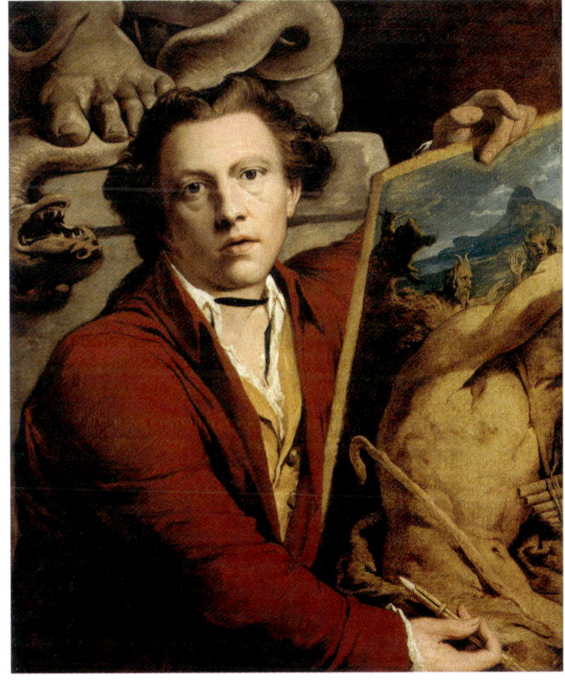

2 James Barry, *Self-portrait as Timanthes*, 1802, oil on canvas.

Samuel Beckett, even though, by the 1960s, modernism itself was well on the wane.

For le Brocquy, Joyce or Beckett the distance from Ireland prompted a kind of 'self-estrangement' that involved a re-engagement with Irishness refracted through the prism of modernism.[22] Something similar can also be seen at work in the paintings of another important artist, Mainie Jellett, although her gender was also an important factor. Contemporary notions of respectability, apart from anything else, meant that Jellett's encounters with the Parisian avant-garde took place on territory far removed from bohemia. At home also, as an Anglo-Irish woman her class and gender separated her from the political imperatives of post-independence Ireland, contributing to a degree of estrangement that also underpinned her development of a modernist visual language. Later in the century the particular features of Ireland's transition through post-modernity and the breakdown of the former certainties of nationalism also provided the conditions for the emergence of a generation of independent and articulate women artists. In the work of Alice Maher, Dorothy Cross or Alanna O'Kelly during the 1980s issues of female identity became particularly visible at a time when women's legal rights over their own bodies became a matter of national concern.

By the end of the twentieth century, however, old forms of nationalism in Ireland were becoming increasingly redundant in the face of forces of globalization and the rise (and subsequent demise) of the Celtic Tiger's economic prosperity, or the apparent resolution of the conflict in the North. Like the darkened Irish waters lit up by the phantasmic glow of the *Ghost Ship*, the certainties of the past became defamiliarized; art in post-nationalist Ireland, whether North or South, continues to cast an oblique view over past and present, making their fissures and contradictions more visible.

Art in twentieth-century Ireland and beyond

From the very start of the twentieth century, nationalist aspirations were for the whole of Ireland to be free of British rule. By 1900, the political impetus was being reinforced by an interest in the use of Irish culture – particularly literary forms – as an important site of the assertion of an independent Irish identity. Significantly, this process was not unique to Ireland at the time. An interest in indigenous folklore, language and music was common within the development of cultural nationalism found elsewhere at Europe's peripheries, yet what separated Ireland from similar movements in Scandinavia or the Baltic states was the experience of colonialism.[23] In Ireland the initial phase of cultural

nationalism was focused around the revival both of the language and of sporting activities. Under its founder Douglas Hyde, the Gaelic League became a popular mass movement for the promotion of the Irish language, which had largely fallen into disuse after centuries of British colonial rule. This contributed to the ethnographic project of Lady Augusta Gregory, collecting and recording Irish folktales and mythology, largely from the peasantry on her Galway estates. This formed part of the basis for the poetry and drama of the Cultural (or Literary) Revival, within which the work of W. B. Yeats and Lady Gregory's own activities with the Abbey Theatre in Dublin played such a prominent role.

In spite of their fascination with the oral narratives of the rural peasantry, the majority of the key figures of the Cultural Revival were distanced from this culture by both their class and their religion. There was a major contradiction between their role in the present and that in the past; members of the class that had previously expropriated the peasantry were now involved in reconstituting them as heroic subjects. As Terry Eagleton has observed, 'If the forefathers of the colonial class in Ireland had been a little less intent on undermining the native culture, their emancipated sons and daughters would have needed to busy themselves rather less with restoring it.'[24]

Yet visual culture also had a part in the Revival, even if marginal to literary concerns. In addition to John Millington Synge's photographs of peasant communities on the Aran Islands, or the paintings of Jack B. Yeats, the art dealer Hugh Lane developed the idea of a national collection of modern art for Ireland, to be permanently housed in a gallery in Dublin. As Augusta Gregory's nephew, Lane was well placed to do this, and began to assemble a collection of both mid-nineteenth-century French painting and the work of more recent artists, including both John Butler Yeats and William Orpen.[25] On 28 January 1908 the Municipal Gallery opened in Clonmel House in Harcourt Street. Its collection of early French modernism – including Manet's *Music in the Tuileries* (1861) and Berthe Morisot's *A Summer's Day* (1879) – was particularly well received, with an enthusiastic review by Synge in the *Manchester Guardian*.[26] Yet the project soon became dogged by controversy as Lane struggled to find a permanent home for the collection, ultimately bequeathing it to London's National Gallery.[27] He subsequently revoked the decision in an unwitnessed codicil, and the situation remained unresolved by the time of his death on the *Lusitania* in 1915.

Lane's project, the formation of a national collection of modern paintings that would inspire artists in Ireland, was an important step in the development of a visual dimension to cultural nationalism. This book begins two years after the initial opening of the Municipal Gallery, with the arrival in 1910 of the painters Paul and Grace Henry on Achill Island off the coast of Mayo. Hugh Lane's aspirations were inextricably bound up with his position within the Cultural Revival, while his collection was assembled along the lines of Edwardian notions of taste. In focusing on the work of Paul and Grace Henry on Achill, my intention is to identify a more modernist consciousness, whereby issues of place and ethnicity are filtered primarily through visual frames of reference, rather than through their associations with the literary.

Chapter One looks at significant changes in art practice during the early part of the century, at a time of major political and historical change. In addition to a focus on the emergent importance of visual constructions of ethnicity at a time of cultural nationalism, the impact of both the First World War and the Easter Rising of 1916 are considered in relation to the work of artists such as John Lavery, William Orpen or Seán Keating. Chapter Two examines the role of painters such as Jack Yeats (the son of John Butler Yeats and brother of William Butler Yeats) and Estella Solomons – in addition to Lavery – during both the War of Independence and the subsequent Civil War. This is followed by a discussion of the role of art in both shaping and engaging with conditions in newly independent Ireland, especially in relation to the two apparently conflicting tendencies of modernity and modernization versus an archaic ethnicity through a comparison of the work of Keating and Mainie Jellett, generally credited with introducing modernism to Ireland in the 1920s. This discussion continues in chapter Three with a consideration of the role of art practice in the Free State during the following decade. However, at this point distinct identities for art in Northern Ireland begin to take shape, drawing to some extent on the very different background of the importance of the ethics of Protestantism in Ulster-Scots culture, underpinning the work of painters such as John Luke, who was one of the artists contributing to the short-lived avant-gardism of the Ulster Unit, supported by the poet, critic and curator John Hewitt.

The outbreak of war in 1939 had contrasting consequences for cultural practice in Northern and Southern Ireland, bound up with the very dissimilar policies of the Free State and Northern Ireland as part of the United Kingdom. These are considered in chapter Four. In addition to the role of war artists such as William Conor in documenting the experience of the Blitz in Belfast, the degree of isolation from Britain meant that other painters such as Colin Middleton began to develop their own version of the avant-garde. However, this was also the time when a formulation of ethnicity undermining the representation of the West began to emerge in the practice of Gerard Dillon. In the South, meanwhile, Ireland's neutral status also facilitated the work of refugees from Britain in the work of the White Stag Group, and in the emergence of the annual *Irish Exhibition of Living Art*.

In chapter Five, the major shifts occurring in the 1950s are examined. These take the form of significant challenges to the myth of the West, in the context of the erosion of the heroic ideology of the Free State with the Republic of Ireland's full independence from the Commonwealth in 1948. A new emphasis on the local and the overlooked began to characterize the work of artists such as Tony O'Malley or Nano Reid both in the Republic and in Northern Ireland. However, the investigation of regional identity and the meanings of the rural by artists like the young Basil Blackshaw also took place in a context where the meanings of specific locations were closely bound up with deeply entrenched religious and political affiliations. By the 1950s, a significant number of Irish artists were also active in British art circles: chapter Six discusses work by a range of practitioners including, among others, Francis Bacon, Louis le Brocquy and Gerard Dillon.

In Ireland itself conditions changed rapidly over the next decade through processes of modernization at work in both North and South discussed in chapter Seven. Although the effects were slow to be felt in art in the North, in the Republic a less insular outlook also informed attitudes to art practice, whether through the work of individual painters such as Micheal Farrell, or the attempts to situate Ireland within international modernism through the instigation of the first *Rosc* exhibition in 1967. However, as chapter Eight explains, within a few years, in spite of an increasing engagement with trends in art practice beyond Ireland, the conflict in the North preoccupied many artists on both sides of the border; Northern artists in particular had to come to terms with a situation unprecedented in their experience, and find a way of representing a response. As the conflict continued into the 1980s, addressed in chapter Nine, the work of artists in the North increasingly drew on a range of practices associated with postmodernism, which was beginning to have a global impact. This ranged from deconstructive strategies to neo-Expressionism as a means of articulating a response to the overwhelming situation they were working within. In the South, neo-Expressionism's associations with gender became particularly apparent at a time when the politics of the Irish body began fundamentally to undermine a sense of nation, and which also contributed to the emergence of independent, highly visible women artists such as Alanna O'Kelly, Dorothy Cross and Cecily Brennan.

During the 1990s, as the remainder of the nationalist project began to unravel and Ireland's economic status changed dramatically, the historical narratives that had secured the role of the state were increasingly subject to interrogation. This is the focus of chapter Ten. Art projects played a significant role in this, whether in the group exhibition *In a State* at Dublin's Kilmainham Gaol in 1991, or the body of work by Alanna O'Kelly that engaged with a groundswell of cultural memory around the trauma of the Famine. Cultural memory was also one concern of artists in the North, providing a knowledge of the past that challenged official versions of controversial events, especially the killings on Bloody Sunday in Derry in 1972. Yet this was also a decade during which the importance of emigration as a facet of Irish nationhood became inescapable; for Irish people living in Britain, the ongoing Peace Process in Northern Ireland also brought about a greater acceptance. For a significant number of Irish artists in Britain, such as Kathy Prendergast and Elizabeth Magill, this resulted in work where a highly nuanced engagement with Irishness became subsumed into issues of displacement of identity. This was a process continuing into the new millennium, in a context where globalization and migration were increasingly eroding old concepts of nationalism. Chapter Eleven examines the ways in which artists in post-nationalist Ireland and beyond engaged with these changed circumstances. In the North, meanwhile, the massive economic and political impact of the 1998 Good Friday Agreement registered on a critical level in art practice, with a sense of artists as both a part of, and yet estranged from, times that were once more in ferment.

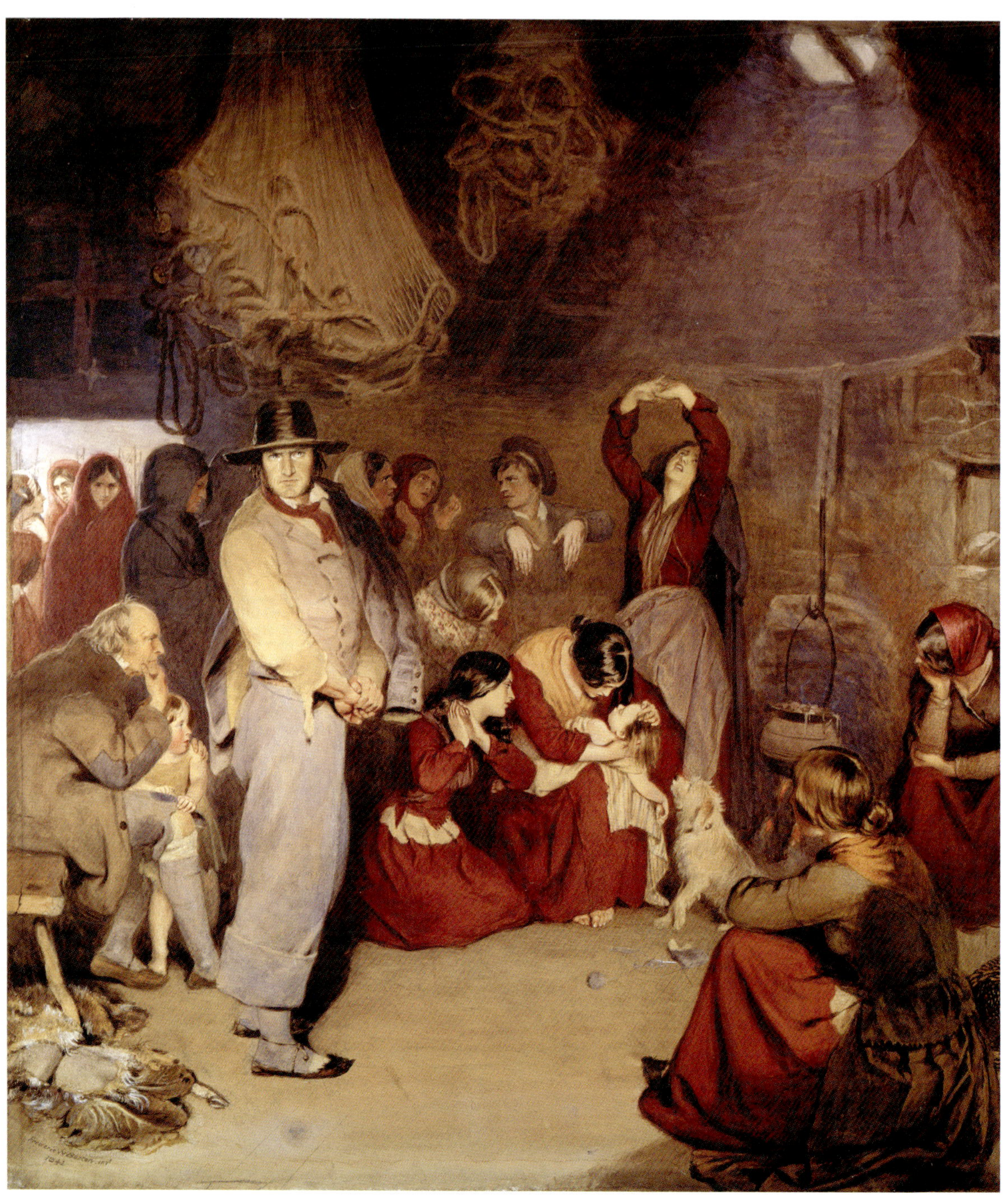

3 Frederick Burton, *The Aran Fisherman's Drowned Child*, 1841, watercolour on paper.

ETHNICITY, REVOLUTION AND THE MODERN, C. 1910–1918

In the summer of 1910 two painters, Paul Henry and his wife Grace, arrived on Achill Island, just off the coast of Mayo in the west of Ireland. They had travelled by train and boat from London initially for a fortnight's holiday; instead, in spite of the financial strain, they stayed intermittently until 1919. As Paul Henry later observed in his autobiography, *An Irish Portrait*, 'Here I intended to stay by the Grace of God. And by the Grace of God it had to be, because I had no money.'[1] Both artists set about painting scenes of the island's rugged landscape not only surrounded by a changeable sea, but inhabited by peasantry attempting to make a living in frequently difficult circumstances. This in itself was not unique at that time. There were precedents in similar representations of peasant communities elsewhere in Europe in the late nineteenth and early twentieth centuries. Gauguin and the Irish artist Roderic O'Conor, amongst others, had painted in rural Brittany in the 1880s, while other artists' colonies included both Newlyn in Cornwall and the more recent Worpswede in northern Germany. The west of Ireland itself had also been a major attraction for artists from the early nineteenth century, an ethnographic nationalism featuring in paintings such as Frederick Burton's *The Aran Fisherman's Drowned Child*. The more recent photographs of the Aran Islands taken by John Millington Synge between 1898 and 1902, and Jack Yeats' slightly later romanticized depictions of the peasantry of the West, helped to confirm this trend.

Yet Paul and Grace Henry's presence on Achill provides a degree of focus for the pervasive changes beginning to take place within Irish art in the early years of the twentieth century. The revival of Irish culture was largely identified with a section of the Anglo-Irish elite who had wielded power since the end of the seventeenth century, and much of whose wealth was derived from hereditary land ownership. Attempts to establish a distinct 'Irish school' of painting were also inseparable from both the predominant literary and dramatic interests of the Cultural Revival and the values of the class from which it was derived; the paintings of 'AE' (George Russell), for example, inhabited the same quasi-mystical Celtic twilight as many of the poems of W. B. Yeats. In common with both Synge and Jack Yeats, the paintings of Achill by Paul Henry suggested an idealization of the peasantry of the West. Yet Henry's interests were not identified with those of the Cultural Revival. Both Paul and Grace Henry were from non-conformist middle-class Ulster and Scottish families, from backgrounds with no stake in Ireland's decolonization, even though Paul Henry's work was to play a major role in the development of a visual discourse capable of articulating the concerns of post-independence Ireland. What is instead significant is that their presence on Achill marks a point when what it meant to be an Irish artist began to change, as notions of artistic identity became increasingly democratic over the following decades.

In addition to the cataclysmic effects of the First World War, the Easter Rising and the subsequent struggles around decolonization, the erosion of the political and cultural power of the Protestant Anglo-Irish elite was also to have considerable consequences for art in Ireland. The shifting grounds of political allegiance greatly affected the work of established society painters such as William Orpen and John Lavery, just as they opened up a range of opportunities for younger artists such as Seán Keating and Charles Lamb. For some women artists, such as Mary Swanzy and Mainie Jellett, the possibilities for artistic innovation were clearly identified as existing outside Ireland itself. However, a closer look at Paul Henry's work provides an initial engagement with the visualization of Irish ethnicity that became deeply embedded in the processes of decolonization and the formation of an independent Irish state for much of the next 30 years.

Paul and Grace Henry and the formation of ethnicity

Paul Henry's paintings on Achill had much in common with notions of the primitive also emerging in contemporary European culture, as peasants generally became characterized as both ruled by intuition and at the mercy of natural forces of weather or the sea. These representations of indigenous and frequently colonized peoples suggested an authentic response lost elsewhere in the alienation imposed by capitalism on its subjects. Something of this is visible in the pre-capitalist labour of

Henry's *Launching the Currach*, painted during one of his early visits to Achill; it was shown at Leinster Hall in Dublin in October 1911, where work by both Paul and Grace Henry was included in a joint exhibition with George Russell, Casimir Markiewicz and Frances Baker. Paul Henry's views of life on Achill were radically different from Russell's concern with an arcane Celtic mysticism. In *Launching the Currach* five men are depicted dragging the boat through the surf into a bluish-grey sea. Their uniform anonymity is reinforced by the scene's bleakness, as the sea stretches towards the empty horizon; men, boat and shore merge in a watery reflection, reinforcing a sense of the island-dwellers' affinities with nature. *The Lobster Fisher* also focuses on this relationship, although here it is a still summer's night with a single male figure at work setting lobster pots in a calm sea. Its blue and purple overall tonality is indebted to Henry's studies in Paris, which included a period at Whistler's Académie Carmen between 1898 and 1900; it also indicates a further concern for some degree of modernist technical radicalism in the depiction of an archaic way of life.

In these paintings, and many others dating from Paul Henry's early visits to Achill, a new language for the representation of the West begins to emerge. Although many of his landscapes subsequently drew heavily on Whistler's soft, muted range of colour tones, Henry's iconic, heroic peasant subjects derived from a combination of Millet and early Van Gogh, both artists whose work he knew from his time in Paris. The application of a model derived from nineteenth-century French realism to contemporary Ireland was important in challenging existing representations of the western seaboard. As opposed to the sentimentality of earlier depictions such as Samuel McCloy's *Mother and Child by the Sea*, Henry proposed a strong, heroic peasantry. His simplified compositions and palette, in addition to an

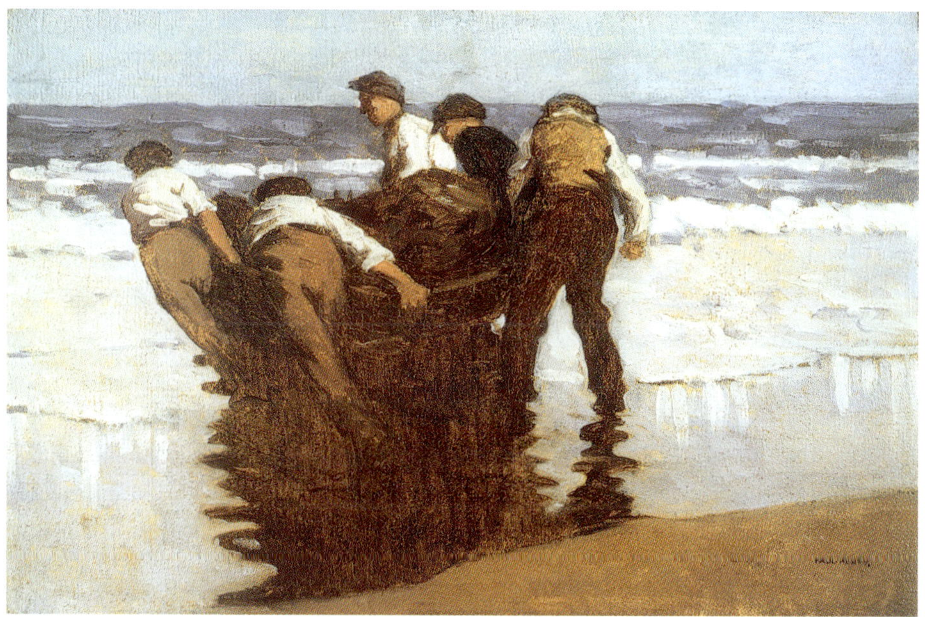

4 Paul Henry, *Launching the Currach*, 1910–11, oil on canvas.

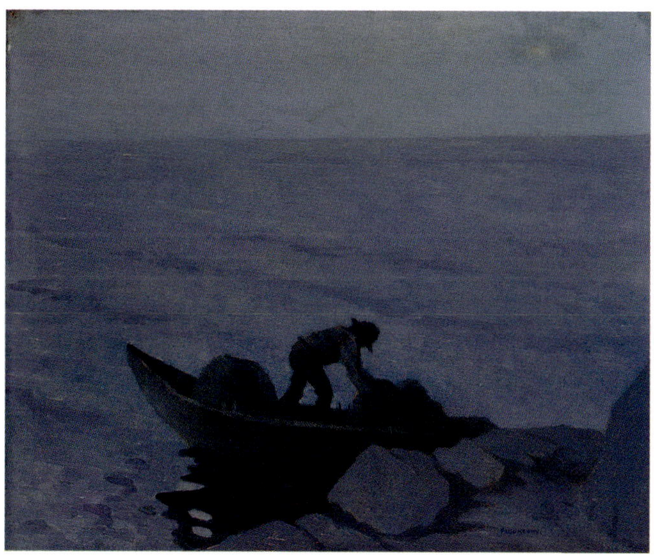

5 Paul Henry, *The Lobster Fisher*, 1911–13, oil on canvas.

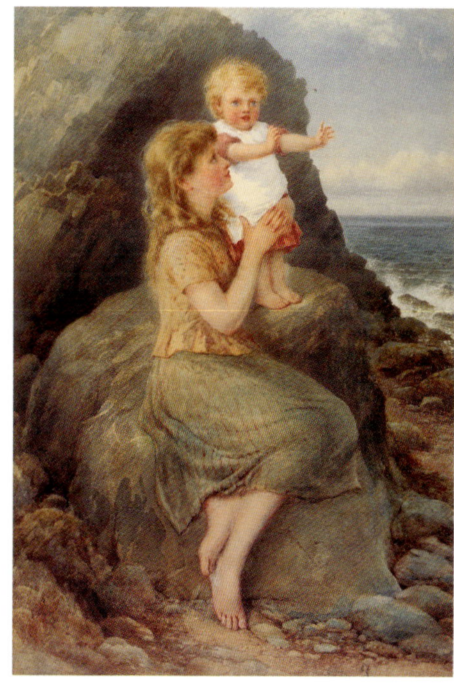

6 Samuel McCloy, *Mother and Child by the Sea*, 1880s, watercolour.

apparently crude handling of paint in works such as *Launching the Currach*, helped to convey a sense of authentic representation of the harsh realities of peasant life in the West; the roughness of brushstroke also indicates a modern technique as inseparable from the directness of approach to the subject.

Henry acknowledged a range of literary influences for this project. During his adolescence in Belfast the remoteness of a solitary rural existence in Thoreau's *Walden* had made a great impression on him, while more recent influences included Synge's play *Riders to the Sea* (1904), based in the Aran Islands. There were also recent Irish visual precedents for the imagery of the heroic western peasantry. As the son of a Northern Baptist minister, Henry's background was very different from the cultured elite of the Literary Revival, and his interests stopped short of the preservation of the Irish language or mythology. Nevertheless, he shared with Synge and Jack Yeats a desire to convey a sense of authenticity of contemporary life in the West, as in Synge's photographs of the Aran Islands. Yet the processes whereby Synge obtained his photographs indicates the degree to which the representation of authenticity was itself constructed; the boy seated on the wall in *Islanders of Inishmaan* wanted to be photographed in his Sunday best rather than the working clothes that Synge preferred as conveying a sense of typicality of the islander's daily existence.[2] Yeats's small watercolour and chalk drawing *The Man from Aranmore* also suggests a highly selective typology of island life in the heroic stance of the fisherman posed at the end of a pier, the mast of his hooker visible behind him. Framed by the

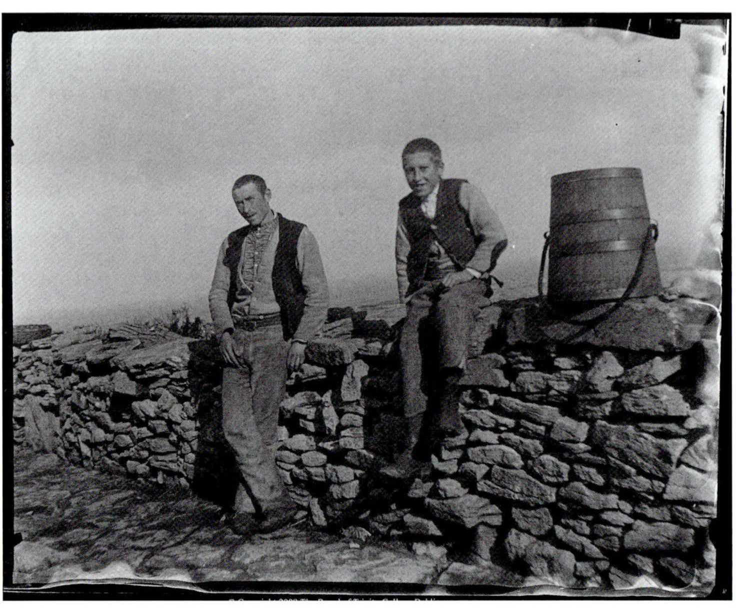

7 John Millington Synge, *The Islanders of Inishmaan*, black and white photograph.

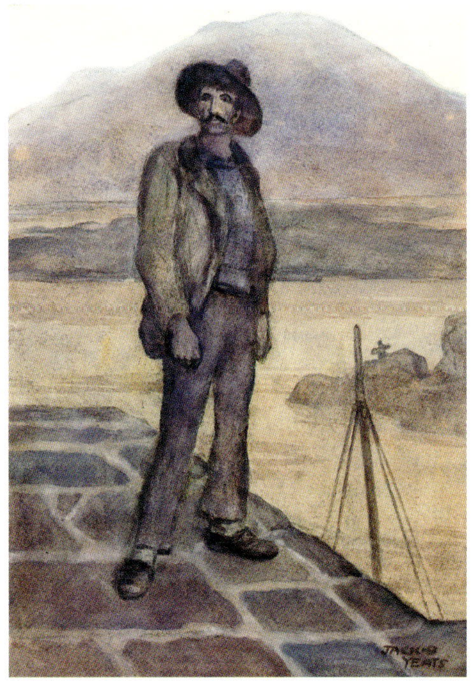

8 Jack Butler Yeats, *The Man from Aranmore*, 1905, black chalk and watercolour on board.

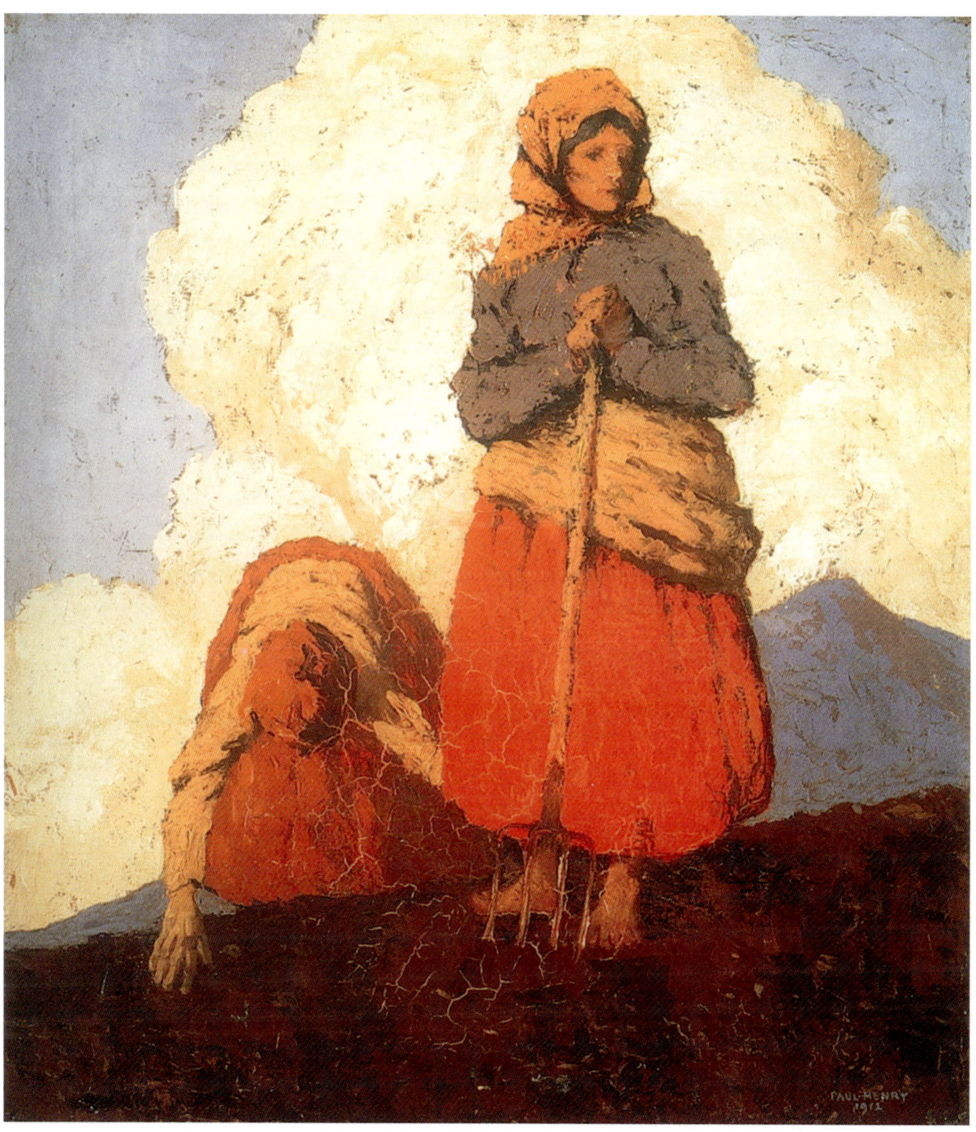

9 Paul Henry, *The Potato Diggers*, 1912, oil on canvas.

mountain beyond, this is a man in harmony with his environment.[3]

It is, however, in Paul Henry's encounters with Achill women that the lure of the primitive emerges most clearly. In *The Potato Diggers* Henry kept representational details to a minimum. The low viewpoint frames the two women against a pared-down background of blue mountain and towering cumulus cloud. Both are dressed in the distinctive clothing of western women, with their shawls, headscarves and bright red skirts dyed with madder. The sight of women working in the Achill landscape fascinated Henry; as he recalled in his autobiography, 'a group of women working in the fields with a background of rich brown earth, made the strip of earth they were working on a riot of gay colour'.[4] In spite of their aestheticization, Henry's potato diggers are heroic female subjects, yet rooted firmly in the soil of a geographical region noted also for its resistance to British rule. A mark of this was the common use of the Irish language, which Henry did not speak. His fantasies of Achill as a primitive outpost were perhaps expressed most strongly by his response to the spectacle of working women: 'The influence of these strong personalities who spoke in a language which I did not understand, the women in their colourful barbaric clothes, made a deep impression on me.'[5] Henry's version of Achill was a remote, timeless region dominated by an atavistic sense of territory; on stumbling on a deserted village, for instance, he delightedly referred to it subsequently as 'the ancestral home of the tribe'.[6]

It was not entirely accurate to depict Achill as isolated either geographically or from contemporary events. Regular rail connections to Dublin were available, and Achill was also part of a larger territory west of the River Shannon whose picturesque scenery had attracted both artists and other tourists since the early nineteenth century.[7] Neither was Achill the home of a peasantry who stoically accepted their fate at the hands of God and the elements; as Mary Cosgrove has shown, the years of Henry's early visits were characterized by recurrent protests over rent and land ownership.[8] Women played a major role in the struggles around eviction; these acts of collective resistance were far removed from the isolated objects of fascination appearing in paintings such as Henry's *The Solitary Digger* (1912–15). Significantly it is in Grace Henry's engagement with life on Achill that a less idealized type of representation of these women begins to emerge. Grace Henry (formerly Mitchell) was a Scottish painter who had also trained in Paris in the late 1890s, and it was here that she and Paul Henry first met. However, her Paris-based observations of post-Impressionist primitivism were put to somewhat different effect in

The Top of the Hill, depicting three women in conversation. Although composed in a similar way to Paul Henry's depictions of Achill – a low viewpoint allowing the focus on an expanse of sky beyond – both the figures and clouds are contained in a heavy *cloisonné* outline reminiscent of Gauguin. There is also a degree of exoticism in the rich layering of shawls and skirts worn by the figure on the left. Two of the women have their backs to the spectator, denying any illusion of access; during her time on Achill, Grace Henry bitterly missed London life. What for her husband became a source of fascination – the women's costume, their shared language and labour – would have only excluded her, as a woman artist who presumably spoke only English and whose working life was very different from the islanders she depicted. In spite of such poignant images as *The Top of the Hill*, it was a male gaze that provided the dominant view of the West, conveying an isolated community pitted against the elements. The inscription of the West within a masculine narrative was further secured by Paul Henry's publication of *An Irish Portrait* in 1951. Following their bitterly contested divorce in 1929, he wrote Grace out of his autobiography completely; nowhere is there any implication that his apparent discovery of Achill was anything other than a solitary experience.

During their years on Achill Paul and Grace Henry would not have been unaware of the significance of events taking place elsewhere in Ireland. In Ulster in 1912, the place of Paul Henry's birth, the possibility of Ireland's Home Rule prompted considerable unease among Unionists, who began to organize in opposition. In April the Liberal leader Asquith announced the Home Rule Bill as a means of maintaining Irish nationalist support for his party in the Commons. Even though it only gave Ireland a relatively small degree of autonomy, Unionist opposition gathered against the

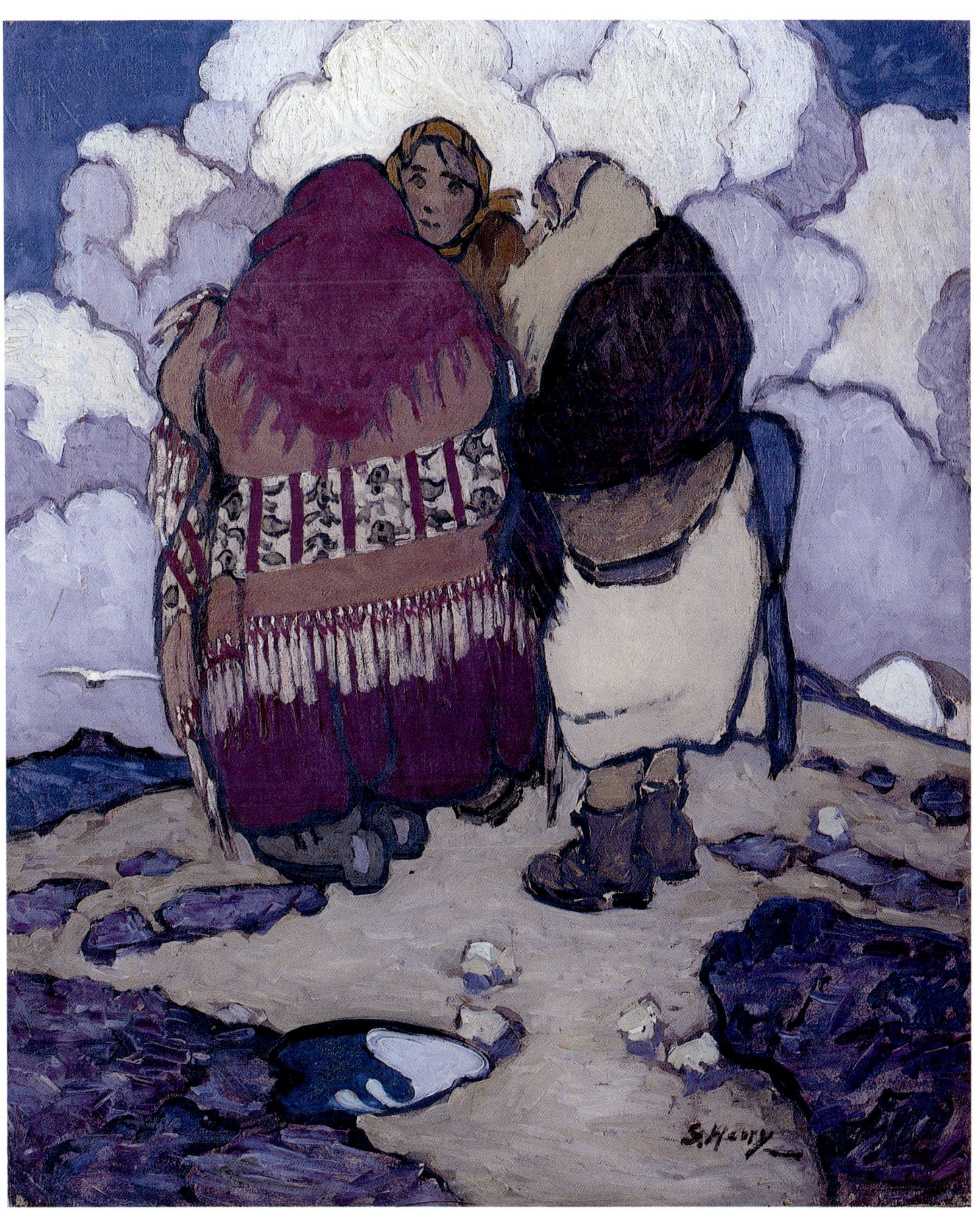

10 Grace Henry, *The Top of the Hill*, c. 1920, oil on linen.

Bill, backed by British Tories. Under the leadership of Sir Edward Carson (the former prosecutor in the trial of Oscar Wilde) and James Craig the campaign quickly escalated with the staged mass swearing in, in Belfast, of the Solemn League and Covenant, promising loyalty to the British Crown; in only a few days nearly half a million people signed the two petitions at the City Hall and Ulster Hall. Militarized opposition crystallized in the formation of the Ulster Volunteer Force (UVF) in 1913, once more supported by Carson and armed through gun-running from Germany. Military organizations were also emerging among nationalists, partly in response to the moves by loyalists in the North. These included the Irish Citizen Army under the leadership of James Connolly, emerging during the Dublin Lockout of 1913. This was a series of mass strikes around the issue of union membership organized by James Larkin, which also attracted the support of artists and writers, organized by George Russell, including William Orpen. Meanwhile, under the leadership of the former painter Constance de Markiewicz, the youth movement Na Fianna Éireann ('Warriors Ireland') was becoming increasingly structured along military lines. With the backing of the Irish Republican Brotherhood (IRB), the Irish Volunteers also emerged in late 1913, rapidly growing in numbers; by the following May there were 129,000 members. The Irish Volunteers were also armed through gun-running organized from London by a group that included the historian Alice Stopford Green and the former diplomat Roger Casement. The arms purchased once more from Germany were landed at Howth, just north of Dublin. Intervention by the authorities had tragic consequences: three people were killed and many injured when soldiers opened fire on a crowd of civilians at Bachelor's Walk in the city centre.

The First World War, the Easter Rising and Irish art

The years that Paul and Grace Henry spent on Achill also included those of the First World War. As he rhapsodized over the spectacle of the alien peasantry, thousands of young Irishmen – particularly from the Protestant North – were enlisting and dying at the Front. In this context, Henry's decision to remain right at the very edge of Europe takes on a new significance at a time when the fields of France were central to the consciousness of the majority of his kinsmen. Awareness of the war must cast new light on his decision to continue his re-enactment of strategies developed within the avant-garde elsewhere in Europe. It is important that we re-evaluate the significance of the war, not just for Irish political developments, but in terms of its deep impact on Irish cultural history as well.[9] In Ireland, significantly, it was the work of Henry, Keating and Yeats – all non-combatants – which was to coalesce into a template for the future development of Irish art.

In the absence of conscription, probably around 210,000 men enlisted in units formed in Ireland – a figure that excludes others who joined other units elsewhere in the United Kingdom or the Empire. Of these probably 30,000 to 35,000 died as a result of their involvement. Other than the obvious Unionist support for the United Kingdom, they volunteered for a number of reasons. Not only did the forces provide economic security at a time of fluctuating employment, but also, for moderate Irish nationalists such as the poet and essayist Tom Kettle, the moral cause of support for small nations such as Belgium and Serbia carried considerable weight. This was reinforced when the Irish Home Rule Bill became law in September 1914, although it was suspended until the end of the war. However, it is important to be aware that the events of

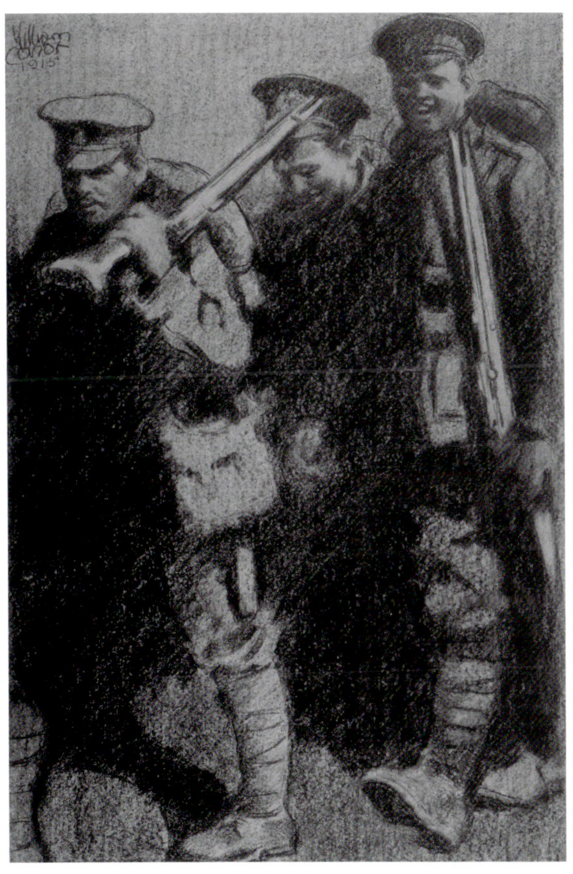

11 William Conor, *Off: The Ulster Division*, 1915, charcoal and chalk on paper.

this period have a distinctly ambivalent status in the formation of national identities in Ireland. This is clear from the selective representation of the events of 1916 within cultural memory. Nationalists have focused on the commemoration of the Easter Rising to the exclusion of the First World War, even though the state (reluctantly at times) continued to debate the issue of appropriate memorials to the war dead for many years after Ireland's independence.[10] In the mythologies of Ulster Unionism, by comparison, the Battle of the Somme occupies an equally prominent position, due to the massive loss of life among the soldiers of the Ulster Division in the first two days of battle in July 1916. The sense of trauma stems also from the fact that the 36th (Ulster) Division was a close-knit 'pals' formation, recruited exclusively from Ulster Protestants, many of whom had already gained military experience in the UVF, and who came from small communities across the North. This sense of camaraderie is perpetuated visually by William Conor's drawing of three young recruits

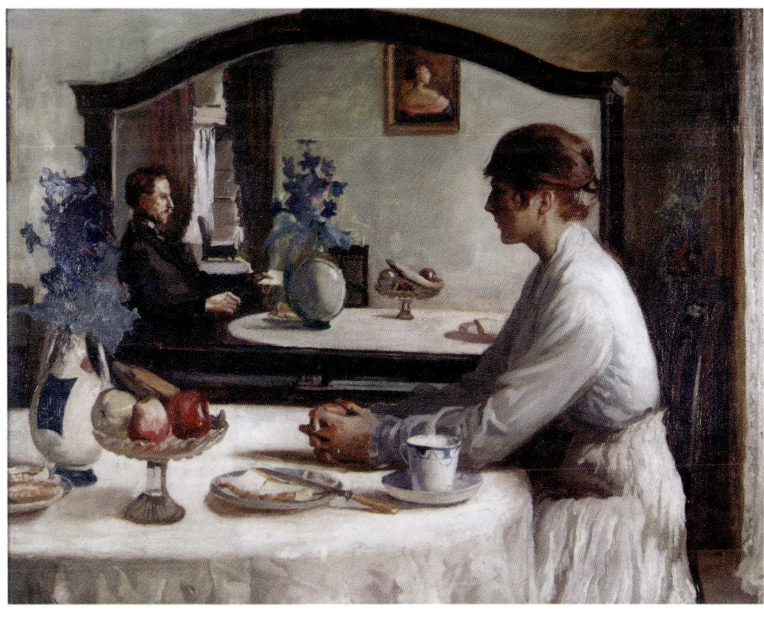

12 William Sheehan, *The Consultation*, 1917, oil on canvas.

preparing to leave Belfast, *Off: The Ulster Division*. However, the focus on the Division's martyrdom for the British state also ignores the sacrifice of other Irish units. These include both the Gallipoli landings of the previous year, when two-thirds of the troops died when they reached the beaches, and the loss of many of the 16th (Irish) Division also at the Somme in September 1916. The devastating effects of soldiers' deaths on their families are suggested in William Sheehan's painting *The Consultation*. Although ambiguous, there is a sense of loss resulting from the news brought by the man reflected in the mirror; the seated woman's stoic attitude provides a rare representation of the female experience of the First World War in Ireland.

For the first two years of the war, meanwhile, William Orpen carried on the role of society portraitist that had made him so successful in England. When conscription was introduced there in 1916, he rejected his former pupil and studio assistant Seán Keating's encouragement to return to Ireland, opting instead to become involved in a non-combatant capacity on the British side. In April 1917 he arrived in France under the war artists scheme set up by the Ministry of Information. Unlike the majority of other war artists who were allowed to stay only for three weeks, Orpen's fame and status meant that he was allowed to stay indefinitely. He spent the hot summer of 1917 on the former battlefields of the Somme, mostly around Thiepval, scene of some of the heaviest fighting the previous year, producing a large number of drawings and paintings that documented the life and death of both British and German soldiers and the devastating effects of the war on the landscape they inhabited. The amount of time available to Orpen was invaluable in developing his observations and gaining a deeper understanding of the effects of the combat. Additionally, as Keith Jeffery has suggested, a characteristic of

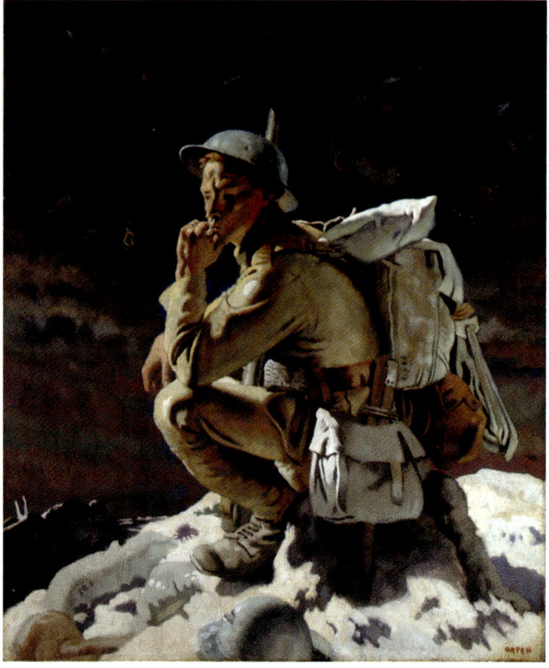

13 William Orpen, *The Thinker on the Butte de Warlencourt*, 1917, oil on canvas.

Irish identity at the time was a 'sometimes ambiguous and qualified enlistment in the war effort'; Orpen's early war images, such as *Thiepval* (1917), have a definite sense of detachment from their subject-matter.[11]

However, Orpen's continued exposure to the relentless destruction of the war on the Western Front had also begun to produce a darker, bleaker vision. As he commented in his memoir, *An Onlooker in France*:

a hand lying on the duckboards; a Boche and Highlander locked in a deadly embrace at the edge of Highwood . . . the shell-holes with the shapes of bodies faintly showing through the putrid water – all these things made one think terribly of what human beings had been through.[12]

This more reflective view is epitomized by *The Thinker on the Butte de Warlencourt*, with its obvious reference to Rodin's thinker in the seated pose, the figure bent forward with chin in hand. The horror of the Front is implied here, rather than depicted. Increasingly, in these later war pictures, the detachment that previously resulted in a desire to record becomes a signifier of deep-rooted trauma that escapes representation, whether in the reclining figure regarding the embracing couple in *Changing Billets, Picardy* (1918) or the central figure of *The Mad Woman of Douai*.

John Lavery's First World War experience was very different. His initial attempts to join the Artists' Rifles were thwarted by the realization that at the age of 58 he was no longer fit enough for strenuous physical drilling. He did, however, hope to travel to the Western Front to record the conflict; these aspirations were also dashed, by a car accident in Park Lane when his wife Hazel was quite seriously injured. In 1917 he was appointed Official war Artist to the Navy; his depictions of naval bases in Scotland and England subsequently appeared in *British Artists at the Front*, published by *Country Life* in 1918.[13] It is, however, a different painting by Lavery that remains his best-known depiction of the war, *Daylight Raid from my Studio Window, 7 July 1917*. This depicts Hazel half kneeling on a chaise longue apparently watching the German aircraft. Her winsome pose conveys a sense of feminine detachment from the masculine business of war, but the original version of Lavery's painting was very different. Here, Hazel, terrified by the raid, was depicted praying before a statue of the Virgin Mary. This figure was subsequently painted out by Lavery before he donated the picture to Belfast

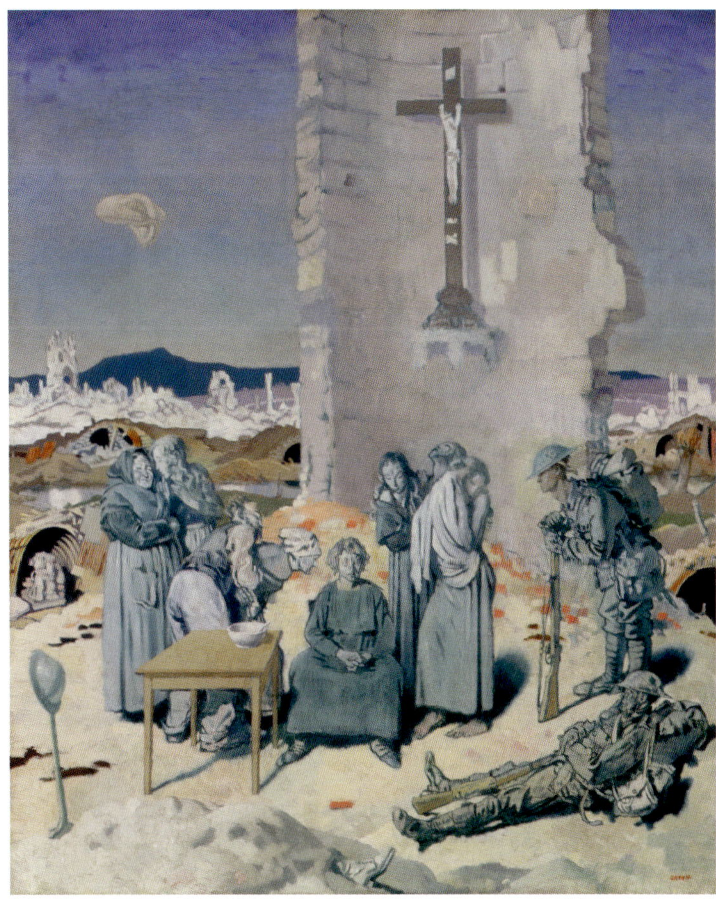

14 William Orpen, *The Mad Woman of Douai*, 1918, oil on canvas.

Municipal Museum and Art Gallery in 1929, so as not to publicly expose Hazel's fear. In doing so, however, what remains is an impression of Hazel Lavery as charming and frivolous, entirely consistent with her husband's numerous depictions of her as a society lady and hostess, such as *Hazel in Black and Gold*.

In spite of their apparent similarities as painters of British high society, the careers of Orpen and Lavery and particularly their relationship to Ireland took very different paths after the war. Orpen's Anglo-Irishness had enabled him to carve out a reputation on both sides of the Irish Sea. This became unsustainable as the Easter Rising and subsequently the War of Independence in 1919–20 affected the meanings of

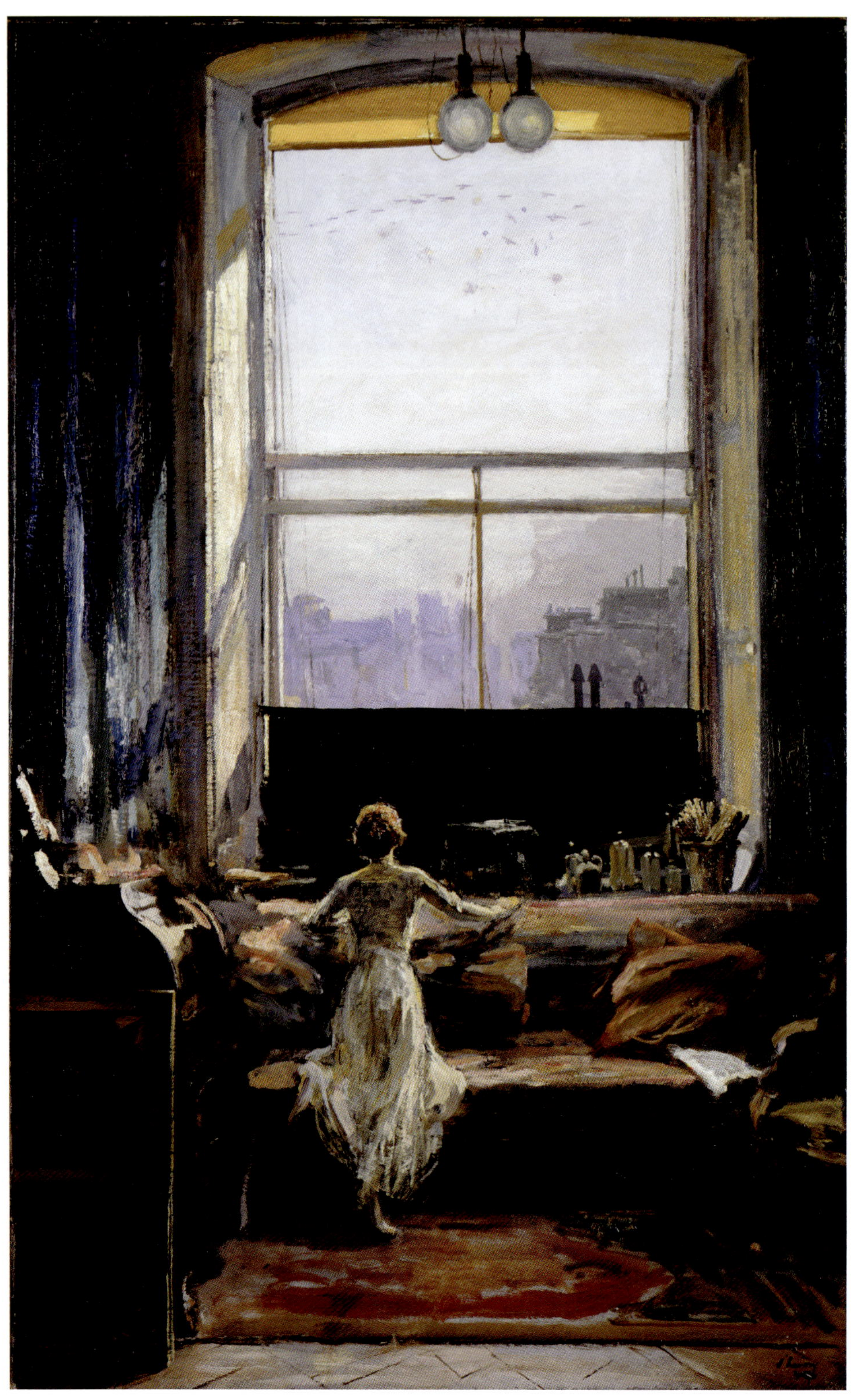

15 John Lavery, *Daylight Raid from my Studio Window, 7 July 1917*, 1917, oil on canvas.

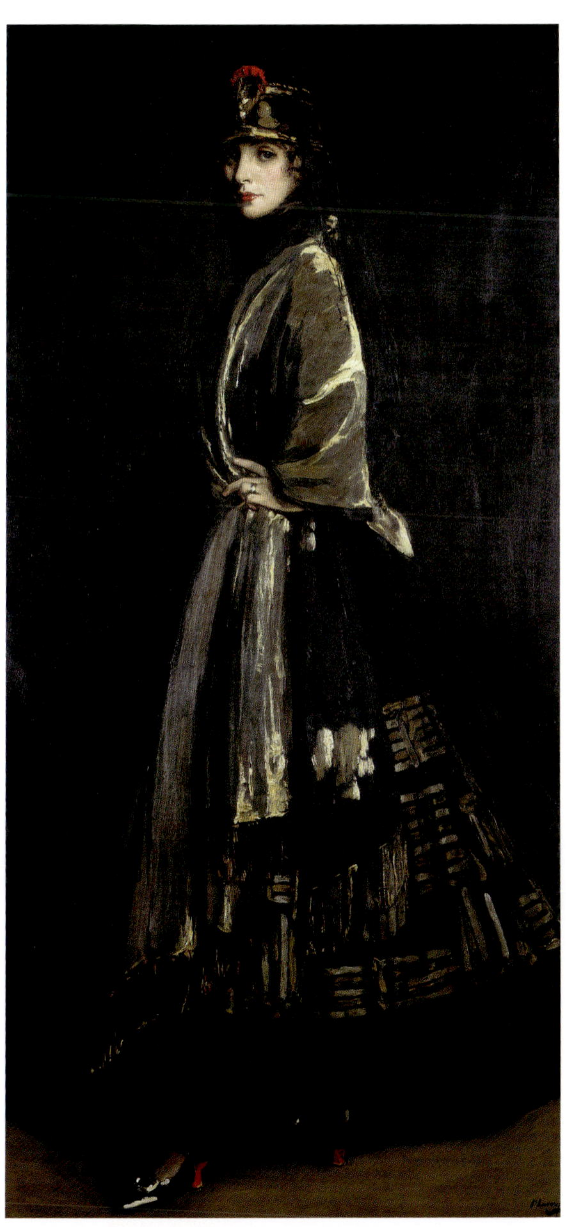

16 John Lavery, *Hazel in Black and Gold*, 1915, oil on canvas.

'Irishness' in Britain. Orpen's war work also served increasingly to identify him with Britain during these volatile years, and his precarious duality could no longer be maintained. After a brief family visit in 1917, he never returned to Ireland again. By comparison, during the post-war years Irish subjects gained an unprecedented importance in Lavery's career; but then his class and cultural background had always produced a much more ambivalent relationship with British cultural hierarchies even though he and Hazel Lavery mixed in aristocratic social circles.

For the wealthy Anglo-Irish, the source particularly of Orpen's patronage, the First World War marked a further moment in their decline in conjunction with their changed economic situation after the Land War of the 1880s. A significant proportion of families of the nobility lost their heirs during the conflict. This affected both the social circles and the artistic aims of the Cultural Revival. Lady Augusta Gregory's son Robert, also a promising painter, was killed in 1918, his demise memorialized in Yeats's poem of the same year, *An Irish Airman Foresees His Death*. This followed the death also of Augusta Gregory's nephew, Hugh Lane, who was sailing to New York on the *Lusitania* in May 1915 when it was torpedoed by a German submarine off the coast of Cork. As a result, the controversy over Lane's bequest of his Impressionist paintings to the new Municipal Gallery remained unresolved. Lane had originally intended to leave his collection to the Gallery, but his frustrations over the delay in the establishment of a permanent home for the paintings led him to change the bequest in 1913 to the National Gallery in London. However, in a further codicil to the will Lane revoked this later version, leaving the paintings once more to Dublin, on the condition that a suitable building was found for them within five years of his death. The codicil remained unwitnessed, resulting

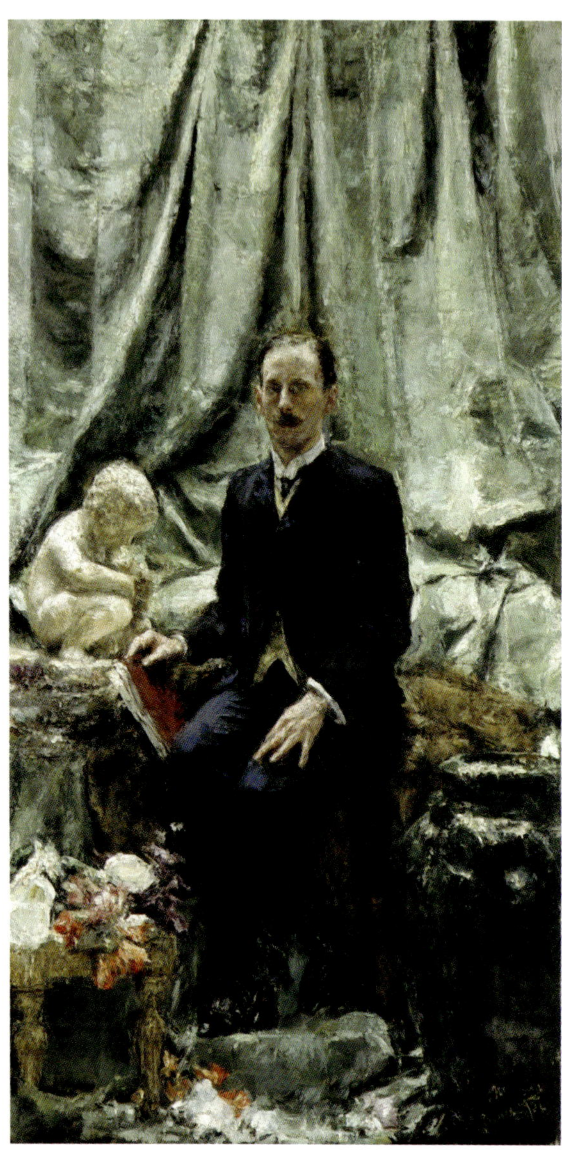

17 Antonio Mancini, *Sir Hugh Lane*, 1913, oil on canvas.

in conflicting claims to the paintings by both Dublin and London. The terms of Lane's bequest were a matter of considerable discussion for much of the century, finally reaching a satisfactory resolution in 1993. Thirty-one of the paintings have remained in Ireland while the remaining eight, including works by Manet, Degas and Morisot, have been divided so that four at a time are lent to Dublin for six years while the others remain in London.

The war provided both opportunity and model for the Rising's use of violent action.[14] In 1915, Patrick Pearse began planning for military combat and in April 1916 the Rising became a full-scale military operation, but without the troops necessary to sustain the occupation of the General Post Office and other key sites throughout Dublin. After one week the rebels surrendered, after scenes reminiscent of the War elsewhere, such as the trenches dug on St Stephens Green by the Irish Citizen Army under the command of Countess Markiewicz where they were picked off by snipers from the Shelbourne Hotel. About 500 people died in the Rising, mostly civilians caught in crossfire, and although only 60 rebels were killed this number would have been swelled considerably by the issuing of 96 death sentences by the British. In the event, with the execution of the Rising's leaders, only fifteen were carried out; Markiewicz's sentence was commuted to life imprisonment on the grounds of her gender, while Éamon de Valera, the future Taoiseach of the Free State, escaped because he was an American citizen. Up to this point public opinion had been largely against the Rising, seeing it as a betrayal of the Irish troops fighting for the British in Europe. This was to change radically after the executions at Kilmainham Gaol in May 1916, especially when it became known that the wounded James Connolly had to be tied to a chair so he could be shot. However, in Jack Yeats's depiction of a race meeting, *On Drumcliffe Strand*, a continued conflict of allegiances underpins the dramatic tension between the two men in the foreground, one of whom is an Irish Volunteer, and the mixed responses of the race-goers they encounter.[15]

It is important not to underestimate the confluence of political and cultural aspirations in the Rising. The

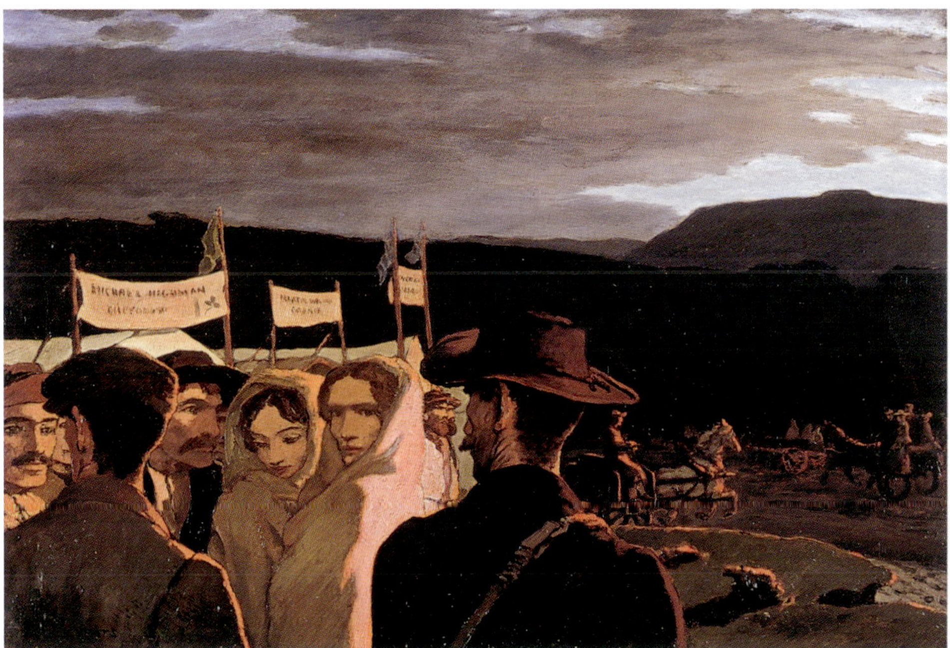

18 Jack Yeats, *On Drumcliffe Strand*, 1918, oil on canvas.

cultural nationalist aims of the Revival became transposed into military action in 1916, and a significant proportion of the Rising's leaders were also participants in Dublin's cultural circles. The commitment to armed insurrection that remained implicit in W. B. Yeats joining the IRB in 1896 became fully articulated in the acts of the poets Patrick Pearse, Thomas MacDonagh and Joseph Plunkett, and the painter Constance Markiewicz. Pearse's act of the reading of the Proclamation of the Irish Republic in front of the Post Office on Monday 24 April 1916 can also be seen on another level as a kind of performance of revolution. A particular type of identity was being enacted at this moment, with far-reaching consequences for the twentieth-century struggles of Irish nationalism. Pearse drew upon a conflation of the mythological figure of Cuchulainn, the legendary champion of Ulster, and the Christian sacrifice embodied in the Catholic celebration of Easter, in order to communicate a clear sense of the redemptive power of heroic masculine self-sacrifice in the cause of Irish freedom.

These values became clustered around the Symbolist sculptor Oliver Sheppard's statue *The Death of Cuchulainn*. Earlier, as editor of the Gaelic League journal *An Claidheamh Soluis* (The Sword of Light), Pearse had approvingly reviewed Sheppard's sculptural group *Inis Fáil* (Island of Destiny; 1902) as embodying a similar ethos of blood sacrifice for political idealism. The Cuchulainn myth itself had a particular resonance for Pearce; in his 1912 pamphlet *The Murder Machine* he described his founding of the boys' school St Enda's as intended to 're-create and perpetuate in Ireland the knightly tradition of Cuchulainn'.[16] The iconography of Sheppard's sculpture is closely derived from the interests of the Cultural Revival, accurately replicating the version of the hero's death given in Augusta Gregory's book *Cuchulainn of Muirthemne* (1902), with its description of the dying hero tied to a pillar to face his

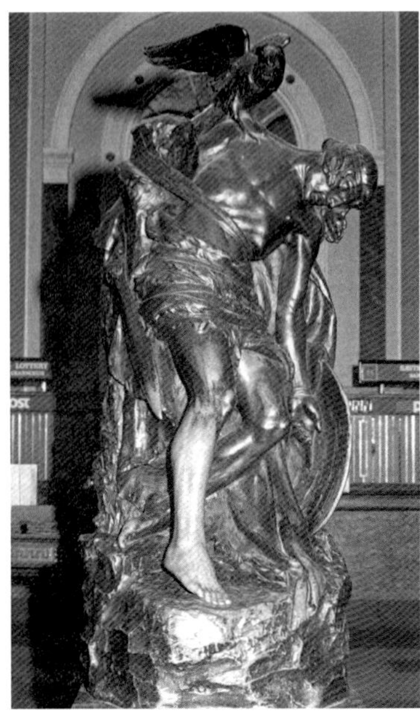

19 Oliver Sheppard, *The Death of Cuchulainn*, 1911–12, bronze.

final enemies. The continued relevance of the statue as public symbol of republicanism is apparent in its subsequent history. Until 1934 it remained in Sheppard's studio, in spite of an abortive sale attempt to the Belfast Museum and Art Gallery. As Turpin points out, its political associations would have been hard to reconcile with the gallery's Unionist-dominated management.[17] In the early 1930s, however, de Valera selected *Cuchulainn* as the official memorial to the Easter Rising, and a bronze cast was subsequently installed in the General Post Office in December 1934.

In comparison with *Cuchulainn*'s use of a past language associated with the Cultural Revival, Seán Keating's painting *Men of the West* deploys a different set of meanings in its engagement with the conjuncture of politics and culture in 1916. Although probably painted after Keating had spent a year in London as Orpen's studio assistant, there is no evidence of an engagement with

any of the forms of avant-garde painting current in London at the time, such as Vorticism or the Bloomsbury post-Impressionism practised by Duncan Grant or Vanessa Bell. The visual language of *Men of the West* distances itself from modernism in its combination of both academicism and realism in the depiction of its three figures; it is, however, an important work whose power derives from its dramatic engagement with a founding moment of Irish modernity in a joining of the emergent myth of the West with the unfolding of political events. The three figures, recognizable as westerners by their clothing, were actually posed by Keating, his brother and a friend. However, rather than evoking the self-contained archaism of Henry's *Launching the Currach*, their collective presence suggests an awareness of a forthcoming role in Ireland's history. The self-consciousness of the man at the left, whose eyes meet the gaze of the viewer, reinforces this sense of both imminence and menace. In spite of the similarity of staging and accessories – hats, waistcoats and rifles – that invites misreading in terms of the much later Hollywood Western, Keating's painting is actually closer to what Luke Gibbons has argued convincingly to be a predominant trope of *Irish* western identity – that of the outlaw. This appears frequently in Synge's representations of the life of the West, from Christy Mahon in *The Playboy of the Western World* to his accounts of his visits to the Aran Islands.[18] In Keating's painting the presence of the tricolour, the flag of the Irish Republic, transforms the isolated outlaw into a political subject, united with others in a circular composition radiating from the flag itself. As James White observed of *Men of the West*, 'For the first time Ireland is presented not as a romantic landscape but as a vision of men united, with a country worth fighting for.'[19]

Seán Keating himself posed the figure at the left of *Men of the West*. Originally from Limerick, Keating was

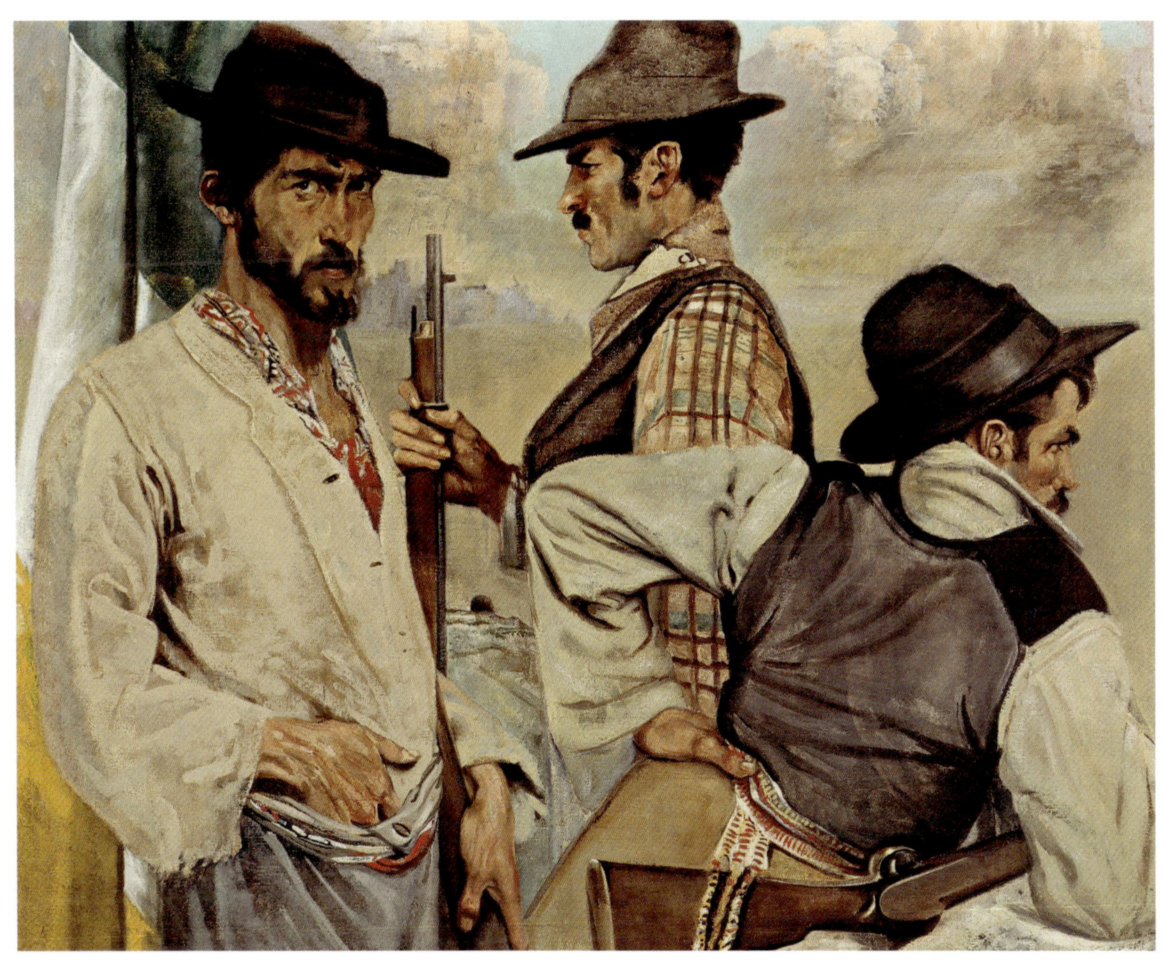

20 Seán Keating, *Men of the West*, 1915–17, oil on canvas.

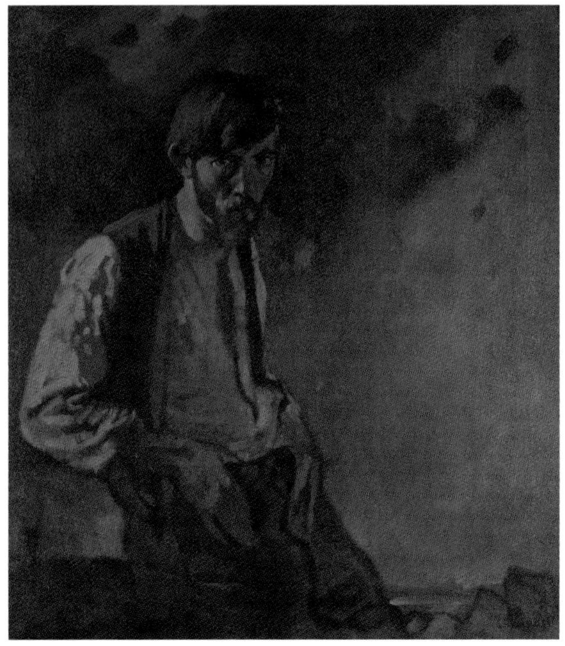

21 William Orpen, *Man of the West*, 1913, oil on linen.

a regular visitor to the Aran Islands, although his visual identification as defiant westerner was formulated in Orpen's depictions of him. Orpen's tellingly entitled *Man of the West* shows him in a pose that pre-empts the self-portrait in Keating's later painting; although the rifle is lacking, the hands tucked into the waistband and the brooding stare contribute to a similar reading of romanticized defiance. Identification of the grouped figures in *Men of the West* with the struggles of the rebels against British rule is something that also helps to date this painting more securely. In 1963, the catalogue to Keating's retrospective exhibition at the Municipal Gallery claimed that it had been painted in 1915 and exhibited at the Royal Hibernian Academy (RHA) that year.[20] The destruction of the RHA's records when the building was burned during the Civil War makes this impossible to confirm. It was, however, definitely included in the RHA's annual exhibi-

tion of 1917 and was more likely to have been painted shortly before then. Political events would seem to support this reading; it was only after the execution of the leaders of the Easter Rising and the release of the other prisoners in 1917 that the rebels gained mass public support. As Joan Fowler has argued, it was only then that Keating 'could have imagined such a strident republican statement'.[21]

Keating's *Men of the West* and Sheppard's *Cuchulainn* visibly indicate that comradeship and self-sacrifice for the nation were both firmly identified with masculinity. The role of women in the Easter Rising was largely undervalued for many years, until the work of feminist historians from the end of the 1970s onwards.[22] The main organization that took part, Cumann na mBan (the Women's Brigade), was founded in 1914 initially to provide support for the male Irish Volunteers through fundraising and first-aid training; some branches (notably in Belfast) later began to include rifle training.[23] In Dublin, the women preparing for action included both the poet Kathleen Goodfellow and her friend the painter Estella Solomons, who came from a prominent middle-class Dublin Jewish family. The 60 women of Cumann na mBan who actually took part in the Rising were confined to more conventionally feminine but equally vital roles as couriers, cooks and nurses; they were joined also by a small number of women in the Citizen Army under the leadership of Countess Markiewicz and Connolly. However, the crucial involvement of the majority of these women has largely been marginalized in relation to the prominent figure of Markiewicz.

Constance Markiewicz was born in 1868 into a long-established Anglo-Irish family, the Gore-Booths, whose home was at Lissadell in Sligo. Through her background as a liberal within Ireland's ruling elite she also had strong links with the Literary Revival. Markiewicz met her husband, an impoverished Polish

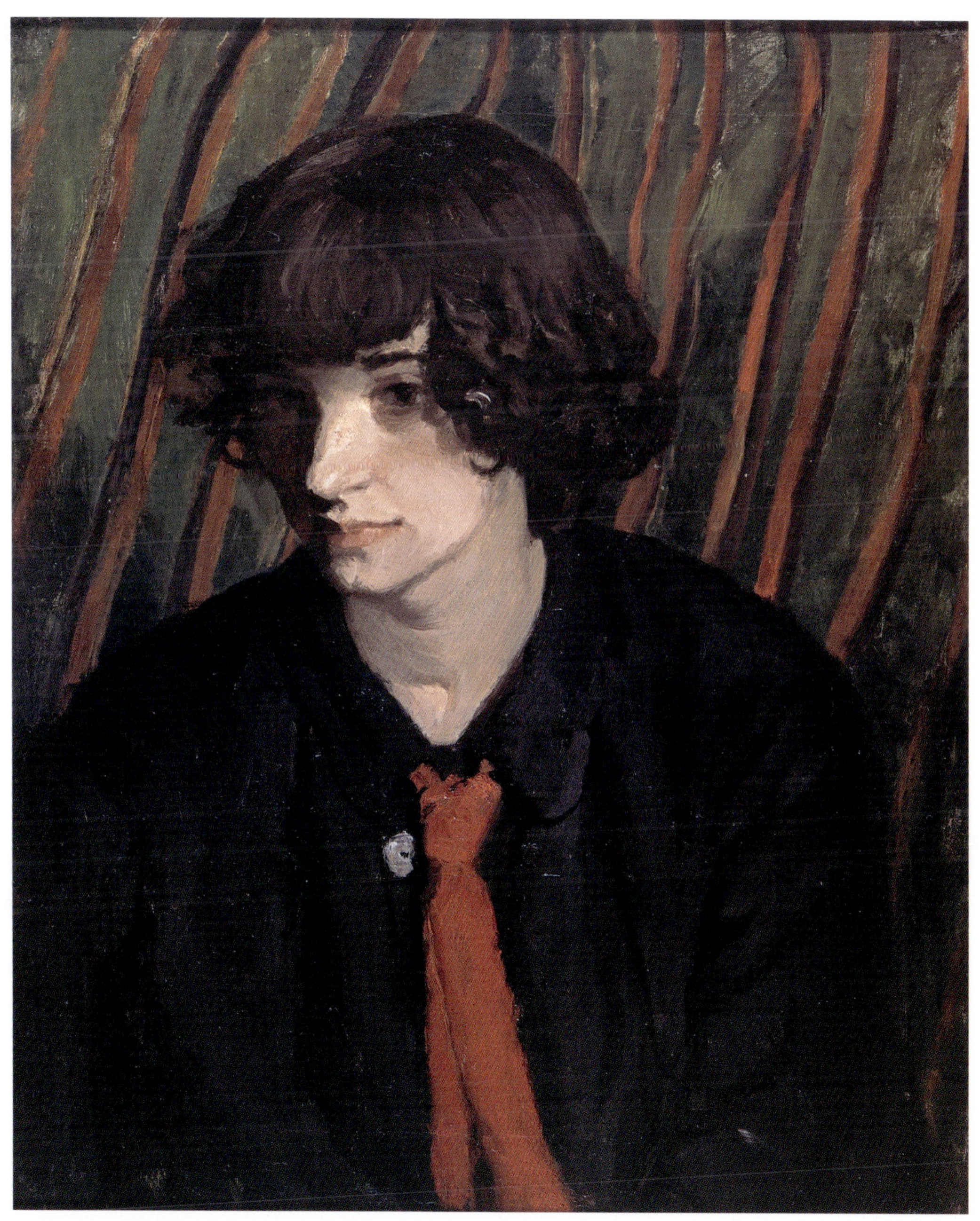

22 Estella Solomons, *Woman in a Red Tie*, n.d., oil on canvas.

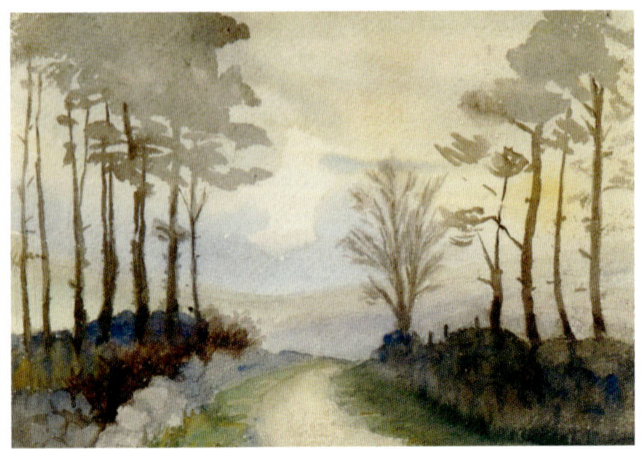

23 Constance Markiewicz, *Wooded Laneway at Dusk*, n.d., watercolour.

aristocrat, in Paris, where, following a period at the Slade, she had been studying at the Académie Julian from 1893 onwards. In the early years of the twentieth century Constance Markiewicz painted the usual range of portraits, landscapes and genre scenes prevalent in Dublin. Until 1908, she and her husband were both part of the Dublin art scene focused around the relatively bohemian United Arts Club, which they founded jointly with Ellen Duncan in 1907. They also frequented more conservative Anglo-Irish social circles around Dublin Castle, the seat of British administration. The increasing radicalism of Markiewicz's politics made such conventional allegiances unsustainable as she became involved in Sinn Féin and the Inghinidhe na hÉireann (Daughters of Ireland) founded by Maud Gonne. Her commitment to painting also became supplanted by training the Fianna in preparation for revolution; in 1916, many took an active part in the Rising. Constance Markiewicz's surrender to the British forces at the College of Surgeons after the Rising's disintegration became the subject of a painting by Kathleen Fox, who accidentally witnessed the event. She recognized Markiewicz from her attendance at

Dublin's Metropolitan School of Art and made some thumbnail sketches on the spot. As Fox later worked these up into a finished painting she began to learn more about the Rising; the finished work includes her self-portrait whose eye contact with spectators, according to Sighle Bhreathnach-Lynch, 'invites their participation in this historic event'.[24] Like many others, Kathleen Fox became radicalized by the executions of the Rising's leaders; her painting *The Arrest of Countess Markiewicz* was finally completed in secret and sent to New York to avoid confiscation by British authorities.

The Rising and its consequences also profoundly affected another artist, the cartoonist Grace Gifford. Originally from a strongly Unionist middle-class Dublin family, both Grace and two of her sisters became politically involved with the nationalist cause to a greater or lesser degree. Although Gifford was not politically active herself at this point, her sister Muriel was married to Thomas MacDonagh, while another sister, Nellie, was a member of the Citizen Army contingent at St Stephen's Green.[25] Grace Gifford married Joseph Plunkett in Kilmainham Gaol the night before his execution on 4 May; some weeks later she suffered a miscarriage.[26] This double trauma was compounded by the death by drowning of her sister Muriel the following year. Prior to the Rising, Grace Gifford's work had tended to satirize gently figures from Dublin's cultural life such as George Moore. In her publication of 1919, however, *To Hold as Twere*, these were augmented by more politically astute cartoons of de Valera as a shamrock-spangled tightrope performer, or Sir Edward Carson manicuring his nails while 'about to rebel'.[27] Significantly, this collection was published under her married name, Mrs Joseph Plunkett.

Both the Easter Rising and the First World War had brought about profound changes in the lives of the

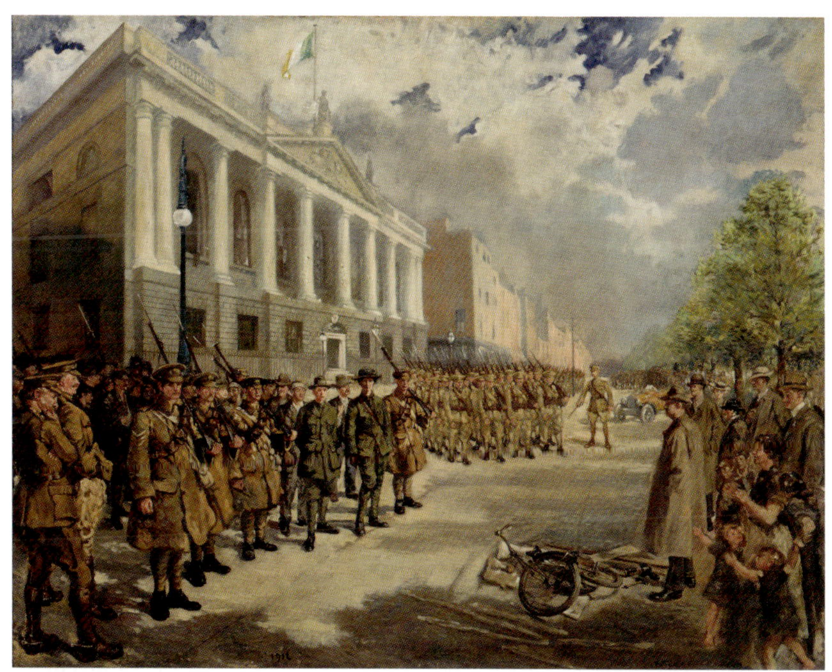

24 Kathleen Fox, *The Arrest of Countess Markiewicz*, 1916, oil on canvas.

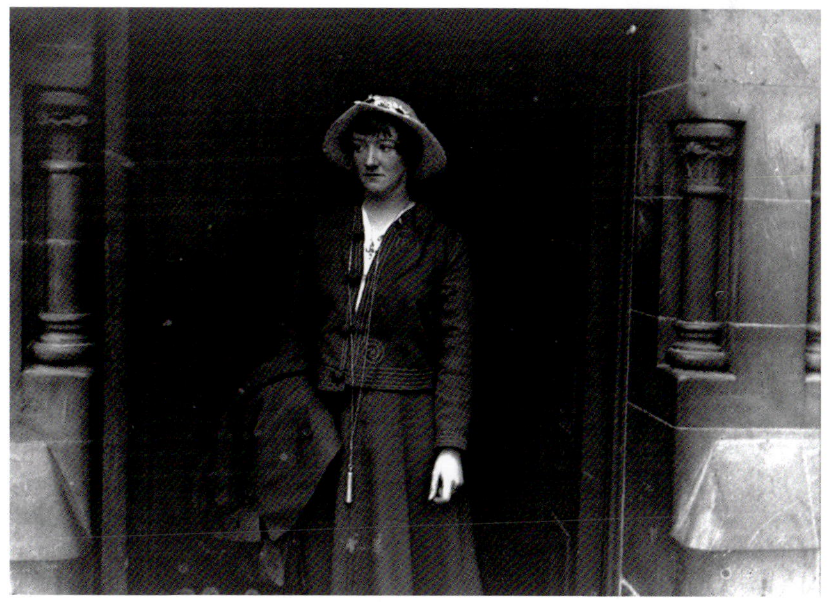

25 Joseph Cashman, *Grace Gifford at Kilmainham Gaol*, 1916, photograph.

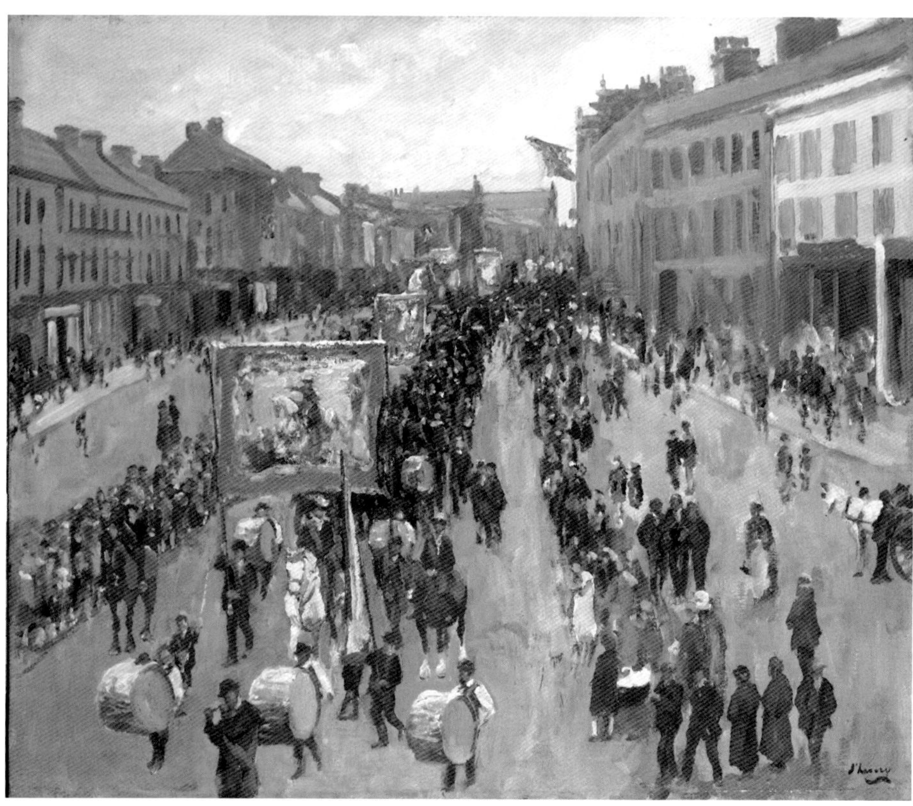

29 John Lavery,
*The Twelfth of July
in Portadown*, 1928,
oil on board.

a further factor into Lavery's sometimes complex set of allegiances and relationships.[9]

Lavery was unwilling to publicly identify himself with political or religious opinions. Yet his autobiography, *The Life of a Painter*, indicates a shift in his position when he became aware of the reports of British brutality during the War of Independence: 'and the Black and Tans were given carte blanche to do their damnedest – which they did – the desire to fight stirred in my blood for the very first time'.[10] In this published account, however, any sense of partisanship is quickly suppressed in favour of the studied impartiality that enabled the cultivation of his aristocratic clientele, and the suggestion that he 'might be some use in making [his] studio neutral ground where both sides might meet'.[11]

Lavery painted portraits of key figures on both sides of the debate around Irish independence, including two of Edward Carson (1916, 1921) and one of Éamon de Valera (1921). In 1928 the painter who began life as a working-class Belfast Catholic also painted *The Twelfth of July in Portadown*, depicting the annual celebration by loyalists commemorating the victory in 1690 of King William of Orange over the Catholic King James, a key event in securing Protestant hegemony within the British state. In 1921 attempts at impartiality were swayed by John and Hazel Lavery's friendship with Michael Collins, who was a frequent visitor to their house during the Treaty negotiations, where he also sat for a portrait. There is also strong evidence to suggest that Collins and Hazel Lavery had an affair at this time;

after his death, letters from her and a piece of her jewellery were found on his body.[12]

Another painter continued to have an even more direct engagement with the republican struggle. During the War of Independence, Estella Solomons sheltered republicans in her studio at 26 Great Brunswick Street in Dublin, where she had moved from premises further down the street in 1918. The description of her earlier studio by her future husband, the writer Seumas O'Sullivan (James Starkey), suggests, without any apparent irony, a particular combination of continuing political commitment and the expectations of middle-class ladies of this time. The studio was

> not only a centre of artistic activity and goodly conversation, but it was also a centre of quiet, of calm; a place of refuge for many whose political and national activities had brought them a very undesirable amount of notice in 'the bad times'. Here many a man, whose name was later to be inscribed on Ireland's Roll of Honour, has enjoyed a respite over a cup of tea and those delectable dishes which the ever generous hostess seemed to be able to concoct at a moment's notice.[13]

Yet Solomons also painted portraits of the fighters who took refuge in her studio; many had to be destroyed as the identity of her sitters and whereabouts could have been revealed. One that has survived is *On Parole*, a depiction of a man in unremarkable clothes against a background so blank that clues to identity or location are difficult to pin down.[14] The effects of the ongoing political situation also permeated the lives of other artists who were differently positioned through allegiances of class or family. A former fellow student of Orpen who remained a friend of Solomons was the painter Beatrice Elvery who, after her marriage to Gordon Campbell in 1912, adopted

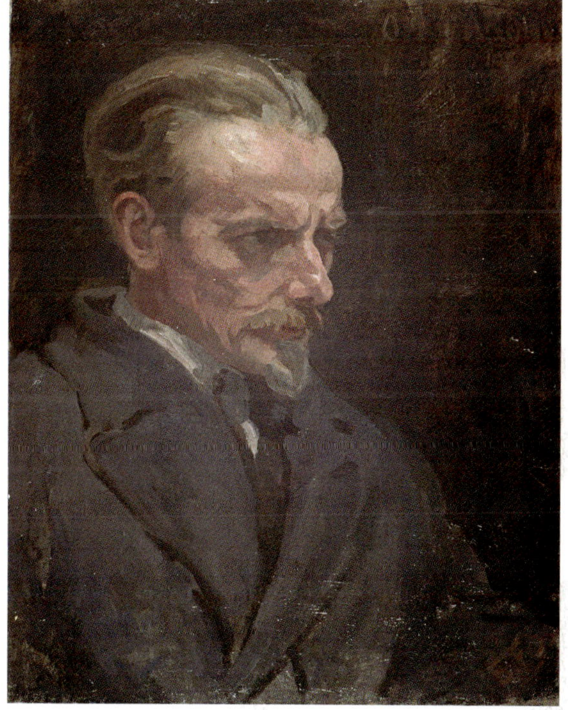

30 Estella Solomons, *On Parole*, 1920, oil on canvas.

his hereditary title and became Beatrice Glenavy. Her husband was regarded as a target during the Civil War and republicans burned the family out of their house in 1922.[15] Another of Solomons's peers, the painter Mary Swanzy, left Ireland after the killing of her cousin, District Inspector Oswald Swanzy, in Lisburn, August 1920. This was a particularly audacious assassination by one of Michael Collins's undercover teams in revenge for Swanzy's probable involvement in the killing of Tomás Mac Curtáin some months earlier. Following a visit to Yugoslavia and Czechoslovakia in 1922 or 1923, the independently wealthy Mary Swanzy embarked on a journey around the Pacific, visiting Hawaii, Samoa and New Zealand, before spending some time in California. Significantly, she spent little time in Ireland after this, settling permanently in 1926 in South London at Blackheath.[16]

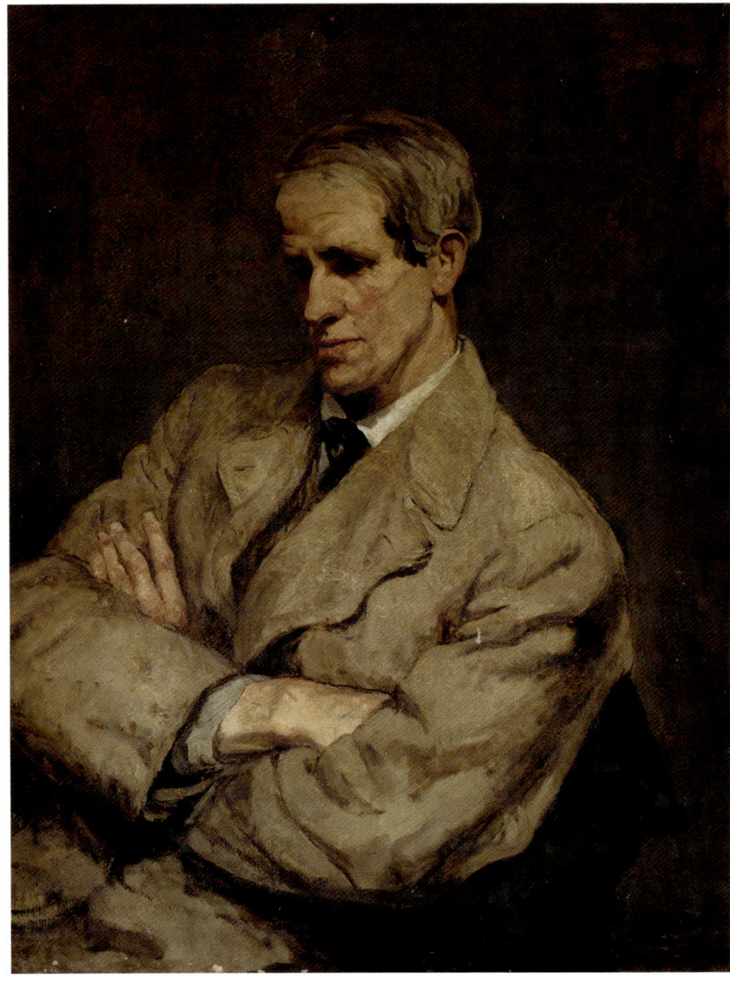

31 Estella Solomons,
Jack Yeats, 1922, oil on
canvas.

By 1920, the predominance of western subjects in the work of Jack Yeats had already begun to shift. Something also seems to have happened to Yeats's concern with memory in this process. The Edenic nostalgia of early works such as *Memory Harbour* (1900) has crystallized into an awareness of subjectivity – in this case that of the new nation – as emerging through profound loss. The melancholia permeating the Symbolist format of the painting *In Memoriam: Bachelor's Walk* (1915) may well have been a product of the severe depression from which Yeats was suffering at this time, but it is transposed from a subjective state onto an actual historical event. The almost spectral presence of the pencil sketch *The Lying in State of O'Donovan Rossa*, dating from the same year, depicts the funeral of the nineteenth-century Fenian, who had been exiled to the United States, where he died in 1915. His body was then returned to Dublin to lie in state at the City Hall before burial. Yeats attended the City Hall and subsequently drew the scene from memory; the

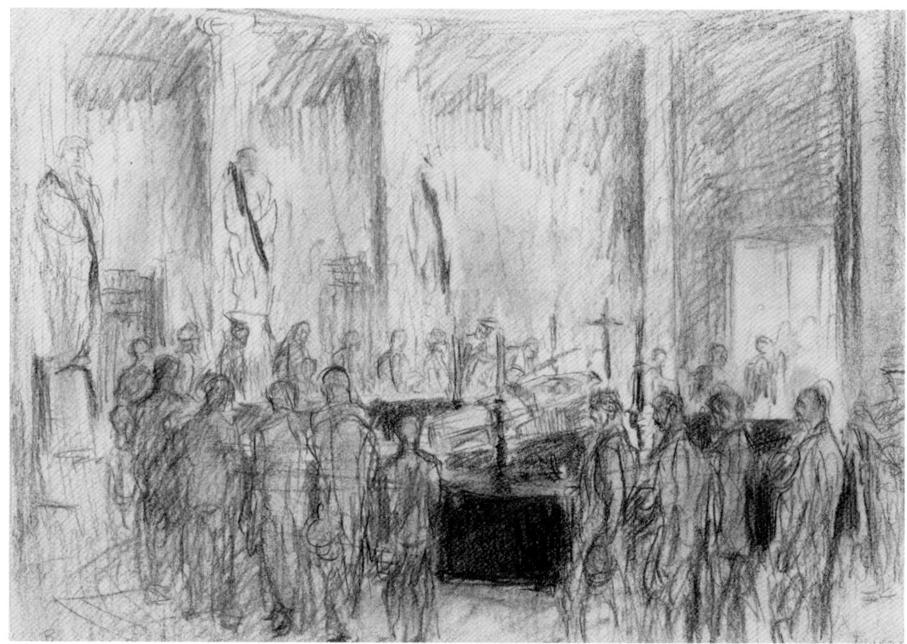

32 Jack Yeats,
*The Lying in State of
O'Donovan Rossa*, 1915,
graphite on paper.

procession filing past the casket suggests a sense of collective mourning that is the public counterpart to the private act of commemoration of *In Memoriam: Bachelor's Walk*, which was painted in memory of the events arising from the authorities' interception of the guns landed at Howth in 1915.

By the early 1920s Yeats's painting technique was beginning to move away from the flatness and heavy outlines derived from his early work in watercolour, and which he was still using in *On Drumcliffe Strand* (1918). A more fluid handling of paint and emphasis on the expressive associations of colour permeates the composition of *The Funeral of Harry Boland*. Viewers are invited to participate in a public grief and loss shared with the IRA members standing at the grave and, a little further back, the women of Cumann na mBan bearing wreaths. Boland, a former close associate of Collins, was strongly opposed to the Treaty; in July 1922 he died from wounds received when he was arrested leaving the Grand Hotel in Skerries, a small seaside town north of Dublin. Unlike the elevated, distant spectacle of Lavery's depiction of Collins's funeral in the Pro-Cathedral, there is a sense that the viewer, like Yeats, is a part of the crowd of mourners bearing witness to a significant historical event. There is a further comparison. In the omission of any clear references to the rituals of Catholicism, Boland's funeral is not only commemorated here as a secular occurrence, but his opposition to the Treaty meant also that his death, unlike that of Collins in Lavery's posthumous depictions, could not be sublimated into martyrdom for the new Catholic state.

For one commentator, IRA member later turned art critic Earnán (Ernie) O'Malley, Yeats's depiction of 'the funeral of a man who has suffered in the national fight' possessed an 'impressive ordered intensity' that was evidence of the painter's 'understanding and devotion'.[17] Yeats's own sympathies with the republican cause had

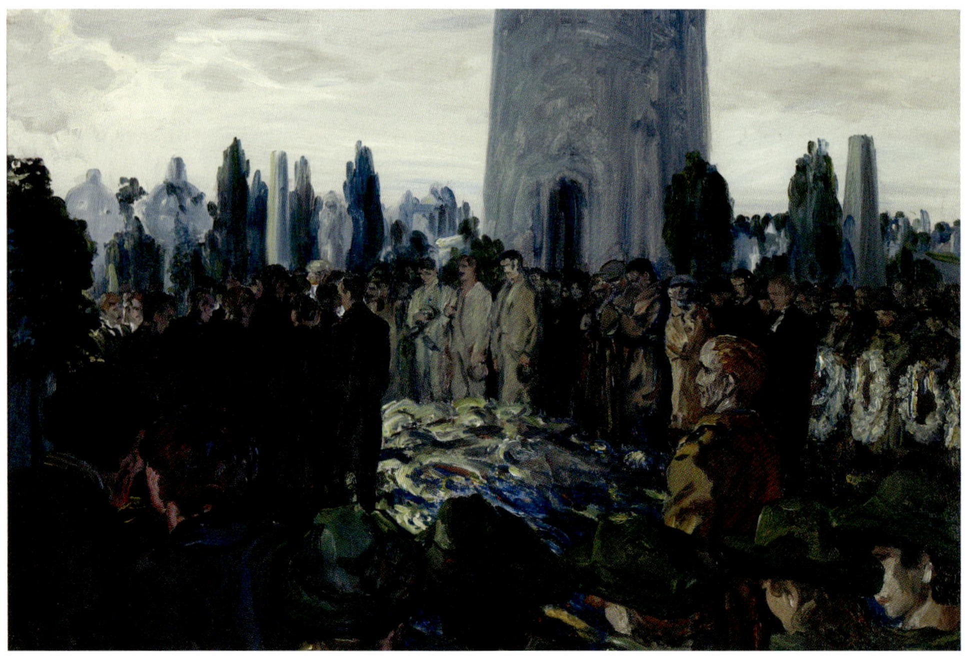

33 Jack Yeats, *The Funeral of Harry Boland*, 1923, oil on canvas.

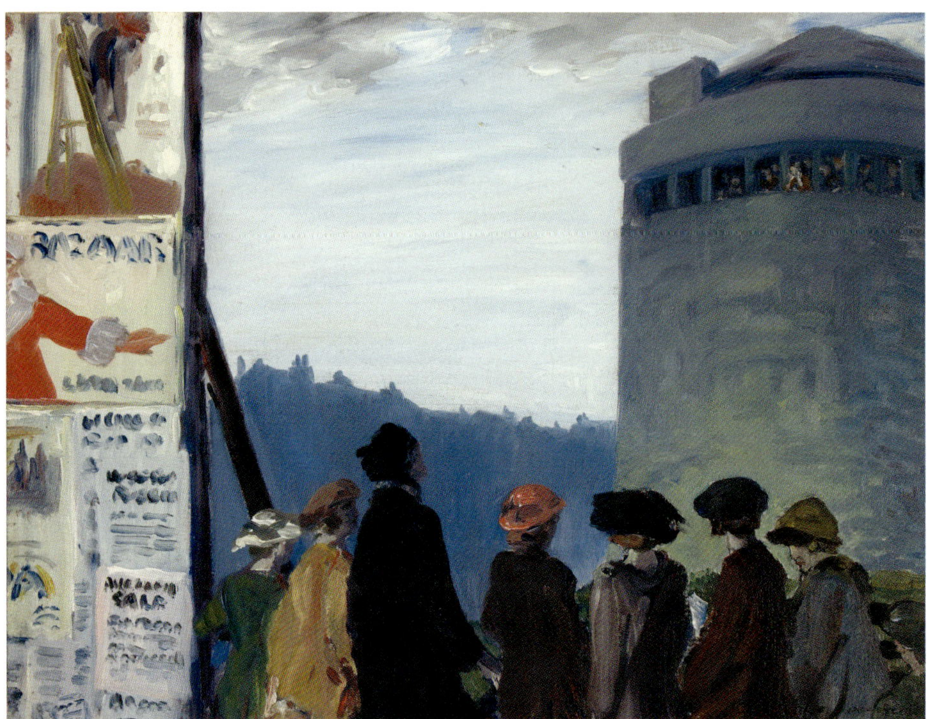

34 Jack Yeats, *Communicating with Prisoners*, 1924, oil on canvas.

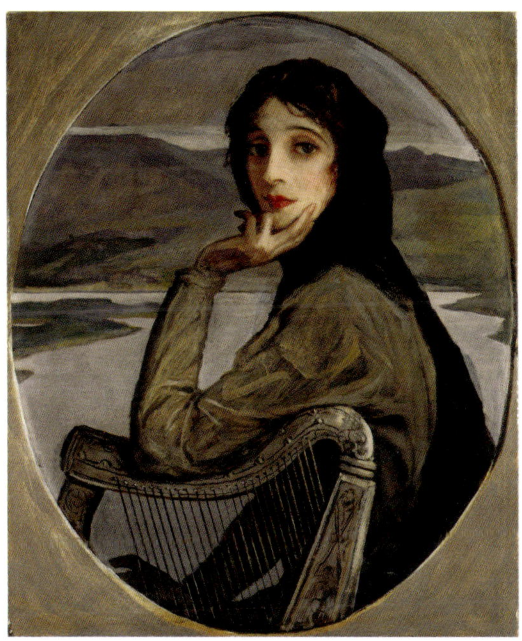

35 John Lavery, *Lady Lavery as Kathleen ní Houlihan*, 1928, oil on canvas.

begun to emerge from about 1914 onwards, when he heard Patrick Pearse speak at political meetings, and became steadily more pronounced over subsequent years.[18] In 1920, he decided to close his Dublin exhibition as a contribution to the national strike in protest at the British authorities' refusal to recognize political prisoners. The issue of prisoners also emerges in a painting from 1924 that refers to recent events during the Civil War. At this time Treaty forces imprisoned numerous republicans, and many of them were summarily executed. Many women from Cumann na mBan who had strongly opposed the Treaty were imprisoned in Kilmainham Gaol, where Grace Plunkett was also held. Conditions in Kilmainham and Mountjoy Gaol – which also held many republican women – were notoriously bad; on at least one occasion women prisoners were beaten severely when resisting a transfer to another prison. Yeats's painting *Communicating with Prisoners* (1924) depicts a scene outside Kilmainham, where a group of women are holding a shouted conversation

with the female prisoners pressed against their cell windows; one prisoner appears to have broken the glass so that she can lean out further. The immense gap between the punitive conditions within the prison and more recognizable lives of women outside is emphasized by the poster hoarding advertising fashions and sales.[19]

Women also had political aspirations within the new state. However, as Mary E. Daly has indicated, the relatively small number of women elected to the Dáil were related to 'dead nationalist heroes', while increasingly legislation was enacted that undermined women's rights through the banning of divorce and contraception and restricted their opportunities for employment.[20] Yet the large-scale disappearance of women from public life was, in one area at least, masked by an increased visibility of female symbolism. In 1927 Lavery, whose work was becoming increasingly popular on both sides of the border, was asked for a design for the Free State's new banknotes. Unsurprisingly, this was to be based on yet another depiction of his wife, *Lady Lavery as Kathleen ní Houlihan*. Here she becomes identified with one of the key figures of Irish nationalist tradition, celebrated in W. B. Yeats's and Lady Gregory's one-act play *Cathleen ni Houlihan*, written in 1902. In this version Cathleen is a symbolic female presence who becomes the catalyst for rebellion and sacrifice as she incites young men to join the nationalist cause to reclaim the 'four green fields' of Ireland's stolen provinces. The female personification of Ireland is deeply embedded within the history of nationalist struggles, allied not just to the mythical figure of Cathleen ni Houlihan but to the image of the suffering Virgin, an important symbol for the Catholic peasantry under British rule.[21] In Lavery's depiction the religious identifications of Mother Ireland as the Madonna are absent, with what Kenneth McConkey has termed Hazel Lavery's 'dark eyes and wistful looks' incorporated within the increasingly popular trope of the Irish peasant woman, closely identified with the land itself.[22] The potency of this symbolic image of the nation is evidenced through its continued use by the Bank of Ireland until 1975, yet in spite of the banknote's symbolism of the financial autonomy of the nation, the economic situation of the majority of actual Irish women was far from similarly independent for much of this period.

Struggling for modernity in the 1920s

In Jack Yeats's *Communicating with Prisoners* the peeling posters suggest the identification of consumerism as part of the spectacle of the modern city. They emphasize the contemporaneity of what we are looking at: this event takes place in the capital of the new modern Irish state, whose emergence has been brought about through such traumatic struggle. Yeats's interest in a kind of Baudelairean modernity during the early 1920s also manifested itself in paintings of aspects of Dublin life, many of which, such as the depiction of the annual *Liffey Swim* (1923) or *In the Tram*, stress a sense of community, of social reconstruction after the Civil War. Like the Baudelairean artist in Haussmann's Paris, the painter takes on the role of the *flâneur* who wanders the streets of a city remade after war or revolution. In spite of the similarities in the Expressionist treatment of subject-matter, this emphasis on community distinguishes Yeats's depictions of modern Dublin from other earlier European avant-garde practices, such as the depictions of the city as a site of alienation in the work of the German artists of the Brücke group, and goes beyond the more frequent painterly comparisons with Kokoschka, whose loose brushwork Yeats's work was beginning to resemble.[23] There are also comparisons that can be made with another virtually contemporaneous set of representations of Dublin as

a modern city – those of Joyce's *Ulysses*, in which Leopold Bloom is only one of many *flâneurs*. Yet *Ulysses*, although written between 1914 and 21, the most important years of the anti-colonial struggle, reconstructs a city on one day in 1904.[24] It is also a book whose specificities of place were reconstructed in exile, as a defence against forgetting: Yeats's observations of Dublin, by comparison, were first-hand.

Yeats's interest in subjects and techniques also found in European avant-garde practices makes the distinctions with other attempts at contemporaneity elsewhere in Ireland more acute. In Belfast in the early 1920s, William Conor was producing sentimentalized depictions of working-class life such as *The Street Dance*. Conor (originally 'Connor') was a working-class Protestant who had Gaelicized his name in response to his encounter with the Celtic Revival in Belfast at the start of the century.[25] In the 1890s he had undertaken the only form of art education then available in Belfast, training at the Government School of Design and subsequently working as a lithographer for a stationery firm. After periods in both Paris and London he settled permanently in Belfast in 1921, where he continued for the rest of his career to depict scenes of contemporary working-class life through a form of academic realism. In the early 1920s, however, working-class life in Belfast was riven by the sectarian conflict that accompanied Partition. Increased IRA activity in the North during the Truce with the British had been answered by brutal reprisals against Catholics, especially in Belfast. Sectarian conflict was reinforced by the expulsion of Catholic workers from the shipyards, the mainstay of the city's economy. In the two years prior to July 1922, 257 Catholic and 157 Protestant civilians were killed in Belfast, while a quarter of the city's Catholics lost their jobs and 23,000 lost their homes.[26] None of this is visible in Conor's *The Street Dance* or

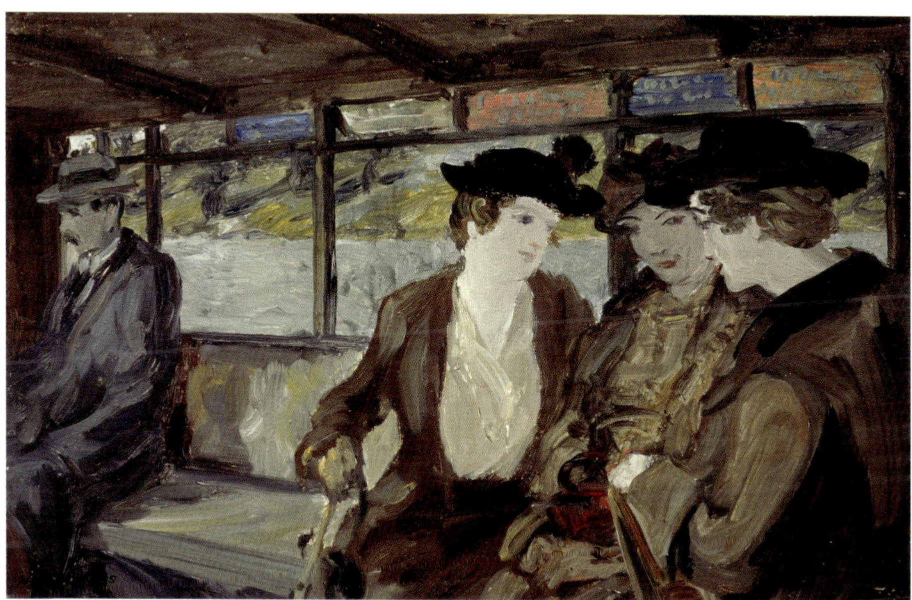

36 Jack Yeats, *In the Tram*, 1923, oil on board.

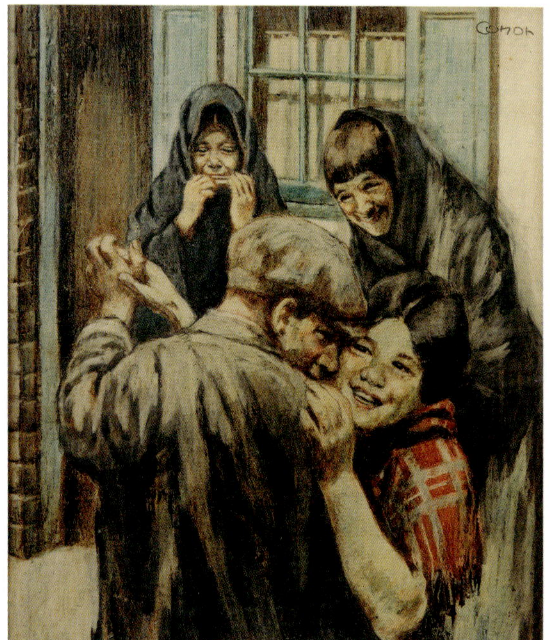

37 William Conor, *The Street Dance*, n.d., coloured chalk.

other works, and indeed the acknowledgement of conflict would have had little appeal to the conservative clientele on which he was dependent.

Yet an engagement with modernity was only one aspect of the representation of the new Free State. As I suggested in discussing *Lady Lavery as Kathleen ní Houlihan*, a strong current of archaism and fetishization of the peasantry was also a major tendency of representation in Ireland during the 1920s. It should be emphasized that two contradictory forms of cultural engagement with the newly independent Ireland were beginning to emerge at this point; on the one hand an interest in processes of modernization and modernism, and on the other a primitivist fascination with archaic modes of production and ways of life. A similar contradiction existed at the end of the nineteenth century, between the aims of the Cultural Revival to preserve the remnants of what was perceived as a dying culture, and attempts to modernize agrarian practice through the introduction of mechanization.[27] However, in the 1920s these opposing forces were embedded in the social, economic and cultural conditions of the new state. The predominant conservatism of a mainly agrarian, Catholic society was reinforced by the stagnant economic conditions of the early years of the Free State, with major economic problems caused by Partition and the Civil War. Ireland's main heavy industry, for example, was in Belfast, now part of a different country. The Catholic middle classes, who were the newly powerful grouping in the early Free State, were both nationalist and culturally conservative; they provided the clientele for a plethora of representations of the archaic West, whose hardworking, Gaelic-speaking peasantry were seen as the antithesis to British rule. This was the legacy of the visual typologies put into currency by the early work of Jack Yeats and Paul Henry. Although Yeats had moved on considerably by the 1920s, these conservative tropes of Irishness continued to be perpetuated by the work of Henry and other artists such as Charles Lamb and Patrick Tuohy, who had fought in the GPO in 1916.

The pressing issues of modernity and modernization affected the new state in a range of different ways. State-funded initiatives such as the Agricultural Credit Corporation and the Electricity Supply Board (ESB) were intended to revitalize the country's economic infrastructure, while in cultural terms the engagement with modernity could take wildly different forms. In addition to Yeats's urban subject-matter of the early 1920s, these include Seán Keating's depictions of the ESB's ambitious scheme to dam the River Shannon to provide electrification for much of Ireland. They also include the encounters with European modernist painting by Anglo-Irish women artists, which were to play such a crucial role in the development of artistic identity in the Free State for years to come.

An appeal to the interests and fantasies of the Catholic middle classes, or indeed the associations of imagery of 'the West' with pre-revolutionary cultural nationalism, are not the only explanations for the popularity of paintings of the region. The philosopher Étienne Balibar has drawn attention to the role of representation – or 'fabrication' – in the construction of a 'fictive ethnicity', whereby

> as social formations are nationalized, the populations included within them . . . are ethnicized – that is, represented in the past or in the future as if they formed a natural community, possessing of itself an identity of origins, culture and interests which transcends individuals and social conditions.[28]

This idea helps to explain the role of visual imagery in the construction of identities for the citizens of the new Irish nation, whereby the effects of historical processes, as Balibar indicates, are naturalized in such a way as to actually appear outside history. The proliferation of imagery of the west of Ireland during the highly conservative pro-Treaty Cumann na nGaedheal government of the 1920s, I would suggest, was one of the ideological means that helped to create a distance from the hugely traumatic experience of the War of Independence and Civil War, by proposing instead a timeless zone of stoic peasants in harmony with nature.

The trope of heroic westerner in harmony with the rugged native landscape that characterized Charles Lamb's work was formulated while he was still a student at the Metropolitan School of Art in 1920. *Dancing at a Northern Crossroads* (1920) shows the influence of his teachers Keating and Tuohy, both of them former students of Orpen, whose depictions of western subjects Lamb admired.[29] Lamb, who was originally from Portadown, first travelled to Carraroe on the west coast of Galway in 1919, where he was deeply impressed by the sense of tranquillity in contrast to 'the dark northern provincial town' of his birth.[30] The painting, which

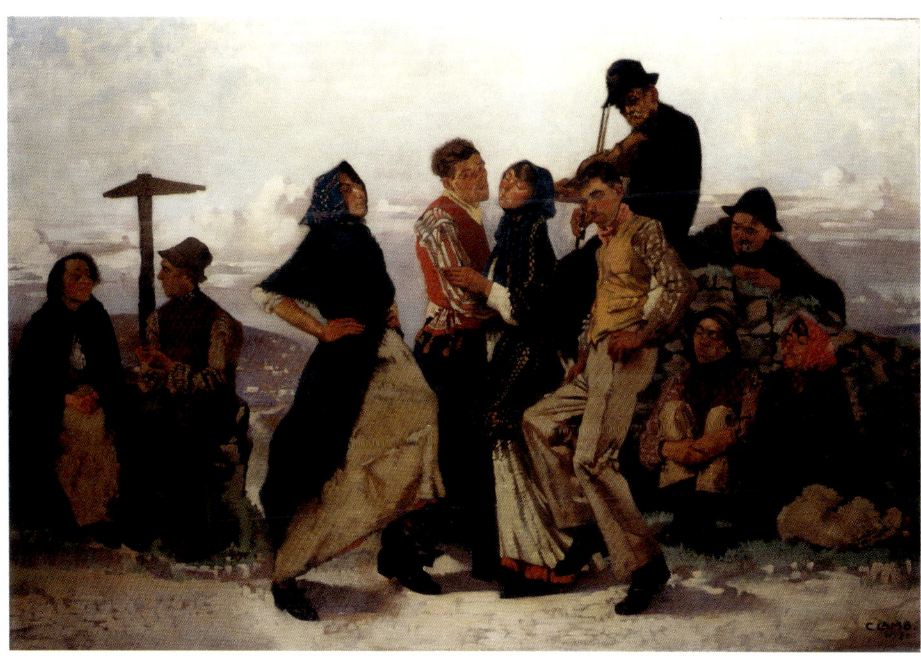

38 Charles Lamb, *Dancing at a Northern Crossroads*, 1920, oil on canvas.

was exhibited at the RHA in 1921 with a price tag of £300, depicts an outdoor scene of a group of peasants dancing to the sound of a lone fiddler while others watch. Although the inclusion of 'Northern' within the title might indicate a different location, the barren landscape is recognizably that of Connemara; another overlapping of North and West occurs in the costume of the man in the red waistcoat. As Marie Bourke has pointed out, this was more typical of Northern costume at the time, as is apparent in another painting by Lamb from the same year, *Lough Neagh Fisherman*.[31] Significantly, although Lamb worked on *Dancing at a Northern Crossroads* during the worst year of the War of Independence, none of its conflict disturbs the rhythmic harmony of the dancing peasants.

Lamb's views of the Atlantic seaboard became increasingly popular both in Ireland and abroad with a growing Irish-American audience addressed through exhibitions in Boston in 1928, and New York in 1929 and 1930. Paul Henry's work was also becoming increasingly well known outside Ireland. In 1925 his painting *Connemara*, an iconic blend of mountain, cumulus and cottage, was used as a poster by the London Midland and Scottish Railway (LMS) to promote holidays in Ireland. The geographical area of Connemara itself thus acquired a further layer of meaning, as the embodiment of 'Ireland' in the tourist imagination. In August 1925 the *Irish Times* claimed that

if thousands of people in Great Britain and America have been led this summer to think over the claims of Ireland as holiday ground, it is largely through the lure of Mr Paul Henry's glowing landscape of a Connemara scene.[32]

Paintings such as Lamb's *A Quaint Couple* continued to perpetuate the existing typology for at least another decade.

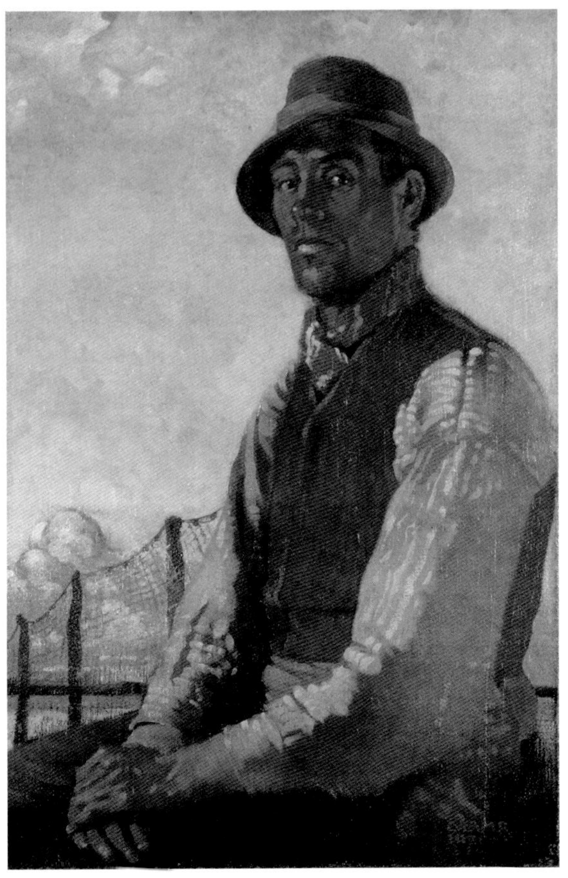

39 Charles Lamb, *Lough Neagh Fisherman*, 1920, oil on canvas.

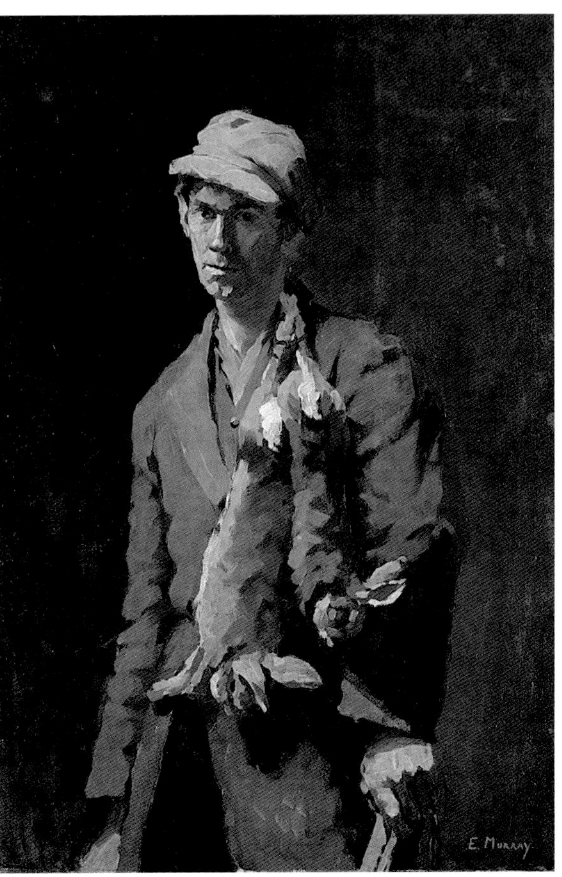

40 Eileen Murray, *This or Emigration*, 1926, oil on canvas.

There was, however, also a degree of resistance to these representations. Compared with Lamb's painting, the two ageing figures of Michael Power O'Malley's *Himself and Herself* convey a sense of the profound isolation and loneliness that actually characterized the remote rural communities of the West. Since the Famine, many of these areas were increasingly depopulated by emigration; many families owed their economic existence to the money sent home by sons and daughters in Britain or the United States. The threat of an uncertain future is also present in Eileen Murray's *This or Emigration*, which emphasizes the effects of rural poverty. The western

seaboard, meanwhile, was not the only location for landscape painting during the 1920s. Although she produced paintings of the West, Estella Solomons also focused on identifiable locations around Dublin such as *The Lake at Marlay, Rathfarnham* (1928), or several views that included her husband such as *Seumas Reading by the Coast*, reminiscent of her teacher Orpen's coastal scenes such *as Howth Head, Looking towards Dublin across Dublin Bay* (1910). The political resonances of Solomons's previous work evaporated in the early Free State's cultural climate of conservative reconstruction, and at a time when women were disappearing from public life she

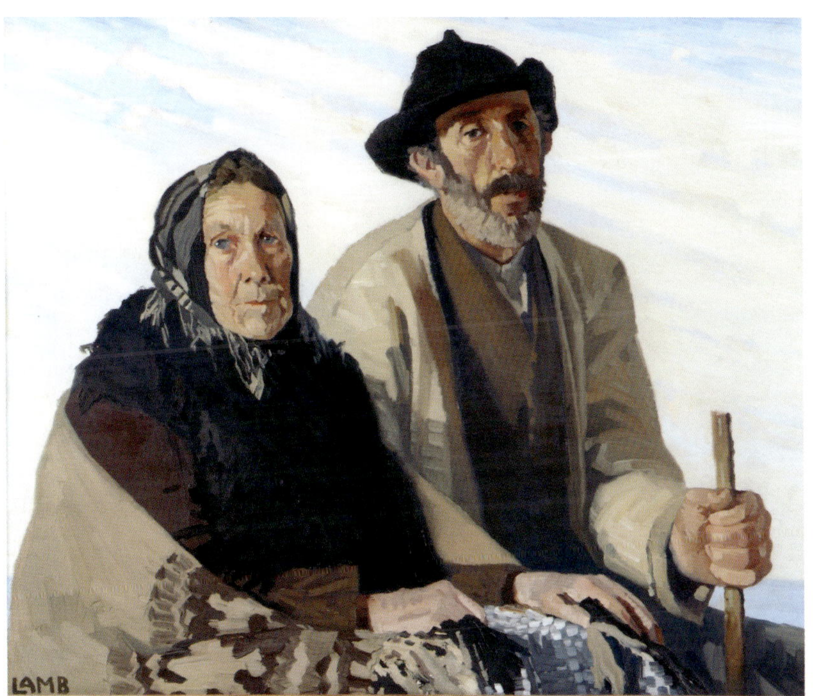

41 Charles Lamb, *A Quaint Couple*, 1930, oil on canvas.

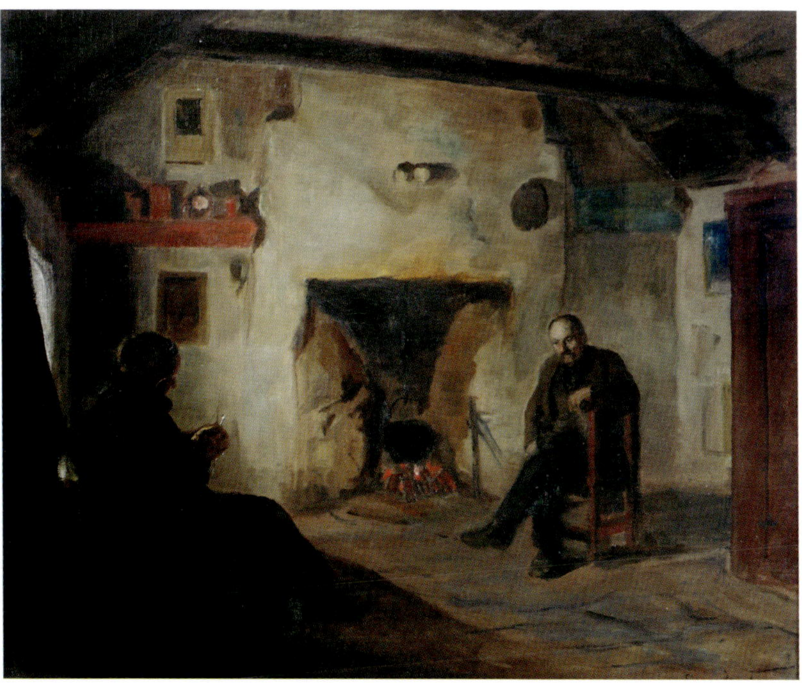

42 Michael Power O'Malley, *Himself and Herself*, c. 1930, oil on canvas.

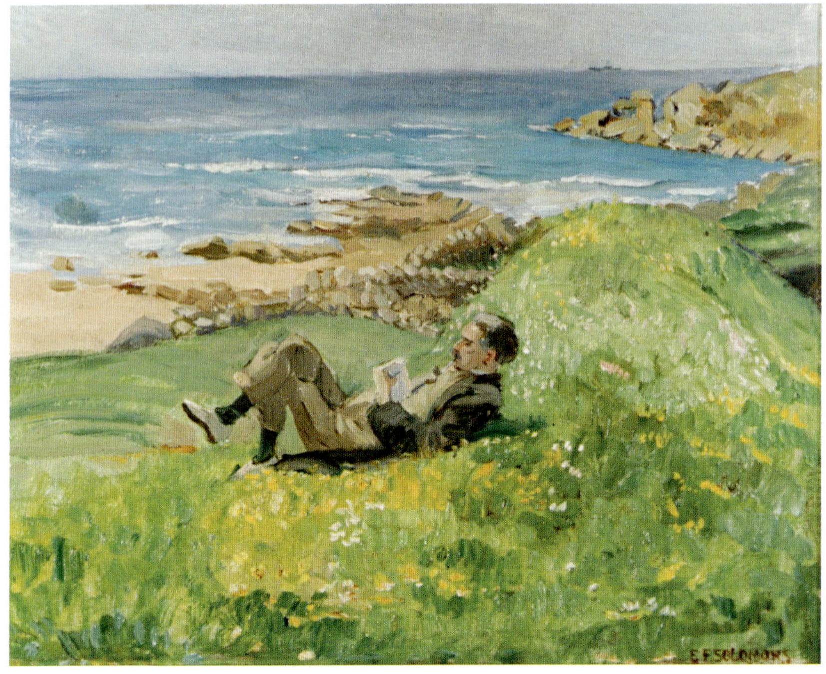

43 Estella Solomons,
Seumas Reading by the Coast,
n.d., oil on board.

faded into the establishment, exhibiting mainly at the RHA until her death in 1968.

In addition to the work of Paul and Grace Henry or Charles Lamb, in the 1920s landscape also became a focus for painters from Northern Ireland such as Frank McKelvey and James Humbert Craig. The emergence of a 'very distinct group' of Northern landscape artists was commented on by Thomas Bodkin in a review for the *Studio* in 1923, who also characterized their landscapes as 'always emotionally sincere, closely observed, firmly and clearly handled.'[33] Significantly, this group of artists were all Northern Protestants, whose ideas were formulated in a culture that valued industry, empiricism and rationality above metaphysical ideals. McKelvey's landscapes of the 1920s fall into that category, such as the direct observation of his paintings *On the River Bann* or *Evening, Ballycastle* (c. 1924). Like much of McKelvey's work throughout his career, these are reminiscent of a late nineteenth-century naturalist sensibility, associated in Ireland with the early landscapes of Walter Osborne. Humbert

Craig, meanwhile, worked mainly in the Glens of Antrim, although he also painted extensively in Connemara and, like McKelvey, in Donegal. In paintings such as *Figures Making Hay, Glendun, Cushendun,* he evolved a practice that relied closely on observation of meteorological changes and their effects on a landscape of dramatic hills and sea.

Although only 50 miles from Belfast, the Glens was an area that appeared remote and timeless to visitors. John Hewitt later characterized its appeal as 'a roughly modelled landscape inhabited by what seemed to the city folk a romantic race of fishermen and sheepfarmers of an older, more Gaelic culture than theirs'.[34] Similar to Bodkin's earlier review, S. B. Kennedy has claimed the work of this group of Northern painters as 'more concerned with the landscape itself and . . . not at all interested in socio-political interpretations of it'.[35] Yet whatever the intentions of painters, meanings are always constructed at least in part at the point of reception. Even McKelvey's bucolic studies of the Bann and Lagan valleys largely painted for a prosperous

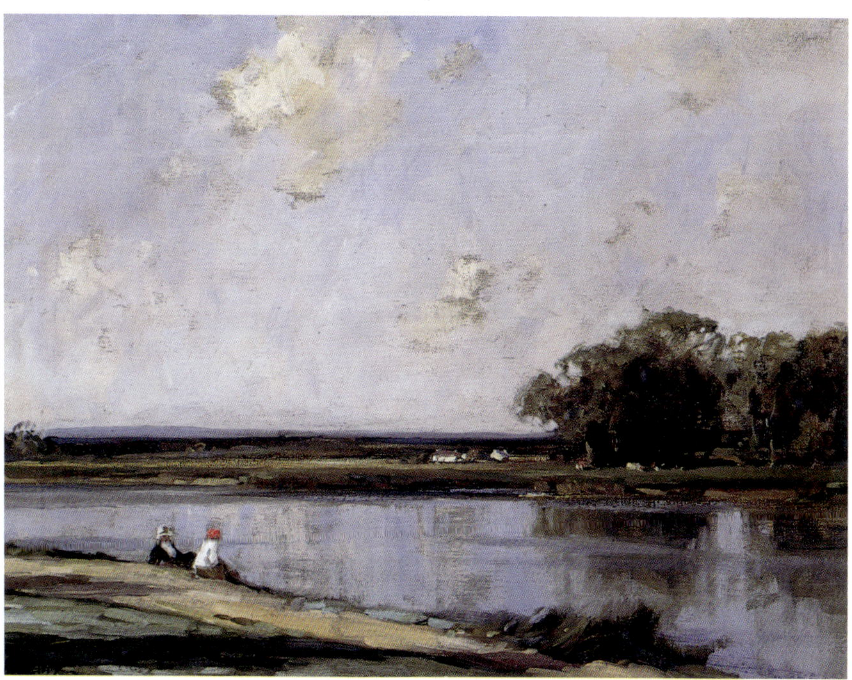

44 Frank McKelvey, *On the River Bann*, 1923, oil on canvas.

Northern Protestant clientele can be read as politically meaningful by the very absence of signifiers of territory or identity. The implicit message is that, in spite of the sectarian violence that continued throughout the decade in Northern rural areas as much as urban, this is a very different type of landscape, politically and geographically removed from the legacy of conflict elsewhere in Ireland as a whole.

It also appeared to be far removed from the pressing questions around modernity affecting the work of painters elsewhere in Ireland, including Seán Keating's depictions of the electrification of the Shannon. In 1925 the Irish government awarded the contract for the Shannon Scheme to a German engineering company, Siemens, a move not without controversy; any anglophile sympathies that emerged during debates in the Dáil were swiftly rejected.[36] Work began in August of that year and lasted until 1929, a massive undertaking that involved a series of dams and artificial waterways to be constructed along the Shannon above Limerick, with the main barrage and hydroelectric generating

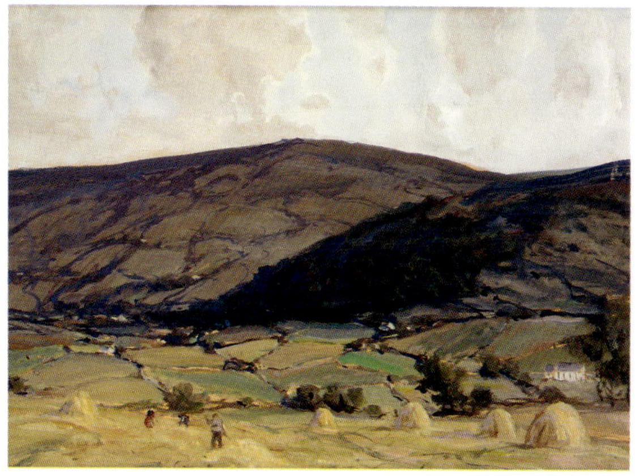

45 James Humbert Craig, *Figures Making Hay, Glendun, Cushendun*, 1920s, oil on board.

station located at Ardnacrusha.[37] The vast scale of the Shannon Scheme marked it out as central to the government's plans for the Free State's economic regeneration, and its vital status was further constituted by a public relations programme that included guided tours, press reports, film footage and the production of postcards. As Andy Bielenberg has noted, Keating's paintings should also be regarded as part of 'this effort to bring the scheme into the public sphere, and to promote it as the flagship of nation-building and economic modernization'.[38] Keating mainly worked on site at Ardnacrusha, painting and taking photographs. Bielenberg has also argued that, contrary to general belief, Keating was not actually commissioned by the ESB to produce the series of paintings and drawings. The Board subsequently acquired many of these works, such as *Wagon Train at Ardnacrusha* (n.d.), at some point in the early 1930s. The best known of the series, *Night's Candles Are Burnt Out*, was, however, purchased by Oldham Art Gallery in 1931.[39]

In its representation of the modernizing forces at work in the Free State, this painting needs to be compared to an earlier work by Keating, *An Allegory*, that relates more closely to the recent traumas of the Civil War. In the earlier painting nothing bridges the gap between the ruined 'Big House' – the country mansion of the Anglo-Irish landed class – in the background, a sign of the destruction of the old order, and the motifs of social disintegration in the foreground: the gunman and soldier digging a grave for a tricolour-covered coffin predominate over the passive, apathetic family, which, for the traditionalist Keating, was the basic social unit. In the marginal figures of businessman and priest, meanwhile, the forces of capitalism and religion have been sidelined. Three years later, Keating's vision had shifted considerably. *Night's Candles* (its title derived from Shakespeare's *Romeo and Juliet*) contains a similar

cast of figures, although the balance of power is different. In the centre of the composition a lone gunman bows obsequiously beneath the disdainful expression of a portly contractor – a triumph of reconstructive capitalism over the forces of revolution. And although the figure of the priest remains relatively marginal in the bottom right-hand corner, the opposite side of the canvas also contains a series of icons of outmoded Irishness – the alcoholic and idle labourers under the hanging skeleton. Yet the role of the family has undergone the most dramatic change. Far from the listless group of the earlier painting, they now perform a much more dynamic role that bridges the compositional gap between foreground and background seen in so many of Keating's paintings. Instead of the lacuna between past and present, present and future have become seamlessly joined through the actions of both mother and father pointing out the features of the large hydro-electric dam at Ardnacrusha to their two children. Keating's identification with this utopian view of modernity – not unlike the forms of Socialist Realism then currently emerging in the Soviet Union – was such that he included himself as the family's father, placing himself firmly on the side of the reconstructive conservatism that predominated in the Free State of the late 1920s. And as Fintan Cullen has argued, the representation of this young healthy family who are the inheritors of the Free State also helps to emphasize the vast distance from the deformed physiognomies of Irishness that prevailed in the nineteenth-century British press.[40]

Yet the continual difficulties and dangers of painting in the middle of a large building site means that the famous photograph of Seán Keating at Ardnacrusha, assertively posed before the easel in his wellingtons, was almost certainly staged.[41] This degree of artifice is the nearest that Keating ever got to an avant-garde

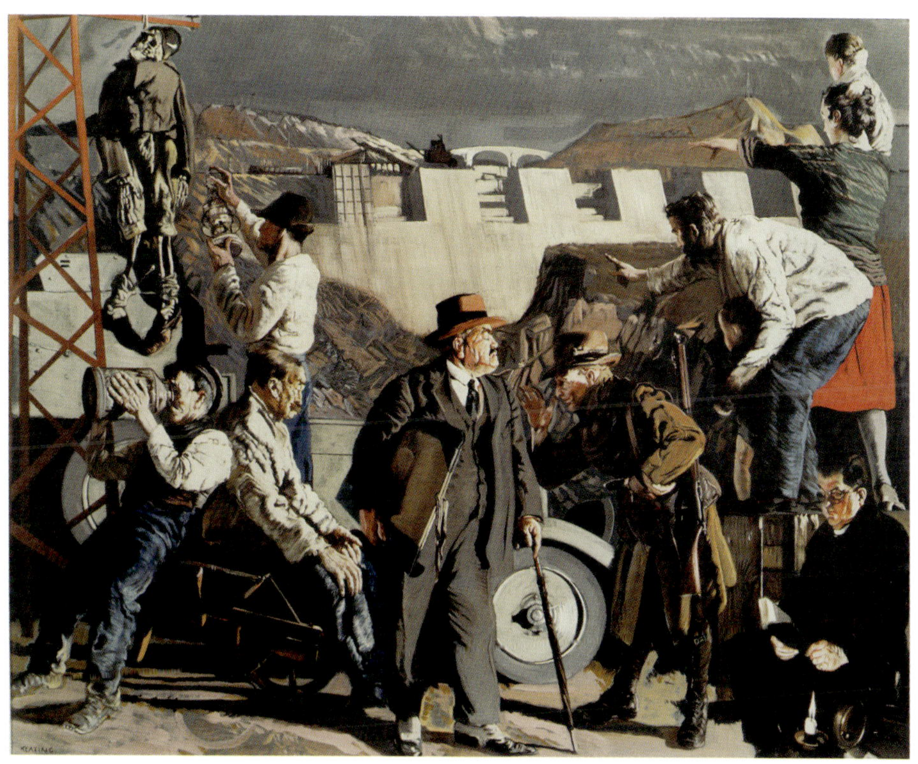

46 Seán Keating, *Night's Candles Are Burnt Out*, 1928–9, oil on canvas.

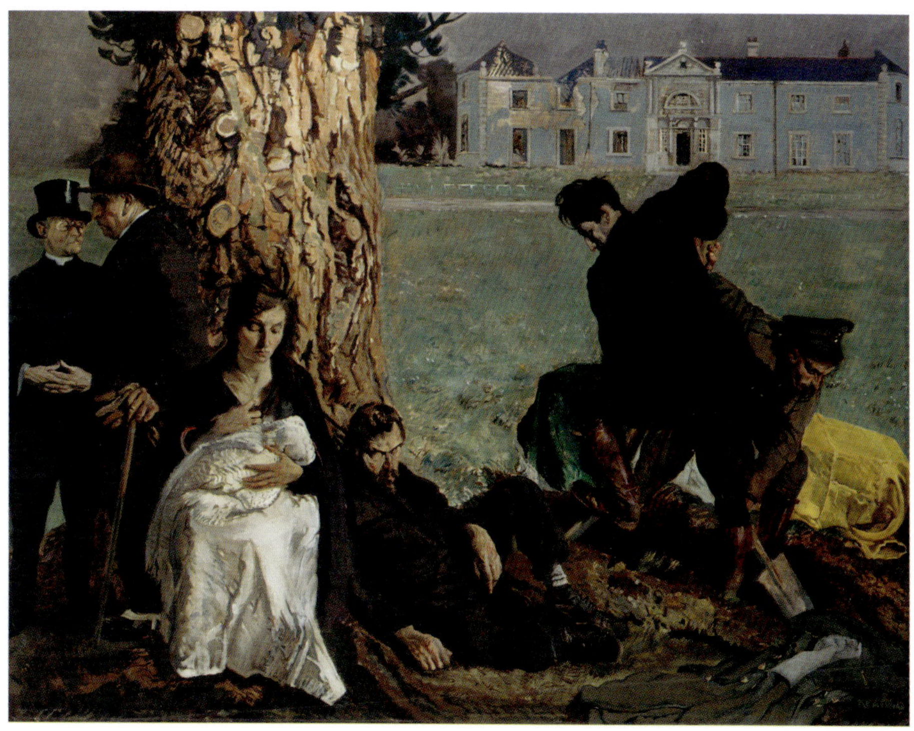

47 Seán Keating, *An Allegory*, c. 1922, oil on canvas.

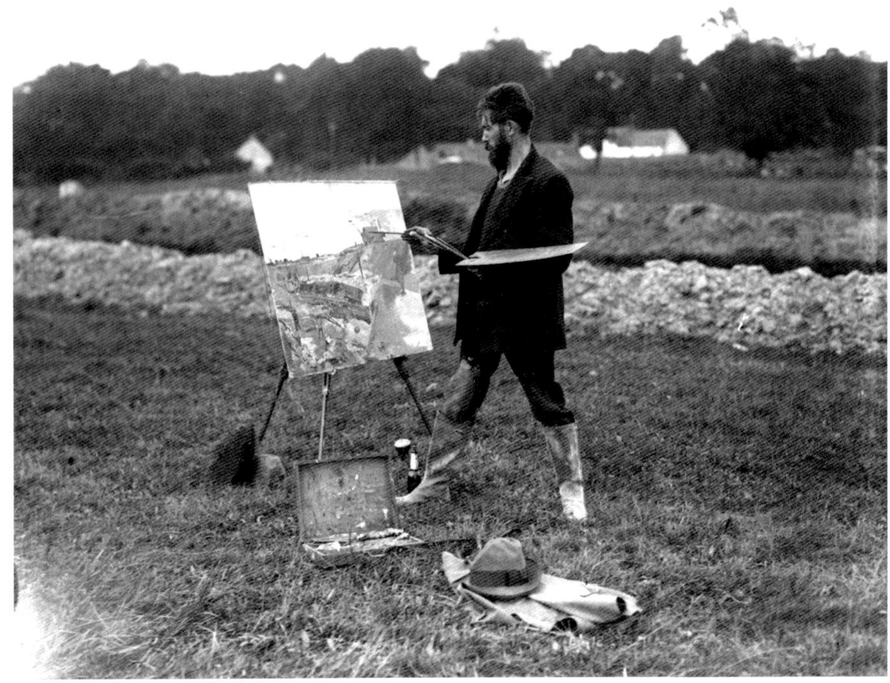

48 Joseph Cashman, Seán Keating painting at Ardnacrusha, c. 1926.

sensibility, yet what is deployed here is an image far removed from the models of post-Baudelairean urbanity and detachment evolving outside Ireland as a dominant feature of modernist artistic identity. In Ireland itself, the cultural and political conditions of the Free State resulted in an eclectic and loosely affiliated avant-garde. This became focused around the Society of Dublin Painters, established in 1920. Both Paul and Grace Henry were founder members, and Charles Lamb joined in 1923. The Society's establishment was, in a sense, a typical avant-garde gambit in its rejection of the exclusivity of the RHA, and a desire to provide an alternative exhibiting venue for young artists at its gallery at 7 St Stephens Green. As S. B. Kennedy suggests, the Dublin Painters 'quickly became a catalyst for all artists who had leanings towards the Modern Movement'.[42] These included Jack Yeats, Mary Swanzy and Mainie Jellett, all of whom were at some time members of the Dublin Painters during the 1920s.[43]

Mainie Jellett: Anglo-Irishness and the modernist woman artist

From its mid-nineteenth-century beginnings in the commodity capitalism of Haussmann's Paris, modernism has involved a mode of representation dependent on a degree of alienation from the culture within which it is produced. As members of an increasingly marginal class, the Anglo-Irish artists Yeats, Swanzy and Jellett were clearly in a situation where their interest in modernism could well have seemed appropriate also to the articulation of a sense of reality that was both fractured and isolated. Furthermore, both as the products of Unionist families and as *women*, it could be argued that Swanzy, Jellett and her collaborator Evie Hone were even stronger candidates for painterly investigations of alienated identity within the Free State. Any implication that their work can be seen as a direct reflection of the trials of Anglo-Irish class-consciousness is undermined by the fairly conservative approach to painting adopted by the majority

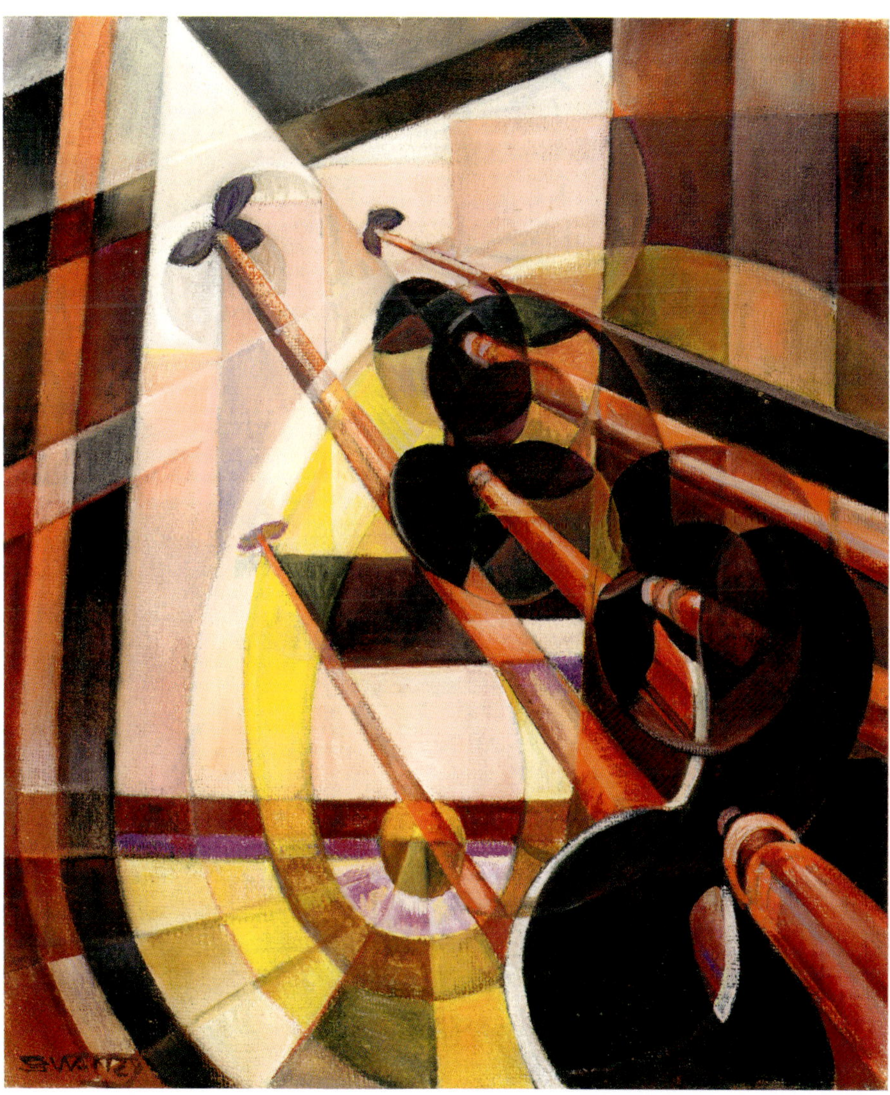

49 Mary Swanzy,
Propellers, n.d.,
oil on canvas.

of the Anglo-Irish women, such as Harriet Kirkwood, who followed their example of studying in Paris during the latter part of the decade.

Within the histories of Irish art, Mainie Jellett, and to a lesser extent Evie Hone, are generally recognized as 'pioneers' who introduced modernism to a generally uncomprehending Irish public in the 1920s.[44] Certainly their role as innovators within a highly conservative cultural climate of the Free State must not be underestimated, but there are precedents for their involvement with modernism in Paris during the early 1920s. In 1913, at the invitation of John Quinn, Jack Yeats had participated in the Armory Show, the first comprehensive attempt to introduce artistic modernism to the United States, where he exhibited several of his early oil paintings including *The Circus Dwarf* (1912). Irish painters, particularly Anglo-Irish women, had also been studying in Paris since the mid-nineteenth century. An earlier forerunner was Sarah Purser, who studied in Paris at the Académie Julian in

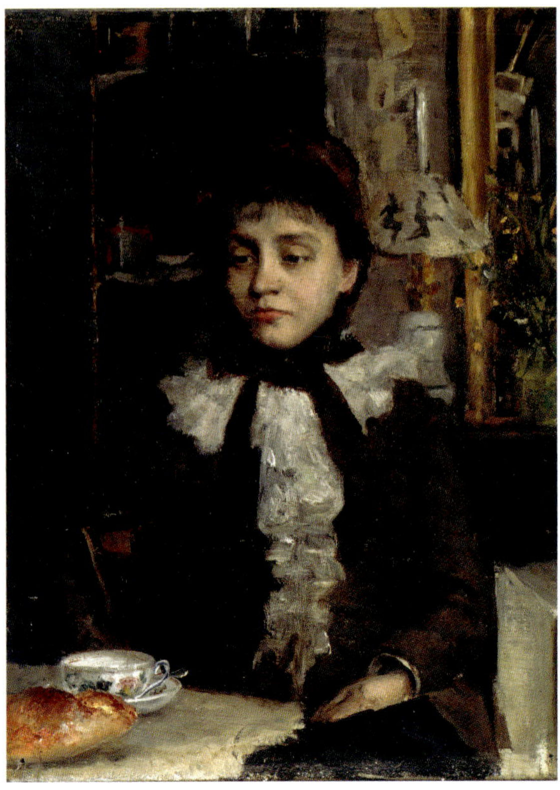

50 Sarah Purser, *Le Petit Déjeuner*, 1881, oil on canvas.

1878–9. Until her death in 1943 Purser was a significant figure in Irish art circles, holding regular salons at her Dublin home, Mespil House, while continuing to paint the kind of 'modern life' subjects that she had embarked on during her early years in Paris. Mary Swanzy was also active in avant-garde circles in Paris prior to Jellett and Hone's arrival in 1921. In 1914 and 1918, she exhibited at the Salon des Indépendants, and although the dating of much of her early work is uncertain, around this time she began to engage with aspects of both Orphism and Futurism in paintings like *Propellers*. Swanzy was also a frequent visitor to the home of Gertrude Stein and Alice B. Toklas at the rue de Fleurus; in 1925 a letter from Stein congratulated her on the success of her exhibition at the Galerie Bernheime Jeune, which included some paintings from her visit to Samoa in 1923.[45]

As an Irish artist participating within the Parisian avant-garde, Mainie Jellett's position suggests comparison with writers such as Joyce or Beckett, but in practice there are few similarities. In spite of her regular visits to France during the 1920s and early 1930s, Jellett did not embrace exile in the manner of either of these writers; her base was still the family home in Dublin. Gender was clearly a factor here. Prior to 1932, Jellett and Hone in effect chaperoned each other during their prolonged stays in Paris. In spite of the long-established practice by young Irish artists of studying in European art centres, in the case of women a return to Ireland was always expected. This was largely due to the tacit enforcement of respectability within the Anglo-Irish bourgeoisie, the requirements of family duty and the maintenance of sexual propriety. By comparison, a male writer from the same background could get away with a lot more; flagrant challenges to bourgeois morality through heavy drinking and regular visits to prostitutes were part of Samuel Beckett's normal routine, whether in Dublin or Paris. Anglo-Irish women such as Jellett, Hone and Swanzy had limited opportunities for being bohemian, a requirement of full participation within the European avant-garde.[46]

After study at the Metropolitan School of Art in Dublin and with Sickert at Westminster, in 1921 Mainie Jellett moved to Paris to join Evie Hone in working with the painter André Lhote. His method involved an application of Cubist notions of the breakdown of formal structure to what was generally a fairly recognizable, naturalistic format; Jellett's *Seated Female Nude* (1921), for example, painted during her time with Lhote, shows a breakdown of the human body into a schema of three-dimensional geometric forms that draws on Lhote's conservative reading of Cubism. However, both she and Hone soon became dissatisfied with Lhote's approach. Their second choice of teacher, Albert Gleizes,

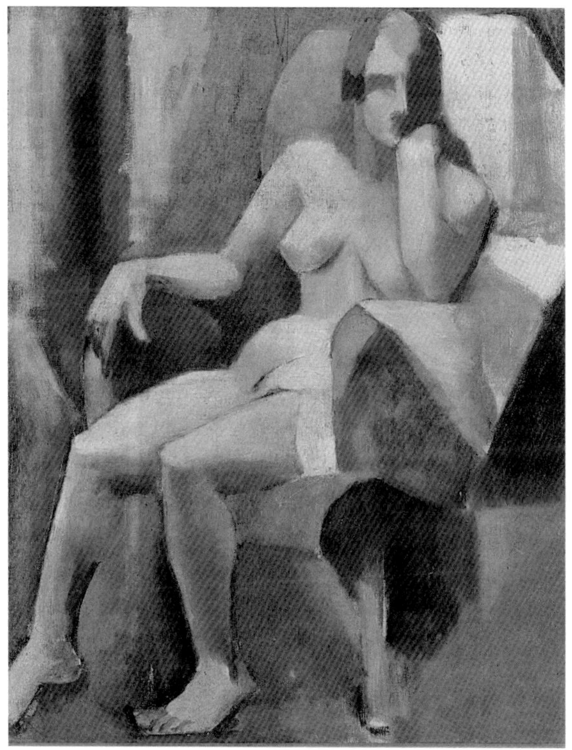

51 Mainie Jellett, *Seated Female Nude*, 1921–2, oil on canvas.

offered a more rigorous engagement with abstract painting, which Jellett and Hone had identified as being at the forefront of modernism. Late in 1921, Jellett and Hone arrived on Gleizes's doorstep and insisted, in spite of his reluctance, that he take them on as pupils. What resulted instead became much more of a collaboration in the rigorous investigation of formal principles; as Gleizes acknowledged in 1948, in a posthumous tribute to Jellett, 'I owe to Mainie Jellett and Evie Hone, and even today my feeling of gratitude to them shows no sign of leaving me.'[47]

In spite of Jellett's enthusiasm for first Lhote then Gleizes (she later described Lhote as 'one of the outstanding influences in the art world of Paris'), by 1921 both were relatively marginal figures.[48] They had been involved with Cubism, the most innovative form of avant-garde practice before the First World War, and

Gleizes had developed a role as a major theoretician in his joint authorship with Jean Metzinger of the analytical essay 'Du Cubisme' in 1912. Some nine years later the interests of the main innovators of Cubism, Braque and Picasso, had shifted considerably; Picasso, in particular, was now more concerned with the development of a form of neo-Classicism. So what Jellett and Hone encountered in 1921 was a form of abstraction largely superseded by other forms of avant-garde activity, such as the nihilism of Dada, and subsequently the confrontational strategies of Surrealism. Gleizes was concerned with the production of an art of balance and harmony, close to the interests of the emergent 'Return to Order' tendency focused around Jeanneret (later le Corbusier) and Ozenfant, but without any reliance on the representation of nature through illusionist perspective. Gleizes proposed not only what later became recognized as a modernist solution of an adherence to the picture plane in the pursuit of flatness, but he also advocated the increased involvement of the spectator through the perception of movement within the painting, in identifying the logical development of colour and form in relation to a pivotal point. Gleizes used the terms 'translation' and 'rotation' to explain how this might be achieved.[49]

By 1923 Mainie Jellett was using these new techniques with a degree of confidence. Translation involved the establishment of horizontal and vertical rectangles in relationship to the picture plane; in her painting *Decoration* this practice is interpreted through black and grey geometric forms that echo the shape of the frame. The second principle, rotation, superimposes a series of forms onto this base – a further arrangement of tilted rectangles and curvilinear shapes suggestive of movement against a static background. Colour is also particularly important; both the gold surround and contrast between layered planes of

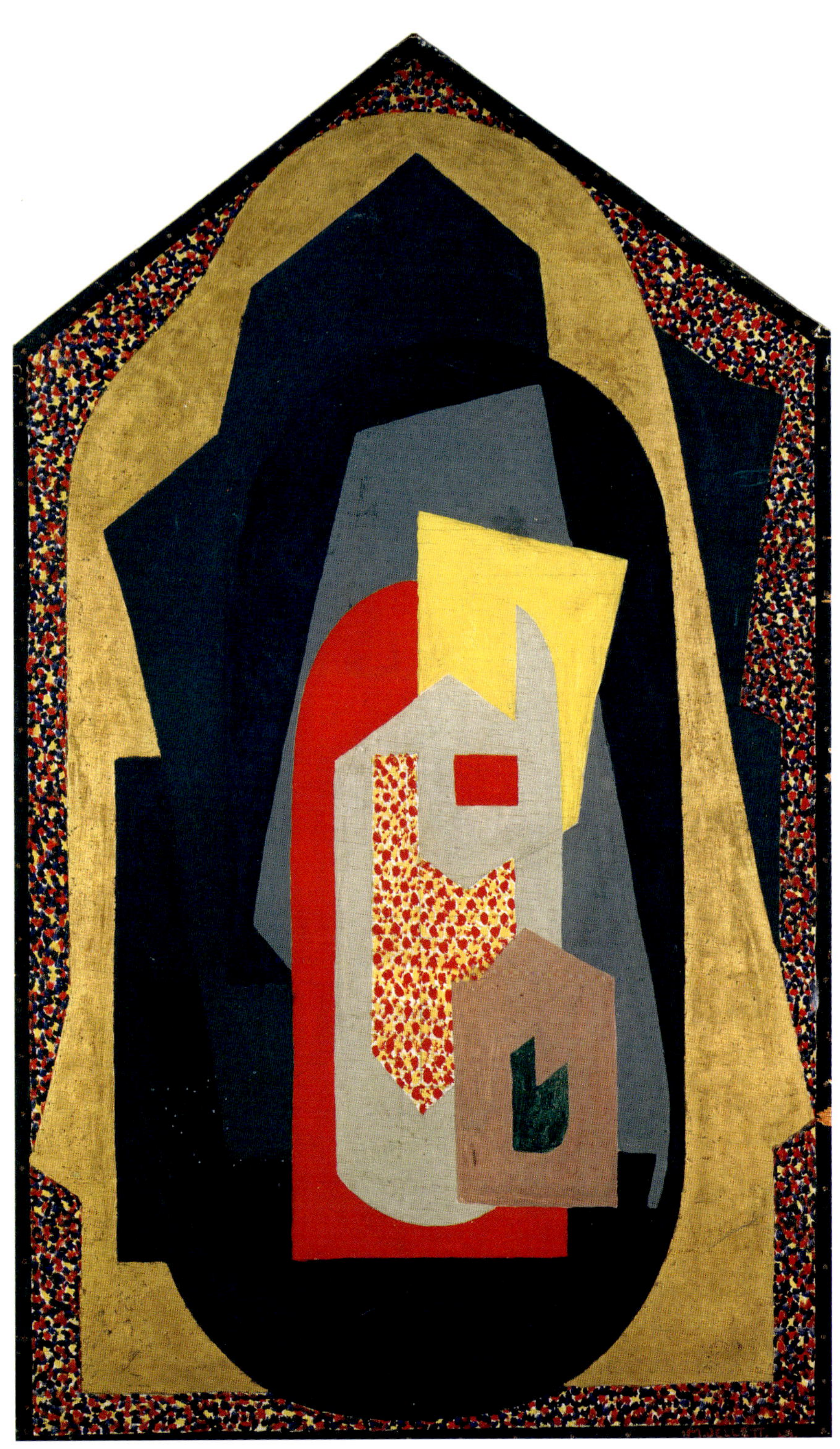

52 Mainie Jellett,
Decoration, 1923, tempera
on panel.

bluish-grey and vibrant tones of red, yellow, white and pink produce further expressive resonances. *Decoration* was shown at the exhibition of the Society of Dublin Painters in October of that year; the critical response was directed almost exclusively towards Jellett. George Russell in the *Irish Statesman*, for example, described her as 'a late victim to Cubism in some sub-section of this artistic malaria'.[50] Although a fairly typical reaction to modernist abstraction, this also needs to be placed in a context more specific to Ireland: the increasing cultural and political hegemony of forms of ethnic nationalism.

As Jellett and Hone continued to work with Gleizes throughout the decade, the formal and tonal interrelationships in their paintings became more complex and confident. A later work by Hone, the hand-finished pochoir print *Abstract Composition*, contains a multiplicity of overlapping and interlocking planes in a range dominated by muted tones of mauve, greens and blues with contrasting accents of red and yellow. The complexity of this work is similar to Jellett's abstracts of the late 1920s, but there were differences in the way both artists painted. Hone's brushwork is much looser and more expressive than Jellett's precise strokes, with the result that Hone's painting becomes much more an essay in tonal relationships. In James White's later opinion, 'All questions of atmosphere, movement or literary content were to her irrelevancies standing in the way of direct communication of feeling.'[51]

Modernist abstraction was a priority for both Hone and Jellett. Like Gleizes, they also believed this to be in the service of a spiritual reality. In the 1930s Hone spent some time in a convent, later converting to Catholicism; a significant part of her subsequent career involved the design of stained-glass windows. Jellett, by comparison, tirelessly campaigned for the acceptance of modernism in Ireland, painting, writing and lecturing until her premature death in 1944. Yet in

spite of her involvement with the modern, much of Jellett's work was based on her admiration of early Renaissance religious painting; her major work *Homage to Fra Angelico* was based on the fifteenth-century painter's *Coronation of the Virgin*.[52] Her attraction to Fra Angelico's work was its combination of 'organic rhythmic movement' with 'pure and exquisite colour schemes like a beautiful crescendo in music'; for her, this sense of harmonious rhythm was also linked to Byzantine and early Irish Christian art.[53] The early Renaissance format of Madonna and Child was also present in *Decoration*, a reading emphasized by the shape of the frame and extensive use of gold, suggesting both the rich surface and compositional format of a Byzantine altarpiece.

Later in her life, Jellett argued that 'the main character of our age is that of mechanical reproduction. The artistic effect, such as it is, is striving to free itself and to rise again with fresh vigour from its decadent torpor.'[54] Although undated, the short essay from which this is taken typifies her views on the function and meaning of abstract art, found in her writings and lectures from the early 1930s onwards, and developed through her practice as a painter during the previous decade. In advocating a rejection of the reproductive processes of capitalism, Jellett proposes a return to an earlier mode of production, an art associated with a pre-industrial age, and which she identified at least in part with Celtic art. To some degree, this is very much in keeping with the discourse of the primitive within the avant-garde milieu of early twentieth-century Paris, with which she was familiar. Yet this statement, I think, also points up some of the inevitable contradictions that surround Mainie Jellett's work. Her partial immersion within Parisian cultural cosmopolitanism was sharply distinct from the double alienation of class and gender in Ireland, a state to which nevertheless she

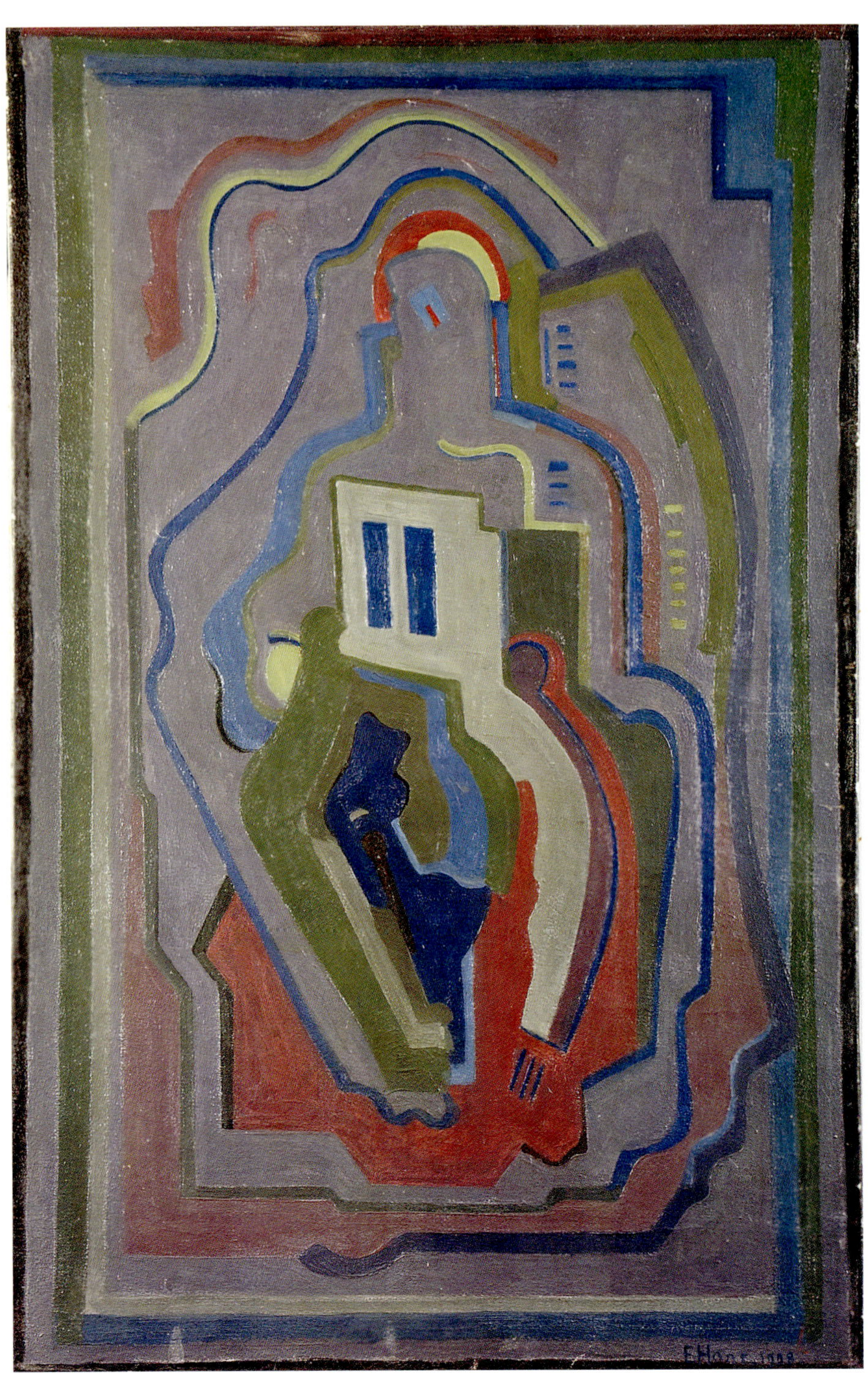

53 Evie Hone, *Abstract Composition*, 1928, pochoir.

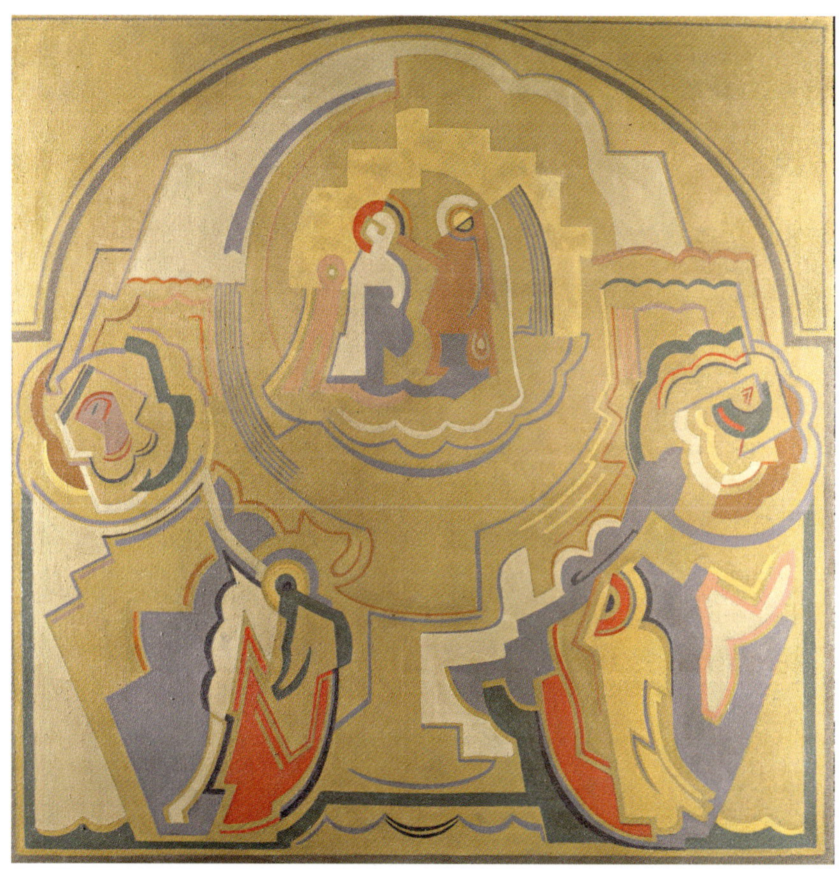

54 Mainie Jellett,
Homage to Fra Angelico,
1928, oil on canvas.

was continually drawn back – not least by the umbilical cord of her family's financial support. In a sense, Jellett could not have escaped if she had wanted to, in that she was committed to the forging of a new sense of artistic identity in the emergent Irish nation. Yet even her championing of an Irish modernism was still marked by the hegemonic concerns of the Free State. Although embodied in a form of painting far removed from the naturalism of Keating or Lamb, her evocation of a pre-industrial spirituality is also reminiscent of the self-conscious primitivism identified with the under-developed West. And in spite of the radical strangeness of her paintings when first exhibited in Ireland, the complexity of their relationship to the dialectic of modernization and archaism invites closer investiga-tion. Mainie Jellett was far from alone in being caught

in this contradiction; the different trajectories of Seán Keating's work during the 1920s also make this clear. The forces at work in the cultural domain of the new nation were much more pervasive than they might initially appear.

THREE

THE WEST, THE SOUTH AND THE NORTH: ART IN IRELAND IN THE 1930S

By 1932 Ireland had been partitioned for eleven years, with separate governments installed in Belfast and Dublin. In comparison with the isolationist nationalism of the Irish Free State, the Unionist government in Northern Ireland retained close links with Britain; these vastly different political positions ultimately affected art in North and South. This was more obvious in the case of Southern Ireland, where an explicit cultural agenda was part of the process of decolonization in the Free State, resulting in the overt and deeply ideological celebration of an entire geographical area, the western seaboard. The West was celebrated by Ireland's Taoiseach, Éamon de Valera, as embodying the values of ethnic nationalism. It was remote, Catholic and a rugged landscape of thatched cottages populated by a hardy, Irish-speaking peasantry. However, the prevalence of imagery of the West in the work of Paul Henry, Seán Keating or Maurice MacGonigal resulted in difficulties for the establishment of an avant-garde related to wider tendencies of international modernism. Significantly, the main instigator of modernism in Ireland, Mainie Jellett, embodied two of the marginalized constituencies of the Irish Free State – the Anglo-Irish, whose political power was declining rapidly, and women. Less overtly, art in Northern Ireland during this period can also be seen as shaped by the political position within the Union. Drawing on their own experience of art education, when artists of the Ulster Unit looked elsewhere for an avant-garde model they chose London rather than Paris. Some years later, in wartime, the volatile nature of Northern Ireland's internal politics meant that the conscription applied elsewhere in Great Britain was not attempted there. As in the South, for different reasons, one result was a flourishing art scene with artists throughout Ireland beginning to articulate identities not bound by the requirements of cultural nationalism.

Art in the Free State

In 1932 Éamon de Valera's Fianna Fáil party gained victory in the election, narrowly defeating Cosgrave's Cumann na nGaedheal. De Valera's immediate intention was the removal of the continuing colonial legacy of the Treaty settlement of 1921, by abolishing the Oath of Allegiance to the Crown. This was accompanied by a policy of economic nationalism, intending to gain Ireland's self-sufficiency through measures such as the high tariff imposed on English goods. In practice it caused serious problems for Ireland's rural economy, given that Britain's response was to impose a corresponding tariff on the importation of Irish agricultural produce. In 1933 a tax on imported newspapers followed, reinforcing the

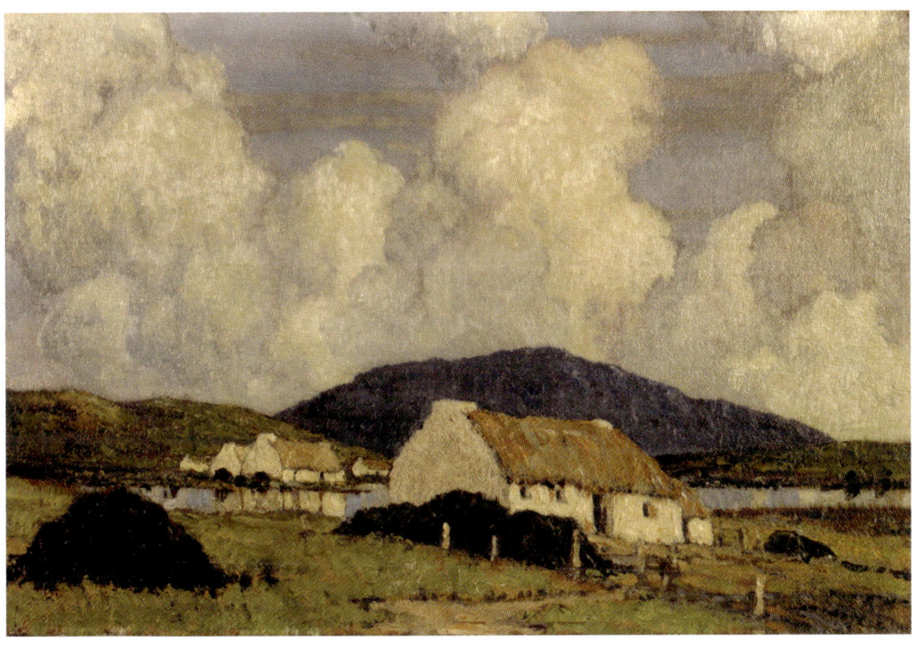

55 Paul Henry, *Lakeside Cottages*, 1929–32, oil on canvas.

existing censorship legislation that had a profound effect not just on the work of Irish writers, but on the Irish reading public's access to contemporary fiction published abroad.[1] This economic and cultural protectionism was reinforced by the firm instatement of Catholicism as central to Irish national identity. In 1932 the international conference of the Catholic church, the Eucharistic Congress, took place in Dublin to an overwhelming popular response; the following year, in a radio broadcast, de Valera described Ireland as 'a Christian and a Catholic nation'.[2] Yet his view of modern Ireland was anachronistic, dependent on a fantasy of a rural utopia populated by Irish-speaking Catholic families, rather than as a secular nation taking its place within industrialized Europe. The irony, however, was that large numbers of young people continued to leave the land in favour of secure employment within the industries of Ireland's former colonial ruler. Emigration to Britain continued at a high level throughout the 1930s and 1940s; the 1951 British census recorded an increase of almost a quarter of a million Irish-born workers in England and Wales since 1931.[3] Rural communities in Ireland stagnated through the high rate of late marriages among those who remained. Yet the project of decolonization was reinforced further by the declaration of the Free State's Constitution in 1937, affirming Ireland's status as 'a sovereign, independent, democratic state'. The central role accorded to Catholicism ensured the continuation of conservative political and social agendas for several decades.

In Britain, the Artists International Association, initially known as the Artists International, had formed in 1933 in response to the deteriorating political conditions of the 1930s, drawing on the broad popular alliance of the Communist Party, the Labour Party and trade unionists. Within Ireland's nationalist politics a similar left-wing basis of support for art opposed to fascism was lacking. Unlike in Britain, the events of the Spanish Civil War did not evoke a collective response by artists in the Free State, whatever their individual opinions may have been. As Beatrice Glenavy observed in her memoirs, the 1930s had been 'one of the most tragic periods of the whole history of Europe', but 'in Dublin it was a time of memorable parties'.[4]

In Ireland during the 1930s the articulation of a political response meant taking up a position in relation to the process of decolonization, or more specifically, in relation to the development of a highly conservative national identity that was becoming prevalent within the Free State. During Ireland's vigorous decolonization of the 1930s and 1940s, privileged interpretations both of the West and its associated way of life became particularly significant. The human interdependence with the physical environment through fishing or the subsistence agriculture of small farmers and labourers became revalued through de Valera's advocacy of rural poverty as generative of a kind of moral integrity; this was stressed in a speech of April 1932 by his claim that 'If a man makes up his mind to go out into a cottage – he had to make up his mind to put up with the frugal fare of that cottage.'[5] As Anthony Smith has argued, the power of the nation is greatly strengthened through its invocation of myth and symbol; by the 1930s this was no longer the ur-narrative of Cuchulainn's sacrifice but a less clearly defined rural archaism identified with a particular location.[6] Nostalgia for a disappearing ethnicity became a predominant feature of a type of painting that came to be closely identified with de Valera's vision for an independent Ireland, often through its ability to provide the multi-layered evocations of myth, history and territory invaluable to the nation in formation.

Although reinforced by the priorities of the Fianna Fáil government during the 1930s and 1940s, the visual template was already in place in the work of Henry, Lamb and others during the previous decade. According to S. B. Kennedy, by the end of the 1920s Henry had 'defined a way of seeing and an attitude towards the Irish landscape that was convincing . . . and . . . helped to formulate a popular vision of Irish identity'.[7] This apparently uncontradictory account of the West became increasingly formulaic in Henry's work of the

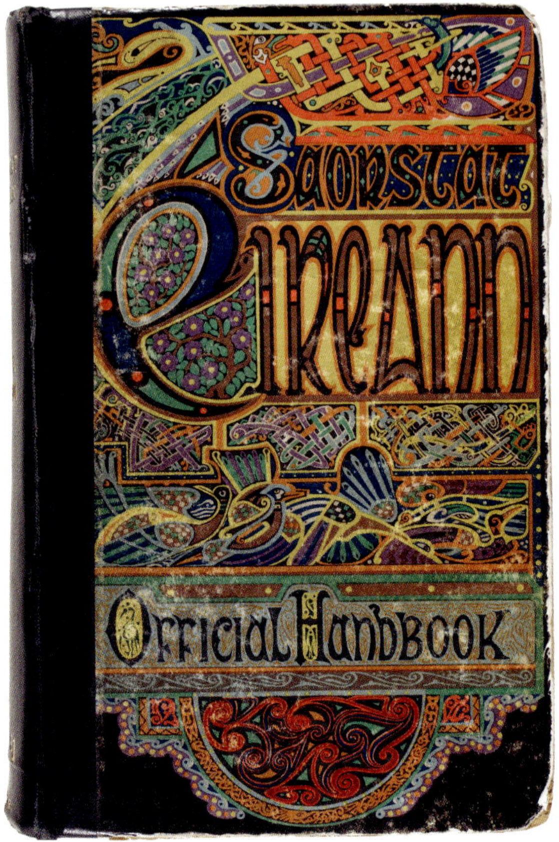

56 Art O'Murnaghan, cover of *Saorstát Eireann* [Irish Free State] *Official Handbook* (1932).

1930s, with innumerable paintings characterized by a contrast of smoothly worked clouds with the relative impasto of the hills and thatched roofs. Visual imagery also played a significant role in constructing cultural forms of nationalism in the official publications of the new state. The *Saorstát Eireann* [Irish Free State] *Official Handbook*, published in 1932, attempted to provide a comprehensive survey of both the material infrastructure and social and cultural features of Ireland, ten years after the Treaty. The editorial committee appointed by the Minister for Industry and Commerce assembled a collection of short essays commissioned from figures recognized within their own field; the art historian Thomas Bodkin, for example, wrote the section

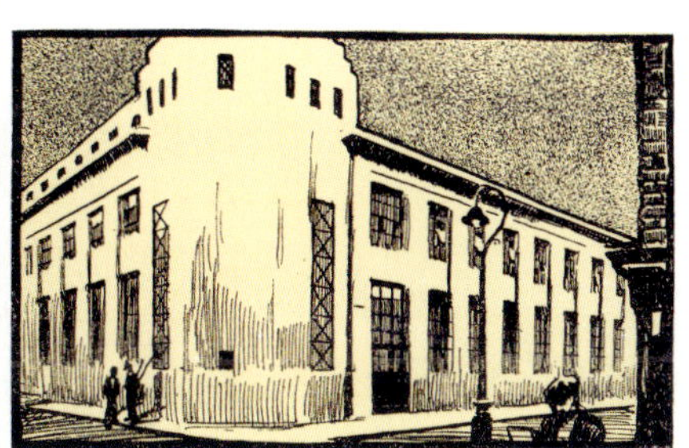

POWER SUPPLY IN THE IRISH FREE STATE

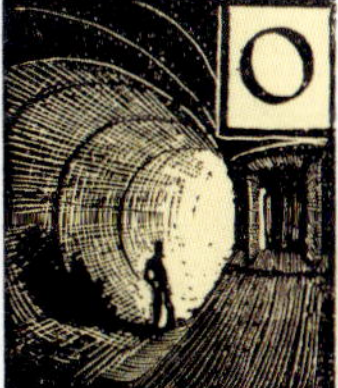

NE of the first economic problems dealt with after the establishment of the Irish Free State was that of power supply. By the hydro-electric development of the River Shannon, power derived from water as distinct from imported fuel, which until then was practically the sole source, was made available on a large scale. The distribution of this power throughout the country was provided for by the construction of a national network. The control and administration of the system was by the Electricity (Supply) Act, 1927, entrusted to a Board nominated by the Executive Council. The monies for the enterprise (over £10,000,000) are provided on loan to the Board from the State Exchequer.

The construction of the Shannon Power Station at Ardnacrusha near Limerick city began in August, 1925, and was completed towards the end of 1929. This power station is situated at the end of a $7\frac{1}{2}$-mile head race canal which conveys the water from a weir situated near O'Brien's Bridge on the River Shannon. A tail race of $1\frac{1}{2}$ miles long returns the water used in the power station back to the Shannon at the village of Parteen, near Limerick.

The head race is about 300 feet wide at water level and 35 feet deep, and ships' locks are provided in the power station dam to allow shipping

Illustrations—I. New Transformer Station at Fleet Street, Dublin. II. Interior of Turbine Spiral, Ardnacrusha Power Station, from drawings by Seán O'Sullivan, R.H.A.

57 Seán O'Sullivan, *Power Supply in the Irish Free State*, from *Saorstát Eirann Official Handbook* (1932).

on modern Irish art.[8] Yet the visual also played a more active role in the discursive formation of national identity within the *Handbook*. The work of eleven artists was included, with a full-colour cover by Art O'Murnaghan, a frontispiece by Paul Henry and numerous illustrations throughout the text.[9] Yet the representations of Ireland's national identity that emerged were both modern and archaic, ranging from Maurice MacGonigal's depiction of cumulus, cottages and peasant women for an essay on land ownership, to Seán O'Sullivan's drawings of a new transformer station in Fleet Street, Dublin, or the interior of a turbine spiral at Ardnacrusha as illustrations for the discussion of the Free State's electrification programme.

In O'Sullivan's illustrations for the *Handbook*, the celebration of modernity implicit in the depiction of Ireland's electrification was modest in comparison with Seán Keating's more grandiose cycle of paintings based on different aspects of the Shannon scheme. As a boundary to the counties of the western seaboard, the Shannon delimited an area primarily associated with ethnic nationalism; the river itself had also become identified as the key site of Ireland's progressiveness as a modern nation. Nevertheless, in spite of its important role in the construction of an identity for the Free State, there were clearly going to be times when painting would not overtly bear the signs of either archaism or modernity. The RHA President Dermod O'Brien's *The Estuary of the Shannon* is an academic, pastoral depiction that omits the major technological and environmental shifts associated with the area. Even its location is disengaged from the Shannon as a conduit for Ireland's modernity; O'Brien depicted a scene at Foynes, some miles downstream from the electrification scheme, the open estuary stretching beyond the foreground stacks of corn.

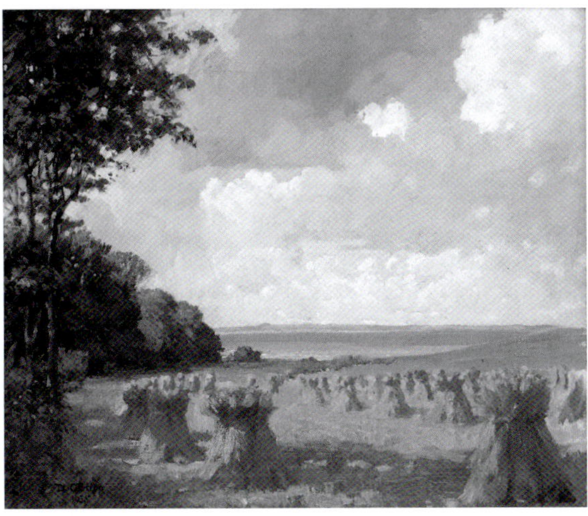

58 Dermod O'Brien, *The Estuary of the Shannon*, 1936, oil on canvas.

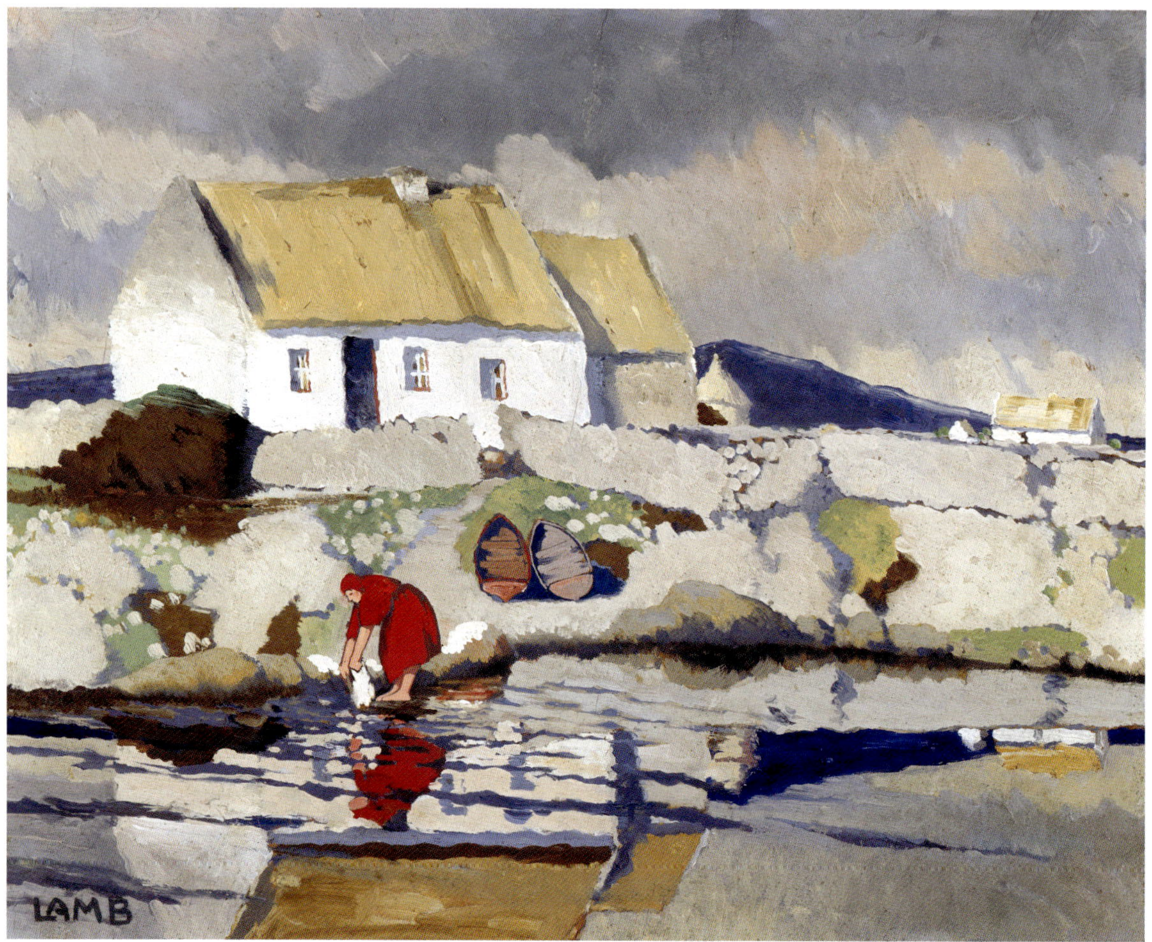

59 Charles Lamb, *Loch an Mhullinn*, early 1930s, oil on board.

The visual construction of an archaic national identity in the cottages planted firmly within the landscapes of the *Handbook*, or the paintings of Henry or Lamb, also conflicted with aspects of Fianna Fáil's modernizing project. When de Valera gained power in 1932, large numbers of the cottages in rural areas had fallen into disrepair, in spite of the existence of a building programme designed to address the problem. The remainder of the 1930s saw the intensification of this scheme, with the large-scale building of new cottages throughout Ireland. These were intended primarily for agricultural labourers – the rural peasantry who were to form the backbone of the Free State.[10] In Charles Lamb's *Loch an Mhullinn*, painted near his home in Carraroe, the quiet idyll of a woman washing clothes in a lake is surmounted by a stereotypical thatched cottage with whitewashed walls and half-door. Yet throughout Ireland these were becoming increasingly obsolete, replaced by housing of a very different construction, with brick walls, sturdy doors and window frames and,

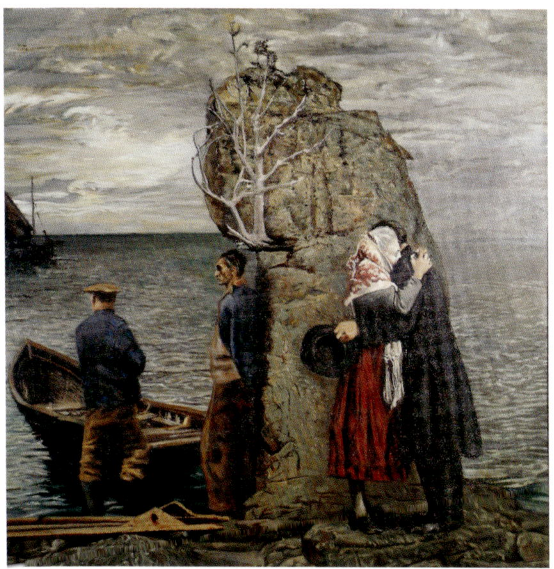

60 Seán Keating, *Economic Pressure*, 1936, oil on board.

above all, a roof made out of concrete tiles. Other depictions of rural communities presented a less idealized view. Poverty and the harshness of subsistence agriculture took their toll through dispossession and emigration. Even in the work of Seán Keating there were occasional references to consequences of the poverty that characterized life in the West. The highly stylized *Economic Pressure* represents a considerable contrast to his other scenes of life in the Aran Islands, depicting an adult son taking leave of his anguished elderly mother as he prepares for emigration, probably to America.

During a period of agricultural crisis induced by the state's protectionist policies, much of the emphasis for the maintenance of rural life fell on women as wives and mothers, whose additional back-breaking roles as workers on farms and smallholdings were generally unacknowledged. The female figure in Lamb's *Loch an Mhullinn* may have been part of a rural idyll, but she was also engaged in hard domestic labour, washing clothes

in the cold waters of a Connemara lake. In spite of the growth in Irish industry during the mid-1930s, women's employment rights became increasingly restricted, culminating in the 1937 Constitution's sanctification of the family as the most important social unit within the Irish state. Both the polarization of gender roles and the role played by the Catholic Church become clear in a comparison of two paintings. Maurice MacGonigal's *Mother and Child* was part of a series of paintings of women of the West that he began in 1938. They mostly feature Aida Kelly, a former model from the National College of Art whom he married in 1940. *Mother and Child* is a portrait of Aida and her first son Muiris, set against the recognizable background of the South Connemara coast. The naturalism of MacGonigal's desire to record the West, combined with the Byzantine frontal pose, result in the attribution of archaic, essentialized qualities to Western women. As Tricia Cusack has observed, there are clear references here to both Mother Ireland and the Virgin Mary.[11] Seán Keating's *Slan Leat, a Athair* (Goodbye Father), by comparison, works through more recognizable codes of realism. A group of islanders stand around a Catholic priest, departing after one of his regular visits to the Aran Islands. The muted palette and low viewpoint impute a degree of solemnity to this scene; for Keating, these islanders were obviously not just ethnic types but heroic subjects, standing at the edge of Ireland against an infinity of sea and sky. The documentary aspects of this painting emphasize this as the cohesive, public face of the island community, cemented together by religious faith. Although Mac-Gonigal represented the female, maternal body as symbolic of abstract principles that underpinned the Free State, this is a *social* body, composed of men, suggestive of a similar polarization within the Free State as a whole. That Keating and MacGonigal were from 1937

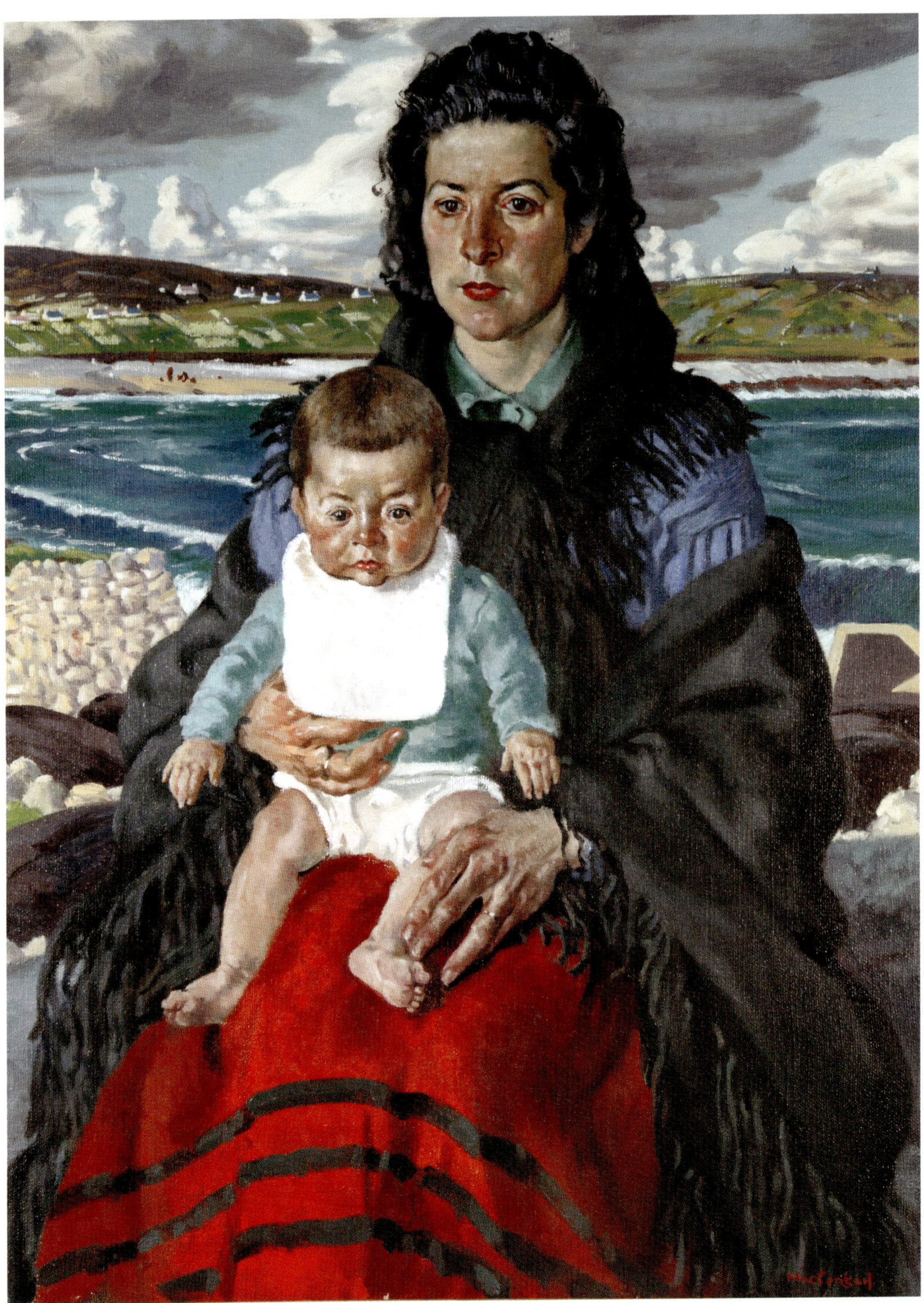

61 Maurice MacGonigal, *Mother and Child*, 1942, oil on canvas.

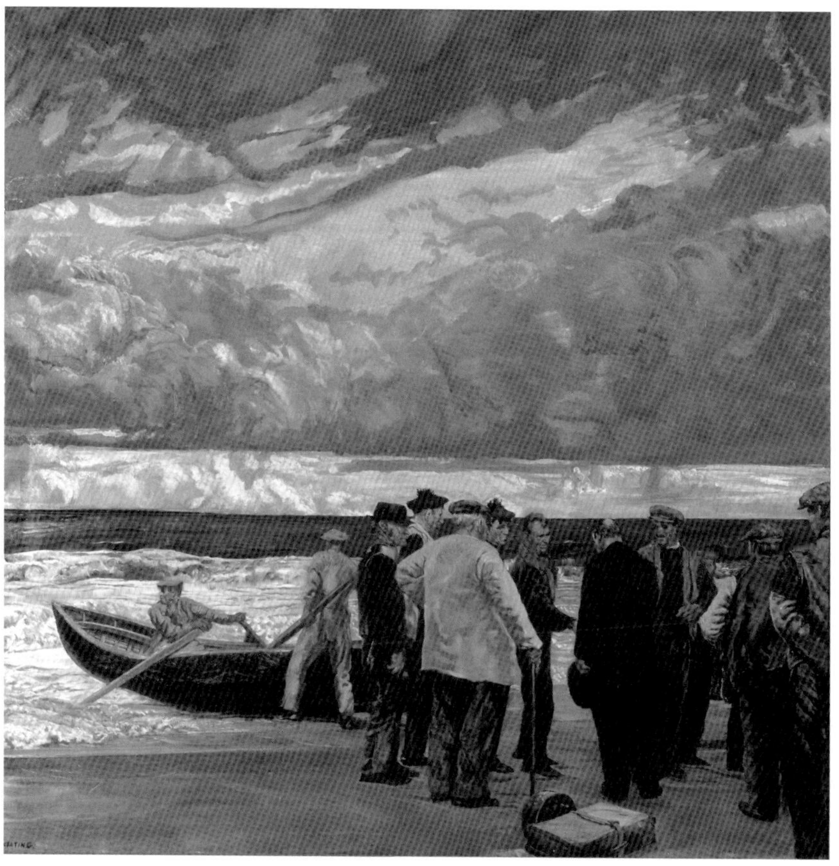

62 Seán Keating, *Slán Leat, a Athair* (Goodbye Father), 1936, oil on canvas.

respectively the Professor and Assistant Professor of Painting at the National College of Art was something that could only ensure the transmission of highly traditional values within Irish art education.[12]

Increasingly ratified by the ideological requirements of the Free State, the reactionary ruralist agenda also had a significant effect on the activities of the Dublin avant-garde. During the 1930s, Jack Yeats painted relatively little. Late in the previous decade he had undergone a major shift in his painting technique, with an increased use of impasto and a greater use of primary colours. This resulted in increasingly expressionistic and subjective works such as *About to Write a Letter*, a painting that also relates to the revival of his literary interests. Partly as a means of increasing his income, during the 1930s

Yeats published several novels, beginning with *Sligo* in 1930. The necessary focus on a different medium involved in the writing of *The Amaranthers* (1936) or *The Charmed Life* (1938) was probably sufficient to reduce his concentration on painting.[13] Although he remained a republican throughout his life (unlike his brother W. B. Yeats) it seems to have been difficult at this time for Jack Yeats to sustain a romanticized view of both the West and recent Irish history in his paintings, given the predominance in Irish visual culture of the reductive imagery of ethnic nationalism. His paintings from the 1930s involved a significant departure from the political subjects of the previous decade, such as *The Funeral of Harry Boland*. Instead, there was an increase in themes with a more mythical interpretation, which was to

75

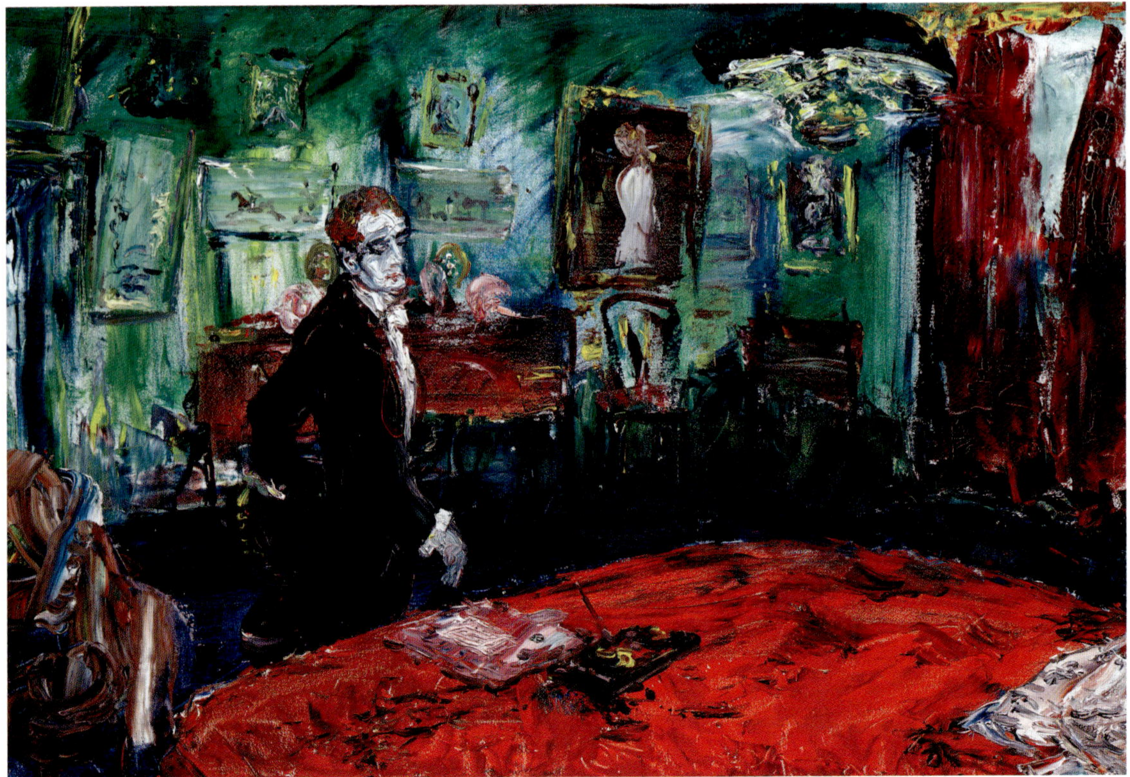

63 Jack Yeats, *About to Write a Letter*, 1935, oil on canvas.

remain a major characteristic of Yeats's work for the rest of his career. In 1938, Samuel Beckett famously remarked to Thomas MacGreevy that Yeats 'grows Watteauer and Watteauer'. Beckett, who already owned the Yeats's painting *A Morning* (1935–6), was referring to the Cythera-like fantasies of paintings such as *In Memory of Boucicault and Bianconi* (1938) or *A Race in Hy Brazil*.[14]

Throughout the 1930s the Society of Dublin Painters' Gallery at 7 St Stephen's Green continued to provide the main alternative exhibiting venue in the city. Yet the Dublin Painters have been criticized for their lack of a radical agenda at this time; Kennedy, for example, describes their work of the early 1930s as 'unadventurous and lacking the rigour of their colleagues of the previous decade.'[15] Issues of gender could be significant here. In spite of the continuing membership of Paul Henry, Charles Lamb, Harry Kernoff and Maurice MacGonigal

during the 1930s, the Society of Dublin Painters was dominated by women; in 1934 approximately fourteen of its eighteen members were female. These included Grace Henry, Mainie Jellett, Eva and Letitia Hamilton, Evie Hone and Harriet Kirkwood, who was also the Secretary.[16] Many of them were Anglo-Irish: Beatrice Elvery, Lady Glenavy, was married to a hereditary peer who had been active within the Cosgrave administration. The great exception, however, was Nano Reid, whose work increasingly became the subject of critical focus from 1939 onwards, with her third exhibition at the Gallery, which was opened by the prominent writer Liam O'Flaherty.[17] Reid came from a very different background; born in Drogheda in 1905, she was the daughter of a Catholic publican. Her consistent rejection of values of middle-class decorum made a significant contribution to the formation of bohemian identities in Dublin of the 1940s,

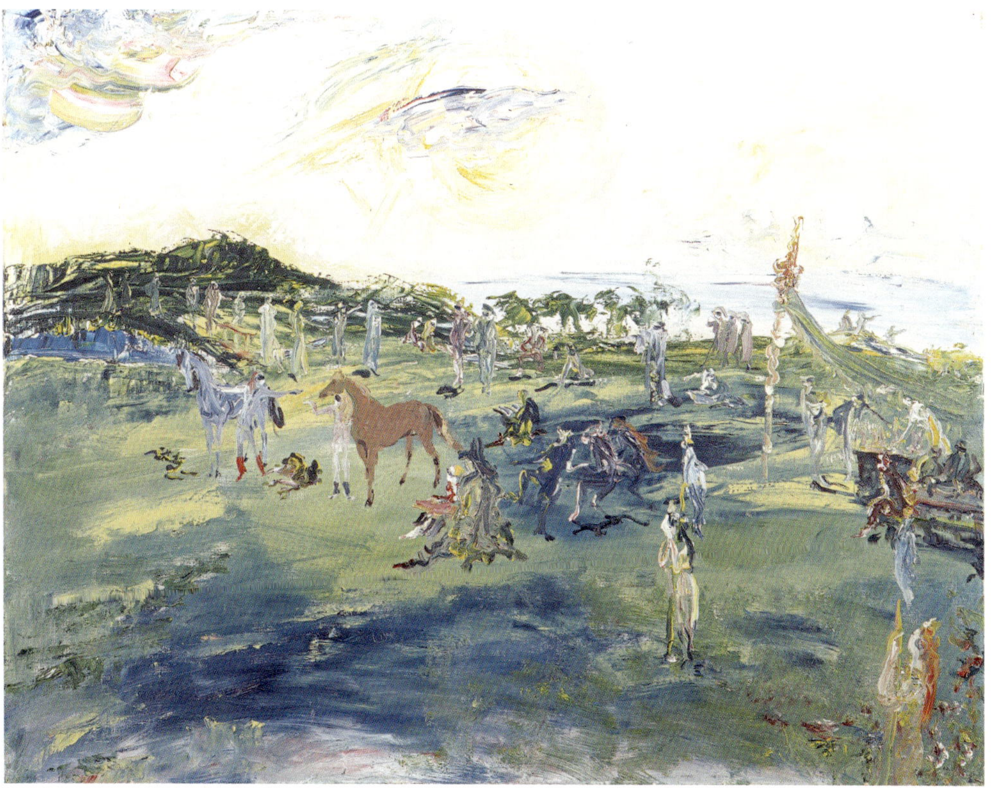

64 Jack Yeats, *A Race in Hy Brazil*, 1937, oil on canvas.

just as her increasingly expressionistic technique and reworking of the imagery of rural Ireland gained in importance in the 1940s and 1950s.

Yet the evaluation of the work of women artists needs to be seen in a specific historical context. The canon of modernism, against which women artists have frequently been judged as inadequate, itself arose within the specific conjuncture of Greenbergian formalism and the historical circumstances of post-war American triumphalism. In 1930s Ireland, the work of Mainie Jellett represented the type of engagement with the modern recognizable within this canon. Her former collaborator Evie Hone was by now increasingly working in stained glass, joining Sarah Purser's workshop Túr Gloinne (the Tower of Glass) in 1933. Jellett's gouache *Abstract*, possibly shown at 'Abstraction-Creation' in Paris in 1934, is but one example of many

works by her that value above anything a sense of both the painting's technical autonomy and the viewer's response to this. In Ireland the public role that Jellett claimed for herself as the instigator of abstract painting was that of a teacher as much as an artist; this pedagogic function was actually quite compatible with contemporary expectations of bourgeois femininity. She exhibited regularly in Dublin during the 1930s, and lectured frequently both in Ireland and Britain on the innovatory role of Cubism. To the extent that she was a woman, a Protestant and through her family had a position in the Anglo-Irish Unionist minority, Mainie Jellett was typical of many artists who occupied a distinctly marginal status within the Free State, particularly after de Valera's election victory of 1932. Yet Jellett's fashioning of her own identity as both artist and teacher was at least in part a negotiation of her position within

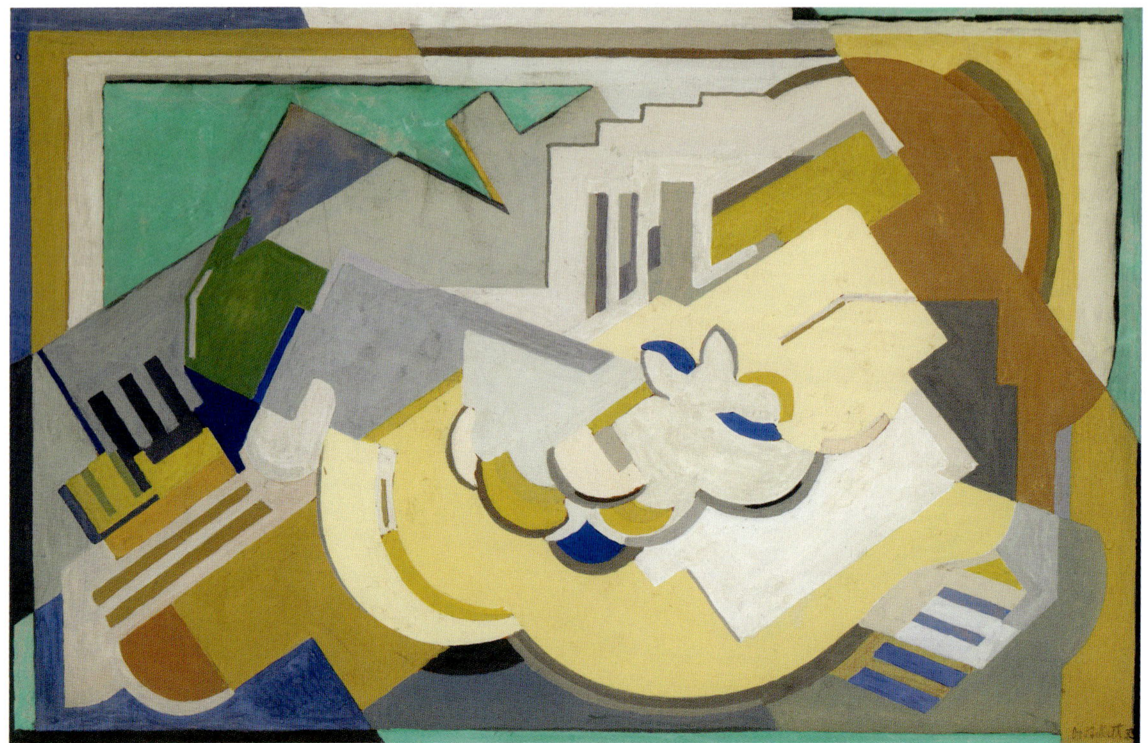

65 Mainie Jellett, *Abstract*, early 1930s, gouache.

a state that was increasingly burrowing its way into an isolated ruralist utopia. Jellett's idealism, on the other hand, was that of an urban modernist with strong links to cultural developments outside Ireland.

However, the involvement of women within the public domain was also highly contentious. It was a commonly accepted belief that only in extreme circumstances should married women work outside the home.[18] In the public exhibition of their paintings, women artists were displaying evidence of their labour, and were liable to criticism and censorship. Although not shown at the Dublin Painters' Gallery, the reception of Glenavy's painting *The Intruder* is a case in point. The painting initially had a favourable reception. When first shown at the Aonach Tailteann exhibition in 1932 the *Irish Times* described it as 'reminiscent of an 18th-century French theme, in which a golden-haired female centaur startles a picnic and bathing party beneath

formalised foliage'.[19] *The Intruder* was also well received at London's Royal Academy in 1934, although it was the subject of a George Morrow cartoon in *Punch* entitled 'The Home-wrecker'. The painting evokes a Watteauesque *fête galante*, with three groups of figures depicted in a woodland glade. Both the imperious, beckoning hand and the pose combined with a female torso suggest an androgynous figure; the centaur rears on its back legs in a manner more usually associated with depictions of the masculine body in classical statuary. Similar to the slightly later work of women Surrealists like Leonor Fini, the irrational, dream-like quality of this painting and its problematization of femininity combine to suggest readings of an active female sexuality within the domain of the unconscious. Yet it was painted in 1932, within a culture where female sexuality and any form of female agency within contemporary social reality were being systematically

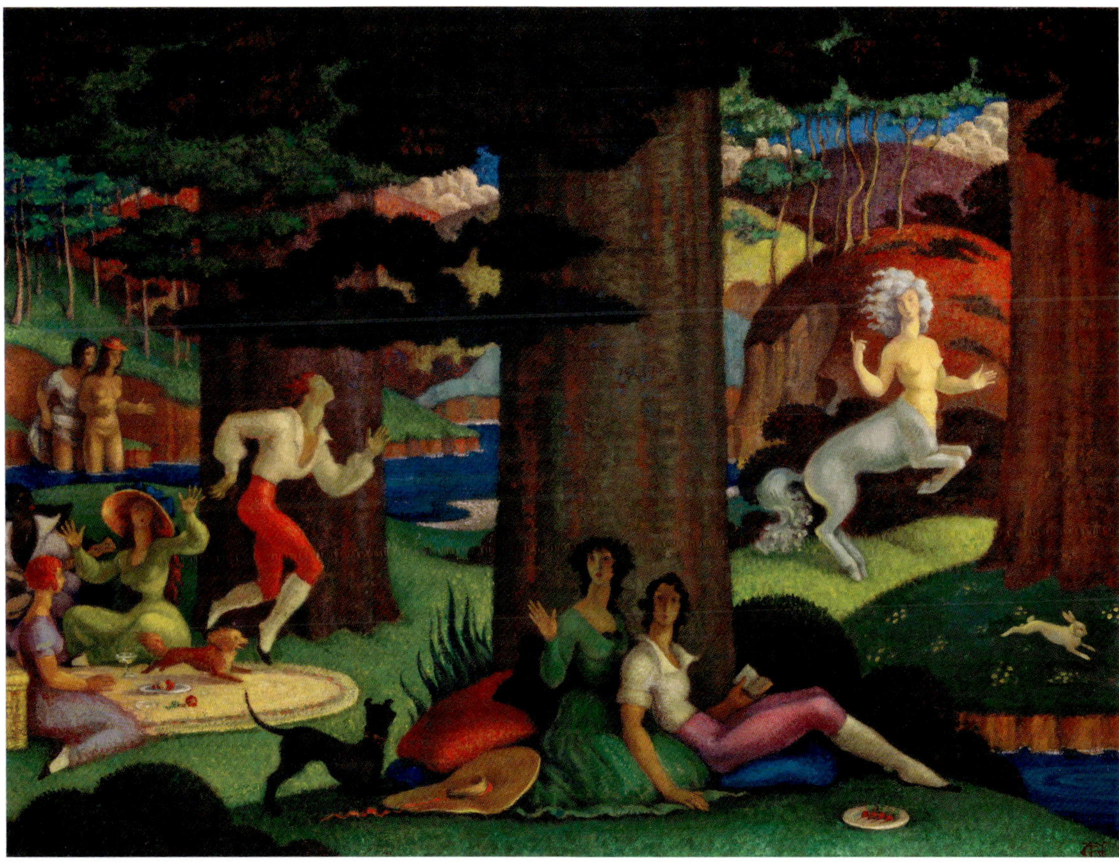

66 Beatrice Glenavy, *The Intruder*, 1932, oil on canvas.

repressed; within this scenario, the unconscious becomes the only possible outlet for the play of female desire. Such a reading is not denied by Glenavy's own view of the painting as indicating 'the unknown as more interesting than the known'.[20]

In 1932, after a further showing, this time at the RHA, William Orpen's brother Richard Orpen recommended it to the Haverty Trust for purchase, but the painting was considered obscene by some members of the committee, which was renowned for its conservatism.[21] Although little appears in Beatrice Glenavy's published autobiography to indicate her views on the position of women in the Irish Free State, she was certainly conscious of the effects of the restrictions on their lives. In 1934, one year after the banning of con-

traception in the Free State, Glenavy planned to do a painting entitled *Birth Control*, depicting two women burying a baby by candlelight.[22] Significantly, the nearest counterpart to Glenavy's representations of unconscious fantasy, Mary Swanzy's paintings of the 1930s were produced outside Ireland. Yet as Declan Kiberd has observed of the writer Elisabeth Bowen, it was Glenavy's very marginalization as Anglo-Irish that enabled her to speak, to articulate a response to the increasing repression of Irish women.[23] Other Anglo-Irish painters were also aware of the implications, especially for peasant women. At some point in the early 1930s, Mainie Jellett wrote to Albert Gleizes that the Catholic Church was forcing women in the west of Ireland 'to have huge families though they have not the means to feed or clothe them . . . the poverty . . . is appalling [,] the babies having to be wrapped in newspapers'.[24]

The North

The cultural themes of ethnic nationalism dominating art practice in the South during the decade had little relevance for painters working in Northern Ireland at that time. In spite of the Free State's territorial claim to the North included in Articles 2 and 3 of the 1937 Constitution, this was an area with considerably fewer connotations of ethnicity than the West. Two-thirds of the population was Protestant, and the Unionist government fiercely rejected any question of reunification with the South. In the early 1930s Northern Ireland was also severely affected by the global economic depression. As the main industrial urban centre, most unemployment was in Belfast, which also became the focus for opposition to draconian government relief schemes. A mass rally of both Protestant and Catholic workers took place in the city in September 1932, with a further demonstration and general strike planned for the following month. However, a fragile alliance of the Protestant and Catholic working class did not last, as sectarian violence erupted in the summers of 1934 and 1935. This was only finally broken up with the intervention of British troops, following the Royal Ulster Constabulary's refusal to become involved. Government ministers from the ruling Unionist party supported sectarianism. In addition to representing established landowning and industrial interests, many of them were also prominent members of the Orange Order. It was at the Twelfth of July celebrations in 1933 that Sir Basil Brooke, the Parliamentary Secretary and future Prime Minister, made his famous remark 'that he had not a Roman Catholic about his own place'.[25] Such officially sanctioned discrimination helped to provide

the impetus for the Orange Order's boycott of Catholic shops and businesses beginning in 1935. By mid-decade, any possibility of Protestant and Catholic working-class unity had been once more submerged by sectarianism, a situation with long-lasting consequences.

None of this unrest registered in current art practice in Northern Ireland; the more remote parts of the Northern Glens of Antrim continued to feature in paintings such as Romeo Toogood's *Dan Nancy's, Cushendun*, with its decorative landscape composition. What was beginning to emerge in the work of some artists was a practice of painting more closely allied to the ethics of Protestantism. After the Reformation and with the availability of print technology, Protestantism replaced the image as an aid to devotion by an insistence on 'the Word' as a signifier of a more private relationship between the believer and God.[26] The discursive connotations of Catholic religious painting became increasingly suppressed in favour of symbol and emblem. Subsequently the values of non-conformist Protestantism became closely associated with the Scottish Enlightenment in an insistence on values of diligence and industry. Given the common nature of Ulster-Scots culture, such values also became deeply embedded within the formation of Protestant identities in Northern Ireland, and as such they also became a factor in the emergence of artistic identities.

In his work of the 1930s, the painter John Luke began to develop a mode of painting that engaged with the ethics of industry in a variety of ways. A fascination with artistic technique led in 1933 to experiments with tempera. The first painting produced by this method was *Landscape Composition* (1933). The process was one that really came into its own in Luke's work of the 1940s, often in combination with oil. Its matte, opaque finish in conjunction with the necessary precision of application reinforced Luke's growing interest in formal

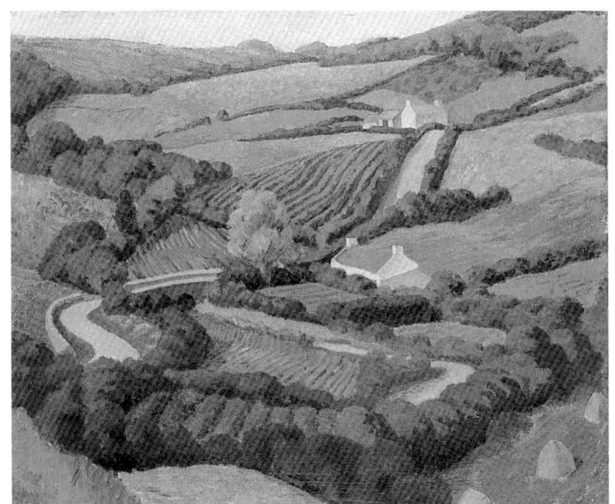

67 Romeo Toogood, *Dan Nancy's, Cushendun*, 1933, oil on canvas.

qualities derived from his reading of Clive Bell and Roger Fry. In the 1930s, this experimentation filtered back into the increasingly decorative and hard-edged features of his landscapes, such as *The Fox* (1937). The laborious process of priming the surface with several coats of gesso and the high level of skill in application of the fast-drying paint evoke the diligence and industry underpinning the formation of Ulster Protestantism, the culture within which Luke spent most of his life. In a more direct way Colin Middleton's early career was also shaped by the requirements of industry. Such little professional training as he received in night classes at the College of Art was mostly design-based, since from 1927 Middleton was required to work in the family business in Belfast. Here he was employed as a damask designer, a rigorous process involving the production of templates on squared paper, which were then worked up onto larger panels. The precision of these industrial processes can be seen as informing many of his paintings during the 1930s and 1940s.

The example of Middleton, however, should indicate the problems in any kind of reductive reading of the relationship between Protestantism and representation; by the end of the 1930s he was experimenting with a range of different pictorial practices such as Expressionism and Surrealism, both of which could be read as implicitly challenging the more puritan aspects of Protestantism. *Spain: A Dream Revisited* (1938) not only suggested a familiarity with the work of Dalí but also was one of the few works by an artist in Ireland to suggest any kind of engagement with the Spanish Civil War.

It was partly his identification of the work of both these artists with the values of industry that attracted the writer and curator John Hewitt to Luke and Middleton in the early 1930s. In 1930 Hewitt was appointed Art Assistant at the Belfast Museum and Art Gallery; until his death in 1987, he was an immensely significant and frequently courageous figure in the various cultural debates in Northern Ireland. His preference was for writers and artists whom he could locate within the Protestant tradition, such as the shipyard poet Thomas

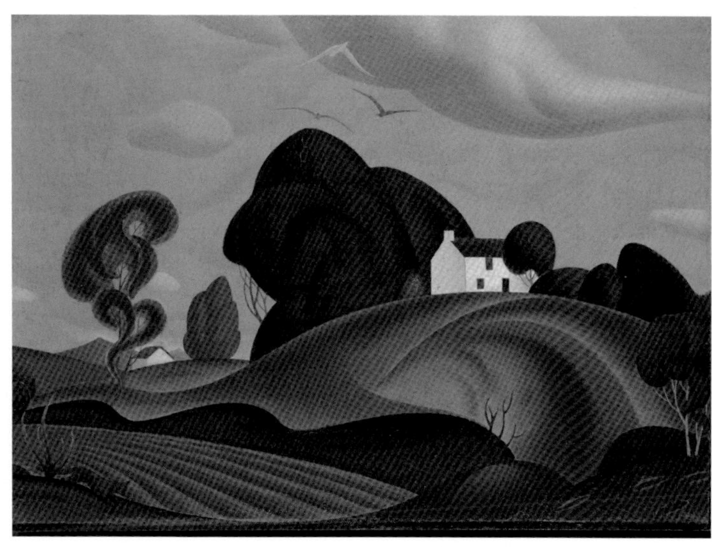

68 John Luke, *The Fox*, 1937, oil, tempera on panel.

Carnduff, and Hewitt clearly identified with what he termed 'his "own kind" – the hardworking, dissenting, skilled tradesmen of Ulster'.[27] Nevertheless, he actively encouraged young artists and writers of either religion until his enforced departure from Northern Ireland in 1953; the Hewitts's house at Mount Charles in the university area was a regular meeting place for artists and writers. The painter T. P. Flanagan recalled the painting collection in Hewitt's living-room in the 1950s as containing works by Luke, Middleton, Humbert Craig, Conor and Dan O'Neill.[28] Hewitt was also a poet of some significance. One of the areas focused on in his work was a response to nature, particularly after he and his wife Roberta discovered the Glens of Antrim in the 1930s, and he was also concerned with historical and genealogical continuity allied to a growing sense of the importance of location. Yet John and Roberta Hewitt combined an involvement with art and poetry with a commitment to political radicalism. In the polarized and bigoted political climate of Northern Ireland in the 1930s they were both anti-sectarian socialists opposed to the Spanish Civil War; John Hewitt was also a member of the Left Book Club at a time when 'the names of [its] committee were said to be displayed on the walls of every police station in the province'.[29]

In 1934, Hewitt was largely responsible for the formation of Northern Ireland's first self-consciously radical group of artists. The Ulster Unit chose its name with reference to Unit One, the main focus of artistic modernism in England in the early 1930s. It consisted of several ex-Slade students, teachers from the Belfast College of Art and a few older, established artists. Their first, and only, exhibition, described by Hewitt as the 'first to consist of avowedly and demonstrably modern work by artists living in the North of Ireland' was held in the Locksley Hall in central Belfast between 18 and 29 December 1934.[30] In addition to the sculptor George McCann, Romeo Toogood and Kathleen Bridle, who showed several landscapes from County Fermanagh, the seventeen exhibitors included Colin Middleton, represented by three abstract compositions and several prints, and John Luke, who included *Co. Down* (1933), one of his first tempera paintings. In the catalogue, which included a Middleton wood engraving on its cover, Hewitt's preface established an ambitious agenda for the group. This acknowledged the specificity of art in Northern Ireland by comparison with the radicalism of late eighteenth-century Belfast, while attempting to avoid the provincialism resulting from the subsequent degree of cultural isolation, through situating the artists of the Ulster Unit in an international context:

In this Unit, Ulster has for the first time a body of Artists alert to continental influence while that influence is still real and vital. It is no vain hope that with a consistent group, bound by more ties than those of mere geographical proximity, working on experimental lines and no longer in an archaic dialectic, Belfast will move step by step not only with Great Britain but with France and Scandinavia.[31]

With the exception of the isolated figures of Jellett and Hone, the internationalist aims of the Ulster Unit were more radical than any other art in Ireland at that time, given the predominance of cultural nationalism. Significantly, the Ulster Unit took a British example as its model of an avant-garde formation, rather than Paris. This is indicative not only of the first-hand experience of the artists such as McCann or Luke who had studied in London, but at a deeper level the political nature of the cultural relations underpinning the study schemes of the 1920s. The press response to the exhibition indicated a degree of confusion, the *Belfast Newsletter* admitting that although

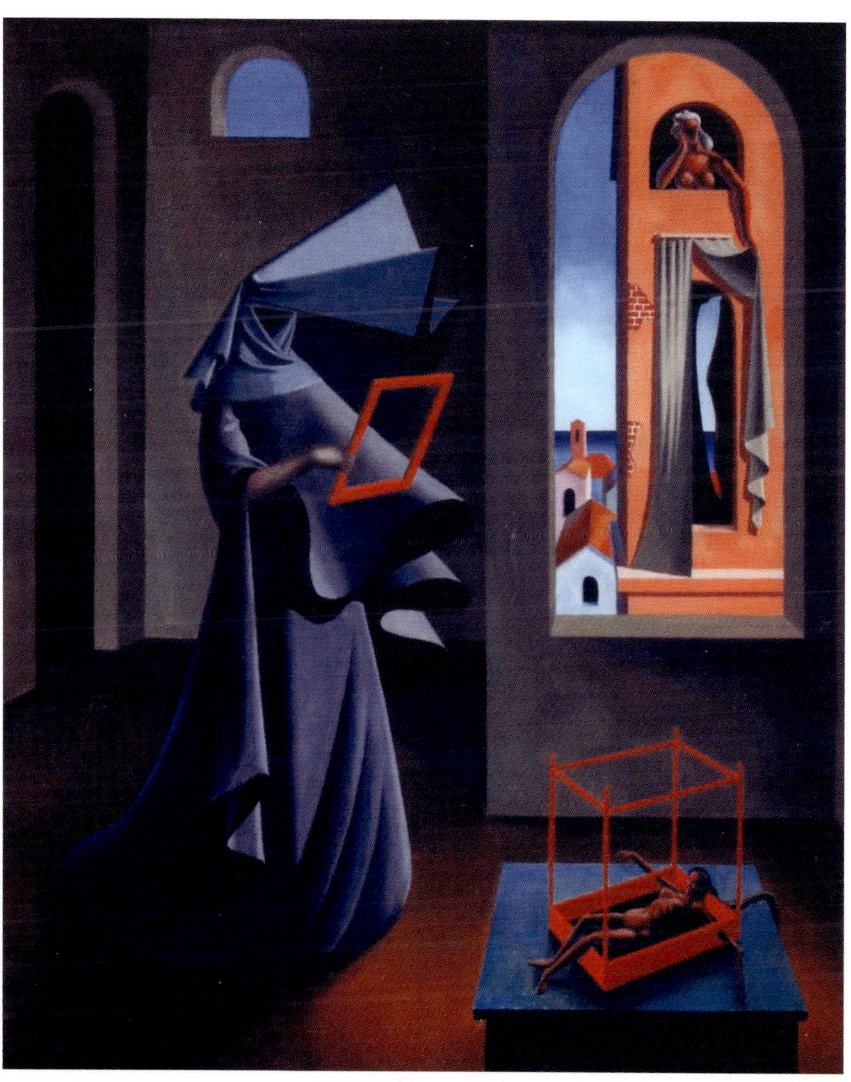

69 Colin Middleton, *Spain: A Dream Revisited*, 1938, oil on canvas.

'a certain amount must be dismissed as hocus-pocus . . . even the most unreal things in it represent honest and worthy experiment'.[32] In spring 1935 the Ulster Unit dissolved amicably, partly due to a lack of money. It had been entirely funded by members' subscriptions and the December exhibition only just paid for itself. The *Unit One* exhibition at the Belfast Art Gallery in March–April 1935 also contributed to this; faced with the collective presence of what was regarded as the most 'advanced' form of art practice in Britain, it became difficult to sustain the Ulster

Unit's existence as a cohesive body in the culturally isolated Northern Ireland.

Not all artists who left Northern Ireland to study in London returned in the early 1930s. In April 1934, Tom Carr became part of the London-based group responsible for the exhibition *Objective Abstractions* at the Zwemmer Gallery. This was an attempt to produce an avant-garde position dependent on a highly autonomous and abstract pictorial language; but it also came at a moment when many artists were questioning

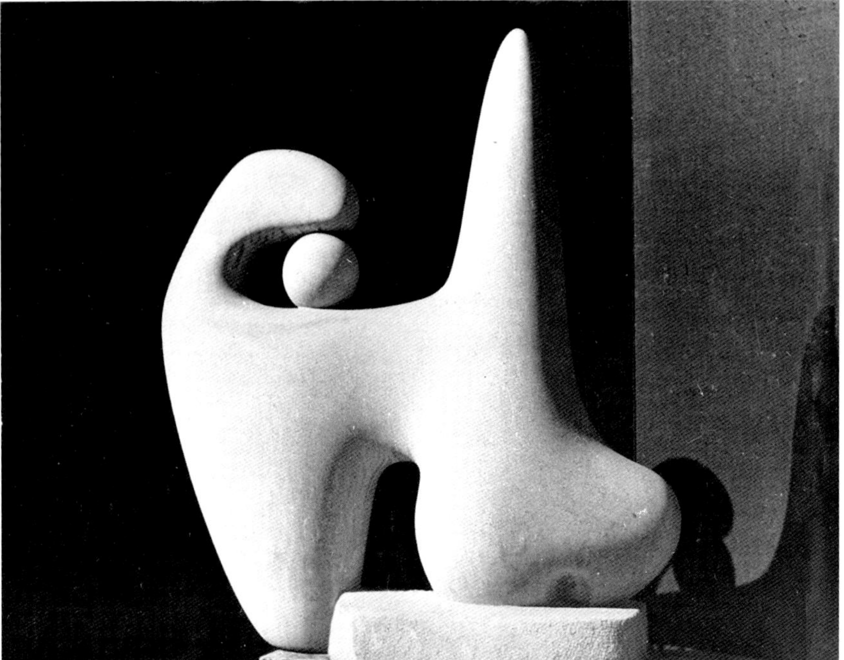

70 F. E. McWilliam, *Eye Nose and Cheek*, 1939, Hoptonwood stone.

the validity of their practice in an uncertain political context.[33] Soon afterwards, in 1936, the sculptor F. E. McWilliam moved back to London after several years of living in relative isolation in Buckinghamshire. He and his wife Beth, also a painter, moved to Hampstead close to the Parkhill Studios associated with Moore, Hepworth and Nicholson. That year his association with the British Surrealist Group also began, following a visit to the *International Surrealist Exhibition* at the Burlington Galleries, which resulted in a series of biomorphic carvings such as *Eye Nose and Cheek*. In 1937 McWilliam, whose early childhood in Banbridge had left him with a 'lasting awareness and hatred of intolerance and religious bigotry', participated in the Surrealist section of the British Artists' Congress exhibition organized by the Artists' International Association (AIA) – a political move that would have been impossible if he had stayed in Northern Ireland.[34]

FOUR

War, its Aftermath and the Visual, 1939–1947

rtists in the North and South soon found they had to formulate a response to the war that broke out in August 1939, but the demands placed on them were very different. As part of the United Kingdom, Northern Ireland declared its loyalty on the outbreak of war with the Unionist Prime Minister Craig's statement 'We are King's men.' Yet despite this claim, the significant proportion of nationalists within the population meant that military conscription operative in Britain was considered too politically sensitive. The severe economic depression of the last two decades had also left high unemployment, yet for many people the war was the beginning of greater prosperity. Sixty thousand went to work in the war industries in Britain, aided by the threat of unemployment benefit being withdrawn if they refused. In Northern Ireland heavy industry underwent a massive expansion. The demands of war production resulted in a considerable development of both the shipyards and aircraft industry in Belfast, although it was only Protestant workers who benefited from this. In Derry, large contracts for military uniforms involved the expansion of the workforce in the textile industries. After de Valera's withdrawal of British access to the Treaty Ports, the importance of Belfast, Larne and Derry as naval bases was vastly increased. With the fall of France in 1940, the role of these ports in securing the Atlantic

shipping routes became vital; the significance of the North as an operational base was further reinforced after large numbers of American service personnel were stationed there from January 1942 onwards.

But the greatest sense of shared experience with those in mainland Britain was the loss of life resulting from the Belfast Blitz of 1941.[1] The city was hopelessly unprepared and undefended; few shelters had been built and virtually all the anti-aircraft guns had been sent to Britain. There were four major air raids in April and May of that year. During the first, on Easter Tuesday (15–16 April), over 700 people were killed and 1,500 injured. Both Protestants and Catholics were affected, resulting in an unusual sense of loss common to both communities. The awareness of suffering shared with other industrial cities in Britain also emphasized Unionist perceptions of difference from the remainder of Ireland, which had opted for neutrality throughout the conflict.

Some figurative artists were employed as war artists. Doris Blair's painting *The Record Breaker* makes visible the role of women in the war effort in Northern Ireland, heroizing its female munitions worker in Mackie's factory. Both Tom Carr, who had recently returned from London, and William Conor were commissioned by the War Artists' Advisory Committee (WAAC) to produce scenes detailing Ulster's war effort; WAAC preferred

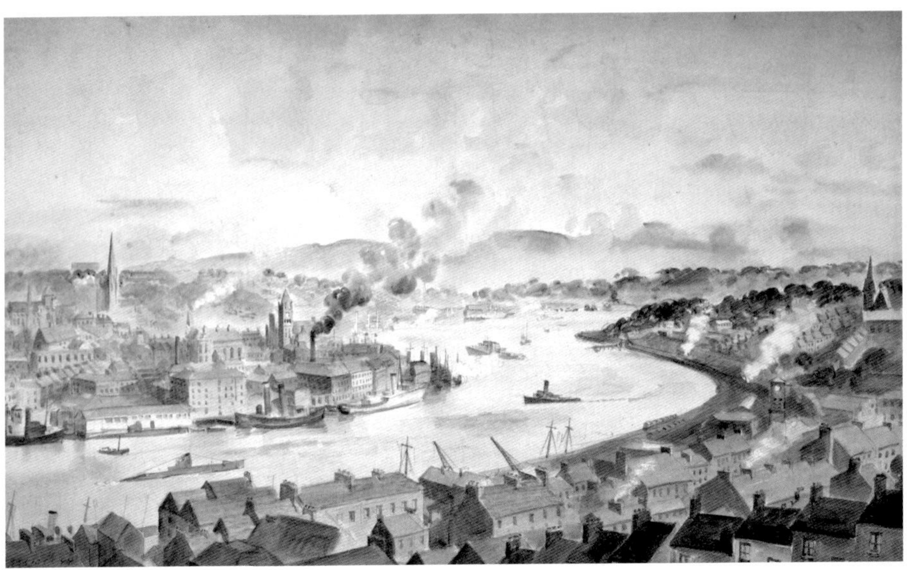

71 Vivian Pitchforth, *Londonderry Base*, 1944, pencil, watercolour on paper.

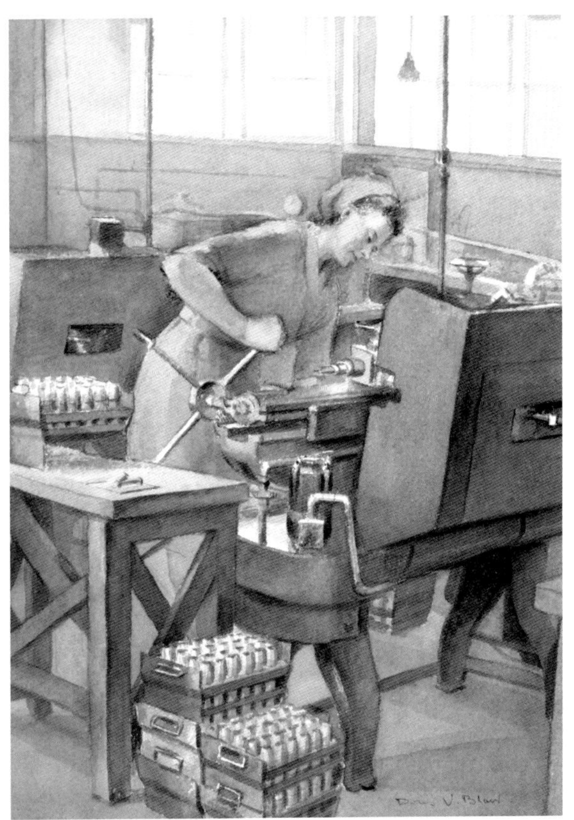

72 Doris Blair, *The Record Breaker*, 1941, watercolour on paper.

figurative artists capable of 'record[ing] the war at home and abroad'.[2] One of Conor's drawings from the early 1940s, *Evacuation of Children, Great Northern Railway Station, Belfast*, was one of only two works by Northern Irish artists to be selected in 1942 for inclusion in *Blitz*, one of a series of booklets publicizing the work on selected themes of British war artists.[3] Appearing the year after the Belfast Blitz, the inclusion of Conor's drawing in this publication also, on another level, imputes a degree of legitimacy to the Unionist claims of Northern Ireland as an integral part of a nation unified by its resistance to enemy bombing.

The lack of conscription inevitably had an effect on the continuing activities of artists and writers in Northern Ireland during wartime. Although some, like the sculptor George McCann, served in British Forces in different capacities, others, like John Hewitt, made several unsuccessful attempts to join up. Hewitt instead became involved in civil defence and lectured on art and Marxism to troops stationed across the North.[4] In the absence of conscription, a degree of cafe culture began to develop in Belfast, focused around Campbell's Cafe in Donegall Square North. This was a regular meeting

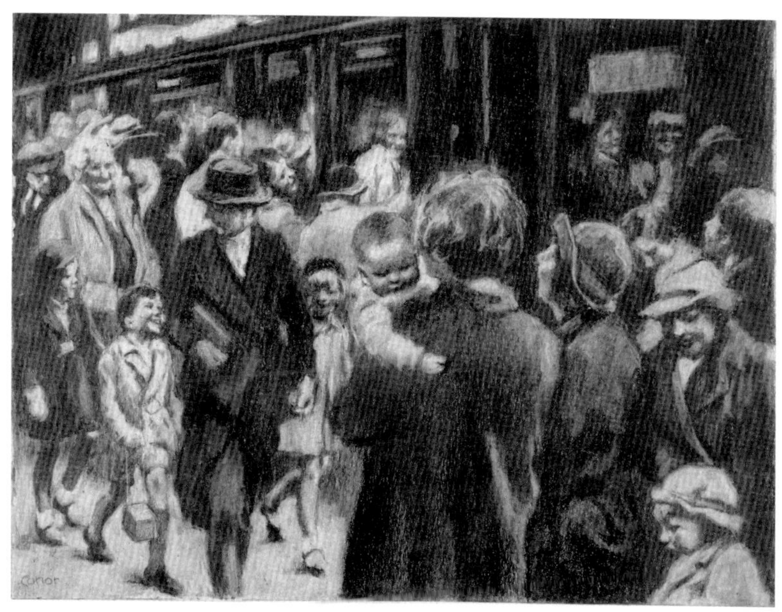

73 William Conor,
*Evacuation of Children,
Great Northern Railway
Station, Belfast,* 1940s,
pencil, crayon on paper.

place for artists such as Dan O'Neill, Markey Robinson and the young James MacIntyre as much as for writers such as Robert Greacen, John Boyd and Sam Hanna Bell. As Patricia Craig has observed, women seem to have been largely absent from the frequent gatherings there.[5] Apart from such established figures as Frank McKelvey, it was also extremely difficult for artists to earn a living from painting. Colin Middleton continued as a damask designer, Dan O'Neill was employed as an electrical engineer and the painter Olive Henry worked as a stained-glass designer in a commercial firm. The largely self-taught painter and former lightweight boxer Markey Robinson continued working as a welder; Robinson was also the basis for the character of the painter Lukey Mulquin in Carol Reed's film *Odd Man Out* (1945), adapted from F. L. Green's novel of the same name.

Belfast's only serious commercial gallery, Magee's, was notoriously conservative, refusing to consider anything other than academic painting. As the War progressed, however, occasional exhibitions at a range of venues helped to provide artists with the opportunity to display their work. In May 1943 this included the *Golden Jubilee Exhibition of the Gaelic League,* held at St Mary's Hall. In addition to established artists such as Paul Henry, Charles Lamb, William Conor and Letitia Hamilton, this large exhibition also included several young Belfast artists; Gerard Dillon showed seven paintings and a sculpture entitled *Slumber,* O'Neill showed two paintings, while George Campbell, who was exhibiting for the first time, included a drawing.[6] Later that year works by George and his brother Arthur were shown in other venues, such as a barber's shop on Royal Avenue and at the Duke of York pub in Commercial Place.[7] In 1943 the newly established Council for the Encouragement of Music and the Arts (CEMA) began to promote art from both North and South; CEMA additionally began to assemble a collection of work by Irish artists. Its gallery at 55a Donegall Place opened in 1947 and helped to provide a focal point for art from both within and outside Ireland.[8]

The year 1943 was also when Belfast Art Gallery reopened, with a major exhibition by Colin Middleton. In 1939 the Stranmillis Museum housing the gallery had been closed, its floors covered in sand and exhibits removed until the danger of bombing had receded. Organized by John Hewitt, the exhibition of 115 of

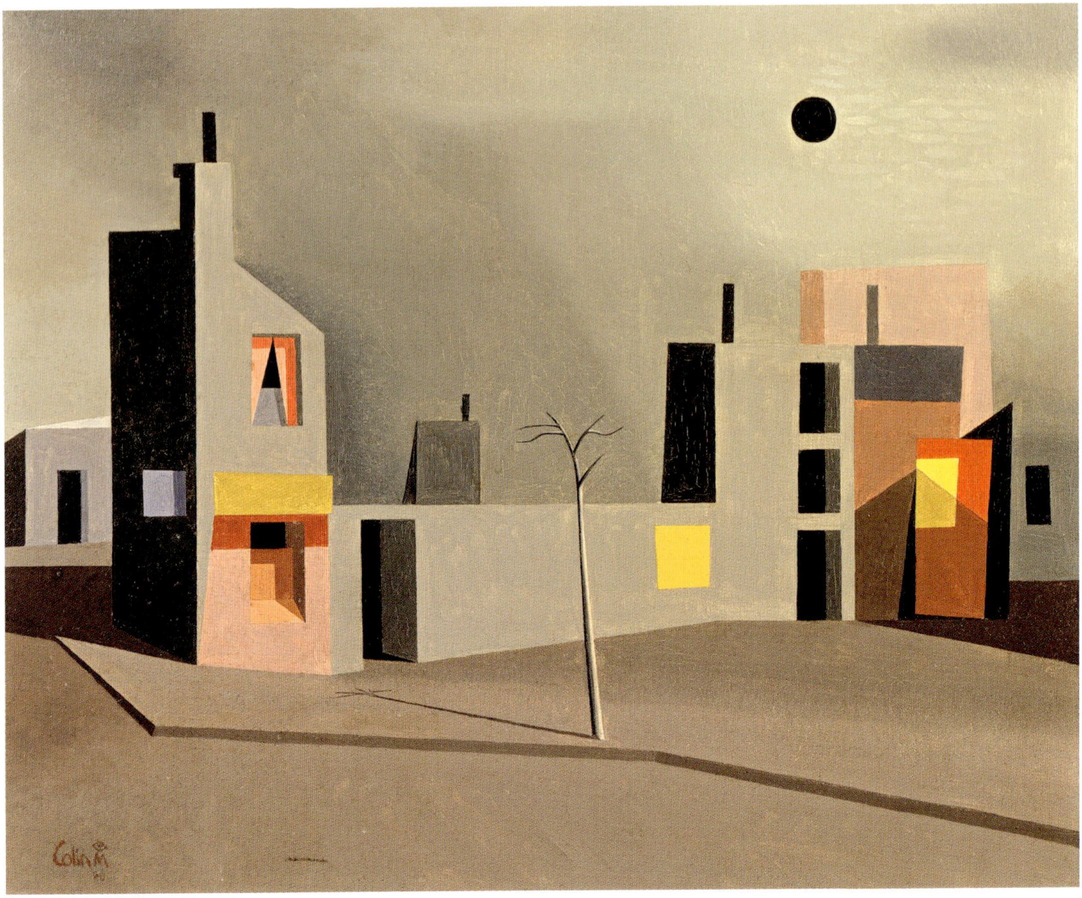

74 Colin Middleton, *Black Sun*, 1940, oil on canvas.

Middleton's paintings established him as an artist of some significance in Northern Ireland. The gallery, however, bought only one work from the show, the fairly conservative *Lagan: Annadale, October* (1941), for which it paid £25. This painting gives little indication of the range of Middleton's work, much of which at the time resembled illusionistic Surrealism. In *Black Sun*, connotations of the uncanny show a familiarity with the work of Magritte or de Chirico. The sense of desolation is also indicative of Middleton's response to the war; the Belfast Blitz profoundly affected him the following year. In this context a different visual language, Expressionism,

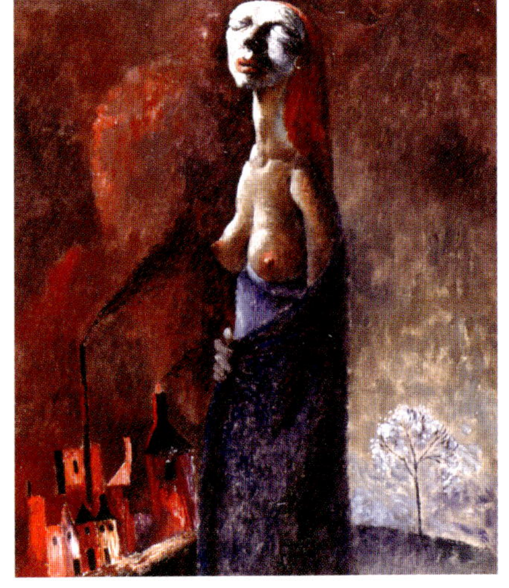

75 Colin Middleton, *The Refugee*, 1944, oil on canvas.

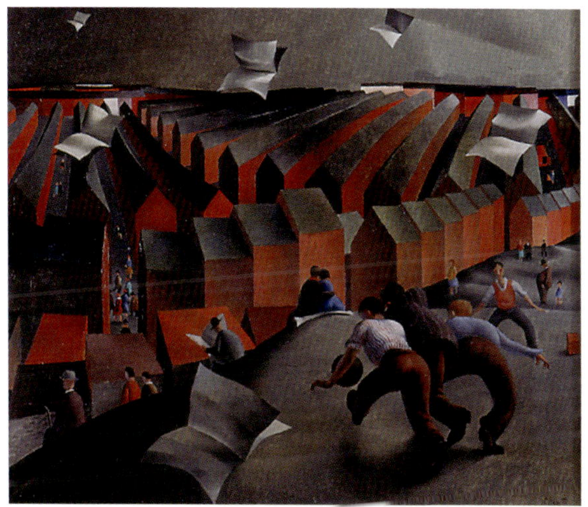

76 Colin Middleton, *The Holy Land*, 1945, oil on canvas.

began to emerge in Middleton's work, offering a means of engaging with a sense of feelings beyond words in the face of historic events.[9] *The Refugee* depicts a lone semi-clad female figure in front of a background of burning buildings, based on the artist's sketches of Belfast during the Blitz, although it also conveys a sense of more universalized suffering.[10] Yet in comparison with this bleak view of Belfast's destruction, a painting from the following year shows the city as a place of working-class community and cohesiveness. Painted in the year the war ended, the distortions of space and figures in *The Holy Land* suggest a reading of Stanley Spencer. Although the title of Middleton's painting uses the local term for this area of south Belfast, its pictorial references suggest a humorous allusion to Spencer's depictions of eccentric Christian belief erupting in rural England.

Colin Middleton's practice veered across a range of styles throughout his career, although this diversity led to repeated accusations of being overly derivative. Brian Fallon, writing in the *Irish Times* in 1974, argued:

One can't help having certain reservations about Middleton's versatility. To keep on the move stylistically . . . is certainly better than being stuck in the rut into which most middle aged or aging Irish painters fall. Picasso, after all, did the same, but Picasso imitated only himself, while Middleton's echoes of other artists have made too much of his work in the past look faintly derivative. He can do almost everything well, but that thing is not always his own.[11]

Middleton, who clearly related the role of the artist to changing social forces, had earlier countered similar accusations in an interview with the poet Michael Longley:

It's accepted that this is one of the most complex periods that the species has ever been through psychologically. And that is why we're getting this unbelievable diversity in styles and so on. But why the heck if a person is aware of this should it not occur in one person instead of one man here and one there all working differently at separate little facets of the same thing? Good heavens, why shouldn't one produce something absolutely different every time one paints?[12]

For John Hewitt, a supporter of Middleton throughout his career, his use of other sources was comparable to the montage of different styles in modernist writers such as Joyce or Eliot.[13] In spite of having little actual contact in the 1940s, Middleton strongly identified with the tendencies he perceived in British and European modernism. His 1967 interview cited Nicholson, Moore, Cézanne and Mondrian as his 'four evangelists', in addition to Piero della Francesca and Vermeer.[14] For an artist in Middleton's position, who wanted to both absorb and be incorporated within modernism, the only

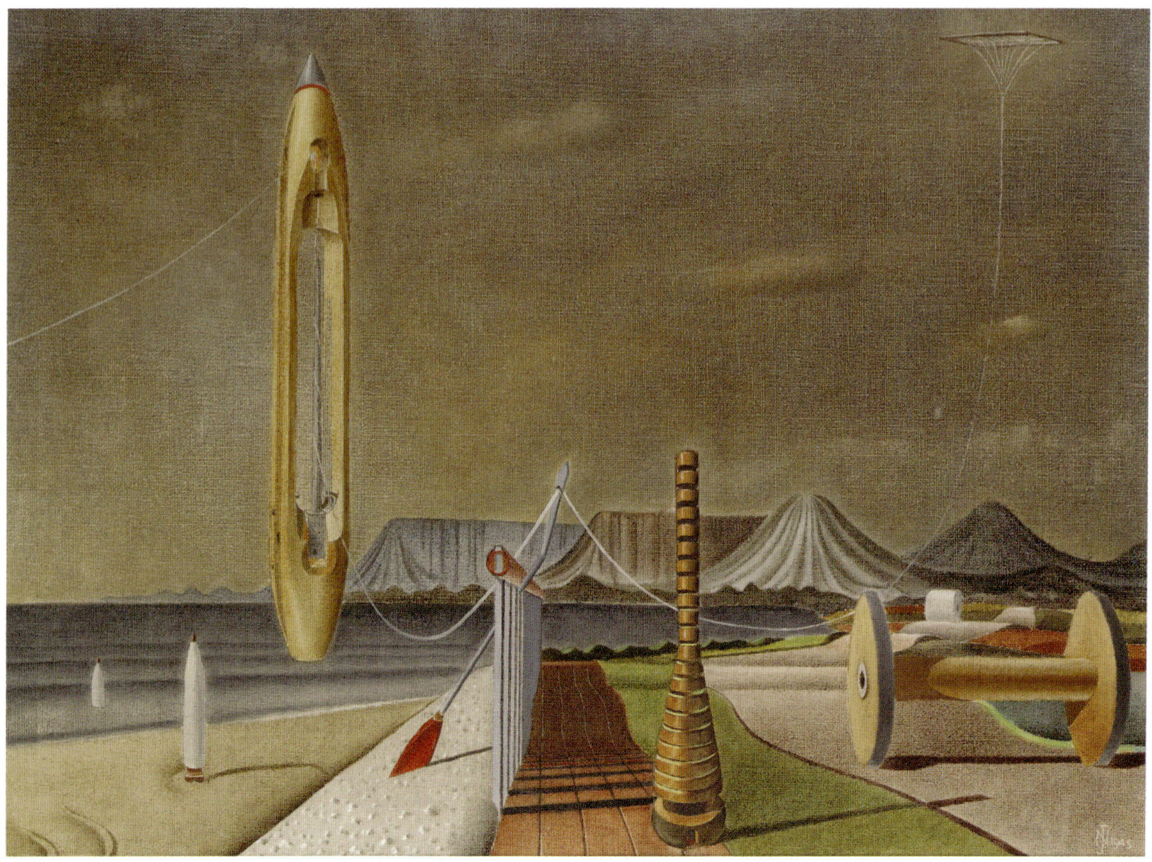

77 Nevill Johnson, *Linenscape*, 1945, oil on canvas.

solution seems to have been to reinvent a succession of avant-gardes for himself.

Surrealism also proved invaluable to the painter Nevill Johnson. Originally from Buxton in the north of England, he moved to Belfast in 1934, subsequently taking painting lessons with John Luke; the two visited Paris, where Johnson's discovery of Surrealism included Ernst, Magritte and Tanguy. Johnson found Belfast oppressive and bigoted, full of 'plebian brick and sixpenny pundits', and regularly escaped to small coastal villages such as Ballintoy in North Antrim or Kilkeel in County Down.[15] Two very different views of the coastline by him indicate how landscape became a means of registering the effects of the war, albeit mediated through the detours of Surrealism. In 1939, Johnson, his wife and baby were staying

in a coastguard cottage at Ballintoy when they heard of the outbreak of war. His painting *Linenscape* depicts the distinctive North Antrim coastline swathed in linen and superimposed by a large spindle and other tools used in textile production, which prospered in wartime Northern Ireland. Even the surface of the painting, with its deliberately rough canvas, draws attention to the significance of the fabric itself. Yet in comparison with the suggestions of security and prosperity, another painting from the same period, *Kilkeel*, offers a hallucinatory vision of a darkened, deserted shoreline populated only by uncanny biomorphic forms and driftwood, which Johnson collected. In spite of the village representing a welcome alternative to the oppressiveness of the city, Johnson also recalled later that his young family had

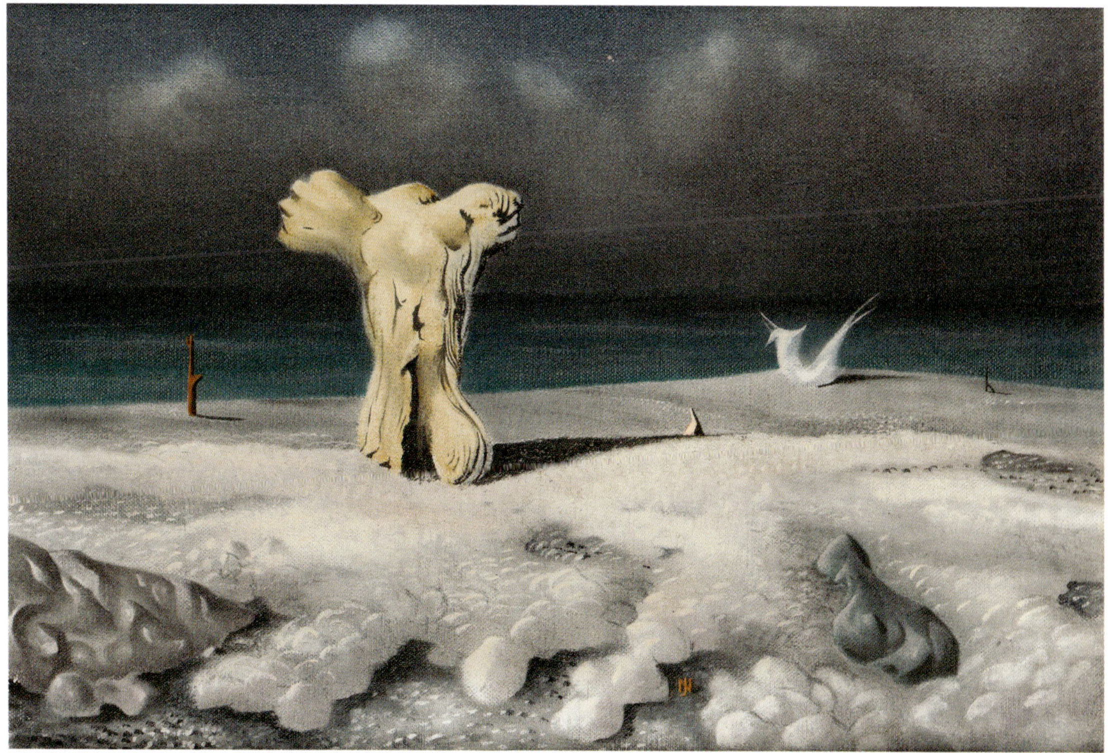

78 Neville Johnson, *Kilkeel*, n.d., oil on canvas.

been picnicking there on the beach as Hiroshima was bombed.[16]

In spite of its relative isolation, the wider effects of the war continued to register in Northern Ireland; John Luke, for example, ceased painting between 1939 and 1943. Living close to the Belfast docks, he experienced the continual disruption and uncertainty of the bombing raids. Eventually, in 1941, shortly after the Belfast Blitz, he moved with his mother to 'Knappagh', a house outside Killyleagh in County Armagh, where Nevill Johnson and his family were already in residence. Luke stayed in 'Knappagh' until November 1950.[17] Here he was able to resume work with the utopian vision of a post-war landscape, *Pax* (1943). The following year *The Road to the West* was commissioned from Luke by John and Roberta

Hewitt to mark their tenth wedding anniversary. This painting was based on a cycling trip to Achill that Luke had undertaken in 1935. It depicts a landscape scene in the west of Ireland, with a road winding its way past peat stacks to the mountains beyond. Two figures, a child and a woman in the traditional clothing of shawl and red petticoat, stand looking towards a male figure placed in the centre of the composition, at the brow of the road. The bulk of the mountains is echoed by the dark brown wedges of peat stacks, which contrasts with the predominantly lighter palette of misty greens and blues. With a contrapuntal rhythm emphasized by the use of colour, this is a highly ordered view of the West. In comparison with Paul Henry's views of the Atlantic seaboard, Luke's version relies on rigorous formal requirements

and isolation more apparent; large numbers of young women especially began to leave, attracted by opportunities elsewhere. Although many went to the expanding conurbation of Dublin, many others continued the emigration to Britain. This crisis of rural identity in Southern Ireland was reinforced by a further failure of Free State ideology in the apparent inability of the Gaelic revival to protect the Irish language; the isolated Gaeltachts (Irish-speaking areas) were also some of the areas suffering the worst depopulation.

Yet despite the inherent conservatism of many areas outside Dublin, 1939 to 1948 was a period of critical reassessment of the political and cultural direction of the Irish Free State. An important site for these debates was the journal *The Bell*, which began publication in 1941 under the editorship of the author Seán O'Faoláin; its first run ceased in 1948, shortly before Ireland gained full independence. *The Bell* was initially subtitled 'A Magazine of Creative Fiction' and included the writers Patrick Kavanagh, Kate O'Brien and John Hewitt among its contributors. In spite of its focus on prose and poetry, it also provided a much-needed engagement with wider issues of Irish culture during decolonization.[23] This included art criticism, which added to the reviews and discussions already appearing in the pages of the *Irish Times* and *Irish Independent* or journals such as *Commentary* and *The Capuchin Annual*. In May 1941 *The Bell* began to publish a short series of profiles of the contemporary artists Harry Kernoff, Cecil Ffrench Salkeld and Nano Reid, written by Anna Sheehy or Elizabeth Curran.[24] Subsequent coverage of visual art became increasingly analytical, such as the assessment of current exhibiting policy in Arthur Power's scathing attack on the 1942 RHA annual exhibition.[25]

One important area of debate in *The Bell* was the increased challenge to the censorship of literature established in 1929; despite his approval of a limited degree of state control, O'Faoláin's own work had been banned under the legislation. Although censorship can be seen as one (particularly extreme) attempt to define the role of culture within the state, its main effect had been to severely curtail the activities of Irish writers: Kate O'Brien's novel *The Land of Spices* (1941) was banned due to a single reference to homosexuality.[26] Wartime had serious consequences in that links with publishers in Britain were virtually cut off. And despite the banning of films like Charlie Chaplin's *The Great Dictator* (1940) on the grounds that they might challenge Ireland's neutrality in wartime, the visual arts, by comparison, were less directly affected by the prescriptive measures of censorship as a means of shaping the nation.[27] There were, however, isolated incidents such the 'Rouault Controversy'.[28] In 1942, Dublin Corporation's Art Advisory Committee refused to accept the gift of Georges Rouault's *Christ and the Soldier* (1930). This painting had been purchased from the Leicester Galleries in London by the Friends of the National Collection of Ireland, who then offered it to the Municipal Gallery. However, the depiction of a religious scene in a modern manner was considered blasphemous by the Committee; ironically, the painting ended up on extended loan to Maynooth College, Ireland's Catholic university. The controversy proved to be particularly long-lasting; it was only in 1956 that the Art Committee agreed to accept the gift, after a further unsuccessful attempt two years previously.[29]

The conflict between Catholicism and modernism in the debates surrounding Rouault's painting is also symptomatic of the major ideological dilemmas characterizing Irish culture during the 1940s. This was no less a problem for the visual arts in the early part of the decade, particularly for painters such as Seán Keating and Jack Yeats. Not only were they older, with careers that had become firmly established during the period of decolonization, but they also both had plausible claims

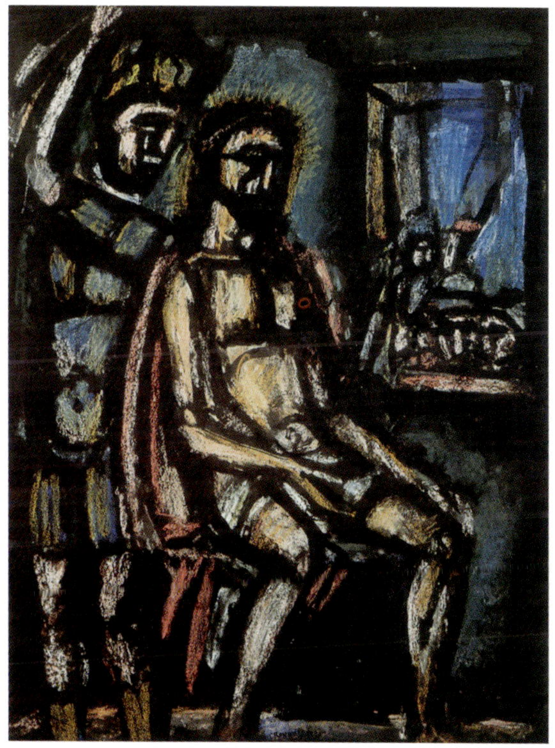

85 Georges Rouault, *Christ and the Soldier*, 1930, gouache, crayon and ink on board.

to being the painter who best represented Ireland's political struggles since the early twentieth century. By 1940, Yeats was also one of the few surviving figures associated with the Literary Revival, especially after the death of his brother William in 1939. Keating, meanwhile, had made a career out of producing social realist tableaux that were easily adaptable to the various ideological requirements of the Irish Free State, whether in the overt ethnicity of *The Race of the Gael* (1939) or the progressive modernization of his cycle of paintings documenting the completion of the Shannon hydro-electric scheme. He had also acquired considerable institutional prestige as Professor of Painting at the National College of Art, a post to which he was appointed in 1934. For many observers, however, Keating's own work had become formulaic by the early 1940s. As Arthur Power commented in his essay for *The Bell* on the

failings of the RHA Annual Exhibition of 1942, 'In Mr Keating's picture everything is of the same texture, the men, the seas, the jerseys, the faces, the trousers.'[30] Power's attack on Keating implicitly acknowledged his prestige within the Academy, also 'symbolic of the state of this country, which lies at present paralysed under moribund authority', a place where everyone 'is cashing in on the Past, on the spirit and genius of the men who went before them'.[31] This approach was consistent with *The Bell*'s policy of a radical critique of all aspects of Free State ideology; it was also symptomatic of a more widely felt unease with the political implications of Keating's practice.

By comparison, although not himself exempt from Power's criticism, Yeats's work in the 1940s was beginning to offer the possibilities of a more nuanced engagement with the grand themes of the emergent nation.[32] In the early 1940s his reputation in Ireland grew considerably, reinforced by a joint exhibition with William Nicholson at the National Gallery in London in 1942 organized by its Director, Kenneth Clark. Things were also picking up for him financially after the lows of the previous decade: in 1943 Yeats was taken up by the dealer Victor Waddington, who continued to represent him until the artist's death in 1957. Before his move to London in the 1950s, Waddington's Dublin gallery was also an important venue for young, radical artists in Ireland: Louis le Brocquy, Dan O'Neill and Nevill Johnson all exhibited there at early points in their career. In addition to developing a lasting friendship with Victor Waddington, however, Yeats's relationship with the dealer provided him with a more secure financial base than previously. In stylistic terms, Yeats's work of the early 1940s continued with the expressive brushwork and heavy impasto of the previous decade, as in *Two Travellers* (1942). In this scene of two figures meeting on a barren road with a mountain looming behind them, a

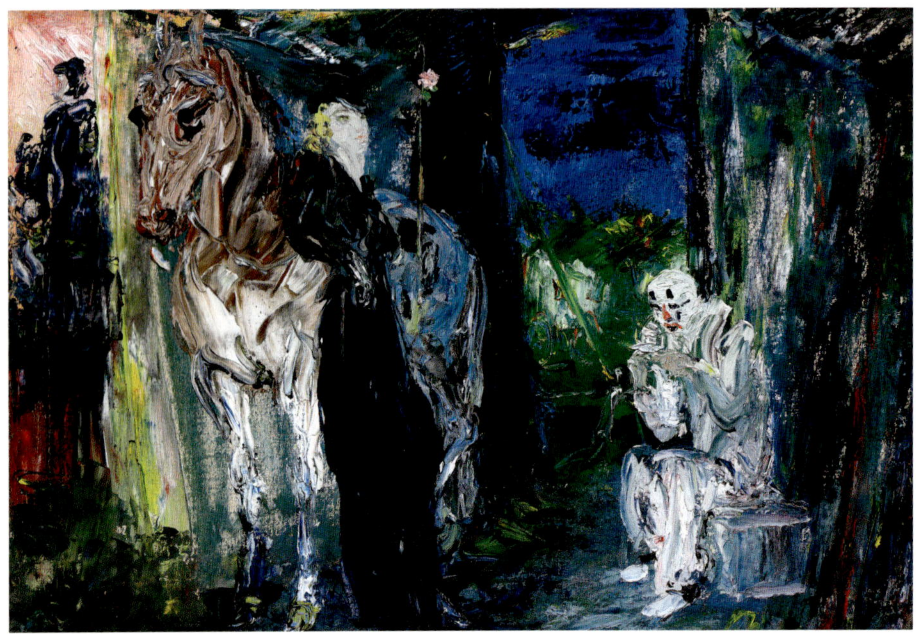

86 Jack Yeats, *That Grand Conversation Was under the Rose*, 1943, oil on canvas.

sense of desolation is reinforced by the low horizon. Other paintings, such as *By Streedagh Strand* (1940), where the figure in the foreground merges with surrounding features, begin to develop themes characterizing the work of Yeats's last decade; the connotations of remote grandeur evoke a peripheral Sublime located within the liminal space between land mass and ocean. Precise references in Yeats's work were becoming increasingly obscure during the early 1940s, due at least in part to his decision no longer to discuss the meaning of his paintings. According to James White, this dated from a specific incident in October 1942 when the United Arts Club held an honorary dinner for Yeats and speeches after the meal treated his work in an insensitive manner. When Yeats and his wife Cottie subsequently returned home, she gave him a paper rose which she had acquired at the dinner. The painter then apparently tied the rose to the easel in his studio, later telling White, 'I made a vow then . . . that from thence forward all my work would be sub rosa; I would never again discuss the meaning of my pictures.'[33] A work from the following year, *This Grand Conversation Was under the Rose*, depicts two

circus performers, the Haute-École rider and the clown, resting in the wings. In Hilary Pyle's reading of this painting, the clown represents the artist and the rider his inspiration or muse; their meeting, the genesis of the work's meaning, thus takes place in a domain away from the public arena.[34]

The indeterminacy of Yeats's work during this period resulted in a malleability of meaning, allowing him to be positioned as a painter within different agendas. In July 1945, the *National Loan Exhibition*, a major retrospective of his work, took place at the National College of Art. Yeats's role as 'national painter' began to coalesce around this exhibition, the opening of which was attended by the Taoiseach, Éamon de Valera. The catalogue essay written by Earnán O'Malley identified Yeats with the ethnicity of the West, the location of both 'an untamed naturalness' and 'a feeling of equality through an understanding of the natural dignity of man', and with the struggles of decolonization, attributing to his work 'the heightened sensibility which could result from the tension of life during the struggle for freedom in Ireland'.[35] This was hardly surprising, given that

O'Malley was an old republican who had been on Michael Collins's staff during the War of Independence. But O'Malley had also begun to collect Yeats's work during the late 1930s, and his essay demonstrated a close awareness of the visual qualities of the paintings, noting an ability to 'create a homogeneous surface with his brush . . . or use the priming of the canvas to aid luminosity of light and shade'.[36] The nationalist reading of Yeats in O'Malley's essay was reinforced by the publication of Thomas MacGreevy's pamphlet *Jack Yeats: An Appreciation and an Interpretation.* Although written in the late 1930s, its late publication took advantage of the success of the *Loan Exhibition*.[37] Yet in a review of MacGreevy's book for the *Irish Times*, Samuel Beckett put forward a very different reading, in effect reclaiming Yeats for modernist autonomy, 'The national aspects of Mr Yeats's genius have, I think, been over-stated, and for motives not always remarkable for their aesthetic purity.'[38] Beckett sought to recover Yeats for a position close to his own interests, where modernist culture was capable of revealing existential truths:

> He is with the great of our time, Kandinsky and Klee, Ballmer [sic] and Bram van Velde, Rouault and Braque, because he brings light, as only the great dare to bring light, to the issueless predicament of existence.[39]

Although these interpretations of Yeats's work in the 1940s were contradictory, they did, however, contribute to the emergent possibilities for readings of Irish art as more complex than previously recognized. This was a factor also bound up with the growth of the avant-garde, and the increasing erosion of the opposition between nationalism and modernism.

For some observers, Dublin during the Emergency was characterized by a combination of insularity and hedonism. As Beatrice Glenavy's son, the writer Patrick Campbell, later commented, 'Dublin seemed to have a special duty, in a world gone grey and regimented, to preserve the gaieties and the pleasures that we felt had vanished from everywhere else', with regular parties fuelled by whisky provided by English expatriates.[40] Both Britain and Germany maintained a diplomatic presence in Dublin throughout the war and their representatives could often be seen at exhibition openings. Ferry crossings between Holyhead and Dun Laoghaire continued to operate, bringing not only a regular supply of English visitors but also Irish painters who had been working abroad, such as Norah McGuinness, Ralph Cusack and Louis le Brocquy. Their reappearance helped to erode the insularity of the Dublin art world. This was reinforced by the arrival of other artists escaping from wartime England, and their presence contributed to the formation of a more recognizable avant-garde.

There were opportunities for the development of alternative, bohemian lifestyles and attitudes to painting in wartime Dublin. Nano Reid's flat in Fitzwilliam Square was a focus for young poets and painters such as Gerard Dillon. It was here that she also painted a portrait of George Campbell, who stayed in the flat for a period with his wife Madge. At this point in her career Reid's Expressionism, developed through paintings such as *Friday Fare*, was regarded as so radical that she struggled to make a living from portraiture. The loose brushstrokes, bright colours and lack of figurative detail in *Through the Studio Door*, depicting Campbell at work at his easel, are there not to fulfil more traditional aims of portraiture but as a pictorial means of signifying the bonds of friendship and common purpose.

A synthesis of bohemian lifestyle and modernist painting closer to aspects of early twentieth-century European avant-gardes became a distinctive feature of the White Stag Group as it began to emerge in Ireland

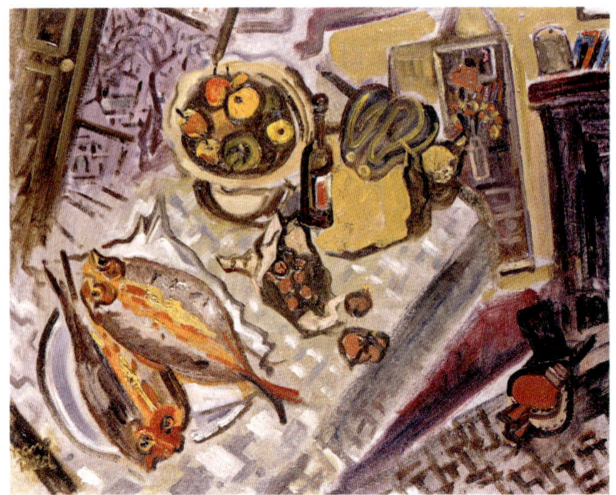

87 Nano Reid, *Friday Fare*, 1945, oil on canvas.

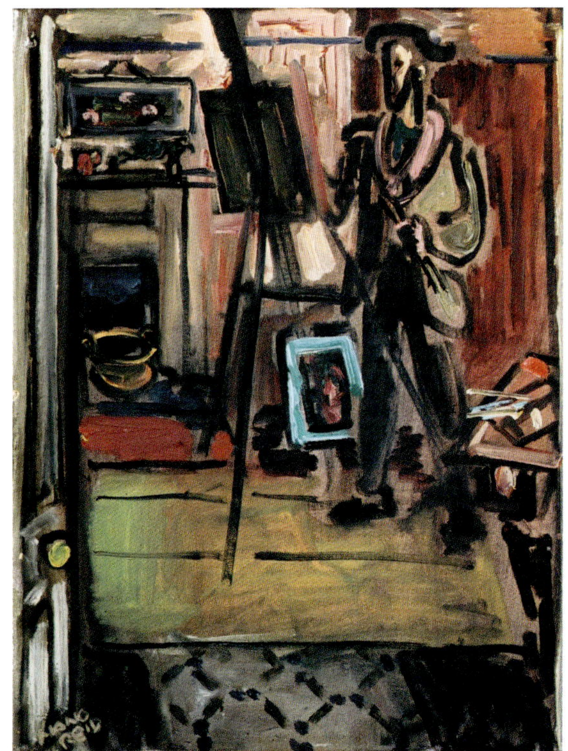

88 Nano Reid, *Through the Studio Door*, 1946, oil on canvas.

from 1939 onwards. This group consisted mainly of English émigrés, central among whom were the painters Basil Rakoczi and Kenneth Hall. A gay couple, both had been conscientious objectors in Britain; Rakoczi had also been responsible with Herbrand Ingouville-Williams for setting up the Society for Creative Psychology in Bloomsbury in the early 1930s. It was here that he and Hall first met in 1935. In the same year they went on to establish the White Stag Group 'for the advancement of subjectivity in psychological analysis and art'.[41] Rakoczi's psychology attempted to combine the study of Freud with that of Adler and Jung; the name of the group was derived from the Hungarian symbol of the white stag on a dark background signifying an archetype of creativity. The group included other English expatriates, such as the painters Nick Nicholls, Phyllis Hayward and Stephen Gilbert, in addition to the Canadian sculptor Dorothy Chewett and the Irish painter Dairine Vanston, who had returned to Dublin from Paris in 1940.

The White Stag Group soon became an accepted part of the Dublin art scene, although for many British and other expatriates, there was always a fear of deportation back across the Irish Sea. As Hall commented somewhat elliptically in his autobiography,

Everybody in Dublin was friendly and nice and in six weeks we were knowing more people than we had known before and they were kind and friendly.[42]

Mainie Jellett was a keen supporter of their activities, participating in both the first and second White Stag exhibitions in 1940. Other young Dublin-based painters such as Patrick Scott became actively involved with the group, showing with them on a number of occasions. On one level the importance of the White Stag Group was that they introduced and promoted modernist

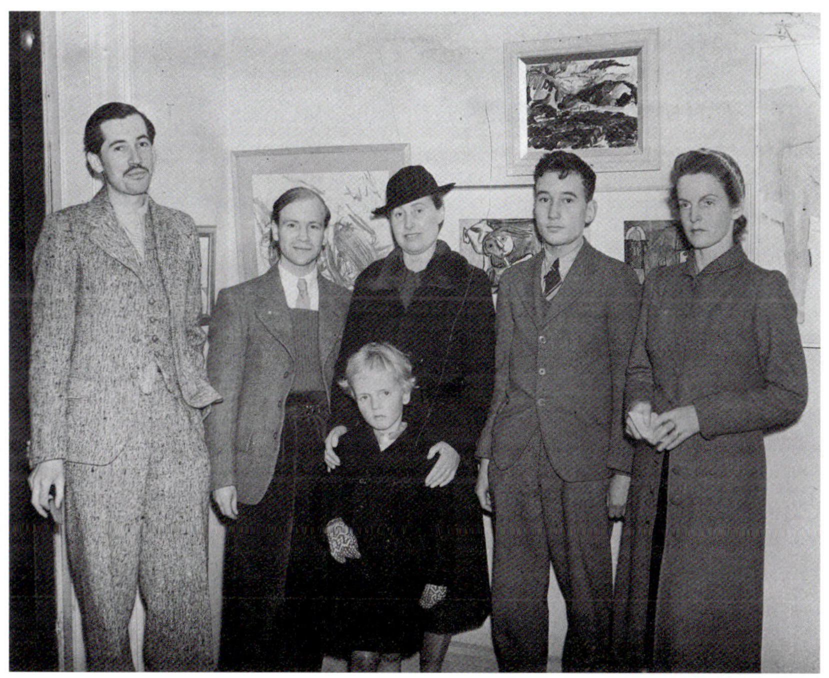

89 White Stag artists at the White Stag Gallery, Dublin, c. 1941–4.

tendencies other than those prevalent within Ireland, which tended to be derived from Jellett and Hone's reading of Cubism. But they also, in some of their work, articulated a degree of engagement with the political events developing outside the neutral Free State. In a political climate where press publication of any material that might challenge Ireland's neutrality was rigorously monitored, the Second World War was only occasionally acknowledged in the work of painters, such as Yeats's *Tinkers' Encampment: The Blood of Abel* (1940). In *Après la Guerre* Kenneth Hall intends to suggest a sense of displacement by the device of the biomorphic form floating in an indeterminate space across washes of colour. This is similar to the non-specific forms found in the work of Surrealist painters such as Miró or Tanguy during the late 1920s; here, in conjunction with the title, it suggests a bleakly pessimistic future of post-war desolation far removed from the perceived complacency of neutral Ireland. The painting is also probably autobiographical: Hall suffered from a recurrent sense of despair and isolation as an exile.[43] Dáirine Vanston's *Dying Animal* is

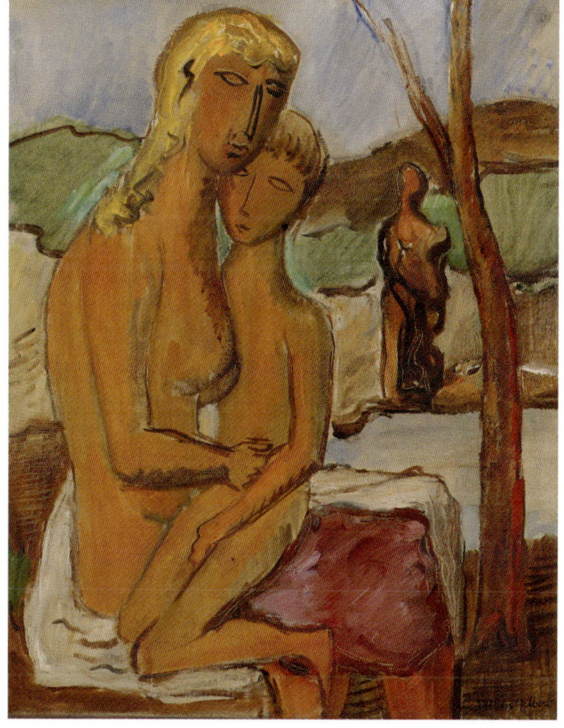

90 Stephen Gilbert, *Mother and Child*, 1940, oil on canvas.

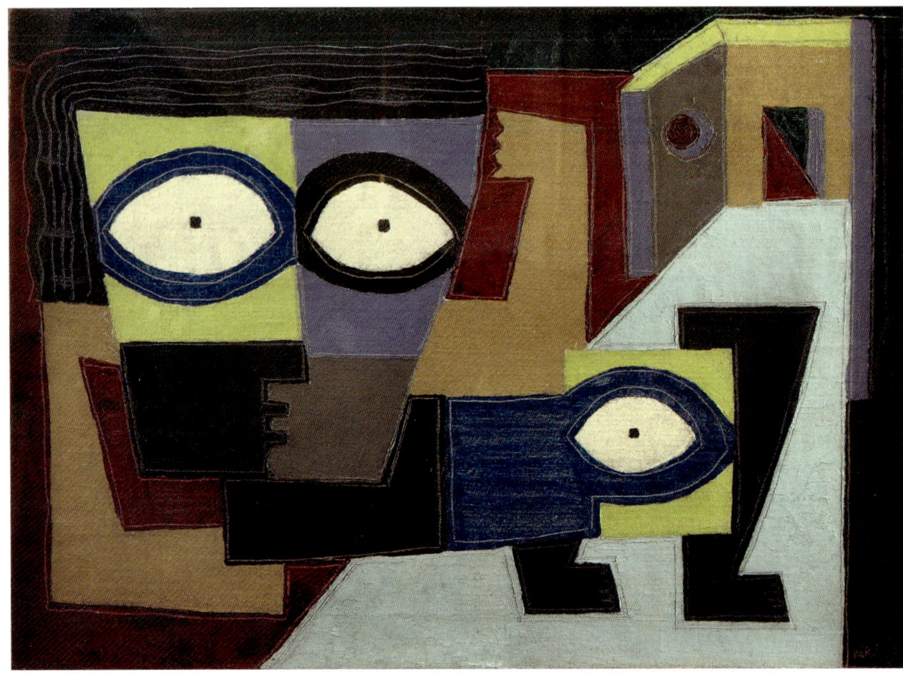

91 Basil Rakoczi, *Prisoner*, 1944, oil on canvas.

more figurative by comparison. Its subject-matter, the contorted form of an animal's death throes, uses a primitivist sense of empathy to suggest suffering on an instinctive level; Basil Rakoczi commented that the painting showed Vanston to be an 'unconscious mystic'.[44] In spite of a brief period of study with André Lhote during the 1930s, the contorted forms of Vanston's painting are more evocative of the Surrealist notion of the convulsive as corresponding to the repressed operations of the unconscious. Significantly, both of these artists, Hall and Vanston, had an awareness of the crisis in Europe quite different from that of most other painters in Ireland at that time. For part of 1938 and 1939 Kenneth Hall and Basil Rakoczi lived in Paris, before returning to Britain. Vanston had probably remained in Paris until the German forces arrived in 1940, when she moved to Cagnes-sur-Mer with the painter Jankel Adler, leaving much of her work behind.[45] From there she made her way to London, eventually returning to Dublin. Both *Après la Guerre* and *Dying Animal* to varying degrees suggest the rejection of

figurative realism as a visual language unable to represent the enormity of the crisis threatening to engulf Western civilization.

A further factor distinguishing the White Stag painters from others in Ireland in the early 1940s is that, as incomers, they did not have the same kind of immersion in the ideology of the Irish West that had permeated Irish culture since the early 1930s. When Rakoczi and Hall arrived in 1939 they lived first near Delphi in County Mayo. Although this was within the western Gaeltacht, their decision was due to the desire to get as far away from the war as possible. Delphi, an early nineteenth-century fishing lodge, was selected because the name reminded them of a visit to Greece in 1938. Yet the White Stag Group functioned much more recognizably as part of an urban avant-garde, distinguished by its orientation towards artistic tendencies in Europe or England, rather than the renewed excavation of familiar themes of Irish culture. This was reinforced by the inclusion in their exhibitions of paintings by French and British artists; the show of December 1940

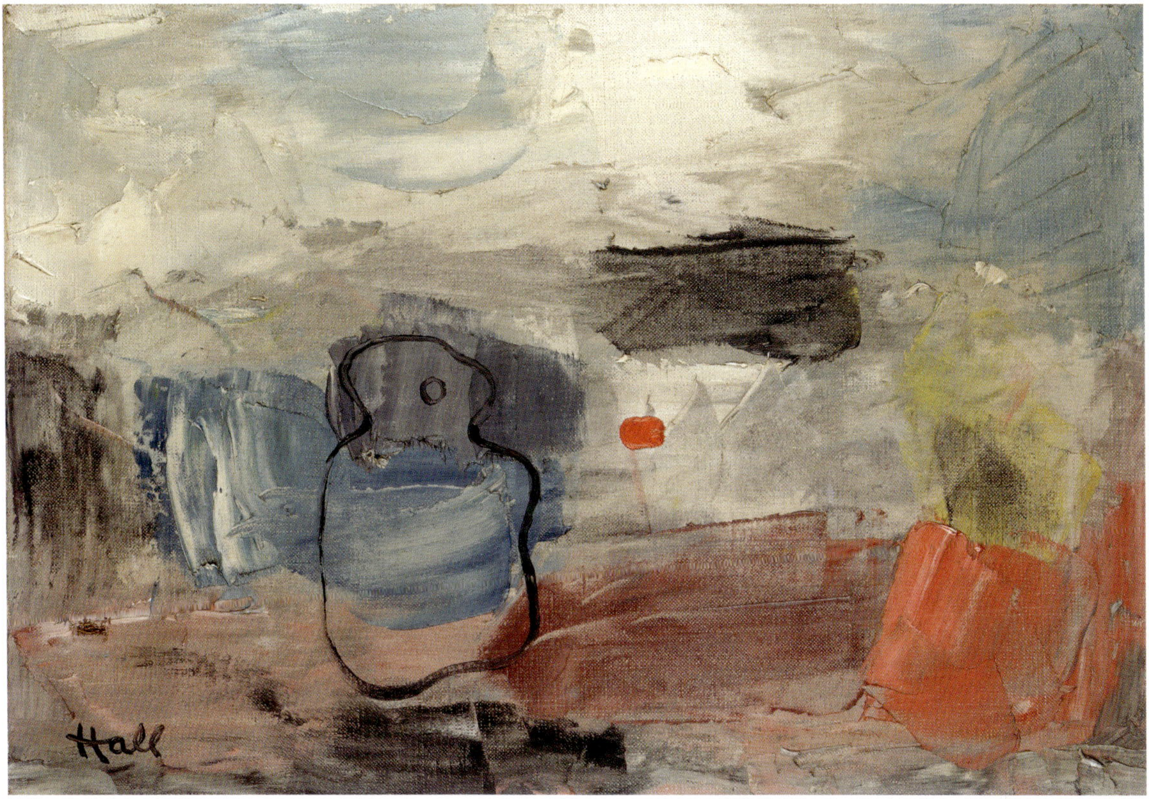

92 Kenneth Hall, *Après la Guerre*, 1941, oil on canvas.

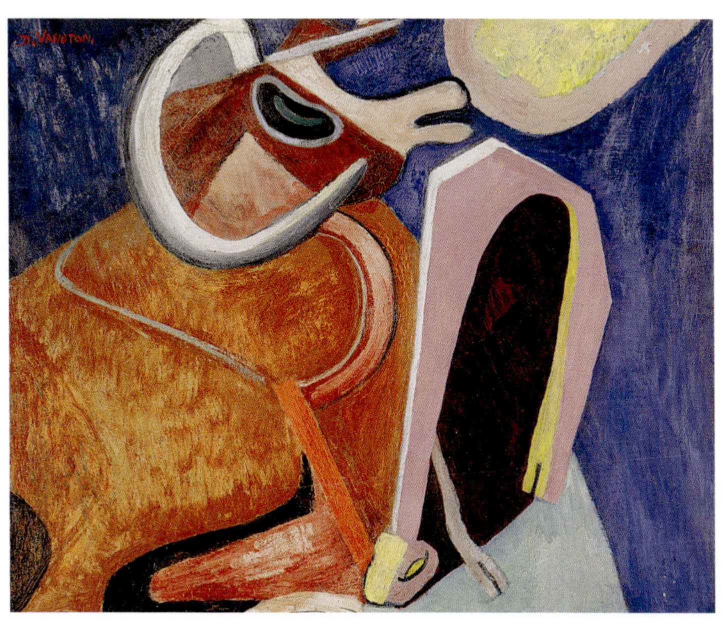

93 Dáirine Vanston, *Dying Animal*, 1943,
oil on canvas.

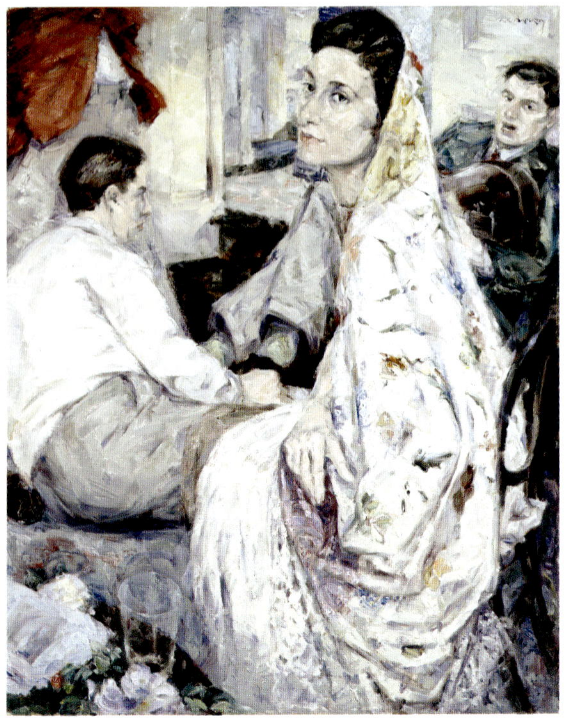

94 Louis le Brocquy, *Spanish Shawl*, 1941, oil on silk.

also included works by Dufy, Gleizes, Picasso, Frances Hodgkins and Christopher Wood, many of which were lent by Evie Hone.[46] In spite of their actual physical isolation from developments outside Ireland during the war, they continued to represent themselves within Dublin as a group which saw itself as part of an international avant-garde.

The activities of the Dublin Painters in the 1930s and the presence of the White Stag Group were, however, part of a context for the instigation of what S. B. Kennedy later termed 'the most consequential art exhibition to have been held in Ireland during the first half of this century'.[47] This was the *Irish Exhibition of Living Art* (IELA), held at the National College of Art between 16 September and 9 October 1943. Like many earlier radical gestures within the European avant-garde, the *Living Art*

(as it became known) grew out of a sense of dissatisfaction with the selection policies of the RHA. Its conservatism had prompted a major essay by Mainie Jellett, published in *Commentary* in May 1942 and entitled 'The RHA and Youth'. Supported by the recent emergence of serious professional art criticism in Dublin, Jellett mounted a critique of the RHA as representative of contemporary Irish art: the issues of Irishness and nationality were paramount here. This was signalled also by the RHA's rejection of two paintings, *The Spanish Shawl* and *Image of Chaos*, submitted by Louis le Brocquy in 1942 for inclusion within its annual show, despite the fact that le Brocquy had exhibited with the RHA on a regular basis since 1937. In 1943, paintings by le Brocquy and other artists were once more rejected by the RHA. Le Brocquy and Jellett were to become key figures in the move to establish an alternative exhibiting venue able to represent the diversity of Irish art, the germ of the idea suggested by Sybil le Brocquy, the artist's mother.

According to Louis le Brocquy, Sybil played a major role in organizing *Living Art*, putting in place managerial strategies to ensure the success of the exhibition.[48] A group of patrons was formed that included the Provosts of Trinity College and University College, the head of the National Gallery (George Furlong) and even the chair of the RHA, Dermod O'Brien. The Taoiseach, de Valera, also attended the opening. To be avant-garde in Ireland in 1943, then, meant something very different from many other European instances. The White Stag Group may have cultivated bohemia, but they were still relatively marginal in Ireland. Radical art was still dominated by the Anglo-Irish Mainie Jellett; other key figures, such as Sybil le Brocquy, were from a similar class, familiar with the operations of power within a relatively small Dublin cultural elite. Also, despite the presence of Waddington and the contemporary picture galleries, there was very little market for radical art. The vast majority of artists could not make a living from their work at this time; Jellett, to the end of her life, was dependent on support from her family. Possibilities for political radicalism, a recurrent feature of European avant-gardism, had also been earlier co-opted by the nationalist hegemony. Anti-academic rebellion in Dublin could only take place within certain predetermined parameters specific to the circumstances of Free State Ireland in 1943; but it was the canny manipulation of these circumstances that, as Louis le Brocquy later claimed, 'made a huge difference to the understanding and the acceptance of this new art – it became a *new force*'.[49]

The organizing committee of nine also included Margaret Clarke, who in addition was a member of the RHA, Evie Hone, Father Jack Hanlon and Norah McGuinness.[50] All of the artists on the committee contributed work to the exhibition, which contained 168 works by 74 Irish painters and sculptors. It thus represented a comprehensive survey of the art being produced in the Irish Free State outside the Academy, ranging from works by the long-established May Guinness and Mary Swanzy to the two paintings by le Brocquy rejected from the previous year's RHA, in addition to works by other young artists such as Gerard Dillon, Nano Reid and Paul Egerstoff. The White Stag Group was represented by Nick Nicholls, Patrick Scott and Doreen [sic] Vanston, whose *Dying Animal* was one of her five included works. Older, established members of the Dublin Painters such as Harriet Kirkwood, Joan Jameson, Beatrice Glenavy and Grace Henry also took part, as did some members of the RHA. In addition to Glenavy, who was also an academician, works by Yeats and Dermod O'Brien were also shown, as was Seán Keating's *The Wagons at Poulaphouca*. Part of his series on the electrification of Ireland, this had probably been borrowed from the ESB without Keating's knowledge, since he was greatly opposed to any form of

radicalism in art. The thirteen sculptural works included four by Melanie le Brocquy, the sister of the painter, and *Woman* (n.d.) by Hilary Heron, a young sculptor whose work was to develop a critical reputation in the 1950s. There was also an accompanying memorial exhibition of the work of Jerome Connor. An academic sculptor who had died in 1943, the themes of his commemorative works, such as *Supreme Sacrifice – 1916* (included in *Living Art*) were well suited to the Free State's project of cultural nationalism.

The *Living Art* was an outstanding success, attracting over 5,000 visitors in three weeks.[51] The critical reception was generally favourable: according to the *Irish Times* reviewer, *Living Art* was the 'most vital and distinguished exhibition of work by living artists that has ever been held'.[52] By comparison, Máirín Allen argued in the *Father Matthew Record* that 'rightly or wrongly one gets the notion that the strange foreign-ness . . . is the result of an absence of contact between the artists and the normal, native, cultural background.'[53]

Such insularity, however, was what might have been expected in a Church-sponsored journal in the 1940s. The exhibition of 1943 clearly indicated that a ajor shift had taken place in the reception of radical art in Ireland. *Living Art* subsequently became an annual event, and in 1944 Norah McGuinness was elected as Chair (later President), a post she held until 1972. Earlier in 1944, in January, another group exhibition of radical art took place: the *Exhibition of Subjective Art*, organized by the White Stag group. Like the *Living Art* exhibition later that year, this also involved an attempt to break down the insularity of Irish culture in the 1940s by inviting Herbert Read's participation – an alliance with radical tendencies outside Ireland. Read's introduction to the catalogue was published in *The Bell* in February 1944.[54] With the end of the war, however, many of the White Stag Group left Ireland. In 1946, Rakoczi and Hall returned to London, where Hall committed suicide the same year.

The *Living Art* continued to provide a focus for anti-academicism in Dublin for the remainder of the decade. There was also evidence of a growing internationalism in Irish art that would develop more fully in the modernist art practices of the 1950s. Following the Republic of Ireland Act in 1948, Ireland finally left the Commonwealth the following year and became a fully independent state. By this point, the cult of ethnic nationalism had largely done its job. Far from disappearing, however, the imagery of the West proved to be durable, mutating into forms more closely related to Ireland's identity after independence. Mainie Jellett did not live to see this; in 1944, at the age of 47, she died of cancer. The rigorous, Cubist-derived modernism she had practised had relatively little influence on subsequent art practice in Ireland. What Jellett did achieve, particularly in conjunction with the other organizers of the *Living Art*, was an increasing acceptance of avant-gardism as a valid practice that would have been unimaginable twenty years previously.

FIVE

The Significance of the Overlooked

The rural environment was the mainstay of Ireland's economy in the post-war years, although not without problems. In contrast with de Valera's earlier goal of a rural self-sufficiency, in practice the farming population was ageing as young people continued to leave the land, and electrification and running water were still rarities. Ireland was highly dependent on imports, mainly from Britain. In spite of the Free State's non-combatant status, post-war economic recovery was slow, exacerbated by the continual exodus to England and beyond. The power of the Church helped to ensure a highly conservative political consensus within which communism continued to be demonized throughout the 1950s. Ireland's role as part of a European bulwark against the Eastern bloc went some way to make up for the international isolation caused not only by wartime neutrality, but also by de Valera's decision to sign the German book of condolence after the death of Hitler, resulting in exclusion from the United Nations in 1946.

In 1948 Ireland finally left the British Commonwealth under the Interparty Government, the coalition that succeeded Fianna Fáil; the following year the Republic was declared on Easter Monday, the anniversary of the 1916 Rising. Relationships with Britain were far from settled, however; Seán MacBride, Head of the Department of External Affairs, was a veteran of 1916.

In spite of being an avid cold warrior, he also maintained old-style nationalist views on Ireland's partition. The result was Ireland's refusal in 1949 to join NATO on the grounds that Britain, a fellow participant, still maintained sovereignty over the six Northern counties claimed by the Republic. MacBride was, however, more sympathetic towards increased links with the rest of Europe. His qualified internationalism also resulted in the establishment of the Cultural Relations Committee to promote Irish culture and the arts outside Ireland, a move that contributed to the gradual erosion of the marginality of Irish artists within a wider arena.

The local and the insignificant

Within Ireland, however, the situation appeared to be quite different. At the start of the 1950s the common themes of both art and literature were the concerns of small-town Ireland, and it looked as if the West as a mythologized home of heroes had been upstaged by ordinary, overlooked places where nothing ever happens. As Colm Tóibín has suggested, this was a turning away from the grand narratives of the Cultural Revival towards the actuality of existence in a postcolonial state where idealism has been replaced by ennui, and a progressive desire for modernization by stagnation.[1]

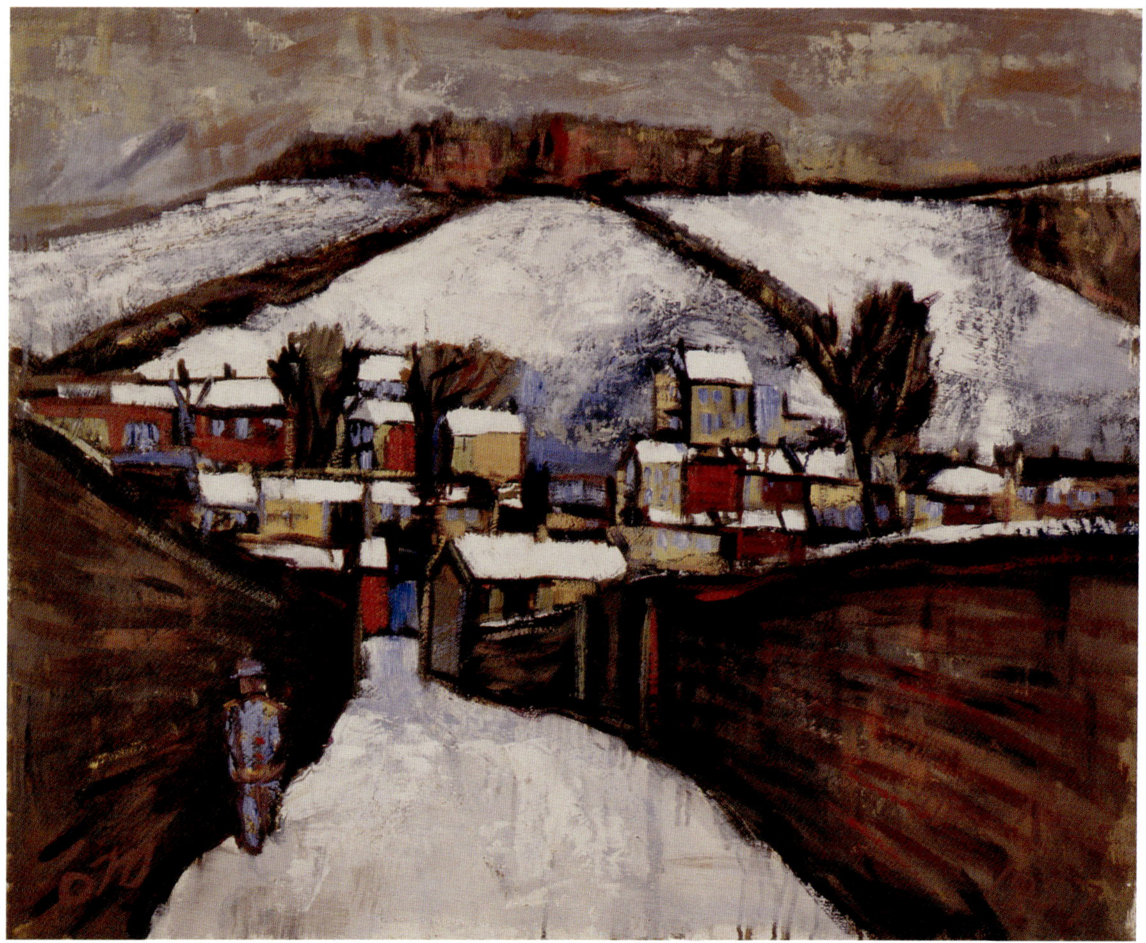

95 Tony O'Malley, *Winter Landscape, New Ross*, 1953, oil on board.

Indeed, at the time, both art and literature increasingly began to address the meanings of spaces marginal to the cultural authority of the West, through the development of themes of the local and insignificant.

In the early 1950s the location for Tony O'Malley's paintings was the rural southeast. A reassessment of the overlooked underpins the saturated vibrancy of *Winter Landscape, New Ross*, where the vivid red of the houses contrasts with the bluish-grey tones and white impasto of snow on the fields. O'Malley was one of the first generation of Irish artists to be influenced by Jack Yeats's Expressionism. This was not only through the looseness of brushwork in his paintings but also due to Expressionism's emphasis on an apparently intuitive response, which O'Malley identified as 'part of my own visionary life'.[2] Colour and brushwork in *Winter Landscape, New Ross* show that he was also looking closely at Vlaminck and other post-Impressionist painters. The fusion of these with a Yeatsian sensibility produced something that for Tóibín was close to writer Patrick

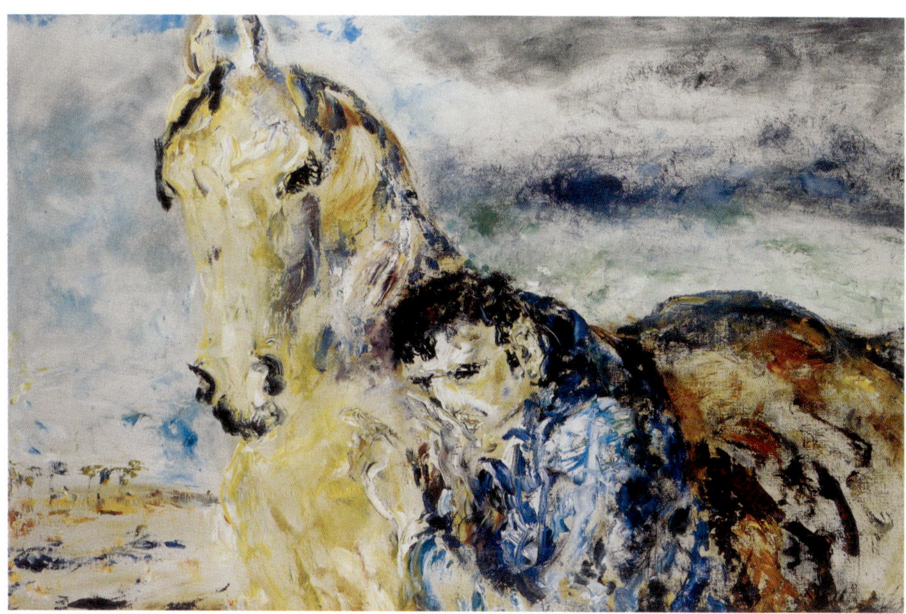

96 Jack Yeats, *My Beautiful, My Beautiful*, 1953, oil on canvas.

Kavanagh's view of rural Monaghan, 'a way of reclaiming for art what had been seen before as dull, establishing for the first time the idea that common experience in the new state could be made into poetry'.[3]

From about the late 1940s onwards what it meant to be an Irish artist underwent considerable changes. Apart from Jack Yeats, who died in 1957, there were few remnants of the Anglo-Irish art culture represented previously by Jellett and Hone and in the 1950s by the declining fortunes of the Society of Dublin Painters. Artists who became prominent in the Republic at this time came from very different class and cultural backgrounds. A self-taught artist from Callan in Co. Kilkenny, O'Malley did not start painting until 1945, while recovering from tuberculosis at the age of 32. Almost until his move to St Ives in Cornwall in 1960, he continued to make a living as a bank clerk in various places across the southeast. Another artist who was to emerge as a major figure in 1950s Ireland, Patrick Collins, had a similar background. Meanwhile, Nano

Reid's family had been Drogheda publicans, and Gerard Dillon came from working-class West Belfast. Norah McGuinness was from a family of Northern coal merchants, and in spite of a successful career as both painter and administrator in her role as Chair of Living Art, for much of her life she also worked at Brown Thomas department store in Dublin as a window dresser. Rather than being supported by old money and an established network of cultural contacts, Irish artists in the 1950s began to operate much more as entrepreneurs, facilitated by dealers such as Victor Waddington (until his move to London in 1957) and Waddington's former assistant Leo Smith at the Dawson Gallery.

When interviewed later in his life O'Malley often referred to the alienation from other workers in the bank as he attempted to lead a dual existence, painting in a bedroom at his lodgings:

You had no one to talk to. That part of your life you kept secret, kept it hidden from them. There was a certain fear also of ridicule – that you were setting yourself up as an artist and only someone with a very foreign name would make a pretence of being that. And in Ireland in the fifties, there was a general feeling that art or painting didn't matter.[4]

In spite of O'Malley's evident difficulties, a strong sense of the importance of the local was beginning to emerge at this time in Irish art; Nano Reid's explorations of the resonances and history of the Boyne Valley are a further example. Reid was in a very different position to O'Malley at the start of the 1950s. Since her first exhibition in 1934 at the Dublin Painters' Gallery, her work had gained increasing recognition to the point where, in spite of baulking over her gender, one reviewer identified its 'profound realisation of structure, whether in figure or landscape, which is all the more astonishing since she is a woman'.[5] In paintings such as *The Hanging Gate* (1945) shown at her solo exhibition at the Dublin Painters' Gallery that year, Reid had developed a practice characterized by a thick impasto and Expressionist handling of paint. Within the conservatism of Irish cultural circles, this still prompted a measured response by an unnamed reviewer of her major exhibition at Waddington's in 1950, suggesting that 'the inexperienced viewer would be puzzled by the extremely shorthand methods she adopts.'[6] Although Reid never fully abandoned other subject-matter, many titles for works in this exhibition – such as *Boyne at Slane* and *River Valley* (both n.d.) – indicate an increased focus on the prehistoric and monastic sites surrounding her home town of Drogheda in County Louth. Significantly, however, her engagement also began to wane as the archaeological excavations of the Neolithic sites around Newgrange attracted a wider interest and, in turn, became implicated in later constructions of Celticism. In an interview of 1969 she claimed, 'I don't paint

the Boyne Valley anymore. Somehow the place isn't the same since they started all that excavating. To me the mounds were interesting when you didn't know what was inside them.'[7]

Jack Yeats, the evacuation of history and the avant-garde

Yet within this climate, which in many ways seemed to become increasingly bleak as the decade wore on, important cultural initiatives were still able to emerge. In 1949 the government commissioned an assessment of culture within the new Republic from the art historian and curator Thomas Bodkin, to be entitled *A Report on the Arts in Ireland*. Bodkin's report was highly critical of institutions such as the National Museum and the National Gallery, where he found only six postcards of works from the collection for sale.[8] Bodkin's desire to promote awareness of the arts within the country was in part prompted by the prominent role of the Department of External Affairs in championing Irish culture abroad. With this in mind, he proposed the inception of an Arts Council based on the successful model of the Arts Council of Great Britain, established in 1945. It was not until 1952, however, that the inaugural meeting of the Irish Arts Council (An Chomhairle Ealaíon) took place.

In spite of the repressive atmosphere of heavy-handed literary censorship and the precarious financial situation of most artists, Dublin offered some kind of alternative to the cultural sterility of small-town Ireland. This was apparent, for example, in the visibility of art criticism in literary journals, following the earlier *The Bell*. The self-consciously avant-garde concerns of the journal *Envoy*, edited by John Ryan, encompassed a commitment to showcasing contemporary Irish artists from its first issue in December 1949 until July 1951, including essays on Reid, Middleton and le Brocquy.[9] The essays helped to establish the avant-garde credentials of these artists and they suggested analogies with European modernism in the placing, for example, of Thurloe Conolly and Middleton in the context of Surrealism. The regrettably brief incursions by the short-lived *Kavanagh's Weekly* (12 April–5 July 1952) into art criticism also showed an acute perception of the ways in which painting could have become identified with a discredited political agenda. In spite of a measured approval of younger painters such as le Brocquy and subsequently Dan O'Neill, Patrick Kavanagh remained highly critical of the work of Jack Yeats:

> There is little that one can say about the new works of art that have been shown in Dublin recently. Jack Yeats, a romantic conception derived from Burne-Jones and Matisse, is a sacred cow who has long since been whisked away out of the field of criticism into that of nationalism, or morality or finance.[10]

After years of criticism and relative isolation, Yeats's status as cultural icon had been more or less assured by three exhibitions of the previous decade: the hugely successful joint exhibition with William Nicholson of 1942 at London's National Gallery, the *Loan Exhibition* of his work at the National College of Art in Dublin in 1945 and a major retrospective at the Tate Gallery in 1948. In spite of this degree of public acclaim, Yeats's work in his old age retreated further into a domain of personal memory. Many of his subjects referred back to his early life in Sligo at the home of his maternal grandfather George Pollexfen. His grandfather infused Yeats with a great love of horses, which he retained throughout his life; romantic equestrian subjects frequently surface in Yeats's work towards the end of his career in

paintings such as *My Beautiful, My Beautiful* (1953) and *Of Ancient Lineage* (1950). He also retained an interest in cultural features of the west remembered from his youth, in paintings like *Clown of Hats* (1954) related to the travelling circuses common throughout the west of Ireland in the late nineteenth century. Yeats's experience of personal loss from the mid-1940s onwards also infuses many of these works with a sense of melancholy and nostalgia. His wife Cottie, to whom he had been married for over 50 years, died in 1947, and the following year his brother's body was returned from France for burial at Drumcliffe; although the family declined a state funeral, W. B. Yeats's coffin was brought to Sligo by Irish naval corvette. In 1949, his remaining sister Lily also died.

In spite of his increasing fragility, until 1955 Jack Yeats continued both to paint and to attend his exhibitions at Waddington's; in this year he left the flat in Fitzwilliam Square for the Portobello Nursing Home, where he remained until his death in 1957. In spite of differences in subject-matter, Yeats's method of painting has considerable affinities with Kokoschka's Expressionism, especially as both artists became older. Herbert Read, in his review of the National Gallery exhibition, indicated the analogy between the two painters, observing that 'the paint is slashed on in a frenzy which can only (in technical jargon) be called "Expressionist", and it is to Expressionist painters such as Oskar Kokoschka that we must go for an adequate comparison.'[11] Indeed in 1955 Kokoschka paid a brief visit to Yeats, escorted with his wife from Dublin Airport to the Portobello Nursing Home by Victor Waddington.[12]

In the 1950s, Yeats was perhaps uniquely placed in relation to Ireland's history in that his representation of personal recollection becomes at times indistinguishable from a broader collective memory. The Pollexfen home at Rosses Point was situated within a landscape laden

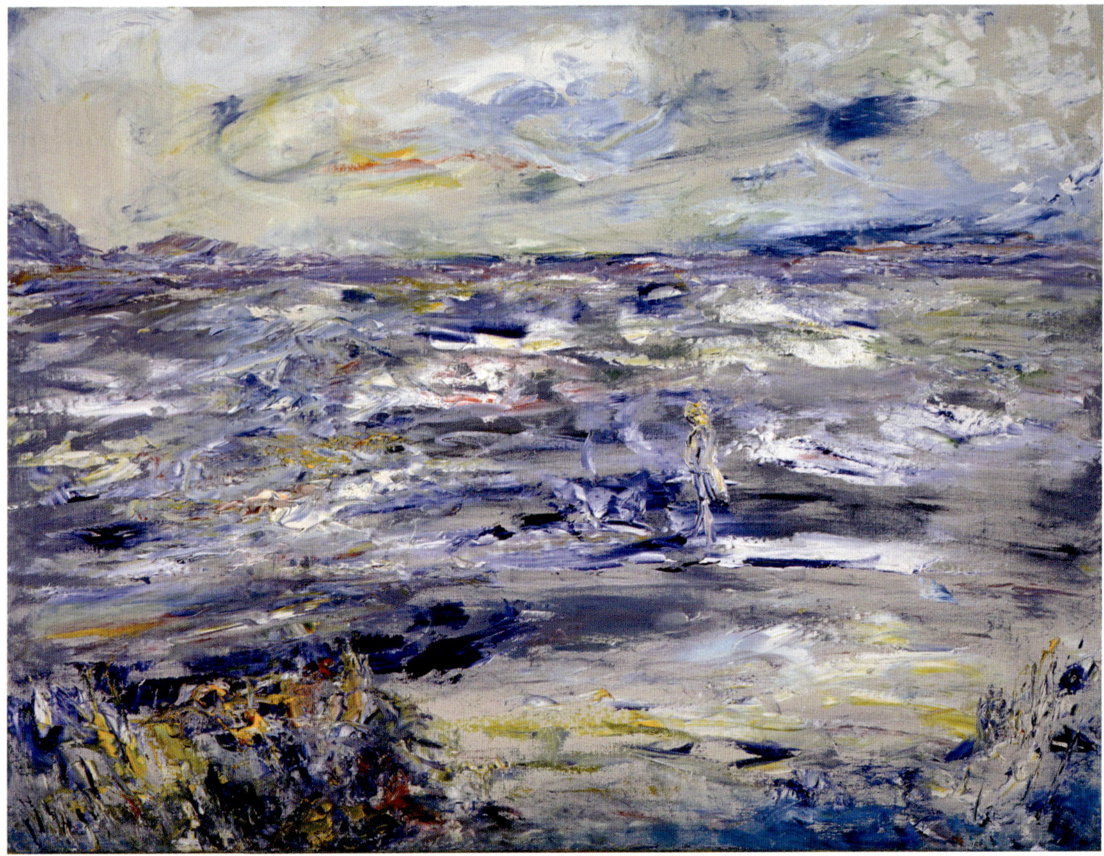

97 Jack Yeats, *Queen Maeve Walked upon This Strand*, 1950, oil on canvas.

with meaning. Looking out onto the Atlantic, this location is overlooked by one of the most striking geological features of the region, the massive escarpment of Ben Bulben. This is also a mythological landscape. In Celtic legend, Ben Bulben figures in the story of Diarmuid and Grainne as a resting place of the lovers in their flight from Finn MacCool, the warrior leader of the Fianna, and to whom Grainne was betrothed. The view towards the southwest, meanwhile, is dominated by the hill of Knocknaree, topped by a massive unexcavated cairn reputed to be the grave of the warrior queen Maeve. Both of these legends feature as subjects in Yeats's late work, whether in *The Path of Diarmuid and Grainne* (1945) or *Queen Maeve Walked upon This Strand*. Hence the landscape features that dominate the surrounding area can also be seen as a link with the mythological cycles of sacrifice and loss that had inspired the conflation of culture and political action in 1916. Yet it is not history but myth that is represented here, and this was an important aspect of Yeats's practice that would contribute to the approach adopted by Irish artists during the next decade. Brian O'Doherty identified this as an

atmosphere characterised by a mythical rather than historical sense, an uneasy and restless fix on the unimportant, and a reluctance to disclose anything about what is painted, let alone make a positive statement about it. Its evasiveness summarises a whole defensive and infinitely discursive mode of existence in Ireland in the forties and fifties.[13]

But then with the death of the republican dream of 1916 in the cold climate of the 1950s, what place was there for the representation of history?

O'Doherty's claims could also apply to Patrick Collins. Largely self-taught, he was born in Dromore West in Sligo, subsequently moving to Dublin where he worked for many years as an insurance clerk. In 1950 Collins exhibited three paintings at the *Irish Exhibition Living Art*, although his first solo show did not take place until six years later, at the newly established Ritchie Hendricks Gallery in Dublin. Collins continued the same romanticized depictions of the West as both Yeats and Paul Henry, who he claimed 'gave me a feeling of dignity about Ireland . . . the only painter in all of Irish painting in a way that I have any respect for'.[14] Collins's painting *Travelling Women* is one of his earliest depictions of travellers, widely believed to be the itinerant descendants of the peasantry dispossessed of their lands during the Famine. The tinkers, as they were commonly known, had featured in Yeats's work as early as 1905 in his illustrations for John Millington Synge, while in the mid-1940s Louis le Brocquy had also painted a series of works engaging with this subject. Retrospectively Collins identified the travellers with childhood memories of Sligo, where 'you would see them on the long roads making from place to place, wearing strong, blatantly different colours, as if to claim their difference.'[15] For Collins, the role of the artist was strongly identified both with these displaced people and the sense of otherness evoked by his western subjects. The centralized motif of figures emerging from an indeterminate space was a compositional feature that Collins developed to great effect during the 1960s, but it also suggests a temporal ambiguity similar to the abstraction of the late Yeats.

In an essay discussing Irish artists of the 1950s, Brian Fallon identified 'a whole generation of Nano Reid,

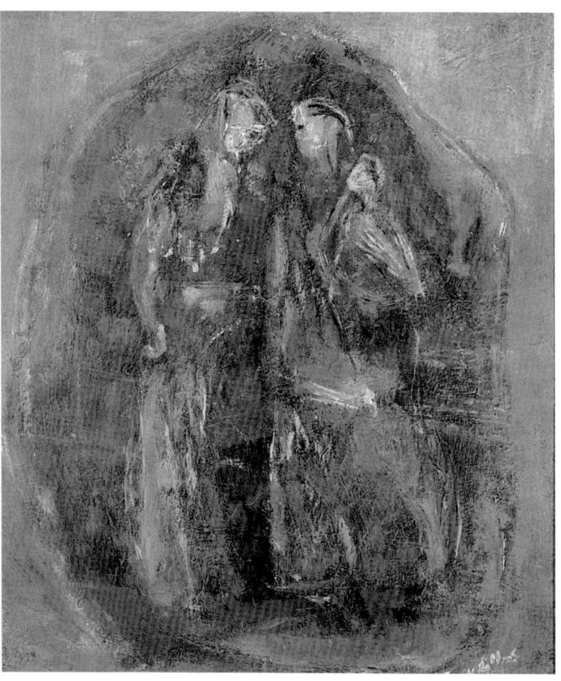

98 Patrick Collins, *Travelling Women*, 1957, oil on board.

Patrick Collins, Tony O'Malley, Colin Middleton *et al.*' as 'to a large extent post-Yeatsian . . . After Yeats, Irish painting had changed and its sensibility altered.'[16] It is hard to dispute the significance of Yeats's practice as a watershed in twentieth-century Irish art, especially in any discussion of landscape painting in the decade after his death. There were, however, alternatives. In the spring of 1951, George Campbell made the first of many visits to the island of Inishlacken, off the Galway coast, in the company of Gerard Dillon and James MacIntyre.[17] In paintings such as *Stormy Day, Connemara* Campbell developed a close visual sensitivity to the landscape of stone and bog and its extreme weather conditions. This was a modernist approach, emphasizing the painter's intuitive response and interpreting it in rhythmic, semi-abstract compositions of dark browns and greys yet rather than mythologizing the landscape, Campbell's Connemara paintings suggest an engagement with its material conditions. Norah McGuinness had also evolved a practice characterized by close

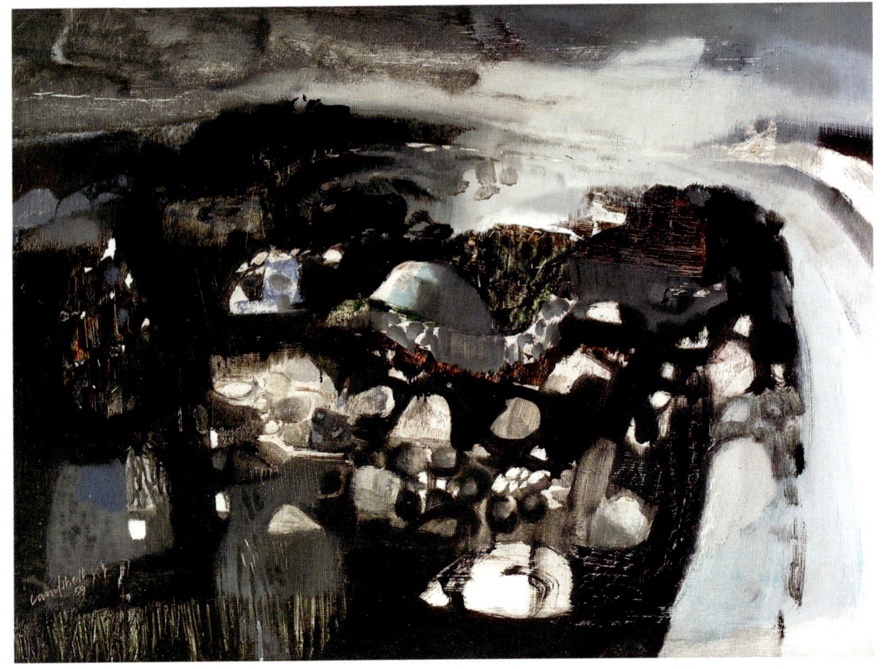

99 George Campbell,
Stormy Day, Connemara,
1959, oil on board.

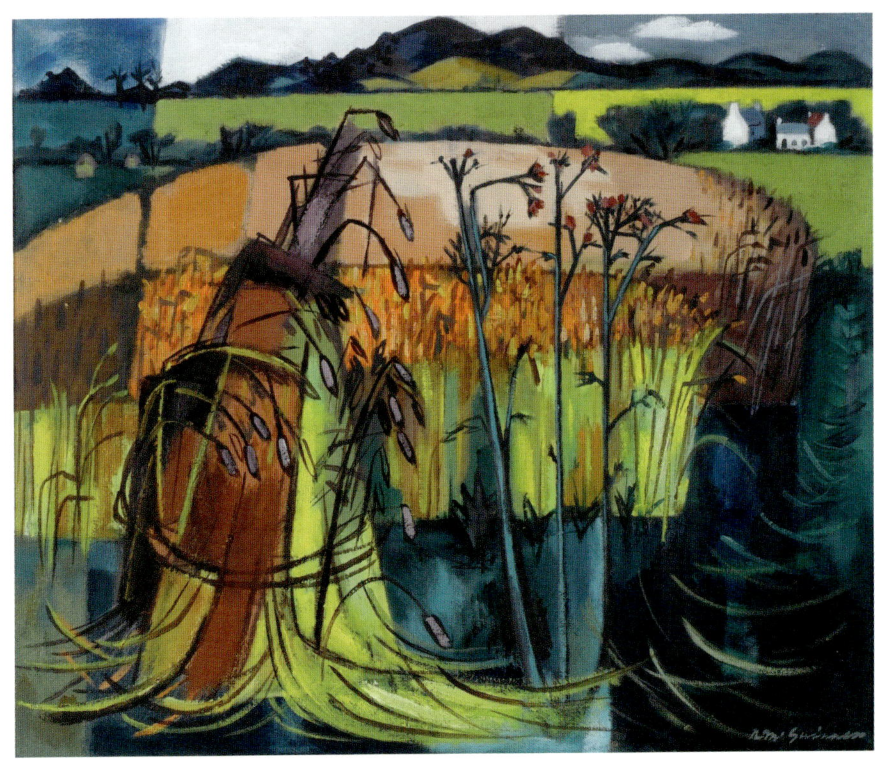

100 Norah McGuinness,
The First Sheaf, 1950s, oil
on canvas.

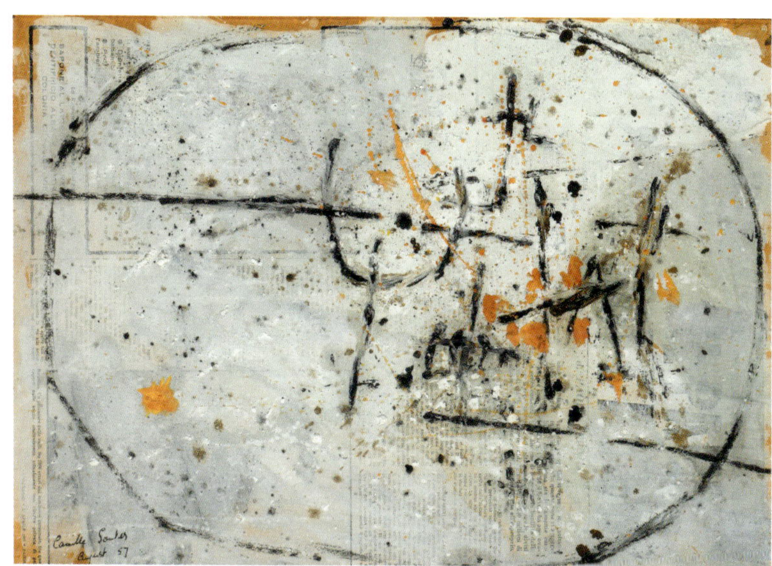

101 Camille Souter, *Untitled*, 1957, oil on Italian newspaper.

102 Camille Souter, *Achill '59*, 1959, oil on paper.

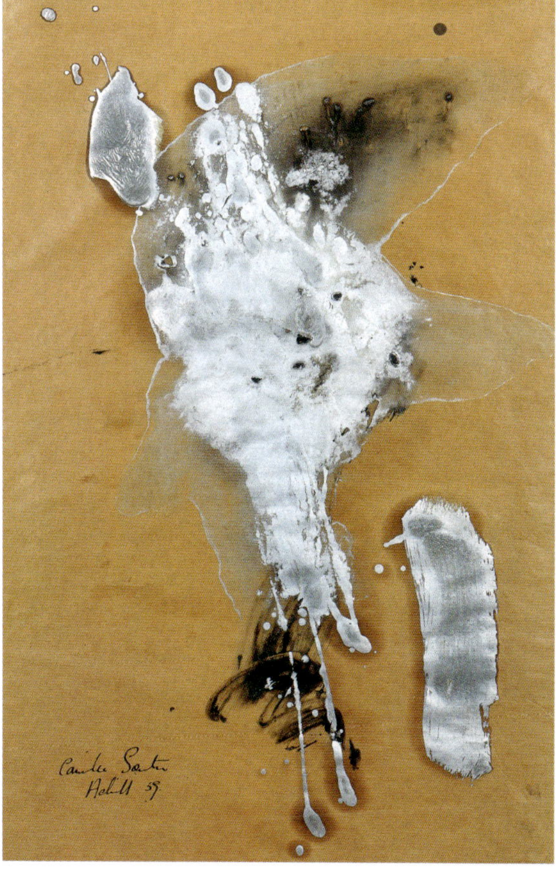

attention to tonal values underpinned by a Cubist-inspired sense of structure, derived from her earlier training with Lhote in Paris.[18] Figurative works such as *The First Sheaf* demonstrate her richly tonal palette within a highly structured format. As Elizabeth Bowen observed, 'in themselves her Irish subjects are bare and factual, myth-defying'.[19] And in fact the close focus and saturation of colour suggest a visionary quality closer to a contemporary British neo-Romanticism rather than the self- conscious archaism of discourses of nationalism.

Another example is Camille Souter.[20] In contrast with an emphasis on an expressive, intuitive model of artistic subjectivity, Souter self-consciously constructed her own identity.[21] Virtually self-taught, she led a bohemian lifestyle, painting and cycling around Italy with her young daughter in the early 1950s. Back in Dublin in 1956, she was taken up by the Ritchie Hendricks Gallery. Unlike much of what was being shown in Dublin, her abstract paintings from the late 1950s indicated her awareness of both European and American avant-gardes, particularly the influence of Tachisme and Abstract Expressionism. The painting *Achill*, with its evocations of Pollock's drip technique, dates from the year in which Souter went to live on the island. In this work there is no evidence of earlier representations of the West with their burden of political significance; Camille Souter's marginality to this history contributes to a fundamental re-reading of the imagery of the West based on her own observations and articulated through an international avant-garde language of abstraction.

There is, however, a range of explanations for the critical marginalization of Irish women artists at this time, which also needs to be read in conjunction with an awareness of their material circumstances. Both the continued conservative influence of the RHA led by Keating and the perilous economics of the Irish art market at a time of overall stagnation during the decade meant that things were difficult for all artists. Women also faced pressures from the social conservatism that tried to restrict their sphere of activities to the nuclear, Church-sanctioned family; for independent women it was difficult to survive in this context. The earlier prominence of Anglo-Irish women was to a greater or lesser extent supported by family finance; women artists of the 1950s had to adopt different strategies to survive. In spite of her critical reputation, Nano Reid faced continual financial difficulties, although occasional portrait commissions provided a means of addressing these. The discourse of Irish art writing of the period, such as it was, reinforced this marginalization. One example is the almost complete silence surrounding the role of McGuinness and Reid as the first artists ever to represent Ireland at the Venice Biennale in 1950, an important post-war move towards the erosion of the international isolation of Irish art.[22] The ability of women once again to *symbolize* Ireland's national identity was not reinforced by their recognition as actual historical agents. Similarly, in 1956, when the sculptor Hilary Heron jointly represented Ireland with Louis le Brocquy, her presence was completely overshadowed by the acclaim surrounding le Brocquy's painting *A Family* (1951).

In his 1950 essay for *Envoy* Edward de Courcy asserted Heron to be 'our only modern sculptor', a claim that indicates the degree to which sculpture in Ireland was marked by a fundamental conservatism.[23] Jellett and Hone's introduction of modernist ideas in painting had little influence on sculpture, and the National College of Art, which Hilary Heron attended in the late 1930s, was still dominated by the legacy of the academic Oliver Sheppard. Within the depressed Dublin art market of the 1950s it was even more difficult to sell sculpture. De Courcy's observation that Heron's work 'is invariably carved and achieves finality in its chosen material' also helped to identify her practice in modernist terms, given the prominence of a 'truth to materials' identified with Moore and Hepworth.[24] Both of these key figures were influential on Hilary Heron, working in such an isolated field. The use of her sources is apparent in a figure entitled *Virgo* (n.d.), carved from iroko wood and included both in de Courcy's essay and in her 1950 show at Waddington's, the first of two at the Dublin gallery.[25] Yet the smooth, rounded surfaces of Heron's form and others from this time such as *Andante* (n.d.), a seated figure, suggest that the modernist sculpture she was looking at was the figurative work of Moore in the late 1930s, rather than the more abstract aspects of both his and Hepworth's practice. Significantly, as with Jellett and Hone's engagement with Gleizes's Cubism, the modernist sculpture introduced into Ireland through Heron's work of the 1950s was, within the progressive rhetoric of international avant-gardism, already outmoded. Yet it is difficult to see how any sense of a complete break with figuration would have been sustainable in Heron's circumstances, working where and when she did. Her best-known piece, the standing bronze figure of *Crazy Jane*, is in many ways much more compatible with current trends in painting, with its subject-matter derived from a series of late poems by

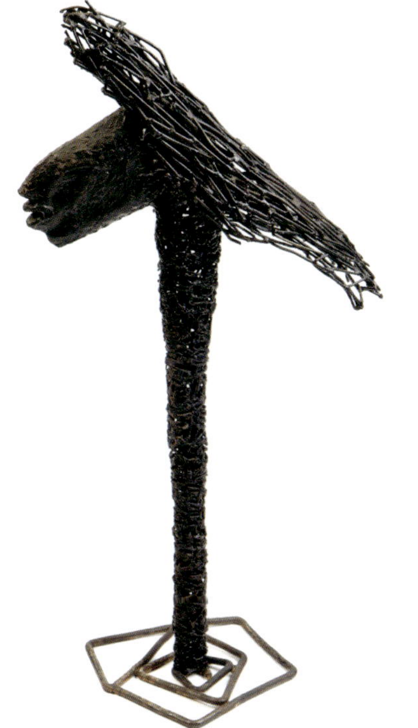

103 Hilary Heron, *Crazy Jane*, 1958, steel.

W. B. Yeats and executed in a manner that derives much from Expressionism.

Modernization, the local and art in Northern Ireland

By comparison with the economic stagnation of the Republic, processes of post-war modernization began in Northern Ireland during a period of high Unionist self-confidence and certainty that Northern Ireland would be rewarded for its wartime loyalty. This not only ushered in the Welfare State and National Health benefits, but also resulted in economic development funded by Westminster. Yet the survival of entrenched divisions meant that modernization in Northern Ireland was far from universally applied. The extension of the 1944 Butler Education Act was delayed until 1947 as the Catholic

hierarchy resisted the loss of control in Catholic schools that were being brought into the State sector, while Protestants challenged the emphasis on non-denominational religious education. The Act eventually made increased educational opportunities available to working-class children, a move whose long-term effects would emerge in major cultural changes in the 1960s, including improved access to art education. There was also a continued heavy reliance on farming. Conditions in the agricultural sector were far from ideal; in 1947, for example, a major survey of rural problems found that 93 per cent of houses still lacked piped water and a toilet.[26] There were major regional differences corresponding to the religious divide: Protestant parts of Antrim were much more prosperous than Catholic South Armagh. Modernization in agriculture in Northern Ireland did succeed in increasing productivity, but at a cost; the widespread introduction of labour-saving tractors resulted in the loss of jobs. In spite of a degree of overall economic progress, levels of unemployment were still the highest in the United Kingdom and religious discrimination remained endemic.

The Stormont government under Lord Brooke financed economic opportunities to replace those lost elsewhere. The new factories, however, were situated in predominantly Protestant areas – Belfast and the Lagan corridor around Lisburn, South Antrim or Coleraine. Like many other Unionists, Brooke considered nationalists too treacherous to be incorporated into the new modern state of Northern Ireland on any but the most basic level, in spite of the lack of widespread nationalist support for the largely unsuccessful IRA border campaign of the late 1950s. This complacency was to have bitter consequences in future years. In the 1950s, however, the construction of a Unionist cultural hegemony took place in a range of ways, often mutually reinforcing. On one level there was the regular assertion

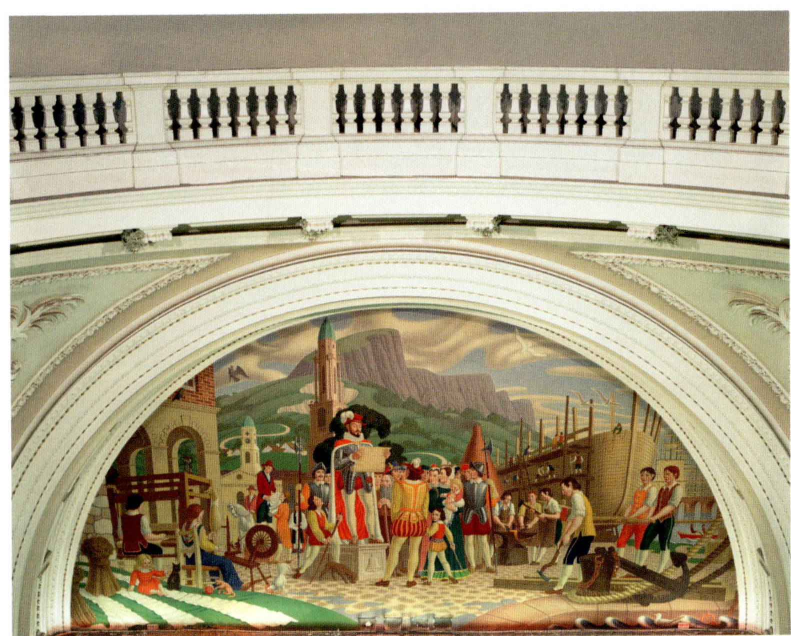

104 John Luke,
*Belfast City Hall
Mural*, 1950.

of apparently ancient rights, as Unionist politicians joined other Orangemen in parading through both urban and rural nationalist areas during the summer 'marching season'. The cultural construction of an Ulster loyal to the Crown was also facilitated through such means as Belfast's participation in the Festival of Britain in 1951 and the celebration of the Coronation of Elizabeth II in 1953.[27] John Luke's mural for the tympanum of the City Hall, commissioned by CEMA in 1950 as part of the Festival of Britain celebrations, played an important role in the assertion of a visual hegemony. Set against the striking landscape of Cave Hill that towers above the city, the mural was intended to 'represent the history of Belfast and its industries'.[28] Yet in spite of the scenes of shipbuilding and the production of linen the compositional focus is on the central figure, that of Sir Arthur Chichester reading the town's charter of 1613. This was an important moment in the early seventeenth-century Plantation of Ulster mainly by Lowland Scots, awarded land in return for their loyalty to the Protestant British throne. The Plantation itself was a process that helped to ensure the bitter divisions over religion and

territory persisting in Ulster for centuries. The depiction of a moment symbolic of Belfast's allegiance to the Crown, bolstered by the city's economic underpinnings, functions, then, as an allegory of a later declaration of loyalty. Notably, the Queen, on her visit to Belfast in May 1951, 'offered her congratulations and expressed her admiration for the mural'.[29]

In spite of the conservatism of a dominant Unionist culture, as Kenneth Jamison suggested, 'a strong awareness of regional identity without a corresponding sense of isolation' was beginning to emerge in art in Northern Ireland during the 1950s and '60s.[30] This was, however, a very gradual process. Artists from the rural North such as Basil Blackshaw and Terry (T. P.) Flanagan had a close familiarity with the shifting character of the landscape, yet the provincialism of earlier Ulster landscapists such as McKelvey or Humbert Craig was slowly being eroded. In addition to a more widespread availability of reproductions in art magazines, improved travel facilities made it easier to see new and influential work at first hand, with regular flights to London and reliable access to Dublin by rail or road. During the 1940s and

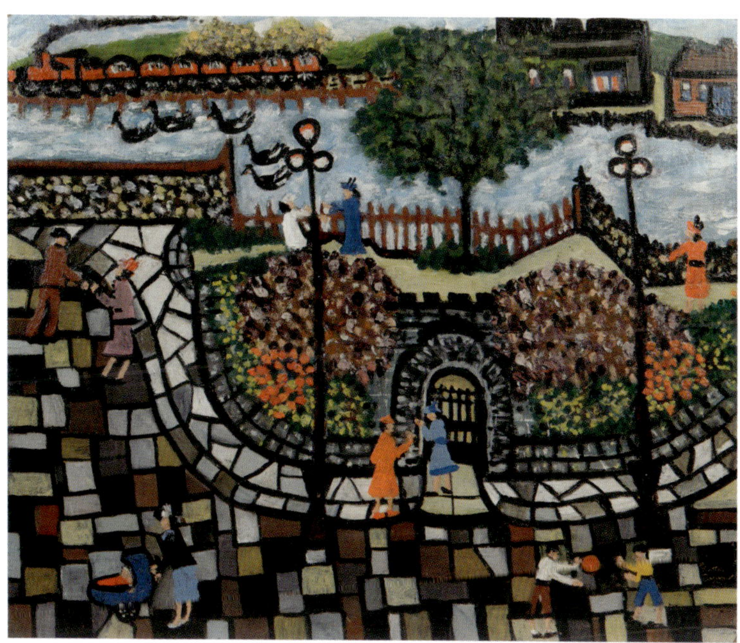

105 Gretta Bowen,
Quiet Sunday by the Sea,
n.d., oil on board.

early 1950s, exhibitions in Belfast were dominated by the academicism of older artists such as William Conor, W. R. Gordon and the sculptor Rosamund Praeger. This was increasingly challenged by the development of CEMA after 1943, subsequently becoming the Arts Council of Northern Ireland in 1962. Until its closure in 1958, the CEMA gallery at 55a Donegall Place in the heart of Belfast's commercial area not only showed a range of local artists but also brought travelling shows from London and elsewhere. Prior to its own gallery's reopening in Chichester Street in 1960, CEMA also continued to support the small Piccolo Gallery set up by Tom Carr and the architect Robert McKinstry.

Yet occasionally art practice slipped through the net of cultural conservatism. In 1955 the first exhibition by the Belfast-based Gretta Bowen took place at the CEMA gallery in Belfast. Bowen was 75 years old at the time and had only been painting for five years, encouraged by her sons, the artists Arthur and George Campbell. However, her small, naive depictions of aspects of Belfast street life and other subjects rapidly became popular, with all 36 paintings sold in a solo show at

Waddington's in 1956. Victor Waddington also supported the emergence of another Belfast-based artist, Dan O'Neill, who achieved critical and commercial acclaim with the success of his first solo show with the gallery in 1946, when 21 out of 23 paintings sold.[31] In 1948, O'Neill spent several months in Paris. In addition to the Irish landscape subjects such as *Knockalla Hills* (1951) that he painted for the rest of his career, his work suggested a closer engagement with European modernism.[32] In 1951 the Belfast Museum and Art Gallery purchased his painting *The Blue Skirt*, whose statuesque draped nude is reminiscent of Picasso's neo-Classical figures of the 1920s, yet also has an eerie luminosity found in other works by O'Neill from this time, such as *Place du Tertre* (1949). His painting *Birth* depicts a scene that Hewitt suggested drew upon the painter's memory – birth in the family home before the reforms of the National Health Service resulted in a dramatic reduction of maternal and infant mortality.[33] In this case the birth is successful, with the mother lying exhausted in the bed. As the doctor closes up his bag, the main focus is on the small boy in the foreground

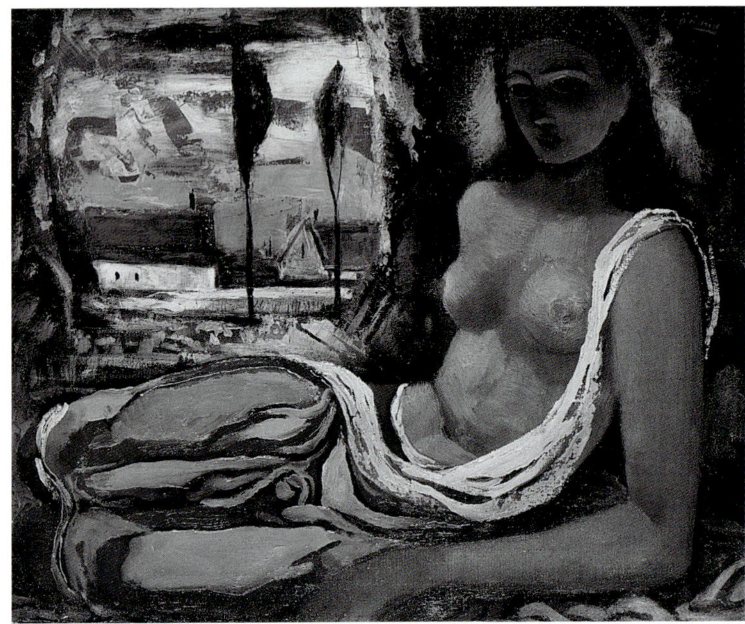

106 Dan O'Neill,
The Blue Skirt, 1949,
oil on canvas.

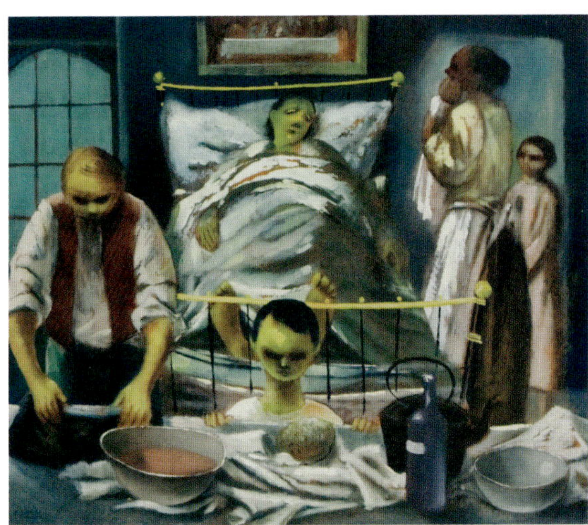

107 Dan O'Neill, *Birth*, 1952, oil on canvas.

gazing at the makeshift equipment, including kettle, sponge and blood-filled basin. Yet instead of the intimacy of O'Neill's earlier *The First Born* (1949) there is a sense of the duration and pain of labour, indicated as much by the air of resignation as the blood-smeared sheets and pillow.

In 1948 Colin Middleton and his wife Kate returned from England, having spent a year in the community set up by John Middleton Murray at Thelnetham in Suffolk. Colin Middleton was still dependent on teaching to make a living, in spite of his steadily growing reputation as an artist. Waddington represented him between 1944 and 1955, during which time he also showed work in London and the United States. Victor Waddington's patronage declined after his move to London, and in 1958 Middleton was taken up by the Ritchie Hendricks Gallery in Dublin. His well-established eclecticism continued with the Expressionist handling of the biblical subject-matter of *Give Me to Drink* (1949) that contrasts

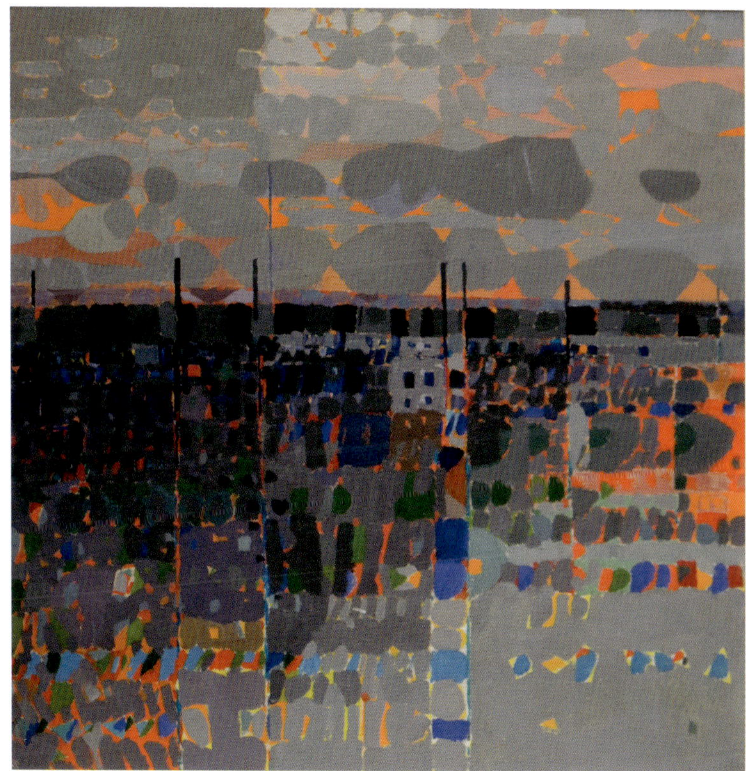

108 Colin Middleton,
*Winter Sundown
Carnalridge*, aka
Sundown, Carnalridge III,
1960, oil on board.

with the contained structure of scenes such as *Winter Sundown, Carnalridge*, just inland from the North Antrim coast. In this painting the strong sense of compositional order imposed upon the landscape is reinforced by the carefully placed brushstrokes. As Liam Kelly has suggested, this is a feature of Middleton's work derived from his early years as a damask designer, a fascination with the 'vertical/horizontal structure of textiles – the weave/weft system'.[34]

During this period of wider attempts at educational reform by the Stormont government, the provincialism of art teaching was also changing. Many artists who had benefited from state funding to study in London during the 1930s, such as Kathleen Bridle, were now teaching in Northern Ireland. Bridle was a former member of the short-lived Ulster Unit during the 1930s, the sole attempt at an earlier avant-garde art practice in Northern Ireland. Her encouragement was an important influence on both the young William Scott and T. P. Flanagan. Meanwhile Basil Blackshaw, Kenneth Jamison, Flanagan and Cherith Boyd (later McKinstry) were all part of a generation of students taught at Belfast College of Art by the painter Romeo Toogood, another former Ulster Unit member. Although Toogood's own practice suffered from his emphasis on teaching, Jamison later paid tribute to his approach as 'an extraordinary compound of allusion and metaphor patiently contrived for the individual'.[35] The significance of order and construction that Blackshaw derived from Toogood's teaching was reinforced by his interest in Cézanne,

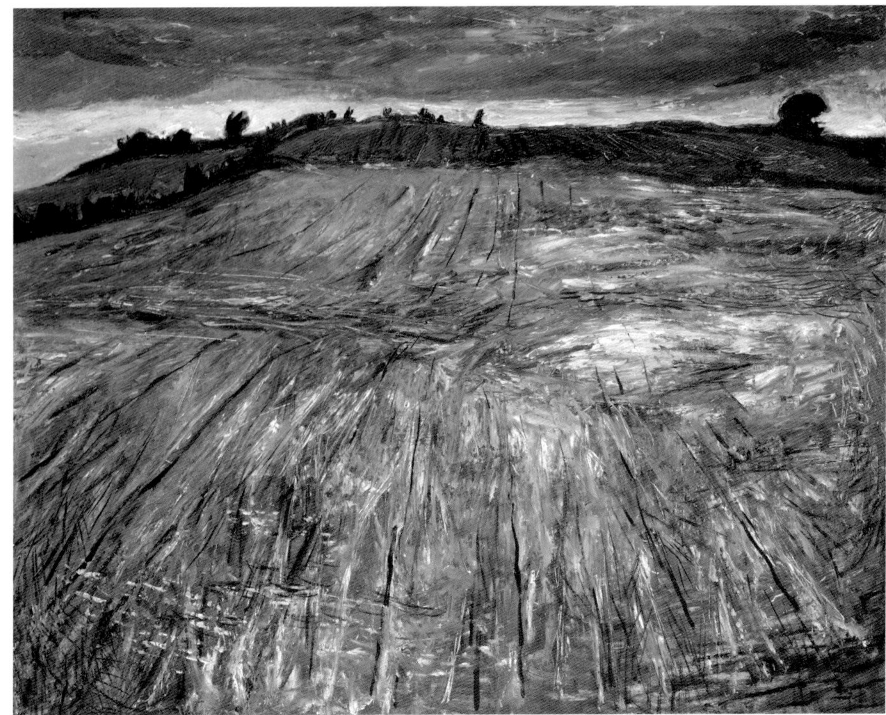

109 Basil Blackshaw,
The Field, 1953,
oil on board.

whose paintings he was able to observe at first-hand as the recipient of a CEMA travel scholarship to London and Paris in 1951. Blackshaw soon developed enduring interests in landscape and the people and animals that inhabit it; the pervasive influence of Cézanne's obsessions with Mont St Victoire emerged in his continued preoccupation with the Colin Mountain overlooking Belfast. In a manner also similar to Cézanne, Blackshaw suppressed narrative implications in favour of an interest in landscape structure in paintings such as *The Field* and the slightly later *Dromara Landscape* (1955). Both paintings were shown at the 22-year-old Blackshaw's first solo exhibition at the Belfast Museum and Art Gallery in 1955; they have in common a low viewpoint, looking up the slope of a worked field to the horizon line. In *The Field*, especially, receding plough tracks and field boundaries stress the empty distance, while the

dull bronze of the sky echoes the tones of the ground beneath. This focus on the ground facilitated by the low viewpoint also emphasizes that this is a land that, like the painted surface, has been worked repeatedly. Like many of Henry's earlier depictions of Connemara, this is a depopulated landscape, but its emptiness suggests the landscape as the product of rural labour rather than an aestheticized escape for the urban traveller.

Blackshaw returned frequently to paint the land around Dromara near where he lived in County Down, a relatively barren area unlike what John Hewitt described as 'the tamer and fatter farmlands ringing it'.[36] In spite of its relative proximity to Belfast and the modernization of the Lagan corridor, this was an area that still retained a rural, remote character, a place that lacked mains electricity until the mid-1950s. And in spite of the almost pre-industrial appearance of these landscapes, Blackshaw's depictions of the Down hinterlands in the 1950s are actually modern in ways beyond their Expressionist surfaces. They differ from earlier Ulster landscapes such as Craig's picturesque glens, paintings that suggest a desire for a cultural remoteness similar to depictions of the West. Blackshaw's paintings of this time also feature the figures of those who work upon the land, but these are far removed from the authentic Northern ethnicity of Charles Lamb's *Lough Neagh Fisherman*. They tend to be horse trainers or 'doggymen', out exercising their greyhounds, both aspects of rural life with which Blackshaw had a long personal involvement. In a sense, Blackshaw's paintings are a further instance of the focus on the local, the overlooked, characterizing the work of his Southern contemporaries such as Reid or O'Malley. But in 1950s Northern Ireland, 'local' meant something different, whether through Hewitt's advocacy of a cultural regionalism or on the level of entrenched political identities, where territorial distinctions between Protestant and Catholic are significant at even the most microcosmic level. These are factors that cannot be overlooked in an assessment of the significance of Basil Blackshaw's depictions of rural Down and Antrim.

Writing in 1957, Hewitt was able to proclaim Blackshaw as 'clearly the most promising of the Northern painters of his age-group. He has, in spite of his youth, cleared a corner for himself among the artists of this country'.[37] In the late 1940s and early 1950s, in addition to the focus on his poetry that produced the collection *No Rebel Word* in 1948, Hewitt was highly active in the promotion and support of contemporary art practice in Northern Ireland. As Tom Clyde observed, this could take a variety of different forms, which might at times be considered incompatible:

On more than one occasion in the early 1950s it is possible to find an art exhibition which Hewitt presented at the art gallery, for which he produced the catalogue, and then proceeded to write the reviews of the event in both the *Belfast Telegraph* and the *Irish Times*.[38]

However, Hewitt's tireless role in the promotion of painting in Northern Ireland suffered a serious setback. Post-war Unionist cultural hegemony was also fully compatible with Cold War paranoia around left-wing politics, as John and Roberta Hewitt discovered. In 1953 John Hewitt's failure to be appointed to the post of Director of the Belfast Museum and Art Gallery was generally perceived to result from him having been 'branded both as Communist and pro-Catholic'.[39] The experience was profoundly traumatic for Hewitt, bringing him close to suicide. As a consequence he left Northern Ireland in 1957 to take up the directorship of the newly opened Herbert Art Gallery in Coventry. Being sent to Coventry was not, however, the exile that this might imply; Hewitt's socialism found a ready home in the city's left-wing climate. His advocacy of regionalism in Northern Ireland during the Second World War would also have facilitated this move to the British Midlands. In regionalism, the awareness of Northern Ireland's colonized past had developed into a historically changing relationship of both poetry and painting to their place of production. Unlike London, or St Ives, 1950s Coventry was distinctly peripheral to the main developments in British art. Hewitt's experience in Belfast, a city whose identity was also at least partly derived from its industrial base, would have encouraged him to take up a post in a place with both a similar economic foundation and degree of cultural marginality. During the fifteen years before his retirement and return to Belfast in 1972, Hewitt established the gallery's collection of work by contemporary artists from both Britain and Northern Ireland, including works by Blackshaw, Middleton and McGuinness. The post-war reconstruction of Coventry, heavily bombed during the war, also attracted a large number of Irish working-class immigrants; Hewitt's autobiographical essay 'No Rootless Colonist' (1972) stressed a connection to the wider experience of the Irish in Britain.[40] It was his awareness of the dialectic of alienation and assimilation within Irish diasporic communities that ultimately helped to provide Hewitt with the sense of rootedness so crucial to his own cultural identity.[41]

SIX

IRISH ART AND DIASPORA IN THE 1950S

From the mid-1940s onwards numerous artists began to leave Ireland, mostly settling in England. As a result there is an increasing sense of Irish culture as beginning to be constituted outside Ireland's national boundaries, shifting and challenging the parameters that existed in Dublin or Belfast. This sense of a cultural shift rather than just the movement of people is usefully conveyed by the term diaspora. However, rather than replicating what has been left behind, diaspora also implies a more selective process of cultural formation situated and enacted in a different location. As a result, diasporic culture can take a variety of forms and involve different constructions of identity. These can include both nostalgia and the creation of tight-knit communities as a substitute for the dynamics of a lost home and, conversely, a receptivity to new experiences and concepts difficult to sustain – or even to imagine – in a more repressive social climate. As Paul Gilroy suggests, diasporic cultural formation involves a sense of a double awareness, the dialectical combination of characteristics of both 'there' and here'.[1] This dual articulation, itself inflected differently by different artists, is perhaps the one unifying feature among the heterogeneous work of Irish painters and sculptors in Britain during the 1950s.

Establishing a position: Irish artists in Britain

For many, the move to England was an outcome of both the dire economic situation and the cultural stagnation of Dublin. Tony O'Malley recalled a dual sense of isolation, first of all from his location in the rural hinterlands, and secondly from the established world of the Dublin art scene. In 1960, after two visits to St Ives in 1955 and 1957, he moved to Cornwall to become a full-time painter, remaining there until his return to Callan in 1990. However, artists from Ireland both became involved with the British art scene and negotiated forms of Irish identity through a variety of ways; there is no set pattern. In addition to those who arrived from the mid-1940s onwards, there were also artists who had left Ireland at various points before the Second World War. These included Francis Bacon, William Scott and F. E. McWilliam, all of whom featured prominently in the British art of the 1950s, but there were also lesser-known artists such as Mary Swanzy. In 1945 she returned to England from Dublin where she had spent three years of the war after her house in Blackheath, southeast London, was bombed. Here she remained until her death in 1978, painting regularly, but exhibiting rarely.[2]

Swanzy's seclusion only serves to emphasize the lack of visibility of women within this group of diasporic Irish artists in the post-war period. In some ways,

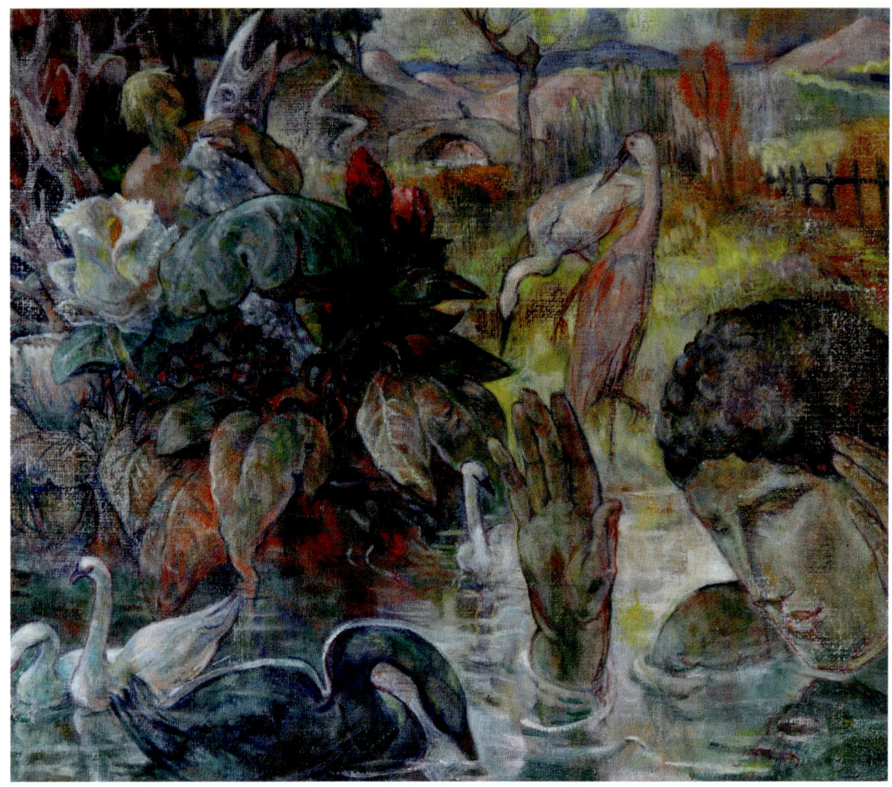

110 Mary Swanzy,
Swans, 1930, oil
on canvas.

this echoes the experience of a more widespread gender division among Irish immigrants at this time; the post-war period was also one of large-scale migration of working-class Irish people seeking employment in Britain's industries. As Bronwen Walter has suggested, since the nineteenth century the visibility of Irish men as builders and labourers has meant that the public construction of diasporic Irishness has tended to be male; women, by comparison, were employed mainly in the domestic sphere and were hence less visible.[3] A further factor during the 1940s and 1950s within the polarized gender politics of the Cold War was the highly masculinized nature of the avant-garde; in Britain, other than Barbara Hepworth, there were few prominent women artists at the time. Mary Swanzy's marginality was also typical of other lesser-known Irish artists in Britain, who had little connection to the London art scene in spite of living and working in the city. These

included the group of mainly Northern artists associated with the dealer Victor Waddington. His decision to relocate to London in 1956 influenced similar moves by Campbell and O'Neill; their friend Gerard Dillon, meanwhile, had already been in London since the 1930s.

Dillon's position had much in common with other male, working-class Irish emigrants to London in the post-war period, with his experience of manual labour and dependency on family support characteristic of diasporic communities. Early in 1945 he returned to London to work for a builder on repairs to bomb-damaged properties; throughout his career Dillon needed to supplement his income through similar work. In 1945 he moved into the basement flat of his sister Molly's new house in the predominantly Irish area of Kilburn, where he remained for approximately twenty years. The house in turn became a focus for Belfast artists in London; at various times the pianist

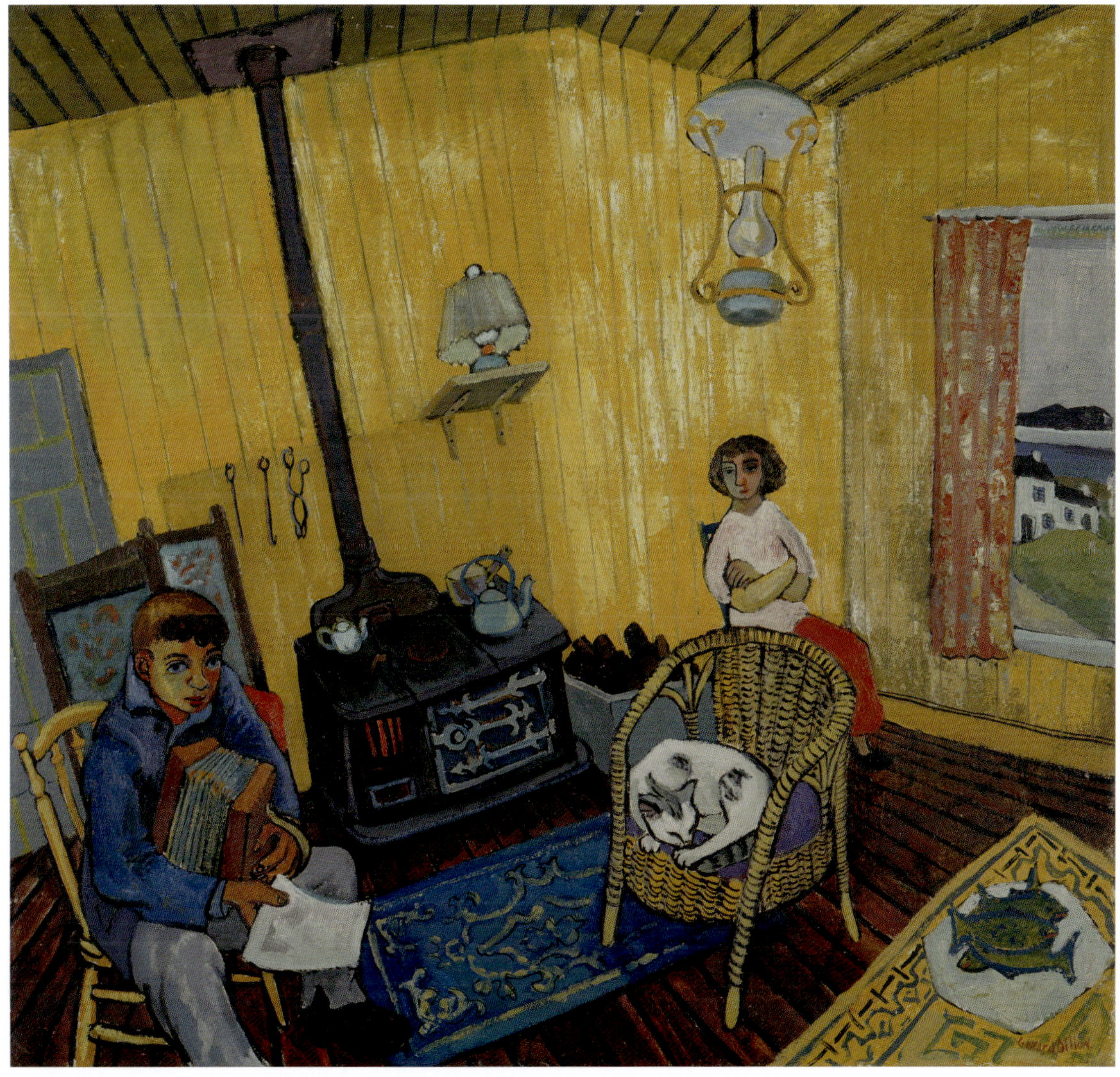

111 Gerard Dillon, *The Yellow Bungalow*, 1954, oil on canvas.

Tom Davidson and painters Arthur Armstrong and Noreen Rice also lived there, while George and Madge Campbell and the writer Aidan Higgins visited. James MacIntyre, by now working in London as an illustrator, lived close by.[4] Yet in spite of the occasional shows at Waddington's new gallery in Cork Street, as MacIntyre recalled, there was no contact either with English painters or with more successful Irish artists such as Scott or McWilliam.[5]

In addition to numerous group shows of Irish artists in Britain and elsewhere, Dillon was by now exhibiting regularly in Dublin. His solo shows at Waddington's in 1950 and 1953 were followed by annual exhibitions at the Dawson Gallery after Waddington's return to London. Dillon painted as frequently as possible in Connemara, financed by his additional jobs in London. Both geographical and cultural distance, however, contributed to a view of the West far removed from the identification

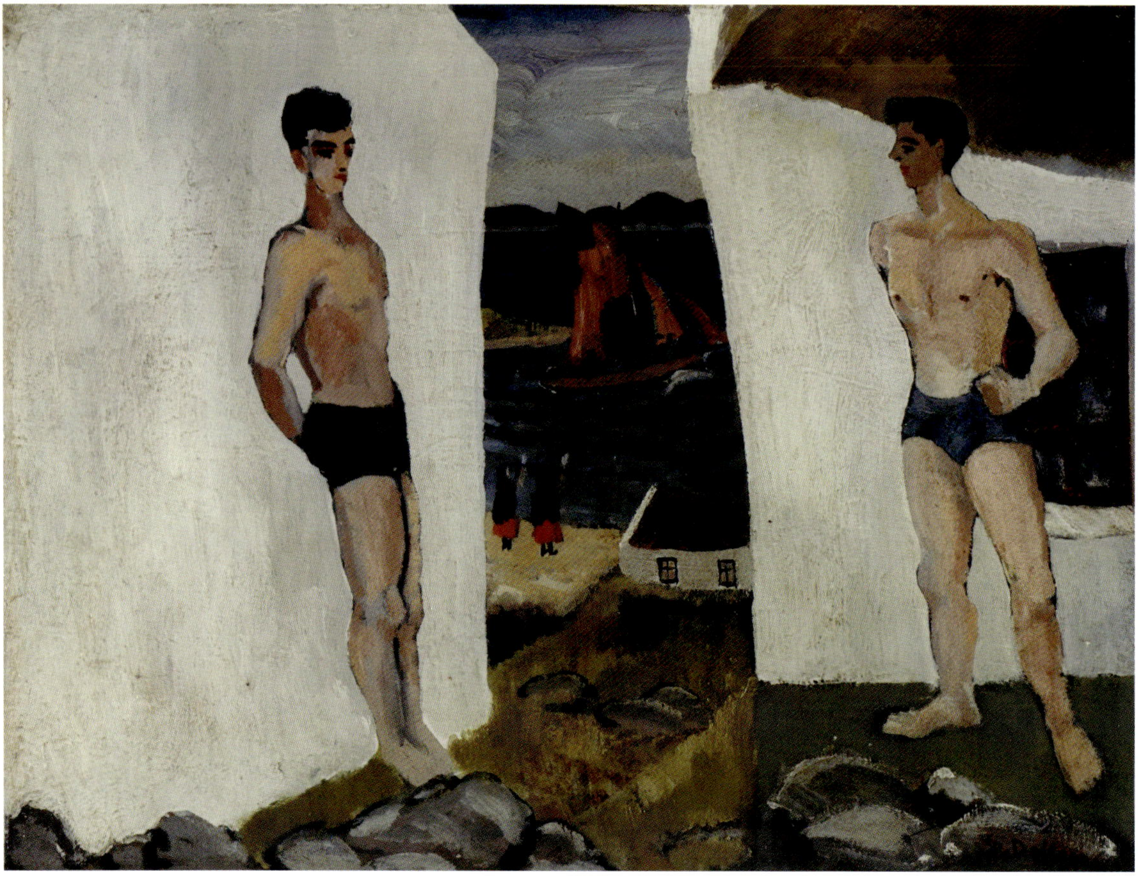

112 Gerard Dillon, *The Cottage Gable*, 1950, oil on panel.

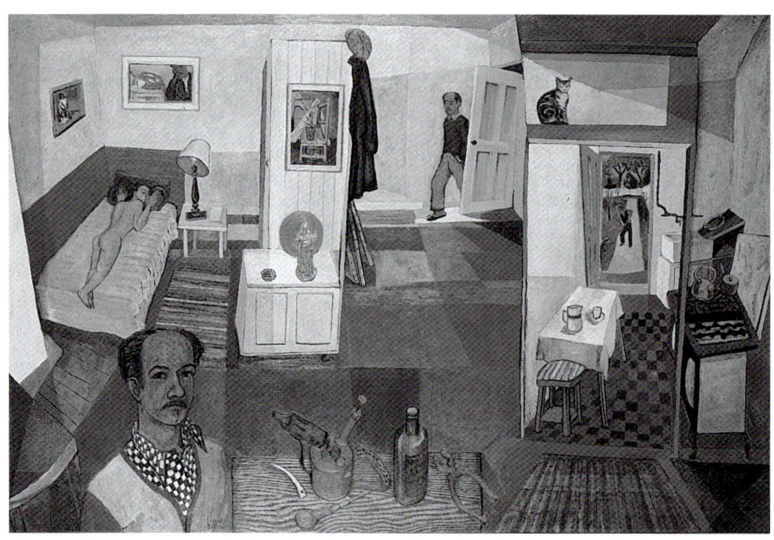

113 Gerard Dillon, *Self-contained Flat*,
n.d., oil on hardboard.

suggested by the work of Yeats or Collins. Defending himself in 1951 against criticisms that he saw 'the people and the landscape of the West with the eyes of a visitor', Dillon's response was:

> think of the West and the life lived there. Then think of my childhood and youth in the middle of industrial Belfast. Is not the West and the life lived there a great strange kind of wonder to the visitor from the red-brick city?[6]

The accentuated naivety of Dillon's approach in paintings like *The Yellow Bungalow* (1954) also evokes both Gauguin's depictions of Brittany and Chagall's recollections of his early life in Vitebsk. Its suggestion of the simplicity of peasant life, combined with the vibrancy of colour and the tilted perspective, produce a primitivist re-reading of more literary accounts of the West in Free State realism. Yet Dillon was caught between a desire for narrativity and its identification with Irish cultural identity and the forms of abstraction becoming more prevalent in both European and American contemporary art.[7] Although, like Mainie Jellett, he identified Celtic religious art as an example of a more formal aesthetic response, in paintings such as *Fast Day* (exhibited 1950), with its depiction of monastic life, this was a contradiction that Dillon never fully resolved. Yet his view of the West as a site of fantasy was also infused with a subversive eroticism that challenged the morality and sobriety of MacGonigal or Keating's heroic peasantry. This emerges in the spatial and sexual tensions between the two young men in swimming trunks depicted in *The Cottage Gable*, or the sleeping figures of *On the Beach* (both 1950). Other paintings, most notably *Self-contained Flat*, also contain encoded allusions to Dillon's homosexuality, incorporated within a fragmented representation of the basement flat in Abbey Road. The

sexually ambiguous reclining figure face down on the bed is not only a quotation from Gauguin's *Manao Tupapao (Spirit of the Dead Watching)* (1892). It also points towards the opportunities offered to gay men by London's metropolitan anonymity, and the construction of an identity difficult, if not impossible, to sustain in the context of Belfast's religious and political conservatism.

Irish artists and the post-war avant-garde

Other more prominent Irish artists in London, F. E. McWilliam, William Scott and Francis Bacon, had a longstanding involvement with British avant-garde practice. They all exhibited at the Hanover Gallery opened by the German refugee Erika Brausen in 1948. Unlike the more conservative Leicester Gallery (where, for example, Norah McGuinness showed), the Hanover had a strong commitment to both new developments in art in Britain and to contemporary art from Paris, including Giacometti and Vasarely. The same generation as Moore and Hepworth, McWilliam's work benefited from the increased visibility of sculpture in the post-war climate. In common with many of his younger contemporaries such as William Turnbull or Reg Butler, McWilliam's practice of the early 1950s used a vocabulary derived from Giacometti and the French sculptor Germaine Richier to articulate a sense of angst and alienation in the post-war climate. In McWilliam's case this resulted in a range of attenuated figurative sculptures with weathered-looking pockmarked surfaces. Unlike these other sculptors, however, he had first-hand experience of Surrealism, another key source of imagery at this point. A fascination with the mythic and archaic as able to express on some primal level the horrors of modern life was a major feature of art practice in the

United States, Britain and some parts of Europe during the early years of the Cold War. The titles of some of McWilliam's works at this time indicate an engagement with a Judaeo-Christian primitivism similar to that of the American Abstract Expressionist painter Barnett Newman – *Patriarch* (1953), *Eve* (1953) and *Cain and Abel*.[8] This last, depicting the biblical murder of one brother by another, was McWilliam's submission for the international competition to design a Monument to the Unknown Political Prisoner, won by the more abstract design of Reg Butler.

F. E. McWilliam still maintained an interest in Irish themes, as is clear from two very different pieces, *The Irish Head* and *Princess Macha*. The archaic classicism of the fragmented *Irish Head* is partly derived from McWilliam's interest in archaeological remains. Yet it also suggests a further form of primitivism, an interest in the Celtic cult of the head later taken up to great effect by Louis le Brocquy. *Princess Macha* was commissioned by the architect Eugene Rosenberg for Altnagelvin Hospital in Derry, the first newly built NHS hospital in the United Kingdom. For McWilliam, who had avoided the immediate post-war involvement in public sculpture by Moore or Hepworth, it was his first public commission. *Princess Macha* was exhibited at the Tate prior to installation in front of the hospital in 1960. The subject-matter of the seated hieratic bronze figure was also archaic – an Ulster princess who reputedly founded the first hospital in Ireland.[9] McWilliam further stressed the Celtic significance of the statue's heavily worked surface: 'The complicated richness of

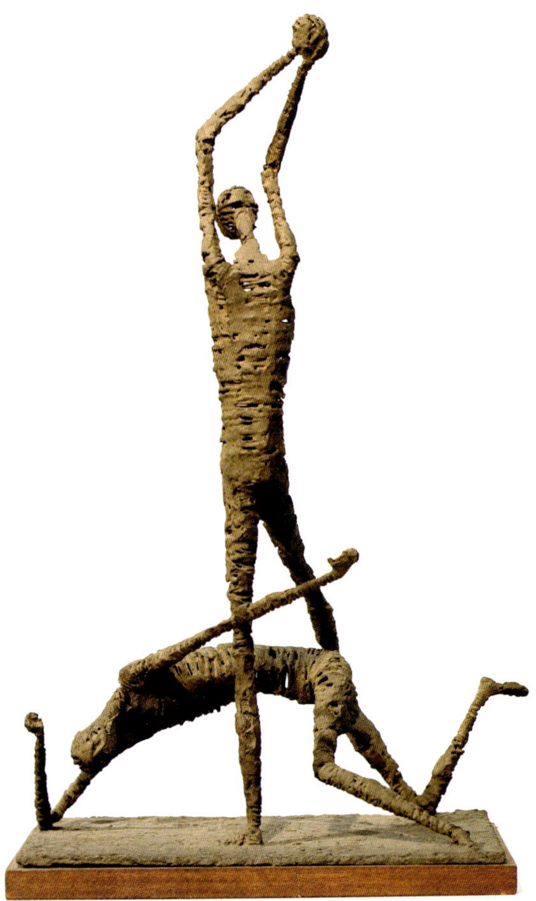

114 F. E. McWilliam, *Cain and Abel*, 1953, metal.

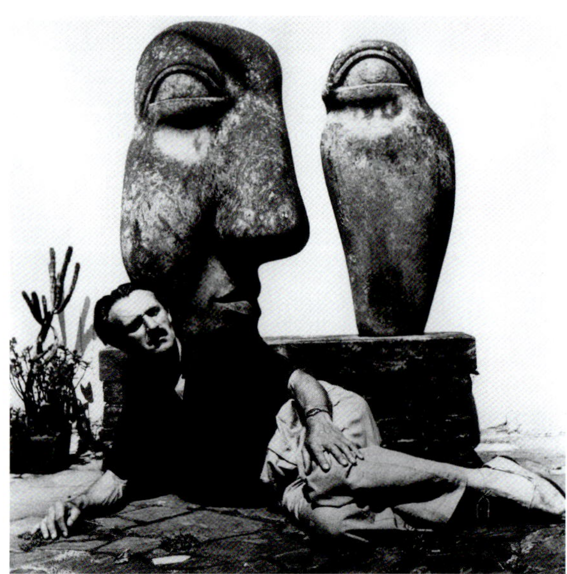

115 Ida Kar, McWilliam with *The Irish Head* (1949), 1955.

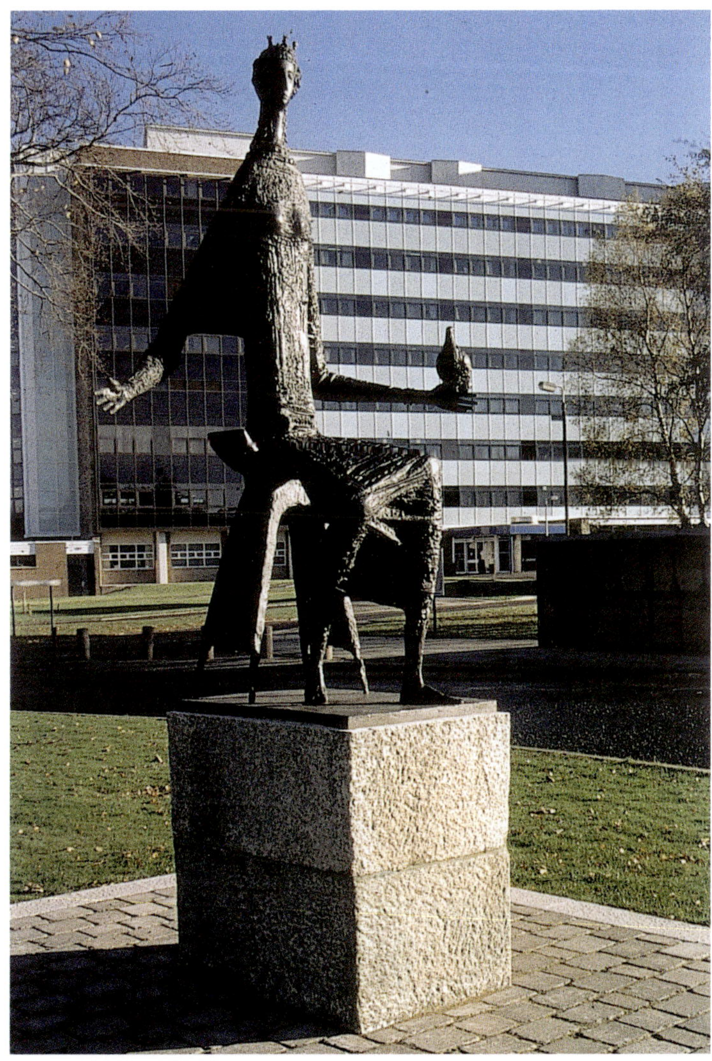

116 F. E. McWilliam,
Princess Macha, bronze,
installation shot,
Altnagelvin Hospital,
Derry, 1957.

the surface treatment is meant not only as a foil to the almost geometrical simplicity of her overall shape, but also as an allusion to the complexity of Celtic design.'[10] As Roy Wilkinson has shown, however, a reading of the press coverage of the statue's installation indicates that neither nationalists nor Unionists in Derry responded in the way that the sculptor had intended. In addition to a predictably blank response to the Celtic imagery by the Unionist *Londonderry Sentinel*, the nationalist *Irish News* also took issue: 'This is no image of Irish motherhood or comfort, her body encased in its bronze armour is as unyielding a motif as it is possible to imagine.'[11] As Wilkinson suggests, the crucial problem was that the statue had violated 'the prime category of Irish femaleness' – the Catholic imagery of the Virgin Mary, which it closely resembled.[12]

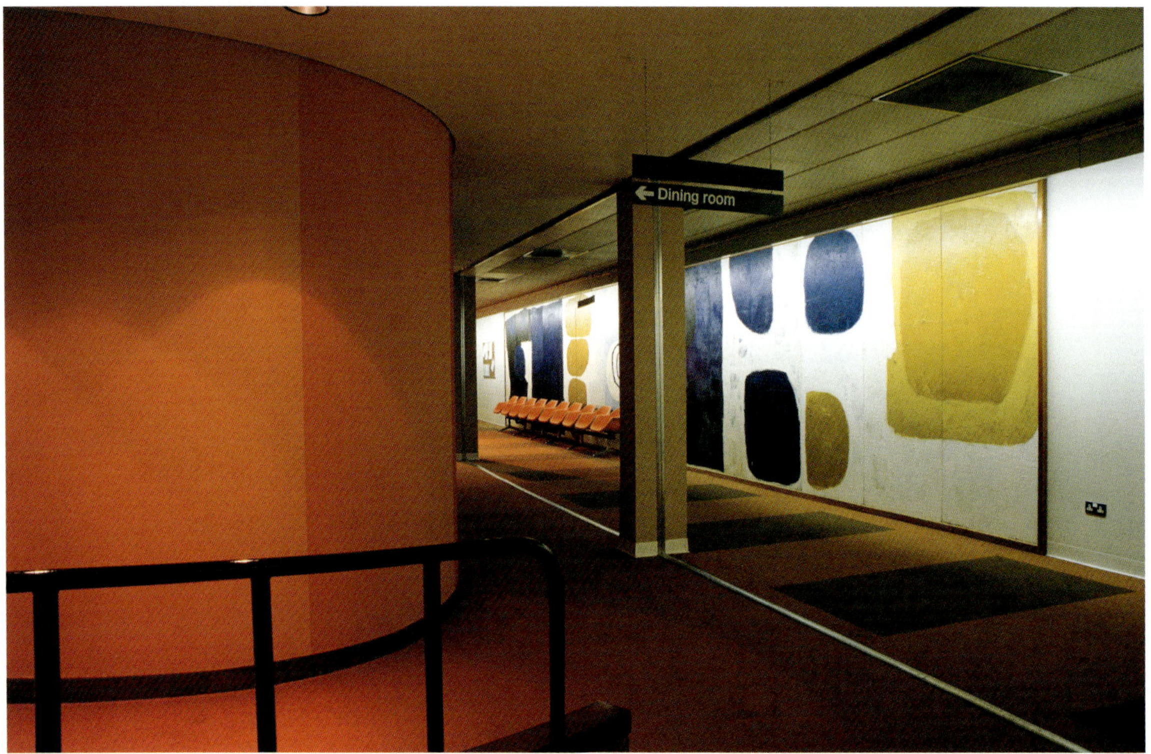

117 William Scott, *Four Seasons* mural, Altnagelvin Hospital, Derry, 1958, oil on plywood panels.

The mural by William Scott commissioned for Altnagelvin, *The Four Seasons*, also received a fairly dismal reception. Indeed the response to both of these works, by two of the leading practitioners of British modernism, indicates the depth of conservatism of reactions in Northern Ireland to contemporary art practice beyond a fairly limited range. Scott's mural was commissioned in 1958 by Rosenberg for the hospital entrance hall. Unlike *Princess Macha*, Scott's theme had no direct relevance to aspects of Irish identity. It was also far removed from the Secretary of the local Hospital Authority's preferred subject, whose references to Derry should include 'the traditional shirt factories, naval associations, the apprentice boys of course and . . . more recent organisations including cadets, boy scouts, girl guides and

others'.[13] Unlike the affirmative response to the mural's exhibition in the Tate in 1961, in Derry it was greeted with a lack of comprehension, a response similar to that caused by the purchase of Scott's *Brown Still Life* by the Belfast Museum and Art Gallery in 1959. In the same year as the Altnagelvin commission, 1958, Scott also represented Britain at the Venice Biennale. The hostile reception of his work in Northern Ireland must have been particularly galling for Scott who, as Norbert Lynton suggests, 'it will have pleased . . . in the year of Venice and his being widely received abroad as an "English" artist, to be asked to create a major public work for the region he considered his home territory'.[14]

By the late 1950s, William Scott had established a distinct position for himself in the British art scene. In

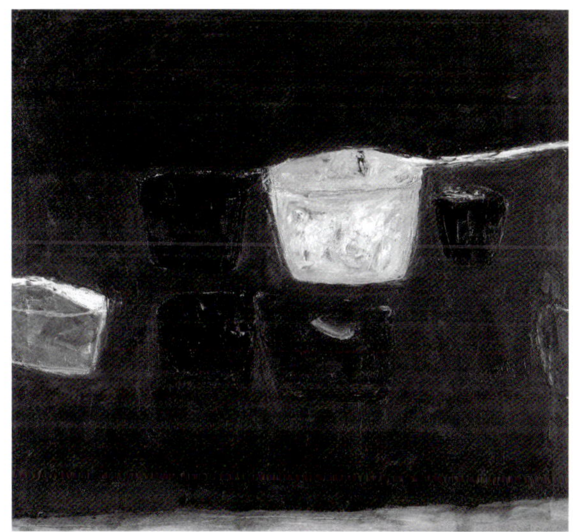

118 William Scott, *Brown Still-life*, 1958, oil on canvas.

1958 his friend, the painter Patrick Heron, described him as 'the senior figure in a generation of British painters – now in their late thirties or early forties – which is fast becoming known to an international audience'.[15] In spite of a friendship with American Abstract Expressionist painters such as Mark Rothko, dating from his visit to the States in 1953, Scott's work was primarily identified with issues of the domestic derived from a selective reading of French painting. Both Chardin and Bonnard informed his preferred themes of still life and nude respectively. These were rooted in his observations of the everyday and the human experience of objects as a basis for painterly exploration, although the austerity of Scott's earlier work, such as the *Still-life* (1948) in the Ulster Museum, can also be seen as derived from the Protestantism of

his upbringing. Yet even at this stage, sobriety was undercut by a richness of paint and a concern for aspects of pictorial surface. In the late 1950s, the dialectic of austerity and sensuality continued to underpin Scott's attempts to break down figuration in his paintings, although it would be misleading to view this as any kind of inevitable progression to abstraction. In one example, the *Gouache Abstract* subsequently shown in Venice, the forms more recognizable in the *Brown Still-life* as saucepans have become the basis for the rectilinear patterning that cover the picture plane. In 1958 the artist later described the process of making this work: 'I kept altering it, obliterating parts of it and the struggle I had to paint it all went to give it a life and vitality that gouache on paper doesn't usually have.'[16] The warm, vibrant colours also contribute to the painting's presence – a range of orange, red, yellow, white and magenta.

At a time when the influence of the abstraction associated with post-war American painting was beginning

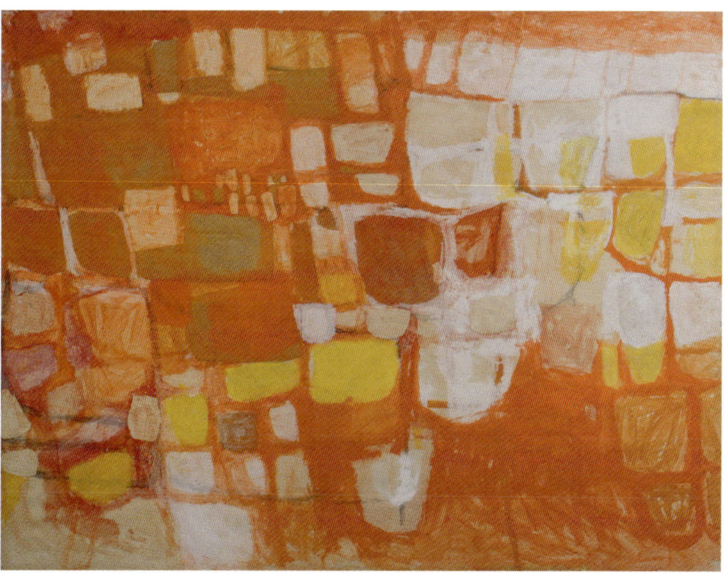

119 William Scott, *Gouache: Abstract*, 1957, gouache and collage on paper.

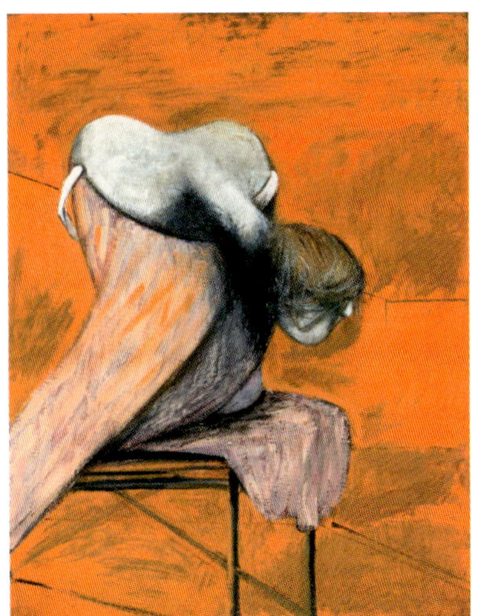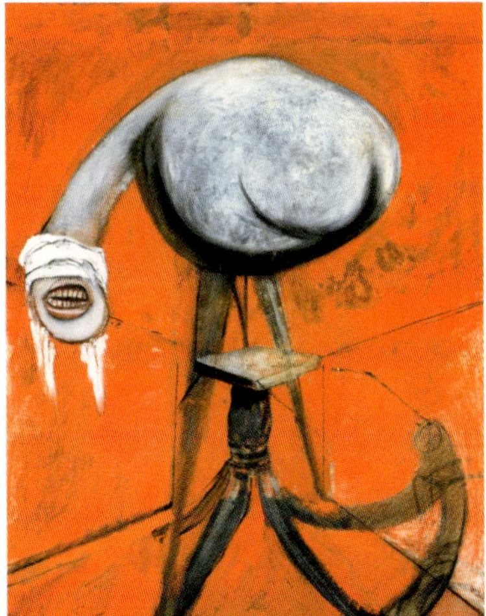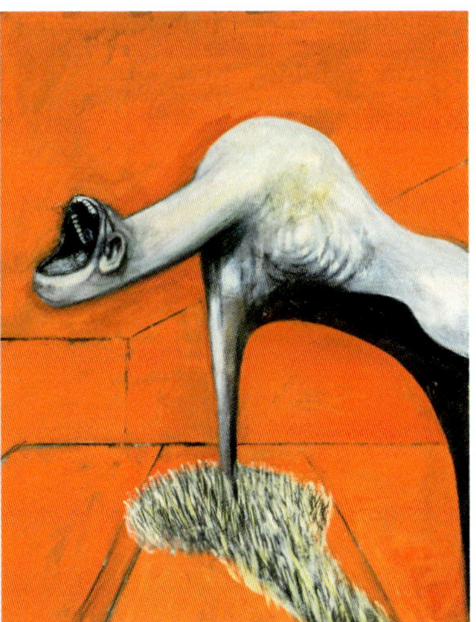

120 Francis Bacon, *Three Studies for Figures at the Base of the Crucifixion*, 1944, oil and pastel on hardboard.

to be felt strongly in London, two other Irish artists, Francis Bacon and Louis le Brocquy, were also producing work that could be read as pushing the body to its limits, albeit in different ways. This process, in both cases, can also be read as inflected and modified by Irish identifications, but with very different outcomes. Bacon not only played a major role in the emergence of a post-war Soho-based bohemia, but his work also involved the inescapably confrontational destruction of the human figure linked to an enactment of sado-masochistic homoeroticism in his personal life. Born in Dublin in 1909 to Anglo-Irish parents, Bacon's early investigations of transvestism led to his expulsion from the family home at the age of sixteen; he is generally believed never to have returned to Ireland.[17] After a period living in Paris and Berlin, he established himself in London as an Art Deco designer in 1930, a practice soon abandoned for experiments with painting. In spite of the menace of his *Crucifixion* (1933), infused with the destructive Bataillean aspects of Surrealism, he only began to emerge as a major painter some eleven years later with the triptych *Three Studies for Figures at the*

Base of the Crucifixion (1944). Bacon's reputation as a leading innovative painter was secured, however, with a series of depictions of the screaming figure from the late 1940s and early 1950s; so much so that in 1949 the critic Robert Melville was able to place him on a par with other modernist figures such as Eisenstein, Dostoevsky, Kafka and Picasso.[18] In a related work, *Pope I* (1951), the patriarch is restaged as a figure of terror that draws as much on the existing climate of Cold War anxieties as on Bacon's fascination with the memory of his own tyrannical father.[19]

Increased recognition of Bacon's work throughout the 1950s culminated in his major Tate retrospective of 1963. However, his reputation as a leading innovator of *international* modernism causes problems for his positioning within a history of Irish art, which remains resolutely marginal to such grand narratives. This is compounded by Bacon's ambivalence to the significance of his Irishness. In spite of his upper-class background, as Michael Peppiatt observed, Bacon frequently represented himself 'as an inspired misfit from the wilds of an Irish stud farm'.[20] And in an interview

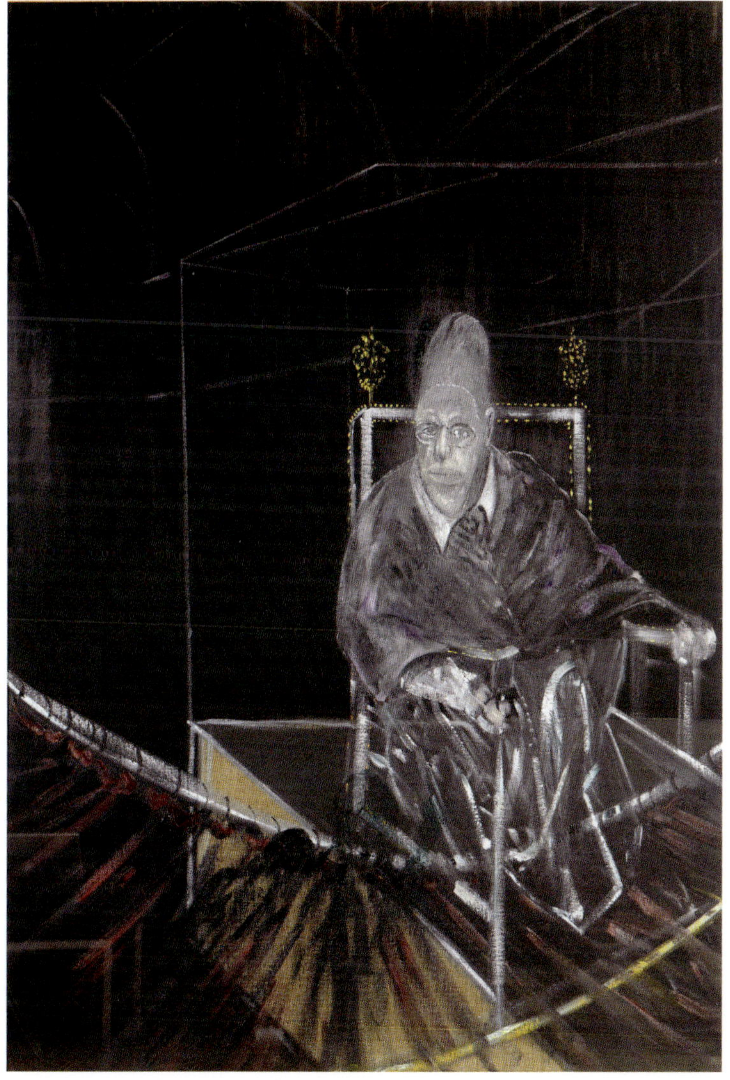

121 Francis Bacon, *Pope I*, 1951, oil on canvas.

this was not the same as the 'violence in painting'. Clearly any suggestions of the significance of Irishness in relation to Bacon's work need to be carefully nuanced.[22]

Of all these artists who attained a significant career outside Ireland in the immediate post-war period, Louis le Brocquy has probably has the greatest impact on art within Ireland itself. In 1946, le Brocquy moved from Dublin to London in the hope of a more congenial reception after the repeated academic rejection of his work in Ireland. His first show in London, containing some 40 works, was at Gimpel Fils, who became his permanent dealers. Just over half of these paintings were of Irish subjects, many of whom were tinkers. Le Brocquy became preoccupied with this subject after his move to London. One of the earliest of the resulting series of paintings was *Tinkers Resting*, whose flattened picture plane revealed a close reading of Picasso – a degree of avant-garde experimentalism that would have been difficult in Dublin's repressive atmos-

with David Sylvester, he attributed his interest in violence at least in part to his early life in Ireland. During the War of Independence he lived for a while 'in a sandbagged house' with his grandmother and her husband, the Commissioner of Police for Kildare; when they went out 'ditches were dug across the road for a car or horse-and-cart to fall into, and there would be snipers waiting on the edges'.[21] However, Bacon, a strong believer in art's autonomous life, was also at pains to stress that

phere. For le Brocquy, the theme of the Irish outcast became a metaphor for the artist. This interest in the tinkers was not only reinforced by knowledge of their historical dispossession within Ireland; the travelling people also came to signify for him the refugees in post-war Europe. The rediscovery of Irish issues through the stimulus of a different culture is also characteristic of le Brocquy's practice. Of Belgian descent, his first discovery of an Irish identity was concurrent also with a discovery of European culture when he first left Ireland in 1937. As

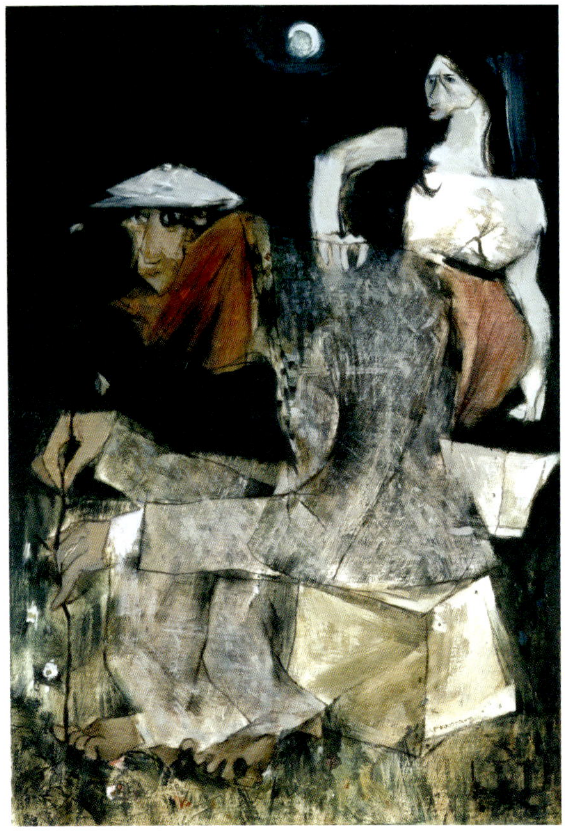

122 Louis le Brocquy, *Tinkers Resting*, 1948, oil on hardboard.

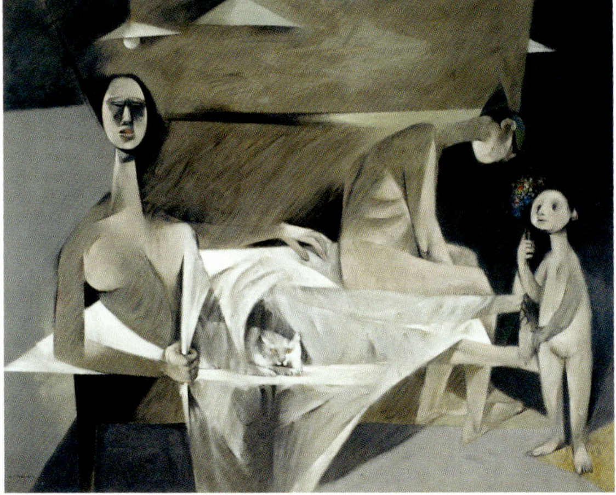

123 Louis le Brocquy, *A Family*, 1951, oil on canvas.

he later claimed, 'Alone among the great artists of the past, in these strange related cities I became vividly aware for the first time of my Irish identity to which I have remained attached all my life.'[23]

Le Brocquy's paintings received fairly immediate public recognition in Britain. He was frequently included in British Council touring exhibitions, and in 1958 *Tinkers Resting* was the first of several of his paintings to be bought by the Tate. Irish themes soon began to disappear from his work, although they did re-emerge in a big way in the 1960s. Instead le Brocquy's work began to feature the apocalyptic Cold War themes that also preoccupied him and which involved an apparent

universality more recognizable to a British and European public. One such piece was *A Family*, le Brocquy's major work of the early 1950s. In addition to its combination of elements of both Picasso and Moore, the family group also involves a reworking of Manet's *Olympia*.[24] The painting is dominated by the reclining figure of the mother with a half-feral cat, a motif also appearing in related works from the same year, the much smaller *Two Rooms* and *Indoors, Outdoors*. Yet the darkness of *A Family* suggests a claustrophobia absent from either of these paintings. A light bulb quoted from Picasso's *Guernica* only helps to evoke the post-apocalyptic scenario, while le Brocquy also identified the relevance

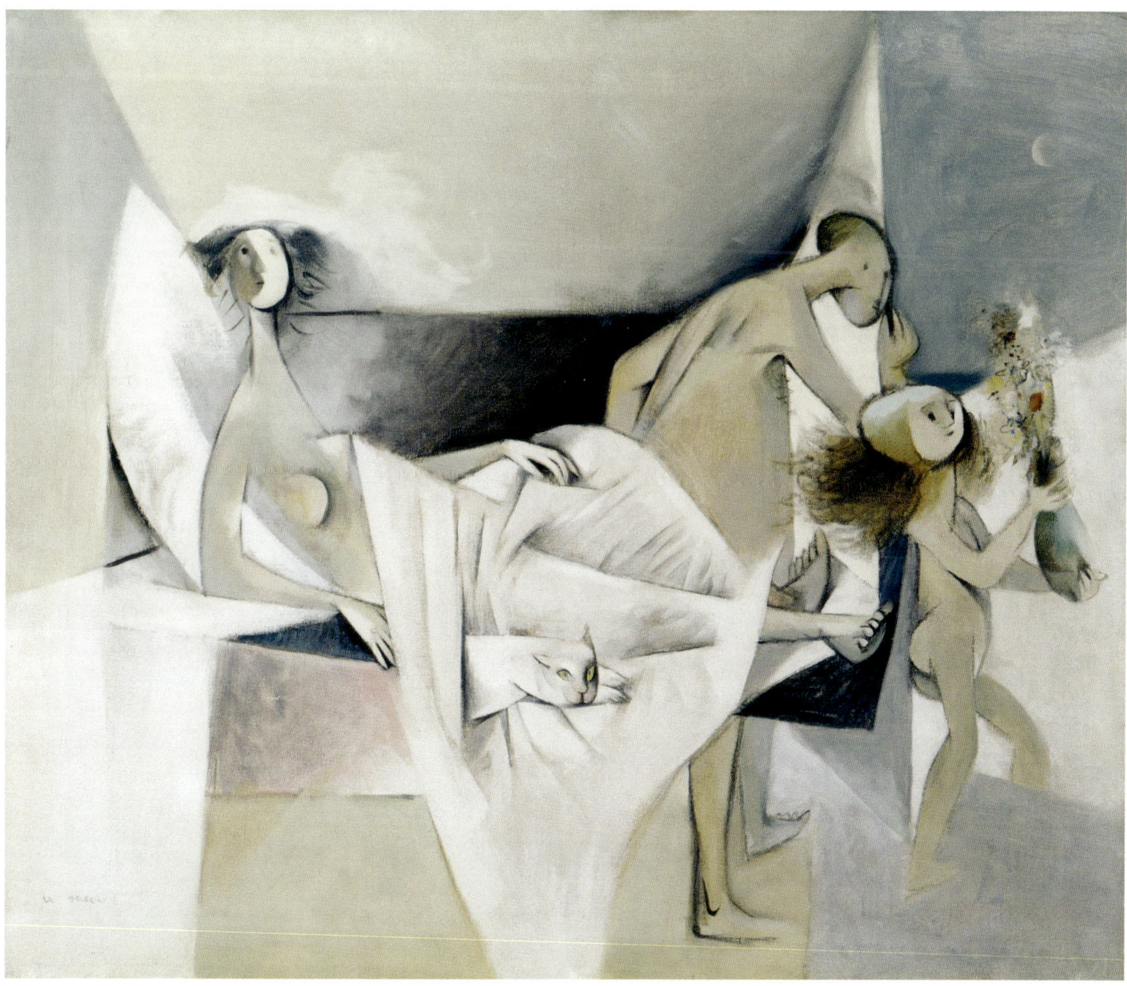

124 Louis le Brocquy, *Indoors, Outdoors*, 1951, oil on canvas.

of his reworking of Manet's painting to 'very different circumstances, in the face of atomic threat, social upheaval and refugees of World War Two and its aftermath'.[25] During the 1940s and early 1950s, the fear of unknown cataclysm manifested itself culturally in a preoccupation with mythology rather than history as offering explanations for a sense of primal terror unleashed first through war and subsequently through an awareness of the destructive power of the atomic bomb.[26] The dominant mother in *A Family* is similar to the Jungian female archetypes that populate the paintings of Colin Middleton and American Abstract Expressionism, notably early Pollock or the work of de Kooning, to whose depictions of women during the 1940s le Brocquy's *Travelling Woman with Newspaper* has been compared.[27]

Both the large scale of *A Family* and its references to Manet indicate it to be a kind of *morceau de réception*, in

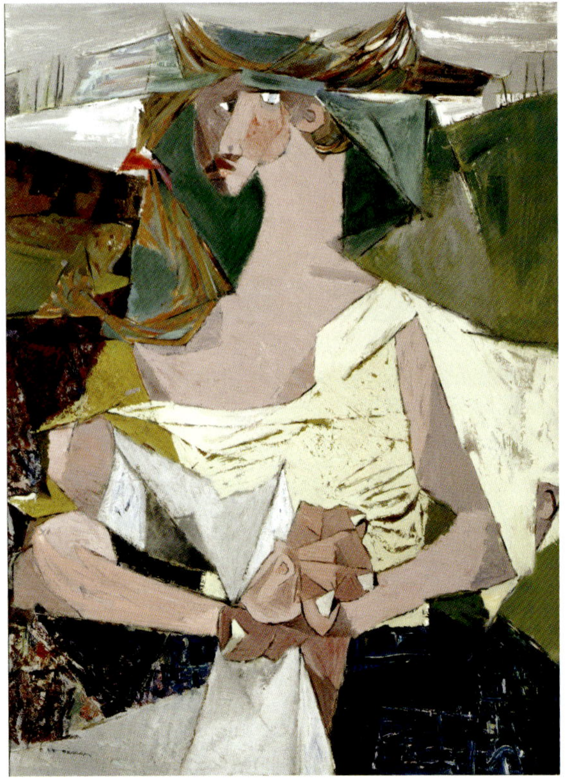

125 Louis le Brocquy, *Travelling Woman with Newspaper*, 1947–8, oil on hardboard.

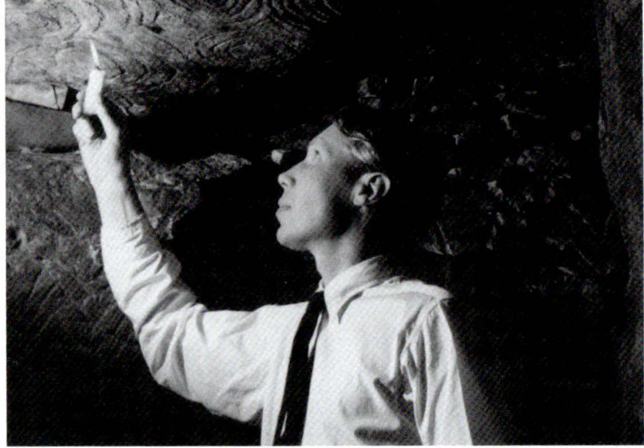

126 Louis le Brocquy revisiting the inner chamber of the megalithic passage tomb at Newgrange in the Boyne Valley, 1952.

this case the act of the displaced artist, displaying his confidence and skill in an adopted culture. But it also helps to suggest a reading as a modern history painting, an advocacy of retrenchment to the most basic form of social organization, the family, as a moral response to contemporary events. In 1956, le Brocquy and Hilary Heron represented Ireland at the Venice Biennale. In addition to a selection of the tapestries he had also been working on since the late 1940s, le Brocquy was represented by a group of paintings from the early 1950s, including *A Family*. That the painting subsequently won the grand painting prize is an indication not just of his proficiency, but also of the timeliness of the theme. It also marked increased public recognition outside Ireland of le Brocquy and of Irish art on a more international scale.[28] All this was in sharp contrast to the situation

inside Ireland. In 1952 a small group of supporters of modernist painting in Dublin offered to buy the painting for the Municipal Gallery.[29] The offer was refused and in 1956 the painting was bought from the Biennale for the corporate collection of Prealpina-Nestlé in Milan. In 2001, in a very different atmosphere around the reassessment of Ireland's involvement with modernism, the painting finally entered the Irish state collection when it was donated to the National Gallery.

During the late 1950s, Louis le Brocquy's practice began to shift radically from the grey paintings of a few years previously. On one of his frequent return visits to Dublin he met the young Irish painter Anne Madden. In 1958, the couple were married in Chartres Cathedral and moved to the South of France, where the climate was better for Madden's health: she had recently undergone a series of operations for a painful spinal injury. They remained there until 2001. Prior to this, on a trip to Spain in 1955, le Brocquy had also experienced a profound realization that would have a major effect on his painting. In Ireland, the blurred edges of landscape produced by the softness of light can lead – as in Patrick Collins's handling – to a sensuous relationship to what is depicted. In the harsh light of southern Europe, le Brocquy became aware of form as flattened and dissolved into a profound whiteness, rather than being revealed and defined. Any solidity in this inversion of the norm was found only in shadows, as matter appeared to dissolve in the light.

The question for the painter, then, becomes one of how to bring matter and form out of that primordial whiteness. Le Brocquy later described the process of making a picture almost as a form of automatism, as

> a peculiar use of oil paint; not to symbolise, not to describe the object, nor to realise an abstract image but rather to allow the paint, while insisting on its own palpable nature, to reconstitute (if it will) the object of one's experience.[30]

One result was the series of 'Presences', a theme that preoccupied le Brocquy from around 1956 until 1964, which depicted the human figure emerging out of a generally white ground. It is not consciousness that is represented here – not yet – but a sense of immanent being, where matter becomes dynamized in the upright, existential human figure reminiscent of Giacometti's isolated figures. In the Tate's *Woman*, the figure hovers on the edge of abstraction. The elongated form is focused around the exposed vulnerability of the spinal column, with a further suggestion of breasts and shoulders. Yet it is its echo, the dark shadow emerging from the pale ground, that provides an uncanny sense of the more normative perception of the body, rounded and complete.

These nude human presences are mainly female, but far removed from depictions of the female body as conventional object of desire. Herbert Read described the body in these paintings as 'reduced to a clotted ganglia of blood and nerves, but recorded so discreetly that the full force of the erotic imagery is only revealed to quiet contemplation'.[31] In the Tate *Woman* the artist's knowledge of a specific, wounded female body becomes the catalyst for a more universalized investigation of an existential humanity. These images also draw upon unconscious associations of femininity for their effect, and hence invite psychoanalytic readings to articulate these meanings. On one level these women are the successors of the archetypal mother of *A Family*, suggestive of primitivist readings of the female body as the giver of life, closer to nature in its fecundity. Yet here it is the repressed desire for the maternal body that structures the viewer's engagement, almost at a somatic level. Drawing on Kleinian readings, Read also identified the ambivalence of desire for the mother's body: 'the good object, milk-white and beneficent … is also associated with erotic envy, aggression and sadism'.[32] The other face of immanent presence shaped by the power of the viewer's desire is the abject eviscerated body, whose proximity to death suggests a very different relationship to undifferentiated matter.

In addition to developing an engagement with primitivist concerns characteristic of earlier cultural responses to the Cold War in their dematerialization of human form, the 'Presences' also invite comparisons with the concerns of French painting during the 1940s and '50s – the Inform (*l'Informe*). Derived from Bataille's earlier notion of formlessness as undermining the very basis of representation, the work of the artist Jean Fautrier during and after the Second World War, in its focus on the disintegrating body, attempted to depict the consequences of torture and destruction during the Occupation and the Holocaust. Fautrier's paintings

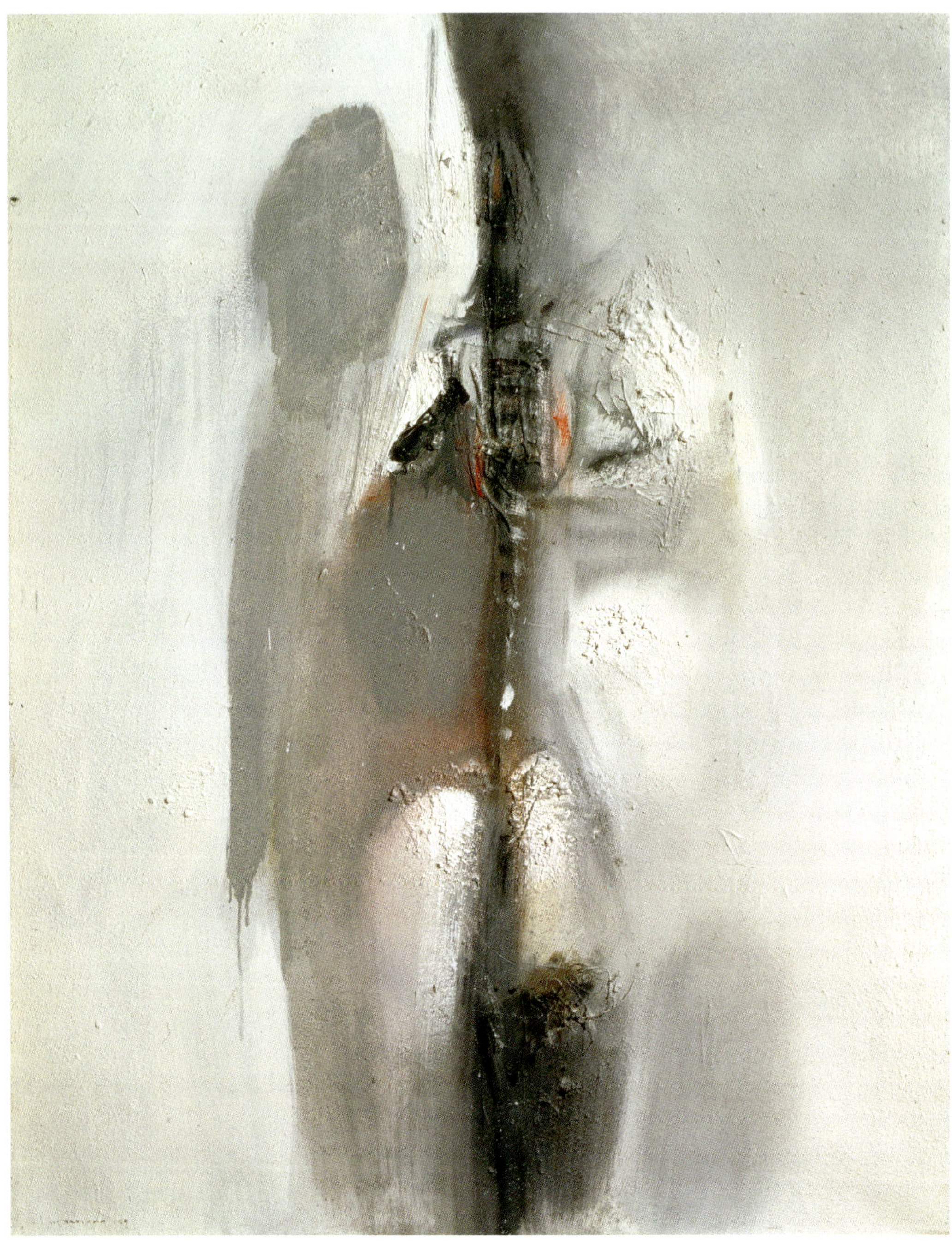

127 Louis le Brocquy, *Woman*, 1959, oil on canvas.

carry a sense of the human presence on the edge of extinction: Serge Guilbaut described them as 'like raw wounds, open for investigation in their beautiful display, but accompanied by an abstract type of repulsion, a nausea ever present through association'.[33] Le Brocquy's 'Presences' also display their open wounds, but they have a sense of immanence not available to Fautrier. In this sense of meaning deferred but still present elsewhere they are similar to the tendencies identified by Brian O'Doherty as characteristic of art within Ireland during the 1950s.

However, rather than linking le Brocquy's work more firmly with its origins, to identify it in this way can also be read, conversely, as a sense of engagement with European art in a new and radical way for an Irish practitioner. The 'Presences' develop a form of painting that had resonances of two very different – and in fact oppositional – cultural precedents: primitivist notions of the unconscious female archetype associated with Abstract Expressionism painting and the disintegration of matter associated with the French Inform. A key feature of the cultural politics of post-war Europe was the debate around the encroaching cultural presence of the United States during the Cold War and strategies of resistance to this: a debate in which Irish art had remained resolutely marginal.[34] Yet it is possible to read the 'Presences' as one instance where certain features of Ireland's isolation, represented through practices that repeatedly deferred meaning, actually allowed the articulation of a 'third space' (to borrow Homi Bhabha's term), one where a new hybrid identity replete with previously unimaginable cultural possibilities could begin to emerge.[35] It is at this point, with Louis le Brocquy's work of the late 1950s and early 1960s, that aspects of Irish art began to take on a very different relationship to the wider features of European culture.

SEVEN

MODERNIZATION AND ITS CONSEQUENCES: THE 1960S

During the 1960s, the conditions within which art could be made, or viewed, began to change radically within Ireland. This was partly a consequence of the effects of modernization in both Northern Ireland and the Republic that brought an end to the isolationism of previous decades. Yet one of the ongoing characteristics of modernity is that it is constituted through contradiction: between past and present, local and global. To be a modern artist in Ireland in the 1960s could also mean, paradoxically, to have a high investment in the representation of the past. Yet it could also involve an increased awareness of the major post-war shifts in the cultural politics of international modernism. This was something that affected not just Ireland but art in a whole range of nations across Europe and beyond.

The isolationism characterizing political life in the Republic since 1922 was increasingly dismantled during the 1960s in a major programme of modernization initiated by Seán Lemass. Rather than adherence to an archaic nationalism identified with the leadership of de Valera, his managerial style promoted progress through unfettered free enterprise. In 1959, after Fianna Fáil won the election again under the leadership of Lemass, more rigorous approaches to economic planning were combined with considerable incentives to foreign businesses to set up in Ireland. The boost to the economy was to have consequences both for the art market and patronage in a climate of increasing contacts with other global powers. Economic optimism was also echoed by the liberalization of censorship legislation in place since the early years of the Free State, with the removal of film censorship in 1964 and that of literature three years later. In spite of such initiatives as the founding of Ardmore Film Studios in 1958, the overall drive towards modernization was not always positive. While the newly founded Kilkenny Design Centre (1963) promoted a sense of a forward-looking Irish design and craft identity, the eradication of other aspects of Ireland's cultural history was well underway. Rampant property speculation and inept planning controls ensured the destruction of some of the best-preserved Georgian architecture in Dublin. After a bitter two-year controversy the Electricity Supply Board, in an act initially supported by the Arts Council, demolished a large part of Lower Fitzwilliam Street to make way for a modernist office building; this was perhaps the most notorious incident to attract a huge amount of hostile publicity.

Landscape, intuition and the Celtic

As David Harvey has suggested, the progressive drive of modernization is also bound up with other contradictory forces that undermine its optimistic rationality in the insistent destruction of the past.[1] It is because the past can act as a brake on progress that it is perceived as such a threat. In the Ireland of the early 1960s, almost 50 years after the Easter Rising, the past and its traditions had become identified with nationalism as a regressive force. Rather than being something that can be purged from the body of modernity, traditions can also be perceived as dialectically bound up with the present, helping to produce a more complex sense of what it means to be both Irish and modern.

These inbuilt contradictions of nationalism and modernization are very relevant to a discussion of the meanings of Irish art at the start of the decade.[2] In a catalogue essay for the exhibition *The Irish Imagination* in 1971, Brian O'Doherty argued that the self-imposed isolationism of the period from the beginning of the Second World War until the end of the 1950s was important in allowing Irish art to develop a specific character, removed from outside influences. Yet the consequent insistence on a kind of poetic 'atmosphere' as the dominant tendency in Irish art of the 1960s 'could be considered a last examination and confrontation of a certain minority or subject [sic] mentality that never responds to anything directly'.[3] And it is more than this. Rather than just being a hangover from the miasmic 1950s, there is a sense of deeper emotional, cultural and political roots for notions of the intuitive invoked by many Irish artists during the following decade. Landscape continued to dominate, yet its meanings had undergone a series of transformations since the early part of the century.

In the old Free State nationalist project, the values of ethnicity identified with the depiction of the West had been intended to promote a sense of belonging to the nation. Derived from this, authenticity continued to be important; but rather than being dependent on

naturalistic depiction in the manner of Keating, the legacy of Yeats meant that it became an authenticity of feeling – a *sense* of Irishness, a new modernized form of ethnicity. Although the West still remained privileged as subject-matter, this was increasingly as a site of resistance to modernization rather than colonialism, although the historical significance of these locations was far from lost. The traces of the pre-industrial in Patrick Collins's paintings are evidence of this, as is the fascination with the prehistoric in the increasingly abstract work of Anne Madden. Yet this type of work can also be read as privileging an intuitive response underpinned by associations of the primitive and the unconscious. It is one of modernism's fundamental contradictions that a visual language employed to articulate the fractured experience of modernity has itself been dependent on notions of the archaic, whether as apparently historically outmoded or as pre-linguistic. These intuitive responses in the visual art of the 1960s in Ireland helped to construct a sense of Irishness that at once escapes and is fundamentally bound up with the progressive logic of modernization.

These were tendencies with different inflections in Irish landscape painting of the 1960s. Writing in 1982, Frances Ruane identified key features of Patrick Collins's practice as

> looking . . . for an art that reflects the nuances of Celtic life. His art goes beyond recording the surfaces so frequently identified with the archaeological remains of the Celtic past. It is rather more profoundly found in aspects that include a fascination with the mythical, a fix on the past, a sense of isolation, a brooding spirituality and an intense love of the land.[4]

All of these were characteristics with a particular resonance in the 1960s, a period when Collins's work

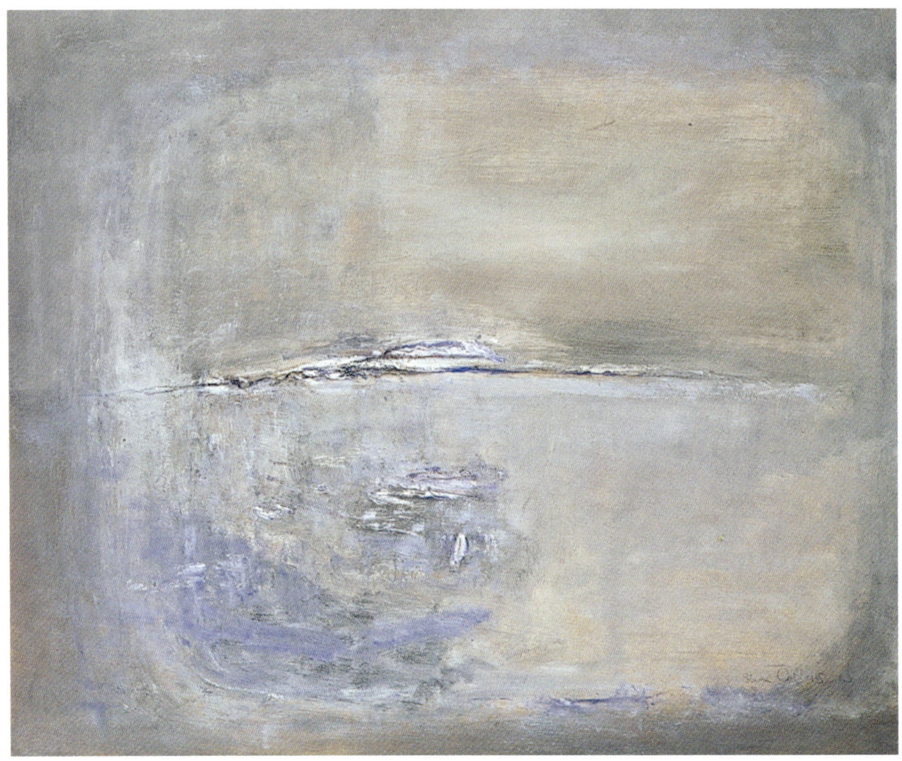

128 Patrick Collins,
Hy Brazil, 1963, oil
on board.

continued to gain recognition. His painting *Hy Brazil* depicts a mythical land reputed to exist off the coast of Ireland, the physical embodiment of Tír na n'Óg, the Land of Eternal Youth. Collins depicts Hy Brazil as an elusive physical presence. A glimpse of high ground emerges above the horizon line that bisects the picture plane, while rocks also appear to break the surface of the sea. These traces of materiality help to anchor Collins's work in figuration amidst the abstract washes of paint – a repeated strategy in his practice. A sense of displacement is also amplified by another recurrent device, the indication of a frame within a frame, suggesting the perception of another reality within the painting. The void from which land emerges in *Hy Brazil* became a further feature of Collins's work of the 1960s. It also contributes to Ruane's description of *Hy Brazil* as 'a highly abstract

vision that dematerialises matter in an effort to make contact with the symbolic character of the subject'.[5]

On the one hand, the negotiation of figuration and abstraction is suggestive of more contemporary international concerns in modernist painting after Abstract Expressionism. On the other, there is a concern for the articulation of a Celticness closely bound up with definitions of more specifically Irish cultural identity in the 1960s. A prevailing tendency in the work of Irish modernist artists throughout the twentieth century was to represent the Celtic in terms of a deferral of meaning that dovetails neatly with a lack of specificity opened up by moves away from naturalism in painting. As Mainie Jellett argued, modernism's destruction of illusionistic space is, in this sense, reinforced by the use of cyclical modes of Celtic decoration, a form of representation that never experienced the Renaissance.[6] Celtic epistemologies have also been interpreted within the practice of Irish modernism as perceiving material objects as less important in themselves than as catalysts for the experience of a more metaphysical reality.

Yet these are claims applicable to some artists more than others. Although, like Collins, the work of Nano Reid or Anne Madden also reveals an interest in the archaic, there is a sense with both these artists during the 1960s that the materiality of the landscape was not just a pretext for the evocation of elusive meaning. The earthy tones of Reid's *Ancient Land* (1962) describe a loose grid arranged around a central ochre panel incised with one of the hieroglyphic signs that increasingly characterized her work.[7] Like the earlier painting *Rubbish Dump* (1958), whose title indicates Reid's interest in more overlooked subject-matter, this can be read as an aerial view of a patchwork of small fields. Yet there are also elements that convey a sense both of geological depth and of a land shaped by human use; the skull in the lower central panel, enclosed within its tomb, is directly below the figure of a man bent over his shovel. This figure is also dug into the ground of the field he works, incised into the painted surface. Other panels include chevroned patterning similar to that found at the Neolithic passage graves of the Boyne Valley, near Reid's native Drogheda. The shifting, jerking perspective of this painting was one that Reid had used from the mid-1940s onwards in more naturalistic works like *Friday Fare* (1945). Here, however, in combination with the grid's disruption of linear narrativity, it becomes a means of suggesting a pre-industrial or Celtic cycle of death and rebirth.

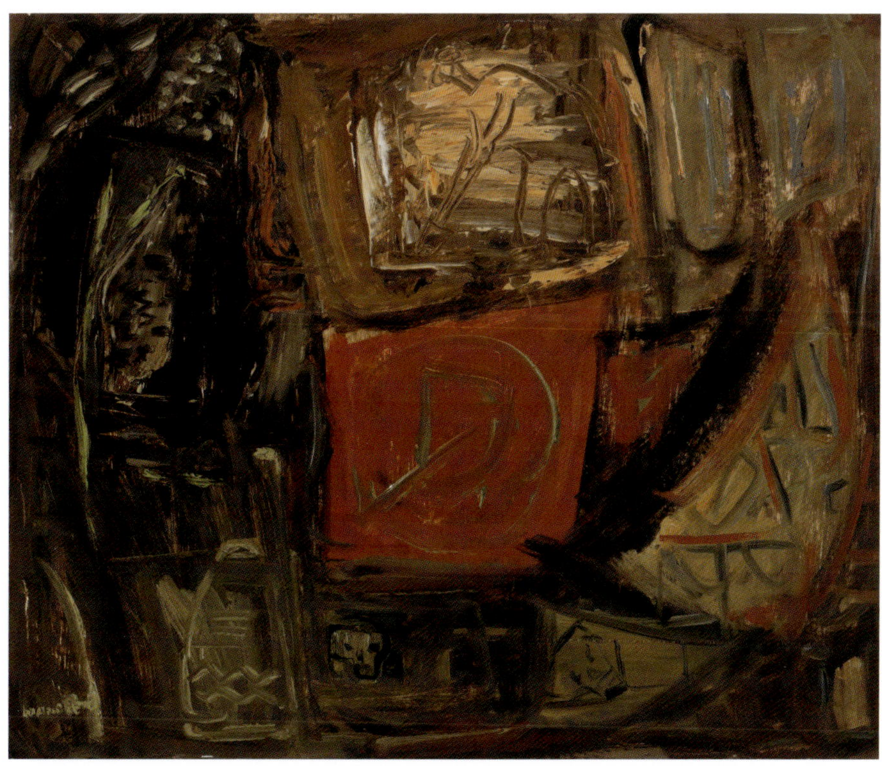

129 Nano Reid, *Ancient Land*, 1962, oil on board.

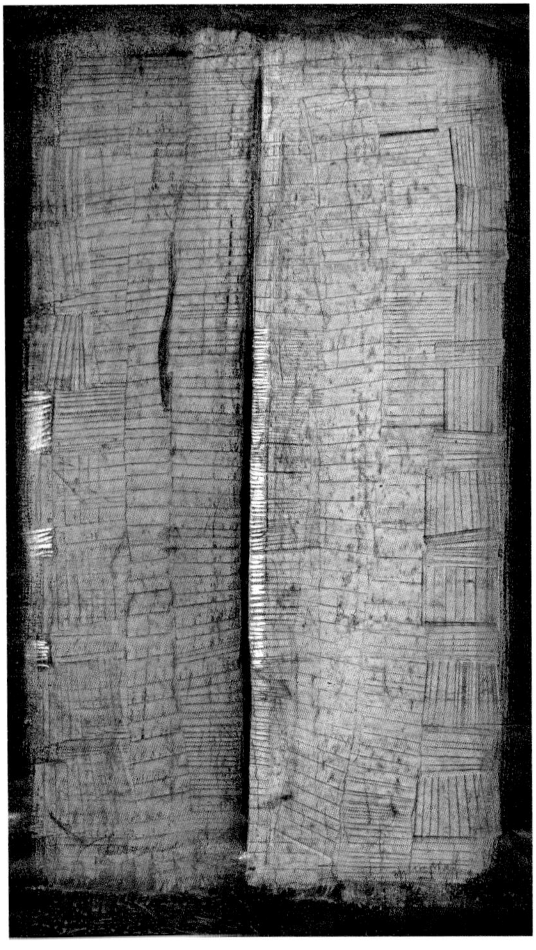

130 Tony O'Malley, *Winter Silence I*, 1967,
mixed media on toned paper.

Landscape as a means for engaging with memory and melancholia also pervaded much of the work of Tony O'Malley throughout the decade. By 1960 he had moved to the artists' community of St Ives in Cornwall; the abiding influence of the earlier generation of Gabo and Nicholson meant that St Ives was much more conducive to the development of abstraction than was common in Ireland at the time. Gradually O'Malley's work became increasingly abstract, frequently incor-

porating the use of incised surface derived partly from a reading of Nicholson, but also from the sgraffito technique of the ceramicist Bernard Leach.[8] The titling of many of these works still retained explicit references to the observable world of nature. These include paintings such as *Winter Silence* I and II, mixed-media works on paper that combine a loose repetition of rectangular elements incised into the surface with a restricted sombre palette of white, blues and black. Throughout the 1960s O'Malley's work relied increasingly on form and colour to convey a sense of melancholia, related to his own experience of personal loss and illness. In 1961, he suffered a serious heart attack, three years after his younger brother died from the same cause.

Frequently mediated through O'Malley's depictions of the stark Penwith landscape, the romantic themes of winter, hovering birds and an ever-present solitude coalesced in his painterly response to the death of the artist Peter Lanyon in 1964. For O'Malley, there were evident affinities between Cornwall and Ireland as Celtic countries with similar histories of poverty and oppression.[9] It was one aspect of his friendship with Lanyon, who was unusual among the St Ives painters in that he was actually born there and had the same close familiarity with the Penwith region as O'Malley did with the landscape around New Ross. In 1964, Lanyon was killed at the age of 46 in a gliding accident in Somerset. O'Malley commemorated his death in two paintings, both derived from his observations of a hawk flying above a quarry. *In Memory of Peter Lanyon* is by far the more abstract. The high horizon line and green vortex emerging from darkness suggest the bird's view as it plummets into the void. These compositional strategies of the Sublime suggest the attempt to convey the painter's immense grief in the immediacy of Lanyon's death. Albeit in different ways, both works combine to articulate a powerful sense of loss and mourning.

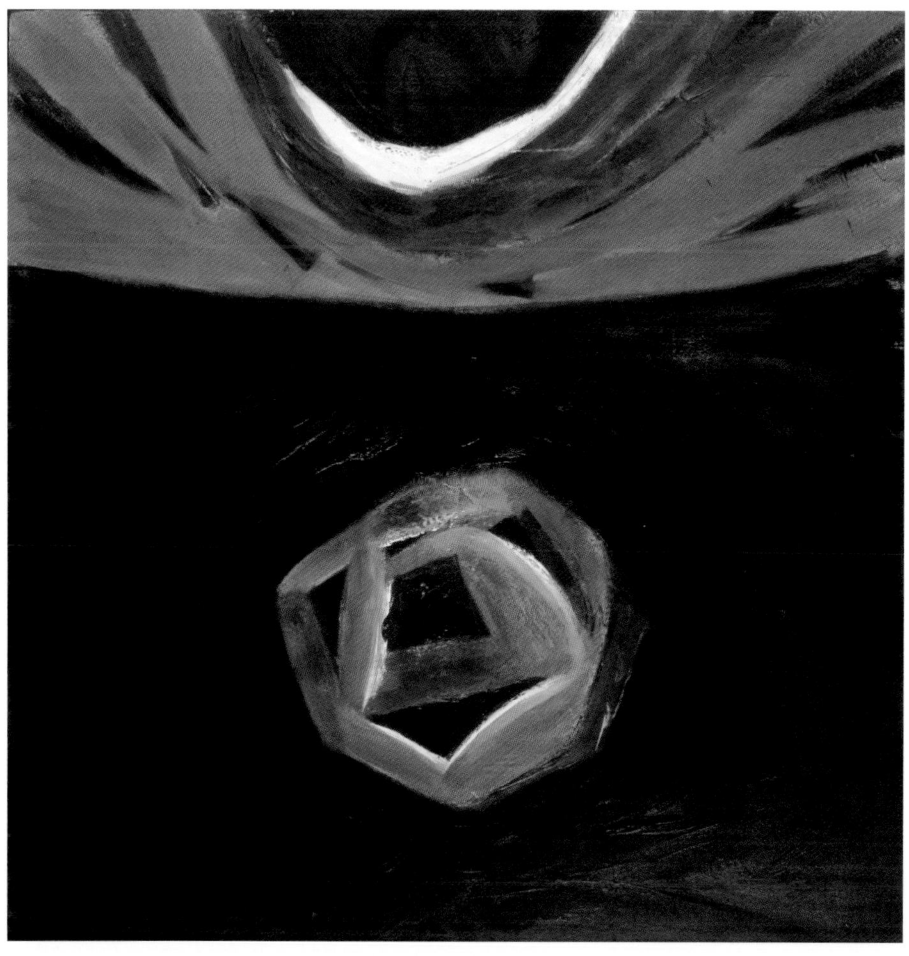

131 Tony O'Malley, *In Memory of Peter Lanyon*, 1964, oil on board.

Yet Romanticism was not the only means of engaging with the landscape as a subject. A former fisherman, James Dixon was already well into his sixties when he began to paint the scenes of Tory Island exhibited from the mid-1960s onwards. As part of the Atlantic seaboard, Donegal was well-established on the landscape painters' circuit; its remoteness and rugged scenery offered plenty of opportunity for idealized interpretation. Tory was particularly inaccessible, especially during winter months, when the small community could be cut off from the mainland by storms for days on end. During the early 1950s, the wealthy landowner and painter Derek Hill began to visit Tory on a regular basis. His picturesque view of *Tory Island from Tor More*, depicting the island receding into the distance and framed by the light reflected off the sea, is characteristic of the works he produced as a result of these visits. Yet Hill was also instrumental in the subsequent fashioning of James Dixon as a publicly recognized artist. The story of Dixon's 'discovery' by Hill has been widely circulated in accounts of his work and plays a large part in the popular reading of Dixon

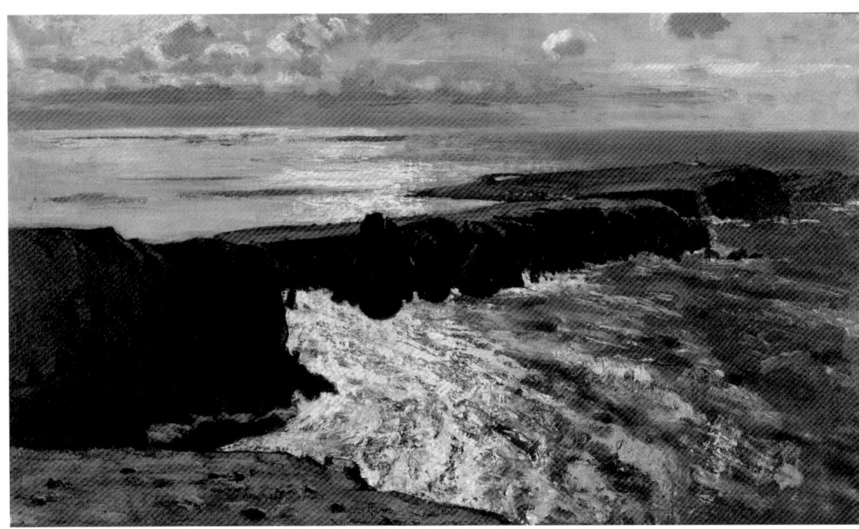

132 Derek Hill, *Tory Island from Tor More*, 1958–9, oil on canvas.

as an untrained naive painter. At some point in the late 1950s, Hill was on a regular painting trip to Tory Island. According to Hill, one Sunday he set up his easel in the West End village:

> A crowd gathered round me after Mass, and Jimmy said, 'I think I could do better'. I encouraged him at once and promised to send him paints, size and paper . . . but he refused brushes, saying he could make his own out of donkey hair.[10]

Hill took on the promotion of Dixon's work, and subsequently that of other untrained Tory painters such as his brother John, and Patsy Dan Rogers. As Matthew Gale has pointed out, Derek Hill was fully conscious of the avant-garde interest in the 'primitive' art of the untrained artist.[11] Due to his age, lack of tuition and preoccupation with the sea, the work of James Dixon has also invited comparisons with that of another 'naive' painter discovered late in life, Alfred Wallis, whose work was first encountered in St Ives by Christopher Wood and Ben Nicholson.[12]

Dixon's depictions of life on Tory could be seen as possessing a sense of authenticity born of an experience lacking from the itinerant gaze of visiting artists. He was also at pains to challenge misrepresentations of seafaring, arguing that 'there is nothing romantic about little boats fighting with crashing waves and winds'.[13] Yet his work also contained reflections on modernity and the cultural memory of events that he himself would not have experienced. These include the wreck of HMS *Wasp* on the rocks surrounding the island in 1884 and *The Sinking of the 'Titanic'*, and extend to more recent events relevant to a seagoing community, such as Sir Francis Chichester's yacht, *The Gypsy Moth Rounding Cape Horn* (1968). Dixon's depiction of agriculture on the island is also far removed from the timelessness of Paul Henry's iconic figures outlined against the cloudscapes of the West. The stylized, decorative format of *Digging Potatoes in Dixon's Farm* is an aerial view of the field with filled sacks to the right, and potatoes waiting to be lifted by the working figures in the lower part of the composition. But what really distinguishes Dixon's painting from earlier versions of this theme is the inclusion of the tractor turning the earth. The most 'authentic' aspect of Dixon's work is not the representation of an unchanging way of life but the very opposite – the encounter with modernity, the mechanization or increased communication that will make life on the island easier. It is indeed the very moment of transformation that he wanted to record – the

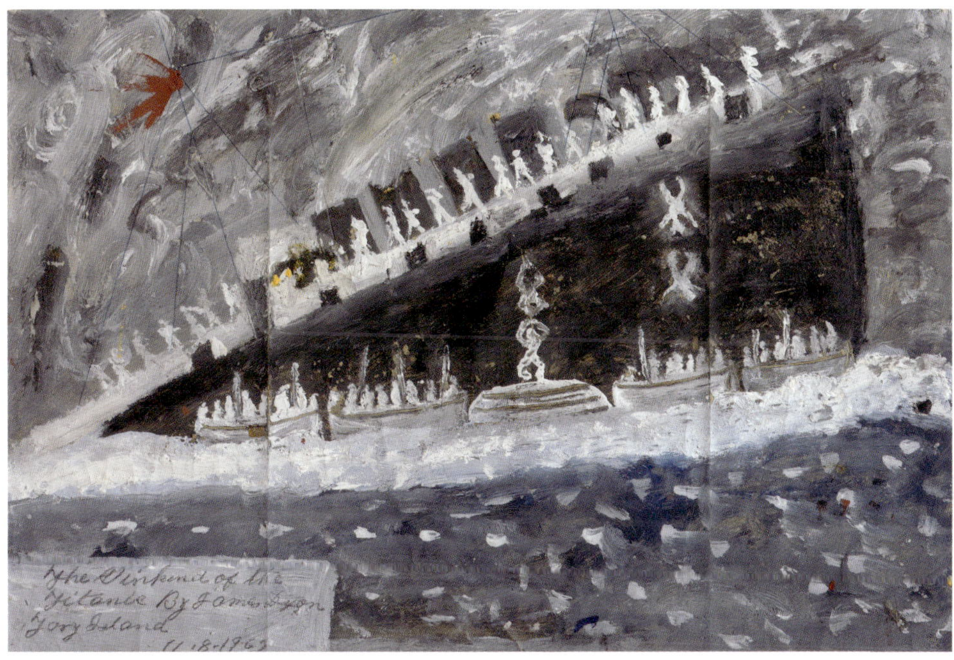

133 James Dixon, *The Sinking of the 'Titanic'*, 1967, oil on paper.

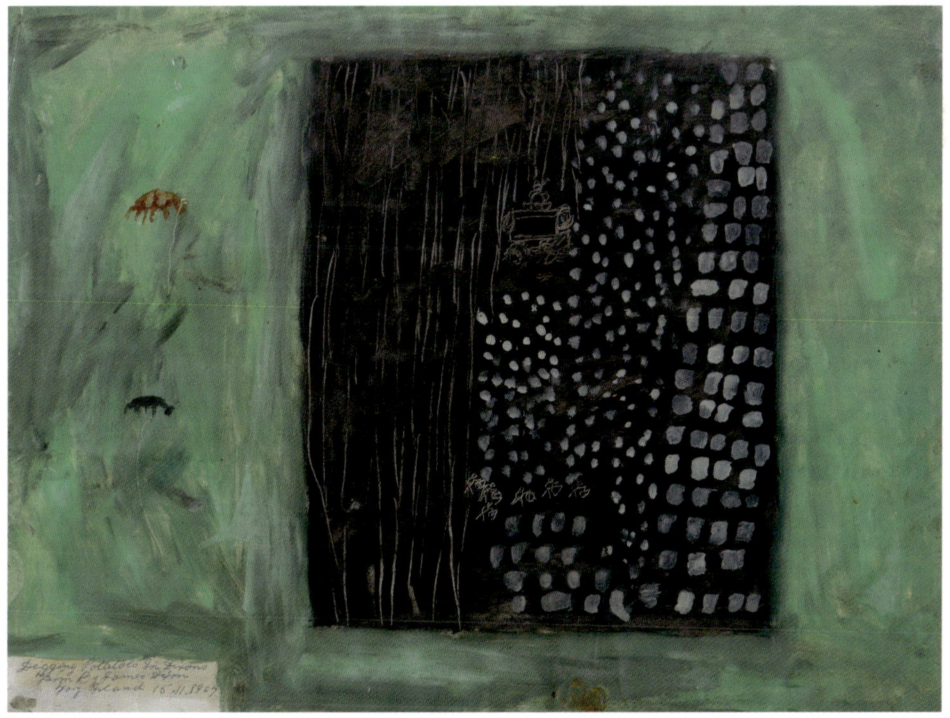

134 James Dixon, *Digging Potatoes in Dixon's Farm*, 1967, oil on paper.

first tractor, the first motor boat or *The First Time the Helicopter Came* (1967).

Irish art and international avant-gardes in the 1960s

There is a further crucial factor here that is more specific to the role of art practice on an international scale – its significance within the cultural politics of the Cold War. During the Second World War the focus of the avant-garde shifted from Paris to New York. In the very different climate of the Cold War that followed, American modernist painting played an important role in asserting the values of individualism within capitalism as opposed to the perceived totalitarianism of communism articulated through socialist realism. The assertion of the United States's cultural hegemony was an important basis for the promotion of American artists such as Pollock and later Rauschenberg within the international arena of the Venice Biennale throughout the 1950s and 1960s – a scenario within which art from Ireland and other marginal nations remained virtually invisible.[14] American Cold War influence also informed the staging of the *Documenta* exhibitions first held in Kassel in 1955; situated right on the border with East Germany, they effectively showcased art in the 'free' Western world. Yet these attempts at cultural domination were far from unchallenged as numerous European artists – such as Pierre S. Soulages, Alberto B. Burri and Asger J. Jorn – made it a priority to define their own avant-garde practice independently from both American and Russian influence. These initiatives contributed to the development of an alternative continental European focus during the 1960s that provided an alternative to ongoing American attempts at Cold War cultural hegemony.

Within Ireland, the climate of progressive modernization meant that the economic infrastructure for art was slowly beginning to improve. Throughout the decade the Arts Council increased its support for visual art: a degree of public rehabilitation was necessary, given its tarnished image after the ESB demolition fiasco.[15] The Council also appointed an exhibitions officer and brought international touring shows to Ireland in an attempt to increase the audience for contemporary art. Significantly, at a time of expanding American cultural hegemony, this included the *Art: USA: Now* exhibition at the Municipal Gallery in 1964. State intervention was reinforced by the involvement of the private sector. In 1962 a group largely comprising businessmen and collectors was set up to purchase works by living Irish artists to be donated to underfunded public galleries. Chaired by the collector Basil Goulding, the original nine members of the Contemporary Irish Art Society (CIAS) included Michael Scott, James White and Cecil King, a businessman and, at that time, amateur painter.[16]

CIAS committee members were also involved in ambitious moves to introduce both Irish artists and a wider public to tendencies in contemporary art practice from outside Ireland. This resulted in the first *Rosc* in 1967, a major international exhibition whose name means 'poetry of vision' in Irish. Michael Scott and Cecil King played major roles in its organization, with James Johnson Sweeney as adviser. A former Curator of Painting and Sculpture at the Museum of Modern Art in New York, Sweeney also chaired the jury selecting works for inclusion.[17] Over half a century since Hugh Lane's campaigns for a Gallery of Modern Art, Ireland still lacked a contemporary art museum; the intention of *Rosc* was to bring what the jury considered the best of current international work to Dublin.[18] In 1967 this included not only established American artists such as de Kooning,

Lichtenstein and Rauschenberg but also a range of European artists. In addition to the ageing avant-garde stalwart Picasso, *Rosc* included post-war artists such as Antoni Tàpies, Soulages and Karel Appel, who had been involved in the development of avant-garde identities in Europe independent of the United States. In bringing international post-war avant-gardism to Ireland, *Rosc* was hugely successful; once installed in the Main Hall of the Royal Dublin Society (more usually used for the Dublin Horse Show) there were approximately 50,000 visitors between October 1967 and January 1968.

The impact of the exhibition on a generation of young Irish artists was considerable, yet *Rosc* was also marked by major controversy. The jury led by the New York-based Sweeney did not select any contemporary Irish practitioners; a range of Celtic and Bronze Age art and artefacts installed separately in the National Museum of Ireland represented the country instead.[19] There are at least two ways in which these decisions could appear problematic. First, the recourse to archaic forms of Irish art in the absence of the contemporary can only work to *deny* Ireland's modernity, an uneasy echo of colonial designations of Ireland as primitive and outside history. Second, the work of many Irish artists during the 1960s involved the development of a range of artistic strategies that suggest a nuanced relationship with both the processes of modernization and ongoing shifts in what it meant to be Irish. However, as far as the jury for *Rosc* was concerned, their work failed to signify within the discourses of international avant-gardism, hence reaffirming the marginal and provincial status of Irish art. The dazzling diversity of post-war practice temporarily transported to Ireland for *Rosc* also had the effect of highlighting Dublin's peripherality – and not just to New York but, within the new spatial configurations of the avant-garde of the 1960s, to Milan or Cologne also. Perhaps inevitably, *Rosc* also failed to live up to the expectations of Clement Greenberg, the

doyen of American modernist criticism. Although he wrote approvingly of the exhibition of Celtic and Bronze Age art and artefacts, for Greenberg *Rosc* was too reminiscent of the 1950s – an impression formed by what he saw as too much contemporary European work and not enough from New York.[20]

Meanwhile, the combination of post-war American painting with more local themes was beginning to characterize some aspects of Irish art practice. Obviously there were exceptions to this, as in the hyper-realism of Edward McGuire's portrait paintings or the more subjective work of Gerard Dillon, concerned for his own mortality as his three brothers died in the early 1960s from the heart condition from which he also suffered. Increasingly his work began to feature the figure of a masked, white-clad Pierrot. Originally a *commedia dell' arte* character, by the twentieth century the Pierrot figure had acquired associations of the alienated and misunderstood artist.[21] In Dillon's *The Brothers* three skeletons lie buried in the earth while above them, in a Connemara landscape, a Pierrot is crouched on the ground as if listening to what is beneath. Throughout the 1960s Dillon became increasingly isolated in London, and returned to Ireland in 1968.

Engagements with American painting continued to be enacted through landscape. Barrie Cooke's *Current*, part of a series of water paintings begun in 1957, uses a vocabulary derived from American gestural painting to convey the force of water rushing down the Lower Caragh River in County Kerry. The muted use of colour, mainly greys and greens and browns, suggests a reworking of forms of Irishness identified with the remoteness of the landscape: its lowering clouds and the surrounding bog glimpsed through the mists of roaring water. Patrick Scott's perceptions of the softness of evening light on the peat bogs of the Midlands also used a technique of soaking and staining the canvas

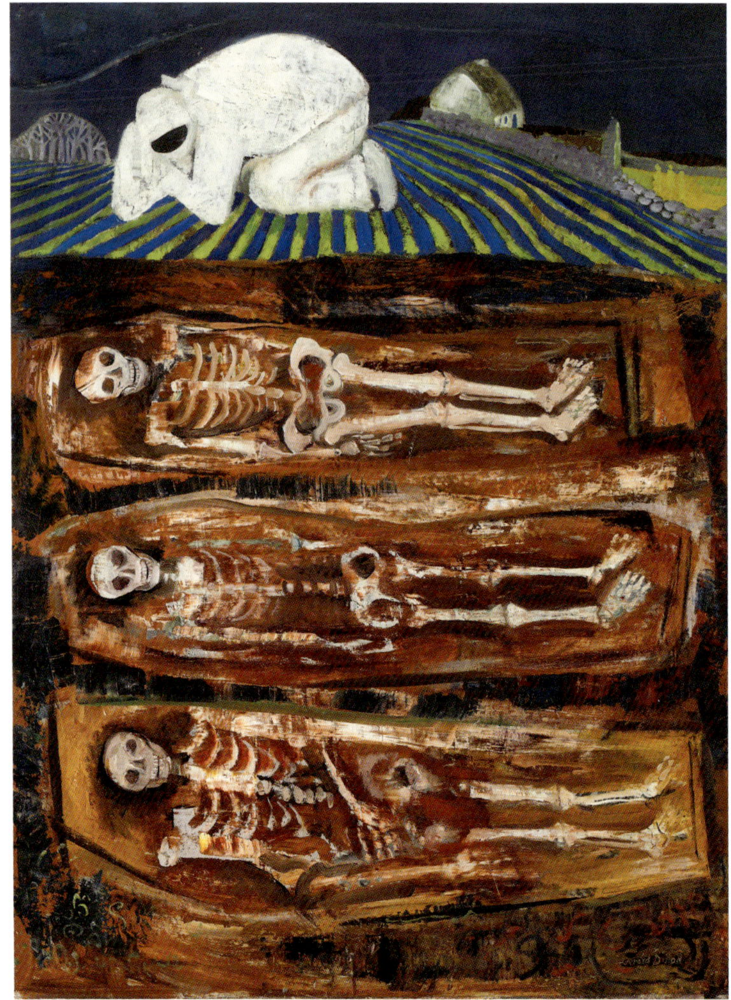

135 Gerard Dillon,
The Brothers, c. 1965,
oil on canvas.

136 Barrie Cooke,
Current, 1962–3,
oil on canvas.

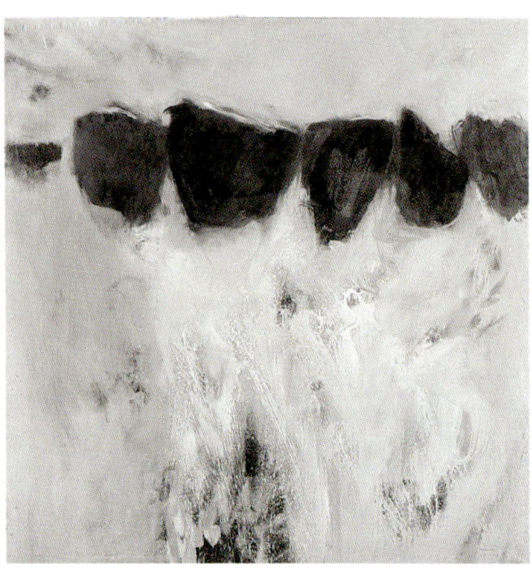

similar to that of Morris Louis or Helen Franken-thaler.[22] Scott soon began to focus on his series of 'Device' paintings; *Large Solar Device* (1963) was given to the Municipal Gallery by CIAS as their first pur-chase.[23] The circular motif of dazzling explosion or disintegrating sun also had significance in relation to both international and Irish concerns. In a shift from the perceived affinities with recent American paint-ing, the formal simplicity of these works was derived more from Scott's interest in Japanese art and philoso-phy. The use of gold leaf on unprimed canvas also evokes the prevalence of gold as a material in Irish

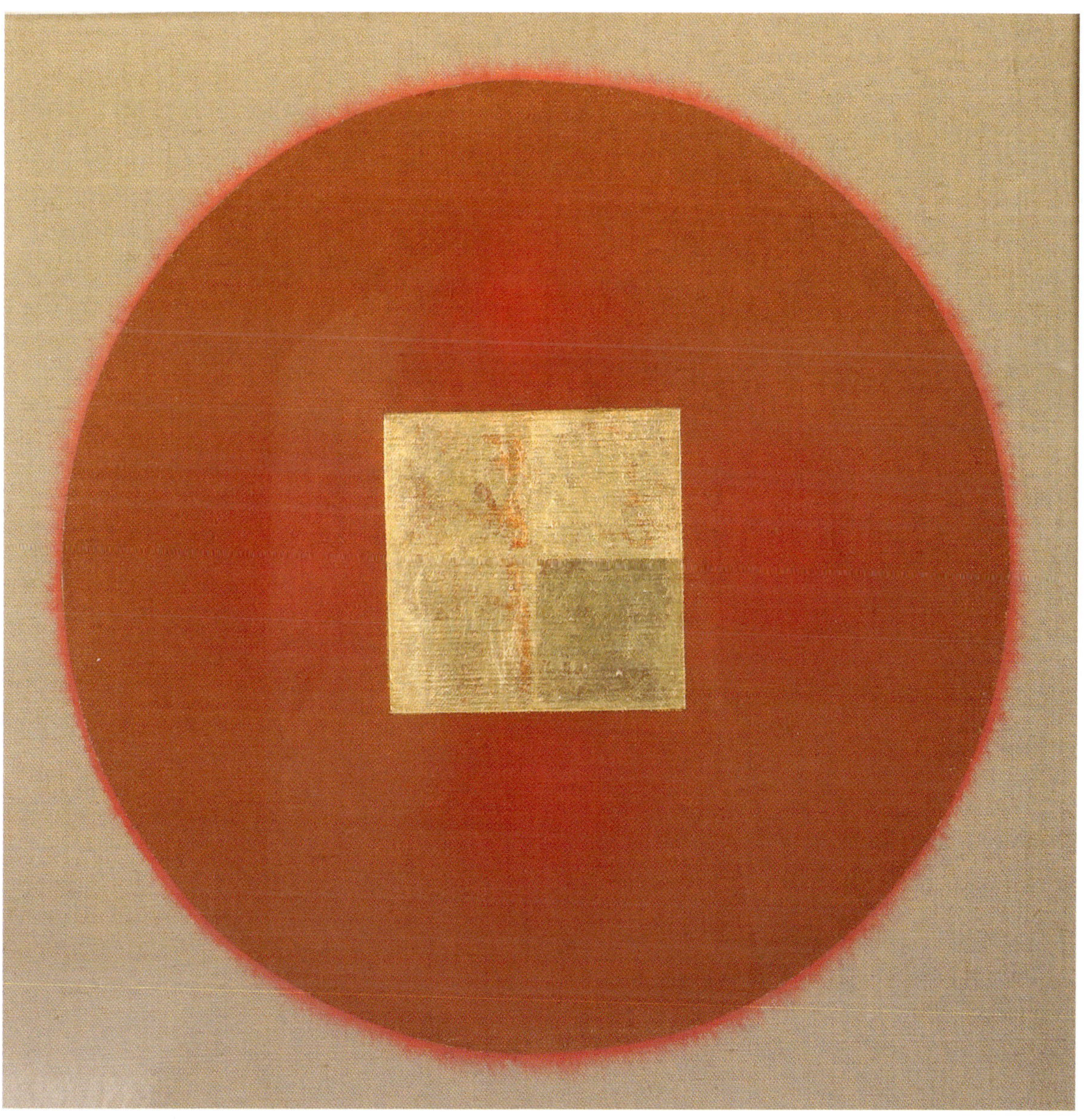

137 Patrick Scott, *Gold Square on Red Sun*, n.d., gold leaf and tempera on unprimed canvas.

Bronze Age ornamentation; similar to le Brocquy's depicted heads, these are paintings that evoke a sense of both the contemporary and the archaic.

In the case of Anne Madden, there are other factors at work in the development of a more nuanced engagement with the Irish landscape. Born in Chile to Irish and Anglo-Chilean parents, she initially trained at Chelsea College of Art and Design and showed at the *Living Art* in 1952. Her earliest encounters with Ireland were during childhood visits, when the dramatic topography and megalithic remains of the limestone Burren in County Clare had a profound effect. Added to this was her discovery of Abstract Expressionism through the seminal exhibition *Modern Art in the United*

States at the Tate in January 1956. As a young painter in London, open to new influences, Anne Madden was one of the Irish artists who most thoroughly assimilated the impact of post-war American painting. At a time when, in Ireland itself, Patrick Collins was suggesting Irish painting's autonomy from all other influences, Madden was developing a more hybridized engagement with landscape that opened up a range of different meanings. In the late 1950s this included work that quite directly took on the practice of the American painter Sam Francis or the Canadian Jean-Paul Riopelle. *Blue Landscape* shows the influence of Riopelle's slashes of colour applied directly with the palette knife to build up a calligraphic grid, while *Aran Field* (1957) draws on Francis's interest in aerial views of landscape.[24]

In a range of works from the mid-1960s Madden's assimilation of features of post-war American painting had moved beyond the earlier direct references to a subtle incorporation of both the scale and fluid gesture of Abstract Expressionism to produce an increasingly complex engagement with Irish motifs. The almost biomorphic forms of some works, such as *Land near Kilnaboy* or *Slievecarran* (1963), however, contrast with the more composite depictions provided by Madden's use of multiple panels, as in the later *Big Red Mountain Sequence* (1967). Positioned on the edge of abstraction, these half-glimpsed slopes and contours also return to the sensory experience of landscape – a walk remembered not as a whole but as a sequence of discontinuous fragments. Sensory experience and reconstructions of the mountain's presence also extended, in some of these works, to incorporation of elements of landscape itself, as in the use of grit and flint fragments in the painted surface of *Slievecarran*.

In spite of their exclusion from the first *Rosc*, Irish artists increasingly began to participate in high-profile

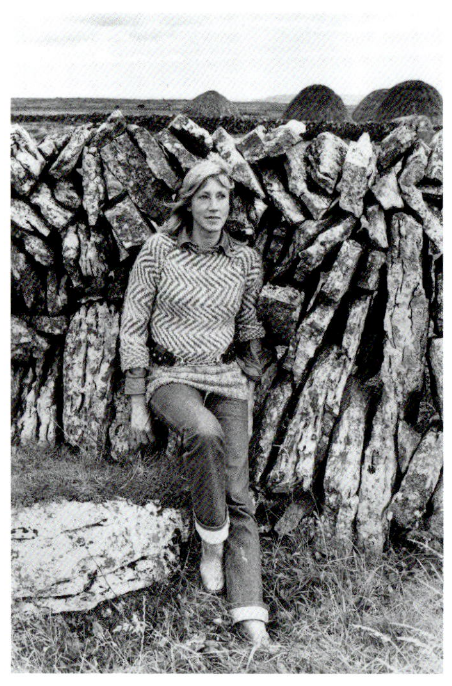

138 Anne Madden photographed in the Burren, Co. Clare, 1979.

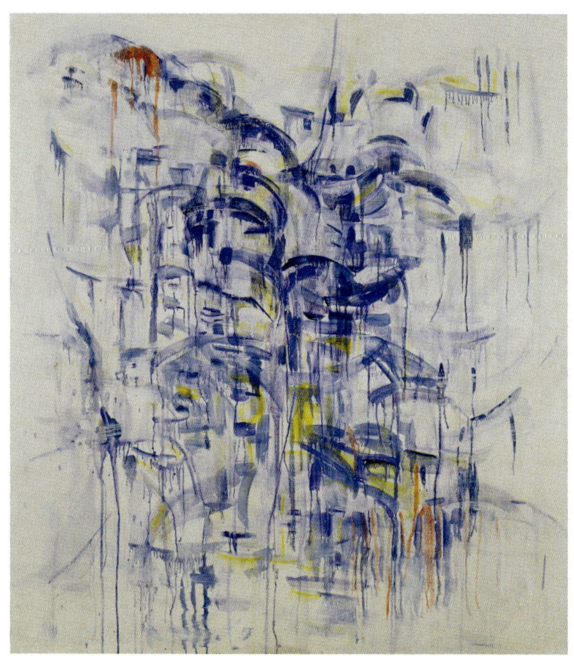

139 Anne Madden, *Blue Landscape*, 1958, oil on board.

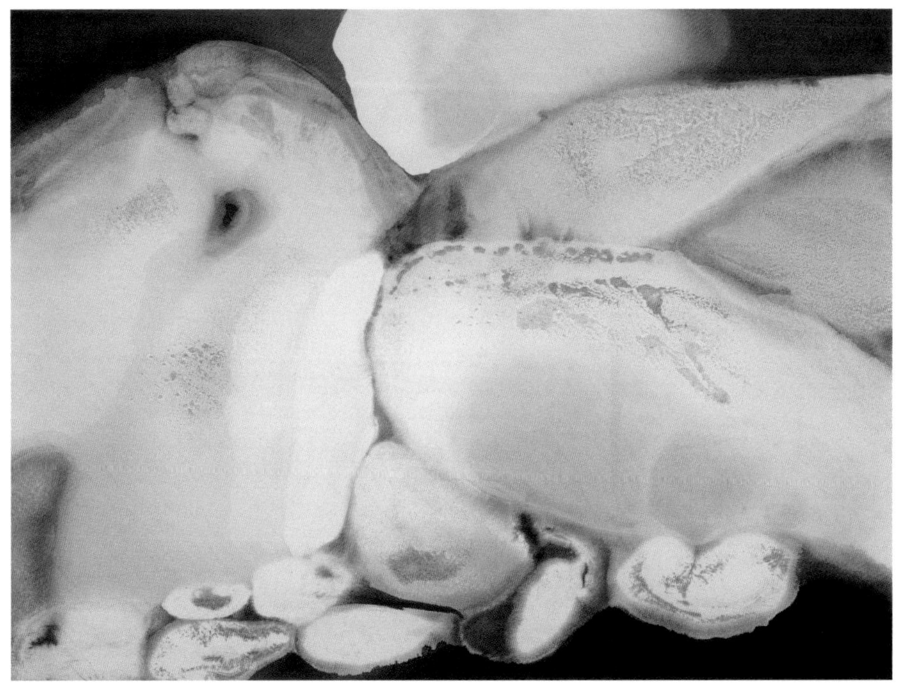

140 Anne Madden, *Land near Kilnaboy*, 1963, oil and sand on canvas.

international exhibitions throughout the decade. In 1963, following Ireland's withdrawal from the Venice Biennale the previous year, Barrie Cooke represented Ireland at the Paris Biennale, followed in 1965 by Anne Madden and Micheal Farrell in 1967. Yet the predominance of Expressionism as a response to the rural still represents the continuation of a poetic sensibility that redefines rather than challenges visual constructions of Irish identity. Other possibilities began to be suggested by art from the 1960s and 1970s. An important figure in this shift was Micheal Farrell, who studied commercial art in London at St Martins School of Art, subsequently meeting some of the emergent British Pop artists, such as David Hockney, Peter Blake and Patrick Caulfield. Farrell's work during the early to mid-1960s attracted prestigious awards – the (British) Prix de Rome in 1963 and a Macaulay fellowship to New York in 1966, where he was particularly impressed by the hard-edge abstrac-

tion of Frank Stella. His training in commercial art and familiarity with Pop Art proved to be significant both for the development of his practice as a professional painter in the early 1960s and the contribution made by this to the ongoing redefinition of Irish visual identities.

In retrospect, Farrell described himself at this time as 'a hardedge Celtic painter'.[25] Painted in the mid-1960s, many of his 'Cairn' series used acrylic paint to reduce the components of the Irish landscape down to a basic series of elements. The randomness of the expressive gesture is replaced by a tightly controlled compartmentalization of rectangular forms with interlocking circles sandwiched between. These works suggest both the forms of the Irish landscape, where cairns of piled stones emerge out of rectilinear fields, and the layout of Celtic manuscripts, where closely defined blocks of text interact with areas of ornament and intertwining imagery. In pictorial terms this represents a significant break with

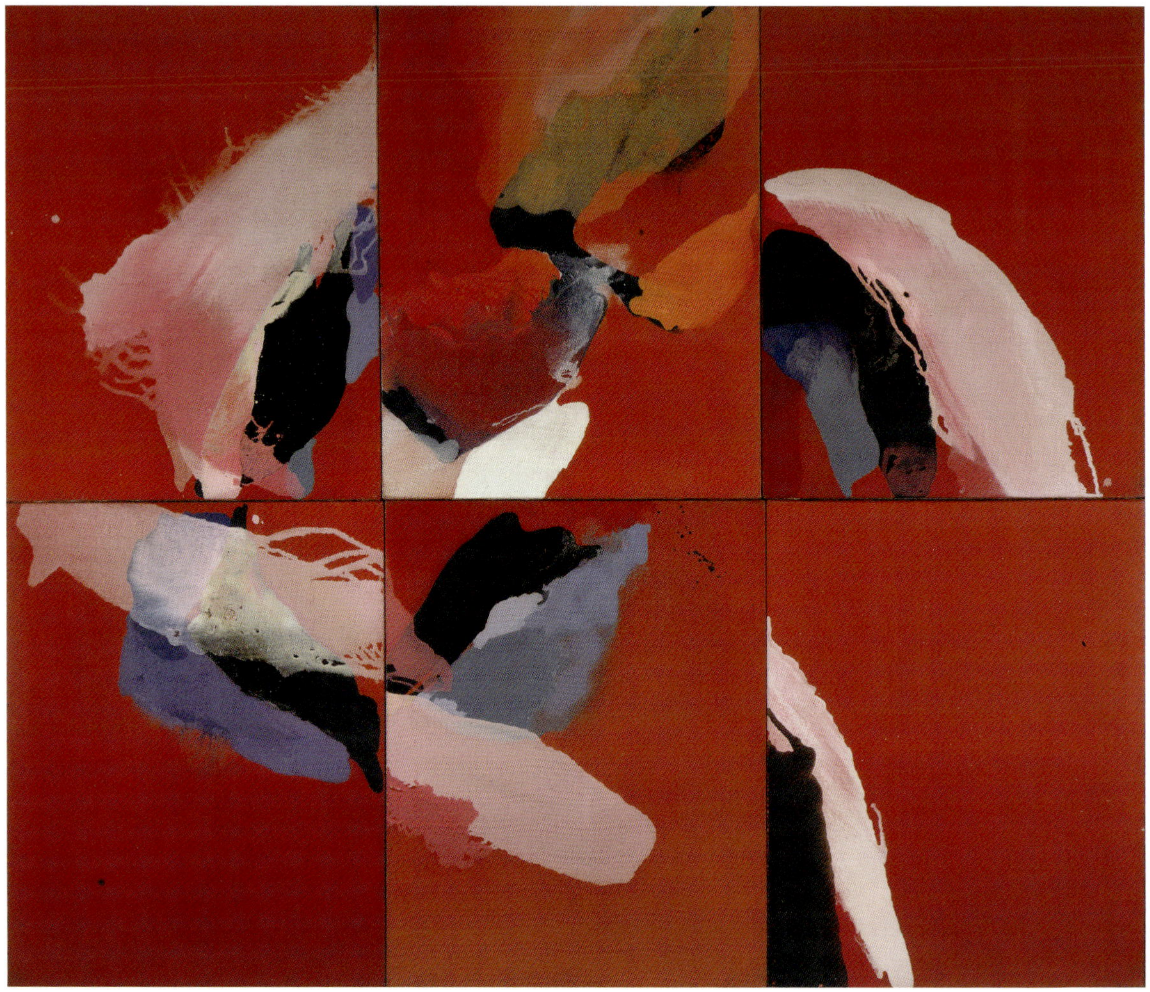

141 Anne Madden, *Big Red Mountain Sequence*, 1967, oil on canvas.

Expressionism; nothing is left to chance and intuitive ways of engaging with the landscape or Celtic text are rejected. Traces of 'the Celtic' itself still remain, particularly suggested by the interlocking rings, but its meanings have become even more deferred and encoded, as in a related work, *Wheel of Fortune*, which relates more closely to the decorative imagery of Celtic manuscripts. For Farrell these works involved

no conscious superimposing of social, satirical or literary comment, they are simply about the solving of pictorial problems . . . Having no Celtic tradition in painting for over 1,000 years one has to go back to when Celtic art was at its greatest and most important, for it is true that no pictures of any value concerned with the real problems of picture-making have been made in Ireland since the book of Kells, a masterpiece devoid of all mist, wind and whimsy – perfect in harmony and uncompromisingly direct.[26]

Yet in spite of Farrell's insistence on the visual autonomy of the 'Cairn' series, historically validated by

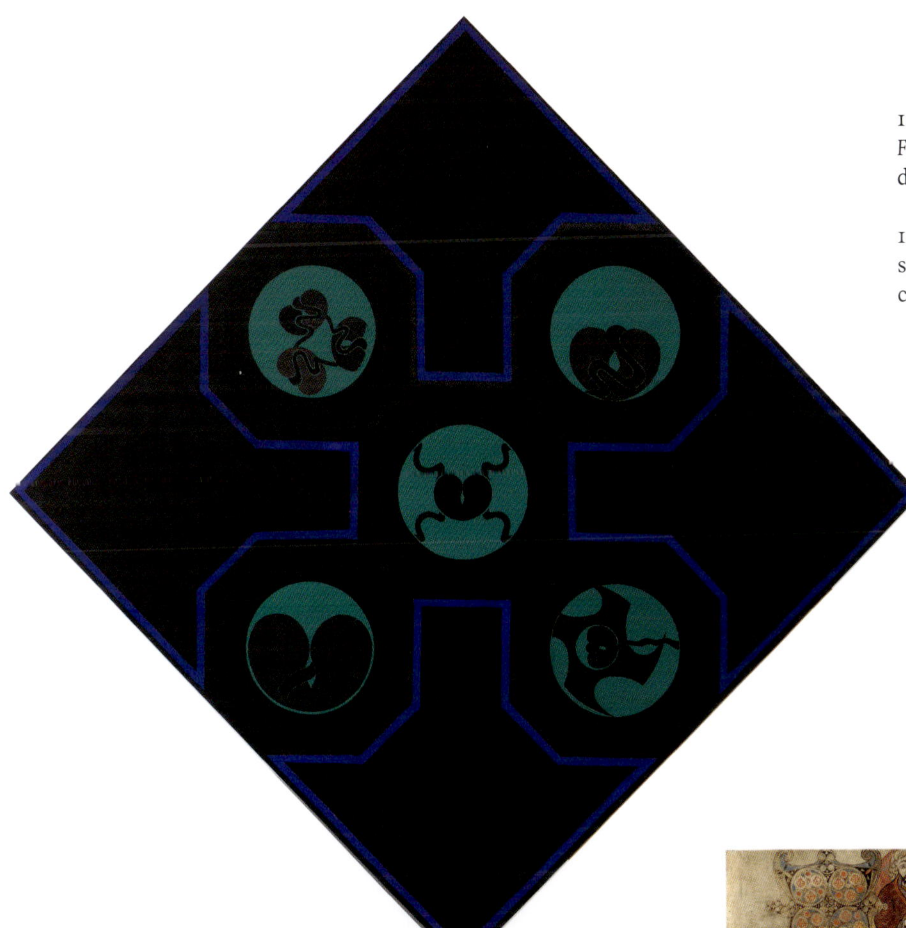

142 Micheal Farrell, *Wheel of Fortune*, 1964, oil on cotton duck.

143 Book of Kells, folio 292, start of St Johns Gospel, 8th century, painted vellum.

its engagement with the pictorial concerns of the Book of Kells, there are ways in which the paintings' contemporary relevance is very apparent. The hard-edged, airbrushed style of this series, combined with the use of acrylic, also derives from the rhetoric of Pop Art. Underpinning Rosenquist's airbrushed scenarios or Lichtenstein's reduction of imagery to a language of basic signs, the fascination with commodification in Pop Art suggests both capitalism's elusive promise and its unattainability. In a similar manner these paintings by Micheal Farrell also evoke the commodification of the Celtic, whose authenticity becomes even more unattainable, and hence desirable, in the process. In the rapidly modernizing Ireland of the 1960s, the dialectical relationship of ancient tradition and a new language of consumerism were once more helping to forge new forms of identity.

On his return from New York in 1967, interlocking circles and also triangles began to feature in Farrell's murals for the National Bank (now the Bank of Ireland) in College Green, Dublin. It was not just the formal design of the murals that was appropriate to the scale of their location in the National Bank. Farrell was using a Pop-based visual language, although adapted to the resonances of the Celtic. Pop's associations with the exchange of commodities had also shifted to a location dedicated to the accumulation of capital – and *Irish* capital at that. During the 1960s, corporate sponsorship of art began to appear in Ireland. In 1964, the tobacco company P. J. Carroll began to sponsor a regular prize at the *Living Art* annual exhibition from which young artists – including Farrell – were able to benefit. Advised by the architect and collector Ronnie Tallon, they also began to buy art; as Dorothy Walker observed, the 'continuing absence of a museum of modern art' meant that corporate collecting was a valuable source of support for contemporary art in Ireland.[27]

Modernism and the Celtic in the work of Louis le Brocquy and Brian O'Doherty

These two tendencies – an engagement with the distant past and a response to external influences – also informed Irish artists working outside Ireland, as is apparent in the earlier discussion of Tony O'Malley and Anne Madden. Yet a further comparison also helps to emphasize the contrast: the use of the Celtic

in the work of two of the most significant Irish artists, Louis le Brocquy and Brian O'Doherty.

For le Brocquy, Celtic themes provided the beginnings of a re-engagement with Irishness that helped to focus his concerns about the trials of a universal humanism marked by the cultural politics of the Cold War. In 1963, a period of profound crisis led le Brocquy to destroy over 40 paintings. Yet this questioning led to a significant reconnection with Irish themes in a further fusion of the primitive and the existential. On a trip to Paris with Madden, he visited the Musée de l'Homme, where he was particularly struck by the Polynesian ancestral heads – skulls rebuilt with clay, paint and cowrie shells. For le Brocquy they were reminiscent of the significance of the head within Celtic culture, as the place where the human spirit is held prisoner.

Once again, his rediscovery of Irish themes was stimulated by contact with another culture, a combination of primitivism with diasporic nostalgia that reconfigures the past in a selective reconstruction of aspects of Irishness. This was reinforced by his subsequent encounter near Aix-en-Provence with the remains of Celtic civilization in France: the defended hilltop settlement at Entremont, systematically destroyed by the Romans, whose archaeological remains include pillars decorated with numerous incised heads. These ideas crystallized in a series of 'Ancestral Heads', whose various origins included not just the Polynesian and Celtic, but also the Palaeolithic. Le Brocquy saw this as a period of existential loneliness, with no sense of past or future. Floating in an indeterminate space, these 'Ancestral Heads' convey a sense of the immanent existence of universalized man; most of them are male, unlike the majority of the bodies from the earlier 'Presences'.

For Brian O'Doherty, by comparison, the Celtic played a very different role. O'Doherty's essay for *The Irish Imagination* in which he discussed the romanti-

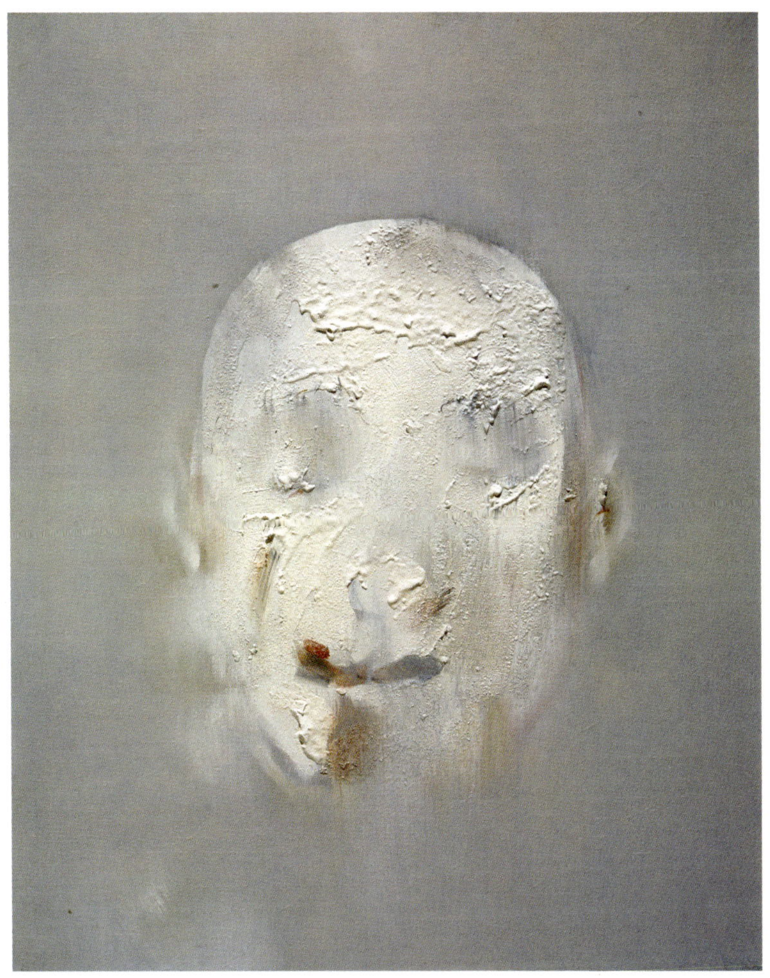

144 Louis le Brocquy,
Ancestral Head (detail),
1964, oil on canvas.

cization of the past suggests a more distanced view. This was not just because he was commenting from New York, where he moved from Dublin in the late 1950s. It is also consistent with his ongoing construction of a detached yet multiple artistic identity: a sense of complexity previously not present in Irish art. Formerly trained as a medical doctor, then artist, writer and curator under different names, O'Doherty's multiple identities have a precedent in Irish culture in the performative identities of Brian O'Nolan, better known as the writer Flann O'Brien, or Myles na gCopaleen. However, the slightly later emergence of a female persona for O'Doherty, the art critic Mary Josephson, also suggests the fluid androgyny of Marcel Duchamp's alter ego Rrose Sélavy. In fact one of O'Doherty's most important works of the 1960s involved both Duchamp and his own medical training. O'Doherty arranged to record Duchamp's heartbeat and then devised a means of displaying the resulting cardiograph, exhibiting it in different forms as a kind of ready-made.[28] Long after Duchamp's death in 1968, the oscillating trace of his heartbeat provides an uncanny survival for the artist who did so much to challenge the romanticization of creative presence.

Diasporic distance also provided a fruitful means of engaging with Irish culture, mediated through

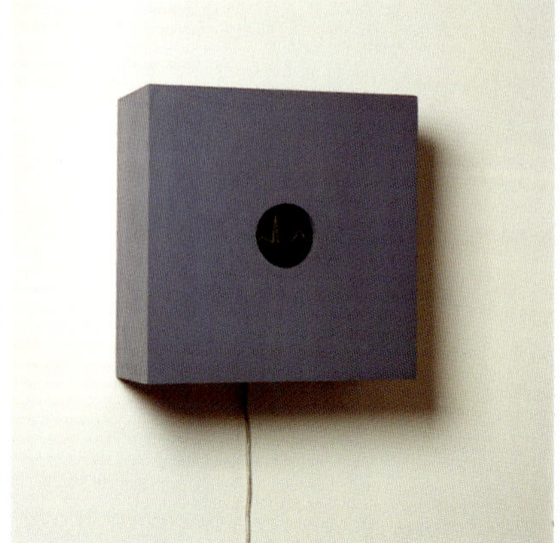

145 Brian O'Doherty, *Portrait of Marcel Duchamp, Lead One, Slow Heartbeat*, 1965, wood, glass, liquitex, motor.

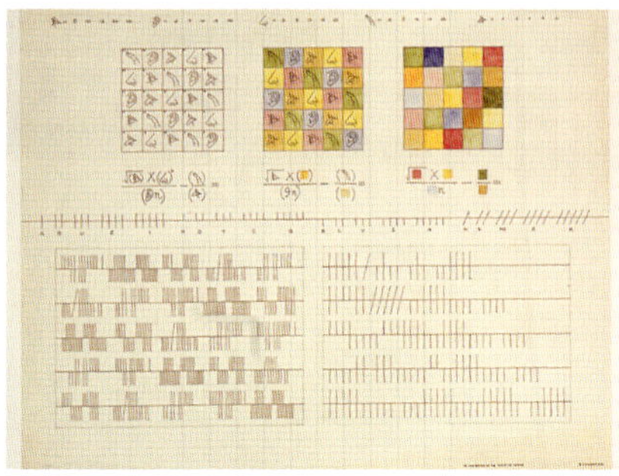

146 Brian O'Doherty, *The Five Senses of the Bishop of Cloyne*, 1967–8, ink and watercolour on paper.

O'Doherty's activities in the New York art scene. *The Five Senses of the Bishop of Cloyne* (1967–8) is an ink and watercolour drawing on graph paper, utilizing the grid format typical of Minimalism's interest in serial progressions.[29] It also investigates the relationship between representation and perception. This was one of the major themes of conceptual art, which, by the late 1960s, was increasingly recognized as a major challenge to late modernism's emphasis on expressiveness and authenticity through a focus instead on the notion of art as idea. O'Doherty's drawing is based on the writings of George Berkeley, the Bishop of Cloyne in County Cork from 1734 onwards. Berkeley was critical of the split between mind and body in Descartes' thinking, proposing instead that knowledge of objective reality is derived solely from sense perceptions. O'Doherty referenced the senses by the three partly figurative drawings in the top half of the composition, accompanied by quasi-mathematical formulae that indicate the relationship between sensation and idea. The lower part of the work is taken up with two drawings that use Ogham, the archaic Celtic language. Ogham is written in serial form using horizontal and diagonal lines: the two lower

drawings contain commands and descriptions that relate to the three drawings above. A key to decoding these inscriptions is provided by the translation of Ogham into Roman script that bisects the work horizontally. Ogham was important for O'Doherty, also providing the basis for a series of wall sculptures that began in 1967, and for other subsequent works. Yet more than this it was, in Brenda Moore-McCann's memorable term, his 'Rosetta Stone' – a means of encoding perception, its serial form midway between the structures of language and synaesthetic emotion.[30]

In the work of both Louis le Brocquy and Brian O'Doherty the deep past provided a means of repositioning their practice, although very differently. O'Doherty's engagement with Celticism played a significant role in aligning his work with conceptualism, and on very different terms from the fascination with the archaic that nourished le Brocquy's modernist sensibilities. For le Brocquy universalism is expressed through his handling of paint: a sense of a timeless immanent presence emerging from the picture plane. O'Doherty, by comparison, used the Celtic to suggest the contingency of meaning. It is not just the comparison

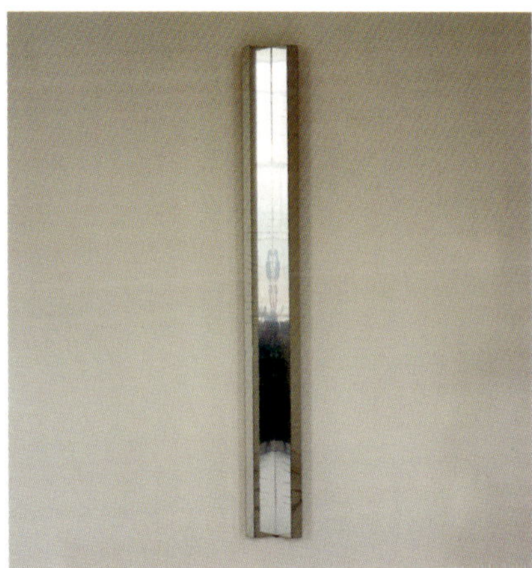

147 Brian O'Doherty, *The Rake's Progress*, 1970, aluminium on wood.

between the works of two very different artists that is highlighted by their engagement with the Celtic, but two completely antithetical approaches to the making of art itself.

The 1960s in the North: modernization and art practice

Similar issues of an engagement with international modernism or a focus on Ireland as location were current in art in Northern Ireland during the 1960s, underpinned also by the beginnings of modernization. Northern Ireland's different political and cultural features meant that the economic and social shifts of the modernizing process took a course different from that in the South, and the forms of art practice that emerged were also different. The effects of Northern Ireland's processes of modernization under the leadership of Terence O'Neill, who succeeded Brookeborough in March 1963, were mediated by embedded sectarianism. The introduction of new industries and investment from outside the province continued to replace the de-

clining traditional industries of shipbuilding and linen, yet once again these were concentrated in Unionist-dominated areas east of the River Bann. Support for the moderate Terence O'Neill was undermined by loyalist suspicions of his meetings with Seán Lemass in 1965, and with the Roman Catholic Primate of All Ireland, Cardinal Conway. Political tensions became increasingly visible as alienated loyalists were drawn to the fundamentalist politics of the Reverend Ian Paisley, leader of the Free Presbyterian Church. In 1966 sectarian attacks by a loyalist paramilitary group, the Ulster Volunteer Force (UVF), killed several people in Belfast. The UVF took the name of one of the key organizations opposing Home Rule at the start of the century, subsequently forming the basis of the Ulster regiments in the First World War. The aims of the revitalized UVF were to overthrow O'Neill's moderate Unionism and destroy the IRA, at this point still largely in decline in spite of the fiftieth anniversary of the Easter Rising that year.

Moves for reform continued throughout the 1960s in spite of the endemic sectarianism, and the black Civil Rights movement in the United States provided a precedent for moves to end discrimination in Northern Ireland. In March 1967 a coalition including both Catholic and Protestant reformers, trade unionists, republicans and students came together under the banner of the Northern Ireland Civil Rights Association (NICRA). Police attacks on a demonstration that October in Derry presented obvious links for some of the students with the uprisings elsewhere in Europe: one commentator observed, 'This was our Paris, our Prague.'[31] RTE television coverage ensured widespread broadcasting of police batoning unarmed demonstrators and the indiscriminate use of water cannons. For the first time, the sectarian nature of the Northern Ireland state, and the lengths to which it was prepared to go to suppress dissent, were visible on an international stage.

At this time very little of the ongoing political developments figured directly within painting in Northern Ireland, although the effects of modernization were themselves being felt to some degree. At a time when no public collection in the South was buying contemporary work, the Belfast Museum and Art Gallery was beginning to assemble a remarkably forward-looking collection under the tenure of Anne Crookshank as Keeper of Art until 1966.[32] The result was a collection that included many of the second-generation American post-war painters: Helen Frankenthaler, Morris Louis and Joan Mitchell, in addition to work by contemporary European avant-garde artists such as Jean Dubuffet and Karel Appel. Crookshank was also responsible for the purchase of the William Scott *Brown Still-life* that caused so much outrage in 1958, in addition to supporting contemporary artists in Ireland.

The market for art in Belfast was still highly conservative, although the New Gallery represented an attempt to challenge this. Run throughout the 1960s by Alice Berger Hammerschlag in association with Mary O'Malley, the founder of the Lyric Theatre, the gallery both supported Irish artists and attempted to introduce contemporary European art to Belfast.[33] Originally from Austria, Berger Hammerschlag lacked the provincialism characteristic of art in Northern Ireland at this time, and as an abstract painter she was also particularly receptive to innovative and divergent trends. Deborah Brown was one artist who benefited from this. Brown's family home was in Cushendun in the Glens of Antrim and, although some of her earliest art lessons were with James Humbert Craig, her work developed along very different lines. In the late 1950s two influential factors combined to radically change Brown's richly coloured realist paintings. Working in stage design for the Lyric Theatre encouraged her to move beyond the standard easel format and scale as

she simplified her ideas; meanwhile, 'sometime about 1958' she also became aware of Jackson Pollock's work.[34] Brown began to develop her own form of abstraction, combining elements of collage with the painted surface in a series of works that emphasized both a sense of the materiality of the painting and its space, indicated initially by her use of sweeping brushstrokes.[35] This extended also to an investigation of the relative role of space beyond the picture plane, in a group of works that combined the pierced canvas with papier mâché collaged elements.

In the cultural conservatism of Northern Ireland in the early 1960s Brown's rigorous modernism was initially developed largely in seclusion, although she showed at the New Gallery in 1964. Like Berger Hammerschlag, who also exhibited frequently outside Ireland, her abstract work more often found a receptive audience in England. Brown's involvement with modernism also extended to the use of modern materials. From 1966 onwards she began to work in fibreglass, and also started to achieve a greater recognition in Ireland with her first exhibition at the Hendricks Gallery that year. In a catalogue essay for Brown's exhibition at the New Vision Centre Gallery in London in 1964 Anne Crookshank emphasized the difficulties facing abstract artists in Ireland:

> It is perhaps hard for those who do not know Ireland to realise the isolation of an abstract artist in this country, where, taking into account both North and South, there would still not be more than a handful of artists whose work is entirely non-representational.[36]

Meanwhile, at a time when deep-rooted identities were increasingly coming into question in the North, a concern for a notion of 'place' was beginning to emerge in the work of Basil Blackshaw and T. P. Flanagan.

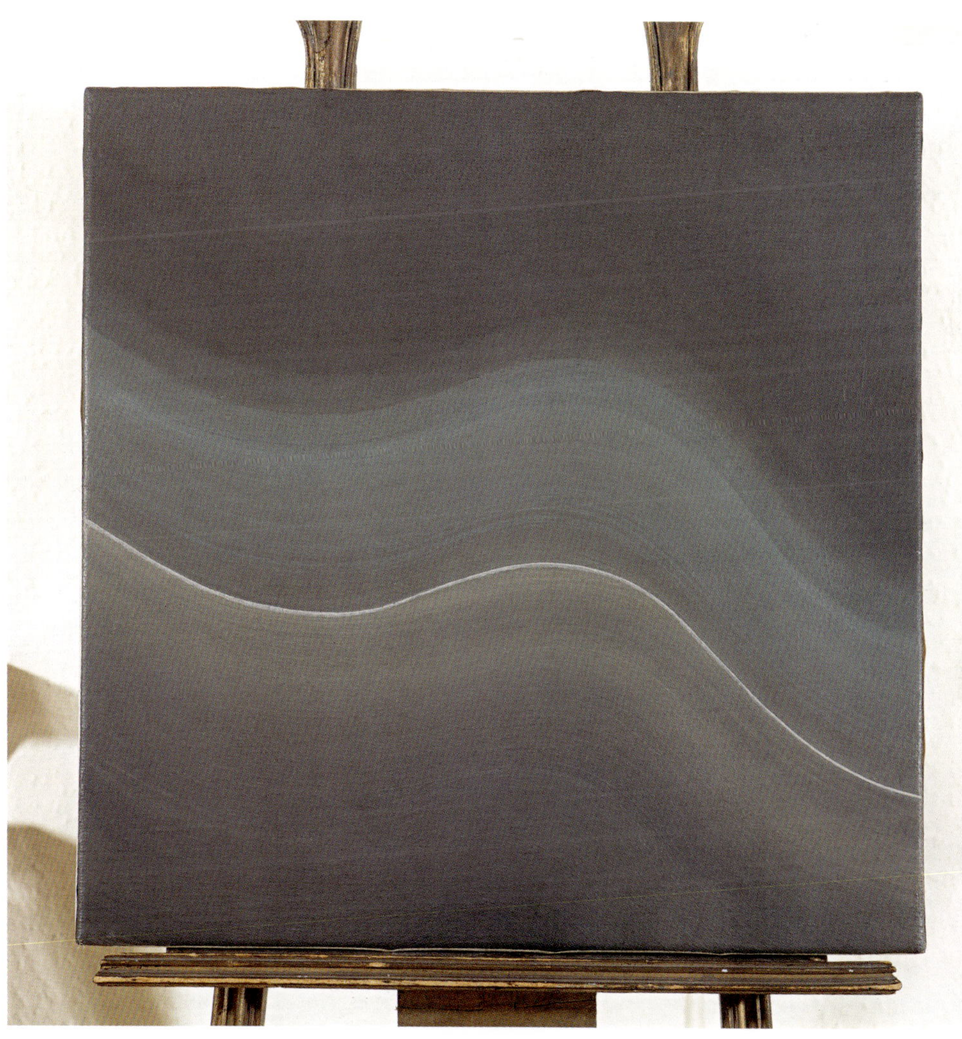

148 Alice Berger Hammerschlag, *Irish Rhythm 4*, 1967, oil on canvas.

Flanagan was part of the same generation as Blackshaw, taught by Romeo Toogood at Belfast College of Art in the early 1950s. Like Blackshaw, Flanagan's work also involved a response to particular locations, yet the places featured have a very different set of resonances from the largely Protestant farmlands of Down and Antrim. Flanagan's childhood was spent in Fermanagh and neighbouring Sligo, where one of his aunts ran a needlework school at Lissadell House, the home of the

Gore-Booth family and birthplace of Constance Markiewicz. As a young boy Flanagan spent numerous holidays there, and Lissadell was later to become a subject of works by the artist from around 1960 onwards. While at school in Enniskillen he took art lessons with Kathleen Bridle. The former teacher of William Scott and a member of the short-lived 'Ulster Unit' in the 1930s, Bridle also had a high reputation as a watercolourist. In depictions of the Fermanagh landscape

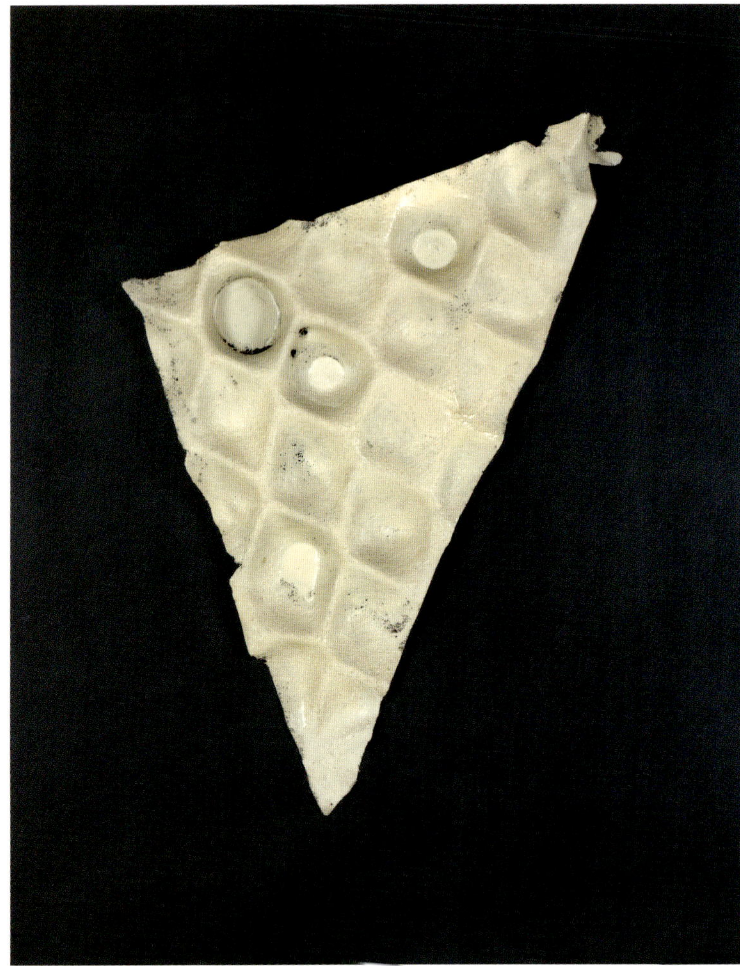

149 Deborah Brown,
Glass Fibre Form on Black,
1967, glass fibre and
canvas.

such as *Lough Erne from Rossfad*, painted when Flanagan was studying with her, she combined a controlled formal composition with a sense of empirical engagement with the scene in front of her. Flanagan's early works of the 1960s, such as *Dawn, Fermanagh Lough* (1960–61), retain similar concerns of subject-matter and handling, both of which he developed in watercolour as well as oil. These, and Flanagan's other depictions of similar scenes, are like tone poems built up through experience and memory of the landscapes of childhood. Yet at the time Flanagan was painting these apparently timeless landscapes the processes of modernization were already underway elsewhere in Northern Ireland, or at

least that part of it east of the Bann and some distance from the lakelands of Fermanagh.

The Lissadell paintings, such as the watercolour *A White Sea* (1967), rework a landscape whose meanings were fashioned into a murky Celtic twilight in the work of Patrick Collins, and they also differ from the mythological Sligo painted by Jack Yeats. The suggested forms of land across the bay evoke the landfall glimpsed in Collins's *Hy Brazil*, but associations of Celtic mythology are checked by a focus on the landscape features of the foreground, with giant hogweeds and undergrowth stretching away to the sea. This is much more securely the territory of the artist's experience.

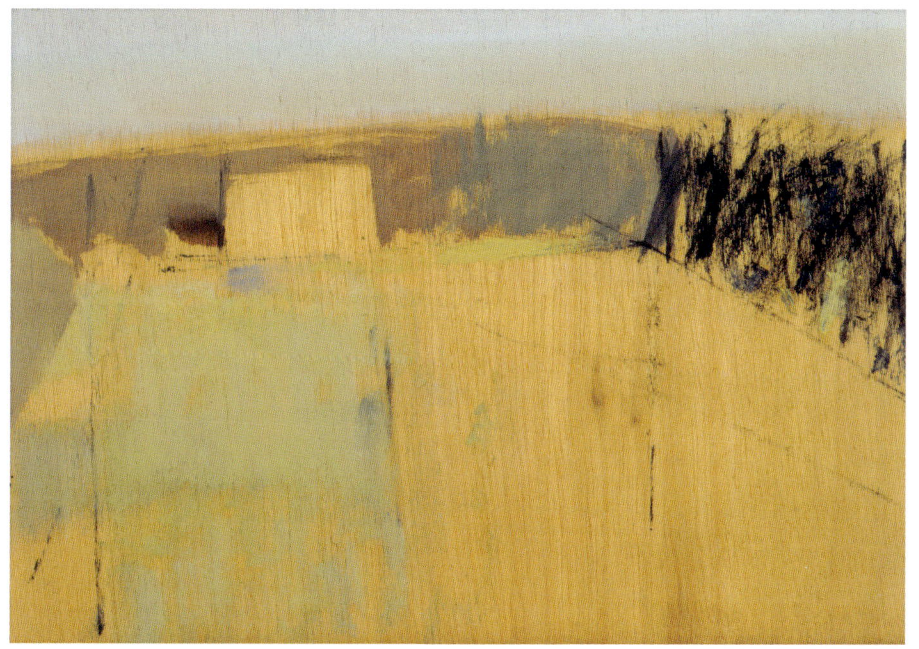

150 Basil Blackshaw,
Cowan's Cottage, 1966,
oil on wood.

Mike Catto has commented upon T. P. Flanagan's preference for 'serial production as offering alternative experimental solutions to a specific thematic problem'.[37] This is evident also in the works painted in Donegal in response to the remote grandeur of the Irish-speaking area of the north coast around Bloody Foreland and the village of Gortahork. Always acutely aware of the interventions of earlier landscapists, such as Craig or McKelvey, who painted in Donegal, Flanagan produced a series of pictures in the mid-1960s that helped to redefine the visual meanings of this region. As with the landscape of Sligo around Lissadell, his depictions did not deny existing meanings, which became part of the cumulative interpretations of 'place' in his work. In Northern Ireland, place is never neutral or unclaimed: it is always the territory of one community or another, even if this is not always apparent in landscape painting. In Flanagan's paintings of the North Donegal boglands over the border in the Republic, by

comparison, the very emptiness of place can draw upon a range of meanings. The area around Bloody Foreland was severely depopulated during the years of the Famine and subsequently through the effects both of emigration and the struggles over land ownership throughout the nineteenth century. Yet Donegal was also one of the three predominantly Catholic counties of the province of Ulster not incorporated into the Northern state under Unionist rule in 1921. Since then, its remoteness for much of the twentieth century has ensured a particular role in the nationalist romantic imagination – particularly for urban Northerners. In this sense the space that opens up within a painting such as *Gortahork I* (1967) can signify a mark of resistance to territorial definitions.

In these paintings the colour scheme of brown and grey, also used by Nano Reid and George Campbell, emphasizes a sense of the materiality of the land itself. In spite of their emptiness, the boglands also signify a

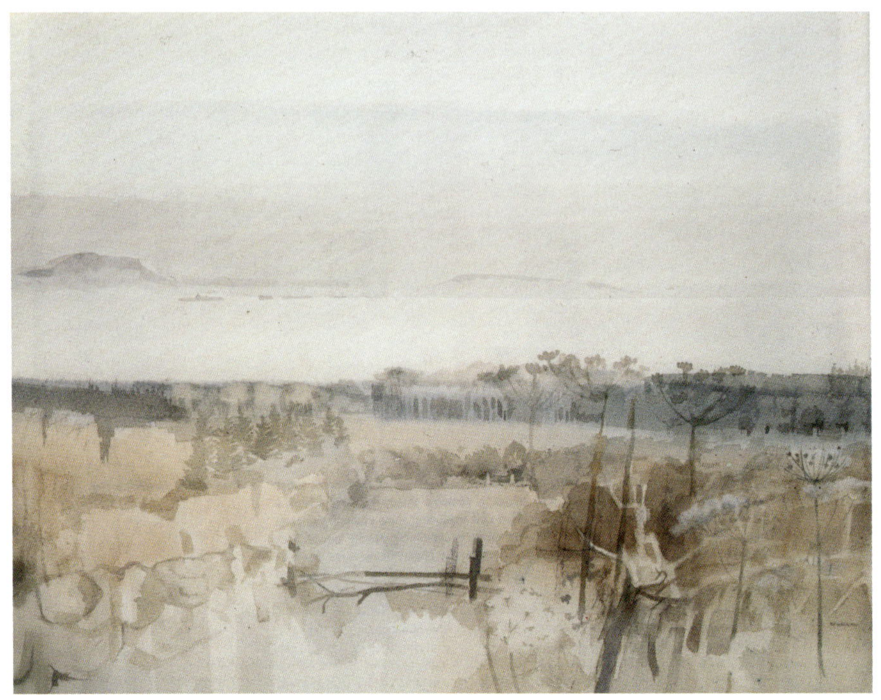

151 T. P. Flanagan,
A White Sea, 1961, oil
on canvas.

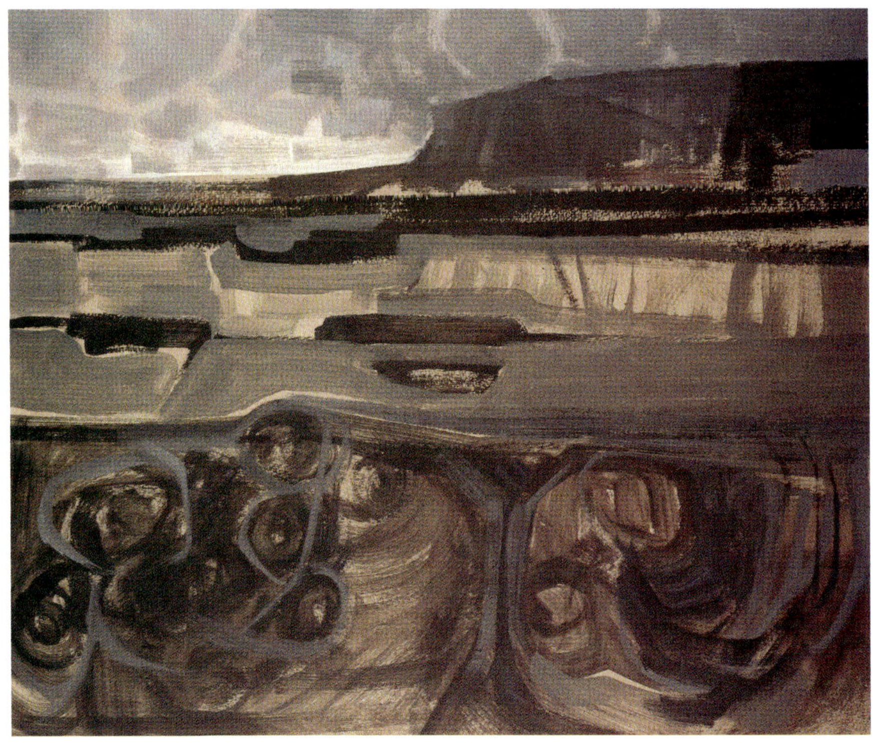

152 T. P. Flanagan,
Gortahork I, 1967, oil and
acrylic on hardboard.

human presence within the painting as the basis of subsistence farming within the region. Turf dug from the bog becomes a source of fuel for remote communities, and its surface bears the marks of cutting over generations. As in the poems of Seamus Heaney, there is a sense in Flanagan's Donegal paintings of the 1960s of the bog as an accretion of human experience. Yet the specificitles of place, sometimes with fatal consequences, were to gain a particular significance for artists in Northern Ireland during the following decades.

EIGHT

THE CONFLICT IN THE NORTH AND IRISH ART, 1968–1979

By the end of the 1960s the hopes and dreams of reform in Northern Ireland were shattered, with on one side the increasing disillusion of the nationalist community and on the other the increasing entrenchment of loyalists as their centuries-old privileges became threatened. Political tensions continued to rise throughout 1969. In April Terence O'Neill was forced to resign, having further alienated loyalists by his concessions of major electoral reform to nationalists. On 14 August the British Army was sent in to Northern Ireland on the orders of the Home Secretary James Callaghan, in a context of growing civil unrest in Derry and Belfast. In 1971, in response to an escalation of violence, internment without trial was introduced, allowing suspects to be detained by the security forces indefinitely without being charged with an offence. During the four years of its operation, internment was used overwhelmingly against nationalists; no loyalists were interned until 1973. Internment was hugely counter-productive, with nationalist communities traumatized by nightly house raids by the security forces. The continued arrests and well-documented allegations of torture only fuelled resistance. Sectarian attacks and bombings escalated throughout the early 1970s, with the effect of terrorizing ordinary civilians. Meanwhile political loyalism was also gaining momentum; in 1971 Ian Paisley founded the Democratic Unionist Party (DUP), finding immediate support among hardline Unionists who saw their position as unrepresented in the Northern Ireland government.

In the midst of this, on 30 January 1972, a mass protest was organized against internment in Derry by NICRA; the march went ahead in spite of being declared illegal. It was entirely peaceful until the Parachute Regiment opened fire, killing thirteen unarmed civilians; the ensuing Widgery Report failed to indict the army in the killings. The effects of what became known as Bloody Sunday were profound and far-reaching, remembered in Derry as a massive trauma that stands out in decades of unimaginable violence. In the months after Bloody Sunday the immediate effects were both mass recruitment by the Provisional IRA and a devastating bombing campaign aimed at commercial targets as part of an overall strategy to remove British interests from Northern Ireland. These bombs frequently detonated with little or no warning. As the random killings, assassinations and bombings continued, the British inability to resolve the problem ultimately shifted into complete intransigence, thanks to the election of Margaret Thatcher as Prime Minister in 1979. Yet the continual violence also had the effect of deterring potential investors in Northern Ireland's economy; the rapid decline was exacerbated by the international oil crisis. Economic survival was frequently only achieved through heavy government intervention, as in the case of Harland and Wolff ship-yards, the mainstay of Belfast's heavy industry since the company's foundation in the mid-nineteenth century. Despite a worldwide boom in shipbuilding, the yards now faced a major economic crisis due to a lack of mod-ernization; government intervention was the only solution at this stage.[1]

Conflict and art practice in Northern Ireland

From 1968 onwards, artists' responses to the worsening political situation in Northern Ireland dominated art practice there to an overwhelming extent. The conflict also had a profound effect on the work of many artists south of the border – although a degree of relative dis-tance made it possible for other concerns to emerge as well. Violence, social breakdown and economic crisis meant that artists in Northern Ireland had to develop a range of means to address the new conditions. This was a process that began early. Belfast College of Art was situated in the city centre, and art education took place in an atmosphere of continual awareness of bomb alerts, threats and evacuations of the building. As the painter Carol Graham, a student there until 1975, later observed:

> Anyone going into Belfast was aware of what was happening, and you were aware that you were likely to become a victim yourself. It was just too big and too powerful and too awful, in the whole sense of the word, to want to think about. There's just too much emotion wrapped up with that.[2]

The direction that Graham took in her work was a conscious response to the political situation outside the college environment. Her paintings abound with im-ages of containment, from interiors hidden within archaeological remains to glimpses of the body within the striped skirt in *Light Falls Within* (1978). This also deliberately represents a world of order in comparison with the chaos dominating everyday life at the time. For some other artists, existing practices of abstraction could take on new meanings in the current circumstances. Deborah Brown's modernist fibreglass sculptures, as Anne Crookshank observed, conveyed a sense of 'calm-ness and peace' in the midst of the violence surrounding them.[3] Yet even this serene practice was not immune from the effects of conflict. In 1972, a no-warning bomb exploded in Donegall Street near Brown's studio, re-sulting in the deaths of two policemen and four civilians. A large quantity of her work was destroyed; afterwards Brown made two sculptures of pared down fibreglass forms containing an embedded roll of barbed wire.

The vast majority of T. P. Flanagan's paintings from the 1970s also had little direct connection with the vio-lence in the North. Much of his work conveyed a distinct nostalgia, a desire for a more harmonious, peaceful time. A cottage at Roughra, near Ardara in South Done-gal, became a place of recuperation for the artist's family. The focus of a group of works on the hearth of the cot-tage suggests a longing for the pre-industrial as offering a respite from the massive contradictions of modernity tearing Northern Ireland apart. On one occasion Flana-gan did engage more directly with the effects of violence, in a work commemorating a friend killed by the IRA in 1974, the judge Martin McBirnie. In borrowing the pose of the marble-like draped fallen figure from Poussin's *Echo and Narcissus*, Flanagan's *The Victim* evokes a sto-icism of mourning also derived from neo-Classical sculpture. His negation of the specificity of McBirnie's death was also deliberate; as Flanagan later commented, 'The shrouded "victim" is not therefore the actual victim, but a symbol of all those who had perished in like circumstances since our "troubles" commenced.'[4]

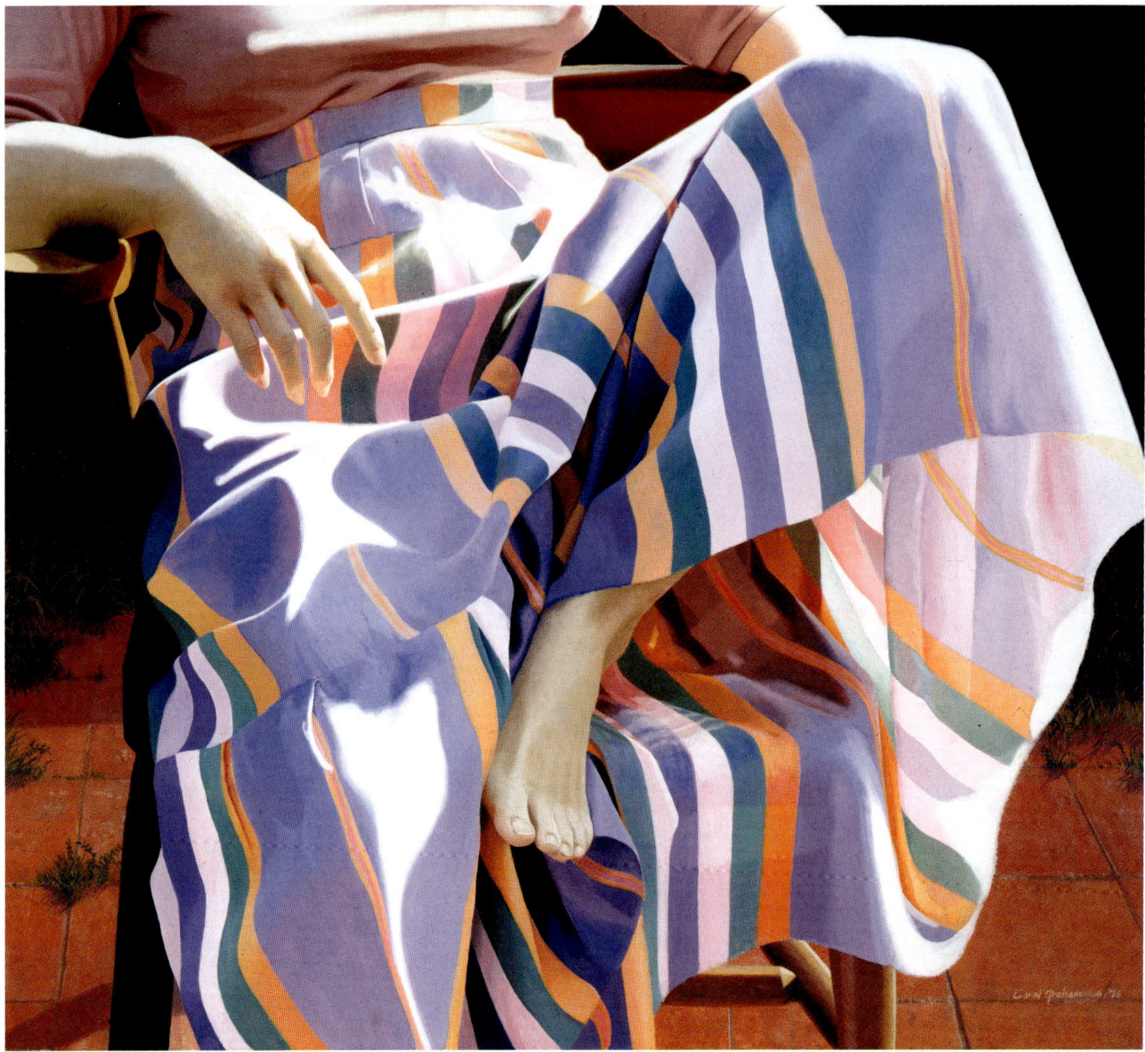

153 Carol Graham, *Light Falls Within*, 1978, oil, acrylic on canvas on board.

Mourning and melancholia also pervade the works of other artists, as in Charles Oakley's depictions of a graveyard in *A View of Ulster '71* (1971) or the abandoned building in Dan O'Neill's *Belfast after the Riot* (1971). Its classicized facade reflected in a pool of water also suggests the architectural uncanny, a deserted scenario evoking unconscious dangers.

The continual city-centre bombings also made it difficult for galleries to function. The Bell Gallery, which had opened in Alfred Street in Belfast's commercial centre in 1964, moved to the safer suburbs of the Lisburn Road during the early 1970s. The relatively short-lived McClelland Gallery was also badly affected by the situation. George McClelland was a former CID

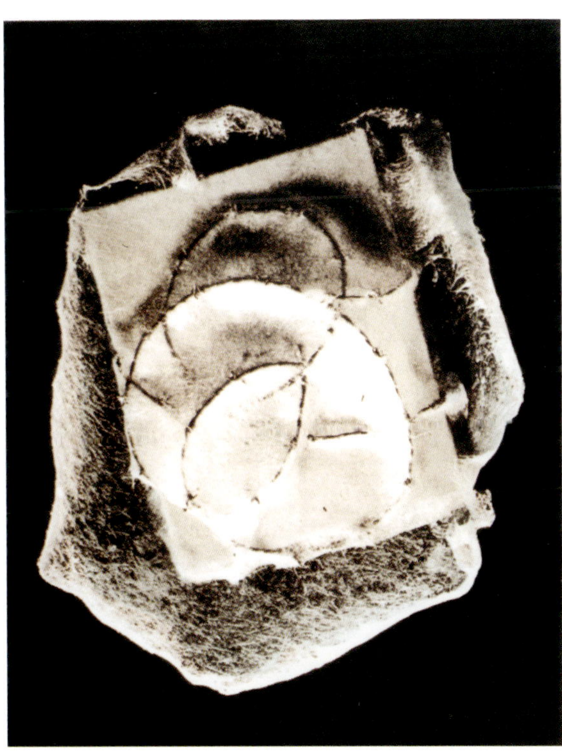

154 Deborah Brown, *Barbed Wire and Glass Fibre Form I*, 1972, glass fibre, barbed wire.

man who had made a private collection of fairly conventional Irish art – Keating, Craig, Conor – in addition to a range of antiques. In December 1966, intending to emigrate to Australia with his young family, he hired premises at 33 May Street to sell off the entire collection before departure. The venture was so successful, however, that George and Maura McClelland abandoned their plans and the McClelland Antiques and Art Galleries opened in the same premises in 1967. Throughout the galleries' entire existence it was the sale of antiques and artefacts that financed the exhibitions by contemporary artists including, in 1969, Dan O'Neill's first exhibition in Belfast in eighteen years.

In December 1971 a bomb destroyed the premises next door to the May Street galleries. After selling off his antiques stock at Rosses Auction Rooms in May 1972 – an event poorly attended due to further bombings – McClelland reopened his gallery at 11 Lisburn Road, slightly out of the city centre. His family, meanwhile, had moved to the relative security of Dublin. The new McClelland Galleries International reopened in May 1973 with a show by Colin Middleton, featuring a large

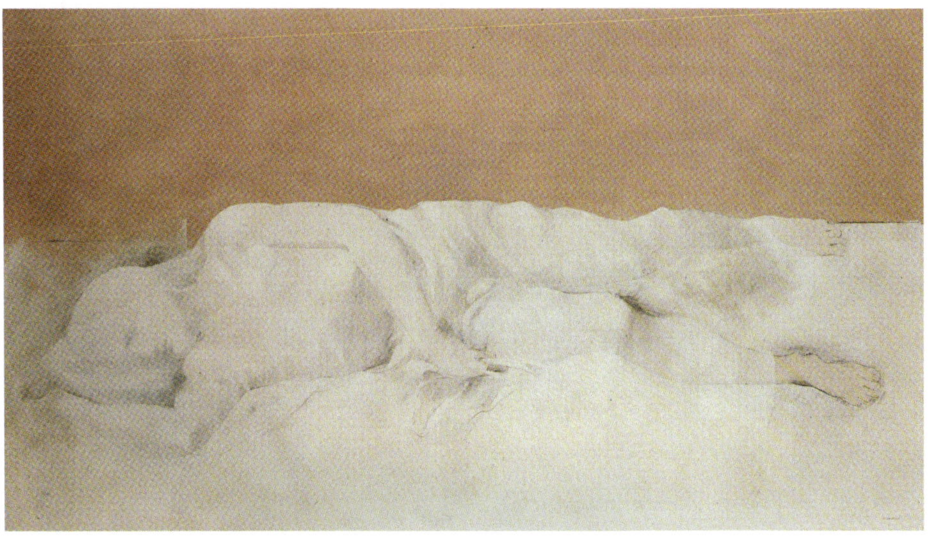

155 T. P. Flanagan, *The Victim*, 1974, oil on canvas.

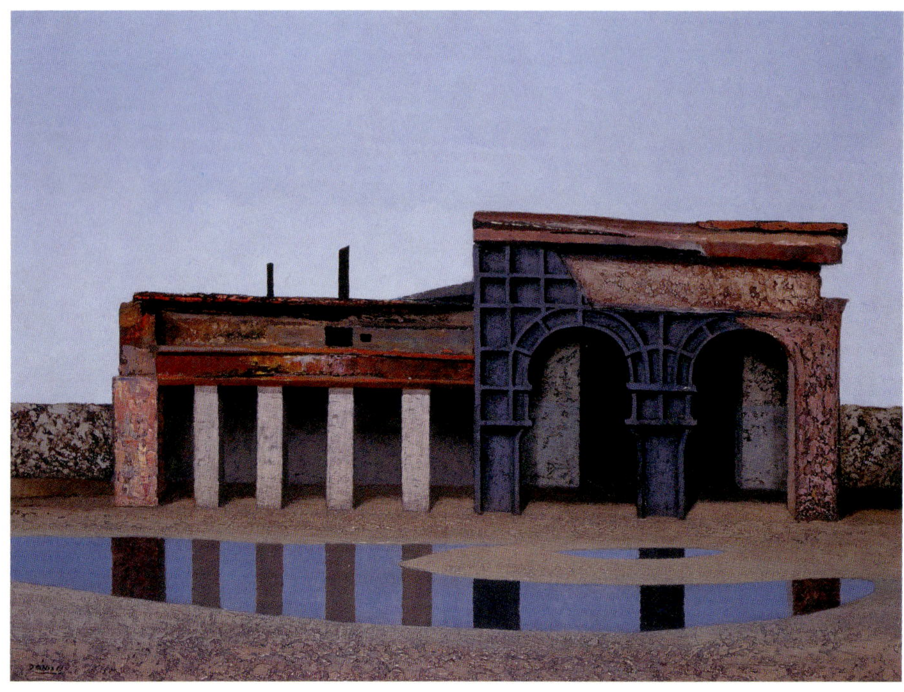

156 Daniel O'Neill, *Belfast after the Riot*, 1971, oil on board.

number of Surrealist and Expressionist works from the 1930s and 1940s that McClelland had bought from the artist's studio, where they had remained unsold. Louis le Brocquy's *Táin* tapestries followed, and other exhibitions included the work of Tom Carr, and F. E. McWilliam's *Women of Belfast* (1972). In the early 1970s the city remained an immensely difficult commercial environment, with regular bomb scares and threats of assassination that frequently turned into the real thing; often people felt it was too dangerous to venture out to art openings in the evenings. George McClelland's health was beginning to suffer, and in early 1974 his galleries closed down. The site was subsequently destroyed by a bomb. McClelland moved to Dublin, eventually beginning a new life as a student at the National College of Art and Design.

Although some artists were able to negotiate a practice within which the effects of the conflict were mediated, for others it proved inescapable, resulting in the need to develop visual forms capable of dealing with situations unprecedented in the experience of earlier generations of artists in Northern Ireland. Conflict and intimidation resulted in a highly polarized political geography in Belfast (as elsewhere in the North), with East and West of the city becoming identified as loyalist and nationalist respectively. Yet there are inconsistencies: the loyalist Shankill is in the West, while the mainly Protestant North also contains distinct nationalist areas such as Ardoyne or the New Lodge. Many of these adjoining areas were separated by the British Army's erection of the 'Peace Line', a barrier that was North Belfast's version of the Berlin Wall and intended – not always successfully – to stop attacks by one side or another. Many of Joseph McWilliams's paintings from the early 1970s were specifically situated in the area of the New Lodge, where his parents lived.

Often, as in *Barricades and People: New Lodge* (1971), they incorporate found objects, fragments from the barricades that accompanied nights of rioting after the introduction of internment in 1971, and which McWilliams later described as 'an attempt to replicate the physicalness of the violence and its impact on the people of the area'.[5]

Catherine McWilliams's work at the time, like that of her husband Joseph, was derived from her observations of life in nationalist areas, which were not only experiencing the traumas of political conflict but were also some of the most impoverished in Western Europe. Many paintings, such as *Schoolgirl* (1974) or *Lizzie Mulvenna, Ardoyne* (1973) featured single female figures trapped and isolated by their circumstances. After the introduction of internment, however, nationalist women played active roles

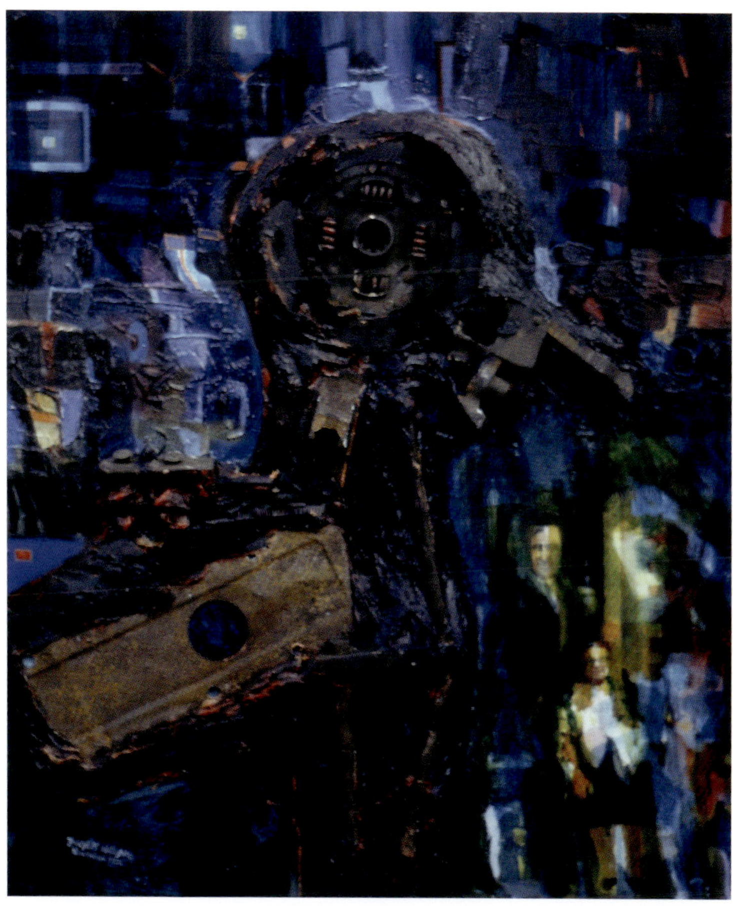

157 Joseph McWilliams, *Barricades and People: New Lodge*, 1971, mixed media.

in maintaining the cohesiveness both of their families and communities. Catherine McWilliams's painting *Girls and Motorbikes* depicts a group of female figures all turned to face the viewer. The painting was based on a photograph taken by McWilliams during the summer of 1972 while visiting her husband's family in the New Lodge. The pose of the riders to the left is protective, turning to meet the viewer's gaze. This is not a comfortable painting: there is a vigilance about these figures, suggestive of a sense of intrusion on their territory. When the IRA began to recruit again in 1969, both women and men joined the organization, yet women were also expected to continue their established roles within families and communities – dual

responsibilities that frequently went unacknowledged.[6] This affects a reading of McWilliams's painting: the young woman on the motorbike to the left of centre was Liz McKee, who on 1 January 1973 became the first woman to be interned. Aged nineteen, she was subsequently charged with IRA membership.[7] Active, strong and resilient, *Girls and Motorbikes* represents an important corrective to the currency of representations of women as 'victims of the Troubles'.

Paintings by Joseph McWilliams, Catherine McWilliams and Brendan Ellis engaged with the effects of conflict on the urban environment and the people who lived there. Other artists, however, began to address issues underpinning the proliferating iconography of

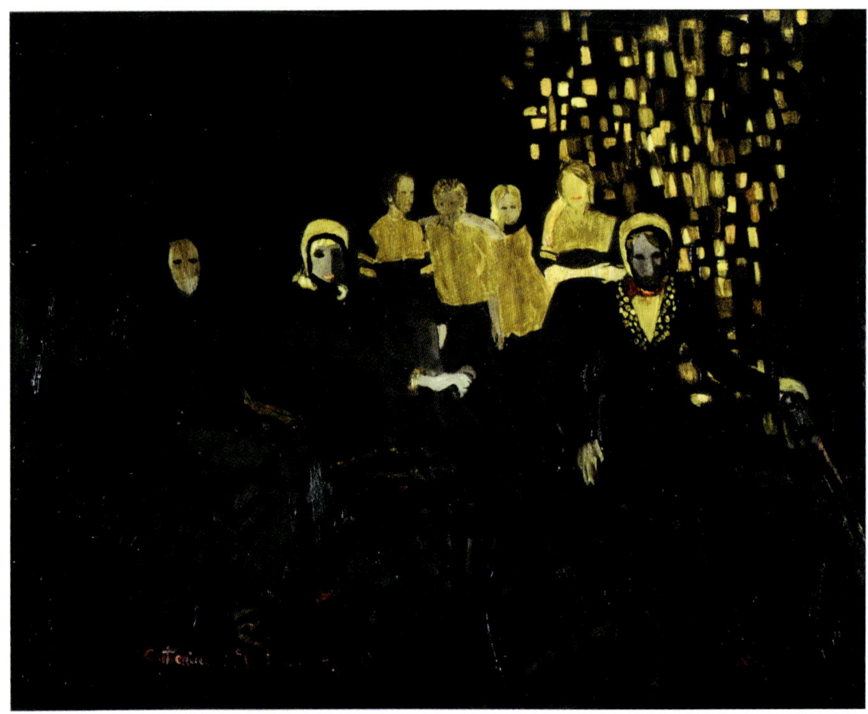

158 Catherine McWilliams, *Girls and Motorbikes*, 1973, oil on board.

the conflict. Although exhibiting from 1960 onwards, in the mid 1970s the painter Jack Pakenham arrived at a symbolic language embedded within the current imagery of violence. A ventriloquist's doll bought for his son provided Pakenham with a potent character recurring repeatedly within his work and enabling him to address the issues he identified as important for artists: 'a duty to respond, to give expression if at all possible to the fears and anxieties of those too afraid to speak'.[8] In the war zones of 1970s Belfast people still attempted to live normally, to impose some sense of rationality upon the chaos and ever-present danger. The uncanny aspects of the ventriloquist's doll allowed Pakenham to penetrate directly to the unconscious terrors underpinning this daily struggle. The doll's ambivalence, both passive and horrifyingly aggressive, represented for Pakenham 'the ultimate manipulated little man whose words are only what someone else gives him'.[9] In *Your Move*, part of the 'Belfast Series' (1975–6), the dolls are controlled by mutilated god-

fathers. Their paramilitary identifications are clear from their uniforms: one wears a balaclava and the other dark sunglasses that hide his identity. On one level they may appear mute and disempowered, but these figures also suggest some of the meanings underlying mass culture's constructions of the 'terrorist': an abject force of destruction, a horror outside language that undercuts the very basis of rationality and the attempts to maintain its hegemony.

Although many people in Northern Ireland at this time had first-hand experience of some of the more horrific effects of the violence, this was supplemented by increasingly prolific media representations. Newspaper journalism and the broadcast media played important roles in providing information and shaping opinion for audiences outside Northern Ireland; although debates around the nature of broadcasting 'the Troubles' continued throughout the 1970s and beyond, an agenda of what was more likely to be represented began to emerge. Between 1972 and 1973 the sculptor F. E. McWilliam,

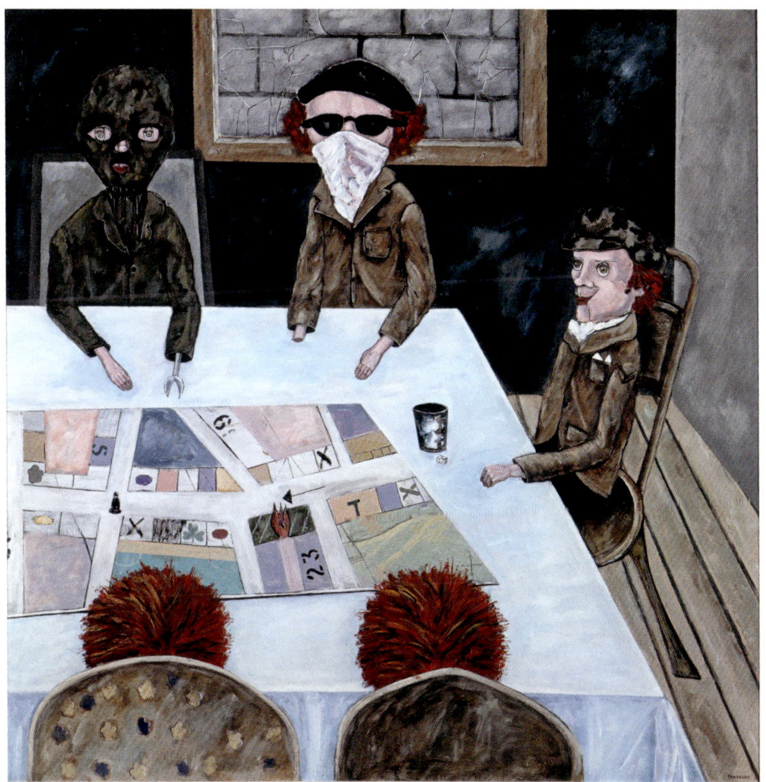

159 Jack Pakenham,
Your Move, 1975–6,
acrylic on board.

based in London, produced a series of works entitled *Women of Belfast*; an additional piece, *Woman Caught in a Bomb Blast*, followed in 1974. The catalyst for this series was also a specific event: the IRA bombing of the Abercorn cafe in Belfast on 4 March 1971, as part of their campaign against commercial interests in the city centre. On a Saturday afternoon the cafe was crowded with shoppers; two women were killed instantly and over 130 people sustained injuries. Unlike George Campbell, who returned to Belfast from London in the 1970s to paint a series of pictures depicting the effects of violence, McWilliam worked from media reports. The outcome was far removed from Catherine McWilliams's paintings derived from everyday observation of the lives of women in Belfast affected by the relentless pressures of both poverty and conflict. *Women of Belfast* was intended to provide visual representations of the effects of a bomb on the human form.[10] Limbs are splayed out or caught off-balance while

frequently the face is obscured, the head shrouded in displaced clothing. In some the mouth is open and eyes stare in an expression of fear or surprise. Less obviously, McWilliam's characteristic pockmarks and striations of the bronze surface here take on the significance of lacerations of the flesh. Swept up by forces beyond their control, the anonymous female figures signify an imaginary shared experience of the 'Troubles' as much as they draw heavily on the well-established iconography of Ireland personified as a passive, suffering woman.[11]

McWilliam's *Women of Belfast* sculptures tread a fine line between the aestheticization of violence and the retreat from the unrepresentable. In reviewing the series at the Waddington Gallery, London, G. S. Whittet singled out 'the range of pose' as adding up to 'a moving and dramatic frieze of events in Ireland's tragic history'.[12] It was precisely a desire to undercut this degree of romanticism and the stereotypes from which it was

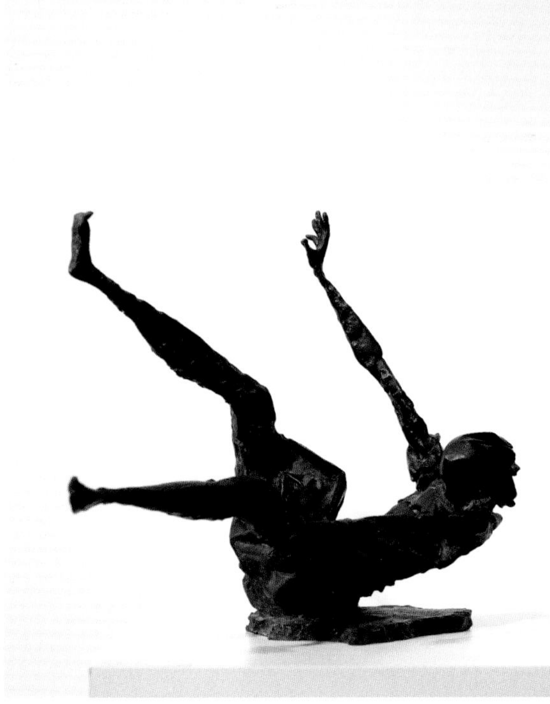

160 F.E. McWilliam, *Women of Belfast 5*, 1972, bronze.

derived that fuelled the interest in Northern Ireland by another British-based artist, Conrad Atkinson. A conceptual artist with an established reputation for politicized engagement with his subject-matter, Atkinson, in common with Rita Donagh, was one of the first artists on the British Left to engage with the politics of Northern Ireland in the 1970s. In 1974 he was invited by the Arts Council of Northern Ireland and the Irish Council for Trade Unions to visit Northern Ireland to research a body of work to be exhibited in Belfast as part of the 1975 May Day celebrations. Atkinson spent several months in the North taking photographs and collecting examples of the visual and material culture from both sides of the conflict, with the intention of providing a different representation from the oversimplified version portrayed in the British media.

A Shade of Green, An Orange Edge (1975) was exhibited at the Arts Council Gallery in Belfast in 1975. A further piece of work emerged from Atkinson's period of research, when he was invited to the Bogside in Derry to be shown the banner for the Civil Rights march in Derry on Bloody Sunday in 1972, still stained with the blood of two of the victims. As Atkinson later recalled:

> The bloodstained banner was unrolled for the first and only time since the day of the shootings, for me to photograph. My assistants and myself will never forget that emotional scene of which we were a part photographing that bloodstained banner in the garden of a council house in Derry . . . The only viable course in Northern Ireland is the withdrawal of the British Army . . .[13]

Atkinson's photograph became the basis for *Silver Liberties: A Souvenir of a Wonderful Anniversary Year* in 1978. Although the title ironically commemorates ten years of the conflict, a significant focus of the work was on Bloody Sunday. The piece consists of four large panels, coloured green, white and orange to signify the Irish flag, while a fourth panel was painted black. Beginning and ending with Atkinson's photograph of the Civil Rights banner, the first panel included photographs of all of the victims on Bloody Sunday, the second reproduced a cartoon graffito of a British soldier copied from a wall in Belfast and the third – the orange – showed photographs of street scenes from loyalist areas in Belfast. The final panel, separated from the others by a length of barbed wire, included, in addition to a quotation from the poet Shelley, photographs of a man who had been the victim of police brutality.

Silver Liberties was shown at the *Art for Society* exhibition at London's Whitechapel Gallery in 1978, and a selection of works from the exhibition were then to be

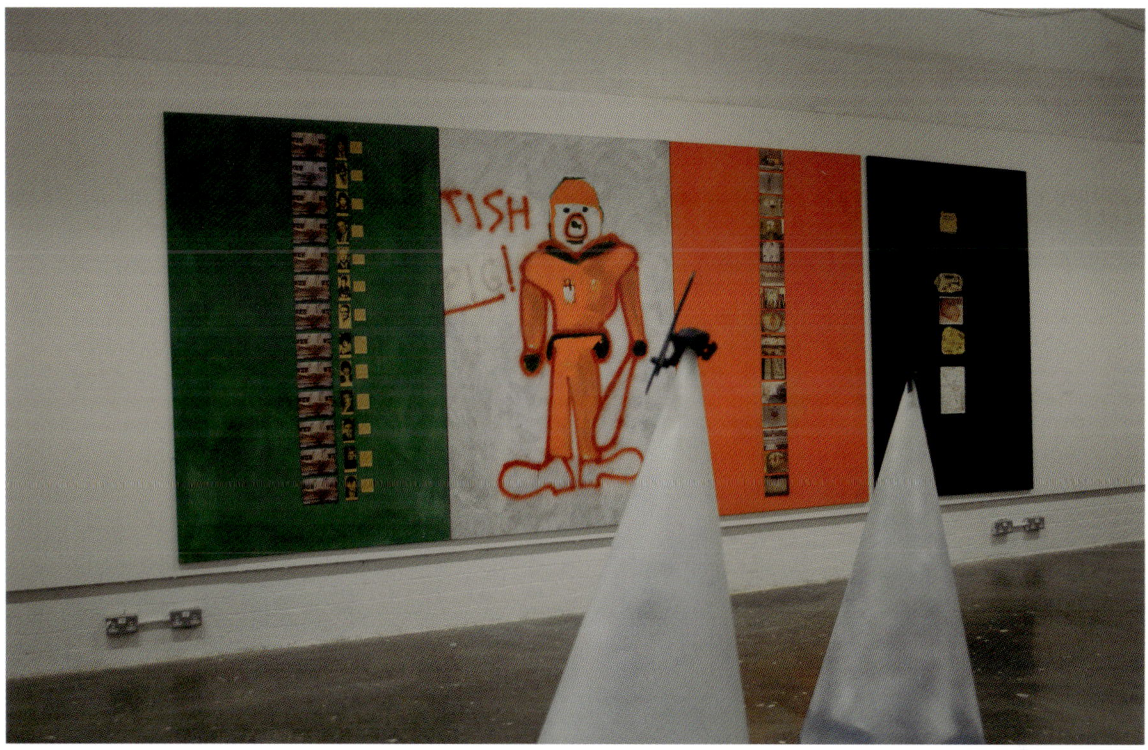

161 Conrad Atkinson, *Silver Liberties: A Souvenir of a Wonderful Anniversary Year*, 1978, mixed media installed at Golden Thread, Belfast, 2012.

shown at the Ulster Museum in Belfast. In keeping with the activist character of the majority of work in the exhibition, *Silver Liberties* was intended to stimulate cultural engagement and political awareness beyond the confines of the gallery. In Belfast, however, unlike at the Whitechapel, the audience for the work was one for whom its subject-matter was already implicated in deeply held and seemingly irreconcilable political ideologies that underpinned and structured everyday life. For the majority of loyalists, Bloody Sunday represented a justified killing, on the (false) grounds that among the victims were armed IRA members. In addition, Northern Ireland's police force, the Royal Ulster Constabulary (RUC), was overwhelmingly composed of Protestants. In spite of the frequent accusations of collusion with loyalist paramilitaries and brutality towards republican suspects, the majority of Unionists vehemently de-

fended the RUC as the defenders of law and order in the face of terrorism. The staunchly loyalist attendants at the Ulster Museum refused to hang *Silver Liberties* in the gallery, supported by the Museum's trustees. After a radio interview during which Atkinson referred to the Museum's staff as 'cultural paramilitaries', the trustees were changed and the exhibition went ahead, minus *Silver Liberties* and several other works, which were shown at the Arts Council Gallery in Bedford Street.[14]

Art practice in Southern Ireland in the 1970s

Meanwhile, in the Republic, Jack Lynch as Taoiseach was put in a difficult position by the unfolding violence in the North. As the leader of a modernizing nation he was unwilling to become involved with the politics of the North, but still wanted to be seen as attempting to alleviate the situation of Northern Catholics. Public feeling ran high, and the news of Bloody Sunday on 30 January 1972 was greeted by mass protests in Dublin, culminating in the IRA's burning of the British Embassy in Merrion Square. Yet this turned public opinion against acts of violence as a solution, a view only reinforced by the horrific bombings in Dublin and Monaghan by the UVF in 1974, in which 32 people were killed.

In 1969 the Republic's growing prosperity began to have a direct effect on artists when the Finance Minister Charles Haughey introduced tax-free status for painters, sculptors, writers and composers in Ireland whose income was derived from 'creative works judged to be of cultural merit'.[15] In spite of the oil crisis of the 1970s that had such a devastating effect on the North, the economic progress of the 1960s continued in the South for much of the decade; with Britain and Denmark, Ireland joined the EEC in 1973. However, towards the end of the 1970s Ireland's economic expansionism was increasingly financed by foreign borrowing, producing debts that would lead to major economic crises during the 1980s.

Meanwhile, over 50 years after the Easter Rising, old loyalties and priorities were being re-assessed in different ways. The revolutionary student politics that had appeared elsewhere in Europe (and in the North to some degree) also emerged in Dublin, in campaigns to reform the existing National College of Art in 1970. After protesting students had been locked out of the college by the Department of Education, the institution itself was closed.[16] When it reopened as the National College of Art and Design in new premises in Thomas Street, significant debates around the nature of art education in Ireland had been initiated. Student protests continued throughout the decade. In 1976 a mass occupation of

listed Georgian buildings in Upper Pembroke Street by architectural students was largely instrumental in thwarting the attempt by Bord na Móna (the Irish Turf Board, founded in 1933 to extract peat for fuel from Ireland's boglands) to have them demolished. After thirteen weeks Bord na Móna finally gave in. On this occasion the Arts Council, under the new radical directorship of Colm O'Briain and mindful of the earlier Fitzwilliam Street fiasco, vehemently opposed the demolition.[17]

Although there was widespread sympathy for the suffering in the North, the majority of people in the Republic were unwilling to get involved. In 1968 Gerard Dillon returned to live in Dublin for the last two years of his life, his nationalist politics largely unmodified by decades in London. In 1969 he made moves – unsuccessfully – to stop the showing of that year's IELA in the North in response to the deteriorating situation.[18] One of the artists who supported Dillon's protest at IELA was Micheal Farrell, Carroll Prize winner for that year. In his speech at the exhibition's opening in Cork, Farrell made his position clear in stating that: 'I am withholding my work from the North of Ireland. I will not let it go to be shown in a gallery supported by that regime.'[19]

He also donated part of the prize money to an artists' fund to help the Catholic refugees fleeing across the border from the North. Farrell's work at this time was focused around the *pressé* theme, referring to a means of mechanically squeezing fruit to extract the juice. There is also a reference to the sexualized connotations of earlier modernist mechanical imagery, Duchamp's chocolate grinder in particular. In these largely symmetrical, highly decorative compositions the juice squirts from between two opposing pestles. At a time when he had begun to feel that abstraction was increasingly depleted as a mode of representation, this suggests, in Gerry Walker's words, 'Farrell's

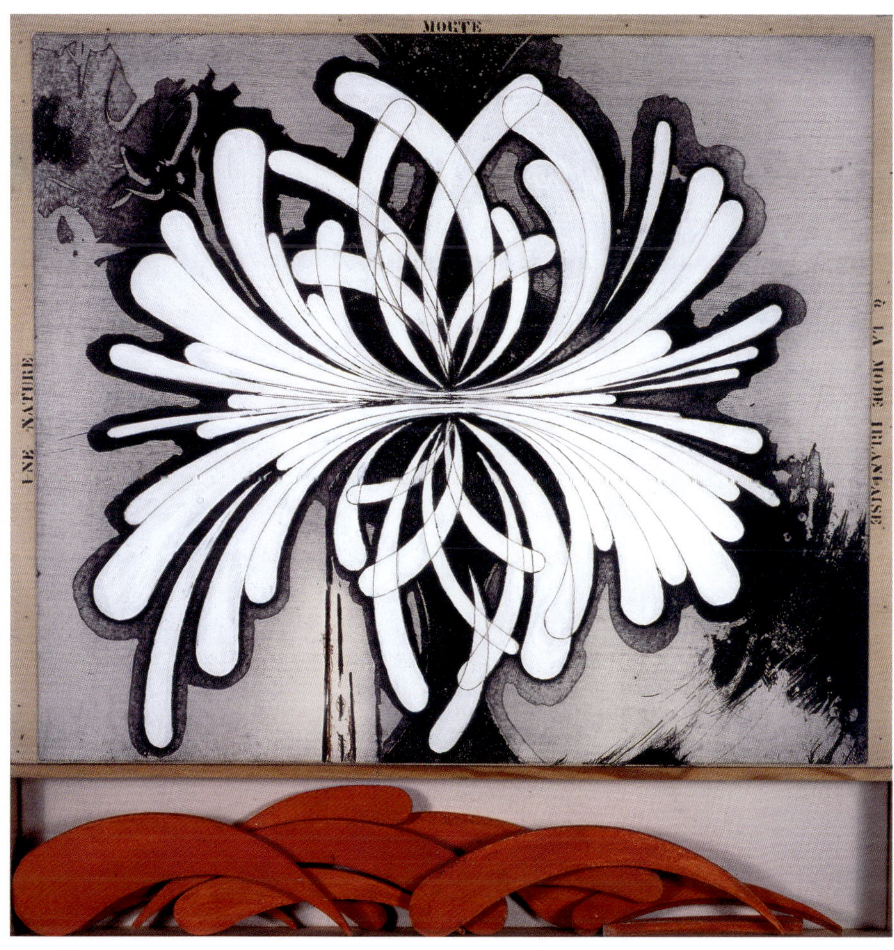

162 Micheal Farrell, *Une Nature Morte à la Mode Irlandais*, 1974, acrylic and paper on board and acrylic on wood.

own bid to squeeze meaning out of an unforthcoming visual language'.[20]

In 1971 Micheal Farrell moved to France with his family. His work was beginning to incorporate an awareness of the political situation in Northern Ireland; the juice squeezed out in the *pressé* paintings had changed from yellow and orange to blood red.[21] In 1974, after the Dublin and Monaghan bombings, the *pressés* became *pressés politiques*. In these, the gobbets of juice spurt out wildly, no longer controlled within a classicized composition. Instead of the slick finish of the earlier works, the stripped-down nature of the materials helps to signify an authenticity of response to a traumatic situation, raw and (apparently) unmediated. Farrell used bare wood as a background for black and white silk-screened collages of newspaper reportage of the two atrocities. Out of this collapse from control to chaos a new visual language emerged, one that was more directly connected with the literary, and which permitted him to engage more readily with issues far beyond the sphere of art practice.

Once again this work took the form of a political commentary on the state of Ireland, in a series of works based on François Boucher's *Nude on a Sofa* (1752), a depiction of Marie-Louise O'Murphy, the mistress of Louis XV. In *Madonna Irlanda* (1977) the move into figuration that characterized Farrell's work for the remainder of his career is fully evident. Farrell later described Mlle

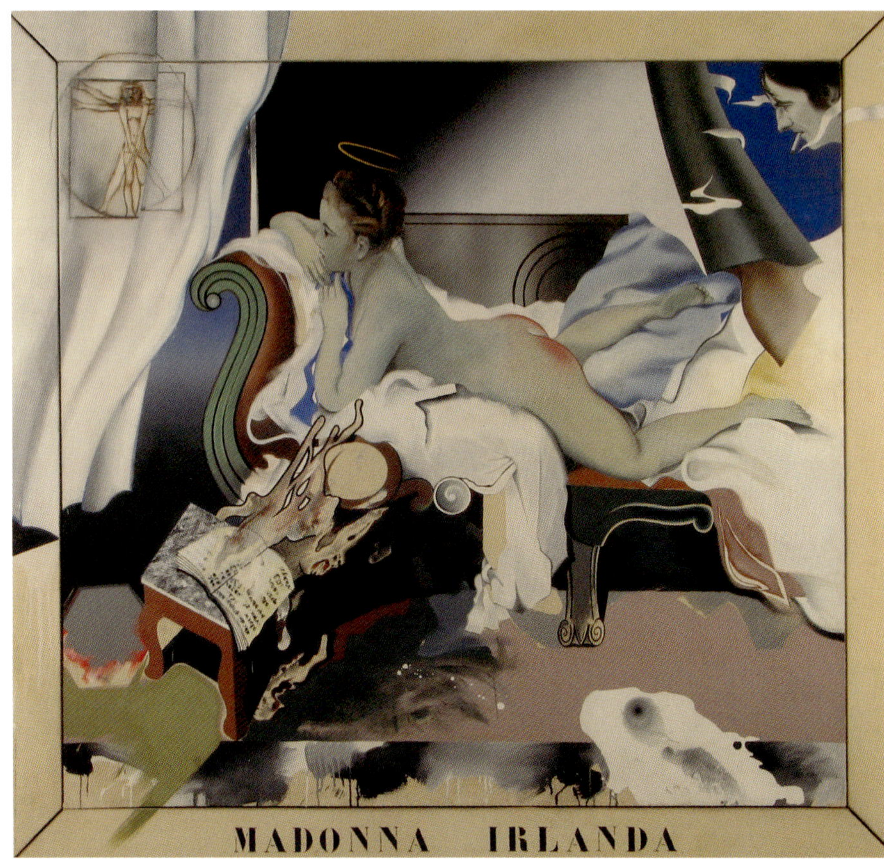

163 Micheal Farrell, *Madonna Irlanda*, 1977, acrylic on canvas.

O'Murphy as a 'Caitlín [Kathleen] ní Houlihan figure'.[22] His engagement with Ireland's female personification shifted it into much more eroticized territory. This is significant on two levels. First, Farrell's version scandalously challenges the conflation of nationalist and catholic imagery of the Virgin Mary represented by such iconic depictions as MacGonigal's *Mother and Child* (1942). Second, it also represents a major shift from the way Brian O'Doherty characterized the representation of the nude in Irish art in one of his short essays for *The Irish Imagination* in 1971. The 'Puritan Nude', according to O'Doherty, was one that signified an indirect approach to sensuality, a 'sense of moderation, a politeness of approach that may be a reflex of the Irishman's terror of sex or his approach to women'.[23] Legs splayed, the female body becomes an object of consumption, whether sexual or otherwise. In other versions of this painting, Farrell, conscious of the meanings of the name 'Boucher', marked out the body as cuts of meat, a carcass ready for carving. In Aidan Dunne's view, 'unquestioning nationalism' has been superseded by 'more ambiguous references to violence', yet in Farrell's shift to figuration this is enacted on a meticulously detailed female body.[24]

His response to the political situation in the North had a transformative effect on Farrell's practice, as for other artists to a greater or lesser degree. Ten months after Bloody Sunday took place in Derry in 1972, the first exhibition organized by a new committee of IELA took place at the Project Arts Centre in Dublin. The Project itself had been set up in 1967 as an attempt to break down the hierarchical distinctions between different

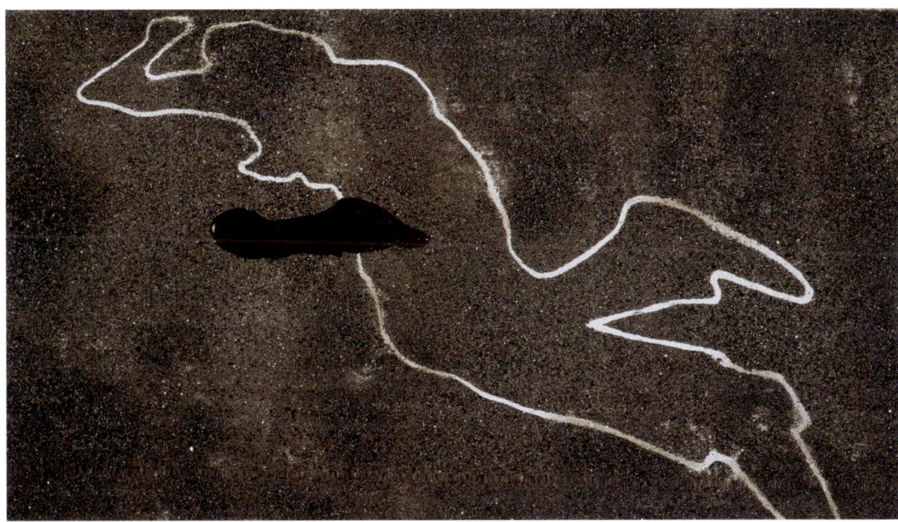

164 Robert Ballagh, *Northern Ireland, the 1,500th Victim*, 1976, print with incised sanded surface with wax.

forms of practice, organizing not only exhibitions but also a range of activities, including poetry readings and musical events. It was also the base for the Independent Artists, a group committed to maintaining a practice of figurative Expressionism in opposition to the modernist abstraction favoured by the Arts Council. The Project Gallery, therefore, was a highly appropriate venue for the 1972 *Living Art*; the work included was much more innovative and experimental than had previously been common practice in Ireland, including a 'sound room' by James Coleman and an installation of folded canvas by the painter Ciarán Lennon. A key focus was the ongoing conflict in the North. In addition to a video by the Dublin-born artist Les Levine about the

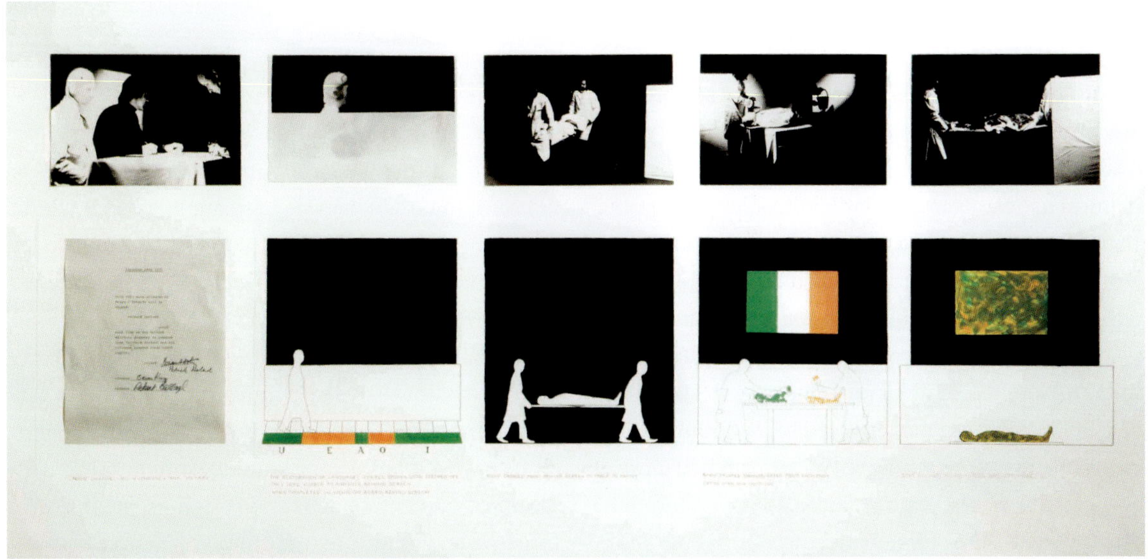

165 Patrick Ireland, *Name Change*, 1972, photographs, ink and gouache drawings on paper, typed text on paper collaged onto poster board.

conflict, Robert Ballagh commemorated the deaths of those killed on Bloody Sunday by chalking their outlines on the floor and filling them with blood.

A further commemoration of Bloody Sunday was also the basis of Brian O'Doherty's piece, originally entitled *Maze* (1972), which, as Brenda Moore McCann observes, was also the 'first "performance art" in Ireland'.[25] During this piece, the documentation of which is called *Name Change*, O'Doherty changed the identity under which his art was exhibited to Patrick Ireland, 'until such time as the British military presence is removed from Northern Ireland and all citizens granted their civil rights'. His critical writings, including the highly influential *Inside the White Cube: The Ideology of the Gallery Space* (1976), continued under the name Brian O'Doherty. The performance, however, both referenced and redefined aspects of O'Doherty's earlier practice in a more politically radical form.

Divergent practices

In raising questions about colonialism, history and identity, albeit in different ways, the work of Patrick Ireland, Micheal Farrell and others helped to situate the political upheavals in the North in relation to ongoing shifts in art practice in the rest of Ireland. These challenges to modernism were also in line with and informed by tendencies in art outside Ireland that would eventually take shape much more explicitly during the 1980s under the banner of postmodernism. One effect of the questioning of modernist painting's concerns for pictorial autonomy was the re-emergence of figuration and realism as alternative modes of representation. The 1970s was the period when the work of the academic portraitist Edward McGuire was most popular; his *Seamus Heaney* depicts the poet seated at a table.

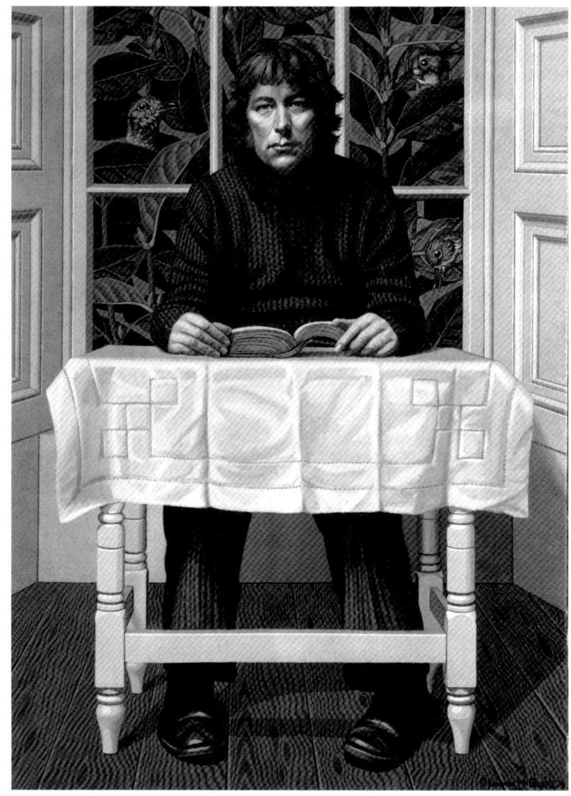

166 Edward McGuire, *Seamus Heaney*, 1974, oil on canvas.

Glimpsed through the window behind him is a tree filled with birds, indicating the image of the poet as Celtic visionary in evoking the late medieval tale of Sweeney, the mad bird-king condemned to wander Ireland because of his rejection of Christianity, yet whose exile enabled him to compose nature poems of great beauty.[26] In spite of the implications of a romantic pastoralism in McGuire's portrait, other paintings that appeared to represent aspects of landscape more directly suggested very different readings. The meticulously rendered surface of Martin Gale's three-panel *Intrusion* (1978) conveys a degree of menace in the presence of the helicopter observed by the three figures beneath: inevitably for Irish viewers in the

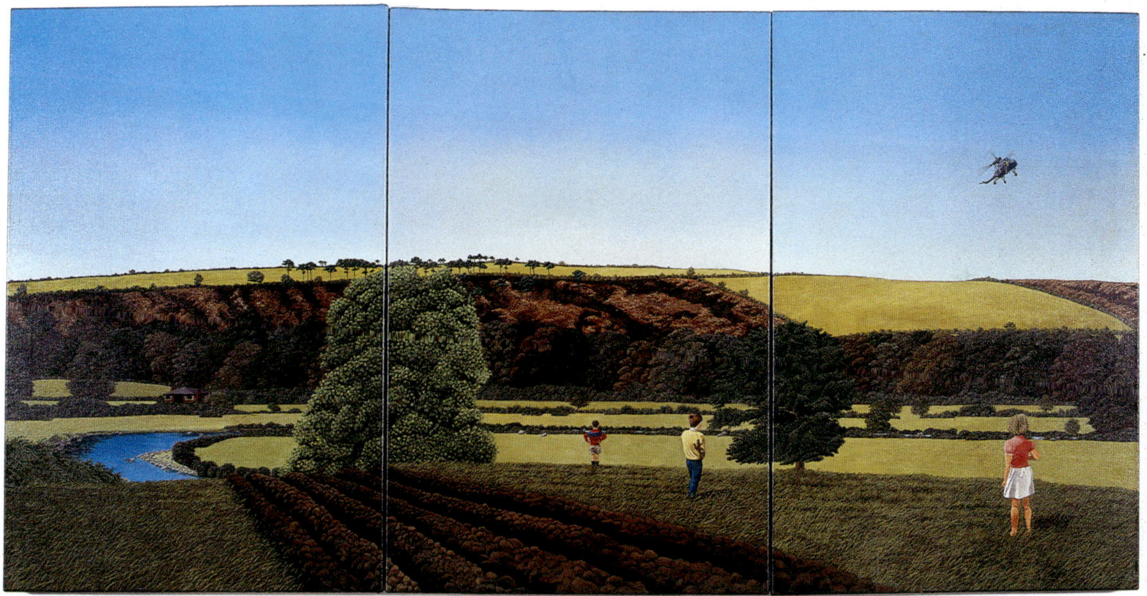

167 Martin Gale, *Intrusion*, 1978, oil on canvas.

1970s this had connotations of the British Army's presence in the North.

In work by Robert Ballagh, naturalistic depiction took on further connotations of the questioning of reality through strategies of self-referentiality and parody. Ballagh's work also embodied a fundamental rejection of the rural as the basis of Irish identity. In common with Farrell, a significant part of the vocabulary of his early paintings was derived from Pop art, in Ballagh's case applied to the reworking of early nineteenth-century political paintings such as those by Goya, Delacroix and David. One aim of paintings such as *Liberty on the Barricades After Delacroix* was to subvert any sense of romanticism or the presence of the artist's individuality. In the context of their unavoidable references to Northern Ireland, however, the deliberate anti-expressiveness also undercuts the romanticism of violence. Ballagh's work has consistently retained a political aspect balanced with an interest in processes of

perception. In 1969 part of his series of depictions of spectators looking at paintings, eventually including replicas of works by Pollock or Soulages in addition to Ballagh's Irish contemporaries such as Patrick Scott or Micheal Farrell, was shown at the Paris Biennale.

A later series of four paintings based around the house in Dublin where Robert and Betty Ballagh lived after their marriage in 1967, 3 Temple Cottages, focused his interests in perception, representation and history through a concern with domestic space. *Inside No. 3* involves a naturalistic parody of Duchamp, with a nude woman descending a spiral staircase into the artist's living-room; all that is visible of him are his white shoes as he also looks in on the scene. On the wall above the hearth hangs a version of Ballagh's reworking of *Delacroix*, while his own face appears on the television screen. As Ciaran Carty has suggested, the claustrophobia of this small, crowded room is evoked by the circular process of looking, set in

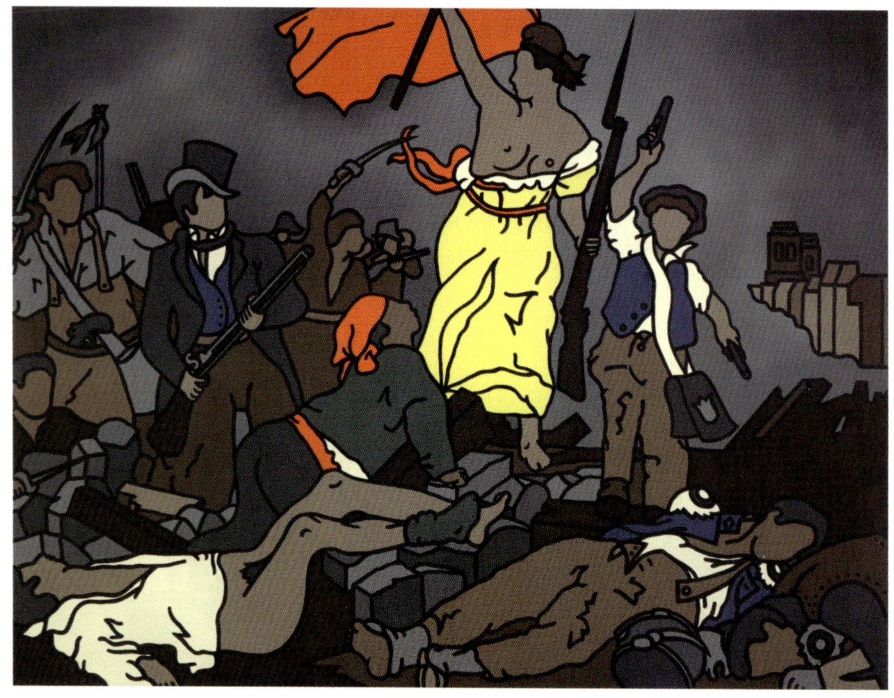

168 Robert Ballagh,
*Liberty on the Barricades
After Delacroix*, 1969–70,
acrylic on canvas.

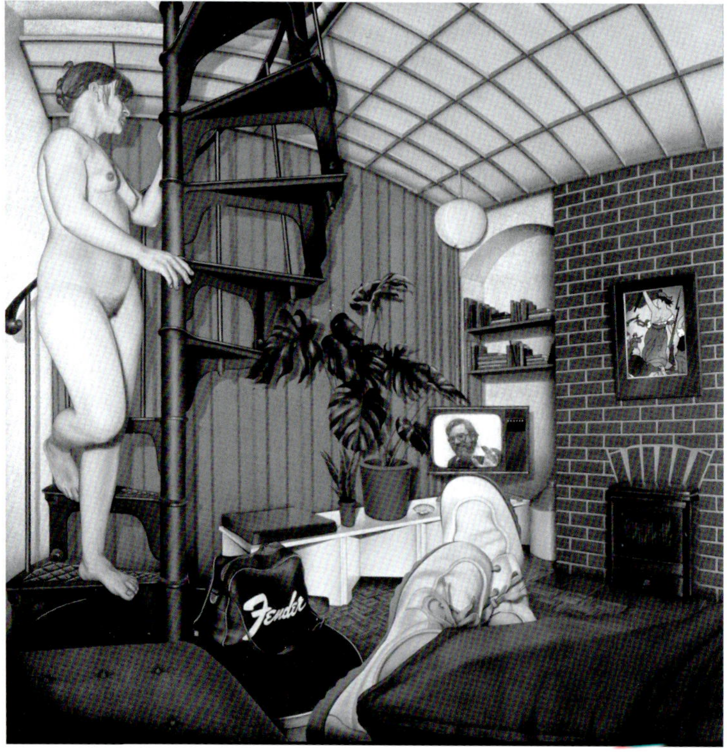

169 Robert Ballagh,
Inside No. 3, 1979, oil
on canvas.

motion by the woman on the staircase, both 'taking in [Ballagh's] own past [and] reflecting the turning around of his own approach to painting'.[27]

In addition to engaging with the politics of the North, the *Living Art* exhibition of 1972 in the Project Gallery had also embodied a move away from conventional forms of representation, concerns also central to the practice of some Irish-born artists working elsewhere. The work of James Coleman is a case in point. In the 1970s, in common with other avant-garde artists such as Vito Acconci or Bruce Nauman, Coleman increasingly began to investigate the representational qualities of time-based media such as video, tape–slide installation and performance. Fundamental to these media-based works was a destabilizing of cinematic conventions of narrative and spectatorship, such as the tape–slide installation *Clara and Dario* (1975), which investigated the selective and partial work of memory. Coleman's work conveys an oblique political commentary through self-conscious strategies of staging – a Brechtian focus on the means of representation that encourages viewers to question the implicit cultural references of the scenes that they observe.

In two works of the late 1970s, *Box (ahhareturnabout)* and *Strongbow*, Coleman engaged with aspects of Irishness in this manner. Yet these are also works that depend for their meaning on a fundamental sense of embodiment. The short film *Box* replays old documentary footage of the world heavyweight boxing championship fight between Gene Tunney and Jack Dempsey in Chicago in 1927. Both of the fighters were from Irish immigrant families; in controversial circumstances Tunney, the outsider, was declared the winner. The sound of a loud,

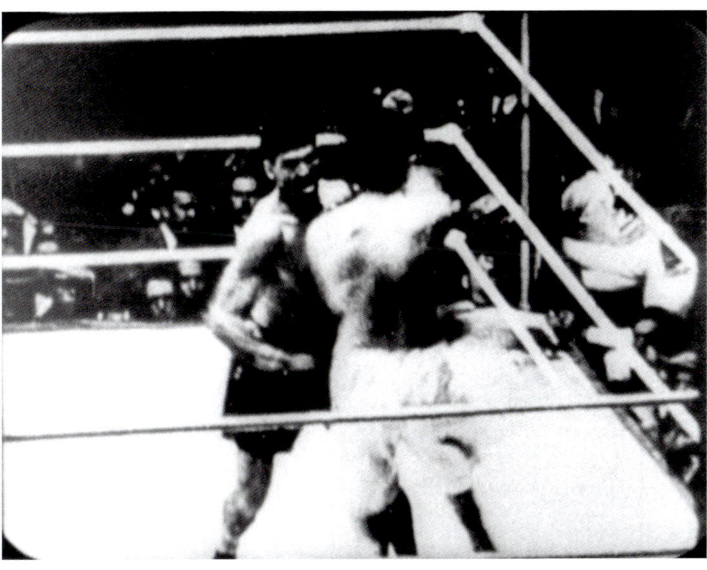

170 James Coleman, *Box (ahhareturnabout)*, 1977, 16mm black and white film, continuous cycle.

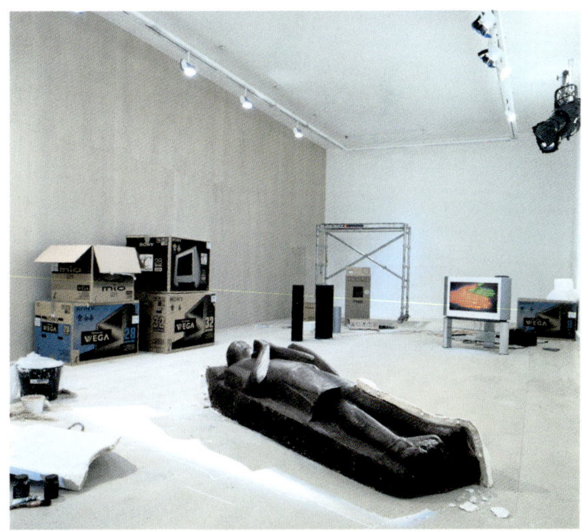

171 James Coleman, *Strongbow*, 1978–2000, plaster cast mould, Sony Art Couture monitor, polystyrene packing, scaffold tower, packing boxes, lighting, speakers, Betamax transferred onto DVD.

rhythmical heartbeat provides the temporal structure for the piece, underpinning the fragmented spoken soundtrack that represents Tunney's internal monologue during the gruelling match, combining references to both his present fight and Ireland's colonized past. As Jean Fisher suggests, part of his anguish is derived from his uncertain status as hero, a concern also raised in Coleman's slightly later *Strongbow*.[28] Here the replica of a twelfth-century tomb effigy, hands clasped in prayer, is juxtaposed with a video of two hands, one red and one green, clapping. As the knight sleeps on, the sound becomes progressively louder and faster; at its crescendo the after-image of the two hands merges the two colours together. In Daniel Maclise's epic history painting *The Marriage of Princess Aoife and Strongbow* the dynastic union of the Norman knight and Irish princess is seen as securing Ireland's colonial status. Coleman, however, suggests a more ambivalent figure, one between cultures, yet the symbolic usage of red and green also refers to Ireland's much later partition and troubles.

Coleman and Patrick Ireland were not the only Irish-born artists closely associated with the development of radical art practices on a more international scale. The conceptual artist Michael Craig-Martin grew up in an Irish Catholic emigrant family in the United States after spending his early years in Dublin. He later described the ensuing experience of displacement as fundamental to becoming an artist – a 'crisis of identity' that involves a sense of 'feeling both comfortable and uncomfortable everywhere'.[29] Yet in the 1970s there were other connections with Irish culture attributable to his practice. One of Craig-Martin's best-known pieces, *An Oak Tree*, consists of a glass of water on a shelf displayed in a gallery. In addition to suggesting Duchamp's belief that everyday objects can be works of art, it also embodies the tendency of conceptualist art to privilege the

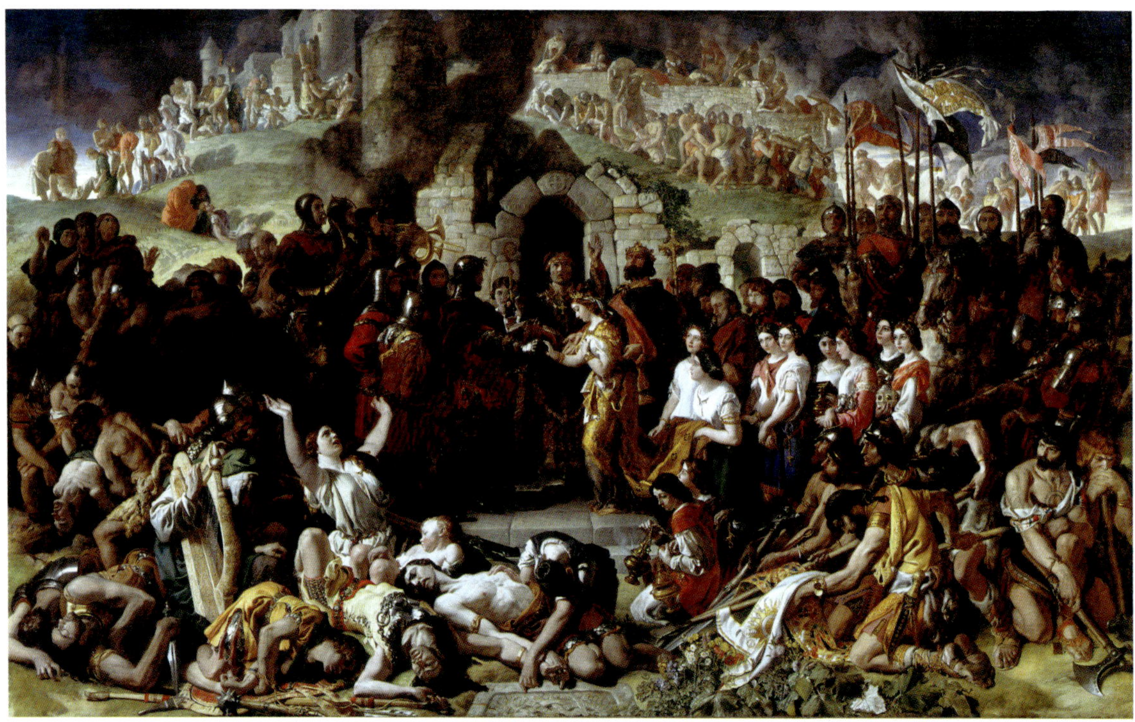

172 Daniel Maclise, *The Marriage of Princess Aoife and Strongbow*, 1854, oil on canvas.

173 Michael Craig-Martin, *An Oak Tree*, Oliver Dowling Gallery, Dublin, 1973, mixed media.

idea behind the art above the object itself. When the work was first exhibited at the Rowan Gallery in London it was accompanied by a leaflet that explained, in the form of a dialogue, that its physical presence is actually something very different from what it appears to be; what looked like a glass of water, the artist claimed, was in fact an oak tree. It has often been noted that, as a former altar boy, Craig-Martin was drawing on the Catholic doctrine of transubstantiation, where the bread and wine of the sacrament are at the same time the body and blood of Christ.[30]

The increasing international visibility of conceptualism also included artworks that did not depend on the gallery space for their existence. Often ephemeral or site-specific, they survive only through their documentation in the form of written accounts, preparatory drawings or photographs. In 1976 the sculptor Brian King, also teaching at the National College of Art and

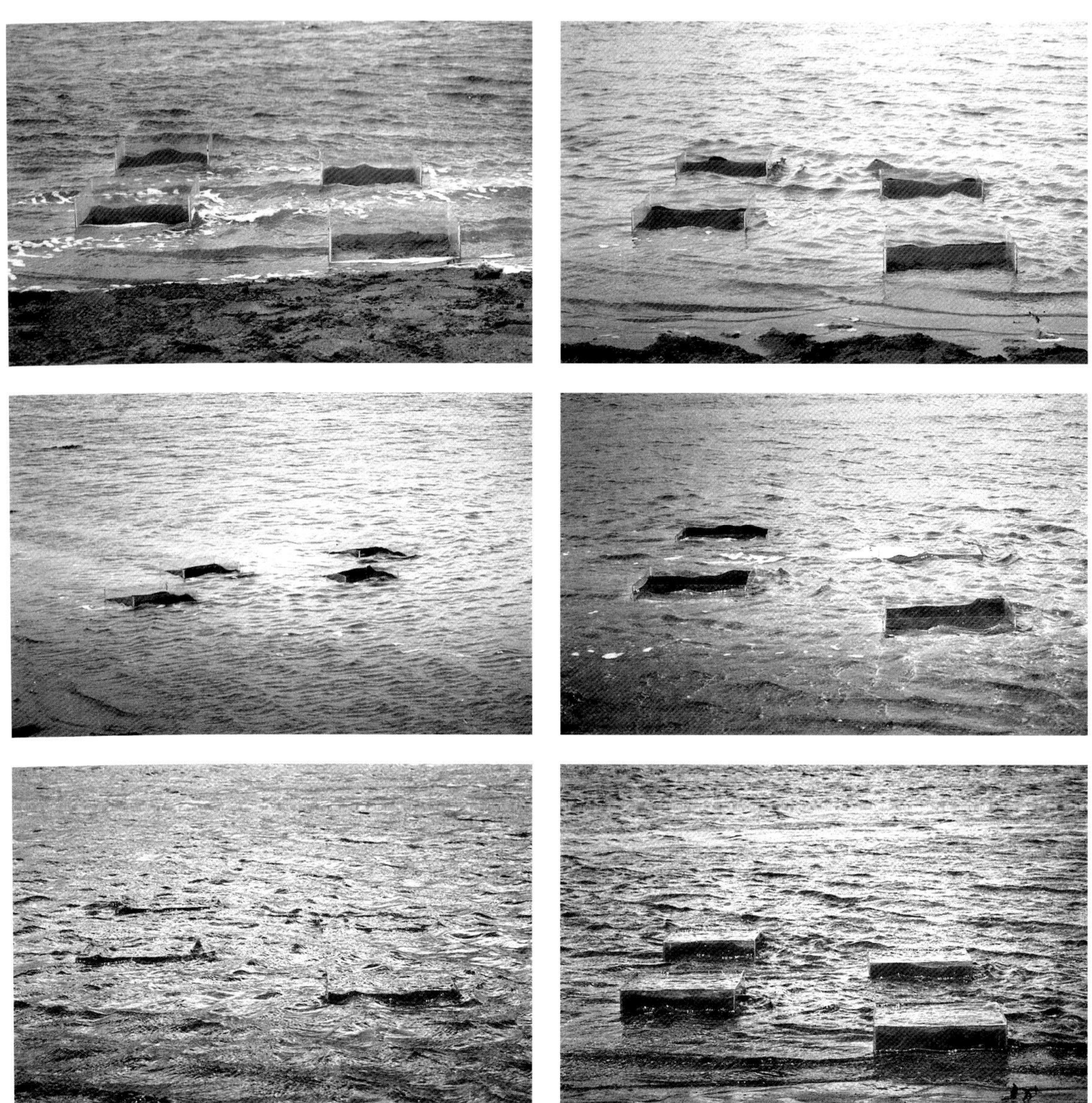

174 Brian King, *Sea Holes*, 1976, glass.

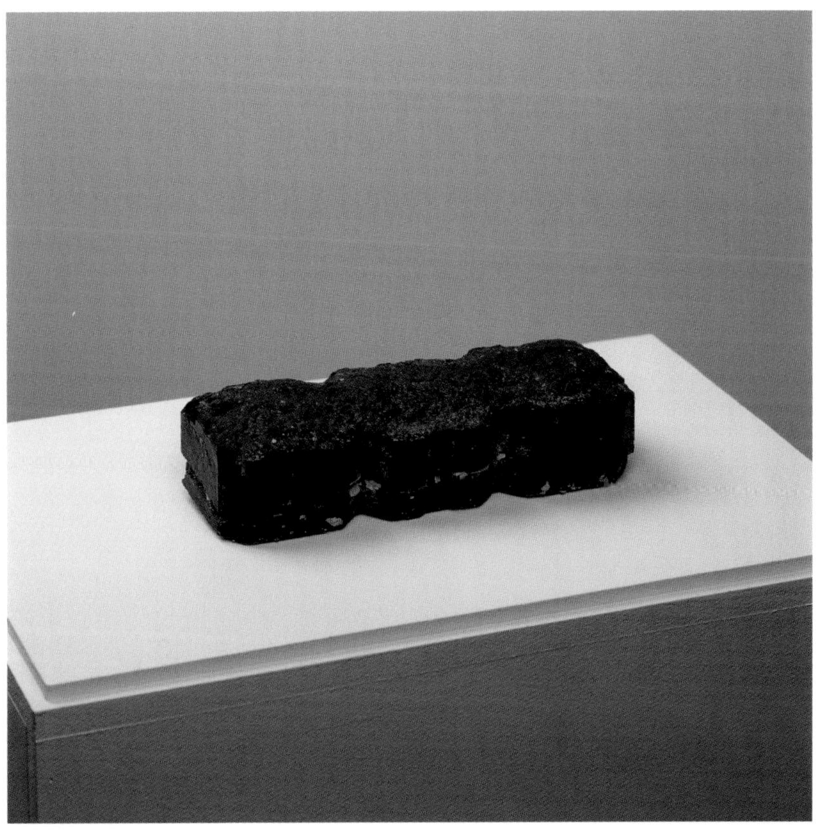

175 Joseph Beuys,
Irish Energy I, 1974,
peat briquette
with butter.

Design (NCAD), took a group of his students to Cumeen Strand in Sligo, where they made a group of site-specific works using the available natural materials. King's own work from this project, however, combined environmental concerns with earlier interests carried over from his hard-edge minimalist sculptures shown at the 1969 Paris Biennale. *Sea Holes* consisted of four glass boxes arranged in a grid format at the water's edge. The incoming tide first surrounded them, leaving four empty spaces in the sea as it reached the top; as water filtered in and the tide receded, the pillars of sea water were left on the beach and gradually drained away. The process was then repeated with the next tide cycle. Although such environmental art projects were influenced by American Land Artists such as Robert Smithson and Walter de Maria, they had a particular significance in Ireland due to the layered meanings of landscape, par-

ticularly in the West. Indeed the concern with prehistory also found in Smithson's earthworks took on further site-specific meanings in King's choice of location in Sligo, where he had long been interested in the numerous Neolithic sites in the area.[31]

The emergence of a range of artistic practices other than painting began to ensure the further erosion of Irish modernism. International precedents were available at first hand through the *Rosc* exhibitions of both 1971 and 1977; the latter included work by Joseph Beuys derived from his perceptions of Ireland. In addition to the photo-work *Northern Irish Tongue*, the piece *Irish Energy I* consisted of peat briquettes sandwiched together with Kerrygold butter. Both works date from Beuys's first visit to Ireland in 1974, when his previously unexhibited drawings collectively entitled *A Secret Block for a Secret Person in Ireland* were shown in Dublin and

Belfast. Beuys was known not only as an artist, but also for his radical ideas on art education, and after his dismissal from his teaching post at Düsseldorf Academy of Art in 1972 he founded the Free International University (FIU). Throughout the 1970s Beuys actively pursued plans to establish a permanent base for FIU in Ireland. Through his charismatic spoken presentations at venues both north and south of the border – a mixture of pedagogy and performance – and the production of talismanic objects from found materials, Beuys provided a model for the breakdown of the polarities of art and life. His visits to Ireland throughout the 1970s were to have lasting effects on art practice.[32] This included the development of performance art in Ireland, through both the practice of Alistair MacLennan and his work at the Belfast College of Art from 1975 onwards, and in the work of Nigel Rolfe, both as performer and teacher at NCAD.

The survival of modernism

In spite of these important developments, modernism was still alive and well in Irish art practice. Sculptural abstraction became a feature of institutional commissions by banks and other corporate patrons, continuing well into the 1980s with works by Michael Warren and Michael Bulfin. This was an area where the influence of sculpture in the United States was particularly apparent, in the minimalist experimentation with materials such as Perspex by Alexandra Wejchert, or the increased use of painted steel by Bulfin and others. *Sails*, Gerda Frömel's commission for Carroll's factory at Dundalk in 1970, also used stainless steel, in the construction of three large wind sails, whose slow movements were reflected in the pool of water in which they stand. In a supportive economic climate, corporate sponsorship enabled the practice of

large-scale sculpture to develop; yet the experimental and at the time radical nature of this was not universal. Public commissions, such as Oisin Kelly's *Children of Lir* for the Garden of Remembrance in Parnell Square in Dublin, still tended to be much more conservative.

Its potential discovered later than many European counterparts, the expressive capabilities of modernism continued to be explored and adapted by Irish artists such as Seán Scully. Much of the critical writing about Scully represents his work in terms of an abstract, self-referential domain: for Donald Kuspit, Scully is 'more of a Greenbergian purist than he might care to acknowledge'.[33] Yet abstract painting is also legible as a highly encoded engagement with aspects of lived experience. Although born in Dublin in 1945, Scully's family moved to London when he was four. In his own account it was the discovery of painting – a reproduction of Picasso's *Child with a Dove* – that helped to compensate for his sense of loss at the time; in his words, 'It was the only thing that gave me any consolation for my sad existence.'[34] This suggests a world separate from the day-to-day existence of an Irish child in a British city of the 1950s where, like other immigrant groups, the Irish experienced relentless racism.

The same sense of an autonomous, self-contained reality also informs the construction of Scully's abstract paintings of the 1970s. These works can be seen as in dialogue with American art practice of the previous decade, as in the minimalist grid that structures *Overlay # 9* (1974), or in the shaped canvas and stripes of the first painting in this series, *Overlay 1* (1973), which is more suggestive of Frank Stella's post-painterly abstraction. During the 1960s, Micheal Farrell had also looked closely at Stella, but unlike Farrell's appropriation of aspects of Stella's technique in the interests of a deconstruction of aspects of material reality, Scully uses

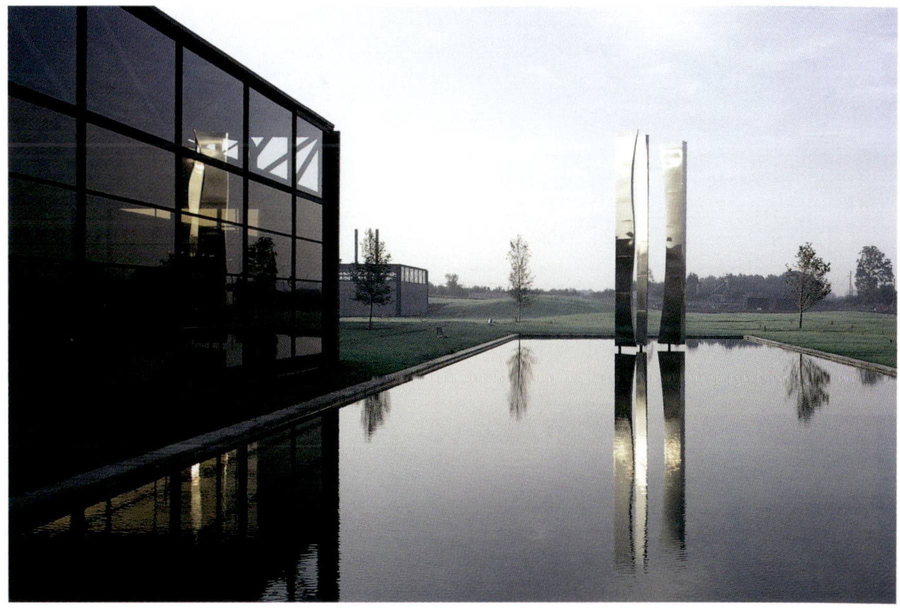

176 Gerda Frömel,
Sails, 1970,
stainless steel.

them here as suggestive of a more spiritual domain. Another, perhaps unlikely, comparison with Farrell is in the two artists' engagement with notions of the Celtic in their work. As Dorothy Walker observed, the densely interwoven textures of Scully's paintings of the 1970s are also suggestive of the 'Celtic interlacing, layered linearity' that characterized Early Christian Irish art such as that found in the ninth-century Book of Kells.[35]

Even work that *appeared* to be securely modernist could also be pulled into frameworks of interpretation related to the situation in the North. James Johnson Sweeney could still describe Cecil King's hard-edge abstraction in thoroughly Greenbergian terms as 'an object complete in itself' that 'speaks to us through the sensibility of its relationships and the compositional order of its parts without requiring interpretation'.[36] In 1970, however, writing about King's *Berlin Suite*, a series of prints, Ethna Waldron also referred to 'a disturbing element, that undermining high-powered tension

which permeates each individual print echoing and re-echoing the artist's complete despondency at the sight of the divided city of Berlin'.[37] Although they reference a different location, concern with political division and tension in Northern Ireland was still very much a part of many artists' consciousness at this time. Dorothy Walker observed retrospectively that much of the abstract painting in Ireland during the 1970s 'relied heavily on the colour black', possibly as a reaction to the deteriorating situation in the North.[38] She included within this both Tony O'Malley's dark, brooding compositions and Anne Madden's hard-edge series based on the megalithic remains embedded within the Irish landscape. This was a theme that preoccupied Madden throughout the decade. The artist was explicit about the relevance of contemporary events to these works:

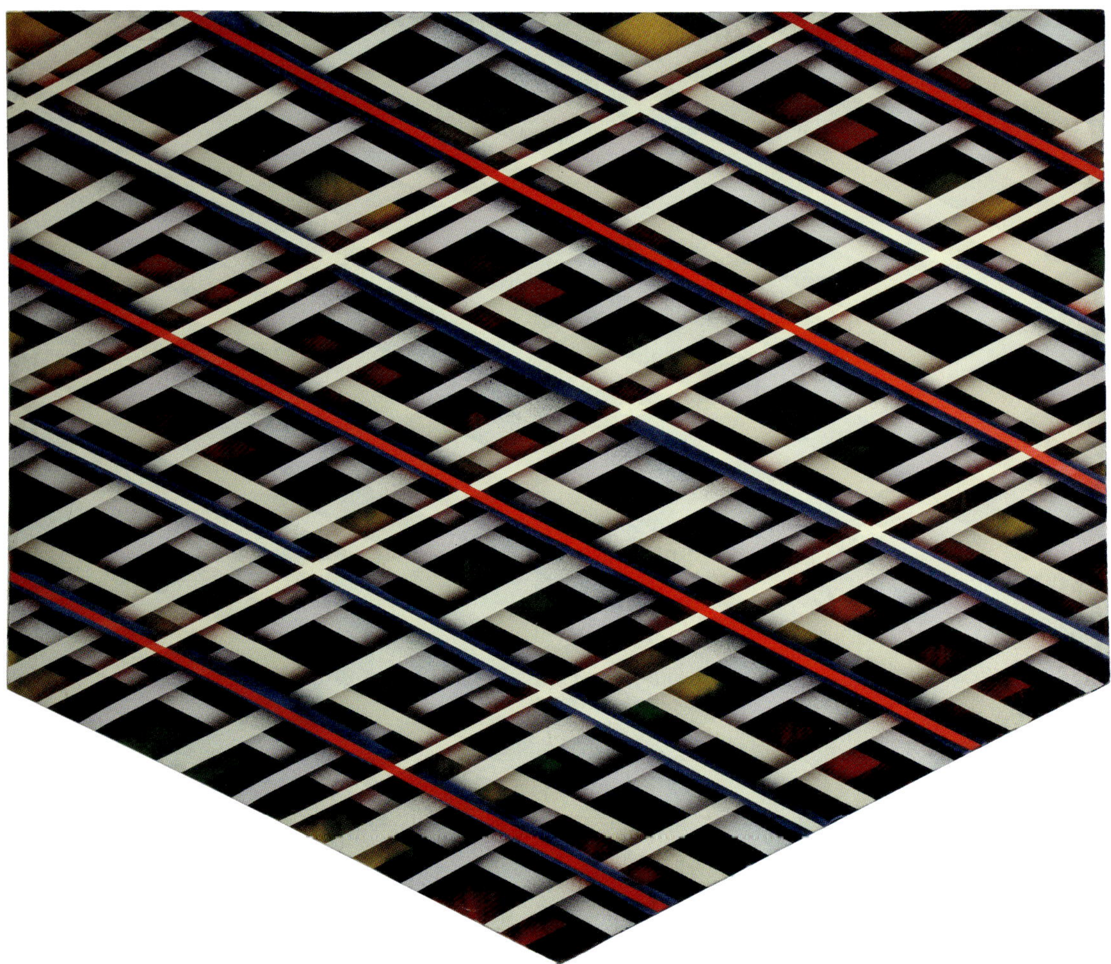

177 Seán Scully, *East Coast Light* I,
1973, acrylic on canvas.

They tended to be dark tonally, reflections of grief, of the Irish landscape, of an instinctive search to find or extract light from darkness; elegies of personal grief but also to the terrible and tragic events in Northern Ireland.[39]

In these large works, such as the triptych *Megalith (Pierres Levées)*, Expressionist features of her earlier paintings are replaced by a tightly controlled, architectural composition. Vertical zips of contrasting colour delineate areas of darkness, suggestive of the bulk of these remains within the landscape.

In the mid- to late 1960s, Louis le Brocquy's work was characterized by the emergence of Irish themes, continuing throughout the rest of his career. The *Reconstructed Head of an Irish Martyr* (1967) suggests Oliver

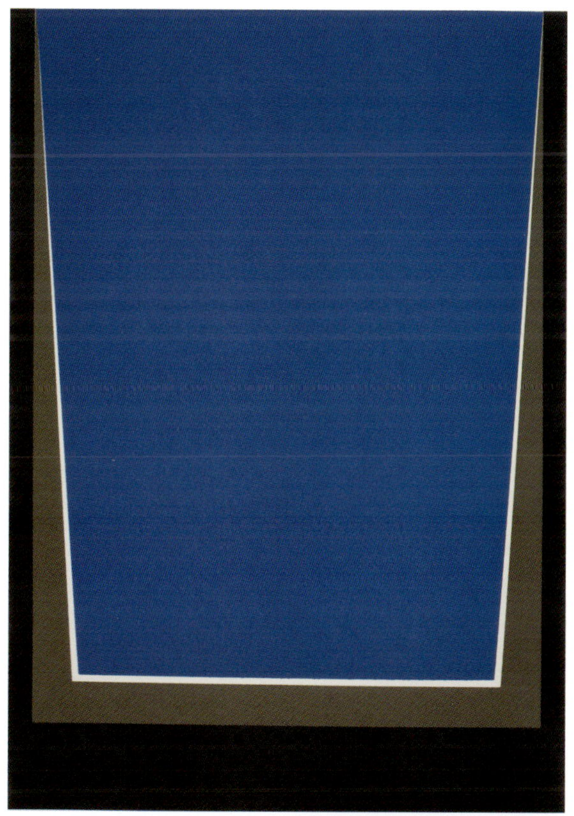

178 Cecil King, *Berlin Suite I*, 1970, screenprint.

Plunkett, the Catholic cleric hung, drawn and quartered by the English in 1680 and whose preserved skull is still kept as a relic in Drogheda Cathedral. Le Brocquy's painted heads increasingly operate in domains of history and language, yet they still retain their atavistic connotations, similar to his brush and ink drawings for *The Tain*. In 1967 Liam Millar of Dolmen Press commissioned the poet Thomas Kinsella to make a new translation of *Táin bo Cuailnge* (The Cattle-raid of Cooley), an ancient Celtic saga surviving only through written sections dating from the eighth century and later. Kinsella's version, illustrated by le Brocquy's drawings, was published in 1969; le Brocquy subsequently used a selection of the images as a basis for a series of tapestries. Anne Madden described the commission as 'an attempt to imbue a series of spontaneous, almost autonomous, brush drawings with the violence and hieratic qualities of the proto-historic myth'.[40] Suggestive rather than descriptive, 'The Tain' retells the story of the attempts by the armies of Queen Medhbh (Maeve) to capture the prized Brown Bull of Cooley, only to be repeatedly thwarted by the Herculean efforts of Cuchulainn, the champion of Ulster, who mercilessly kills and

179 Anne Madden, *Megalith (Pierres Levées)*, 1974, acrylic on canvas duck.

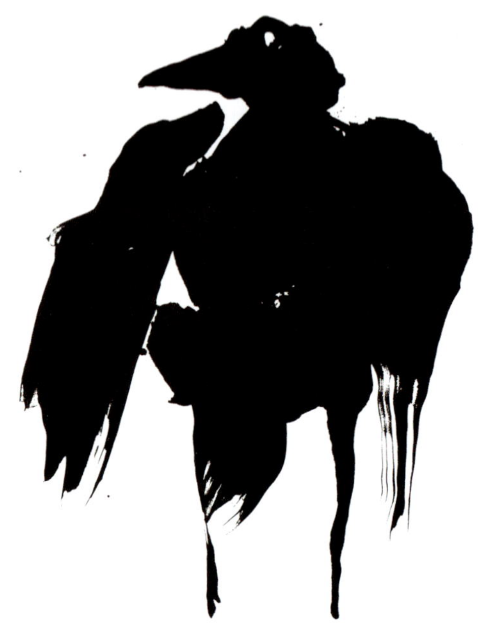

180 Louis le Brocquy, 'The Morrigan', 1967, illustration for Thomas Kinsella's translation of the *Táin bo Cuailnge*.

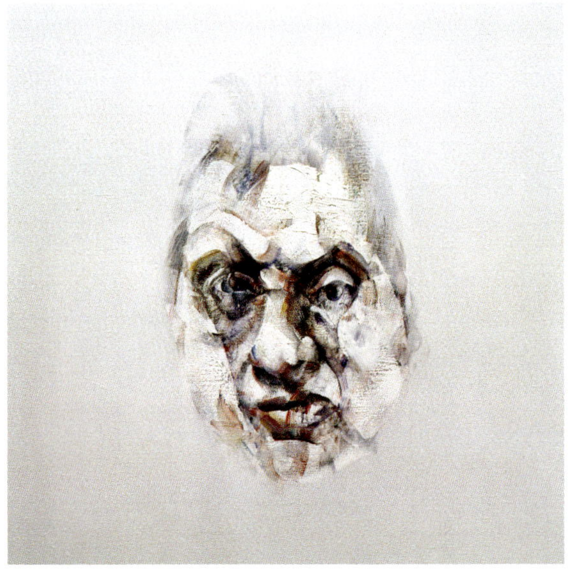

181 Louis le Brocquy, *Head of Francis Bacon* (detail), 1979, oil on canvas.

decapitates swathes of the enemy. One of the areas of fascination of this story for le Brocquy was that it signified 'the earliest memories of the Irish'.[41] Its representation of the savagery of ancient tribal conflict also, in 1969, bore some relevance to perceptions of the deteriorating situation in the North. Other work by le Brocquy also commented on this: open-mouthed heads, some blocked by hands as if in an attempt to ward off the oncoming blow.

Throughout the 1970s and onwards, le Brocquy's work was preoccupied with series of heads of the triumvirate of Irish modernist writers, Yeats, Joyce and Beckett. All expatriates (including Yeats at the time of his death), these figures represent the moments at which Irish writing could be seen to enter the mainstream of

modern European culture. As literary equivalents to le Brocquy's own practice, his engagement with these figures also involves a prolonged meditation on the status and visibility of the modernist artist in exile. Other heads, of Lorca, Bacon and Picasso, also appeared at this time. According to Richard Kearney, the blending of 'ancient and modern' in the heads amounts to a deconstruction of linear temporality, 'an ambivalent co-existence of different time-frames'.[42] This is one of many factors, including a concern for simulation, repetition without a recognizable point of origin, that for Kearney contributes to a reading of le Brocquy as a postmodernist. Perhaps, however, it is accurate to describe these as works in transition, since they still bear hallmarks of a modernist consciousness as well. The well-established appropriation of the archaic and the primitive provides a position from which to comment on the culture of modernity through the obsessive fascination with the intellectual presence of its key figures.

Coda: where are the women?

The 1970s was also the decade that saw the re-emergence of a strong women's movement in Southern Ireland, and the appearance of women playing key roles in constitutional politics for the first time since Ireland's independence. Feminism was becoming established as a significant political and cultural force.[43] Yet in spite of the progressive and gradual modernization of the social status of women in Ireland, what was happening at the level of the image, or in the visibility of women as artists, was somewhat different, suggesting a hegemonic denial of women as actively moving to control their own lives. With the exception of Anne Madden, the work of women artists was marginal to the shifting debates around art practice in Ireland during the 1970s. And as Dorothy Walker observed, the replacement of Norah McGuinness as President of *Living Art* by Brian King in 1972 was followed by a lack of women exhibiting at IELA; by 1975 only three women artists were selected by the all-male committee, in comparison with 28 a decade previously.[44]

As the subjects of representation the visibility of women was also highly contingent. In Louis le Brocquy's work, the inchoate female body of the earlier 'Presences' had largely disappeared, superseded by male cerebrality in his preoccupation with Irish modernist writers. Yet women's bodies were also very much on display elsewhere, as the vehicle for a naturalistic Duchampian pastiche descending Robert Ballagh's staircase, or splayed out for consumption in Farrell's

Madonna Irlanda. It is important to remember that this objectification of women was most fully realized at a time when actual women were becoming particularly visible within Irish culture, and debates around women's control over their own bodies were becoming central to the political agenda.

NINE

Postmodernism and Ireland

On a global scale, the 1980s were a decade when major shifts in representational practices, and ideas about the meaning of representation itself, were taking shape in the context of significant changes to Western society and philosophy. Although modernism took different forms, its key theoretical formulations by mandarin critics such as Clement Greenberg proposed both a significant emphasis on the autonomy and authenticity of artistic experience and a progressive purification of its means of expression.[1] These imperatives had been considerably undermined since the 1960s, with Pop art's and Minimalism's very different strategies for reinstating a relationship with the world beyond the art object. Postmodernism took this further into the emergence of art practices that questioned a sense of progressive development from earlier forms of representation, instead re-visiting them through strategies of pastiche and irony. This was accompanied by the re-evaluation of the hierarchies of art practice that privileged painting and sculpture in favour of relatively marginal forms such as photography and digital or time-based work. Often cited as a breakdown of categories of 'high' and 'low' culture and an increasing eclecticism, these new shifts in art practice investigated the changing notion of identity.

Postmodernism became a means whereby challenges to the progressive logic of modernity could be acknowledged and contested. The situation north and south of the Irish border was radically different, however. Having spent the last two decades or so building a relationship with international capitalism, the Republic's economic decline in the 1980s and accumulated foreign debt signalled a major crisis of modernity. Meanwhile, the accelerating rate of emigration, including that of skilled graduates, could no longer be separated from the decolonizing narrative of nation-building. Economic instability and other crises throughout the decade became contexts for art-making; the potential for both a radical critique of social and cultural institutions and of representational practices themselves emerged in this context. As we have seen, modernism and modernity were experienced very differently in Ireland from metropolitan cultural centres such as New York or Paris. Postmodernism and its relationship to shifting underlying social, economic and political conditions also took on specific inflections.

One place where these were addressed was the magazine *Circa*, a cross-border initiative established in 1981, which increasingly helped to situate Irish art within a critical discourse. Writing in *Circa* in 1989, John Hutchinson recognized a problematic relationship for Irish artists with postmodernism. Hutchinson argued that 'if "critical" Postmodernism remains largely undeveloped in the South, this isn't the case in the North', where artists were working in the context of a major crisis of authority represented by both the ongoing conflict and post-industrial decline.[2] The 1980s also represented a further crisis of authority as the politics of the Irish body became inescapable. This ranged from, in the North, the 'No Wash' protests by both male and female prisoners in the Maze and Armagh gaols and the subsequent hunger strike, to the fierce debates around abortion and women's control of their own sexuality in the South.

In 1983, a proposed amendment to the Constitution that would have legalized abortion was defeated in a referendum by a two-to-one majority, as was an attempt to change legislation banning divorce three years later. In earlier years the consequences of a lack of readily available birth control or access to pregnancy termination remained hidden. In the mid-1980s, by comparison, the death of Ann Lovett and the infamous Kerry Babies case received extensive coverage.[3] In January 1984 a young teenager, Ann Lovett, and her baby died after she gave birth alone and unaided in a religious grotto outside a church in Granard. For the Catholic Church it was safer to focus on the hallucinatory appeal of the allegedly moving statue of Our Lady at Ballinaspiddle in County Cork rather than on the actuality of a young woman dying at the feet of another Virgin, in a small town in Ireland's desolate centre. For many women, in addition to high unemployment, the repressive attempts of Church and state to control their bodies were enough to tip the balance towards emigration. These hotly contested issues were also to form an important context for Irish art practice in the 1980s.

Neo-Expressionism in an Irish context: landscape and the body

Far from undermining painting during the 1980s, the re-evaluation of the hierarchies of art practice provided a context whereby its values could be re-asserted. The legacy of post-war American painters such as Jackson Pollock ensured that brushstroke and gesture were associated with unmediated authenticity of experience and the primacy of feeling – categories challenged by postmodernism. The correlative to the deconstructive practices of postmodernist art was the re-assertion of Expressionist painting. This was a type of representation dependent on precisely the values that postmodernism rejected – painting as a vehicle for the unmediated authenticity of the artist's response at an intuitive level. Yet the global predominance of neo-Expressionism during the 1980s also converged in Ireland with a modernism that had been developed later, and in different conditions, than elsewhere. By this point in the century Expressionism had acquired a deeply canonical significance in Ireland, partly through its associations with the work of Jack B. Yeats, and what this represented in terms of Irish cultural identity. Significantly painting, and particularly abstraction, continued to have a particular sense of cultural validity in Ireland throughout the decade.

Perhaps unsurprisingly, a concern with the western seaboard continued as a focus of art practice during the 1980s. This was the location that played such a major role in the hegemonic construction of modernity in the formation of the Free State: now it became the site for a re-invigorated modernist painting. This could take different forms. At the start of the decade, Camille Souter's paintings of Shannon airport, far from an explicit engagement with corporate modernity, focused on issues of space and formal composition.[4] Yeatsian antecedents, meanwhile, continued to be very

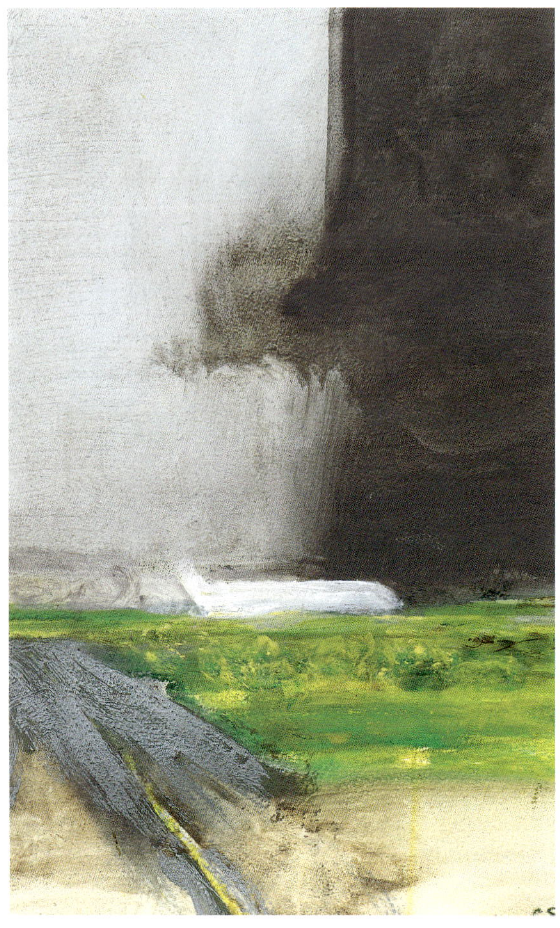

182 Camille Souter, *Storm at Shannon*, c. 1980, oil on paper.

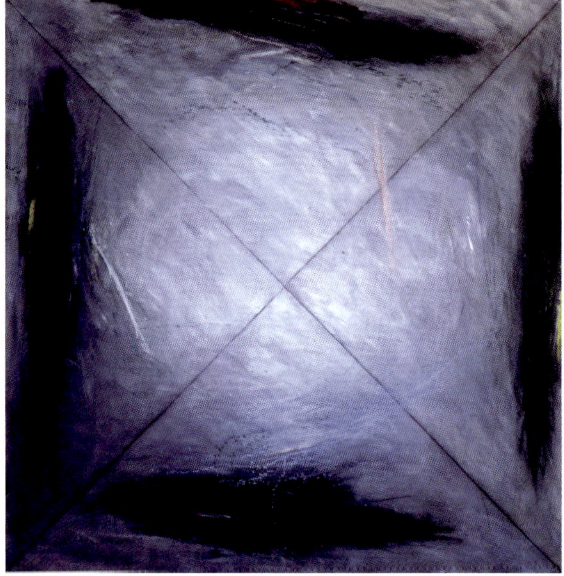

183 Charles Tyrrell, *Slow Turn*, 1987, acrylic on canvas.

much in play in the ongoing lyricism of Patrick Collins's depictions of the West, or in the work of the younger Seán McSweeney and Gwen O'Dowd.

Yet the increasingly pervasive presence of postmodernism meant that abstraction in Ireland also underwent processes of reassessment, largely in the form of what Aidan Dunne noted as 'an expanded realm of referentiality'.[5] Rather than a concern with formal elements alone, for example, painters like Samuel Walsh and Charles Tyrrell increasingly began to incorporate landscape features into their work. In Tyrrell's case this was reinforced by his move to the remote Beara Peninsula in West Cork in 1984. An early interest in Abstract Expres-

sionist painterliness was superseded, as in *Slow Turn* (1987), by a concern for framing and the imposition of a geometric structure on more fluid elements within. This was a feature of Tyrrell's work that he later described as 'a window through to the elemental'.[6]

In the case of other abstract artists, such as Mary Fitzgerald and Felim Egan, the trace of the body was not far from the surface of the works. Egan's inclusion of sculptural contours of neon tubing on the painted surface suggested allusions to the curves of the body and to musical rhythms. These references sometimes became more explicitly figurative in painted works such as *The Battle of Hercules and Antaeus* (1984), also

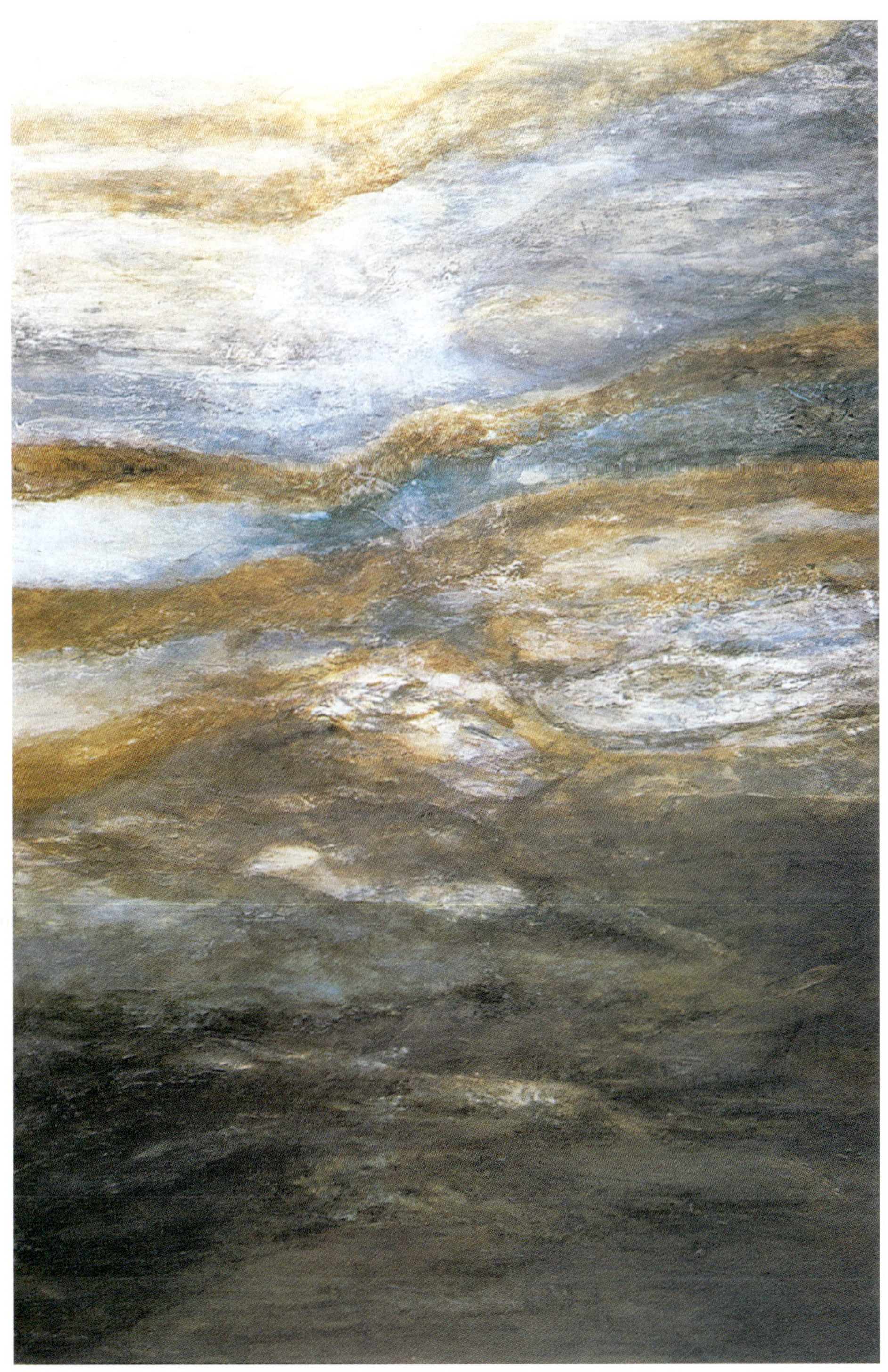

184 Gwen O'Dowd, *Glór na Mara*, 1989, encaustic on canvas.

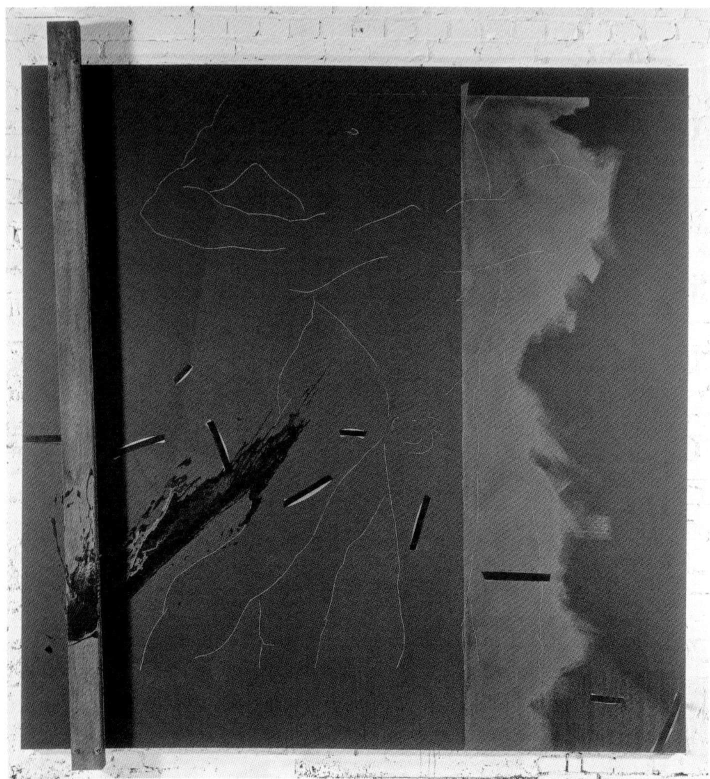

185 Felim Egan, *The Battle of Hercules and Antaeus*, 1984, mixed media on canvas.

Irish cultural identity were once more in flux. Cultural references were beginning to expand beyond the founding narratives of nation to engage with more universal underpinnings of Western culture.

Although neo-Expressionism can be seen as a conservative retrenchment in the face of the new, it also had a more radical potential. In Germany, where another version of Expressionism had been embedded within early twentieth-century modernism, painters such as Anselm Kiefer and A. R. Penck in the 1980s appropriated its means for the interrogation of Germany's recent history and identity. Expressionism, both in its earlier German and post-war American versions, also had deep associations with sexuality. The use of colour and gesture became an index of the painter's emotions as raw, violent and intuitive, capable of conveying sex and anger repressed beneath a civilized veneer. In American Abstract Expressionism the brushstroke with its drips and smears became legible as the trace of (usually) the male artist's presence, an apparent guarantee of his strength of feeling. These two contradictory aspects of Expressionism, both its critical potential and its associations with conservative, heteronormative masculinity, were significant for the development of neo-Expressionism in Ireland during the 1980s. For the Independent Artists, a group associated with the Project Arts Centre in Dublin, which included Michael Kane, Eithne Jordan and Anita Groener, Expressionism had an important role in the investigation of aspects of cultural, social and political identity. However, no women were included in the first exhibition to signal the adoption of neo-Expressionism

underpinned by a mythological subtext. Indeed, the 1980s was a decade when mythological themes in Irish art practice began to derive from sources outside the imagery of the Celtic past that had featured in earlier years. On one level these still persisted, as in Brian Bourke's focus on the legend of Sweeney, but important sources of the mythical and archetypal began to extend to Greek mythology in the work of Egan and Patrick Hall, or beyond, as in Michael Mulcahy's interpretations. Neo-Expressionism's concerns with the unconscious and the intuitive also encouraged the investigation of the mythological. There is a further significance in the case of Irish art practice, suggesting that the strong links between the Celtic and issues of in Ireland, *Making Sense: Ten Painters, 1963–1983* at the Project in 1983.

Critical tendencies also surfaced prominently in the work of Brian Maguire, whose major exhibition of 1988 at the Douglas Hyde Gallery was accompanied by a catalogue written by Donald Kuspit, the American critic primarily associated with neo-Expressionism.[7] The subject of *Divis Flats* was a notorious housing complex in Catholic West Belfast, synonymous with some of the worst features of the conflict in Northern Ireland. The isolated figure hemmed in on three sides by the oppressive grey architecture is a format that recurs also in later works by Maguire dealing with the effects of institutions on individuals. *The Big House* (1990) was derived from his experience of working in Port Laoise Prison, which contained many republican inmates – many also the products of a similar urban deprivation to that evoked in *Divis Flats*. However, as Caoimhín Mac Giolla Léith has observed, without the specificity of its titling this earlier painting 'might be read as an anguished depiction of existential despair'.[8]

Specific references to Irish culture, rather than a generalized state of alienation, are more visibly embedded in neo-Expressionist works by Patrick Graham, such as *My Darkish Rosaleen*. In spite of the title's reference to the popular song with its romantic feminine personification of the nation, like Micheal Farrell before him, Graham represents Ireland's female embodiment in highly sexualized terms. The female figure, clad in stockings and suspenders, is surrounded by shamrocks.

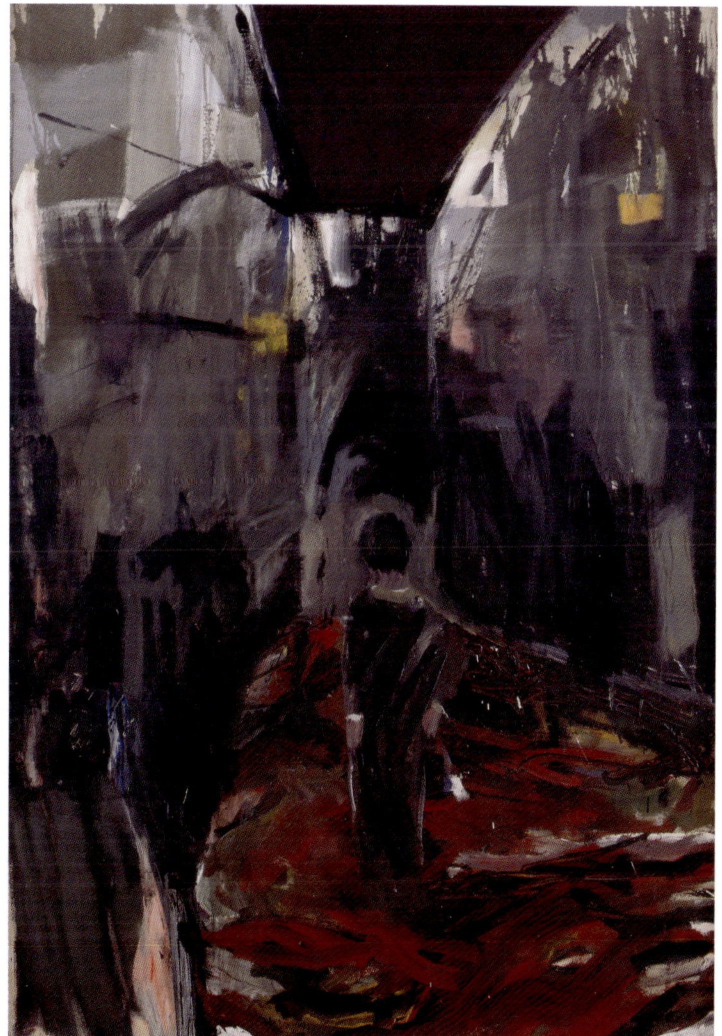

186 Brian Maguire, *Divis Flats*, 1985, acrylic on canvas.

References to the two main political parties, Fianna Fáil and Fine Gael, suggest that Ireland's body politic is available to the highest bidder. The use of the iconic, eroticized female subject is indicative of a time when the representation of sexuality was so firmly on the agenda for Irish artists, within the wider context of the political issues surrounding women's bodies and identities. Much of neo-Expressionism in Ireland was fundamentally conservative, affirming a normative heterosexual masculinity. In the work of Michael Mulcahy this was

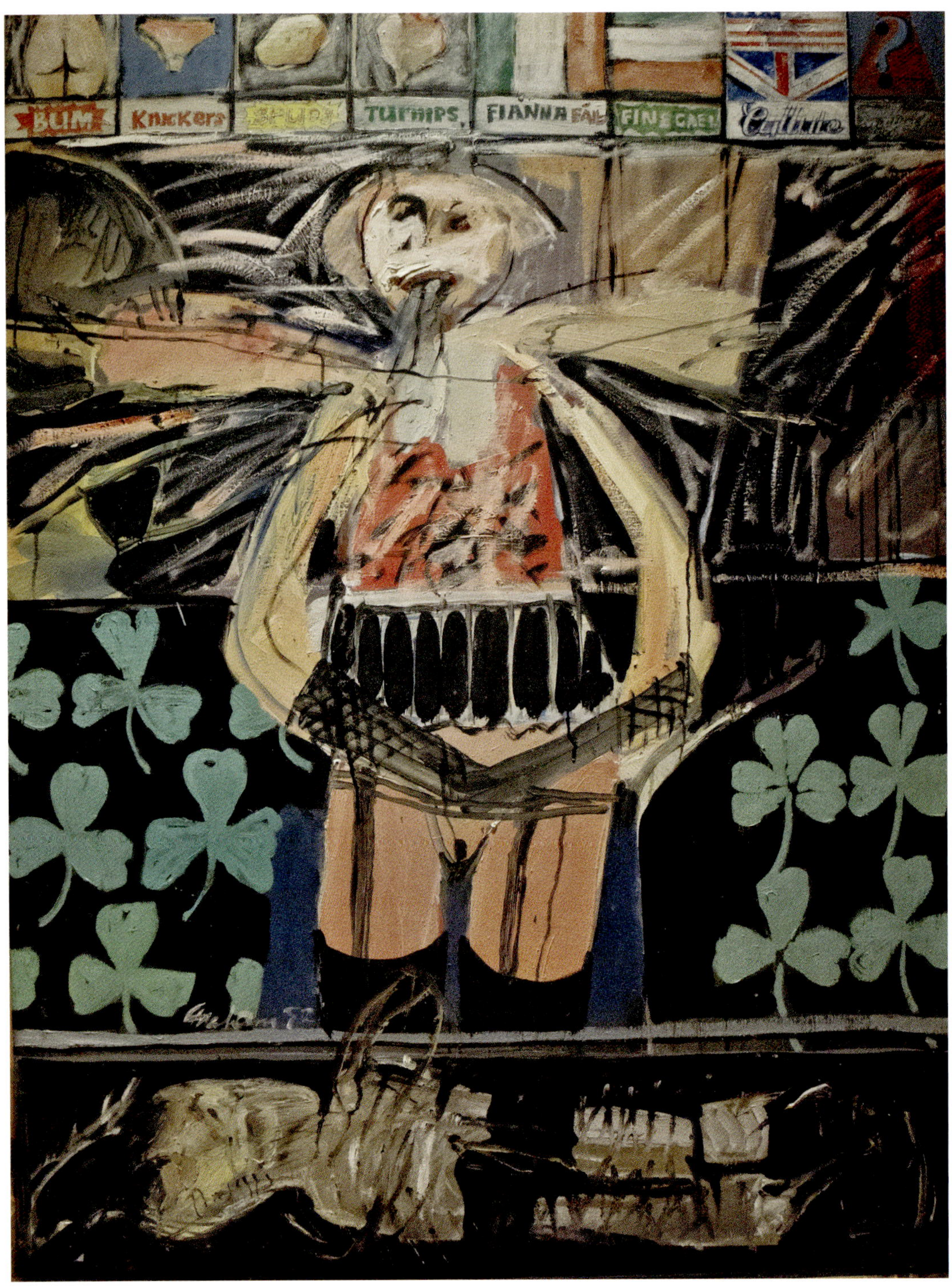

187 Patrick Graham, *My Darkish Rosaleen*, 1982, oil on canvas.

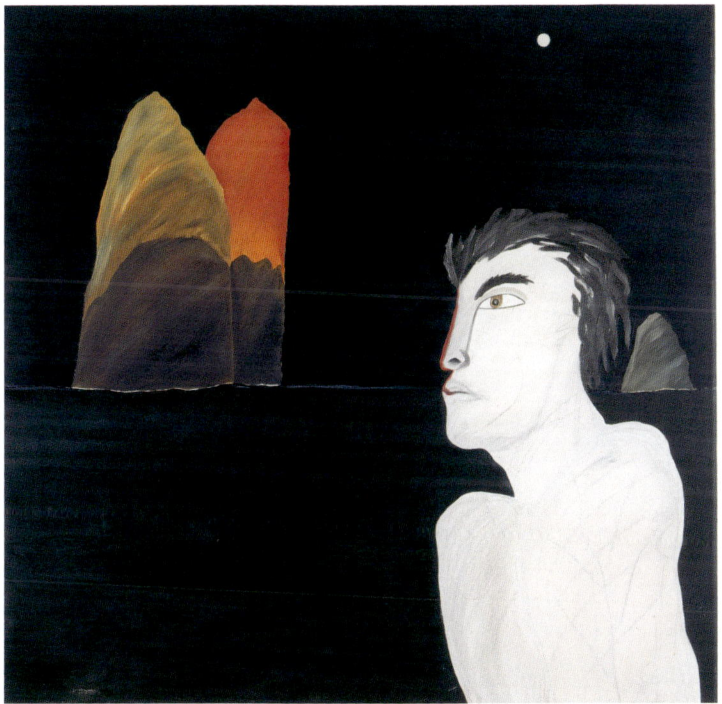

188 Michael Mulcahy, *Navigator*, 1982, oil on canvas.

allied to a shamanic identity, whereby the artist adopts a visionary role. Mulcahy's work was fuelled by periods of time spent with nomadic peoples in Africa and Australia. Remarkably unscathed by emergent debates around race and primitivism in the 1980s, he continued to produce paintings both infused with his own sense of mysticism and reminiscent of contemporary Italian painters such as Francesco Clemente. The title of *Navigator* (1982) recalls the sixth-century Irish saint Brendan, reputed to have explored the Atlantic.[9] However, as an image loaded with sexual tension between the male figure and the breast-like shapes emergent from the dark background, it also suggests woman as the dark continent awaiting penetration.

By comparison, Patrick Hall's paintings offered a more interrogative approach both to the body and questions of masculine identity. Hall's work of the 1980s, such as the series entitled *The Flaying of Marsyas*, used Expressionism as a means of pushing the representation of the body almost to the point of disintegration. John Hutchinson has observed that, 'In Hall's paintings bodily and mental space is internalized in such a way that our familiar conceptions of "wholeness" are split wide open.'[10] The result is a sense of loss of identity, a state that Hall has suggested is fundamental to his process of painting: 'For me lostness is where, in full view of my limitations, I can draw on the necessary energy to paint well.'[11] Yet significantly these were paintings that were also made in the context of a growing awareness of AIDS in Ireland, primarily affecting the male gay community.

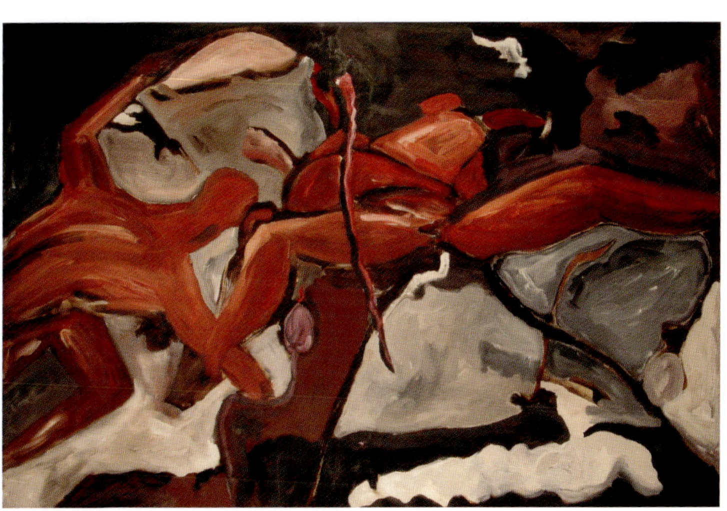

189 Patrick Hall, *The Flaying of Marsyas II*, 1984, acrylic on canvas.

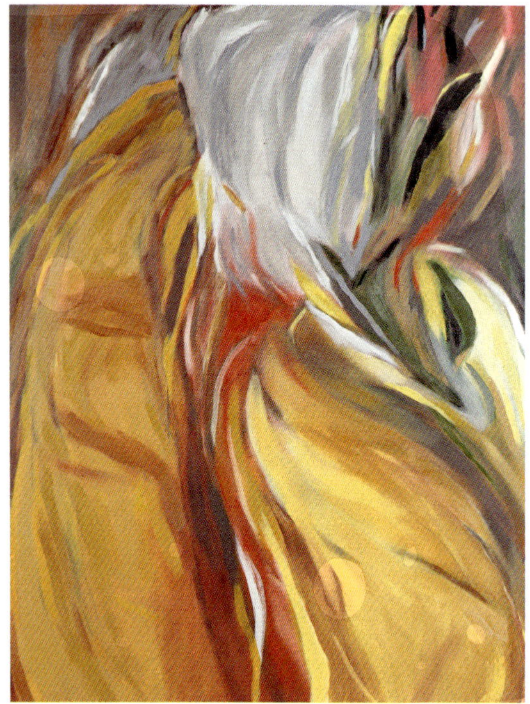

190 Cecily Brennan, *Garden in Autumn*, 1985, oil on canvas.

Similar concerns with mythology and the intuitive were also present in the work of Eithne Jordan in the 1980s; like Anita Groener, Patricia Hurl and Cecily Brennan, she was a woman artist whose work took on aspects of neo-Expressionism. Jordan's dark colours and overt brushstrokes helped to link her work formally with that of her male counterparts, but the subjects of her paintings of the 1980s were much more clearly informed by feminist issues and the debates around female identity. In *Divided Head* (1989) the oversized faces and tiny bodies convey a sense of anxiety that is also a feature of Expressionism. In Jordan's usage, rather than a signifier of isolation, this tension becomes much more legible in terms of the changes facing women in Ireland in the 1980s – a collective rather than individual identity caught up in profound contradiction.

Feminism and Irish women's art

In the summer of 1987, a major exhibition, *Irish Women Artists from the Eighteenth Century to the Present Day*, opened in Dublin. This chronological survey was spread across three venues, the National Gallery of Ireland, the Hugh Lane Municipal Gallery and the Douglas Hyde Gallery. A widely felt anger and frustration at the exclusion of practising women artists from any of the decisions around the curation of these shows was a major factor in the formation of a group explicitly dedicated to the promotion of the interests of women artists in Ireland. Initially chaired by the artist Pauline Cummins, the Women Artists Action Group (WAAG) was also informed by similar developments in London, where Irish women's art was becoming increasingly visible. WAAG rapidly established itself as a significant presence, campaigning for the recognition of contemporary women artists in Ireland.[12] As an alternative to the three exhibitions run concurrently by the three major galleries, WAAG organized an open-submission slide show at the Project that included the work of over 80 women artists from throughout Ireland. This was followed by an inaugural exhibition at the Guinness Hop Store in Dublin in September, in which the work of 90 artists was represented.[13] WAAG continued to campaign for the visibility of Irish women artists until the early 1990s, highlighting repeated instances of discrimination and providing a valuable support network.[14] Increasingly, however, the contradictions present from the outset between feminist aims of collectivity and the necessity of individual artists to develop their own professional practice became hard to reconcile.

In an essay originally published in 1983, the American art critic Craig Owens identified a major focus of feminist postmodernist art as the dismantling of the patriarchal construction of 'master' narratives of

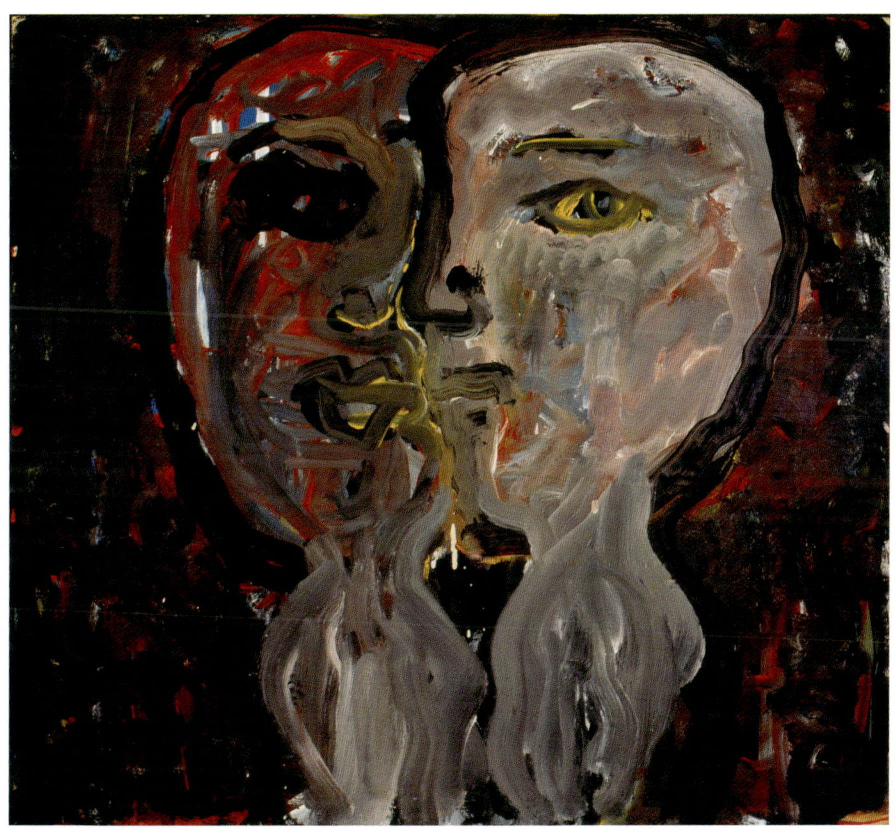

191 Eithne Jordan, *Divided Head*, 1989, oil on canvas.

representation.[15] Similar deconstructive strategies were beginning to appear in work by women artists in Ireland. Three very different projects indicate the diversity of women's art practice critically engaged with aspects of gender. *Ebb*, a sculptural installation by Dorothy Cross at the Douglas Hyde Gallery in 1988, consisted of a range of pieces combining both found objects and fabricated elements. Many of these works were closely related to each other, resonating in a way that was both humorous and unsettling. A central theme in *Ebb* was the breakdown of polarities of gender; the androgynous *Shark Lady in a Ball Dress* (1988) is both phallic and feminine. The shark resurfaces elsewhere, its fin emerging from a bathtub to menace a melodramatically drooping phallus, whose similarity to a church tower also suggests the feminist identification of church and patriarchy embedded in current debates.[16]

By comparison, Kathy Prendergast's 'Body Map' series (1983) situates the representation of the female body within a discourse of conquest and colonialism. Large, delicate pen and ink drawings such as *Enclosed World in Open Spaces* depict the female body mapped out as a landscape according to recognized conventions of cartography, including grid lines and compass points. These drawings also recall the strategies of the British Ordnance Survey's mapping of Ireland in the early nineteenth century, an important means of identifying Ireland as colonized territory within a discourse of empire, reinforced by Ireland's symbolic personification as female.[17] At a time when the patriarchal founding narrative of the Irish state was being undermined by the controversies around the politics of the female body, Prendergast's drawings made visible the interrogation of both nation and Irish womanhood as stable categories.

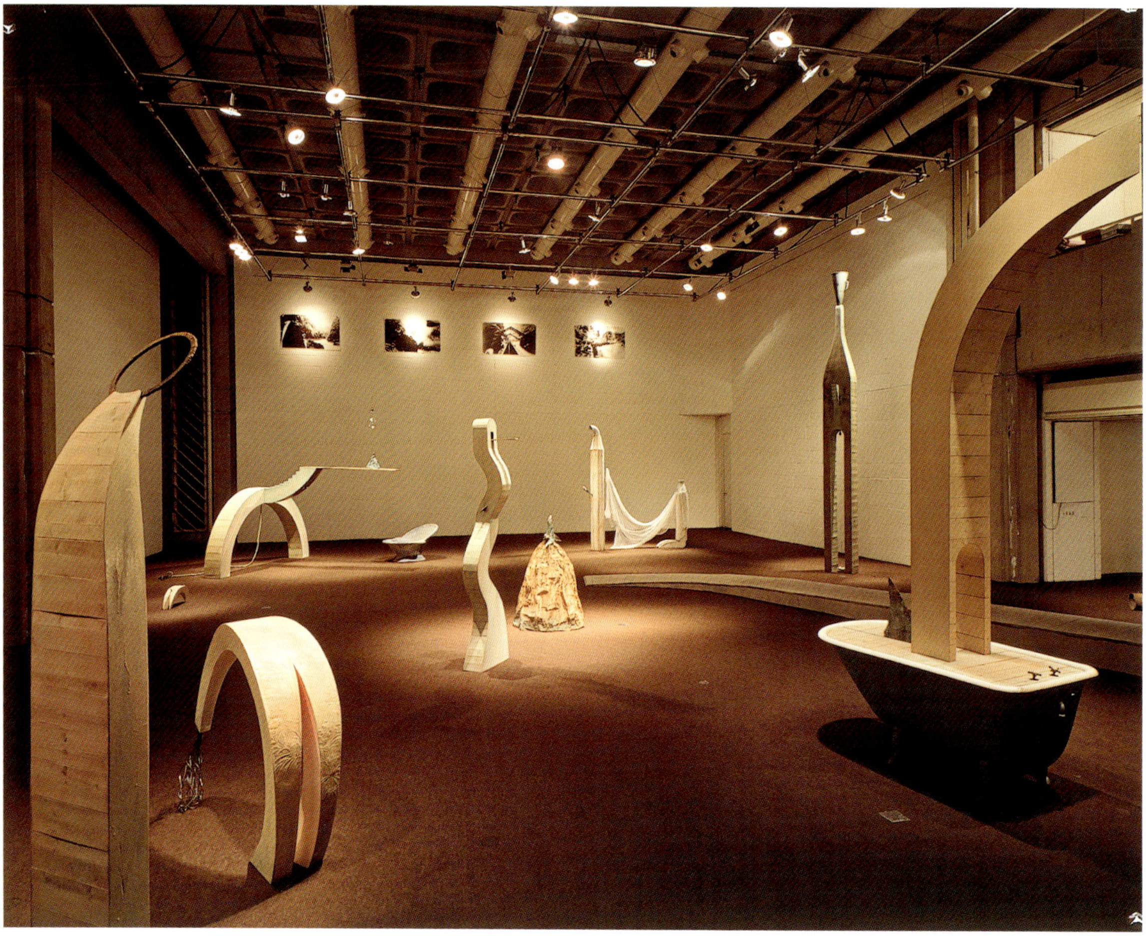

192 Dorothy Cross, *Ebb* installed at the Douglas Hyde Gallery, 1988.

These works by Dorothy Cross and Kathy Prendergast stand out because of their cool deconstructive strategies that lead readily to more theorized terms of analysis. Other feminist work used new technologies to undermine master narratives of both nation and the body, while still privileging an expressive, intuitive response. Pauline Cummins's slide-tape work *Inis t'Oírr* (1985), like Prendergast's drawings, problematizes the relationship between location and the body fundamental to the formation of Irish national identity. Cummins's piece focuses on the traditional work of women in the Aran Islands, including Inis Oírr Island (Inisheer), knitting the distinctively patterned fishermen's sweaters for

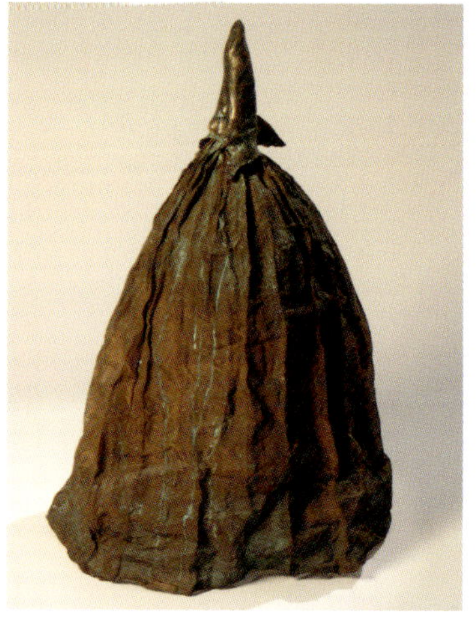

193 Dorothy Cross, *Shark Lady in a Ball Dress*, 1988, cast and woven bronze.

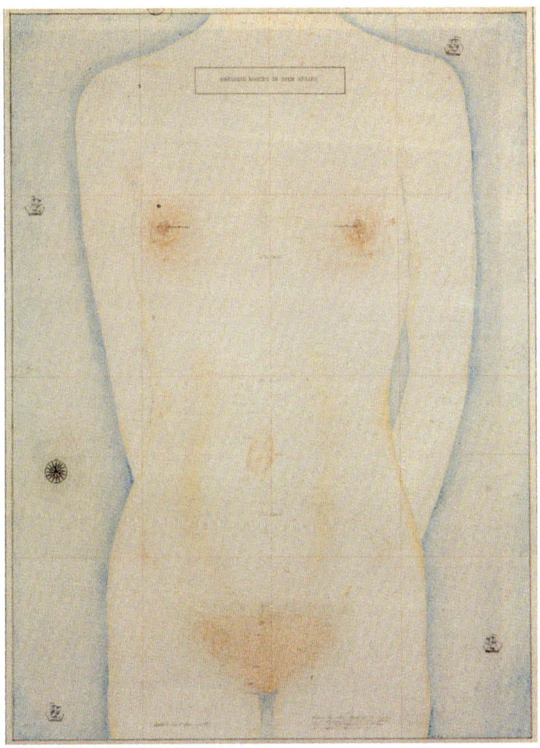

194 Kathy Prendergast, *Enclosed Worlds in Open Spaces*,
1983, watercolour and ink on paper.

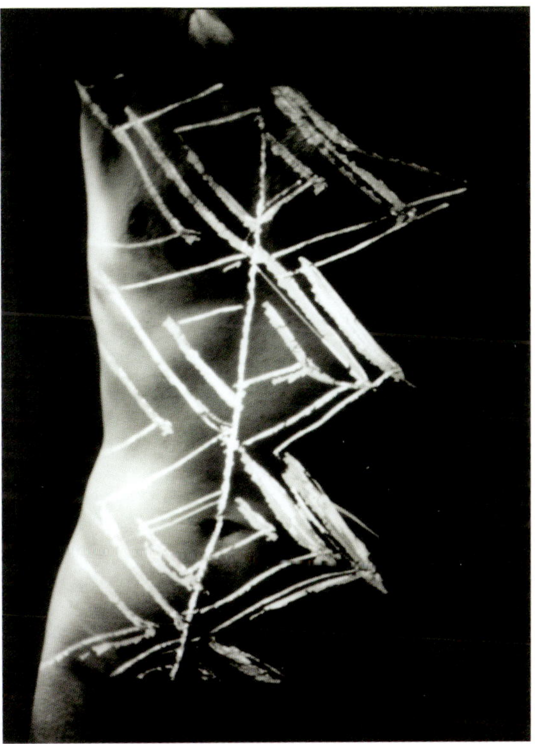

195 Pauline Cummins, *Inis t'Oírr*, 1985, slide-projected
installation with sound.

which the region is renowned. The representation of
the Aran fisherman as ruggedly masculine played a
major role in the iconic status of the West in the formation of nationalist and post-nationalist ideologies. Here,
however, the male body becomes the object of the female
gaze, a sensuously enclosed focus of desire.

The 1980s in the North

In the North, the violence continued on through the
next decade. In the H-Blocks of the Maze Prison, following a prolonged protest by republicans in an attempt to
gain recognition as political prisoners, the Provisional
IRA's commander Bobby Sands went on hunger strike
on 1 March 1981. This eventually led to his death 66 days
later.[18] In all, ten men starved themselves to death in the

face of the British government's intransigence by the
time the strike was called off on 3 October. There was an
upsurge of mass nationalist support, even among the
many who did not agree with the aims and methods of
the Provisional IRA. A sense of outrage that the British
government of Margaret Thatcher was prepared to
stand by as Irish men died of starvation also evoked the
Famine, when approximately one million Irish people
died while the British administration refused to intervene. This support within both Northern and Southern
Ireland was also reinforced by widespread international
condemnation of the British government's decision to
let the men die. However, a major blow to republican
support during the decade came with the IRA's bombing of a Remembrance Day commemoration in the
small rural town of Enniskillen in 1987, when eleven
people died. The massive media coverage that ensued

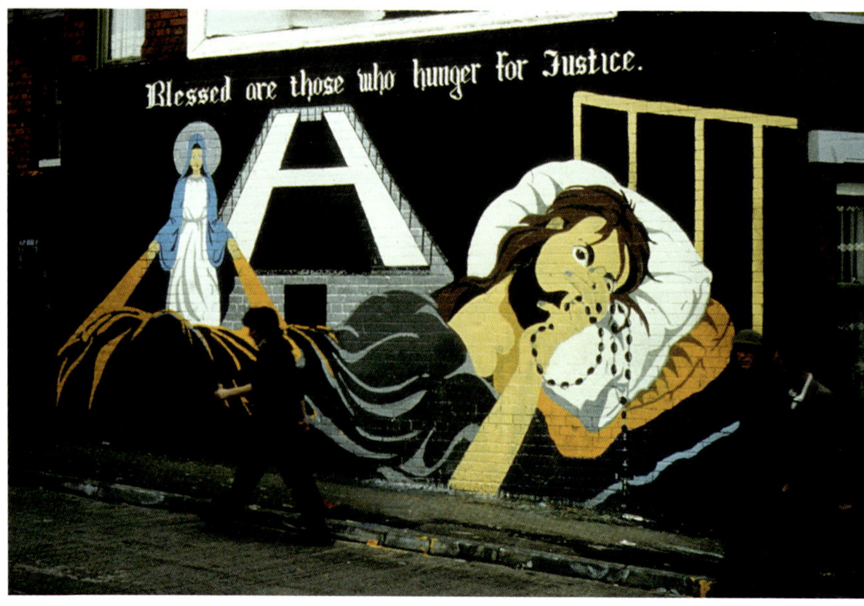

196 Republican mural depicting the hunger strike, Rockville Street, Belfast, 1981.

had a major effect on support for the IRA, particularly among Irish-Americans, many of whom had helped to fund the military campaign.

Media, murals and the politics of representation

The representation of the 'Troubles' by both broadcast and print media was an important factor in shaping the work of many artists in Northern Ireland during the 1980s. Both press photography and broadcast imagery tended to portray a highly selective view of the conflict, within which the subtle contradictions of lived experience were generally elided in favour of sensationalism and stereotypes of bombers and their victims. From the early 1970s onwards, the British media's reporting of the conflict was subject to a range of government-imposed restrictions. The control of visual imagery played a part in establishing the state's hegemonic management of the conflict, outlawing any views that could be considered as partisan and liable to lend support to terrorism. Challenges to official

ideologies that positioned state forces as peacekeepers intervening in a conflict between two atavistic factions were suppressed and marginalized. Claims of an impartial, even-handed approach to the conflict were difficult to sustain in the face of views – and actions – that challenged the state, particularly those of republicans. In the 1980s this took place in the climate of increased marginalization of dissent after the Thatcher government's defeat of the hunger strikers, culminating in a particularly draconian piece of legislation, the Broadcasting Ban of 1988, a series of measures focused on the denial of broadcast access to paramilitaries and their supporters.[19]

During the years of the ban's operation it became common practice for actors to speak the words of Sinn Féin representatives in television interviews, often closely lip-synched. This bizarre simulacrum of reality contributed to a climate for art practice already characterized by a heightened awareness of the codes of media representation. In addition, for many people in Northern Ireland at this time a highly developed consciousness of the politics of the gaze was a part of everyday experience, due to the constant presence of overt military surveillance by helicopters hovering overhead or security cameras at street level, or more covert processes of information-gathering carried out by the British state. For republicans, the constituency most alienated from the state, the development of new means of resistance and affirmation of political identity also took a visual form with the proliferation of murals throughout nationalist areas from the start of the decade onwards. The use of murals to depict political imagery in working-class areas had been a feature of loyalism since the early twentieth-century campaigns against Home Rule; during the 1981 hunger strike it was also adopted for republican purposes. At a time when Sands and the other hunger strikers were being portrayed as criminals in the British media, anonymous, largely self-taught muralists responded with depictions of heroic martyrdom derived from the iconography of Catholicism. Deliberately partisan and lacking in ambiguity, other republican and loyalist murals throughout the decade celebrated paramilitary prowess on one side or another. Also, like the kerbstones painted in the colours of the Union or the Republic, they functioned as a means of defining territory, at a time when knowing exactly where one stood could be a matter of life or death.

Throughout the 1980s, politically referenced art in Northern Ireland took its place among a plethora of representations of the conflict visible within the public domain, whether in the media or in the murals decorating the walls of working-class republican and loyalist areas in Belfast and beyond. In many ways, both media and murals established discursive parameters against and through which fine art practice sought to define itself. There is an important difference, in that an artwork is both produced *for* and consumed *within* very different conditions from a mural on a gable-end or an image in a newspaper. Artists in Northern Ireland at this time developed a range of strategies to negotiate these often complex conditions of representation.

Two very different projects are indicative of attempts to challenge the apparent impartiality of press photography. In Victor Sloan's 'Entering the Field, Armagh' (1986), part of a body of work depicting the Orange parades on the Twelfth of July, the deliberately scratched negative and bleached surface of the print removes the photograph from the realm of the documentary, suggesting also the impossibility of a mere observation of events. In Paul Seawright's series *Sectarian Murder* (1988), however, it is the camera's viewpoint that helps to suggest alternative readings. Seawright photographed a number of locations where assassinations had taken place some fifteen years previously. In each case he provided a short text that describes what happened at each location; the image combined everyday elements with a viewpoint that disrupts normal expectations of spectatorship. In one example, the prehistoric remains at the Giant's Ring outside Belfast are seen at ground level and almost obscured by the large head of a dog being walked by its owner. Not only does this suggest the viewpoint of the dying, but it also indicates the interweaving of horrific events with the commonplace.

A group of paintings by Micky Donnelly, by comparison, explicitly take as their subject-matter the visual and material culture of Irish nationalism. These include the image of the phoenix, the Easter lily and James Connolly's hat with its bullet hole (a relic of the Easter Rising preserved in the National Museum in Dublin), all of which regularly feature in the construction of twentieth-century nationalist tradition. In these works by Donnelly, such as *Connolly's Hat with Lilies* (1987), irony and ambiguity operate as means of destabilizing the certainty of meaning and opening up a discursive space where history and identity are called into question.

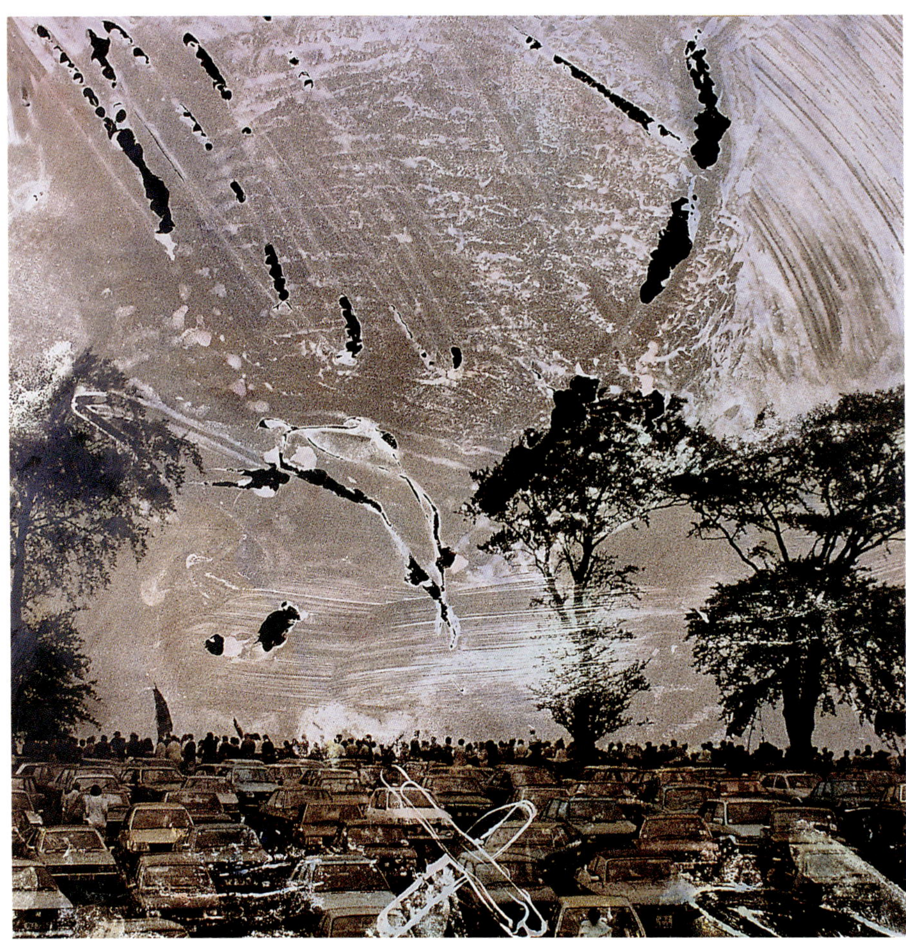

197 Victor Sloan, 'Entering the Field, Armagh', from *Drumming* series, 1986, silver gelatin print, toner and gouache.

Other artists, such as the sculptor Locky Morris, questioned how art could intervene within the dominant set of visual meanings to provide alternative readings. An early piece by Morris, *Town, Country and People* (1986), drew attention to the continued presence of surveillance in a series of three solid cones made by the beams from military helicopters. Morris developed a sculptural language often using cheap, found materials – bin lids, an old suitcase or cardboard – to suggest readings that challenge notions of both 'high' art and accepted media representations of events. Although there were precedents for Morris's practice in both the formal and political strategies of the Italian art movement Arte Povera in the 1960s, this was work closely engaged with the realities of the current situation in Northern Ireland. In *Twist* (1989), for example, a helix of rectangles cut from the frame of a battered suitcase spirals out onto a tabletop like a hand of cards. Although visually intriguing, the reference is to the case of the Birmingham Six, wrongly convicted in 1975 on the basis of traces of explosives allegedly found on playing cards used by the men on a train journey to Heysham to catch the ferry back to Belfast.[20] The men's apparent guilt was reinforced by the representations of republican terrorists as crazed psychopaths that predominated in the British media throughout the 1980s, yet these were also challenged by an active campaign to establish their innocence. In *Twist* it is as if the

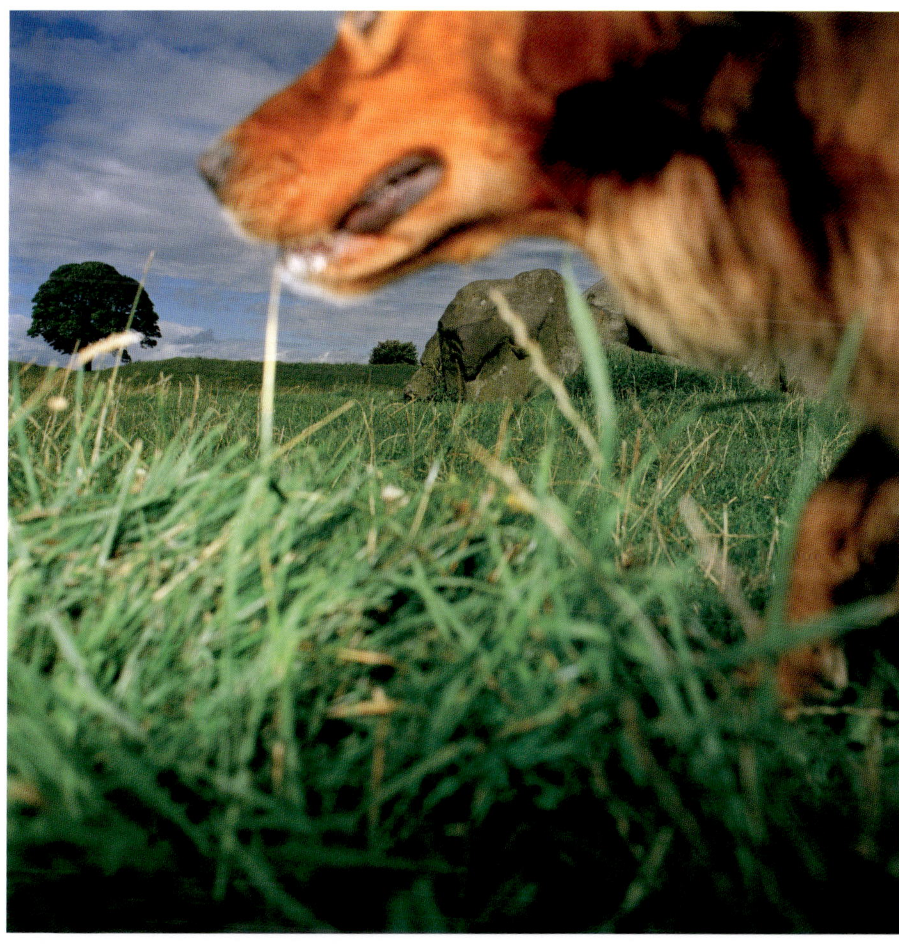

198 Paul Seawright, from *Sectarian Murder*, 1988, colour C-type print.

story spills out of its frame, spinning into fantasy far removed from the actual events.

The links between surveillance, power and paranoia also featured in Dermot Seymour's *A Lysander over Ballymacpherson, County (L)Derry* (1984). In this painting a spy plane overshadows the land below, accompanied by the omnipresent helicopter; the body of a young woman on the ground, the object of such detailed military voyeurism, appears as a dizzying juxtaposition. At a time when ambushes and assassinations on remote country roads or at beauty spots were not uncommon, Seymour, like Paul Seawright, showed landscape as a place of danger rather than enjoyment. Although for an older generation of artists, including Basil Blackshaw,

it was the painter's response that continued to be important in depicting landscape, Seymour's enigmatically entitled depictions of rural Northern Ireland – such as *Do You Ever Think of Daniel Ortega* (1985) – are equally full of disquietingly contradictory visual elements that draw upon strategies of irony and heavily encoded meaning. All of these are recognizably postmodern features, but they also took on a particular significance in the lived experience of political conflict. In an atmosphere of uncertainty and paranoia underpinned by the real threat of violence, allusion and a displacement of meaning replace direct articulation, and self-censorship becomes a means of survival.

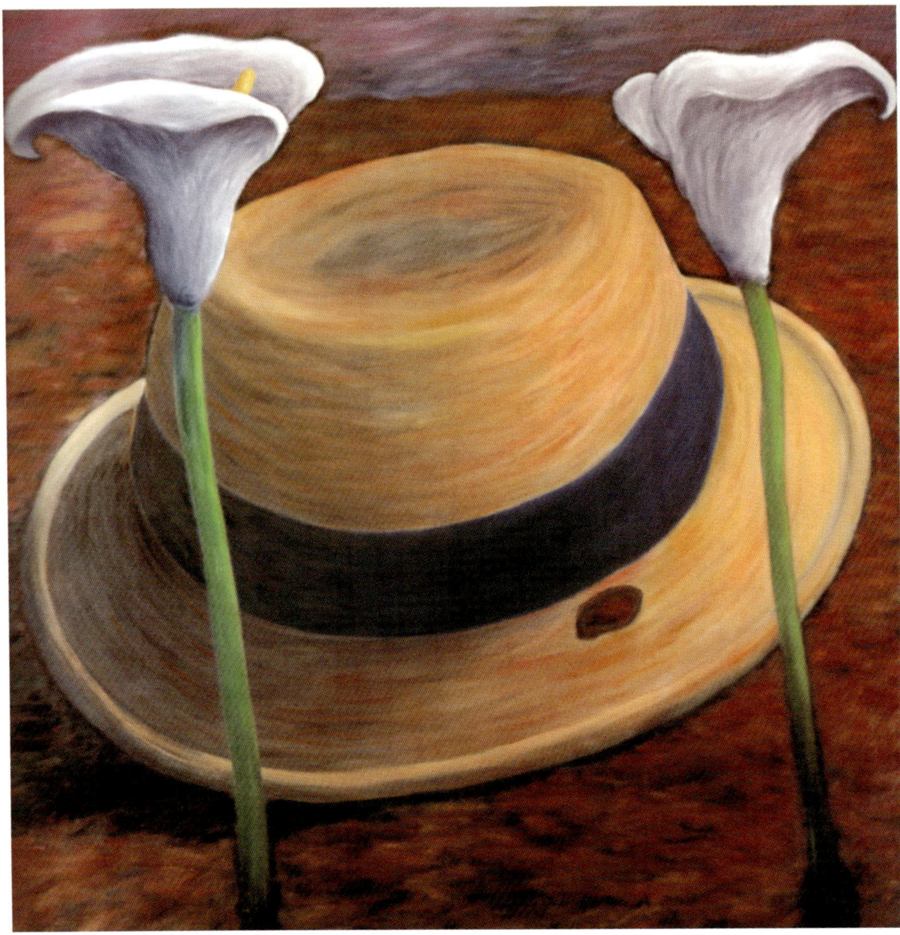

199 Micky Donnelly, *Connolly's Hat with Lilies*, 1987, oil on canvas.

The body, Expressionism and gender

In the work discussed in the last section, the representation of the body is generally absent, or present only by implication in a play of postmodernist strategies of irony and displacement. Yet the violence alluded to in Paul Seawright's *Sectarian Murder* is always enacted upon the body, even if it is not depicted. For other artists in Northern Ireland the actual depiction of the body as either agent or object was particularly significant. For Alastair MacLennan, the performing body became a vehicle for channelling an engagement with conflict that articulated a response intended to move beyond the current political impasse. MacLennan's performances and installations worked on a variety of levels, at once

referenced to the immediate situation yet also engaged with a deeper level of experience. The black balaclava that he often wore during performances, for instance, evokes both the uniform of paramilitaries and his study of Zen during the early 1970s.

Increasingly from 1982, MacLennan's durational performances included references to the conflict. These frequently included a range of common elements, such as the use of a grid to define the performance space that in turn contained installations of found objects, either specific to the location of the performance or part of the artist's collection of disparate artefacts signifying aspects of the conflict. MacLennan also frequently incorporated dead animals (pigs' heads, in particular,

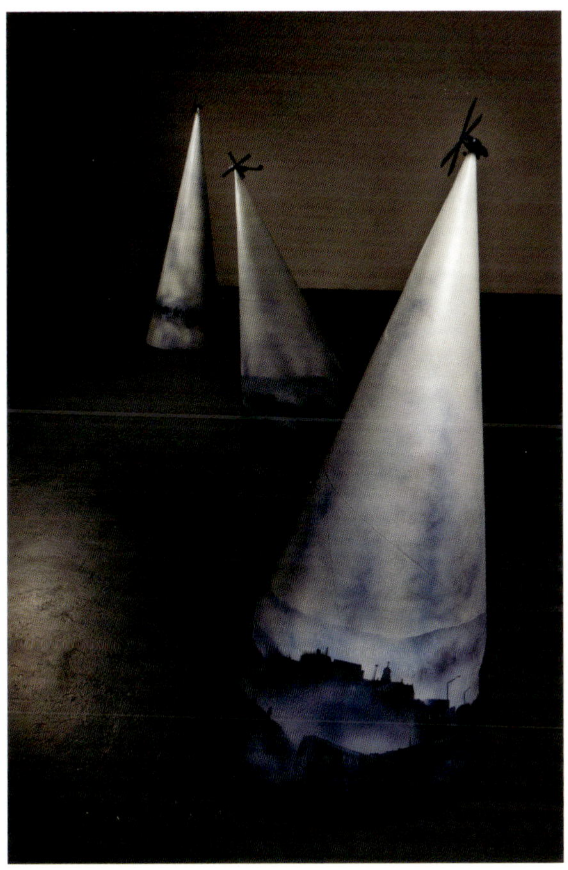

200 Locky Morris, *Town, Country and People*, 1986, mixed media.

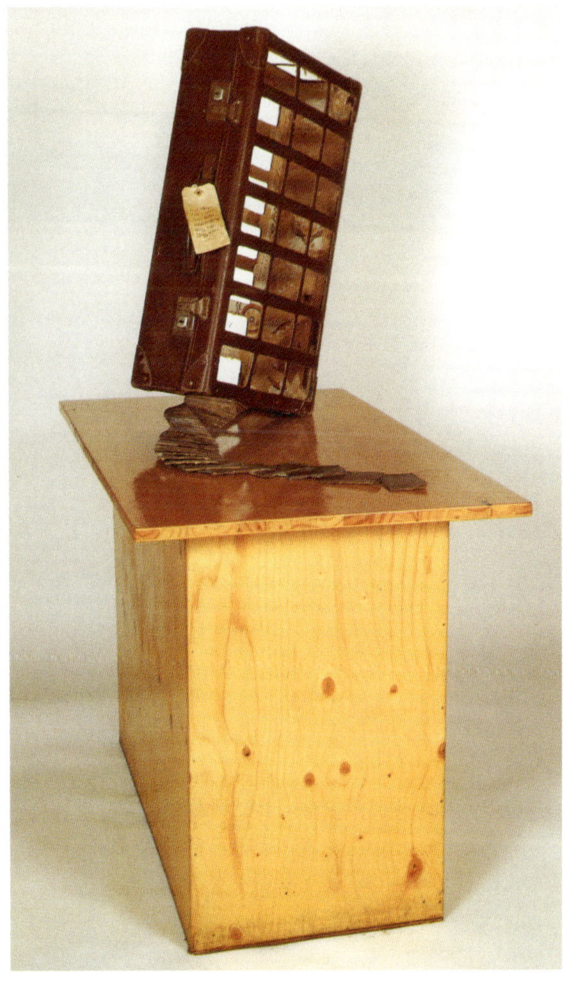

201 Locky Morris, *Twist*, 1989, suitcase, bolts, wood resin and lock.

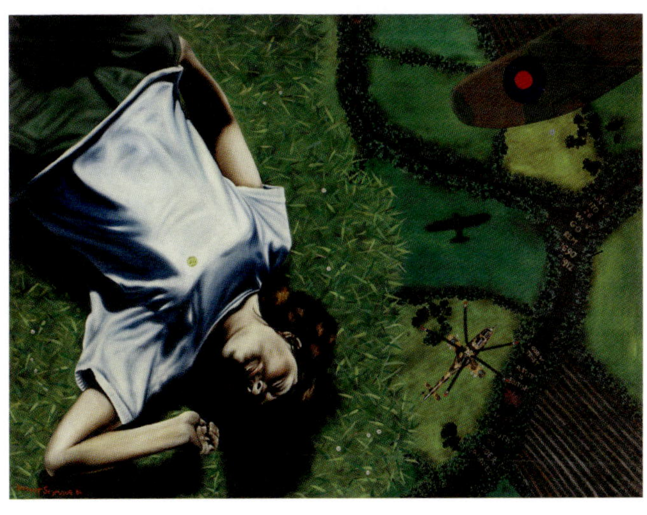

202 Dermot Seymour, *A Lysander over Ballymacpherson, County (L) Derry*, 1984, oil on canvas.

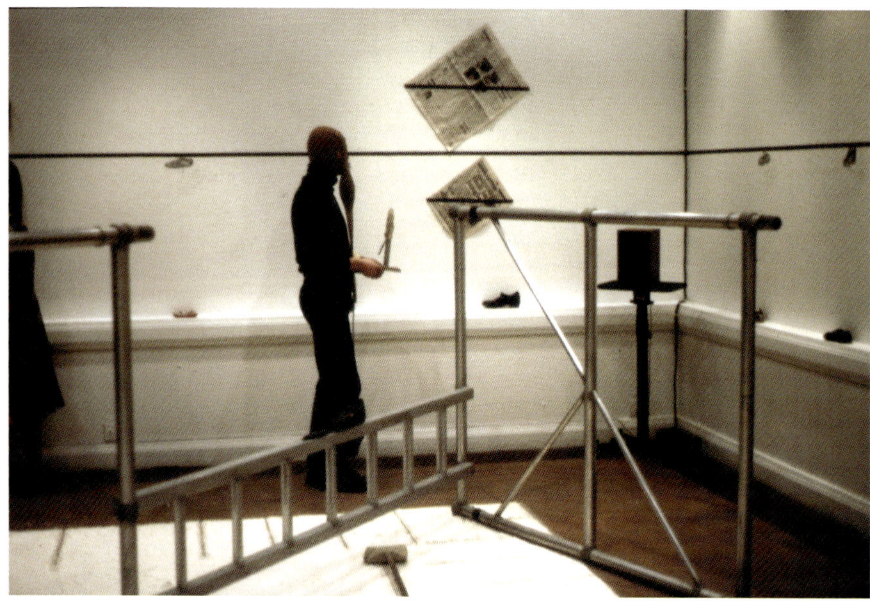

203 Alastair MacLennan, *Body Break*, 1984, performance at Mappin Art Gallery, Sheffield.

and fish) that, over the prolonged period of the performance, would begin to decay. The intention was not the sensationalism of the abject; for the artist, fish symbolize meanings not apparent within everyday consciousness, while the use of pigs' heads suggests a kinship with other species, caught up in cycles of violent death.[21] *Body Break*, a 72-hour performance – or actuation, the artist's preferred term – at the Mappin Art Gallery in Sheffield in 1984, incorporated many of these.[22] Confined within a square of flour on the floor and accompanied by a soundtrack of Irish pipes, the cries of seagulls and the ocean, a collection of objects included copies of Belfast's morning newspapers caught between the rollers of an old clothes wringer, their reporting of events literally mangled. Black-clad and with his head and face also covered with a stocking, MacLennan purposefully interacted with these elements over the duration of the piece through a range of slow, repetitive and ritualistic actions.

Reviewing *Body Break*, Robert Ayers called the performance 'great and frightening and poetic'.[23] In MacLennan's work the deprivations of the body during long performances were also underpinned by the knowledge of suffering bodies, victims of torture and abuse in Northern Ireland at this time. A similar sense of unease was also present in the tableaux staged in Graham Gingles's boxes, although in some instances, as in *Tomb 1* (1980), uncertainty spills into complete horror in the depiction of its butchered victim. Neo-Expressionism in Northern Ireland, however, appeared in different forms, and was used to different ends, from the sexual angst of Martin Wedge's painting *Jealousy* (1989) to Diarmuid Delargy's etchings such as *On through the Not So Quiet Lands* (1983), where references to Jack Yeats take on fresh meaning in the current context. Neo-Expressionism, with its privileging of emotion and intuition, acquired a particular significance in the context of Northern Ireland in the 1980s. Expressionist concerns with universal suffering and the artist's angst became mediated through specific circumstances of unease and horror generated by the political situation. The self-conscious tribalism of Gerry Gleason's masked figures, for example, may have evoked Emil Nolde's use of similar imagery to

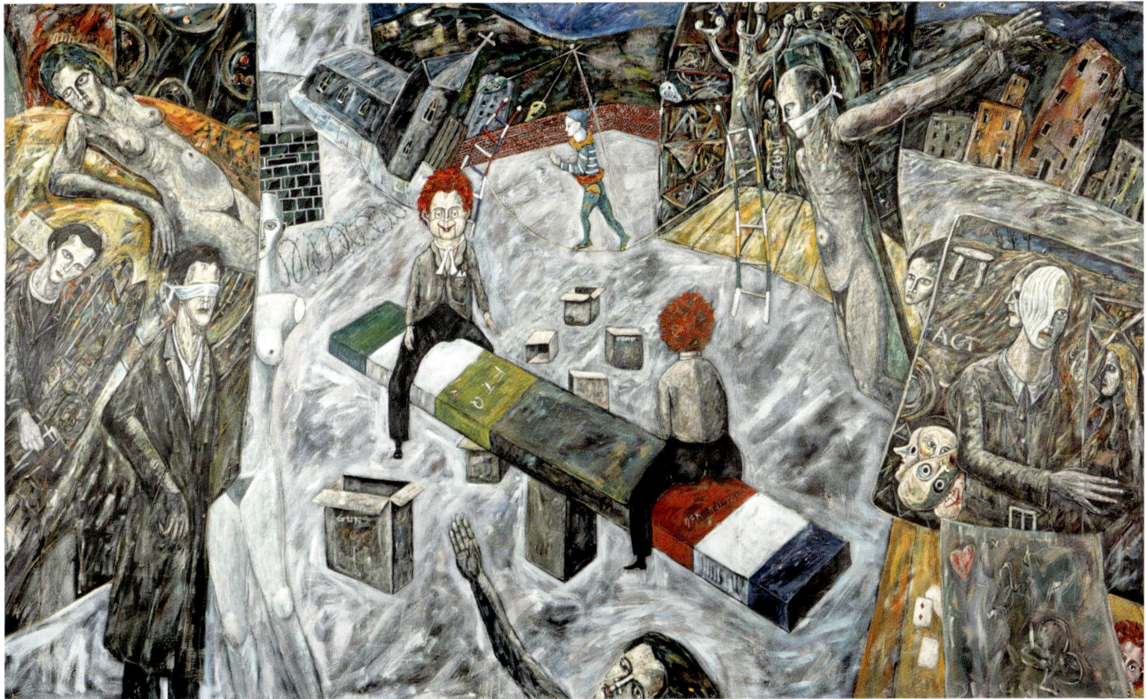

204 Jack Pakenham, *Ulster Playground*, 1989, acrylic on canvas.

articulate the European artist's wonder at the primitive soul, but this is balanced by an awareness of the use of masks and balaclavas by paramilitaries. The displacement and concealment of identity in this way was also referenced by Ann Carlisle's *Blockhead* series.

In the work of some artists, such as Rita Duffy and Jack Pakenham, Expressionism provided a language capable of evoking a response to a situation frightening beyond words. Yet Expressionism's transcendent subject could also become the impartial observer, witnessing without intervening in a conflict between two tribes, as in Pakenham's *Ulster Playground* or Duffy's *The Big Fight* (1989), in which, in a composition derived from Andrew Wyeth, two boxers fight dirty in an illuminated ring. These are works that evoke the deep-rooted nature of the conflict, yet they can also suggest long-established hegemonic views of the Irish as tragic yet barbaric, needing the civilizing hand of the colonizer to intervene and maintain order.

As is clear from artistic practice in the South at this time, Expressionism's associations with an active masculinity could prove problematic for women artists. They also contributed to a climate where gender divisions in relation to war were apparently clearly defined. War could easily be seen as the business of men, even though women were equally affected – as victims of violence and intimidation, as bearing the burden for maintaining families where husbands and fathers were dead or in prison, or as protagonists themselves. That women could be so easily regarded as not having an active role in defining the *meanings* of war is clear from the case of the *Directions Out* exhibition curated by Brian McAvera for the Douglas Hyde Gallery in Dublin in April 1987. Subtitled 'An investigation into a selection of artists whose work has been formed by the post-1969 situation in Northern Ireland', the twelve painters and sculptors were all

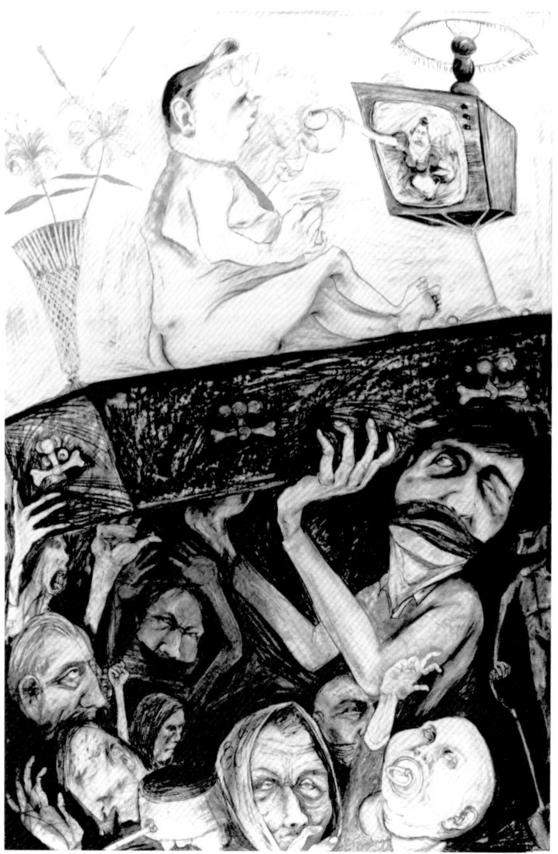

205 Rita Duffy, *The Unheard*, 1988, charcoal on paper.

male. McAvera went to some lengths in the catalogue to justify this exclusion:

> I was very conscious of the need for a woman artist . . . However, I refuse to bow to totemism just to satisfy some numerical notion of representation. The blunt fact is that women do not seem to be working in the areas considered by this show.[24]

The art world in Northern Ireland during the 1980s was small and relatively close-knit; McAvera's decision to exclude women could appear as blatant discrimination. It was also inaccurate to say that women's art was not engaged with the conflict, as examples will indicate. Rita Duffy's early work, produced in the years immedi-

ately after leaving Belfast College of Art, was closely engaged with the observation of a wide spectrum of political events and attitudes thrown up by the conflict; her drawing *The Unheard*, for example, depicts the consequences of the broadcasting ban in stifling the voices of an entire community. Duffy's drawings frequently contained an explicitly gendered perspective, such as in the charcoal drawing *The Marley Funeral* (1988). Similar to Locky Morris's *Cortège* (Morris was included in *Directions Out*), this drawing had its basis in the tight security surrounding republican funerals. A former IRA member from Ardoyne, Marley was killed by loyalist paramilitaries; at his funeral a major confrontation ensued between the dead man's mourners and relatives and the police, who refused to allow the coffin to leave the house covered in the flag of the Republic. During the two days that they battled it out, Duffy, who was teaching domestic science in a nearby girls' school, was struck by the irony of attempting to prepare girls for a future of apparent normality. This highly expressionistic drawing combines both horror and the absurd in the broad sweeps of charcoal depicting the emaciated corpse pulled both ways by mourners and police, while in the foreground a uniformed schoolgirl attempts to boil an egg.

Rita Duffy's politically engaged drawings and paintings of the 1980s also implicitly challenged the gendered associations of Expressionism; for other women artists the conflict registered in their work in relatively subtle ways. The formal, classicized containment of Deirdre O'Connell's sculptures and drawings involved a more oblique engagement through the representation of architectural structures that articulate power and control. In the large-scale series of drawings *No Fire in the Hearth, No Sun in the South* (1985–7), the partially seen installations in bleak, desolate settings suggest the anonymity of a military power and presence whose scope is also

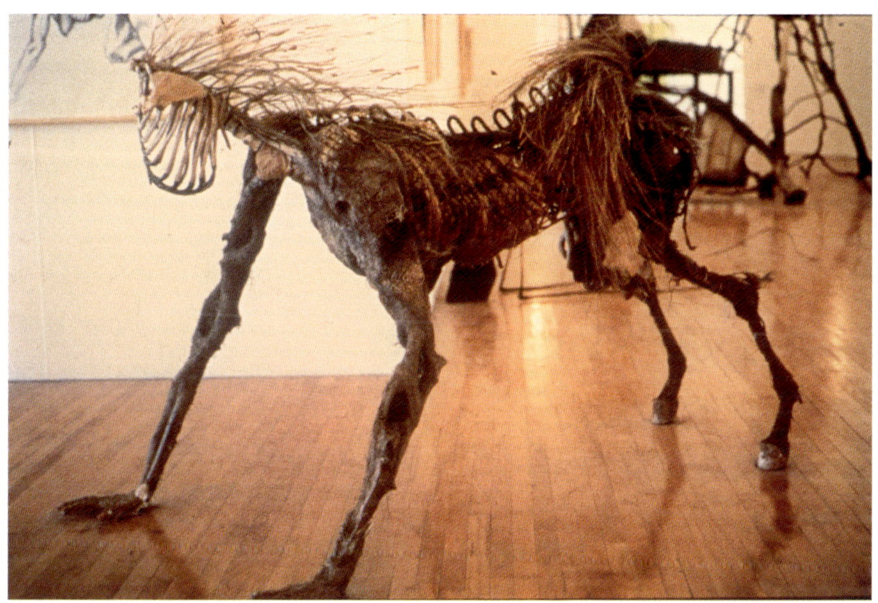

206 Louise Walsh,
Harvest Queen, 1986,
mixed media.

unknown. Unlike Duffy's work, gender is not explicitly referenced, but these are images that work to convey an ongoing condition of unease and paranoia.

The work of other women artists, however, offered opportunities to engage with something different from the surrounding violence. For Barbara Freeman, abstract painting provided the opportunity after her mother's death to explore issues such as a relationship with the maternal body.[25] For Alice Maher and Louise Walsh, both from Southern Ireland but who had come to Belfast for postgraduate study at the University of Ulster, Expressionism offered opportunities to investigate issues affecting women throughout Ireland, albeit in different ways. Walsh's large sculpture *Harvest Queen* combined a bricolage of found natural and synthetic materials to produce a hybrid figure, part woman and part animal, poised on all fours. Walsh's concern was to challenge the representation of woman as a 'beast of burden'; in this sculpture the transformation of cultural analogies between woman and nature rejects any sense of female passivity.[26] For Maher, the ability as an outsider to deal with the 'continual atmosphere of paranoia and fear' became channelled through images that dealt with

'what the Catholic Church was doing to women in Ireland'.[27] This resulted in a series of mixed-media works with collaged elements violently torn out of magazines combined with drawing and painting. These images often involved a reworking of themes from Renaissance painting particularly affecting women, such as the Annunciation: in its reconfiguration as *The Visit*, humour and violence combine to depict a Virgin Mary uneasily awaiting the approach of the Archangel Gabriel, here transformed into a giant lobster.

The spaces of making and consumption

In spite of the difficult circumstances in Northern Ireland, the 1980s was a time when the spaces where art could be made, exhibited and discussed were becoming more diverse. In Belfast an important focus was the Art and Research Exchange (ARE) established in the late 1970s after Joseph Beuys's visit to Belfast, and from which developed both the Artists Collective of Northern Ireland and the magazine *Circa*. These developments also had an effect on *what* was shown.

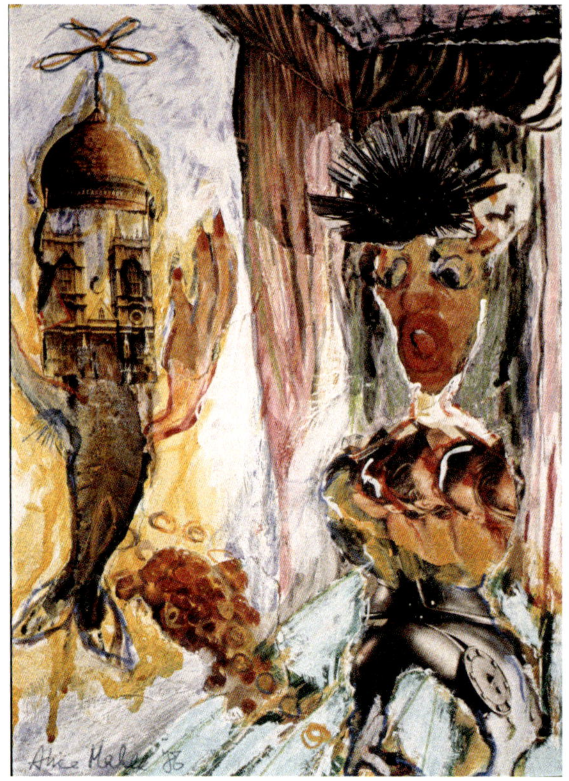

207 Alice Maher, *The Visit*, 1986, mixed media collage on paper.

At a time when the Arts Council of Northern Ireland appeared to be doing little to engage with the significance of the conflict for art practice, ARE provided an important alternative, with exhibitions by young artists such as Micky Donnelly or Willie Doherty, in addition to promoting time-based work including performances by Alistair MacLennan, John Carson and Anne Tallentire. These exhibitions and events were part of a drive to situate art practice in Northern Ireland in a wider context of socially engaged art practice. ARE also exhibited a range of work by practitioners from outside Ireland, such as Helen Chadwick, Mona Hatoum and Barbara Kruger.[28]

The early 1980s also saw the emergence of a range of alternative gallery spaces in Belfast, including the privately run Fenderesky Gallery, and an increase in

local arts centres throughout the province. However, the domination of these by the agendas of Unionist local councils resulted in regular attempts to censor work on political or moral grounds. A significant exception was the Orchard Gallery in Derry, which opened in 1978 under the directorship of Declan McGonagle. Run by the nationalist-dominated Derry City Council, the Orchard provided a further alternative to the Belfast-based hegemony of the Arts Council. Questions of identity have always been paramount in a city whose ambiguity over its own name has political implications; the emphasis in the official name, Londonderry, on Britain's dominion means that this is the version used by Unionists, while 'Derry' is the nationalist designation. Situated a couple of miles from the border with the Republic, Derry's division by the River Foyle also has political significance; the majority of nationalists live in the areas of the west bank, and Unionists on the east. A sense of place was important from the outset to McGonagle's programme at the Orchard, which combined local and frequently highly accessible shows with challenging work, often by internationally renowned conceptual artists such as Victor Burgin, Hamish Fulton, Richard Long and Lawrence Weiner. Yet a further consequence was correspondence to a postmodernist emphasis on decentralization. In spite of being geographically at the furthest edge of the Union, the Orchard refused to see itself as in any way peripheral, effectively bypassing centralized relationships with first Belfast and then London as sites of cultural power. As McGonagle stated, the aim was to make it 'possible for Derry to think of itself as existing in the world, not just in Northern Ireland, not just in the North West of Northern Ireland, or not just in Ireland or Great Britain'.[29]

The policies of the Orchard Gallery during the 1980s were to have long-term consequences for the

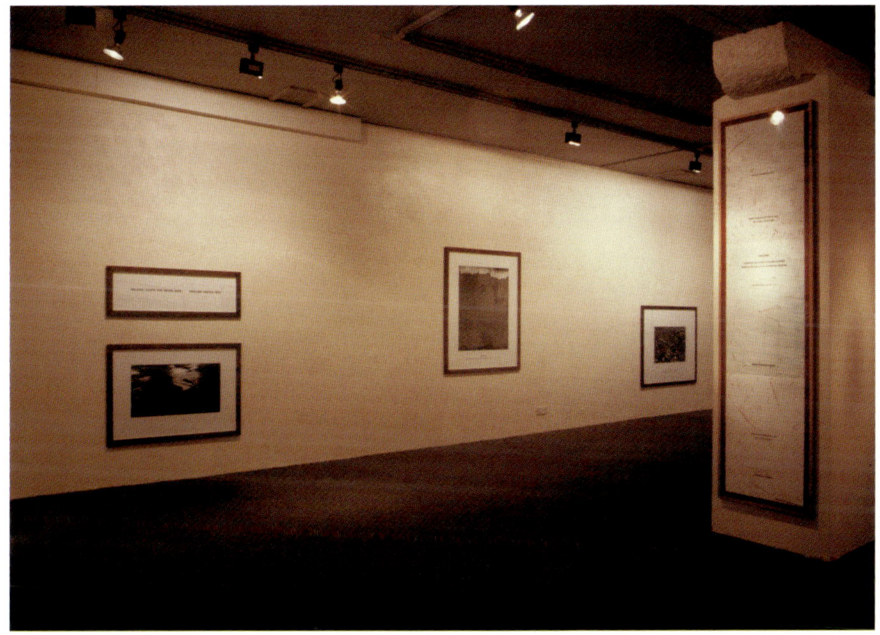

208 A Hamish Fulton exhibition, in 1985, showing the interior of the Orchard Gallery, Derry.

development of art practice in Northern Ireland, particularly in its sense of *situatedness* in relation to a wider international context. But there was also a more immediate effect on artists based in Derry, enabling the development of a locally based but critically informed practice. This included the work of both Locky Morris and Marie Barrett, whose Expressionist drawings emphasized a gendered dimension to the experience of conflict. The specific knowledge of Derry's distinctive political and geographic identity in the context of wider issues of representation was instrumental in shaping the early work of Willie Doherty. In common with other artists, Doherty's work suggests a critical distance from the dominant stereotypes of media representation of Northern Ireland. An early photo-work, *The Other Side* (1988), shows a panoramic view of the city of Derry. Elements of text are superimposed on the image. Although visually reminiscent of Richard Long's readings of the Irish landscape, the textual conundrums used here – 'West is South' and 'East is North' – relate more specifically to the contradictions and subtle elisions of language in conveying lived

experience in Derry as a particular location. Each of the terms defines the parameters of the other, and they also indicate the contested nature of public space within the city itself.

Irish art outside Ireland and the politics of representation

Some British artists also responded to their perceptions of the Northern Ireland conflict. For Rita Donagh, this was a continuation of work from the previous decade, where her interests in the relationship between experience and its conceptualization through the use of mapping and grids became focused on the ongoing conflict. 'Shadow of the Six Counties' (1979–81) was a series that highlighted the British presence in the North through an investigation of cartography. In the wake of the hunger strikes, when the artist was a visiting lecturer at the Belfast College of Art, she became particularly interested in depicting the H-Blocks where the strikes had taken place in the Maze Prison, formerly

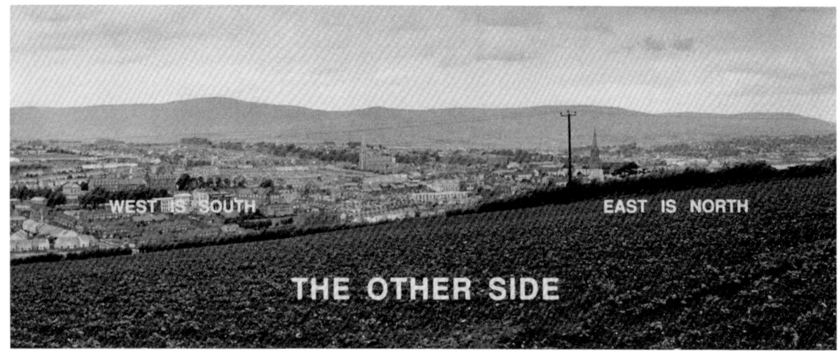

209 Willie Doherty,
The Other Side, 1988,
black and white
photograph with text.

known as Long Kesh ('Long Meadow'). Her sources for these paintings and drawings were both news media and murals: aerial photographs were often used to illustrate reports of the hunger strikes, showing the distinctive shape of the H-Blocks spread out across the site, while the letter 'H' or image of the blocks was a regular feature of republican murals at this time.[30] In the largely monochrome painting *Long Meadow*, the letter 'H' appears in two different forms, in an oblique perspectival alignment across the picture surface reminiscent of aerial photographs, and as a much feinter vertical presence suggestive of its function within the murals. On a discursive level, the clash between what these images represented was a further aspect of the conflict itself, an ideological confrontation subtly encoded in *Long Meadow*.

Rita Donagh's work about Northern Ireland was shown in a joint exhibition with Richard Hamilton at the Orchard Gallery in Derry in late 1983. The main focus of Hamilton's contribution was a large, two-panelled painting, *The Citizen*, also derived from media representations of protests in the Maze, in this case a BBC documentary shown in 1980. The painting depicts Hugh Rooney, a republican prisoner, standing in his prison cell clad only in a blanket and in front of a wall covered in his own excrement. Prior to the 1981 hunger strike, republicans had undertaken a 'no wash' protest

in an attempt to gain political status, refusing either to wear prison uniform or to slop out their cells. Hamilton later described the impact of the scene in the documentary as 'a strange image of human dignity in the midst of self-created squalor . . . endowed with a mythic power often associated with art'.[31] Hamilton's work derived its title from a Fenian character in Joyce's *Ulysses*, and the depiction of the long-haired 'blanketman' has an iconic quality suggestive of images of martyrdom and sacrifice. Yet there are also painterly concerns in the relationship between the figuration of the right-hand panel and abstraction of the left represented by the swirls of excrement, which Hamilton also compared to 'the megalithic spirals of New Grange [sic]' or 'the Gaelic convolutions of the Book of Kells'.[32]

In spite of a generally favourable review of the Orchard exhibition by Belinda Loftus in *Circa*, other critics were less positive: writing from a Marxist perspective John Roberts subsequently denounced *The Citizen* as 'sentimental pathos'.[33] At the start of the decade, Irishness was largely synonymous in Britain with the reductive stereotypes that characterized the media's reporting of the conflict in the North. With the aim of redressing this, a major festival entitled 'A Sense of Ireland', celebrating Ireland's participation across the arts, took place in London between 3 February and 15

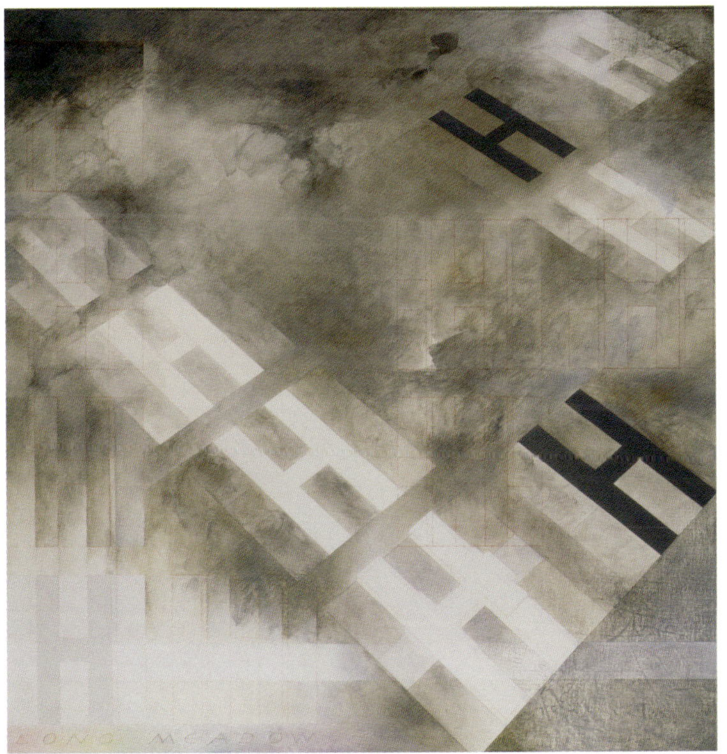

210 Rita Donagh, *Long Meadow*, 1982, oil on canvas.

March 1980. The focus on music, drama and literature was also supplemented by visual art. In addition to exhibitions by Irish artists in commercial galleries, three major group shows were also organized. *The International Connection*, curated by Cyril Barrett at the Round House Gallery, focused on abstract art and included Seán Scully, William Scott and Michael Craig-Martin, while *The Delighted Eye*, an Arts Council of Ireland touring exhibition, was curated by Frances Ruane and *Without the Walls*, organized by Dorothy Walker, showed at the ICA.

The exhibitions organized as part of 'A Sense of Ireland' aimed to make the wide variety of forms of art now current in Ireland accessible to a wider audience as part of a more general project of rehabilitating the

image of Irishness at this time. Yet the festival also spoke to the large population of Irish people in London and in Britain as a whole. Throughout the decade there was a significant change in the pattern of emigration from Ireland to England as an increasing number of skilled professionals left the country. And as Breda Gray points out, the assertive presence of feminism in Ireland during these years made the gendered dimension of Irish migration particularly apparent.[34] Yet whatever their class and gender, the perception of Irish migrants in Britain was still subject to the institutionalized anti-Irish racism of the Thatcher government.

The 1980s was also a time when both feminist art practices and the emergence of groups of black artists explicitly confronting the politics of racism were beginning to become more active in Britain. Within this context Irish artists became visible in very different terms to these that had prevailed previously. In the 1950s, Louis le Brocquy or William Scott were enabled by their class and gender to operate within the mainstream of a London-based art scene; Irish women artists, such as Mary Swanzy or Noreen Rice, remained on the margins. In the 1980s, however, art made by Irish women assumed a collective presence through group exhibitions such as *Prism I* and *Prism II*, part of the London Irish Women's Festival in 1986. *Off the Map*, shown at Chisenhale Gallery in August 1987, also featured the work of six artists from the recently formed Irish Women Artists Group (IWAG) in a more radical deconstruction of gendered Irish identity. It included a performance piece by the artist Anne

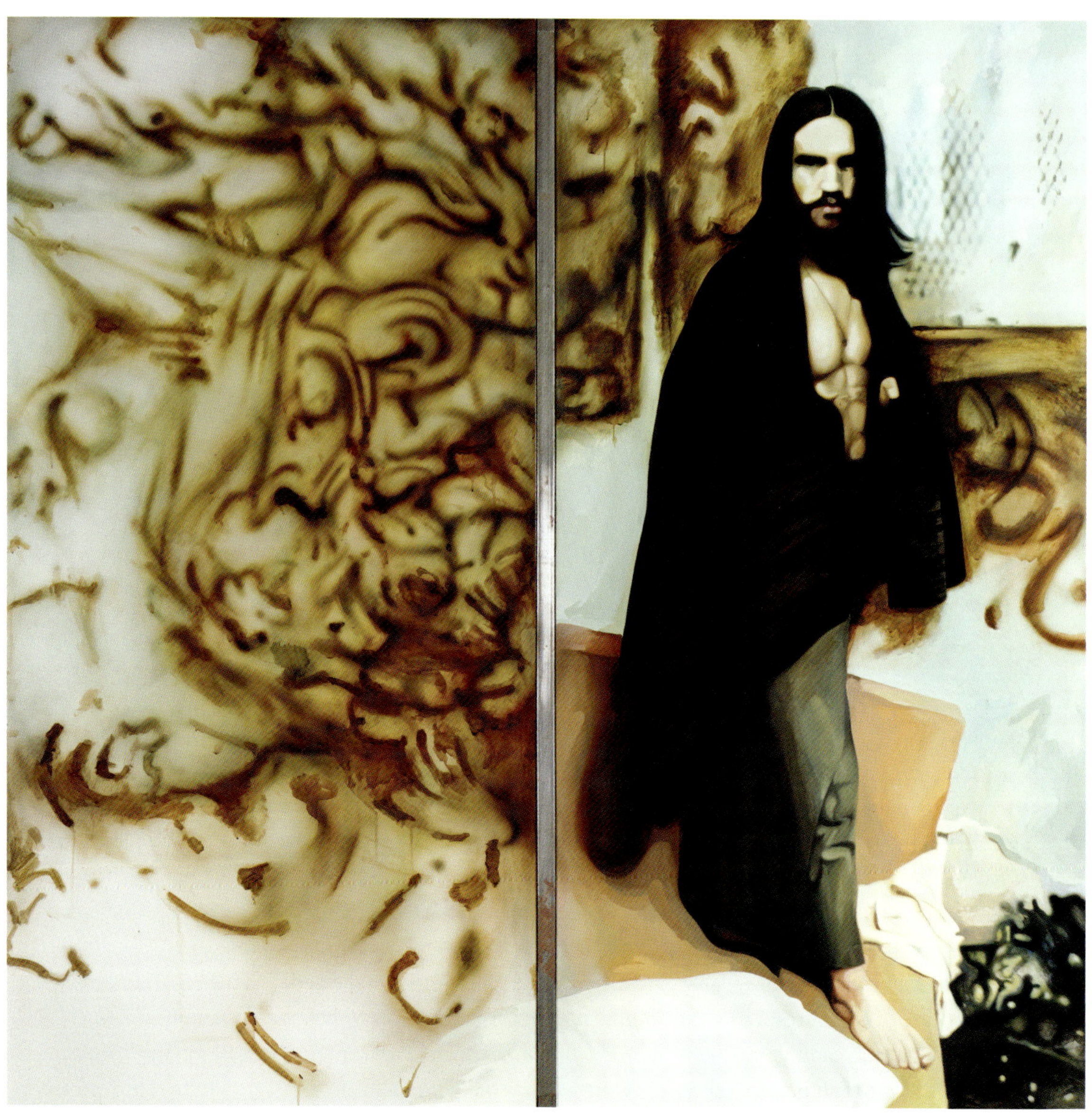

211 Richard Hamilton, *The Citizen*, 1982–3, oil on canvas.

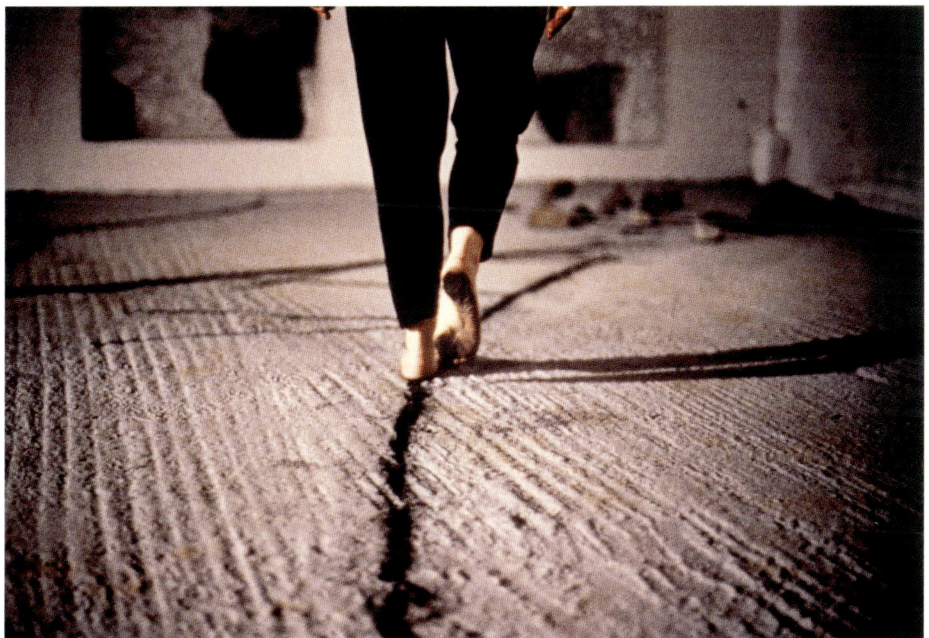

212 Anne Tallentire, *Altered Tracks*, 1987, performance still.

Tallentire. Like her subsequent installations *Bound Words Stolen Honey* and *The Gap of Two Birds* (both 1988), *Altered Tracks* opened up significant questions about colonialism and identity through a focus on the inter-related areas of language, culture and territory. Similar to Brian Friel's play *Translations* (1980), Tallentire's performance focused on issues of cartography, naming and power. During the performance she walked along lines drawn on the floor, placing stones as markers at various points in response to a soundtrack with two pre-recorded readings of the artist's palm, spoken either in an English or Irish voice. The performance space included enlarged photographs of maps of the area of Northern Ireland where Tallentire grew up, their details partially obscured by large stones. The maps displayed Irish place-names rather than their anglicized counterparts, indicative of a history and geography both lost in translation.[35]

The Irish voice also played a major role in a remarkable performance by another member of IWAG, Alanna O'Kelly. *Chant Down Greenham* – in an echo of the Rastafarian chanting down of Babylon – used location sound from the women's peace camp set up at the airfield at Greenham Common in 1981 to protest against the use of the base for cruise missiles. There is a poetic quality to the mingling of women's voices and drumming, interspersed with both periods of silence and the sound of helicopters hovering overhead – immediately reminiscent of the military presence in Northern Ireland as well. O'Kelly's voice cuts across this in a kind of *caoineadh*, the wordless lament whereby Irish women traditionally mourned the dead. Here, however, as Jean Fisher observed, it 'is less a cry of loss . . . than a rallying cry of defiance, to which the women's chanting and laughter becomes a chorus or echo of solidarity'.[36] *Chant Down Greenham* linked

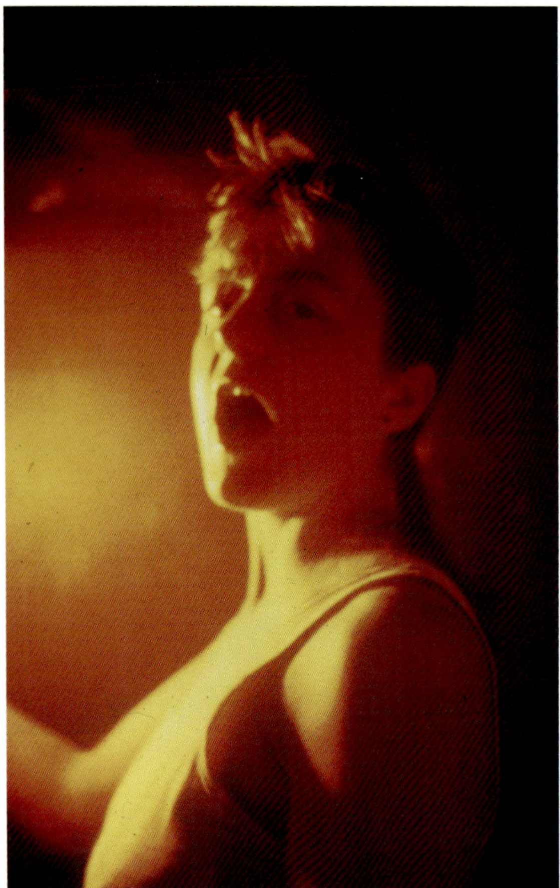

213 Alanna O'Kelly, *Chant Down Greenham*,
performance still, 1987.

together two of the most important concerns of British feminism during the decade – the struggle against colonialism's eradication of Irish identity and resistance to the British military presence in the North. In O'Kelly's performance the elemental power of the Irish voice went far beyond the establishment of cultural difference: this was a position of resistance to the British state at a visceral level.

TEN

THE UNRAVELLING NATION, 1990–1998

After the best part of a century during which constructs of nation had played such significant roles in Irish culture, processes of political and economic change began to encourage the questioning of former orthodoxies, albeit in different forms north and south of the border. In 1990 John Major succeeded Margaret Thatcher as British Prime Minister. His premiership brought in a new willingness to achieve peace in Northern Ireland; talks between British and Irish governments resulted in the Downing Street Declaration of 15 December 1993, whereby both governments stated their commitment to 'the development of an agreed framework for peace', based on the will of the majority of the population of Northern Ireland. The Declaration also involved the renunciation of the Republic's claims to the North, 'in the absence of the freely given consent of the majority of the people of Northern Ireland' – a move with considerable consequences for political ideologies on both sides of the conflict.[1]

The Declaration was an important step towards peace in the North, paving the way for the paramilitary ceasefires of 1994 and the subsequent Good Friday Agreement in 1998. However, with the renunciation of the Dublin government's territorial claims to the six Northern counties, the ideological imagining of the space of the nation became increasingly difficult to sustain on the same terms as previously – especially at a time when Ireland was experiencing a new-found and unprecedented prosperity. Re-evaluations of the meanings of land, history and identity emerged as issues underpinning the work of artists in the South; a focus on memory as undermining the authority of history became a concern for artists both south and north of the border. However, for many artists in the north, where the conflict still dragged on, the relationships between space, visuality and power also continued to be both relevant and pressing.

Mapping, memory and identity

On 31 August 1994, the IRA ceasefire effected the 1993 Downing Street Declaration's intent of a 'complete cessation of military operations'. A similar move was made on 13 October by loyalist paramilitaries. The British government also responded by lifting the broadcasting ban on proscribed organizations, including Sinn Féin. Even after the ceasefires there were repeated attempts to undermine the fragile peace. In addition to the ongoing killings, these included the continuation of the annual standoff between loyalists and nationalists in Portadown during the summer marching season, and IRA bombs in British cities in 1996. Debates over the

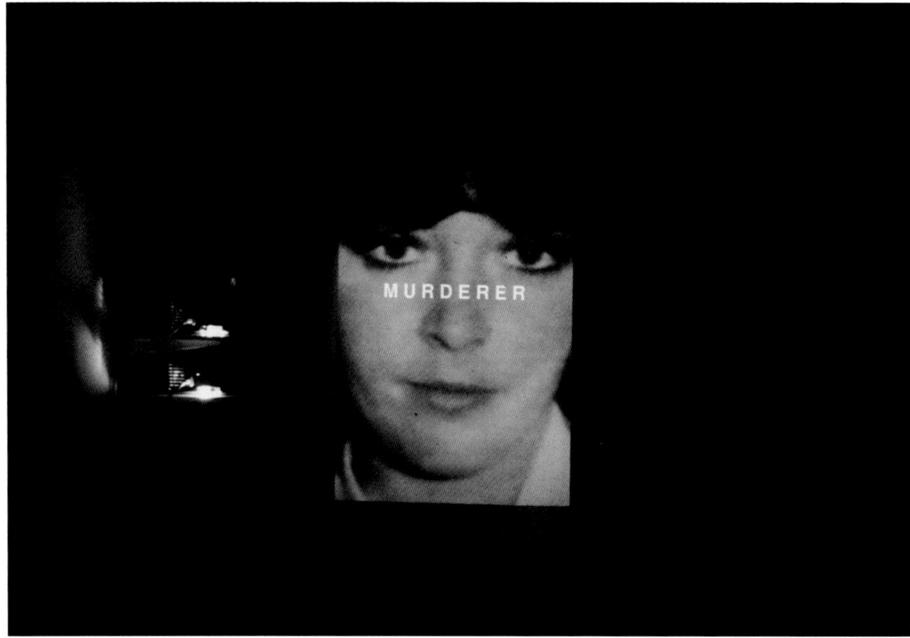

214 Willie Doherty, installation view of *Same Difference*, 1990, installation with two 35mm slide-projected images and changing text.

future of weapons held by the paramilitaries became a key feature of the frequently tortuous peace process that culminated in the Good Friday Agreement.

These were momentous events, with a lasting effect on Northern Ireland's political landscape. Explicit references to conflict in art practice began to be replaced by a focus on the psychological effects of years of violence and uncertainty. Expressionism still lingered on, but there was an increasing interest, especially among young artists, in an expanding range of practices such as installation or the use of lens-based media. In a development from his photo-works of the 1980s, Willie Doherty began a more dynamic engagement with the changing political situation. Two tape-slide installations, *Same Difference* (1990) and *They're All the Same* (1991), were made in the context of the draconian censorship measures of the Broadcasting Ban that had stifled the possibility of dissent by the dominant representations of Irish republicanism in the British media, yet they also drew upon deeply embedded racial stereotypes of 'Irishness'. Each of these works juxtaposed a media-derived photograph of a convicted terrorist (one female, one male) with a range of spoken and written phrases that provided either a positive or negative reading for the image.[2] Although simple in conception, this strategy disrupted the apparently seamless construction of rebel Irish deviancy, and returned a voice to those denied representation following the ban.

This suggests a shift in the way that art practice could envisage the conflict and its effects, a process that continued in Doherty's work as a concern with the role of cultural memory in shaping the past in a manner different from orthodox historical representation. Doherty's first work of this kind – an important development for the artist – focused on the significance of Bloody Sunday in 1972, still a highly contentious issue in Derry some two decades later. The official version of how thirteen unarmed civilians met their deaths at the

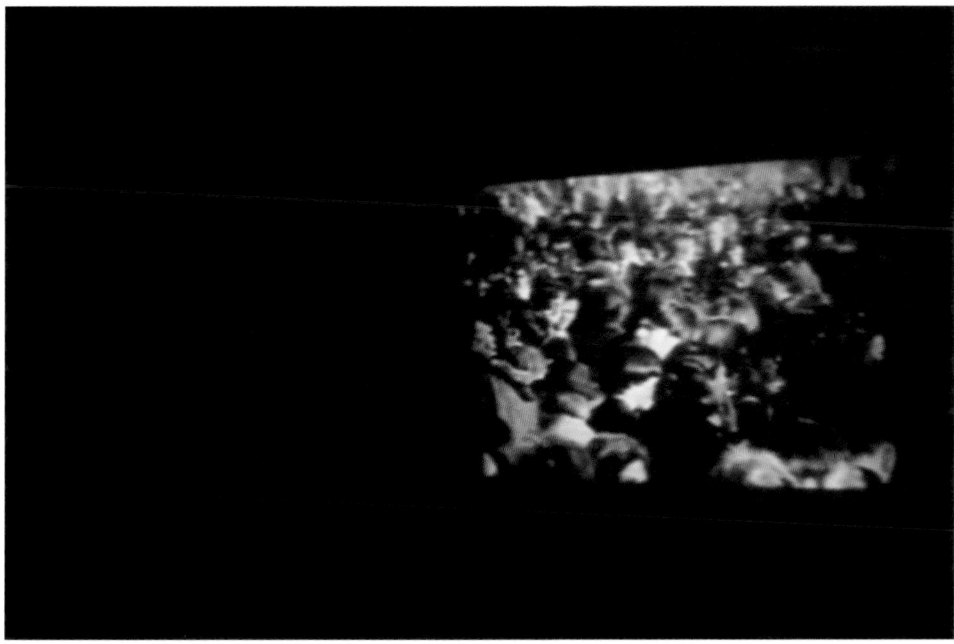

215 Willie Doherty, installation view of *30th January 1972*, 1993, slide installation with two projections on one screen.

hands of British paratroopers was extremely controversial, and continued efforts were made to prove the victims' innocence. Doherty's video installation *30th January 1972*, first shown at the Douglas Hyde Gallery in Dublin in 1993, was begun twenty years after Bloody Sunday and built upon the artist's vox-pop interviews with people in the area of the Bogside where the killings had taken place. These were people who had either witnessed the events or whose knowledge was derived from its representation within the media. In the exhibition space, two images were projected back to back on a freestanding screen, one depicting Glenfada Park, where four victims were killed, and the other re-photographed from television news coverage of the events. These projections were accompanied by three audio tracks, one derived from recordings made during the shootings in 1972, the other two extracts from the interviews. While embodying a technical development from the earlier tape–slide works, *30th January 1972* also showed the increasing emergence in Doherty's work of a concern with often problematic narratives that both acknowledge and challenge the official version of events.[3]

Doherty's work throughout the decade continued to embody a subtle and complex relationship with political events in Northern Ireland. One consequence of the 1994 ceasefires was the increased recognition of the conflict's effects on the survivors, and how the knowledge of terrible events in the recent past resurfaces in the form of traumatic memory. Doherty's video works became increasingly focused around psychological displacement – the undermining of certainty in the narratives of *The Only Good One Is a Dead One* (1993) and *Sometimes I Imagine It's My Turn* (1998). This lack of fixity also meant that although the majority of Doherty's works were still situated in and around Derry with reference to events in Northern Ireland, their themes became increasingly transferable to the traumatic consequences of conflicts

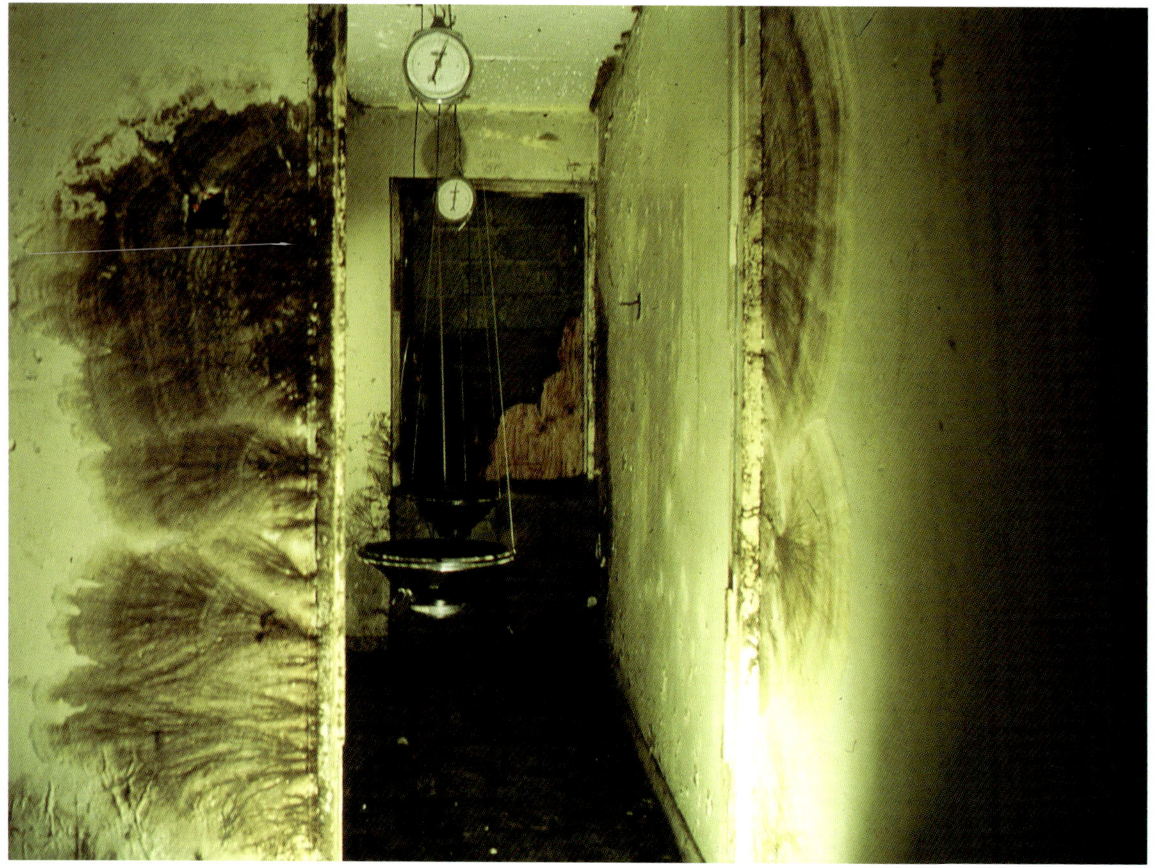

216 Philip Napier, *Gauge II*, 1997, installed at Glenfada Park, Derry, weighing scales, public address system, sound, running water, speakers.

elsewhere. This was also linked to the growing exposure of Doherty's photographs and video installations outside Northern Ireland: in 1993 he represented Ireland at the Venice Biennale and the following year he was short-listed for the Turner Prize.

Philip Napier's two-part installation *Gauge* (1997) also engaged with the events of Bloody Sunday, and was made in the context of the increasing demands for an apology from the British government for the killings. In the Orchard Gallery in Derry, *Gauge II* consisted of a public address system transmitting a repeated apology through fourteen speakers – one for each of the dead. As pools of water from dripping taps formed on the gallery floor, the resonance of the sound across the surface of each speaker triggered the movement of a needle on the dial of a weighing scale. Yet measuring the weight of each apology revealed it to be continually variable and contingent. As Liam Kelly, then Director of the Orchard Gallery, has suggested, the work becomes 'a proposition that language alone cannot be adequate', indicative of a deep traumatic scarring as the legacy of the events of 30 January 1972.[4] The second part of the work, *Gauge II*, reinstalled the speakers and scales in a derelict Housing Executive property in Glenfada Park. Here the addition of Napier's installation had the effect of activating a range of meanings, the already uncanny associations of the abandoned house also underpinning the tragic connotations of its proximity to the site of the killings. The property's imminent demolition, meanwhile, suggested that the need for a resolution to the controversies of Bloody Sunday was all the more pressing.

Although *Gauge* might suggest the use of a specific location as a catalyst for memory, an earlier piece by Napier foregrounded the visceral aspects of trauma. The assemblage *Ballad 1* (1992) combined the plaintive sound of a motorized accordion with an image of

Bobby Sands, not only the leader of the 1981 hunger strike, but also the first man to die. On one level, the inarticulate sound that accompanies the often reproduced photograph of Sands could imply, in the context of the broadcasting ban, the lack of means of coherent self-representation for those who had been silenced. Any romanticization of martyrdom is countered by the ghastly evocation of the starving body, as the air forced through the accordion suggests a final struggle for breath; it also evokes a visceral memory of the deaths of the Famine in the 1840s.

Many artworks made in the 1990s involved a multi-layered response suggestive of the range of effects and interpretations of the conflict. Sandra Johnston's slide

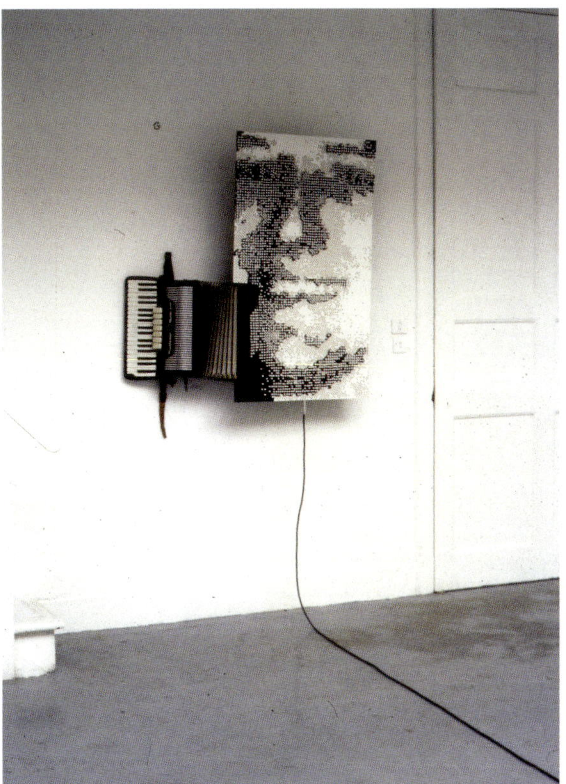

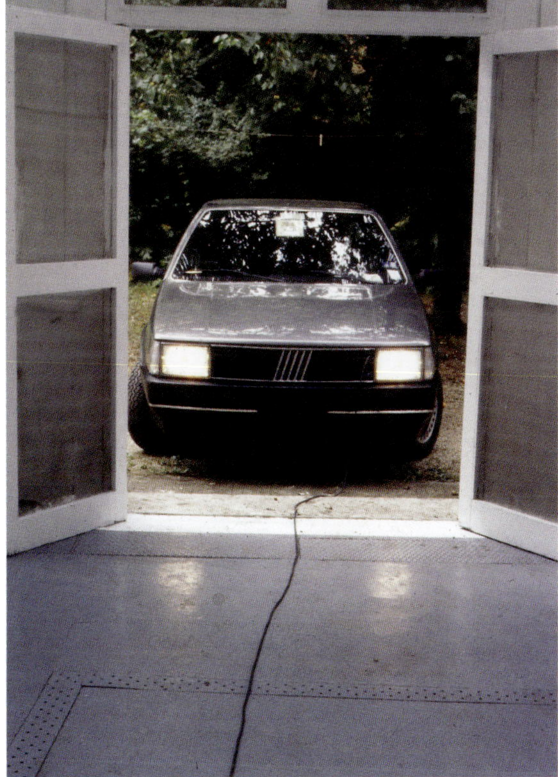

217 Philip Napier, *Ballad 1*, installed at the British School in Rome, 1992.

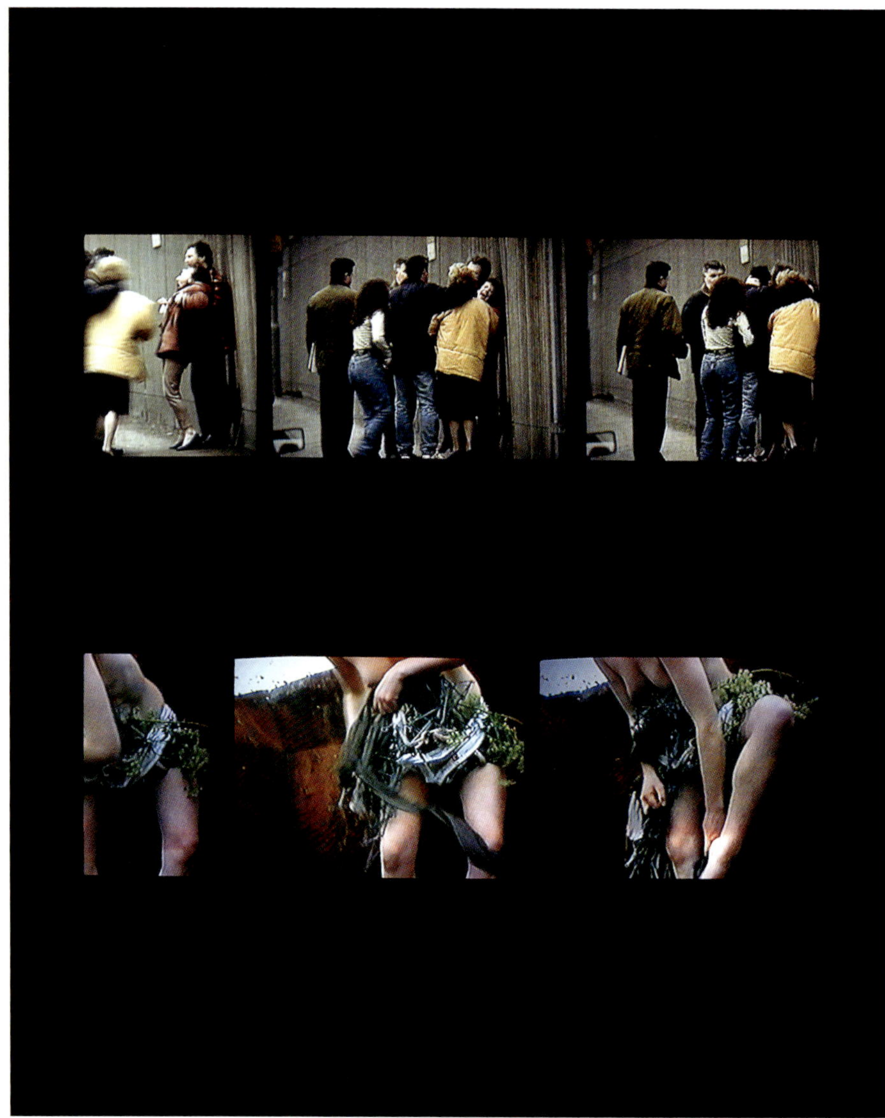

218 Sandra Johnston,
To Kill an Impulse:
mourners (top), and
artist's performance
in a skip, 1994.

installation *To Kill an Impulse* (1994) examined the conjuncture of public grief and personal trauma through a focus on the roles of women both as victims and as mourners at the funerals that occurred so frequently at this time. Two sets of slides were projected onto the same sheet of glass from opposite sides of the room. The first set was of images of women mourners derived from television footage, while the second documented a performance by Johnston in a skip in a public space in East Belfast. Rather than depicting the grieving women as media spectacle, Johnston's interest was in subverting this representation, focusing instead on the management of grief, whereby extreme emotion was shielded from the television camera's intrusive voyeurism.[5] The slides of Johnston's performance documented a series of actions. Climbing naked into a skip full of urban detritus, she began to clothe herself in discarded women's and children's clothing found

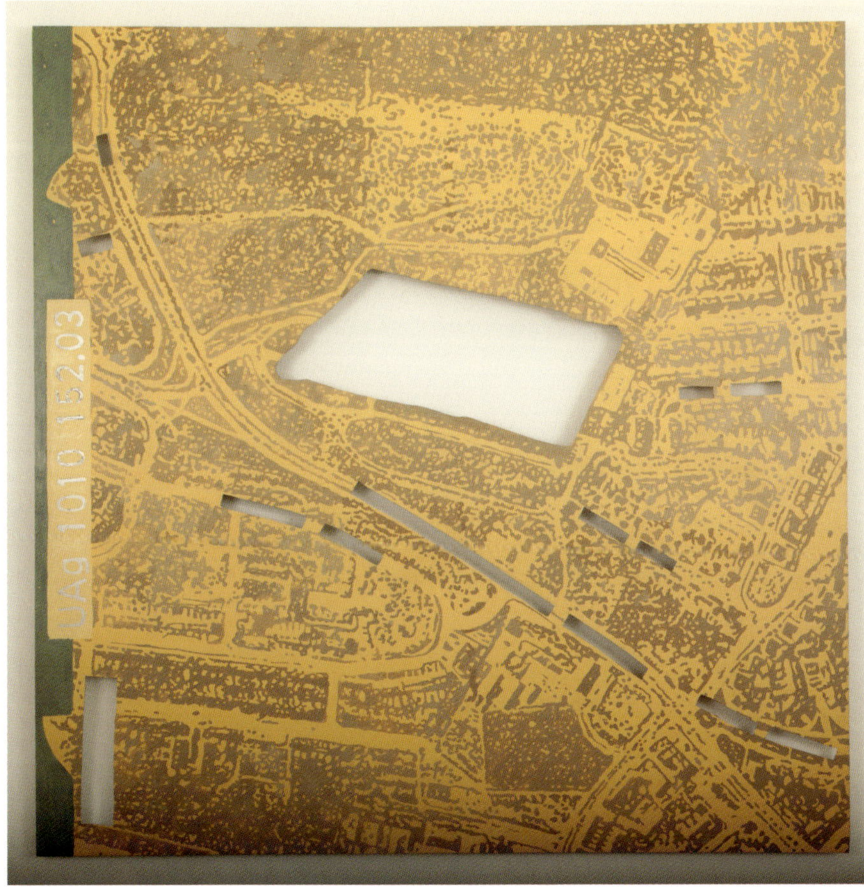

219 Michael Minnis,
Moving in a Given Direction,
1993, oil on aluminium.

there. This suggests a process of catharsis, a working through of rage and grief after a traumatic attack that she herself had undergone. Yet the artist's ritualized actions were also an act of mourning for Margaret Wright, a Protestant woman murdered by loyalist paramilitaries after being mistaken for a Catholic earlier in 1994, and whose body was dumped in the yard of a derelict house.

In Johnston's *To Kill an Impulse* the urban environment functions as a site of trauma and catharsis erupting through procedures for its containment. A further concern for artists in the 1990s was the regulatory mechanisms affecting public life in a war zone. Significantly, at a time when the military presence was becoming increasingly subject to question through the

beginnings of the peace process, there was also a shift in art practice towards an increased interrogation of the links between military power and spectatorship. The experience of urban space in Northern Ireland's cities and towns was subject to a continued regime of military occupation and ongoing surveillance; movement through city streets was frequently curtailed by barriers and roadblocks and always recorded by security cameras on the heavily fortified police stations and army posts, their voyeuristic power reinforced by a blank anonymity. In a painting entitled *Moving in a Given Direction* (1993), the artist Michael Minnis focused on relationships between cartography, surveillance and power. The paintings involved the replication of parts of maps of Belfast on large sheets of aluminium.

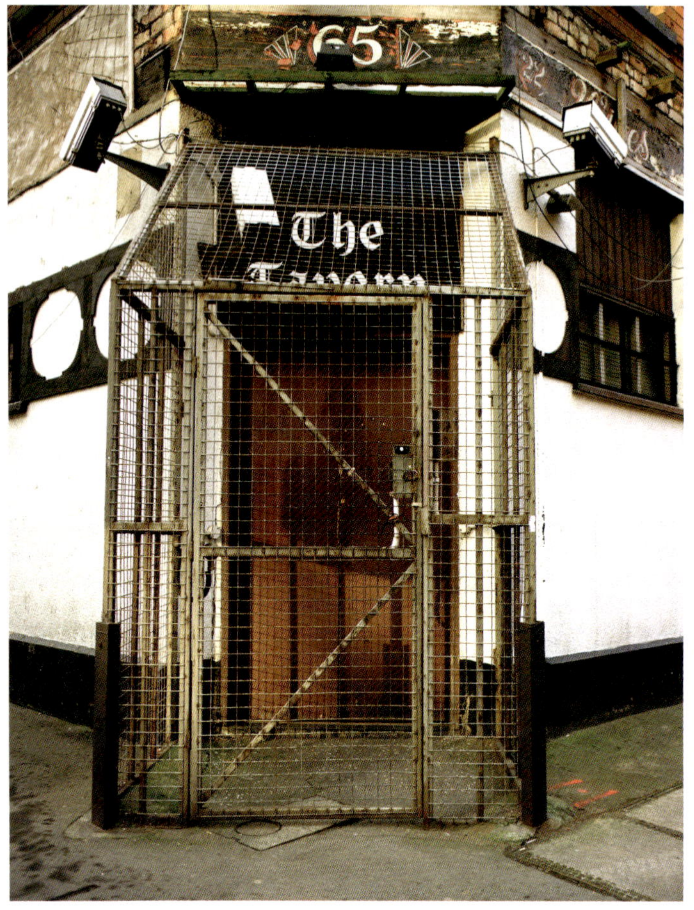

220 Paul Seawright, *Cage II*, 1997, C-type photograph on aluminium.

In spite of the provision of otherwise detailed topographical information, security installations are missing from Ordnance Survey maps of Northern Ireland. In this painting these areas of the map have been cut out from the surface. No longer unseen, the installations now become highly visible, stressing their presence as anomalous and alien to the organic structure of surrounding streets.

An awareness of the panoptic gaze as controlling and regulating the experience of urban life in Northern Ireland in the 1990s was a recurring feature of art prac-

tice. A photograph from Paul Seawright's series 'Police Force' (1995) shows the view out of the upstairs window of a police station on to a street below; a sub-machine gun lies on a ledge in the foreground. The alliance of the regulatory power of the gaze with more coercive forces of containment is particularly explicit in this image, yet surveillance is also a feature of other works by Seawright from this time. *Cage II* (1997) depicts the front door of a bar, heavily fortified and fitted with CCTV cameras. Pubs and clubs were targets of bombings and assassinations from the earliest stages of the conflict, necessitating measures to protect people within.

These bars were the home of hard-drinking men on both side of the conflict yet, as Alvin Jackson suggests, Seawright's photograph evokes the history of fortified houses in Ireland's past.[6] In paintings by Rita Duffy dating from the same year, the relationship between the contemporary conflict, the colonized past and gender identities becomes more explicit. Both *Banquet* and *Plantation* (1997) depict fortified enclosures whose corrugated walls and watchtowers derive from contemporary security installations. This military presence, heavily associated with masculinity, surrounds a feminized domestic space within – a dinner table and chairs, or a manicured kitchen garden. The term 'plantation', however, is also a precise historical reference to the early seventeenth-century settlement of Ulster, mainly by Protestant lowland Scots, to whom the British state gave land confiscated from the Catholic Irish nobility. Plantation settlements tended to be around fortified garrisons to ensure their survival. After

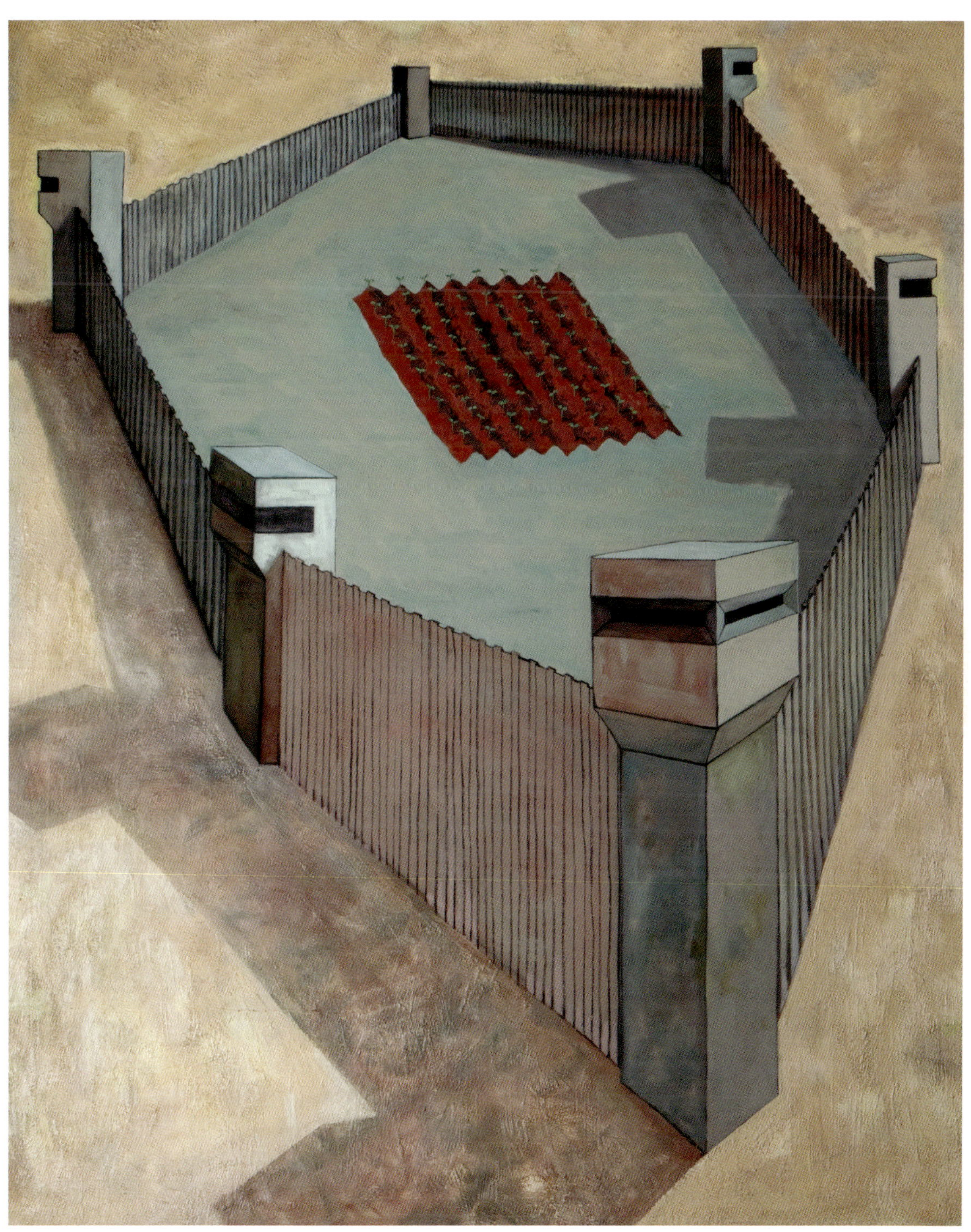

221 Rita Duffy, *Plantation*, 1997, oil and wax on linen.

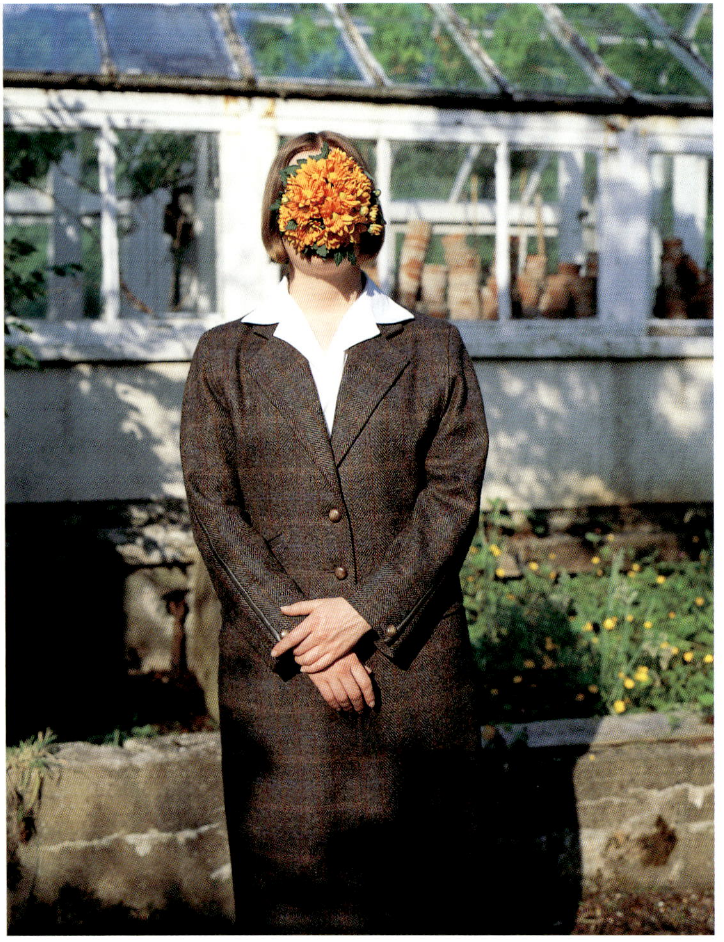

222 Mary McIntyre, *The Great War Continues*, 1993, colour photograph.

a garden in front of an extensive greenhouse. A small gardening fork in one hand, her clothing, demeanour and setting are indicative of understated privilege. Class and wealth are never inseparable in a Northern Irish context from associations of religion that in turn link to demarcations of territory. This photograph suggests lush Victorian gardens in suburban South Belfast tended by leisured upper-middle-class women, relatively untroubled by urban conflict. Yet the security of such readings is destabilized by a strategy borrowed from Magritte (as is the photograph's title), in that the woman's face is obscured by a bouquet of flowers. In common with a slightly later photograph, *Already Seen by Too Many People* (1994), an inverted image of a woman with her head in the ground, McIntyre's staging here suggests a querying of conventional associations of woman and nature. But it also conveys a sense of dislocation and unease, undermining the stability of gender readings in association with

the massacres of the Elizabethan period the Plantation was a relatively peaceful process as the settlers established themselves with their families.[7] Duffy's paintings, however, suggest that urban spatial politics in Northern Ireland are also inseparable from the history of colonization, and that both need to be reconfigured in gendered terms.[8]

The representation of women in urban space is not always straightforward. Mary McIntyre's photograph *The Great War Continues* depicts a woman standing in the subtle signs of place underpinned by class and religion.

Relational art in the urban environment

A reassessment of the ways in which artists could engage with the urban environment had other consequences, with new spaces for the making and exhibiting of work beginning to facilitate more socially

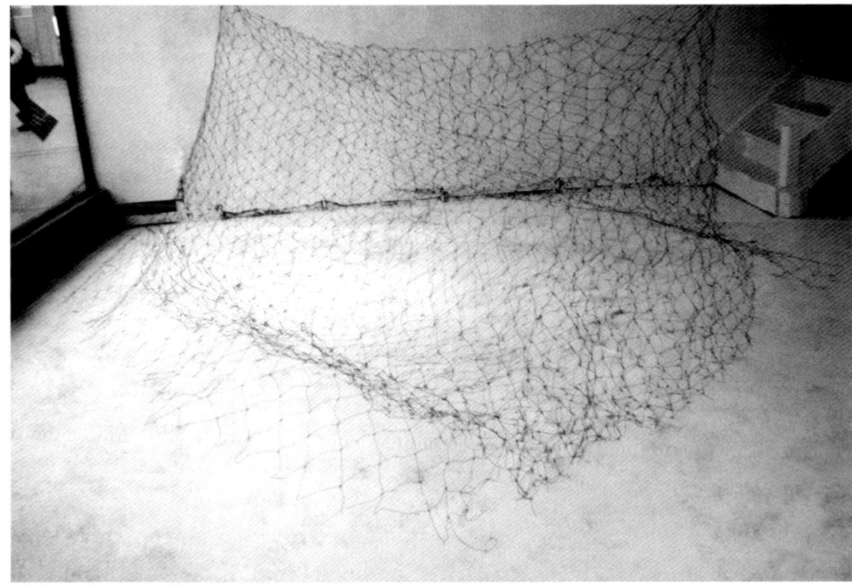

223 Aisling O'Beirn, *Tent*,
1995, copper wire.

engaged or conceptually based forms of practice. Following the precedents of the Beuys-inspired Art and Research Exchange and the Artists Collective of Northern Ireland, these initiatives were essentially artist-led. During the 1980s, the Artists Collective's activities were focused around the Queen Street studios in the centre of the city. By the end of the decade it was becoming apparent that the studios could not support the increasing diversification of art practice. Situated at the top of an old building, the studio environment was more suited to portable easel painting than large sculptural installation.[9] In 1989 the Flax Studios was founded by a group of recent graduates from the MA programme at the University of Ulster as a means of enabling them to continue to make experimental, installation-based work. The studios were situated in a disused linen mill at the Edenderry industrial estate high up on the Crumlin Road to the north of the city; they remained there until destroyed by fire in 2003. The vast spaces of the Flax Studios encouraged

more experimental attitudes towards art practice. As Aisling O'Beirn, who became involved with the studios in 1992, suggested, the Flax 'was not about organising exhibitions but providing a context within which work could happen'.[10]

In this environment, with its vantage point above the city, O'Beirn's own practice became increasingly engaged with issues around architectural space, mapping and the mediation of information. A site-specific piece, *Tent* (1995), was originally situated in a disused arcade that served as a thoroughfare between commercial areas in the centre of Belfast. Like many of O'Beirn's works, *Tent* took the form of a 'spatial drawing', its shape and form constructed out of knotted copper wire; its bizarre appearance in an empty shopping unit served to highlight the incongruity of the outmoded spectacle of display elsewhere in the arcade – no longer a celebration of capital, but indicative of an endemic decline. A significant feature of Aisling O'Beirn's work at this time was a move away from the artwork as a commodified object; more important is its ability to catalyse the viewer's engagement with their surroundings or aspects of the cultural and political environment shared with the experience of other spectators. In common with other artists associated with the Flax Studios, such as Mike Hogg and Philip Napier, O'Beirn's work suggests readings of relational art, a term used by Nicolas Bourriaud to denote 'a set of artistic practices which take as their theoretical and practical point of departure the whole of human relations and their social context'.[11] Although applied to a range of artists who emerged in the 1990s, any notion of the relational in the context of Northern Ireland was always mediated by the specific conditions of a distinct political and cultural history.

A proliferation of studios and other artist-run initiatives followed during the next few years. The most significant of these was Catalyst Arts, established in 1993 near the art college in Belfast's city centre in order to promote a wide range of contemporary art practices in a space removed from the market-orientated concerns of private galleries. Catalyst soon became a focus for innovative and experimental art, often situated outside the gallery itself. This included site-specific installations by a range of artists in *Hit and Run* (1994), situated in Wilmont House, a former nursing home in a park to the south of the city, and live arts events such as *Splatter* on Hallowe'en night in 1996 at the former Crawfordsburn Fever Hospital.[12] These new artist-run initiatives – which also included the Golden Thread Gallery from 1998 onwards – played an important role in revitalizing the city's cultural life at a time when political intransigence was finally beginning to crumble; they also began to attract the interest of artists from outside Northern Ireland.

The nation's time and place

Remarkable as it would have seemed twenty years previously, Ireland at the end of the century was one of the world's richest nations as a result of the economic boom called the Celtic Tiger phenomenon. Unemployment declined considerably throughout the 1990s and wages rose, as did consumer spending. Yet Ireland's new wealth was far from universally distributed. Existing social divisions between rich and poor became even more apparent as already inadequate social services declined further and the wealthy benefited from sympathetic tax schemes. As Fintan O'Toole points out, Ireland was also one of the most globalized nations, with prosperity fuelled by large-scale foreign investment, mainly by American companies.[13] Encouraged by major tax incentives and a skilled labour force, foreign companies began to set up in Ireland in the early 1990s. Ireland's new-found prosperity and reduction of economic dependence on Britain also created a context for a major reassessment of the relationship between the two countries. This was reinforced by the ongoing development of the Peace Process throughout the decade. The renunciation of the Republic's claims to the North also recognized the desire of most of its inhabitants to remain part of the United Kingdom. This major revision of nationalist claims was indicative of a significant shift in public opinion in the South, largely a consequence of the growth of disillusionment with the protracted conflict over the past two decades. Indeed, questions around the meanings of 'nation' were also beginning to emerge on a wider scale after the fall of the Berlin Wall in 1989.

This soon became evident in relation to the commemoration of the founding moment of twentieth-century Irish nationalism, coinciding with Dublin's year as European Capital of Culture in 1991. The 75th anniversary of the Easter Rising passed by, largely without official commemoration. One of the places where the anniversary was remembered, though, was in Kilmainham Gaol, the site of the executions of the Rising's leaders. This also became the venue for a significant exhibition, *In a State: An Exhibition in Kilmainham Gaol on National Identity*. Curated by Jobst Graeve from the Project Arts Centre, works by 21 artists were installed in the ground floor cells encircling the Gaol's Great Hall. Many of the works were highly critical of established constructs of Irish national identity, although in different ways. Alice Maher's *Cell* – a large ball of briars filling all the available space – for example, forcefully suggested a fundamentally dystopian view of the nation.[14] Two other installations challenged discourses of Irish national identity through the politics of the criminalized and sexualized body. In *Caught in a State* by Dorothy Cross, a pig embryo on its bed of straw, bathed in a green light, suggested the forced incubation of unwanted foetuses in a country where abortion was still illegal. Louise Walsh's installation focused more on the meanings of the Gaol itself as a site both of 'criminality and colonialism'. In *Out Laws and In Laws*, photographs of two gay couples kissing were overlaid by the writhing bodies of snakes. Not only were snakes symbols of sexuality allegedly expelled from Ireland by St Patrick, but the entrance to the Gaol itself is surmounted by chained serpents, a motif providing Walsh with a means of bringing 'together these ideas of nationality, sexuality and oppression'.[15] Although decriminalized two years later in 1991, homosexuality was then still illegal in Ireland. Central to Walsh's installation was a sense of anger that,

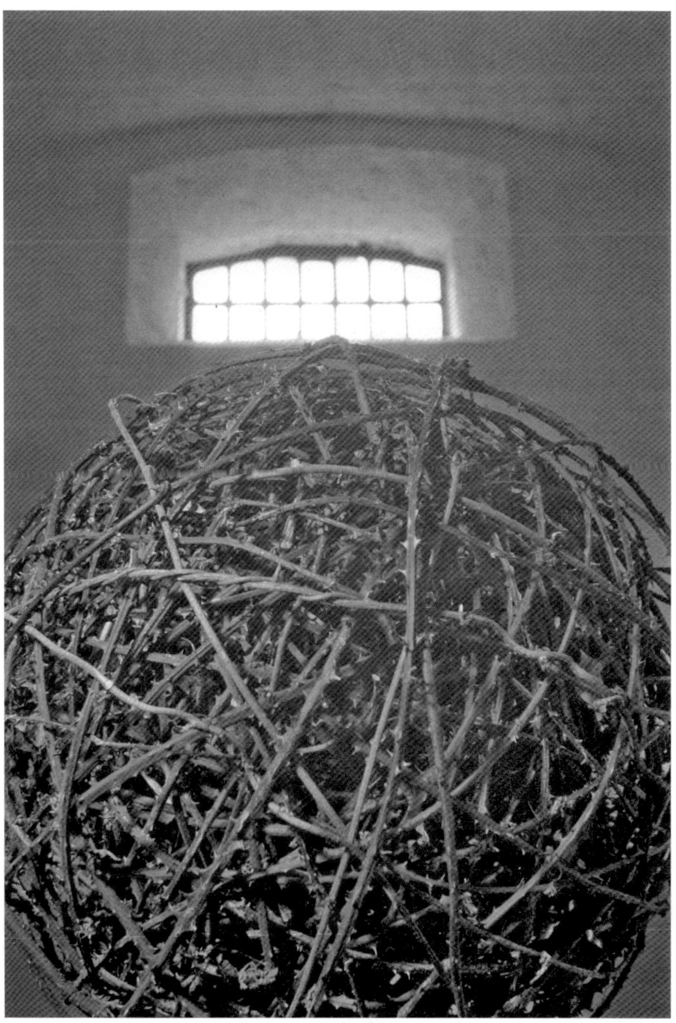

224 Alice Maher, *Cell*, 1991, brambles.

in spite of challenges in the Irish and European courts, 75 years after the Rising's promise of a transformation in the lives of the people of Ireland, gay Irish men were still punished by a law enacted under British rule. In both of these works by Cross and Walsh the body as a site of control, criminality and continued colonization marked out a position of otherness to dominant modes of national identity.

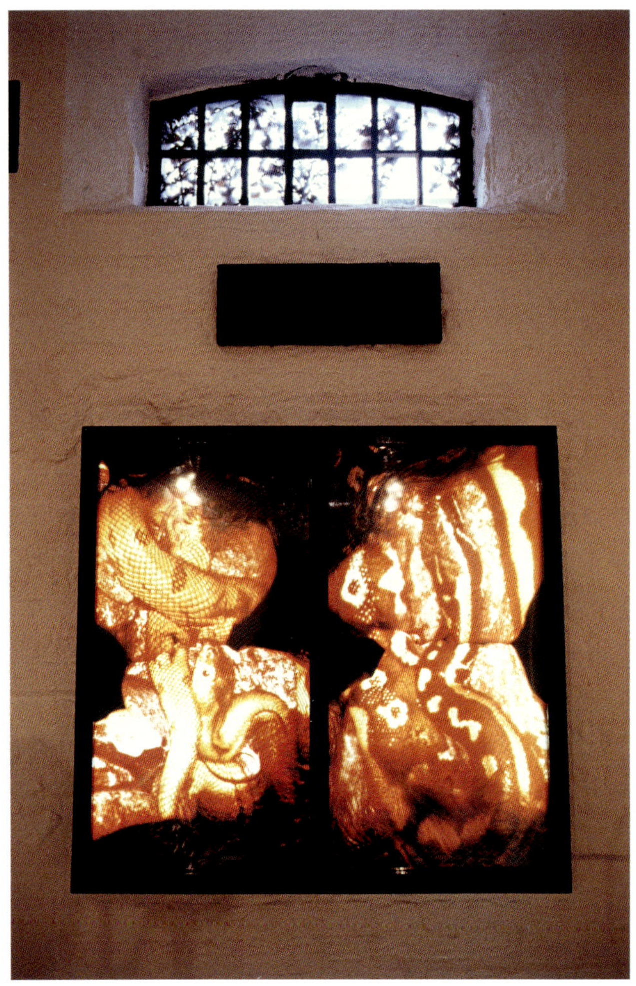

225 Louise Walsh,
*Out Laws and In
Laws*, 1991,
installation.

A transition from the isolationist discourse of nationalism towards a more inclusive cultural identity was also taking place elsewhere. One of the highlights of Dublin's year as Capital of Culture was the opening of the Irish Museum of Modern Art (IMMA) in the seventeenth-century Royal Hospital Kilmainham, with Declan McGonagle as the first Director. The museum's opening collection included a large number of acquisitions from both Irish artists, including Dorothy Cross, Ciarán Lennon and Patrick Ireland, and non-Irish, such as Richard Long and Lawrence Weiner. Some 85 years after Hugh Lane's proposed collection of modern Irish and European art, Ireland finally had an institution that to some degree addressed these aims. However, IMMA arrived in very different political circumstances, with a very different relationship to both Irish nationalism and the culture of contemporary Europe – or indeed the world beyond. This also affected the relationship of the Museum with the building in which it was situated. Widely recognized as one of the finest achievements of

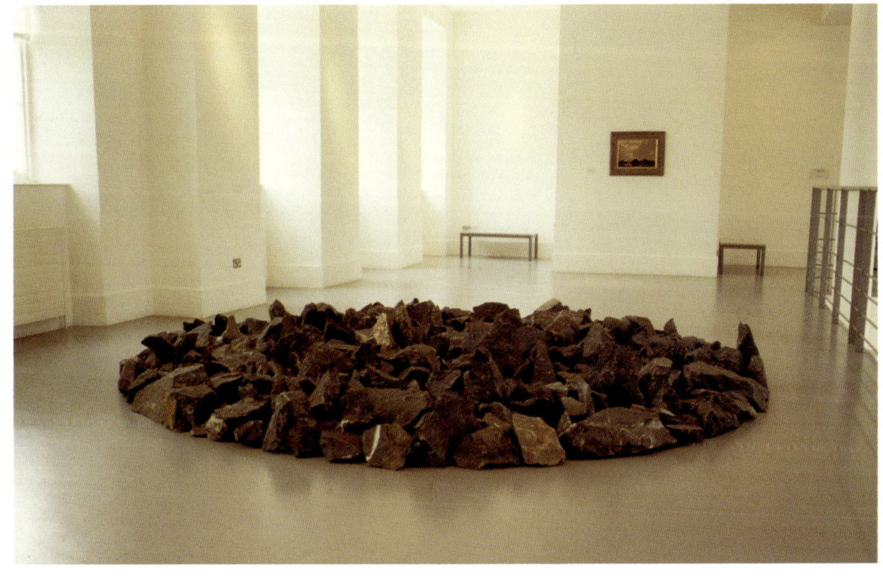

226 Works by Paul Henry and Richard Long displayed together as part of the opening hang at IMMA (the Irish Museum of Modern Art) in Dublin, 1991.

Irish architecture, the French-designed Royal Hospital represented an engagement with classically defined European cultural tradition. Narrow corridors and small rooms around a massive open courtyard made it difficult to suggest continuity between the works on show. For McGonagle, displaying a similar sense of ingenuity as he did at the Orchard Gallery, this became an opportunity for an affirmation of postmodern diversity although, as Joan Fowler pointed out, the outcome was rather more contradictory, embracing both 'the breakdown of linear and hierarchical cultural legacy as defined by the cultural centres, and a reinvestment of meaning in those very legacies'.[16] Strategies of discontinuity and juxtaposition also had consequences for the representation of earlier Irish art. The siting of a Paul Henry painting next to Richard Long, for example, raised questions about the ways that artists engage with landscape. On another level, this and similar curatorial decisions contributed to the continued unravelling of both the cultural discourses of nation and the museum as a repository of the past.

IMMA's collection continued to expand and diversify throughout the decade, acquiring works that included video installations such as Jaki Irvine's *Margaret Again* (1995) in 1996 and Alanna O'Kelly's *Sanctuary/Wasteland* (1993) the following year. Yet the acquisition and display of O'Kelly's installation was one instance of a pervasive re-reading of the past extending far beyond the institution itself. Revision of the nationalist agenda during the 1990s affected not only Ireland's projected future, but also its rehabilitation of the past. An important focus of this was the re-emergence of interest in the effects of the Irish Famine of 1845–9, when it is estimated that approximately one million people of a population of eight million died, largely as a result of the failure of the British authorities to intervene, while a further one million emigrated. Within the discourses of nationalism the memory of the Famine served as a reminder of Ireland's humiliation. Representations of Irish victimhood at the hands of the British were difficult to sustain in the context of Free State rhetoric of independence and the need for positive images of an independent nation. The

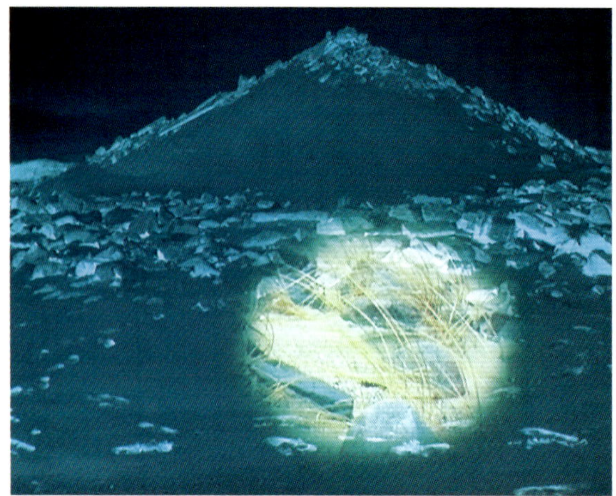

227 Alanna O'Kelly, *Sanctuary / Wasteland*, 1993,
DVD-projected installation.

Famine largely remained uncommemorated, leaving the memory of the cataclysmic events of the previous century to fester as a collective trauma. Significantly, the 1990s was a period of major reassessment of the Famine's status within cultural memory, culminating in 1995 in the commemoration of the 150th anniversary of its onset.

During the decade, Famine memorials began to appear throughout Ireland, often marking significant locations such as the mass graves where the anonymous dead were buried. Others, however, emphasized the suffering of the Famine as the cause of mass emigration. The location of Rowan Gillespie's multi-figure *Famine* (1998) on Custom House Quay in Dublin marked the embarkation point of thousands of destitute emigrants, while the National Famine Memorial, John Behan's *Famine Ship* unveiled the same year by President Mary Robinson in Murrisk, County Mayo, pointed out across the Atlantic to the New World and, ultimately, the transformation of victimhood into a bright diasporic future.[17] Like both of these public commissions, O'Kelly's *Sanctuary/Wasteland* drew attention to the significance of location as a catalyst

for cultural memory, as implied by Pierre Nora's term 'lieux de mémoire'.[18] As a museum-based art installation, however, the piece operated on very different terms and with a much more elliptical and allusive address to viewers than the emotive Expressionism used by Gillespie or Behan.

The interconnected significance of location and the depth of the Famine as cultural trauma were the basis for a tape-slide installation initially made when O'Kelly was shortlisted for the prestigious Glen Dimplex Award in 1994. The site of *Sanctuary/Wasteland* is in Mayo, near Louisburgh at a former Famine burial ground on the Silver Strand beach. At this windswept location at the edge of the ocean, the gradual building of a large cairn commemorated the interment of the nameless victims of starvation. Mayo was an area particularly affected by the Famine: during the 1840s, the population fell by almost 30 per cent. The constant focus of *Sanctuary/Wasteland* is this 'hill of stones', over which images of the surrounding landscape and fragments of bone and other material found at the site are montaged, accompanied by an evocative, wordless soundtrack suggestive of the oral narratives whereby Famine memory was passed on by a non-literate peasantry. Particularly when filtered through the meanings of the landscape of the West, this project invites romanticized readings. *Sanctuary/Wasteland*, however, also draws on a range of associations of the location, which played an important role in the life of the South Mayo community for hundreds of years, first as the site of an early Christian church (whose ruins provided many of the cairn's stones), and second as a burial ground predating the Famine by centuries. This palimpsest of meanings also underpins an emphasis on montage and multivalency within the piece itself. Yet for O'Kelly *Sanctuary/Wasteland* and other works on the same theme indicated the Famine as a point of historical focus, a cataclysmic

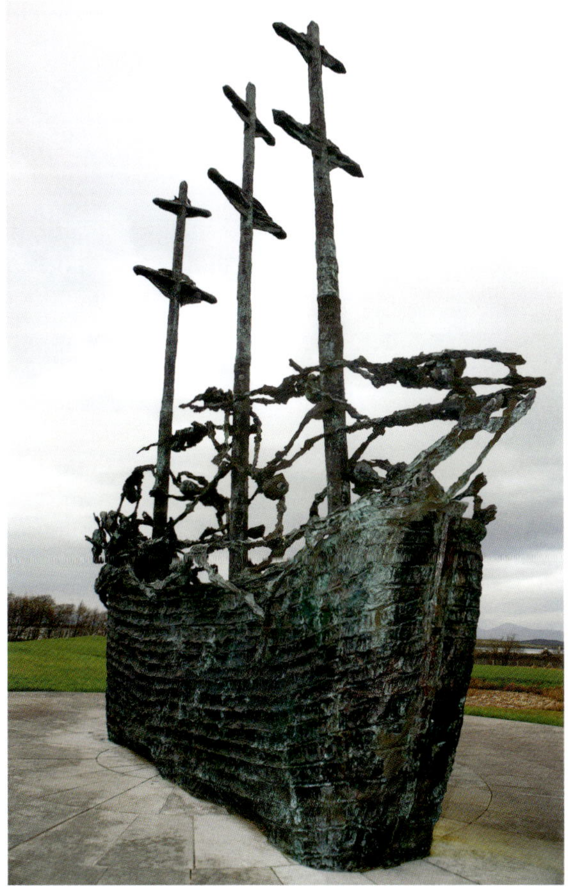

228 John Behan, *Famine Ship (National Famine Memorial)*, 1998, bronze.

moment that initiated significant changes both in notions of Irish identity and culture and in the relationship between Ireland and Britain.

The spectacle of transformation

All aspects of Irish culture and identity were affected by changes that happened so fast that they scarcely felt real. A blending of reality and fantasy permeated a collection of collages by Seán Hillen in which the contradictions of the new Ireland are not so much deconstructed as held up as marvels. The 24 images that made up *Irelantis* were produced between 1994 and 1997, years of unprecedented economic and cultural transformation. The source material for many of Hillen's collages was John Hynde's postcards of scenic landscapes populated by Irish stereotypes: red-haired children loading a donkey in a turf bog or Aran-clad fishermen, for example. Hynde's postcards were hugely popular during the 1960s, purveying nostalgic views of an imaginary Ireland in the fully saturated colours of a remembered dream. In Hillen's fantasies this already highly evocative material was combined with other imagery to suggest an Ireland where the defining visual features of nationalism were eroded in favour of a displaced globalism. Egyptian pyramids emerge from Carlingford Lough, while in *The Oracle at O'Connell St Bridge* an elevated view of Dublin's central thoroughfare is sandwiched between the ruins of the Temple at Delphi and skyscrapers from Los Angeles. As Hillen observed, these were also reminiscent of the new Irish Financial Services Centre then being built in central Dublin.[19]

Increased prosperity led to the expansion of Dublin and other cities, and a proliferation of housing estates, shopping malls and developing road networks contributed to the erosion of distinctions between urban and rural in many areas. Yet the lack of planning regulations meant that remote rural locations, many of great natural beauty, often became densely populated. These changes affecting both the appearance and the social structure of the rural environment took place at the same time as the unravelling of the nationalist project to which representations of rural Ireland had been so central. Throughout the century, landscape painting had played a significant role in the discursive formation of the nation. In the 1990s the representation of the rural in turn became a significant place where the ideological freight of these ideas could be examined. Like

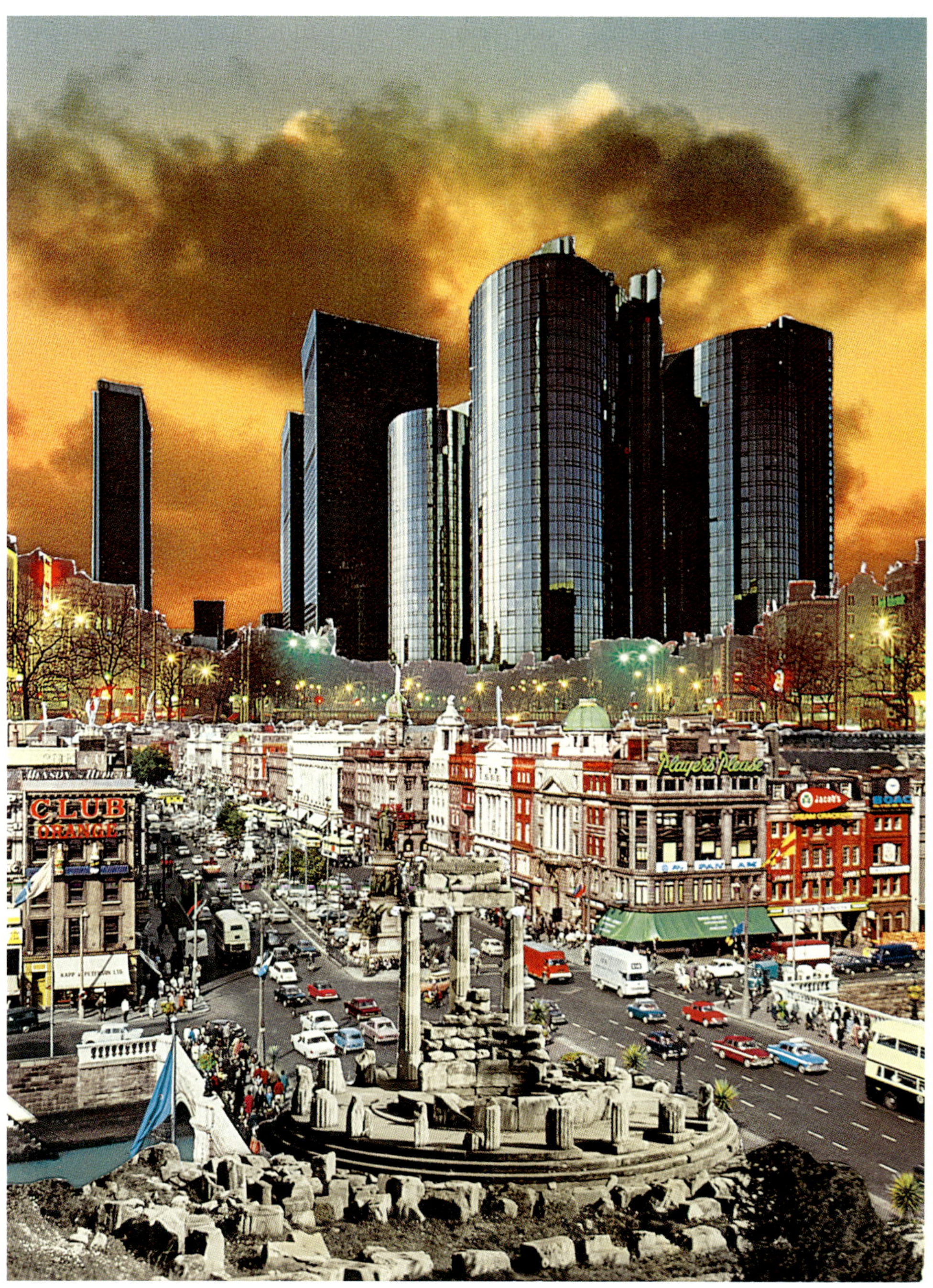

229 Seán Hillen, *The Oracle at O'Connell St Bridge*, 1994–7, photomontage.

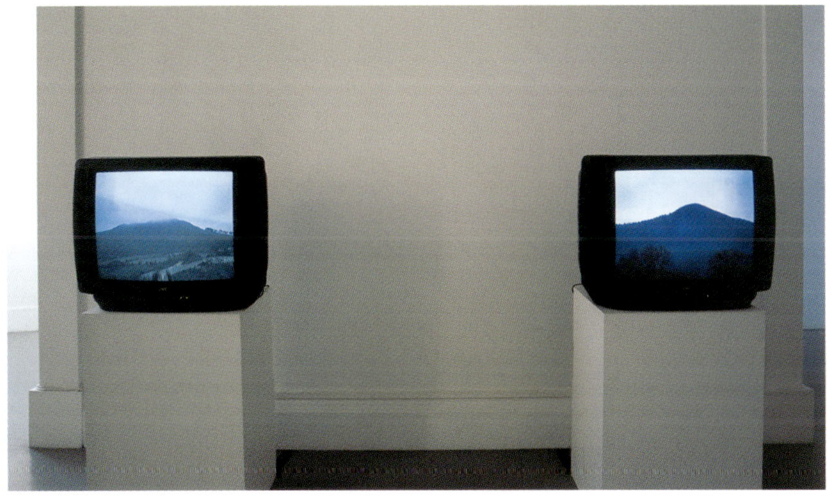

230 Caroline McCarthy, *Greetings*, 1996, video installation.

Hillen's *Irelantis*, Caroline McCarthy's video installation *Greetings* also recognized the power of the picture postcard to frame the landscape within an increasingly outmoded set of assumptions. In *Greetings* a static camera focuses on a distant, misty hillside evocative of a romanticized Ireland; it also records the artist's repeated failed attempts to include herself in this vision as she jumps up and down in front of the camera, the top of her head occasionally coming into shot.

Gender, sexuality and the body

That two women, Mary Robinson and Mary McAleese, could successively become Irish Presidents would have been unthinkable during the polarized gender roles of the Free State earlier in the century. In 1990 Robinson became the first female President of Ireland after a career as a barrister campaigning for causes such as he availability of contraception, abortion and the legalization of homosexuality. Yet in spite of Robinson's public role, the experience of many women in Ireland still left much to be desired. By 1998 women still made up only 38.3 per cent of the workforce, markedly less than in many other European countries.[20] And in spite of increased access to contraception, the continuing illegality of abortion ensured that the body continued to be very much on the feminist political agenda throughout the 1990s.

At the start of the decade it was also beginning to look as if a major change was taking place in the representation of women artists in galleries: in 1992 IMMA's retrospective of the pioneering work of Mainie Jellett earlier in the century was immediately followed by an exhibition featuring the work of two contemporary women artists, *Sounding the Depths*, by Pauline Cummins and Louise Walsh. Indeed throughout the decade women could build on and consolidate the feminist exposure of the 1980s. During the 1990s both Alice Maher and Dorothy Cross began to make work that could be seen less as reacting to immediate, pressing circumstances than investigating deeper themes of identity and sexuality through an expanded range of practice.

Alice Maher's move away from Expressionism came in 1990 with a series of drawings entitled *The*

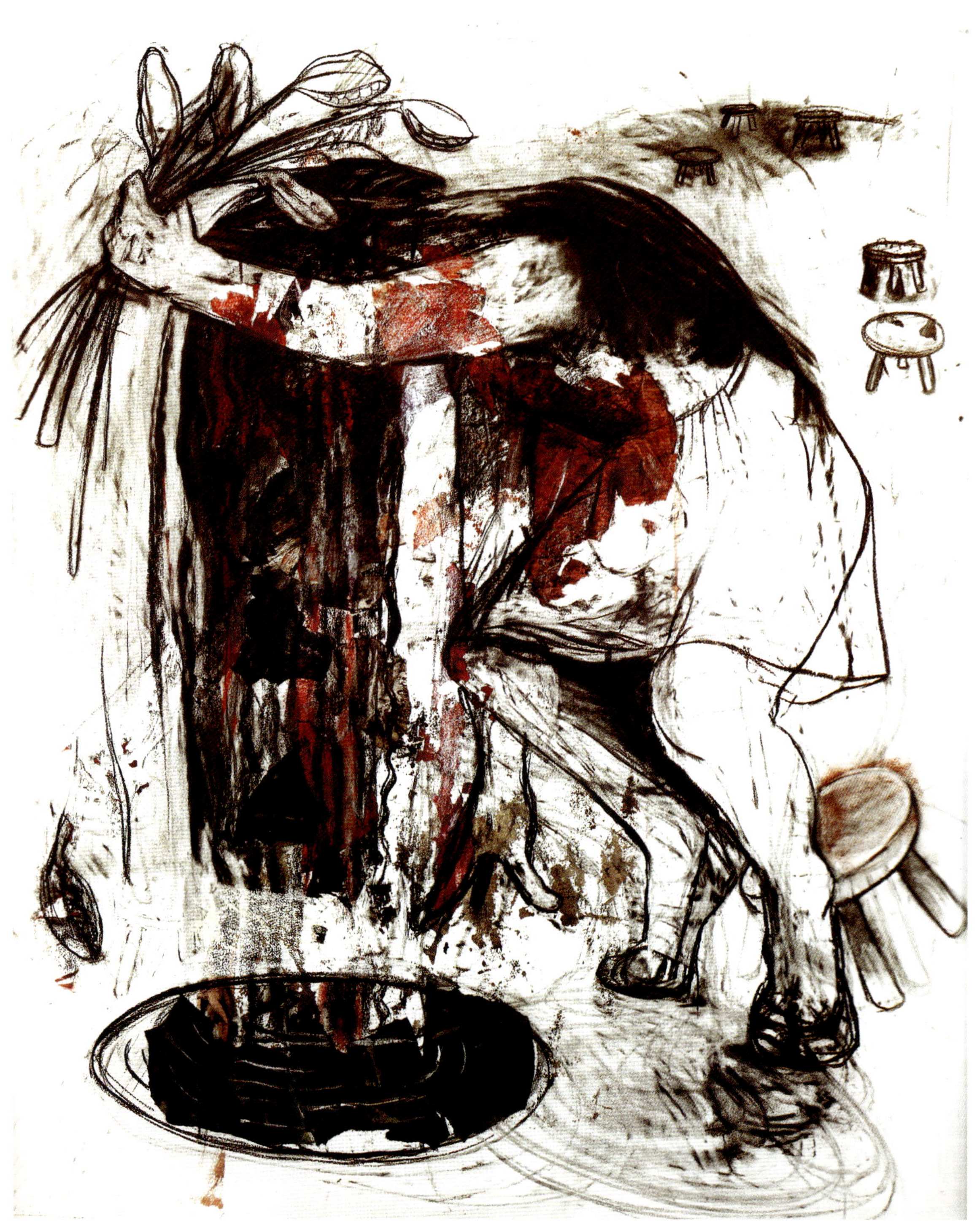

231 Alice Maher, drawing from *The Thicket* series, 1990, charcoal and collage on paper.

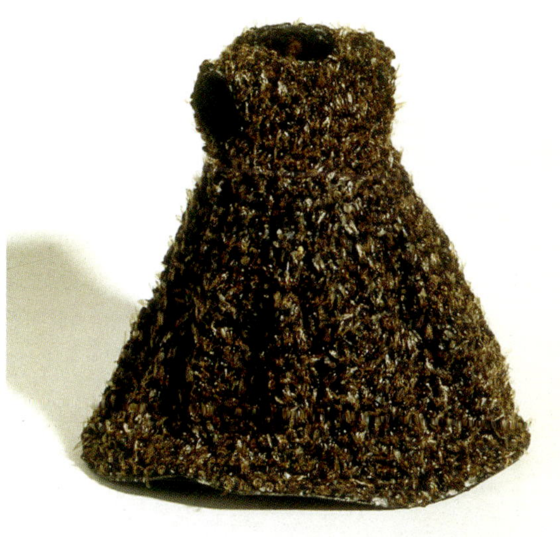

232 Alice Maher, *Bee Dress*, 1994, honey bees, cotton and wire.

Thicket, depicting young girls absorbed in different activities – thinking, walking and weighing and measuring. *The Thicket* also signalled the increased use of drawing in Maher's practice as a technique for interrogative means. The play between a build-up of marks on the paper's surface and their subsequent erasure suggested a shift away from the representation of the female figure as an object of the gaze, and towards a concern with female embodiment – what it means to inhabit the body as a woman. This was a process of identification that continued as a defining characteristic of Maher's practice, through the paintings, drawings and objects of *familiar* (1994) and beyond. In some of these large paintings, such as *familiar 1*, the dizzying perspective focused on tiny figures both fascinates and frustrates the gaze.

Natural materials such as hair or other found objects became a feature of Maher's practice at this time. In *Bee Dress* or *House of Thorns* (1995) the use of

rurally scavenged materials – dead bees or briars – also signified a deep concern with issues of identity. For Alice Maher, whose childhood was spent on a farm in Tipperary, the land was a place of work and sometimes hardship as constitutive of experience. It also, as she later indicated, provided a basis for a sense of scale in her work, recalling the vastness of landscape to a small child, 'when you're a tiny blip moving through it'. This was fundamentally different from the rural as spectacle in the earlier landscape paintings of the West. For

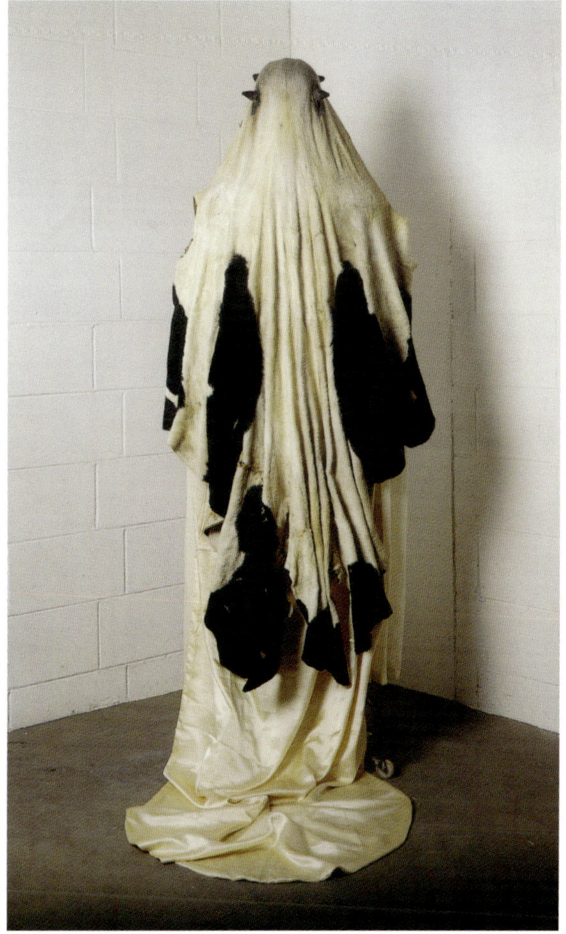

233 Dorothy Cross, *Virgin Shroud*, 1993, mixed media.

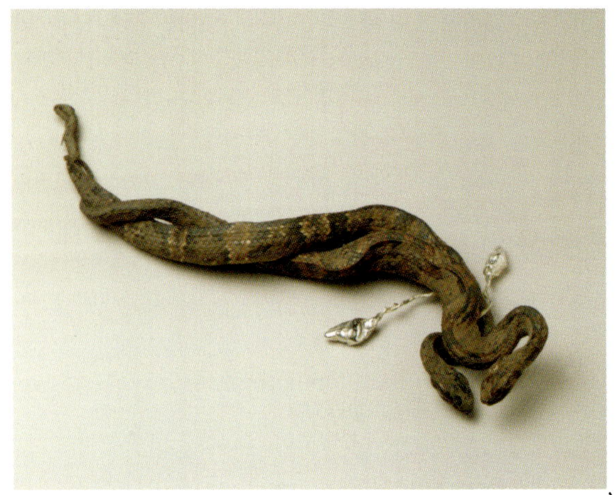

234 Dorothy Cross, *Lover Snakes*, 1995, mixed media.

Maher it was clear that 'land equalled physical discomfort not visual satisfaction'.[21]

In *Bee Dress* Alice Maher produced a talismanic object that was both familiar and menacing. A similar sense of ambivalence, although more erotically charged, also permeated Dorothy Cross's concerns. A group of works made between 1990 and 1994 involved investigation of the suggestive power of the found object, different from her constructed work of the previous decade. These pieces used a combination of cowhide and manufactured artefacts to produce a range of objects that are often both funny and disquieting. In *Amazon* (1992), for example, the cow's udder features as a large nipple protruding from a hide-covered tailor's dummy; both feminine and phallic, its androgynous eroticism also suggests a thematic continuity from the earlier *Shark Lady in a Ball Dress*. Another piece, *Virgin Shroud*, also used a mannequin, but this time draped in cowhide over a wedding dress once worn by Cross's grandmother. There are contradictory signs of the ideal and grotesque, or purity and the bestial; Marina Warner, for example, described these works as 'confront(ing) us with the beast in our

human selves'.[22] In *Virgin Shroud* already insecure readings are further destabilized by the arrangement of the cowhide so that the udder is at the top of the head. Although the falling drapery suggests religious statuary, the Virgin's halo is thus replaced by something altogether more demonic, a complex and powerful image that goes far beyond the artist's earlier critique of Catholicism's attempted control of female sexuality.

The subversive power of these works by Dorothy Cross is also due to their fetishistic quality that has its forerunner in Meret Oppenheim's famous Surrealist object *Le Déjeuner en fourrure*, where a cheap coffee cup, saucer and spoon were covered in Chinese gazelle skin to disturbing effect. Yet the play of meaning in Cross's objects involves verbal as well as visual punning. The making strange of familiar objects – shoes, a shuttlecock or an ironing board – is inflected with references to a problematization of Irishness at a linguistic level: 'the udder' can sound like 'the other' in an Irish accent. An interest in androgyny's instabilities also underpinned a slightly later group of works by Dorothy Cross. *Lover Snakes* consists of two entwined snakes, their hearts removed and encased in little silver reliquaries attached to the preserved bodies. Although sexually differentiated, snakes are believed to be hermaphroditic; the two entwined therefore suggest a common experience of desire. For Cross it was this blurring of boundaries that was important. In describing *Lover Snakes* and related works she asserted: 'I am interested in common mortality, common love and common struggle and the snake provides the perfect metaphor for that communality.'[23] In spite of the snake's far-reaching range of symbolism it also has particular meanings in an Irish context, signifying the banishing of sexual desire by Christian morality. Yet in Cross's imagery – as indeed in Louise Walsh's *Out Laws and In Laws* – there is also the implication of regeneration and rediscovery.

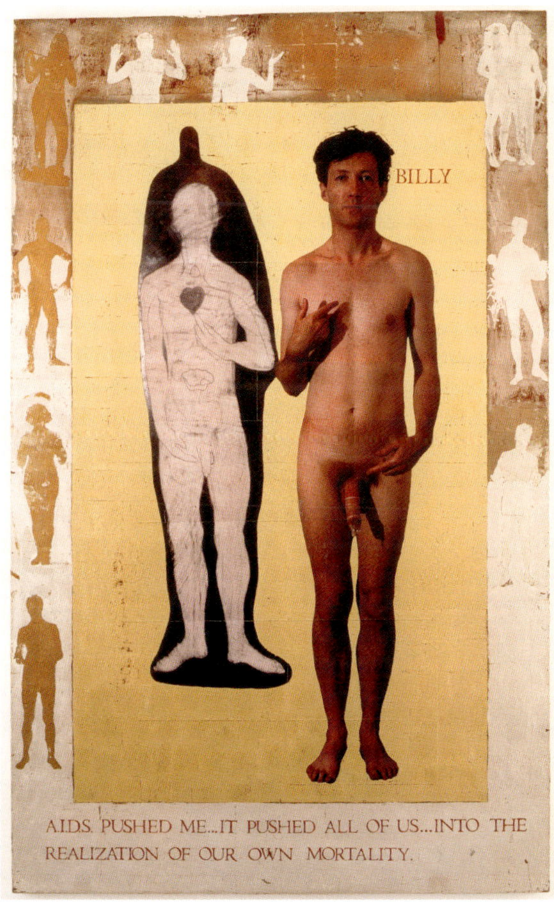

235 Billy Quinn, *Billy*, 1991, laser prints, gold and silver, acrylic on wood.

The increasing fluidity of identity, sexuality and the body in Irish art during the 1990s also took place in a wider context of the liberalization of attitudes to homosexuality. Three years after legalization, the 1996 Dublin Gay Pride Festival also included the exhibition *Pride in Diversity*, featuring the work of fourteen gay, lesbian or bisexual Irish artists.[24] In addition to celebrating a diversity of identity among the artists selected, the exhibition contained work in a range of media, from Mo White's video *My Eye* (1994) to Henry Pim's clay and wood carving *Flight into Egypt* (n.d.). In addition to a range of works engaging with aspects of female identity, the show also included a number of works by Mick Wilson, Andrew Kearney and Billy Quinn. An earlier work by Quinn from 1991, entitled *Billy*, already identified his concerns with the male body as a locus of risk, pleasure and desire. The picture combines photographic self-portraiture with a range of symbolic elements displayed on a gold background and surrounded by a frame containing further figures and text. Naked apart from a condom, the fingers on one of the artist's hands point towards his genitals, while the fingers on the other hand are crossed against his chest for good luck. Meanwhile, behind him a similar figure is drawn in reverse, this time with fingers pointing both to the heart and to the now flaccid penis. The pale corpse-like figure is encased in a black outline that could be either condom or shroud, while the frame's inscription further specifies the work's meaning: 'AIDS pushed me – it pushed all of us – into the realization of our own mortality.' Framing, gesture and symbolism all combine here in the production of a queer iconography of the male body at a time of crisis. Yet there are also clear references to – and a subversion of – the votive imagery of Catholicism. Significantly Quinn made this work while living in London rather than in Ireland, having left in the 1980s due to relentlessly repressive attitudes towards homosexuality.

Irish art in Britain: new belongings

One of the most significant features of Mary Robinson's presidency was the recognition of the role played by notions of diaspora as formative of Irish identity and concepts of the nation. As a means of 'rethinking the boundaries of the nation and how they might be more

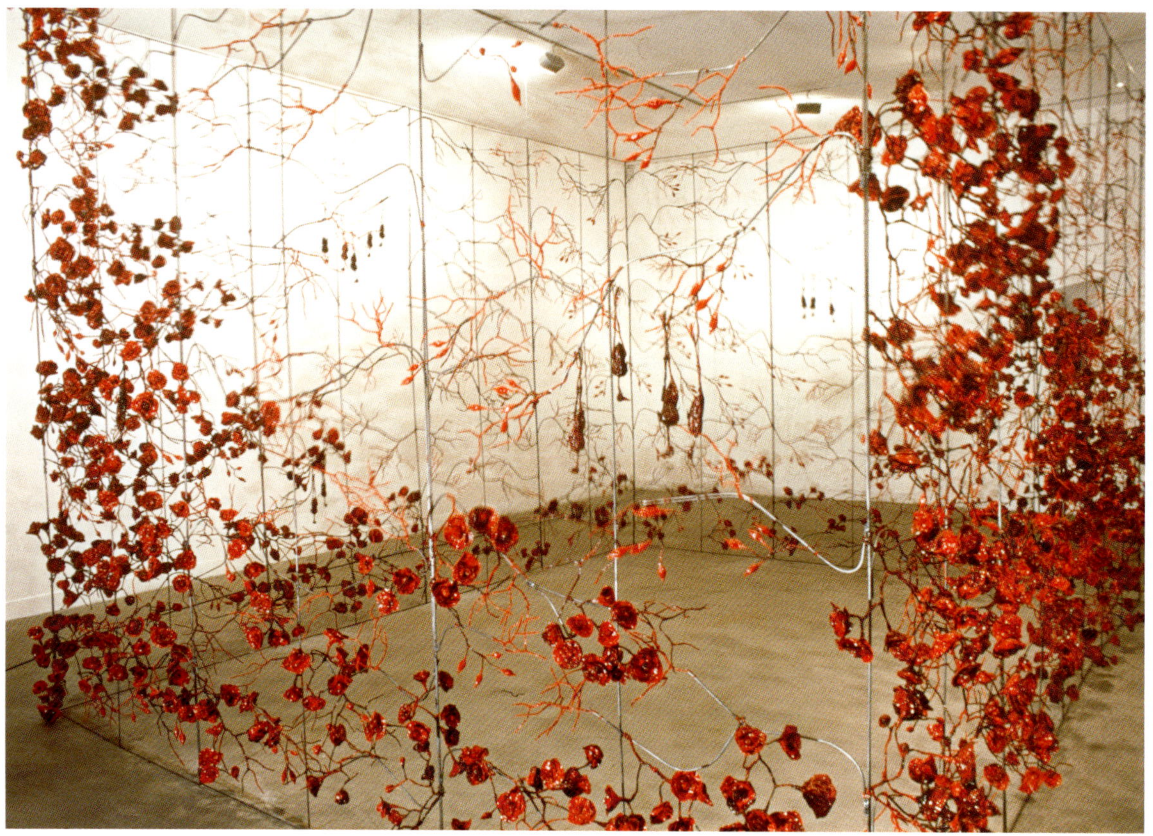

236 Daphne Wright, *They've Taken to Their Beds*, 1997, tinfoil, metal, paint.

openly or progressively defined', diaspora was a term that increasingly gained currency during the 1990s.[25] In a context of increased global mobility across national boundaries, it suggests a more complex formation of identity and subjectivity. Diaspora also implies a sense of a new belonging within a hybrid culture, through an exposure to a range of different influences that help to undermine the old concepts of the nation-state and the static and restrictive forms of identity left behind.[26] These new attitudes began to show up in the work of Irish artists in Britain that was very different from the concerns of works of the 1980s. In a new climate of openness resulting from the changed political relation-

ship between Britain and Ireland, Irish artists in London and elsewhere during the 1990s were able to explore increasingly fluid notions of identity and difference.

For some artists distance allowed a more mediated assessment of aspects of Irish culture to emerge in their work. Coming from a Protestant Anglo-Irish family, Daphne Wright had developed an early awareness of difference from the predominantly Catholic culture of the Republic. As an artist in England this disjuncture became a source for a number of sculptural installations dealing with the uncanny qualities of domestic space. In pre-Independence Ireland the 'Big House' surrounded by its estates was the symbol of the

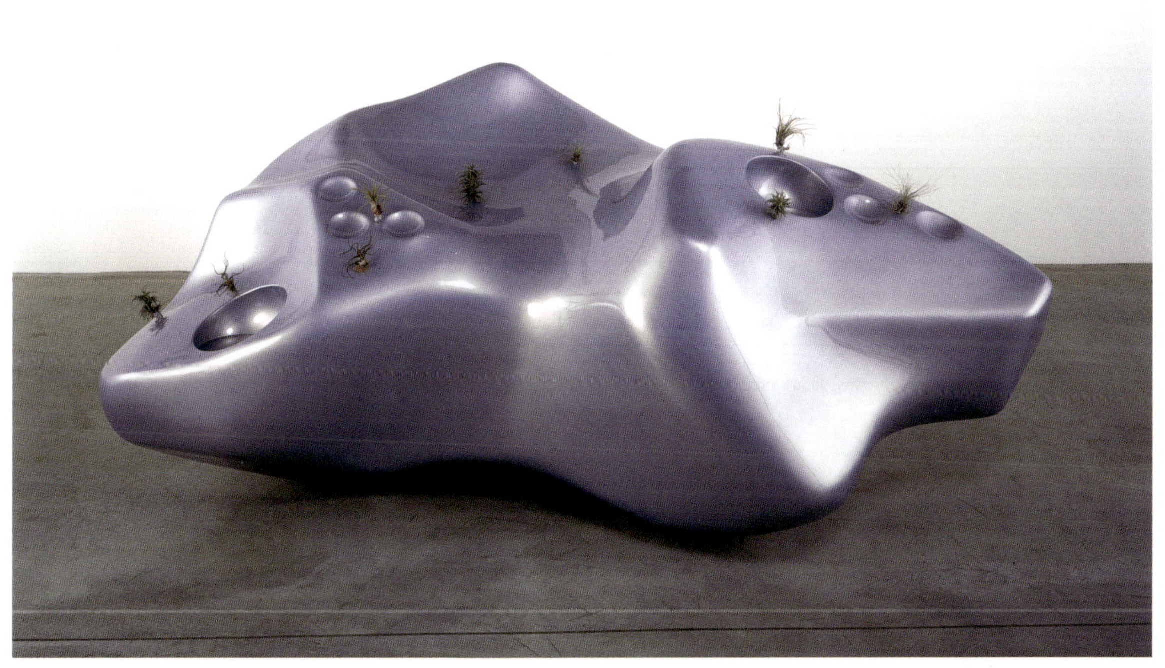

237 Siobhán Hapaska, *Land*, 1998, mixed media.

238 Elizabeth Magill, *View*, 1997, oil on canvas.

Anglo-Irish presence upon the land, a material embodiment of colonial power and control. Wright's installations were made of fragile ephemeral materials. A related group of works from the early 1990s used plaster to produce delicate sculptural forms such as the moulded wallpaper of *Domestic Shrubbery* (1994). She subsequently used painted tinfoil built onto an armature to create the macabre garden space of *They've Taken to their Beds*. Both of these pieces contained elements that undermine the comfort of domesticity through an introduction of the abject: a small eviscerated plaster heart suspended from a wallpaper trellis, or the corpses of birds hanging from the blood-red trees in *They've Taken to Their Beds*. Rather than the benign assertion of authority, the meanings of the 'Big House' are here restaged as horror and decay.

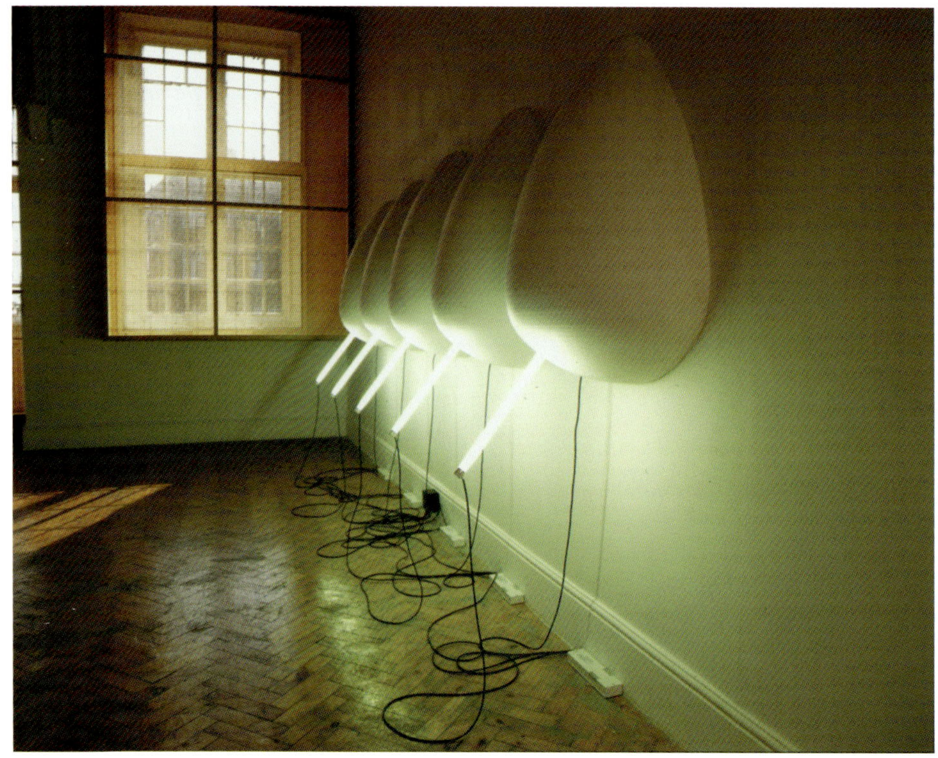

239 Andrew Kearney, *The Policing of Pleasure*, 1995, mixed media.

Other Irish-born artists in Britain at this time also rejected the fixity of Irish identity. For Siobhán Hapaska this was a process that began during her early life in Belfast, where people's names function as a means of identifying their religion. In Hapaska's case, however, her name 'always backfired. It was something else again'.[27] A significant feature of Hapaska's work since the early 1990s was the production of semi-abstract sculptures that often embodied a sense of transition from one state to another. Even the naming of these objects, such as *Hanker* (1997), suggests an indeterminacy borne out by the formal characteristics of the work itself, in this case white fibreglass moulded into the shape of what might resemble a prehistoric bird's head. Yet the objects involve a mismatch that is not just spatial but temporal, in the contradiction between the pristine technology of the works' surfaces and their evocation of something much more primeval. The shiny blue fibreglass of *Land* (1998), dotted with small plants, is interrupted by irregular water-filled craters; its undulating curves appear familiar but are part of an alien topography. The knowledge of Hapaska's Irish origins, however, opens up questions about where – and when – this land might be. The reductive representations of timeless landscape featuring so strongly in the formation of Irish identity are here completely reconfigured into a new hybridity.

The conventions of landscape also inform the work of Elizabeth Magill, although on very different terms than in Hapaska's usage. In a painting entitled *Scenic Route 3* (1997), silhouettes of four people, including a child, gaze up in wonder at what might be the landscape displayed

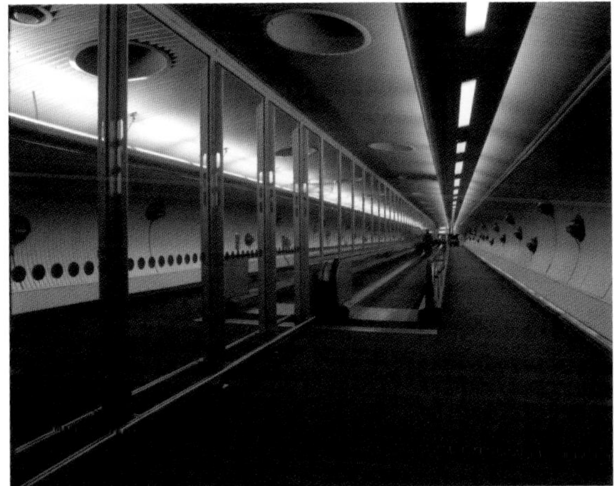

240 Andrew Kearney, *A Long Thin Thread*, 1996–7, installed at Pier 4A, Heathrow Airport, mixed media.

before them or might be a vision of the cosmos. In spite of overt references to German Romanticism and Caspar David Friedrich in particular, the destabilizing effects of the Sublime are reinforced by Magill's use of composite sources. In this painting elements are drawn from sources near her home at different points in her life; one of the figures was photographed in London, while the trees were situated near her family home in the Glens of Antrim. Although Elizabeth Magill grew up in a scenic area of Ireland's northeast coast, she was born in Canada. Aspects of other works, such as the indeterminate vastness of *View* (1997), seem to draw upon the significance of the vista of wilderness in the formation of Canada's national identity.[28] In Magill's handling in these paintings, however, the spectacle of the Sublime, although predicated on a purity of aesthetic response, is in fact derived from a hybridity of experience. As such, as Caoimhín Mac Giolla Léith observed, it resists easy classification in national terms, not 'fitt[ing] comfortably into exhibitions exploring the "the Irishness of Irish art"'.[29]

A significant number of young Irish artists, such as Daphne Wright and Andrew Kearney, moved to Britain

to take advantage of postgraduate educational opportunities. Kearney's large sculptural installations were now informed by often theoretically derived notions of sexuality, identity and power, as in an untitled installation at the Serpentine Gallery in 1992 or the slightly later *The Policing of Pleasure* (1995), shown at Camden Arts Centre.[30] This installation contained a row of five ambivalent objects, whose swelling forms were simultaneously reminiscent of urinals and pregnant bellies, yet were penetrated from beneath by a neon rod. The infrared beam recording the presence of viewers also reinforced the sense of dominance and control. Kearney also used similar technologies of surveillance for a different purpose in a slightly later work, *A Long Thin Thread*, installed 1996–7 at Pier 4A in Heathrow Airport, where all flights to Ireland depart. The passage of travellers, both incoming and outgoing, was monitored by twin infrared barrier beams, and the numbers transferred to a number of rubber-encased digital counters distributed along the pier. Yet the 60 counters displayed different figures, further contributing to the dislocating experience of moving through the anonymous and liminal space of the airport terminal. And in spite of an increased ease of travel between Britain and Ireland at the time, *A Long Thin Thread* was also a reminder of the continued existence of surveillance, monitoring and the gathering of information for apparently arbitrary purposes.

The dislocatory effects of migration, and the ability to unfix identity, were becoming increasingly prevalent features in the work of Irish artists in Britain. Kathy Prendergast's *City Drawings*, an ongoing series begun in 1992, continued to develop her involvement with cartography. Painstakingly executed pencil drawings of maps of the world's capital cities, this series mapped the configuration of streets and routes criss-crossing and defining a view of urban space.

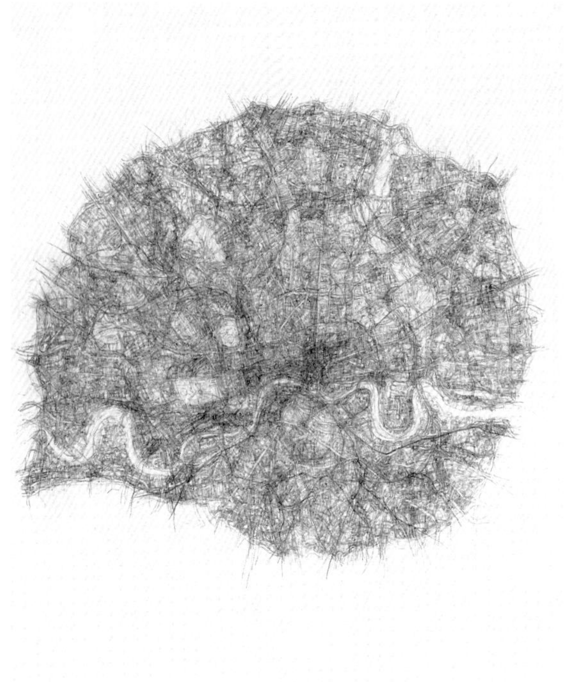

241 Kathy Prendergast, *City Drawings, London*, 1992, pencil on paper.

But with all references to topography omitted, their information value is negated. These cities of the imagination also retain a relationship with the 'body' characteristic of Prendergast's earlier work. Vast conurbations are reduced to a uniformly intimate scale, while the delicately traced streets appear more like arteries and capillaries. In the *City Drawings* the phenomenon of the city becomes a spectacle in its own right, rather than an identification of place, and this undercutting of fixed identity also implies a hybrid cosmopolitanism in its stead. Yet this series was also begun at a time of major geo-political changes such as the break-up of the former Yugoslavia, a time when it was becoming apparent that maps as indices of the territory of the nation-state were themselves open to question.

ELEVEN

After the End of Progress

At the start of the twenty-first century it looked as if the entrenched political polarizations that had also shaped Ireland's economic, social and cultural life were now being transformed into a new and optimistic future. Certainly this was the post-Good Friday view of Richard Kearney, for whom the shifts in 'the Irish-British archipelago' at the start of a new millennium were 'little short of a revolution in our political understanding'.[1] In identifying the Good Friday Agreement of 1998 as marking the end of the power of the nation-state, Kearney also welcomed the emergence of post-nationalism as offering the potential for 'our ineradicable need for identity and allegiance [to] be gradually channelled away from the exclusive focus of the nation-state . . . to supplementary levels of regional and federal expression.'[2] Kearney's focus in this essay was on Northern Ireland, but he advocated the development of different levels of identity – 'regional, national, and transnational' – as undermining the notion of territorial boundaries.[3] Changing conditions would seem to support this; indeed both at home and elsewhere one of the more positive aspects of globalized communications and transnational mobility was the emergence of increasingly fluid and dynamic ways in which Irishness could be defined and experienced. The conflict in the North was ostensibly over, while the South appeared to have settled into an unprecedented prosperity. Yet, as ever, both peace and economic stability were more complex. The Southern economy, rather than secure, actually proved to be quite fragile, while lingering vestiges of conflict haunted the Northern peace.

Irish ethnoscapes and art practice

In June 1999, the exhibition *0044 – Irish Artists in Britain* opened at the PS1 Contemporary Arts Centre in New York, subsequently travelling to the Albright-Knox Gallery in Buffalo before returning to Ireland later in the year, where it was shown at the Crawford Municipal Art Gallery in Cork. The exhibition was initiated by the Crawford's curator, Peter Murray, and featured the work of twenty artists from Ireland currently working in Britain.[4] As Murray stressed in his introduction to the exhibition's catalogue, the emphasis of *0044* was not so much on Irish identity or ethnicity but on 'examining the dislocation that occurs when people move from one country to another'.[5] These 'personal fractures, faultlines and dislocations' themselves become the points of friction from which art emerges, oriented towards a state of identity experienced as a process rather than predetermined, and constantly subject to new influences and encounters within a new set of

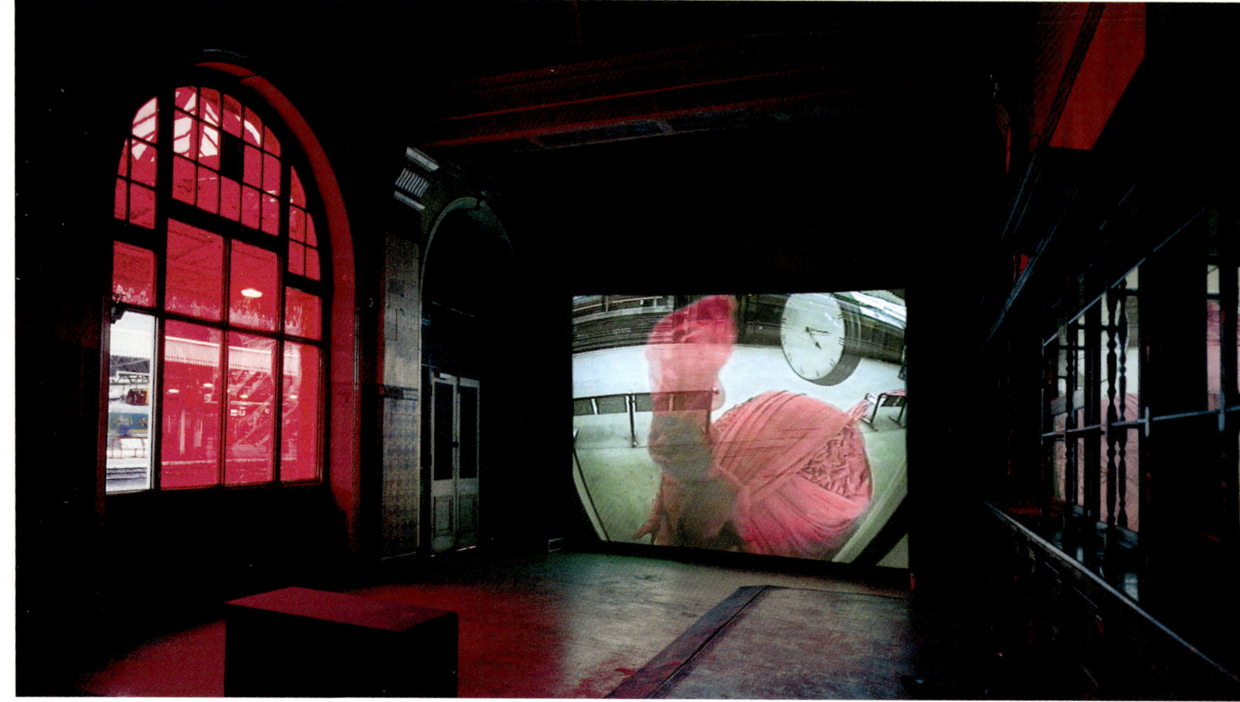

242 Frances Hegarty and Andrew Stone, *Seemingly So, Evidently Not, Apparently Then*, 1997, installation view.

conditions. 0044 itself had been two years in the making, and as such registered changes in the work of Irish artists in Britain that had developed during the latter part of the 1990s; several of these – Siobhan Hapaska, Andrew Kearney, Elizabeth Magill and Daphne Wright – were discussed in chapter Ten.

Significantly, there was very little in 0044 that could be specifically labelled as 'Irish' in terms that would have been recognizable earlier in the century. One work in the exhibition that was pivotal in suggesting readings that queried the stability of Irish identity was *Auto Portrait* (1998), made by Frances Hegarty in conjunction with Andrew Stones and based on the documentation of an earlier live art project, *Seemingly So, Evidently Not, Apparently Then*. This combined CCTV footage from an event staged by the two artists at Sheffield Railway Station with additional filming. It records the spectral presence of a woman (Hegarty) dressed in Victorian costume, descending the stairs to the platform, where she paces up and down. A former member of the Irish Women Artists Group in the 1980s, a significant part of Hegarty's video work of the 1990s explored interrelated ideas around Irishness, femininity and diaspora. *Turas* (Journey; 1990–91), dealt with both the artist's relationship with her own mother and the loss of her mother tongue, the Irish language.[6] *Gold* (1993), filmed partly in Ireland and partly in the Australian desert, opened up more problematic questions about female identity, colonialism and the politics of surveillance.[7] *Seemingly So . . .* developed these concerns, yet rather than trying to claim or retrieve any form of identity, this was a work that queried its fixity. The costume worn by Hegarty, in shocking pink with an excessively large bustle and exaggerated train, was obviously more a pastiche than an accurate representation of middle-class Victorian women's clothing. Putting on this dress allowed Hegarty, who was born in Donegal in the 1940s, to

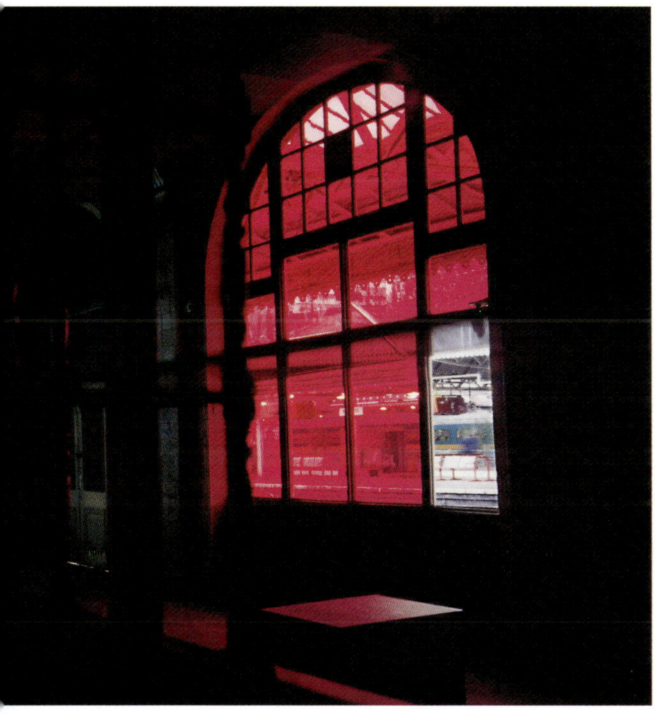

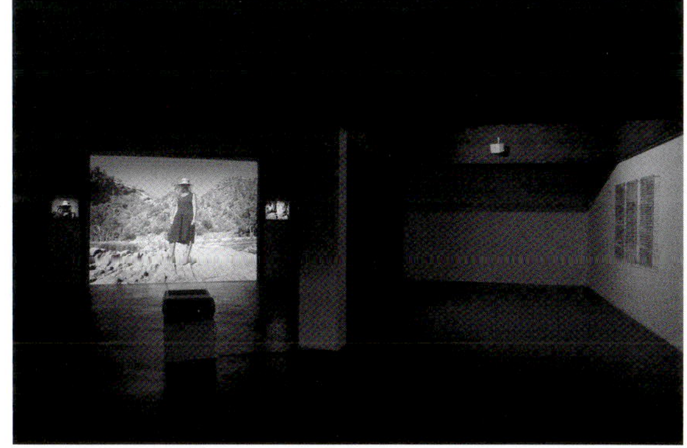

243 Frances Hegarty, installation view of *Gold*, 1993.

masquerade temporarily as a member of the British ruling elite of the previous century; her Irishness becomes invisible, buried by the weight of the fabric she drags behind her. This piece was commissioned by the Site Gallery as part of 'Shunted', a group of public artworks using the station as location. In this context, the hidden labour of the nineteenth-century Irish immigrant men who built the railways also becomes significant, intermingling with readings of travel, mobility and the unfixing of identity characteristic of more recent notions of diaspora.

A similar querying of the role of Irish diasporic identity as a basis for a collective reading of art practice also characterized a slightly later exhibition, *Kin*, curated at the Kerlin Gallery in Dublin by Caoimhín Mac Giolla Léith in 2000. *Kin* featured four American artists of Irish descent: John Currin, Cheryl Donegan, Ellen Gallagher and Sean Landers. The filmed documentation of Donegan's 1993 performance KMRIA (Kiss

My Royal Irish Ass) showed the artist squatting in paint to produce four-leafed shamrock shaped 'buttprints', eloquently satirising the stereotypes of Irish-American identity, just as it undermined the grand gesture at the heart of Jackson Pollock's 'action' paintings. Within this exhibition identifications of diasporic Irishness featured in highly contingent terms, if present at all.

The multi-layered and contradictory identifications of Irishness represented by both 0044 and *Kin* suggest redefinitions of identity in art practice in keeping with cultural shifts extending far beyond the reductive tendencies of nationalism. These shifting definitions also invoke Arjun Appadurai's description of the new global cultural economy as 'a complex, overlapping, disjunctive order that cannot any longer be understood in terms of existing centre-periphery models'.[8] Appadurai instead proposes that the movement of people and ideas be seen in terms of a range of intersecting 'global flows' that continually shape and determine

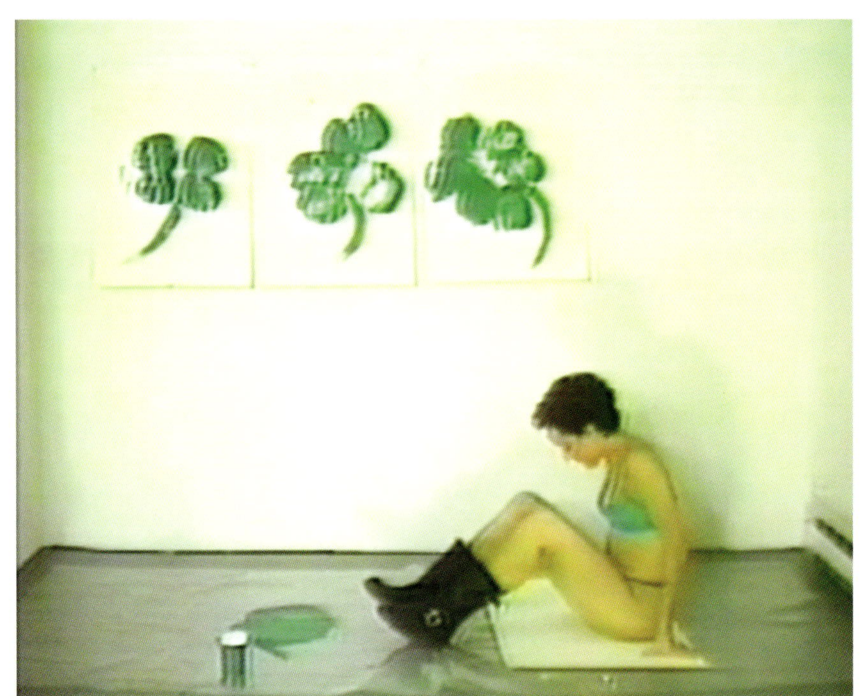

244 Cheryl Donegan, still from *KMRIA*, 1993, video.

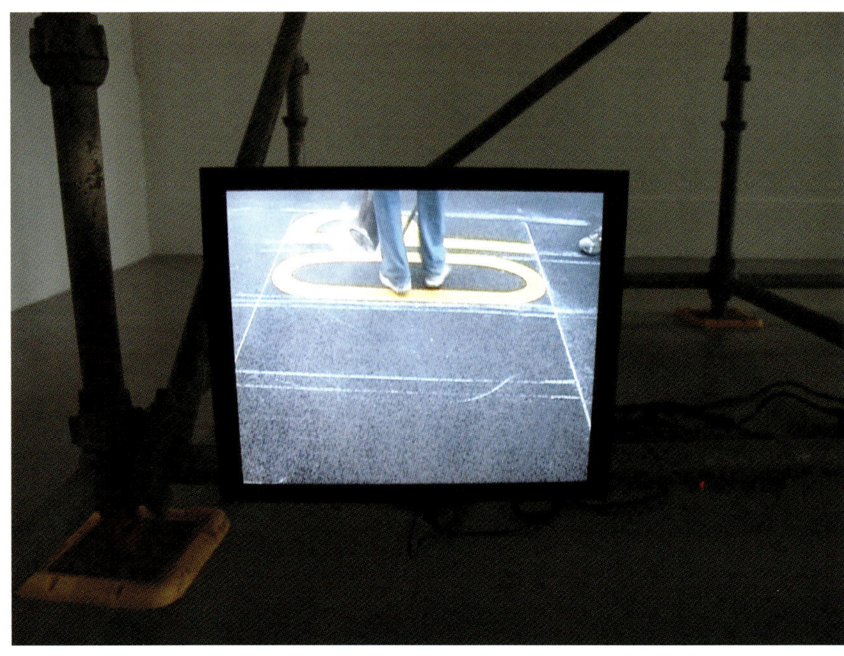

245 Anne Tallentire, *Drift 11.40* installed at IMMA, Dublin, 2005.

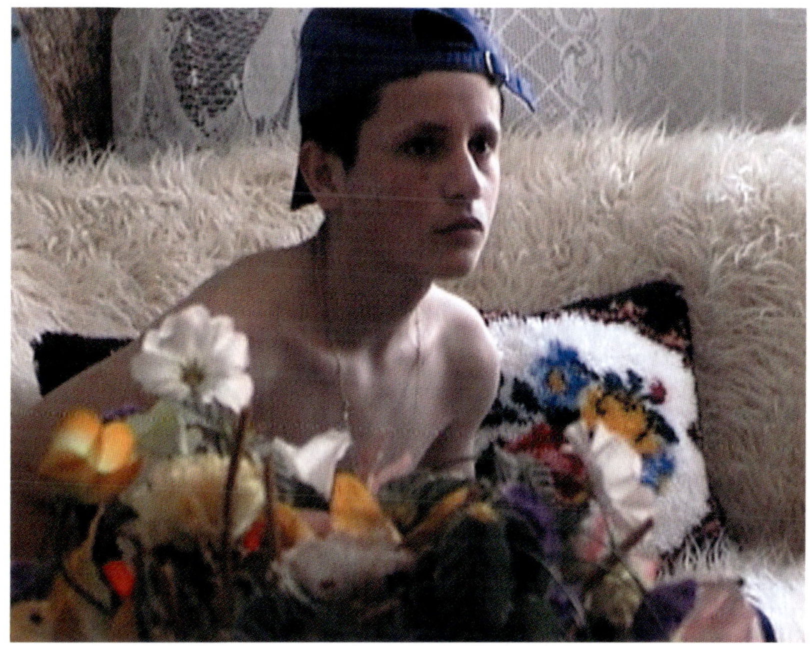

246 Phil Collins, *How to Make a Refugee*, 1999, single-channel video, colour, sound.

one another; the 'ethnoscape', for example, involves 'the landscape of persons who constitute the shifting world in which we live: tourists, immigrants, exiles, guest workers'.[9] These terms help to suggest readings for Anne Tallentire's more recent video work. *Drift* (2005), a collection of short videos filmed in London, detailed the work of people performing simple and often repetitive maintenance tasks – sweeping the streets, cleaning windows or painting road markings. Each video is identified by a time (*Drift* 11.40 records a worker painting a 'Stop' sign on a road, for example), but rather than indicating the duration of the piece this denotes the time at which it was filmed. Tallentire's practice in *Drift* is reminiscent of early feminist art-works informed by conceptualism that also made visible the tedium of labour. One precedent is Mierle Laderman Ukeles's *Touch Sanitation* project (1980), which involved the artist in shaking hands with all of New York's 8,500 sanitation workers over a period of

eleven months. Also, in *Drift* the denotation of time is indexically linked to the worker's day, rather than the viewer's experience within the gallery.

The anonymity of these manual workers – and to the viewer's eye perhaps also their interchangeability – is also indicative of the shifting fluidity of globalized labour as it both coalesces within and diffuses across the world's cities. In Tallentire's *Drift*, however, the cultural dimensions of ethnoscapes are absent – there is no wider sense of the anonymous worker's life beyond repetitive anonymity. In Phil Collins's video *How to Make a Refugee*, by comparison, the emphasis is on the processes of representation whereby identity is stripped away in order to turn displaced persons into fitting subjects for media consumption. This short film was made in 1999 when Collins was living in Belfast, and at a time when the negative effects of Ireland's remarkable prosperity as a result of both the Celtic Tiger phenomenon and the Peace Process were becoming visible in the form of increased racism. In a bitter reversal of the not-so-distant past, this was directed primarily at refugees and asylum seekers. Filmed in refugee camps in Macedonia, Collins's film focuses on the efforts of British television reporters to turn a young Kosovan survivor into a war victim, insisting that he reveals the bullet holes beneath his shirt and shows his broken leg. As Sally O'Reilly observes, this is a piece that reveals 'the ethics of looking and being looked at' as problematic, in that the 'direction and misdirection of imagery often compounds the plight of the oppressed and displaced'.[10]

In Ireland, resentment was frequently focused on an increasingly large number of asylum seekers from Africa and Eastern Europe, mistakenly believed to be benefiting from government support at the expense of the Irish poor. In comparison with other countries in the European Union, Ireland had relatively few asylum seekers until a marked increase at the end of the 1990s, and of these only a very small number were actually granted refugee status or leave to remain.[11] The response of the Irish government was either to deport asylum seekers or attempt to disperse them around the country. The major reception centre was at the former Butlins Holiday Camp at Mosney, north of Dublin, where immigrants from a wide range of different cultures and ethnic backgrounds were housed while awaiting a decision on their status. Between 2004 and 2008 the photographer Anthony Haughey worked on a series of projects with the residents, aimed at countering the frequently inaccurate media representations surrounding asylum seekers. In his portrait series *Between* (2006), the frontally posed images of residents are framed by the incongruous setting of the run-down holiday camp; in spite of the constant uncertainty of their situation Haughey's photographs work to restore some of the residents' lost dignity.

Asylum seekers were often dispersed around small towns where there was little or no experience of incomers, let alone those from a different culture, speaking a different language, and whose frequently traumatic experience of war and displacement made it difficult for them to integrate. Many refugees and migrants had also experienced the dehumanizing and dangerous consequences of human trafficking, smuggled across borders through a variety of means that stripped away both any remaining material wealth and their former identities. In one particularly notorious incident, eight Kurdish asylum seekers suffocated on the journey from Zeebrugge and were found dead in the back of a container lorry in Wexford in November 2001.

That same year, in a time-based artwork, Mick O'Kelly spent eight months travelling around small Irish towns where asylum seekers had been settled by the Irish government. O'Kelly's *Immigrant Vehicle* made visible the processes that preceded the arrival of displaced migrants in close-knit monocultural Irish communities such as Thurles or Wexford. The vehicle in question was an anonymous white container attached to an articulated lorry, the doors opened to enable viewers to enter and listen to a range of audio-narratives made by refugees and asylum seekers in Ireland. *Immigrant Vehicle* simulated the conditions of human trafficking as one means of countering the disturbing growth of xenophobia, yet this piece also contributed to the development of O'Kelly's concerns with the role of the public sphere in democratic society. The sometimes awkward role of artworks as a bridge between private and public space also underpinned a later project, *An Artwork for an Imperfect World*, exhibited in Temple Bar Gallery, Dublin in 2005. The result of collaboration between arts organizations and agencies such as Merchant Quay addressing issues of homelessness in Dublin, the project took the form of a large white van installed in the gallery. Over a period of

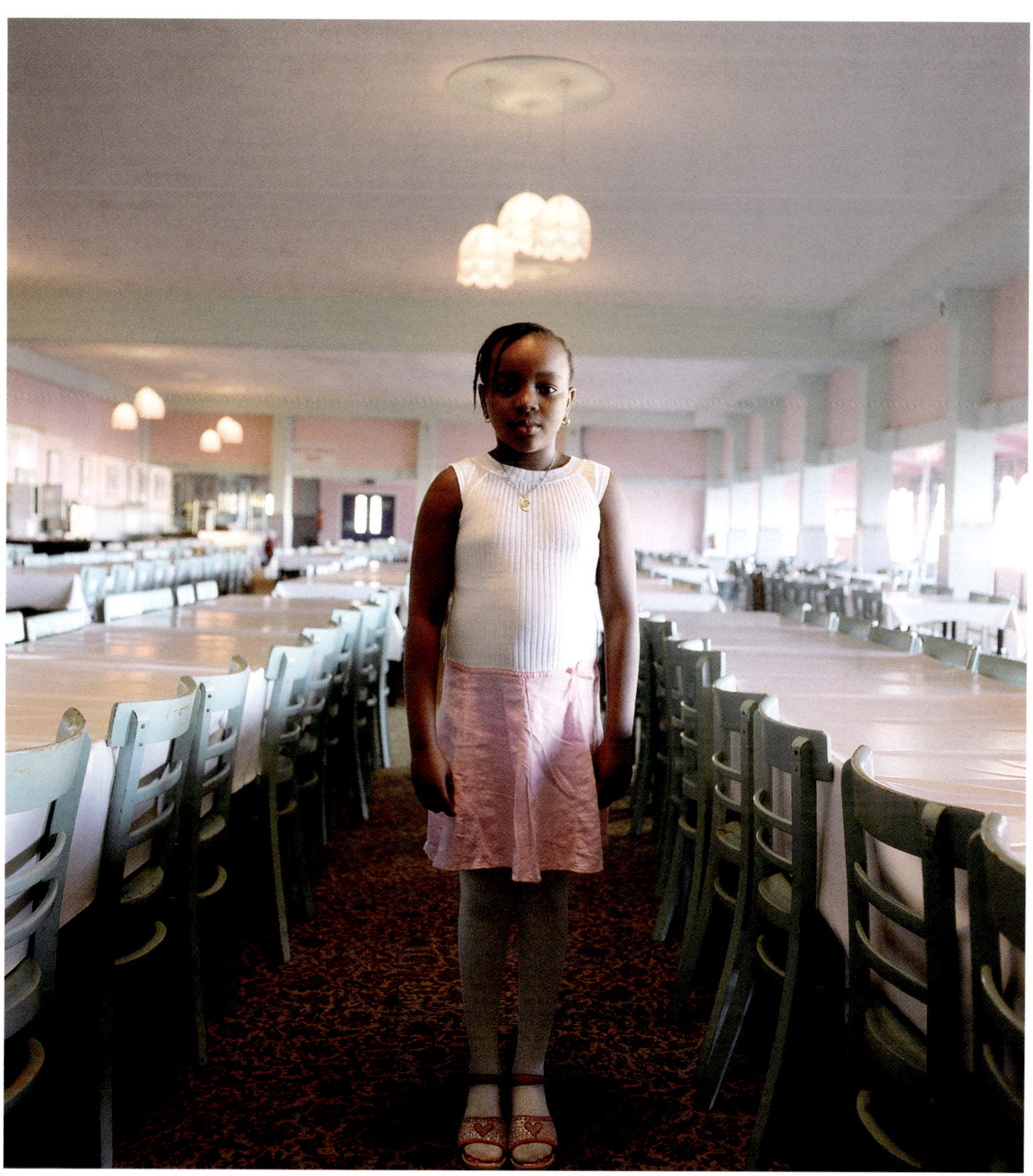

247 Anthony Haughey, *Moji, Mosney Reception Centre, Co. Meath*,
from the *Between* series, 2006, colour photograph.

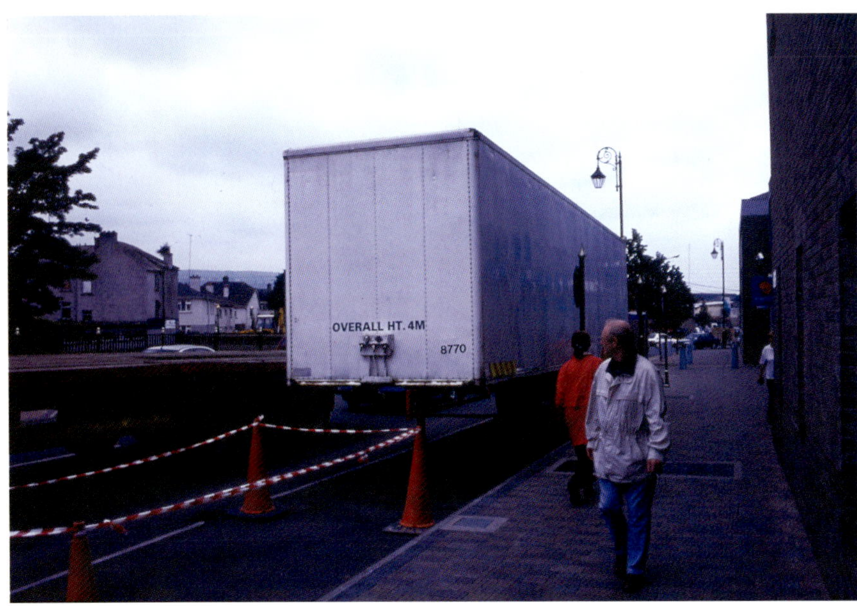

248 Mick O'Kelly,
Immigrant Vehicle,
Carlow, 2001,
colour photograph.

two weeks, the van served hot meals to Merchant Quay's homeless clients in the gallery, screened off from public view in an attempt to undermine the processes whereby poverty could become commodified for aesthetic consumption. As O'Kelly has stated, the project 'disrupts the ordinary function of the gallery as primarily a place of aesthetics', becoming instead a site for a very different type of exchange that questions the nature of social relations determining access to urban space.[12]

Rewriting the past

These shifting ethnoscapes have contributed to a disruption of the fictive space of the nation, but its *temporal* axis, a sense of the nation as constituted through progressive modernity, has also continued to unravel. This has informed art practice in the years after the millennium in various ways.

Amanda Coogan's performances, for example, continue the interrogative practices of an earlier generation of Irish feminist artists such as Alanna O'Kelly or Frances Hegarty, yet they also embody a gendered engagement with the work of canonical male artists such as Beuys or Nauman. *Yellow* (2008) or *The Fountain* (2001) suggest the re-emergence of historical trauma in conjunction with the representation of female bodily experience. In common with her mentor Marina Abramović, Coogan's performances are often lengthy and subject her body to prolonged discomfort. These themes emerge in *How to Explain the Sea to an Uneaten Potato*, performed in a coastal shelter in Clontarf, north of Dublin city centre. The title evokes Joseph Beuys's seminal performance in 1965, *How to Explain Pictures to a Dead Hare*, just as aspects of the performance suggest the talismanic nature of objects collected by Beuys during his visits to Ireland in the 1970s. Although she wore a costume made up of potatoes equivalent to her own body weight, Coogan's head was covered in gold leaf, similar to Beuys; during the two hours of the performance, in spite of the weight of her costume, she sat motionless, staring out to sea.

On one level the use of potatoes in an Irish context inevitably references the Famine. The uneaten tubers imply both unfulfilled potential and the loss of life while across the sea lies England, the first destination

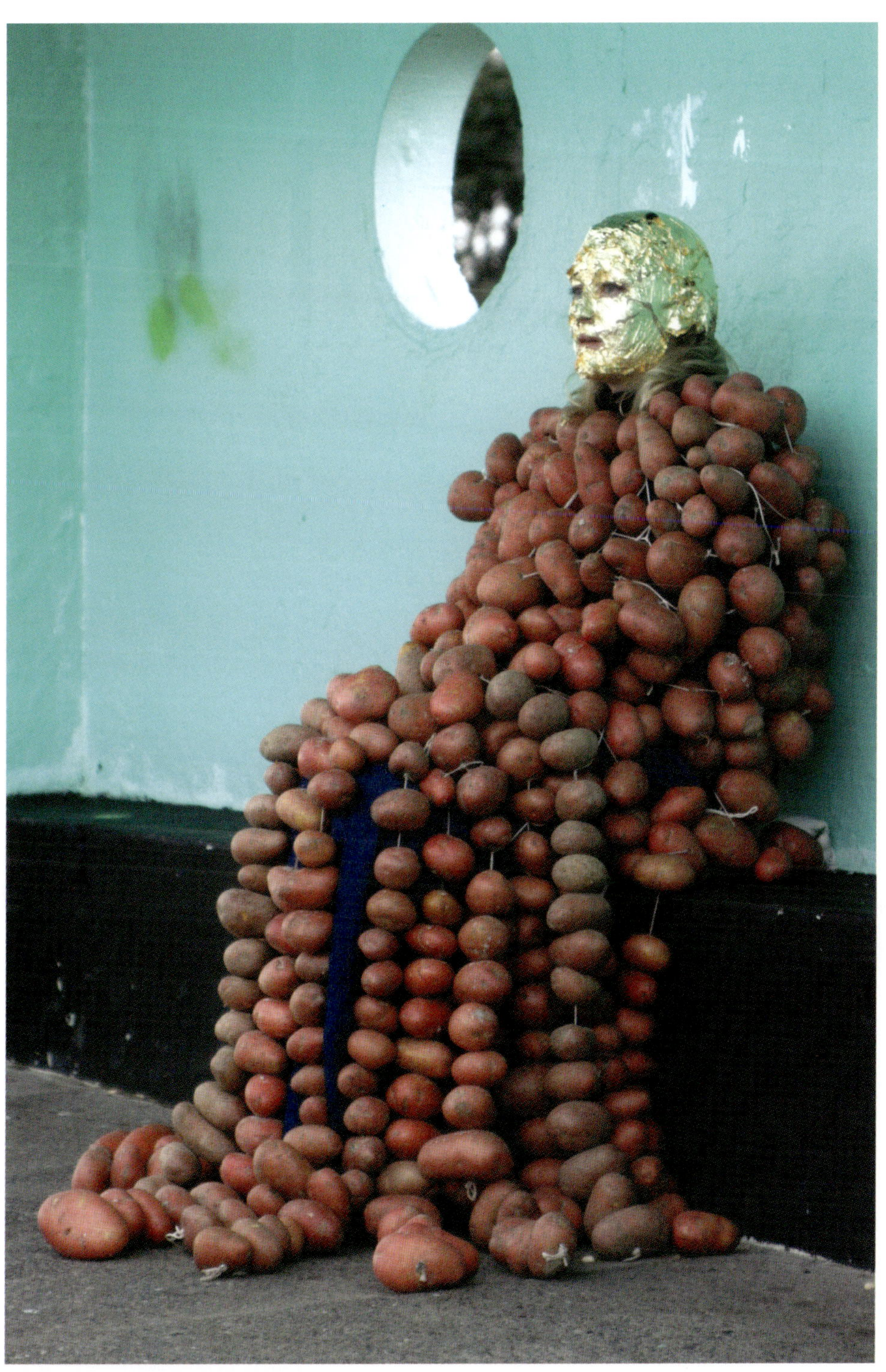

249 Amanda Coogan, *How to Explain the Sea to an Uneaten Potato*, 2008, performance still.

for many Irish emigrants escaping starvation. However, a central concern in Amanda Coogan's practice has also been the politics of Irish women's sexuality. *The Fountain*, its title suggestive of both Duchamp and Nauman, involved Coogan urinating for two and a half minutes in front of an audience at IMMA. With its connotations of shame and transgression, this public enactment of a private function also, for Coogan, alluded to the horrific circumstances of the death of the young Ann Lovett, whose final act of giving birth took place in a public space in Granard in 1984.[13] In reading *How to Explain the Sea to an Uneaten Potato*, Kate Antosik Parsons suggests a further frame of reference for Coogan's concerns with female embodiment and sexuality in the ongoing exodus of Irish women to England for abortions, invoking 'the difficult journeys that women have made across the watery divide'.[14] Certainly, Amanda Coogan's performances continue to raise uncomfortable issues in their undermining of both past and present.

The breakdown of progressive narratives of the modern also permits a return of the past in forms other than the disruptive force of trauma. As Svetlana Boym suggests, nostalgia is also 'dependent on the modern concept of unrepeatable and irreversible time' – if only to interrupt its passage.[15] Nostalgia's objects of desire 'must be beyond the present space of experience, somewhere in the twilight of the past'. The staging of nostalgia as a different return of the past also surfaced within Irish art projects around the turn of the millennium, such as Dorothy Cross's *Ghost Ship* (1999), discussed in the Introduction. Yet as Maeve Connolly has indicated, Irish art museums have become the venues for projects that involve the breakdown of notions of time and space in ways that suggest a multiplicity of narratives.[16] Jaki Irvine's *The Silver Bridge*, begun in 1999 as a proposal for the

Nissan Public Art Project but not completed until 2003, is a case in point. An eight-channel video installation in IMMA's collection, *The Silver Bridge* engages with issues found elsewhere in Irvine's work, through a focus on the ability of memory and fantasy to destabilize perceptions of reality. Based on the Irish writer Sheridan Le Fanu's lesbian vampire story *Carmilla* (1872), aspects of the gothic play a significant part in the installation's disruptions of spatial and temporal continuity, in addition to providing a source for the piece's imagery. Evocative images of bats, massing birds and glimpses of human activities are situated in outmoded spaces from Dublin's nineteenth-century past: Dublin Zoo in Phoenix Park, the Natural History Museum and the Silver Bridge over the Liffey. One of Irvine's recurrent themes – as in the later multi-screen work *In a World Like This* (2006) – is the use of birds and animals to indicate the limitations of human behaviour and the inadequacy of conscious rationality as a means of understanding the world. The vampire provides a further embodiment of these concerns, not only through its legendary ability to metamorphose into animal form, but in its fundamental liminality, hovering between life and death. Sexually transgressive through its oral penetration of the body, the vampire also suggests a desire that can never be fulfilled. This corresponds to the viewer's experience of the work, which is deliberately left as partial. Episodes of a fragmented narrative are projected simultaneously on screens within connected installation spaces; the variable routes through the gallery provide a way of attempting to make sense of this.[17] Yet both the structure and content of *The Silver Bridge* continually suggest melancholia and a romanticized loss. In the final sequence, two women hang, bat-like, beneath the silver bridge; they embrace, and then one figure alone remains.

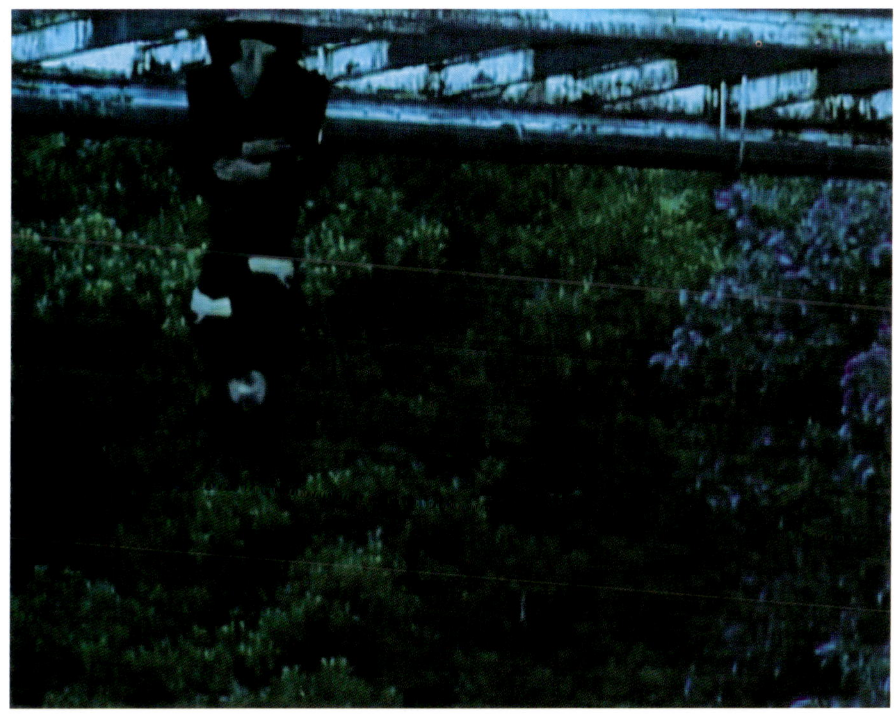

250 Jaki Irvine, still from *The Silver Bridge*, 1999–2003, 8-part video installation.

By comparison with the uncanny evocation of the out-moded past in *Silver Bridge*, in gallery-based works by Gerard Byrne time functions as a means of examining the failure of utopia and loss of idealism. Byrne's four 'magazine projects' use actors to restage the dialogue from debates recorded in magazines between 1963 and 1980. Two of these were from *Playboy*. *New Sexual Lifestyles* (2003) is based on a round-table discussion published in 1973, while a similar event ten years previously featuring a group of science fiction writers was the starting-point for Byrne's next project, *1984 and Beyond* (2005), shown at the 2007 Venice Biennale. Both of these reconstructions were filmed in modernist buildings that were not only completed at the time of the original published discussions but also evoke their utopianism. The piece *1984 and Beyond* used two locations in the Netherlands – Gerrit Rietveld's Sonsbeekpaviljoen now in the Kröller-Müller Museum and the Provinciehuis in den Bosch designed by Hugh Maaskant – while *New Sexual Lifestyles* was filmed in Ireland, at the Basil Goulding Summerhouse in the ravine of the Dargle River in County Wicklow. As Mark Godfrey has noted, Byrne's practice has precedents in the earlier work of James Coleman in that conventions for staging and editing the work's content are derived from its methods of technical production; DVDs can be divided into chapters or a soundtrack channelled through headphones.[18] Also similar to Coleman is Byrne's production of extended tableaux that disrupt narrative convention; discontinuous sections of the same film are screened simultaneously on monitors in the gallery, requiring a considerable degree of input on the part of the viewer.

In *New Sexual Lifestyles* the original debate ranged over subjects including open marriage, group sex and homosexuality, and involved a range of participants renowned for their libertarian attitudes, such as porn star Linda Lovelace, feminist and sexual campaigner Betty Dodson and Al Goldstein, editor of *Screw* magazine. Yet rather than being a faithful replication of the actual event, Byrne's projects involve processes of

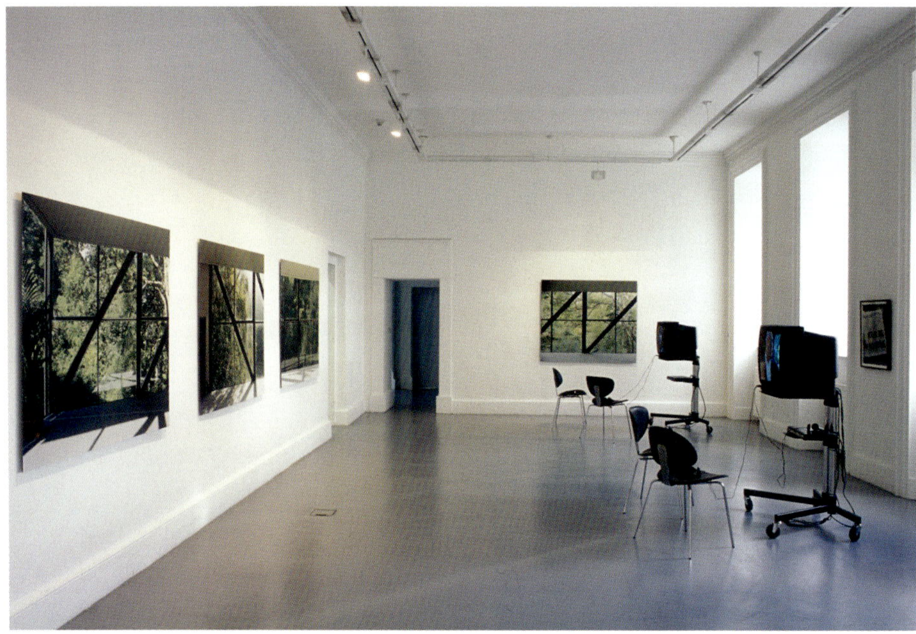

251 Gerard Byrne, *New Sexual Lifestyles* installed at IMMA, Dublin, 2004.

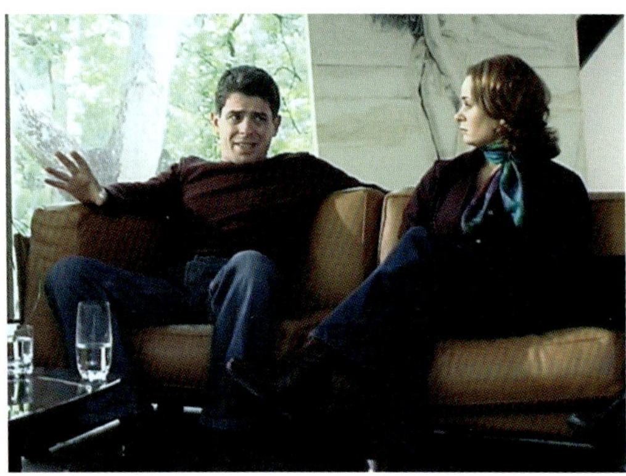

252 Gerard Byrne, still from *New Sexual Lifestyles*, 2003, 3-channel video installation, non-linear duration (approx. 54 mins in total) plus 7 photographs.

defamiliarization, Brechtian strategies that result in a critical distance from the discussions themselves. These include both the location of the reconstructions and the choice of actors. As Godfrey observes, the Goulding Summerhouse 'exudes a kind of austere and tranquil purity quite at odds with the images that are conjured of orgies and sado-masochism'.[19] This is a contrast also stressed by photographs on the gallery walls to accompany the DVD footage: they show the sunlit interior of the empty summerhouse with its canopy of trees beyond. In choosing actors with Irish accents to play the part of American sexual radicals of the 1970s, questions inevitably arise about the massive gap between the practices they describe and the repression of sexuality in Ireland at the same time. Yet the utopianism of the debate in *New Sexual Lifestyles* itself also begins to sound hollow as deeply conservative attitudes also emerge – perhaps unsurprisingly given the original publication in *Playboy*. And temporal distance, bringing with it the knowledge of the global impact of AIDS or the re-assertion of punitive attitudes towards rape victims, also indicates the failure of a sexual utopia envisaged in a very different era.

Similar to *New Sexual Lifestyles*, Gerard Byrne's series of photographs collectively entitled *A Country Road; A Tree; Evening* also open up questions around shifting notions of Irishness. Derived from the stage directions for the opening scene of Beckett's *Waiting for Godot*, the titles of these landscape photographs are each suffixed by their precise location: *Near Cruagh, on the road between*

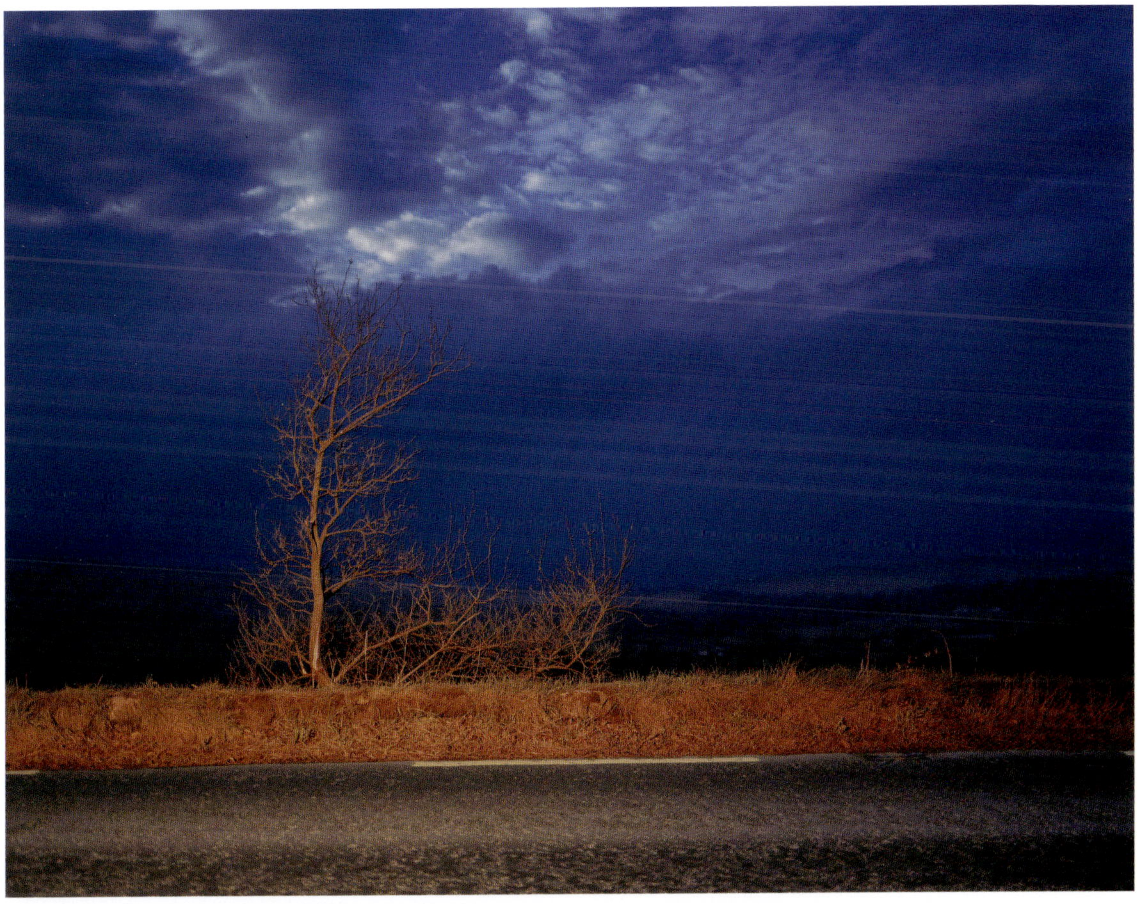

253 Gerard Byrne, *A Country Road; a Tree; Evening near Cruagh on the road between Killakee and Tibradden, above Rathfarnham, Dublin Mountains*, 2005–7, Fuji Crystal archive print.

Killakee and Tibradden, above Rathfarnham, Dublin Mountains is one example. Specific identification, however, only makes more apparent the nature of the photograph's artifice. *Near Cruagh*'s spotlit, technicolour tree against a darkening sky suggests not the natural world but a depopulated stage set. Representations of the empty landscape have a history in Irish modernity, deeply embedded in the formation of a visual identity for the Free State through their currency in the work of Paul Henry and others, yet also far removed from Beckett's involvement with European modernism evoked by Byrne in these photographs. Their staged artifice acknowledges the privileged meanings of the imagery of cultural nationalism, if only to imply the distance also travelled from that time and space. Querying the meanings of a landscape steeped in mythologized connotations was also the basis of another project by Byrne, *Case Study: Loch Ness: Some Possibilities and Problems, 2001–2011*, in which ten years of investigation resulted in an exhibition initially staged at the Milton Keynes Gallery in 2011. The work shown on this occasion combined Byrne's photographs of the Loch with found imagery, objects and other documentation dating back to the 1930s, when the first sightings of the monster began to appear in photographs. The viewer's response to these images hinges on belief in their veracity or otherwise.

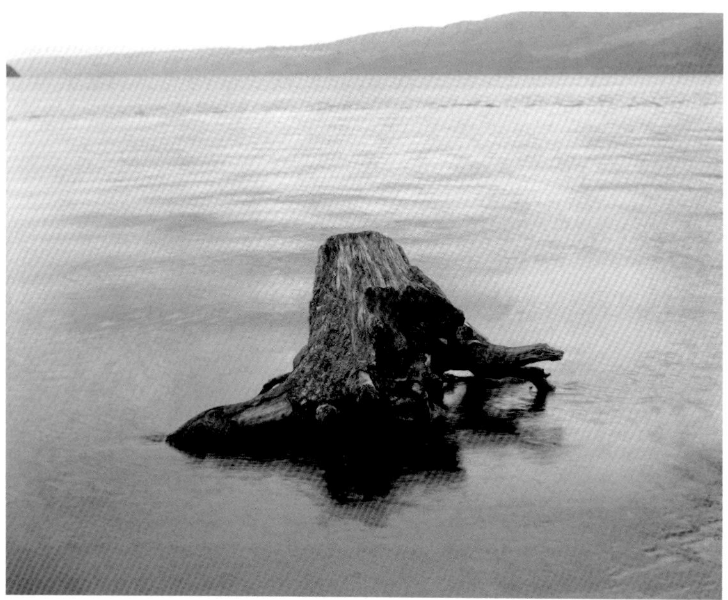

254 Gerard Byrne, image from an installation of 6 photographs, *East, South-south East, North-west, South-south East, Northwest, again East*, from the series *Case Study: Loch Ness: Some Possibilities and Problems*, 2001–2011 (2011).

As with his other projects, *Loch Ness* encourages a querying of the authenticity of the image and what it claims to represent.

As Richard Kearney argued, rather than representing a disappearance of old cultural forms through which nation can be articulated, this shift involves 'a transition from traditional nationalism to a post-nationalism which preserves what is valuable in the respective cultural memories of nationalism . . . while superseding them'.[20] As the previous discussion has shown, museums and galleries can function as places where notions of temporality can be explored through the staging of art projects. They are also places where narratives of national art history have been constructed and which both inform and are informed by formations of nation. The emergence of the post-national has also had an effect on these art historical narratives. The collections of Dublin's National Gallery of Ireland and the Hugh Lane Gallery made major contributions to the formation of Irish twentieth-century art. However, in both instances,

significant gallery acquisitions at the start of the new millennium meant that these narratives could become subject to re-interpretation.

In 2000, Louis le Brocquy, widely acclaimed at that point as Ireland's greatest living painter, and his wife Anne Madden returned to live in Dublin after spending more than 40 years in the South of France. Two years later, in 2002, le Brocquy's painting *A Family* (1951) was donated to the National Gallery of Ireland, returning to Ireland from Italy after an absence of nearly 50 years. The painting was bought for £1.7 million, establishing a record for a living Irish artist. It was also the first work by a living artist to be acquired by the National, and was displayed in the newly built Millennium Wing, for which le Brocquy had also designed tapestries. In common with Manet's *Olympia*, whose composition was the basis for le Brocquy's painting, *A Family*'s initial radicalism has, over time, been replaced by an increasingly canonical status. Its installation in the National Gallery of Ireland parallels the return of its painter, yet in a globalized context both can be seen as symptomatic of the greater fluidity of both Irish people and cultural forms across borders. This, I would suggest, has consequences for readings of Irish art history. The Municipal Gallery's rejection of the painting in 1952 was due at least in part to the radical strangeness of its modernist depiction of the nuclear family, at a time when this was still heavily associated with the visual and political requirements of the recently defunct Free State. In 2002 this same depiction of the family in le Brocquy's painting, with its derivations from French

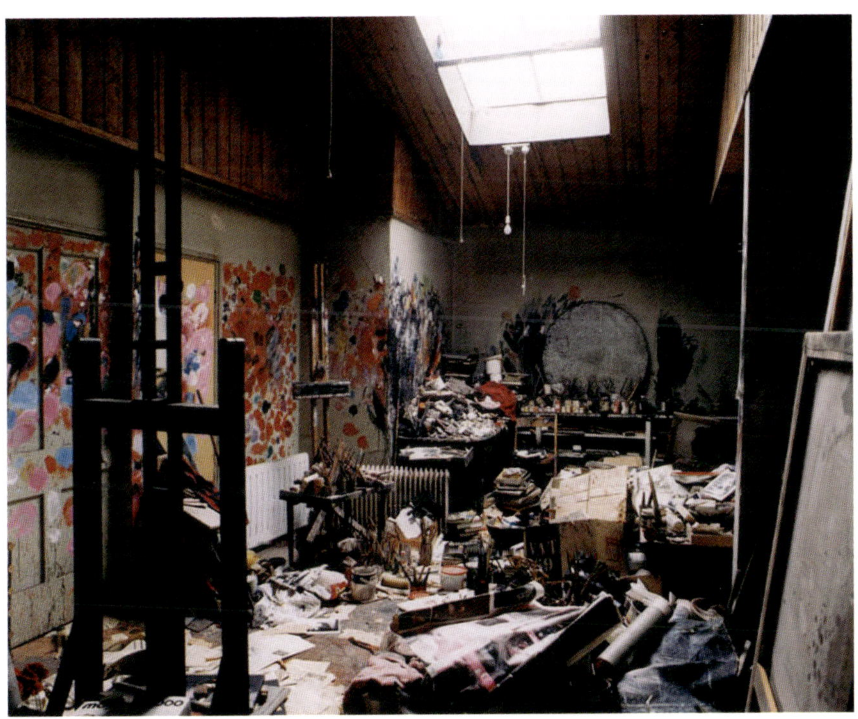

255 Francis Bacon studio installation at the Hugh Lane Gallery, Dublin, 2001.

modernism, could become a symbol of Ireland's European identifications in a way that was unavailable in the isolationist 1950s. It also, as Kearney suggested, re-invokes the imagery of cultural nationalism in a post-nationalist context.

There are different issues raised by another symbolic return from exile, which presents greater problems with institutional narratives. On 23 May 2001 the reconstructed studio of the painter Francis Bacon was opened to the public at the recently renamed Dublin City Gallery as the Hugh Lane Gallery. Bacon's heir John Edwards donated the studio to the gallery in August 1998, six years after the painter's death. Bacon spent most of his life in London, living and working in a flat at 7 Reece Mews in South Kensington from 1961 onwards. In spite of his Irish birthplace, Francis Bacon was renowned as not only the foremost *British* painter, but also as an artist who had dominated twentieth-century art on a global scale. His posthumous return was far from inevitable. Edwards had initially offered

the studio to the Tate; it was only after this approach was turned down that negotiations began with the Hugh Lane. The entire contents of Bacon's studio, including walls, doors and a vast amount of collected detritus, were painstakingly dismantled in August 1998 before being catalogued and reassembled in the Gallery in Dublin.

The Francis Bacon studio played an important role in commemorations of the gallery's centenary in 2008, building on the claim by the director Barbara Dawson that '[t]he studio is the most important acquisition by the gallery since Hugh Lane donated his collection of modern art to Dublin in 1908, and Bacon builds on that legacy of great European painting'.[21] But Bacon's work and the installation of his studio in the Hugh Lane Gallery still sit uneasily with the heroic visual narrative of post-independence Ireland. In a cultural climate dominated not only by the ideology of the family, but also by the Catholic Church, it is hard to see how there could be a place for screaming popes painted by a

Protestant, modernist homosexual. Yet it is perhaps in the acknowledgement of the difficulties posed in attempting to incorporate Bacon within the existing narratives of twentieth-century Irish art that the potential resides for the writing of more inclusive, more pluralistic versions of the same story.

Northern Ireland: post-conflict contradictions of time and place in art practice

In the North, the frequently tortuous peace process ongoing since the start of the decade finally reached its fruition on 10 April 1998 with the signing of the Good Friday Agreement. In a move unprecedented in Northern Ireland's history since Partition in 1922, Unionists and nationalists would share power in a new joint Assembly, which also meant the end to direct rule from Westminster. The Agreement also sought to bring about an end to political violence: an important step was the planned decommissioning of weapons held by paramilitaries and the destruction of arms dumps. Power-sharing proved difficult to achieve in actuality. Unionist distrust and suspicion of nationalists was deeply ingrained, fuelled also by an awareness of the accompanying erosion of 300 years of Protestant hegemony. After a series of setbacks, the Northern Ireland Assembly finally became operational in May 2007. Its principles of power-sharing and reconciliation between warring factions appeared to be personified by the much-publicized friendship of the First and Second Ministers, the Reverend Ian Paisley, leader of the Democratic Unionist Party and Martin McGuinness, not only a Sinn Féin member but a former IRA commander.

These massive political changes were accompanied by considerable economic investment, which was also fuelled by the Celtic Tiger phenomenon south of the border. In Belfast this resulted in rapid urban redevelopment, yet the deeply entrenched meanings of localized urban space meant that the construction of a post-conflict city was problematic. Significantly, development became particularly focused around the waterfront and the commercial areas of the immediate city centre, identifiable as locations unburdened with sectarian associations. A spectacle of consumerism unseen for 30 years was accompanied by a rapid rise in the value of domestic property; in 2006, house prices increased by 37 per cent, more than anywhere else in the United Kingdom.[22] Not all sections of society benefited equally from the new prosperity. The rapid rise in house prices increasingly marginalized and continued to polarize working-class areas of Belfast already scarred by endemic poverty and long-term unemployment; sectarianism continued to flourish in these areas, with former paramilitaries diversifying into drug-dealing.

The major shifts in political and economic conditions derived from the Peace Process registered in art practice in the years after the Agreement. In addition to the problematization of former definitions of the city's spaces through the new imperatives of consumerism and economic investment, there were further consequences in the perception of the role of the past in determining the present. The power-sharing of Protestants and Catholics implied revisions of both loyalist and republican views of history. On the one hand, the historical inevitability of political dominance became subject to question, while on the other, years of political activism and resistance had resulted not in a united Ireland but in a legislative role within the Northern Ireland state. These substantial changes in notions of both time and space, themselves interlocking axes of modernity, became in turn part of the cultural material transformed by art.

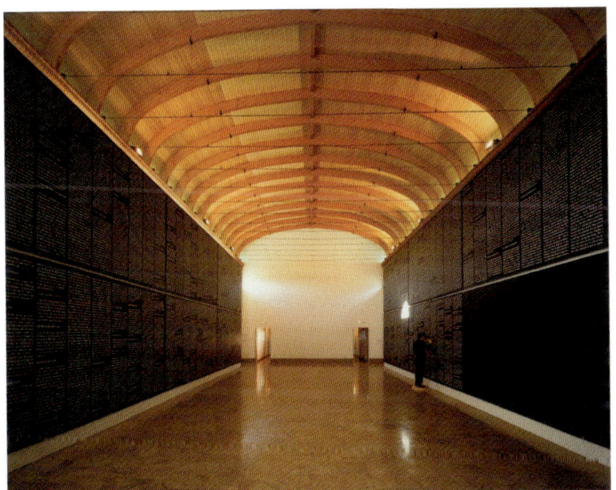

256 Shane Cullen, *Fragmens sur les Institutions Republicaines* IV, 1993–7, painted text, acrylic on 96 styrofoam panels, 12 blocks of 8 panels.

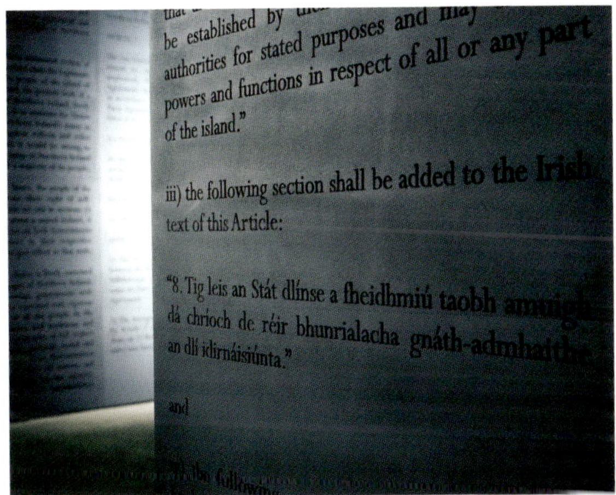

257 Shane Cullen, *The Agreement*, 2002, installation detail, Beaconsfield, London, 11,500 words of the British-Irish Peace Treaty of 1998 digitally routed into 55 HDU panels.

All of this occasioned a need to find forms of representation appropriate to such significant changes. The Dublin-based artist Shane Cullen's *The Agreement* (2002) reproduced the entire 11,500-word text of the Good Friday Agreement, etched mechanically onto 55 polyurethane panels and exhibited in its entirety in a number of venues. There were clear comparisons with Cullen's earlier monumental installation *Fragmens sur les Institutions Republicaines* IV, a 96-panel piece reproducing some 35,000 words of 'comms' – illicit communications smuggled out of the Maze Prison during the republican hunger strikes of 1980–81. An obvious reference point for both of these works is Maya Lin's *Vietnam Veterans' Memorial* (1982) in Washington, DC, while the reliance on language rather than visual imagery also derives from the work of conceptual artists such as John Baldessari during the 1960s. However, the anonymity of industrial practices used in the representation of the text undermines both the status of the artist as unique creator and, by implication, the role of heroic individualism in the making, or writing, of history. As Caoimhín

Mac Giolla Léith has observed, it was significant for Cullen that the text of the Agreement 'bears all the marks of communal effort', rather than sole authorship.[23] It is this degree of communality that in turn suggests a potential for the future of Northern Ireland. Cullen's *The Agreement* opened up a space for later works by other artists that continued to interrogate the recent history of conflict from the changed perspectives of the present, including Duncan Campbell's short film *Bernadette* (2009). A project that used a range of archival and other material to produce a reassessment of the role of Bernadette Devlin as political agent, Campbell's film attempted to move towards a re-reading of the early years of the conflict that went beyond the polarizations of sectarianism.

One aspect of an increasingly assertive and confident public face of new Northern Ireland was its first participation at the Venice Biennale in 2005, with a group exhibition of fourteen artists, *The Nature of Things*, curated by Hugh Mulholland. The exhibition explicitly sought to distance itself from previous representations of Northern Ireland as characterized by

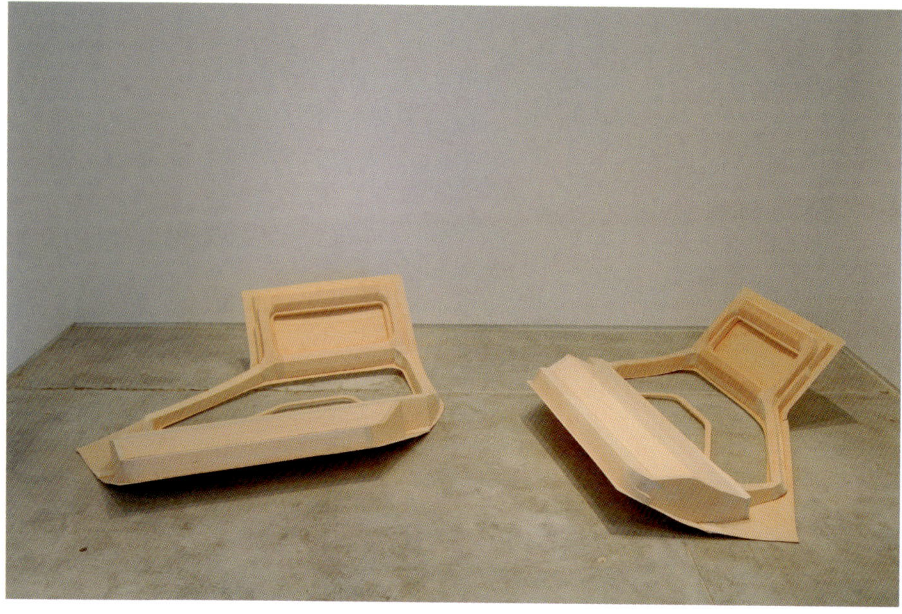

258 Katrina Moorhead, *On or About December 1981*, 2005, basswood, plywood, wood glue, zinc screws and brass plated step 1 screws.

conflict alone.[24] Much of the work, such as Seamus Harahan's video *Holylands* or Ian Charlesworth's paintings, suggested a critically nuanced engagement with Northern Ireland's recent prosperity. Katrina Moorhead's *On or About December 1981*, for example, referenced a lost utopian moment in the midst of conflict. In the late 1970s economic incentives encouraged the American car manufacturer John De-Lorean to set up a factory in Belfast, employing both Catholic and Protestant workers to make a luxury sports car, the DMC-12. In 1982, however, the venture folded when DeLorean was convicted of drug trafficking, and all the prototypes of the car were destroyed. Moorhead's piece reproduced the DMC-12's distinctive gull-wing doors. Made out of plywood and grounded on the gallery's floor, their fragility suggests a lost future, a failed dream of prosperity.

On or About December 1981 was only one of many works made by artists in Northern Ireland at this time that begin to open up questions about a sense of a progressive narrative towards a bright future. Frequently this also involved a querying of the meanings of *place*. In John Duncan's photographic series *Boom Town* (2002), the geography of redevelopment is traced across the city in a seemingly random fashion. Like the gaze of the *flâneur* in Haussmann's Paris, a personage previously invoked in comparison with Duncan's practice, the camera registers the spectacle of rapid urban change.[25] This is more than just the incongruous juxtaposition of new and old. In Duncan's photograph of the decaying Crumlin Road Courthouse superimposed with an estate agent's hoarding, the comparison is between the non-specific future described in the language of real estate and the sense of a past whose meanings are deeply embedded in the history of conflict. The streets in these photographs are strangely depopulated, suggestive of a silence far removed from the bustling modernity that the *flâneur* usually observes. Rather than the confident transition to a new future, the impression is one of temporal collapse and loss of certainty.

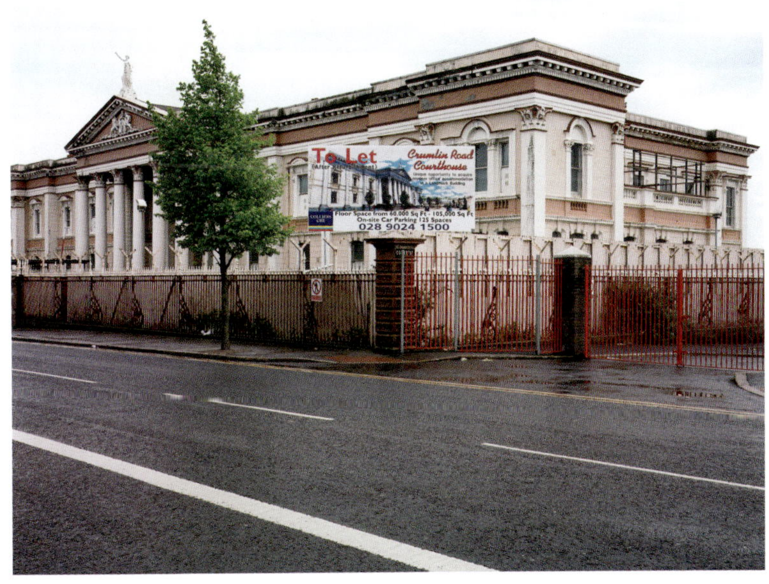

259 John Duncan,
'Crumlin Road Courthouse'
from *Boom Town*, 2002.

The need for loyalist communities to maintain identity in the face of its eradication by an urban development from which they would not be the beneficiaries was a theme that underpinned a later series by John Duncan, *Bonfires* (2004). These photographs depict the massive temporary constructions that populate loyalist areas, which were designed to be set alight on Eleventh Night, preceding the celebrations of the Twelfth of July. They suggest an atavistic survival in the face of the city's renewal and pervasive consumerism, but they are not alone in engaging with the contradictions surrounding the material culture of loyalism. A further group of photographs, this time by Eoghan McTigue and entitled *All Over Again*, appeared to document the post-conflict eradication of paramilitary murals, painted over by members of the same loyalist communities who originally installed them. Although they share a frontality with Duncan's images, McTigue's photographs show that the contradiction between past and present is not staged as juxtaposition but as palimpsest. One example depicts a stage in the oblit-

eration of a gable-end mural in East Belfast. Originally celebrating the prowess of the UVF, similar murals have been repainted in homage to another local hero, the footballer George Best. McTigue's photograph stops the process at the point where traces of previous slogans and imagery – armed figures surrounding the emblem of the Red Hand of Ulster – show through the now whitewashed surface. The public endorsement of sectarian violence is now remade into, as Aaron Kelly termed it, 'a different iconography; the cult of celebrity and fame'.[26]

Documentary photography has deep historical associations with a need to record objectively events happening in front of the lens. Projects by both Duncan and MacTigue, however, suggest a use of this mode of photography to offer a different sense of realism – a querying of apparent truths and revealing of contradiction that underpins the construction of spectacle. For other photographers, such as Paul Seawright, this process of enquiry continued an engagement with the psychological states engendered by the same historical

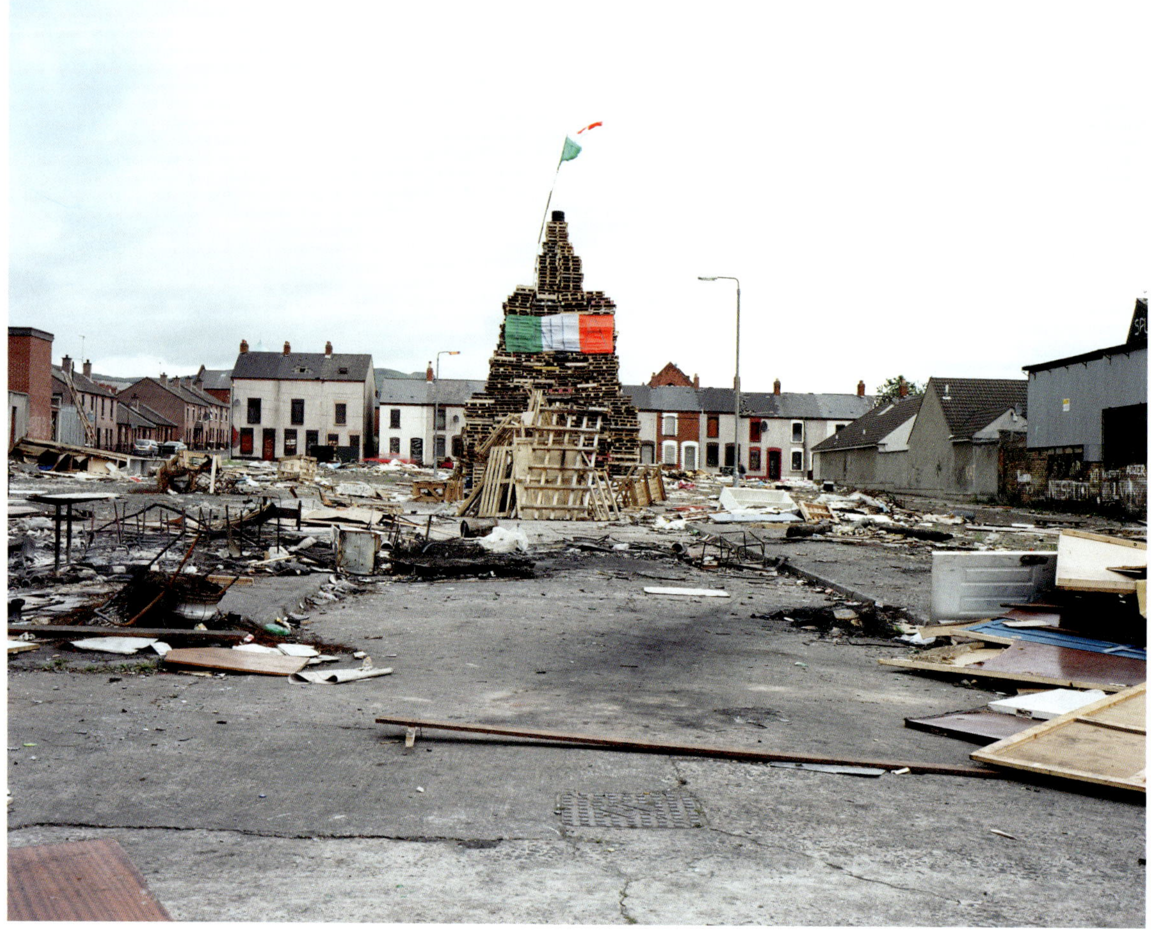

260 John Duncan, 'Keswick Street Belfast 2004', from *Bonfires*, 2004, C-print.

conditions. Like McTigue's photographs in *All Over Again*, Seawright's *Erased Texts* (2008–9) shows over-painted sectarian graffiti, this time on the wall of an anonymous underpass. Yet the dark void that threatens to swallow the whitewashed words suggests more disturbing readings, a malaise at the heart of the city's remaking. On one level this is an example of what Colin Graham described as 'focusing precisely on those marks of nothingness, the unsayable things which the history of the city trails in its wake and embosses onto its materiality'.[27] In post-conflict cultures, however, the unsayable has a habit of resurfacing, even though, as in Belfast, the material traces of the past were actually being eradicated.

Conflict resolution, trauma and the visual

Conflict resolution is increasingly recognized to be a psychic as well as a political process. Years of conflict resulted in a considerable death toll on a small population in a confined geographical area. In the years 1969 to 1998, a total of 3,483 people were killed, the majority of them civilians.[28] A large number of people in Northern Ireland have stories of parents, children and other loved ones killed or maimed, and terrible injustices wrought for one cause or another. During the conflict this contributed to an atmosphere of fear and paranoia, with individual horror suppressed by the need to survive on a daily basis. In post-conflict Northern Ireland processes

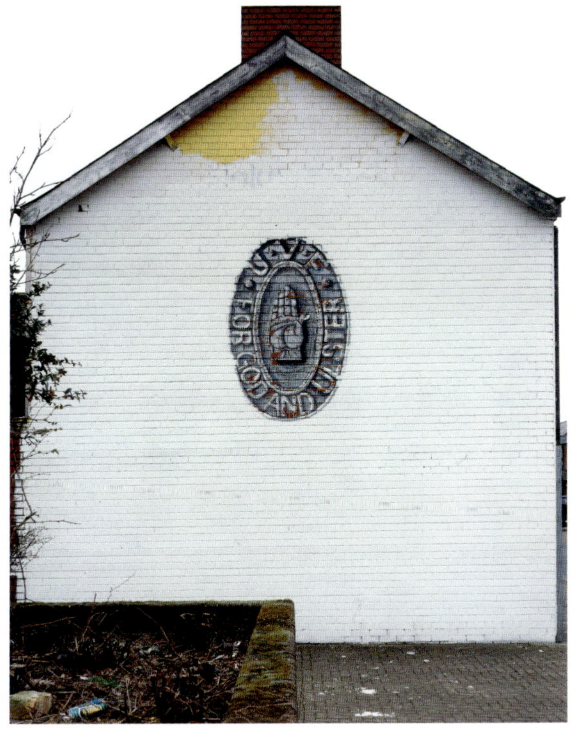

261 Eoghan McTigue, from *All Over Again*, 2004, colour photograph.

of the recovery of the past have been officially sanctioned by such means as the Saville Inquiry, set up in 1998 in the wake of the Good Friday Agreement to reinvestigate the circumstances of Bloody Sunday in 1972. The Inquiry took evidence from over 900 witnesses to the events, finally reporting its findings in 2010.[29] This public acknowledgement of the crucial role of memory in establishing justice became part of a more widespread concern with the need to reconstruct experience of the recent past. The notion of trauma, as a term that refers to a psychic rather than physical wounding, has gained considerable currency in explaining the processes whereby individuals engage with these experiences once conflict is over. As Cathy Caruth observed, trauma involves a degree of psychic damage as a result of experiences so horrific they defy the ability of language to deal with them at the time. As such, the memory of these experiences becomes lodged within the unconscious, emerging only at a later point, when it

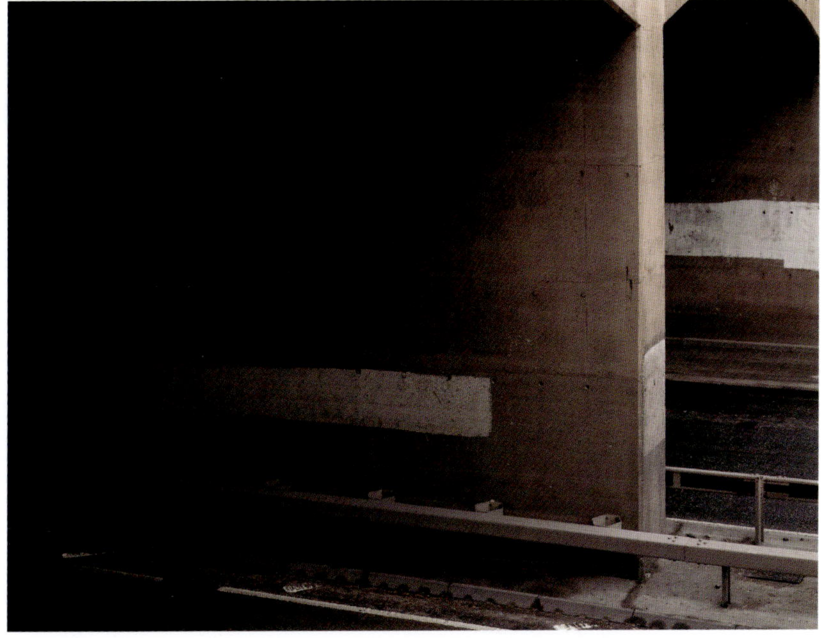

262 Paul Seawright, *Erased Texts*, 2008–9, colour c-type print mounted on Di-bond and Perspex.

is as if it acquires its own agency, insisting on being spoken. Psychological trauma, as Caruth explains, is 'the story of a wound that cries out, that addresses us in the attempt to tell us of a reality or truth that is otherwise not available'.[30] It is difficult not to get a sense of post-conflict Northern Ireland as a society saturated by the need to remember, which has also affected artists living there.

Artists in Northern Ireland, as curator Megan Johnston stated, 'feel the deviant or disrupted interpersonal relationships that impact deeply the psyche of people in the North'.[31] A significant venture in this respect has been Rita Duffy's *Thaw* (2003 onwards), informed in part by her viewing of Dorothy Cross's *Ghost Ship* (1999). For Duffy, the iceberg has become a metaphor for the experience of trauma in post-conflict Northern Ireland, signifying the still hidden and unresolved depths beneath. It also has a key role in one of the founding narratives of the Northern Ireland state – the loss of the *Titanic*, the pride of the Belfast shipyards, in 1912. One of the city's major post-conflict redevelopment schemes has involved the redevelopment of the now largely redundant docklands as the 'Titanic Quarter', supplanting a legacy of industry with ephemeral real estate. A key part of Duffy's project, which includes film, photography and painting, addresses the apparent superficiality of such decision-making, and involves a plan to tow an iceberg from the North Atlantic to Belfast Lough, where its eventual melting symbolizes a process of resolution and healing.[32]

Duffy's project reaches back through layers of Belfast's history. Other artistic projects are more closely focused around the traumatic legacy of locations outside the city, such as the former Maze Prison. After the introduction of internment in 1971, mainly republican prisoners were held in Long Kesh Prison, a facility based on the site of a former RAF aerodrome ten miles from Belfast. In 1976 the Maze Prison, characterized by its

distinctive H-Blocks, was constructed alongside. The majority of republican and loyalist male detainees were later held there. It was the site of the republican hunger strikes and subsequently, in 1983, 38 republican prisoners escaped from one of the H-Blocks. The decision to close the prison in the wake of the Good Friday Agreement immediately opened up debates around the site's future, with a cross-party Maze Consultation Panel advocating what aspired to be a politically neutral solution. This involved the redevelopment of the site as a resource that would serve the interests of the whole community, such as a sports stadium or shopping centre.

The prison's history has meant that it has become a site of heavily contested meanings within cultural memory. As Rebecca Lynn Graff-McRae has observed, 'for both Unionists and republicans, the ghosts of the Troubles are symbolically tied to the Maze'.[33] For republicans the Maze represented a site of resistance to state oppression and should be preserved as such, while for loyalists these same associations amounted to a commemoration of terrorism. Between 2002 and 2004 the photographer Donovan Wylie gained access to the now defunct prison; his images register the deserted and decaying buildings and the spaces that surrounded them. The photographs of empty cell interiors, each with an identical single bed with neatly folded linen, are an uncanny contrast to the depopulated and overgrown roadways edged with barbed-wire fencing and now sightless watchtowers. Wylie's use of documentary's apparent objectivity seems to suggest a degree of neutrality in the contestation of meanings attached to the prison, yet, as Louise Purbrick argues, these photographs evidence an 'architecture of containment', the physical means of exercising the state's powers of incarceration.[34]

Following the Good Friday Agreement, the recognition of rural sites as laden with disturbing associations

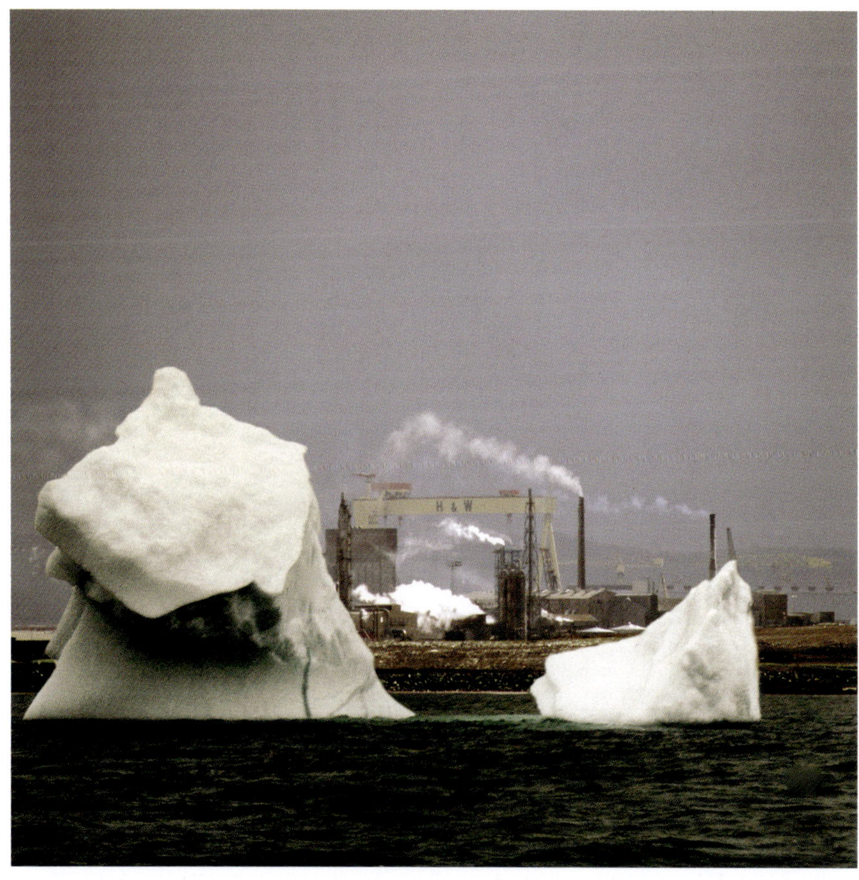

263 Rita Duffy,
Thaw, 2007,
mixed media.

took a further development in searches for the bodies of the 'disappeared', Catholic victims of the IRA in the 1970s, killed on suspicion of being informers or for other reasons. In many instances the bodies were never recovered, although it was generally believed they had been buried in remote rural locations. In 1999 the republican movement agreed to release details enabling the victims' families to retrieve the bodies. A series of photographs by David Farrell taken between 1999 and 2000, *Innocent Landscapes*, depicts a number of burial sites. These are photographs that self-consciously engage with established depictions of landscape in Ireland, while simultaneously subverting these readings. Some examples, such as the photographs taken at Colgagh where the remains of Brian McKinney and John McClory were found, suggest pastoral conventions in their framing and composition, only to disrupt the idyll through the implicit violence of an uprooted tree, or the marks of heavy digging machinery. There is a further significance in these undermined landscapes as all the locations identified as burial grounds and photographed by Farrell are situated over the border in the South. In this context his photograph of the rolling Wicklow Hills, burial place of Danny McIlhone, inevitably recalls the ideological significance of landscape in early formations of Free

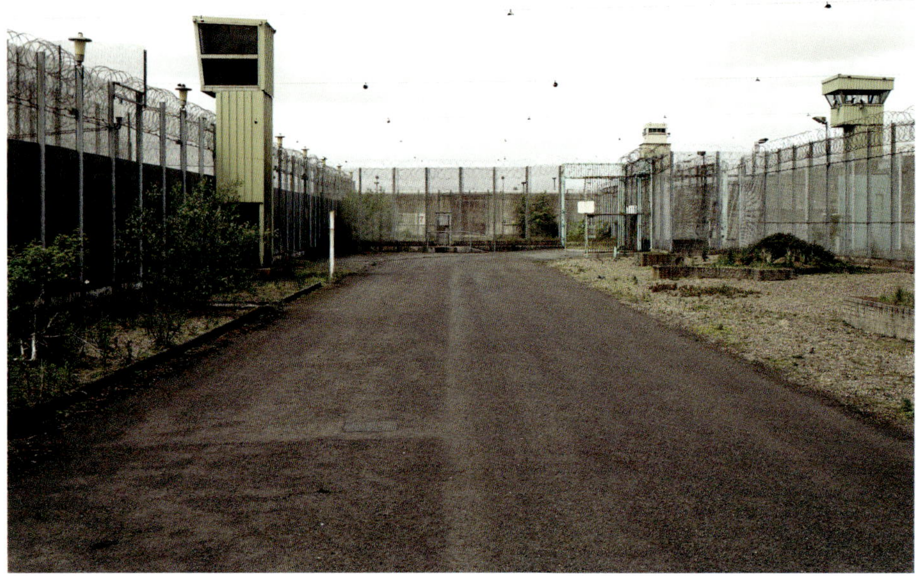

264 Donovan Wylie, *Road*, phase 3, 2004, colour photograph.

State national identity. As the depicted repository of republican violence, this photograph, right at the century's end, also implicitly contributes to the unravelling of the nationalist project.[35]

If Farrell's *Innocent Landscapes* deals with submerged trauma as much as buried bodies, the focus of Willie Doherty's *Ghost Story* is on the more spectral remains of horrific experience in the face of historical change. Shown at the Venice Biennale in 2007 when Doherty represented Northern Ireland, the fifteen-minute film was made at a time when it was becoming apparent that the political and material consequences of the Peace Process were still underpinned by deeply embedded trauma. The film consists of an unseen narrator's passage through a sequence of liminal spaces – a forest path at the edge of a city, an underpass, an alley behind houses, a deserted car park. Doherty's use of Steadicam for the filming means that the viewer is drawn irresistibly on this journey through murky daylight or twilight in a 'gliding, ghostly, disembodied form of motion' that constantly hints at something else that the camera does not see.[36] Trauma as a continual presence within the hinterlands of consciousness is figured through the sense of a haunting, which regularly recurs through the speech of the narrator, recalling both places where terrible things have happened and elusive presences, such as those of the terrified people reminiscent 'of the faces in a running crowd that I had once seen on a bright but cold January afternoon'.[37] We are back once again on the ever-present terrain of the Bogside on Bloody Sunday. Yet Doherty's frame of reference in *Ghost Story* is not just Northern Ireland's past,

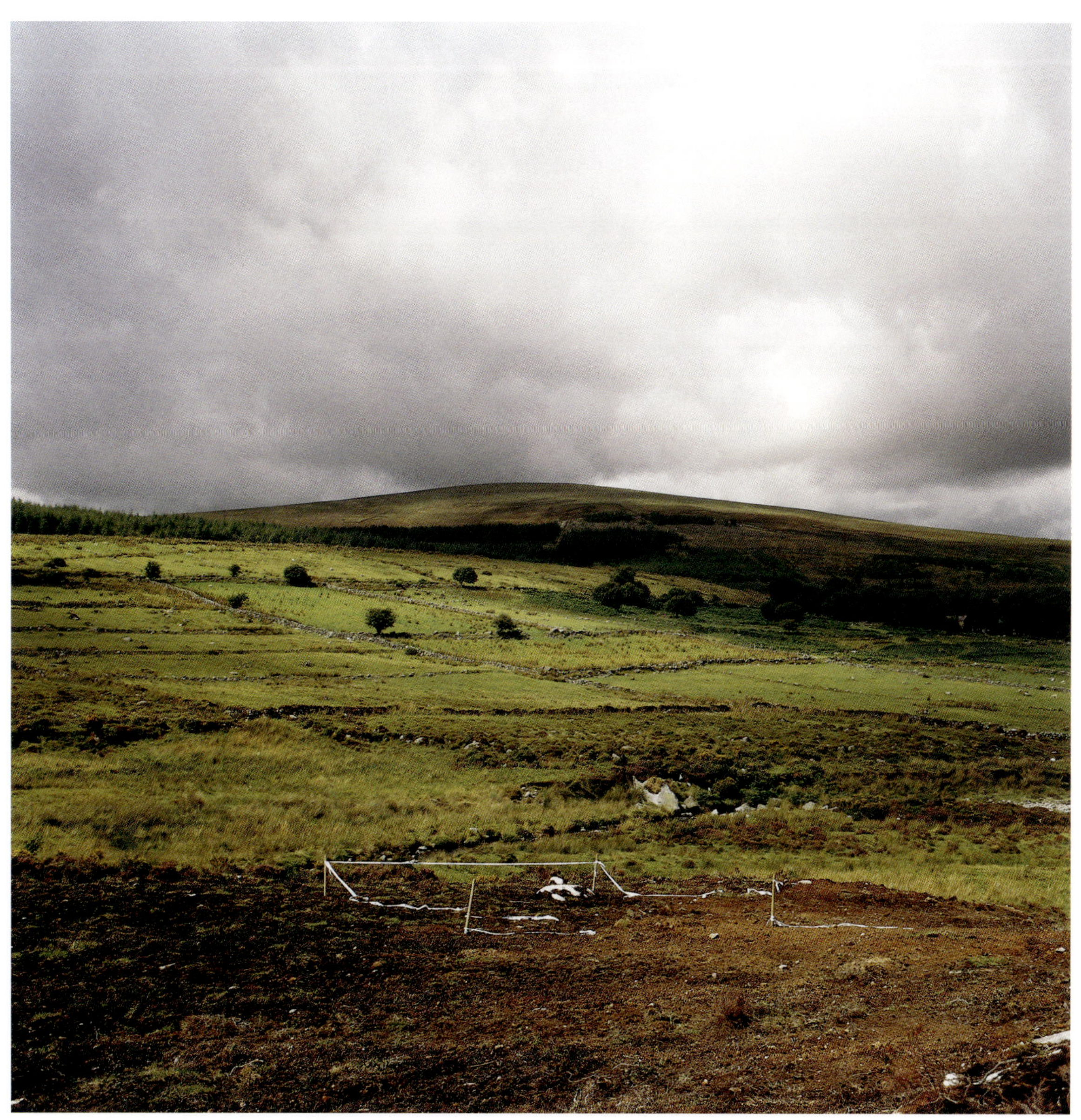

265 David Farrell, 'Ballynultagh', from *Innocent Landscapes*, 2001, colour photograph.

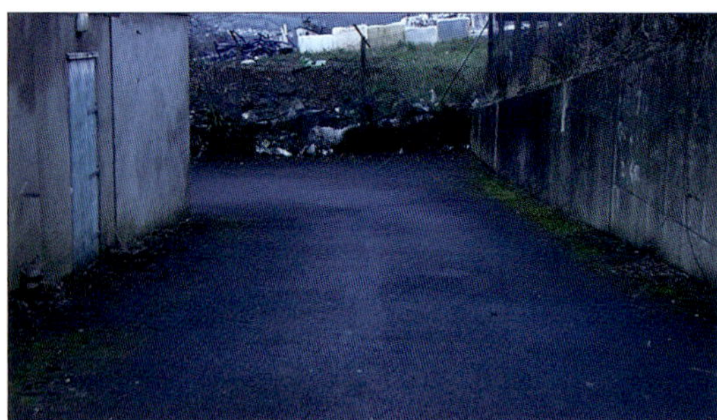

266 Willie Doherty, still from *Ghost Story*, 2007, video.

but spills out into images glimpsed from Abu Ghraib and more recent atrocities elsewhere.

Throughout this entire period, the lived experience of identity, place and time has been a basis for the development of the work of Irish artists that both acknowledges these circumstances and projects them back onto the culture that produced them. After a century in which ideas of the Irish nation have been so closely bound up with the progressive logic of the modern, the boundaries of space and time now appear less finite. In the years after the millennium Irish art practice has re-presented and refracted these deep concerns, opening on to a multitude of possible futures, and a potential for new temporalities and new geographies.

References

Introduction: The Ghost Ship, Nation and Modernity

1 'Ghost Ship to Appear in February 1999', IMMA press release, 3 December 1998, at www.modernart.ie, last accessed 24 May 2012.

2 S. B. Kennedy, *Irish Art and Modernism, 1880–1950* (Belfast, 1991).

3 Ibid., p. 3.

4 Dorothy Walker, *Modern Art in Ireland* (Dublin, 1997), p. 102. See also Walker, 'Traditional Structures in Recent Irish Art', *Crane Bag*, VI/1 (1982), pp. 41–4.

5 Tom Duddy, 'Irish Art Criticism – a Provincialism of the Right?' [1987], in *Sources in Irish Art: A Reader*, ed. Fintan Cullen (Cork, 2000), pp. 91–9. Duddy's essay provides a useful critique of both Dorothy Walker and other writers on Irish modernism, including Cyril Barrett, Brian O'Doherty and Frances Ruane.

6 James Elkins, 'The State of Irish Art History', *Circa* (Winter 2003), at www.recirca.com, last accessed 24 May 2012.

7 One occasion where this became particularly apparent was at the 2007 conference of the Association of Art Historians at the University of Ulster in Belfast, in a session convened by Lucy Cotter and entitled 'Irish Studies and Histories of Art: Impossible Dialogues?' where issues of interdisciplinarity were foregrounded both through papers presented and subsequent debate.

8 David Cairns and Shaun Richards, *Writing Ireland: Colonialism, Nationalism and Culture* (Manchester, 1988).

9 Shaun Richards, '"Our Revels Now Are Ended"· Irish Studies in Britain – Origins and Aftermath', in *Ireland beyond Boundaries: Mapping Irish Studies in the Twenty-first Century*, ed. Liam Harte and Yvonne Whelan (London, 2007), pp. 48–57. Richards's essay provides a history of the critical project of Irish studies in a British context since the mid-1980s.

10 Luke Gibbons, *Transformations in Irish Culture* (Cork, 1996).

11 The impact and extent of New Art History is discussed in Jonathan Harris, *The New Art History: A Critical Introduction* (London, 2001).

12 Fintan Cullen, *Visual Politics: The Representation of Ireland, 1750–1930* (Cork, 1997), p. 2.

13 Anne Crookshank and the Knight of Glin, *The Painters of Ireland, c. 1660–1920* (London, 1978), since republished as *Ireland's Painters, 1600–1940* (New Haven, CT, and London, 2002).

14 My formulation of 'nation' here draws on both Anthony D. Smith, *National Identity* (London, 1990) and Benedict Anderson, *Imagined Communities: Reflections on the Origin and Spread of Nationalism* (London, 1983).

15 Seamus Deane, 'Introduction', in Terry Eagleton, Frederic Jameson and Edward Said, *Nationalism, Colonialism, Literature* (Minneapolis, MN, 1985), p. 9.

16 W.J.T. Mitchell, *Landscape and Power* (Chicago, IL, and London, 1994); Stephen Daniels, *Fields of Vision: Landscape Imagery and National Identity in England and the United States* (Cambridge, 1993).

17 Síghle Bhreathnach-Lynch, 'Landscape, Space and Gender: Their Role in the Construction of Female Identity in Newly Independent Ireland', in *Gendering Landscape Art*, ed. S. Adams and A. Greutzer Robins (Manchester, 2000), pp. 76–86; Belinda Loftus, *Mirrors: William III and Mother Ireland* (Dundrum, c. 1990).

18 Joe Cleary, 'Introduction: Ireland and Modernity', in *The Cambridge Companion to Modern Irish Culture*, ed. Joe Cleary and Claire Connoly (Cambridge, 2005), p. 2.

19 Ibid., p. 9.

20 Tom Dunne and William Pressly, eds, *James Barry: History Painter* (Aldershot, 2010).

21 Edward Said, 'Reflections on Exile' [1984], in *Out There: Marginalisation and Contemporary Cultures*, ed. Russell Ferguson, Martha Gever, Trinh T. Min-ha and Cornel West (New York and Cambridge, MA, 1990), pp. 357–66.

22 David Lloyd, *Anomalous States: Irish Writing and the Post-colonial Moment* (Durham, NC, 1993), pp. 1–2.

23 John Hutchinson, *The Dynamics of Cultural Nationalism: Gaelic Revival and the Creation of the Irish Nation State* (London, 1987).

24 Terry Eagleton, *Heathcliff and the Great Hunger: Studies in Irish Culture* (London and New York, 1995), p. 251.

25 For an account of Lane's early career as an art dealer, see Robert O'Byrne, *Hugh Lane, 1875–1915* (Dublin, 2000).

26 J. M. Synge, 'Good Pictures in Dublin: the New Municipal Gallery', *Manchester Guardian* (24 January 1908), reprinted in J. M. Synge, *Collected Works*, ed. Alan Price, vol. II: *Prose* (London, 1966), p. 390.

27 Jeanne Sheehy, *The Rediscovery of Ireland's Past: The Celtic Revival, 1830–1930* (London, 1980), pp. 107–19; Barbara Dawson, 'Hugh Lane and the Origins of the Collection', in *Images and Insights*, exh. cat., Hugh Lane Municipal Gallery (Dublin, 1993), pp. 13–31.

ONE: ETHNICITY, REVOLUTION AND THE MODERN, c. 1910–1918

1 Paul Henry, *An Irish Portrait* (London, 1951), p. 7.

2 J. M. Synge, *My Wallet of Photographs: The Collected Photographs of J. M. Synge Arranged and Introduced by Lilo Stephens* (Dublin, 1971), p. xii.

3 Yeats actually painted this watercolour after his return from a visit to Connemara and Mayo in the company of Synge, who had been commissioned by the *Manchester Guardian* to write a series of reports on the deprived areas of the West. Accompanied by Yeats's illustrations, these were published between 10 June and 26 July 1905. What emerged from their reports was a typology of the peasantry according to occupation. The heroic anonymity of the figure in Yeats's watercolour is also suggestive of a kind of typicality similar to Paul Henry's slightly later depictions of life on Achill.

4 Henry, *Irish Portrait*, p. 51.

5 Ibid.

6 Ibid., p. 54.

7 This is similar to the situation in Brittany in the late nineteenth century prior to the arrival of Gauguin, discussed in Fred Orton and Griselda Pollock, 'Les Données Bretonnantes: La Prairie de Représentation' (1980), reprinted in Fred Orton and Griselda Pollock, *Avant-gardes and Partisans Reviewed* (Manchester, 1996), pp. 53–88.

8 Mary Cosgrove, 'Paul Henry and Achill Island', in *Landscape, Heritage and Identity: Case Studies in Irish Ethnography*, ed. Ullrich Kockel (Liverpool, 1995), pp. 93–116.

9 In her study of a very different avant-garde formation, New York Dada, Amelia Jones has drawn attention to the marginality of the experience of the First World War to the heroic narratives of modernist innovation. Amelia Jones, *Irrational Modernism* (Cambridge and London, 2004).

10 David Fitzpatrick, 'Commemoration in the Irish Free State', in *History and Memory in Modern Ireland*, ed. Ian McBride (Cambridge, 2001), pp. 191–5.

11 Keith Jeffery, *Ireland and the Great War* (Cambridge, 2000), p. 79.

12 William Orpen, *An Onlooker in France* (London, 1924), p. 18.

13 Kenneth McConkey, *Sir John Lavery RA, 1856–1941*, exh. cat., Ulster Museum and Fine Arts Society

(Belfast, 1984), p. 75.

14 Jeffery, *Great War*, p. 47.

15 Initially under the leadership of John Redmond, the Irish Volunteers split in 1914 over the issue of participation in the War effort, with many subsequently giving their allegiance to more republican leaders and supporting the Rising.

16 Patrick Pearse, *The Murder Machine* (Dublin, 1912), cited in John Turpin, *Oliver Sheppard, 1865–1941: Symbolist Sculptor of the Irish Revival* (Dublin, 2000), pp. 134–42. I am indebted to Turpin's discussion here of the iconography of *The Death of Cuchulainn* and its significance for the conflation of cultural politics and revolutionary nationalism. Pearse's review of *Inis Fáil* is quoted in full on p. 70 Turpin's book.

17 Ibid., p. 139.

18 Luke Gibbons, 'Synge, Country and Western: the Myth of the West in Irish and American Culture' [1984], in Luke Gibbons, *Transformations in Irish Culture* (Cork, 1996), pp. 23–35; J. M. Synge, *The Playboy of the Western World* [1907], in Micheál Mac Liammóir, *J. M. Synge's Plays, Poems and Prose* (London, 1968).

19 James White, 'Introduction', in *John Keating: Paintings – Drawings*, exh. cat., Hugh Lane Municipal Gallery of Modern Art (Dublin, 1963), p. 8.

20 Ibid., p. 11.

21 Joan Fowler, 'Seán Keating: "The Men of the West"', *Critics' Choice*, exh. cat., Hugh Lane Municipal Gallery of Modern Art (Dublin, 1988), p. 17.

22 For example, Elizabeth Coxhead, *Daughters of Erin* (Gerrards Cross, 1979); Margaret Ward, *Unmanageable Revolutionaries* (London, 1983); Ruth Taillon, *When History Was Made: The Women of 1916* (Belfast, 1996).

23 Ward, *Unmanageable*, p. 93.

24 Síghle Bhreathnach-Lynch, 'The Easter Rising 1916: Constructing a Canon in Art and Artefacts', *History Ireland* (Spring 1997), p. 39. I am indebted to Bhreathnach-Lynch's essay for introducing me to this painting by Fox, and my discussion of it here is closely derived from her research in this published account.

25 Marie O'Neill, *Grace Gifford Plunkett and Irish Freedom: Tragic Bride of 1916* (Dublin, 2000), p. 36.

26 Mrs Joseph Plunkett, *To Hold as Twere* (Dundalk, 1919).

27 O'Neill, *Grace Gifford*, p. 45.

28 Ibid., p. 67.

TWO: MODERNITY AND INDEPENDENCE

1 Tim Pat Coogan, *Michael Collins* (London, 1991), pp. 76–84.

2 The name 'Black and Tans' was derived from the colours of their uniform, reminiscent of a pack of hunting hounds.

3 *Irish Art, 1770–1995 – History and Society: Works from the Crawford Municipal Gallery, Cork*, ed. Peter Murray (Cork, 1997), p. 34.

4 S. B. Kennedy, *Irish Art and Modernism* (Belfast, 1991), p. 180.

5 Christine Kinealy, *A Death Dealing Famine: The Great Hunger in Ireland* (London, 1997), pp. 95–6.

6 Joseph M. Curran, *The Birth of the Irish Free State, 1921–1923* (Tuscaloosa, AL, 1980), pp. 237–45.

7 Ibid., p. 184.

8 Sinéad McCoole, *Hazel: A Life of Lady Lavery, 1880–1935* (Dublin, 1996), pp. 63–6.

9 These had led to his depiction of, for example, the trial of Roger Casement, found guilty of treason after his arrest on Banna Strand on Easter weekend in 1916; the painting *High Treason* depicts the scene in the courtroom on 17 July where Casement made an unsuccessful appeal against his death sentence. John McGuiggan, 'A Rare Document of Irish History: "High Treason" by Sir John Lavery', *Irish Art Review*, 15 (1999), pp. 157–9. Lavery had some sympathy for Casement, yet the painting was actually commissioned by Lord Darling, the presiding Appeal Judge, who was not only a friend of the painter but a staunch Unionist close to Edward Carson.

10 John Lavery, *The Life of a Painter* (London, 1940), p. 207.

11 Ibid., p. 208.

12 Coogan, *Michael Collins*, p. 291; McCoole, *Lady Lavery*, pp. 101–02, refers to items donated to Kilmainham

Gaol, Dublin after the death of the widow of Shane Leslie in the 1960s.

13 Seumas O'Sullivan, *The Rose and the Bottle and Other Essays* (Dublin, 1946), p. 96.

14 Hilary Pyle, *Estella Solomons*, HRHA (1882–1968), exh. cat., Frederick Gallery (Dublin, 1999), p. 19.

15 Beatrice, Lady Glenavy, *Today We Will Only Gossip* (London, 1964), pp. 113–16.

16 Julian Campbell, 'Mary Swanzy: Biography', in *Mary Swanzy, 1882–1978*, exh. cat., Pyms Gallery (London, 1986), pp. 21–3.

17 Ernie O'Malley, 'The Paintings of Jack B. Yeats' [1945], in *Sources in Irish Art: A Reader*, ed. Fintan Cullen (Cork, 2000), p. 138.

18 Bruce Arnold, *Jack Yeats* (New Haven, CT, and London, 1998), p. 184.

19 Hilary Pyle and Fran Hegarty, 'Communicating with Prisoners, c. 1924', in *Jack B. Yeats at the Nyland Gallery Sligo*, ed. Donal Tinney (Sligo, 1998), p. 32.

20 Mary E. Daly, 'Women in the Irish Free State, 1922–1929: The Interaction between Economics and Ideology', *Journal of Women's History*, VI/4 and VII/1 (1994–5), p. 99.

21 Belinda Loftus, *Mirrors: Mother Ireland and William III* (Dundrum, c. 1990); also Ann Crilly, dir., *Mother Ireland* (1988); see also Ryan Thapar-Bjorkert, 'Mother India/Mother Ireland: Comparative Gender Dialogues of Colonialism and Nationalism in the Early Twentieth Century', *Women's Studies International Forum*, XXV/3 (2002), pp. 301–13.

22 Kenneth McConkey, *Sir John Lavery* (Edinburgh, 1993), p. 164.

23 Arnold, *Jack Yeats*, p. 248.

24 Enda Duffy, 'Disappearing Dublin: *Ulysses*, Postcoloniality and the Politics of Space', in *Semicolonial Joyce*, ed. Derek Attridge and Marjorie Howes (Cambridge, 2000), pp. 37–57.

25 Martyn Anglesea, *William Conor, the People's Painter* (Belfast, 1999), p. 9.

26 Micheal Farrell, *Northern Ireland: The Orange State* (London, 1980), p. 62.

27 Andy Bielenberg, 'Seán Keating, the Shannon Scheme and the Art of State Building', in *The Shannon Scheme and the Electrification of the Irish Free State*, ed. Andy Bielenberg (Dublin, 2002), p. 137.

28 Étienne Balibar, 'The Nation Form: History and Ideology' in É. Balibar and I. Wallerstein, *Race, Nation, Class* (London, 1991), p. 96.

29 Marie Bourke, 'A Growing Sense of National Identity: Charles Lamb (1893–1964) and the West of Ireland', *History Ireland*, VIII/1 (2000), p. 30.

30 Ibid., p. 32.

31 Ibid., p. 33.

32 'Connemara for the Artist: Mr Paul Henry's Experiences', *Irish Times* (4 August 1925), cited in S. B. Kennedy, *Paul Henry* (New Haven, CT, and London, 2000), p. 95.

33 Thomas Bodkin, 'T.B.', *Studio*, LXXXVI (1923), p. 341.

34 John Hewitt, in Hewitt and Theo Snoddy, *Art in Ulster: 1* (Belfast, 1977), p. 84.

35 Kennedy, *Irish Art*, p. 81.

36 Lothar Schoen, 'The Irish Free State and the Electricity Industry, 1912–1927', in Bielenberg, *Shannon Scheme*, p. 39.

37 At its height in 1928 the scheme employed 5,000 workers, both skilled and unskilled. In actuality working conditions were poor; wages were 32 shillings for a 50-hour week, little more than for an agricultural labourer. The scarcity of accommodation meant that workers were often reported to be lodging in pigsties or other outhouses, while medical care on the massive building site was also largely inadequate. See Michael McCarthy, 'How the Shannon Scheme Workers Lived', in Bielenberg, *Shannon Scheme*, pp. 48–72.

38 Bielenberg, 'Seán Keating', in Bielenberg, *Shannon Scheme*, p. 125.

39 Ibid., pp. 126–7.

40 Fintan Cullen, *Visual Politics: The Representation of Ireland, 1750–1930* (Cork, 1997), p. 168; Catherine Nash, '"Embodying the Nation"– the West of Ireland Landscape and Irish Identity', in *Tourism in Ireland: A Critical Analysis*, ed. Barbara O'Connor and Michael Cronin (Cork, 1993), p. 104.

41 Bielenberg, *Shannon Scheme*, p. 128.

42 Kennedy, *Irish Art*, p. 46.

43 Yeats was a member of the Society of Dublin Painters from 1920 to 1923, Swanzy from 1920 and Jellett from 1923.

44 For example, Bruce Arnold, *A Concise History of Irish Art* (London, 1977), p. 146; Anne Crookshank and the Knight of Glin, *Ireland's Painters, 1600–1940* (New Haven, CT, and London, 2002), p. 296.

45 Campbell, *Mary Swanzy*, p. 23.

46 The great exception to this was the designer Eileen Gray. In addition to other factors, her identity as a lesbian would have precluded her from returning to the restrictions of her Anglo-Irish family background.

47 Albert Gleizes, 'Homage to Mainie Jellett' [1948], in *Mainie Jellett: The Artist's Vision*, ed. Eileen McCarvill (Dundalk, 1958), p. 41.

48 Mainie Jellett, 'André Lhote' (1940) in McCarvill, *Artist's Vision*, p. 52.

49 Ibid.

50 George Russell, 'The Dublin Painters', *Irish Statesman* (27 October 1923), p. 206.

51 James White, 'Introduction', in *Evie Hone, 1894–1955*, exh. cat., University College (Dublin, 1958).

52 Bruce Arnold, *Mainie Jellett and the Modern Movement in Ireland* (London and New Haven, CT, 1991), p. 121.

53 Jellett, 'The Importance of Rhythm in Modern Painting', in McCarvill, *Artist's Vision*, p. 93.

54 Jellett, 'Modern Painting and Some of Its Aspects', in MacCarvill, *Artist's Vision*, p. 82.

THREE: THE WEST, THE SOUTH AND THE NORTH: ART IN IRELAND IN THE 1930S

1 A useful discussion of the effects of these measures on Irish reading habits in the 1930s is found in Elizabeth Russell, 'Holy Crosses, Guns and Roses: Themes in Popular Reading Material', in *Ireland in the 1930s*, ed. Joost Augusteijn (Dublin, 1999).

2 De Valera quoted in Terence O. Brown, *Ireland: A Cultural History* (London, 1985), p. 151.

3 Tracey Connolly, 'Emigration from Ireland to Britain during the Second World War', in *The Irish Diaspora*, ed. Andy Bielenberg (Harlow, 2000), p. 51.

4 Beatrice, Lady Glenavy, *Today We Will Only Gossip* (London, 1964), pp. 144, 146. A branch of the AIA was finally formed in Belfast in November 1944, where the 23 participants in the exhibition *Belfast Commentary* included such important Northern artists as Kathleen Bell, Arthur and George Campbell, Tom Carr and Colin Middleton.

5 De Valera, 29 April 1932, quoted in Anne-Marie Walsh, 'Root Them in the Land: Cottage Schemes for Agricultural Labourers', in Augusteijn, *1930s*, p. 50.

6 Anthony D. Smith, *National Identity* (Harmondsworth, 1991), p. 20.

7 S. B. Kennedy, *Paul Henry* (New Haven, CT, and London, 2000), p. 107.

8 Thomas Bodkin, 'Modern Irish Art', in *Saorstát Eireann [Irish Free State] Official Handbook* (Dublin, 1932), pp. 239–44.

9 The artists included were Paul Henry, Sean O'Sullivan, Sean Keating, Art O'Murnaghan (cover only), Estella Solomons, Maurice MacGonigal, Mary Duncan, Hilda Roberts, Harry Kernoff, Dorothy Blackham and Harry Walsh.

10 Walsh, 'Cottage Schemes', pp. 47–52.

11 Tricia Cusack, 'Janus and Gender: Women and the Nation's Backward Look', *Nations and Nationalism*, VI/4 (2000), p. 556.

12 Sinead Crofts, 'Maurice MacGonigal PRHA (1900–79) and His Western Paintings', *Irish Art Review*, XIII (1997), pp. 135–42 has useful information about MacGonigal as a teacher, in addition to his paintings of the West.

13 Bruce Arnold, *Jack Yeats* (New Haven, CT, and London, 1998), p. 254; see also Norah McGuinness, *The Literary Universe of Jack B. Yeats* (Washington, DC, 1992) for a full discussion of Yeats's literary work during the 1930s.

14 See Hilary Pyle, *Yeats: Portrait of an Artistic Family* (Dublin, 1997), p. 236, for a more detailed discussion of *In Memory of Boucicault and Bianconi*.

15 S. B. Kennedy, *Irish Art and Modernism, 1880–1950* (Belfast, 1991), p. 56.

16 For full details of membership of the Society of Dublin Painters during the 1920s and '30s, see

Kennedy, *Irish Art*, pp. 368–9.

17 'Miss Nano Reid's pictures: Exhibition at St Stephen's Green', *Irish Times* (28 November 1939).

18 Mary Daly, 'Women in the Irish Free State: The Interaction between Economics and Ideology', *Journal of Women's History*, VI/4 and VII/1 (1994–5), p. 108.

19 Quoted in *Irish Women Artists: From the Eighteenth Century to the Present Day*, exh. cat., National Gallery of Ireland and Douglas Hyde Gallery (Dublin, 1987), p. 133.

20 Glenavy, *Today*, p. 148.

21 Ibid. The Haverty Trust was set up in 1930 to buy contemporary Irish art; acquisitions were subsequently donated to public institutions. See Kennedy, *Irish Art*, pp. 85–6.

22 Nicola Gordon Bowe, 'The Art of Beatrice Elvery, Lady Glenavy (1883–1970)', *Irish Arts Review*, XI (1995), p. 174.

23 Declan Kiberd, *Inventing Ireland: The Literature of the Modern Nation* (London, 1995), pp. 364–79.

24 Bruce Arnold, *Mainie Jellett and the Modern Movement in Ireland* (New Haven, CT, and London, 1991), p. 137.

25 Sir Basil Brooke in *Fermanagh Times* (13 July 1933), quoted in Micheal Farrell, *Northern Ireland: the Orange State* (London, 1980), p. 90.

26 David Brett, 'The Reformation and the Practice of Art', *Circa*, 26 (January 1986), pp. 20–24.

27 Geraldine Watts, 'Utility Clashes with Emotion', 'Hewitt', *Fortnight* supplement (1987), n.p.

28 T. P. Flanagan, 'The John Hewitt Collection', *A Poet's Pictures*, exh. cat., Shambles Gallery (Hillsborough, 1987), p. 12.

29 Sam Burnside, 'Preparing Lonely Defences', in 'Hewitt', *Fortnight* supplement.

30 John Hewitt, *Colin Middleton* (Belfast, 1976), p. 9.

31 John Hewitt, 'Preface', in *The Ulster Unit Exhibition of Contemporary Art*, exh. cat., Locksley Hall (Belfast, 1934), n.p.

32 *Belfast Newsletter* (19 December 1934).

33 Other members of this group included Victor Pasmore, Ceri Richards and Rodrigo Moynihan; like Carr, their practice shifted towards forms of realism coalescing in the Euston Road School in 1937.

Charles Harrison, *English Art and Modernism, 1900–1939* (London, 1981), pp. 334–9.

34 F. E. McWilliam quoted in Mel Gooding, *F. E. McWilliam: Sculpture, 1932–1989*, exh. cat., Tate Gallery (London, 1989), p. 15.

FOUR: WAR, ITS AFTERMATH AND THE VISUAL, 1939–1947

1 Brian Barton, *The Blitz: Belfast in the War Years* (Belfast, 1989).

2 Meiron and Susie Harries, *The War Artists: British Official War Art of the Twentieth Century* (London, 1983), p. 161.

3 Both this drawing and Conor's *Building an Air-Raid Shelter in a Belfast Street* were reproduced in *Blitz*, the second in the WAAC-produced series 'War Pictures by British Artists' (London 1942), with an introduction by J. B. Morton. The title is given as *The Evacuation of Children in Northern Ireland*. With the inclusion of James Miller's depictions of the effects of the Blitz in Scotland and John Armstrong's tempera painting of a farm in Wales destroyed by the bombing, these work together to produce a sense of a homogenous experience of war throughout the British nation.

4 Frank Ormsby, 'Tomorrow with his Notes: Editing the *Collected Poems of John Hewitt*', in *Returning to Ourselves: Second Volume of Papers from the John Hewitt International Summer School*, ed. Eve Patten (Belfast, 1995), pp. 388–9.

5 Patricia Craig, 'The Liberal Imagination in Northern Ireland Prose', in Patten, *Returning to Ourselves*, p. 140; see also James MacIntyre, *Making My Mark: An Artist's Early Life* (Belfast, 2001), p. 94.

6 James White, *Gerard Dillon: An Illustrated Biography* (Dublin, 1994), p. 42. Arthur Campbell also exhibited on this occasion.

7 Ibid., p. 43.

8 S. B. Kennedy, *Irish Art and Modernism, 1880–1950* (Belfast, 1990), p. 148.

9 'Biography', in *Colin Middleton: A Millennium Appreciation*, ed. Carlo Eastwood (Belfast, 2000), p. 75.

10 Dickon Hall, *Colin Middleton: A Study* (Belfast, 2001), p. 37.

11 Brian Fallon, 'Middleton Exhibition', *Irish Times* (29 November 1974), p. 15.

12 Michael Longley, 'Talking to Colin Middleton', in Eastwood, *Colin Middleton*, p. 17.

13 John Hewitt, *Colin Middleton* (Belfast, 1976), p. 32.

14 Longley, 'Colin Middleton', pp. 15–16.

15 Nevill Johnson, 'The Other Side of Six', *The Recorder*, XIV/1 (2001), p. 77.

16 Dickon Hall, 'Nevill Johnson', in Dickon Hall and Eoin O'Brien, *Nevill Johnson: Paint the Smell of Grass* (Bangor, 2008), p. 16.

17 John Hewitt, *John Luke (1906–1975)* (Belfast and Dublin, 1978), p. 47.

18 From the cotton cloth glued with skin size to a Masonite Standard Prestwood Board, to details of the glazes and over-painting, which involved 'two and mostly three or four separate glazes, one on top of the other, the medium being sun-thickened linseed oil, dammar varnish, and some Canada Balsam'; ibid., p. 54.

19 James White, *Gerard Dillon: An Illustrated Biography* (Dublin, 1994), pp. 34–5.

20 An account of a slightly later visit to Inishlacken, an island off Roundstone in Co. Galway, by Dillon, George Campbell and James McIntyre can be found in James MacIntyre, *Three Men on an Island* (Belfast, 1996).

21 Roy Douglas, Liam Harte and Jim O'Hara, *Drawing Conclusions: A Cartoon History of Anglo-Irish Relations, 1798–1998* (Belfast, 1998), p. 215.

22 Luke Gibbons, 'From Megalith to Megastore: Broadcasting and Irish Culture', in Gibbons, *Transformations in Irish Culture* (Cork, 1996), pp. 74–5.

23 Gerry Smyth, *Decolonisation and Criticism: The Construction of Irish Literature* (London, 1998), p. 114.

24 Anna Sheehy, 'Harry Kernoff RHA', *The Bell*, 11/2 (1941), pp. 27–9; Sheehy, 'Cecil Ffrench Salkeld', *The Bell*, 11/3 (1941), pp. 48–51; Elizabeth Curran, 'The Art of Nano Reid', *The Bell*, III/2 (1942), pp. 128–31.

25 Arthur Power, 'A Guide to This Year's Academy', *The Bell*, IV/2 (May 1942), pp. 96–107.

26 Kate O'Brien, *The Land of Spices* [1941] (London, 2000).

27 Donal O Drisceoil, *Censorship in Ireland 1939–1945* (Cork, 1996), pp. 35–7.

28 Charles Sidney, 'Art Criticism in Dublin', *The Bell*, IX/2 (1944), pp. 104–10.

29 *Images and Insights*, exh. cat., Hugh Lane Municipal Gallery (Dublin, 1994), pp. 236–7.

30 Power, 'A Guide', p. 96.

31 Ibid., p. 102.

32 Ibid.

33 Yeats quoted in James White 'Introduction', in *Jack B. Yeats, 1871–1957: A Centenary Exhibition*, exh. cat., National Gallery of Ireland (Dublin, 1971), p. 14.

34 Hilary Pyle, *Yeats: Portrait of an Artistic Family* (Dublin, 1997), p. 248.

35 Ernie O'Malley, 'The Paintings of Jack B. Yeats' [1945], in *Jack B. Yeats: a Centenary Gathering*, ed. Roger McHugh (Dublin, 1971), pp. 66, 68.

36 Ibid., p. 70.

37 Thomas MacGreevy, *Jack Yeats: An Appreciation and an Interpretation* (Dublin, 1943).

38 Samuel Beckett, 'MacGreevy on Yeats', *The Irish Times* (4 August 1945), in McHugh, *Centenary Gathering*, p. 73.

39 Ibid.

40 Patrick Campbell, *My Life and Easy Times* (London, 1967), p. 151.

41 Kennedy, *Irish Art*, p. 91.

42 Kenneth Hall, unpublished autobiography, private collection, p. 58.

43 Kennedy, *Irish Art*, p. 265.

44 Letter from Dairine Vanston to S. B. Kennedy, 28 February 1982, artist's file, Ulster Museum Archives.

45 Letter from Dairine Vanston to Heloise Mitchell, 29 December 1971, artist's file, Ulster Museum Archives.

46 Kennedy, *Irish Art*, pp. 94, 356n.

47 Ibid., p. 121.

48 Louis le Brocquy in conversation with the author, 21 February 2002.

49 Ibid.

50 The full list as cited in the catalogue is Laurence Campbell RHA, Margaret Clarke RHA, Elizabeth Curran, Ralph Cusack, Revd Jack Hanlon, Evie Hone, Mainie Jellett (Chairman), Louis le Brocquy and Norah McGuinness.

51 Kennedy, *Irish Art*, p. 121.

52 'Living Art – A New Departure', *Irish Times* (16 September 1943), p. 3.

53 Máirín Allen, 'Irish Post-Impressionism', *Father Matthew Record* (November 1943), p. 10.

54 Herbert Read, 'On Subjective Art', *The Bell*, VII/5 (February 1944), pp. 424–9.

FIVE: THE SIGNIFICANCE OF THE OVERLOOKED

1 Colm Tóibín, 'Public, Private and a National Spirit', in *When Time Began to Rant and Rage*, ed. James Steward (London, 1998), p. 25.

2 Tony O'Malley interviewed by Hilary Pyle, cited in Peter Murray, *Tony O'Malley* (Oysterhaven, 2000), p. 10.

3 Tóibín, 'Public, Private', ibid. p. 25.

4 Brian Fallon, *Tony O'Malley: Painter in Exile* (Dublin, 1984), p. 98.

5 Patrick Swift, 'Contemporary Irish Artists (4): Nano Reid', *Envoy*, I/4 (March 1950), p. 32.

6 'Nano Reid's Pictures', unattributed review of exhibition at Victor Waddington Gallery, 9–20 March 1950, Nano Reid cuttings file, National Gallery of Ireland archive, Dublin.

7 Reid interviewed by Harriet Cooke (1969), cited in Jeanne Sheehy, 'Introduction', *Nano Reid: A Retrospective Exhibition*, exh. cat., Municipal Gallery of Modern Art (Dublin, 1974), p. 5.

8 Thomas Bodkin, *Report on the Arts in Ireland* (Dublin, 1949), p. 20.

9 Cecil Ffrench Salkeld, 'Daniel O'Neill', *Envoy*, I/I (December 1949), pp. 31–43; Patrick Collins, 'George Campbell: Portrait of an Artist', *Envoy*, I/2 (January 1950), pp. 4–50; Noelle Brissac, 'Thurloe Conolly', *Envoy*, I/3 (February 1950), pp. 32–6; Patrick Swift, 'Nano Reid', *Envoy*, I/4 (March 1950), pp. 26–35; Edward Sheehy, 'Colin Middleton', *Envoy*, I/5 (April 1950), pp. 32–40; W. J. White, 'Louis le Brocquy', *Envoy*, II/6 (May 1950), pp. 52–65; John Ryan, 'Patrick Swift', *Envoy*, V/20 (July 1951), pp. 56–7.

10 Patrick Kavanagh, 'Exhibitions', *Kavanagh's Weekly*, I/I (12 April 1952).

11 Herbert Read in *The Listener* [8 January 1942], in Bruce Arnold, *Jack Yeats* (New Haven, CT, and London, 1998), p. 305.

12 Ibid., p. 351.

13 Brian O'Doherty, 'The Irish Imagination' [1971], in *Sources in Irish Art: A Reader*, ed. Fintan Cullen (Cork, 2000), p. 270.

14 Patrick Collins, quoted in Brian Lynch, 'Irish Painting? There's No Such Thing', *Hibernia* (28 June 1979), p. 27.

15 Patrick Collins, letter to S. B. Kennedy, artist's file, Ulster Museum Archives, 20 September 1976, n.p.

16 Brian Fallon, 'Irish Women Artists in the Nineteen-fifties', *Irish Women Artists from the Eighteenth Century to the Present Day*, exh. cat., National Gallery of Ireland and Douglas Hyde Gallery (Dublin, 1987), p. 47.

17 James MacIntyre, *Three Men on an Island* (Belfast, 1996).

18 In 1959, in the introduction to her solo show at Belfast Museum and Art Gallery, Seán O'Faoláin extolled her consistent reputation as a colourist: 'So many of these latest pictures might suggest an abrupt physical release in terms of colour, a painter suddenly letting herself go, but those who know her earlier work will recognise with delight the straight line of descent in these rebellious dark-blue-greens, these broodings in brown and burnt sienna, these gay contrasts of ochre lemon and cyclamen'. Seán O'Faoláin, 'Foreword', *Recent Paintings by Norah McGuinness*, exh. cat., Museum and Art Gallery (Belfast, 1959), n.p.

19 Elizabeth Bowen, 'Preface', *Norah McGuinness*, exh. cat., Leicester Galleries (London, 1957), p. 2.

20 Paula Murphy has also indicated the difficulty of classifying Camille Souter's work in her essay on the artist, 'The Tiny Poems of Camille Souter – A Context', in *Camille Souter Retrospective*, exh. cat., Model Arts and Niland Gallery Sligo and RHA Gallagher Gallery Dublin (Sligo, 2001), p. 14.

21 Born in Northampton as Betty Pamela Holmes and brought up partly in Ireland, a bout of tuberculosis led to her adoption of the name Camille after Dumas' consumptive heroine. She also retained the surname of her first husband, the actor Gordon Souter.

22 Fionna Barber, 'Excavating Room 50: Irish Art and the Cold War at the 1950 Venice Biennale', *A Shared*

Legacy: Essays on Irish and Scottish Art and Visual Culture,
ed. Fintan Cullen and John Morrison (Aldershot,
2005), pp. 207–23.

23 Edward de Courcy, 'The Sculpture of Hilary Heron',
Envoy, 11/7 (June 1950), pp. 50–58.

24 Ibid., p. 54.

25 *Hilary Heron: Recent Sculpture*, exh. cat., Victor
Waddington Galleries (Dublin, 1950); this was fol-
lowed by a second show of the same name on 17–28
September 1953.

26 John Mogey, *Rural Life in Northern Ireland: Five Regional
Studies* (London, New York and Oxford, 1947), cited in
Diarmaid Ferriter, *The Transformation of Ireland,
1900–2000* (London, 2004), pp. 452–3.

27 Harriet Atkinson, 'Putting Reconstruction on
Display: Post-war Exhibitions of Agriculture and
Industry', paper given to the Annual Conference of
the Social History Society, Trinity College, Dublin,
7–9 January 2005; Gillian McIntosh, *The Force of
Culture: Unionist Identities in Contemporary Ireland* (Cork,
1999).

28 Ibid., p. 111.

29 John Hewitt, *John Luke (1906–1975)* (Belfast, 1978),
p. 82.

30 Kenneth Jamison, 'Painting and Sculpture', in
Causeway: The Arts in Ulster, ed. Michael Longley
(Belfast, 1971), p. 44.

31 Gena Lynam, 'Daniel O'Neill (1920–1974): Landscape
and Figure Painting', *Irish Arts Review*, XV (1999), pp.
134–41.

32 Ffrench Salkeld, 'O'Neill', p. 34.

33 John Hewitt and Theo Snoddy, *Art in Ulster: 1* (Belfast,
1977), p. 124.

34 Liam Kelly, 'Colin Middleton – a Consummate
Visionary', in *Colin Middleton: A Millennium
Appreciation*, ed. Carlo Eastwood (Belfast, 2000), p. 11.

35 Jamison, 'Painting', p. 59.

36 John Hewitt, 'Portrait of the Artist as a Young Man',
Threshold, 1/1 (1957), p. 80.

37 Ibid., p. 81.

38 Tom Clyde, *The Prose Writings of John Hewitt* (Belfast,
1985), p. 6.

39 John Hewitt, 'From Chairmen and Committee Men,

Good Lord Deliver Us' [1968], in *Ancestral Voices: The
Selected Prose of John Hewitt*, ed. Tom Clyde (Belfast,
1987), p. 51.

40 John Hewitt, 'No Rootless Colonist' (1972), ibid.,
pp. 146–57.

41 A similar point is made by Eamonn Hughes in his
essay 'Sent to Coventry: Emigration and
Autobiography', in *Returning to Ourselves: Second Volume
of Papers from the John Hewitt International Summer School*,
ed. Eve Patten (Belfast, 1995), pp. 261–75.

SIX: IRISH ART AND DIASPORA IN THE 1950S

1 Paul Gilroy, 'It Ain't Where You're From, It's Where
You're At . . . The Dialectics of Diasporic
Identification', *Third Text*, 13 (1990–91), pp. 3–16.

2 Swanzy's solo show at St George's Gallery, London,
March–April 1947, was her last exhibition for over
twenty years until her retrospective exhibition at the
Municipal Gallery, Dublin in June 1968.

3 Bronwen Walter, *Outsiders Inside: Whiteness, Place and
Irish Women* (London, 2001), pp. 88–102.

4 According to MacIntyre, all members of this group
lived within half a mile of each other (interview with
the author, 15 September 2005).

5 Ibid.

6 Gerard Dillon, 'The Artist Speaks', *Envoy*, IV/15
(February 1951), p. 39.

7 'The Irish are a nation of talkers and storytellers . . .
The Irish painter is trying to fight this storytelling
quality (natural in himself) in his work, because he
knows it isn't "pure painting". It's a hard fight.'
Ibid., pp. 39–40.

8 Both *Patriarch* and *Eve* were included in McWilliam's
exhibition of February–March 1956 at the Hanover
Gallery, which also included the study for *Princess
Macha* and busts of William and Mary Scott.

9 F. E. McWilliam, untitled essay, *Architectural Design*
(September 1958), p. 378. Roy Wilkinson also points
out Macha's significance as a Celtic goddess with
responsibility for tending the war-wounded and
bringing peace; Roy Wilkinson, 'The Place of Public
in Public Sculpture: responses to F. E. McWilliam's

Princess Macha', *Circa*, 45 (May–June 1989), p. 30.

10 McWilliam, untitled essay.

11 *Irish News* (11 April 1960), cited in Wilkinson, 'Place of Public', p. 30.

12 Ibid.

13 Cited ibid., p. 227.

14 Ibid., p. 219.

15 Patrick Heron, 'William Scott' [1958], in *Modern Painters*, III/4 (Winter 1990–91), pp. 22–4, p. 22. This essay was commissioned by the British Council as an introduction to Scott's catalogue for the Venice Biennale, but subsequently rejected and replaced by a piece written by Herbert Read.

16 Excerpt from illustrated lecture (1958) by William Scott, transcript held in artist's file, Whitworth Art Gallery, Manchester.

17 The popular myth of Bacon's self-imposed exile is refuted by Barbara Dawson, based on her interviews with the artist's sister Ianthe Knott; 'All Changed, Changed Utterly', in *Francis Bacon: A Terrible Beauty*, ed. Barbara Dawson and Martin Harrison (Dublin, 2009), p. 8.

18 Robert Melville, 'Francis Bacon', *Horizon*, XX, nos 120, 121 (1949–50), pp. 419–23.

19 Fionna Barber, 'Disturbed Ground: Francis Bacon, Traumatic Memory and the Gothic', *The Irish Review*, 39 (2008), pp. 123–38.

20 Ibid., p. 163.

21 David Sylvester, *Interviews with Francis Bacon* (London, 2002), p. 81.

22 A similarly circumspect approach to reading Bacon also appears in Simon Ofield, 'Wrestling with Francis Bacon', *Oxford Art Journal*, XXIV/1 (2001), pp. 113–30, which focuses on the construction of aspects of homosexuality in relation to his paintings.

23 Louis le Brocquy, 'A Painter's Notes on His Irishness' [1981], in Dorothy Walker, *Louis le Brocquy* (Dublin, 1981), p. 90.

24 John Russell, 'Introduction', in Walker, *Louis le Brocquy*, p. 9.

25 Le Brocquy quoted in Síghle Bhreathnach-Lynch, 'Louis le Brocquy's *A Family*: An Unwholesome and Satanic Distortion of Natural Beauty', at www.recirca.com, last accessed 24 May 2012.

26 Michael Leja, *Reframing Abstract Expressionism: Subjectivity and Painting in the 1940s* (New Haven, CT, and London, 1993).

27 Walker, *Le Brocquy*, p. 23.

28 Fionna Barber, 'Excavating Room 50: Irish Painting and the Cold War at the 1950 Venice Biennale', in *A Shared Legacy: Essays on Irish and Scottish Art and Visual Culture*, ed. Fintan Cullen and John Morrison (Aldershot, 2005).

29 See Roisin Kennedy, 'Made in England: The Critical Reception of Louis le Brocquy's "A Family"', *Third Text*, XIX/5 (2005), pp. 475–86.

30 Louis le Brocquy (1969), 'Notes on Painting and Awareness' [1979], *The Recorder*, XIV/1 (Summer 2001), p. 47.

31 Herbert Read, quoted in Walker, *Le Brocquy*, p. 37.

32 Ibid. See also Riann Coulter, 'Louis le Brocquy's *Presences*, 1954–64: Irish, British or International?', *The Irish Review*, 39 (Winter 2008), pp. 139–56 for an extensive discussion of the significance of Kleinian readings in relation to these paintings.

33 Serge Guilbaut, 'Postwar Painting Games: The Rough and the Slick', in *Reconstructing Modernism: Art in New York, Paris, and Montreal, 1945–1964* (Cambridge, MA, 1995), p. 59.

34 See Barber, 'Excavating' for a discussion of the relationship of Ireland to European cultural politics during the 1950s.

35 Homi Bhabha, *The Location of Culture* (London, 1994), p. 37.

SEVEN: MODERNIZATION AND ITS CONSEQUENCES: THE 1960S

1 David Harvey, *The Condition of Postmodernity: An Enquiry into the Origins of Cultural Change* (London, 1989), pp. 10–38.

2 This section draws on Conor McCarthy, *Modernisation: Crisis and Culture in Ireland 1969–1992* (Dublin, 2000), pp. 16–20; Benedict Anderson, *Imagined Communities: Reflections on the Origin and Spread of Nationalism* (London, 1991); Marshall Berman, All

that *Is Solid Melts into Air: The Experience of Modernity* (London, 1983).

3 Brian O'Doherty 'The Irish Imagination' [1971], in *Sources In Irish Art: A Reader*, ed. Fintan Cullen (Cork, 2000), p. 270.

4 Frances Ruane, *Patrick Collins* (Dublin, 1982), pp. 28–9.

5 Ibid., p. 46.

6 Mainie Jellett, 'Modern Art and Its Relation to the Past' [1931], in *Mainie Jellett: The Artist's Vision, Lectures and Essays on Art*, ed. Eileen McCarvill (Dundalk, 1958), p. 90.

7 Nano Reid's *Ancient Land* was exhibited at ILEA in 1962 and subsequently in New York in 1963 as part of the *Twelve Irish Painters* exhibition.

8 Peter Murray, *Tony O'Malley* (Oysterhaven, 2000), p. 41.

9 Brian Fallon, 'The St Ives Period', in *Tony O'Malley* [1996], ed. Brian Lynch (Dublin, 2004), p. 104.

10 Derek Hill, 'Introduction', in *Dawson Gallery Catalogue* (1967), reprinted in *Two Painters: Works by Alfred Wallis and James Dixon*, exh. cat., Irish Museum of Modern Art (Dublin, 1999), p. 119. (Also at Tate Gallery, St Ives, 2000.)

11 Matthew Gale, 'Artistry, Authenticity and the Work of James Dixon and Alfred Wallis', in *Two Painters*, p. 21.

12 George Melly, *A Tribe of One: Great Naïve Painters of the British Isles* [1981], pp. 120–21.

13 Dixon quoted in Malise Ruthven, 'The Other Tories Earn Their Keep' (n.d.), in *Two Painters*, p. 125.

14 Laurie J. Monahan, 'Cultural Cartography: American Designs at the 1964 Venice Biennale', in *Reconstructing Modernism: Art in New York, Paris and Montreal, 1945–1964*, ed. Serge Guilbaut (Cambridge, MA, and London, 1995), pp. 369–416.

15 Brian P. Kennedy, *Dreams and Responsibilities: The State and the Arts in Independent Ireland* (Dublin, n.d.), pp. 140–41.

16 The other members were Stanley Mosse, Robert Figgis, George Hetherington, Anne King-Harman and Serge Philipson. Campbell Bruce, 'CIAS 1962–2005', in *SIAR 50: 50 Years of Irish art from the Collections of the Contemporary Irish Art Society* (Dublin, 2005), p. 6.

17 The other jury members were French art critic and historian Jean Leymarie and Willem Sandberg, Chairman of the Israel Museum in Jerusalem and a former director of the Stedelijk Museum in Amsterdam.

18 For an account of the history of *Rosc* from its inception until the last exhibition in 1988, see Dorothy Walker, *Modern Art in Ireland* (Dublin, 1997), pp. 110–39.

19 A plan to include them among the exhibits in the RDS was thwarted by the Museum's Director. Ibid., p. 114.

20 Clement Greenberg, 'Poetry of Vision: Ireland Inaugurates "An International Quadrennial Without Prizes"', *Artforum*, VI/8 (April 1968), pp. 18–21.

21 Robert F. Storey, *Pierrot: The Critical History of a Mask* (Princeton, NJ, 1978).

22 Although he had exhibited with the White Stag Group in the 1940s, Patrick Scott subsequently became better known as an architect, only returning to professional painting in 1960, the year he represented Ireland at the Venice Biennale.

23 Over a period of twelve years the gallery acquired 33 works by contemporary Irish artists from CIAS donations. These included the work of established artists such as Nano Reid and Norah McGuinness, Patrick Collins's *Hy Brazil* and early paintings by the young Barrie Cooke and Noel Sheridan. Many members of the rapidly expanding Society, such as Goulding and subsequently Gordon Lambert and Dorothy Walker, continued to develop their personal collections.

24 Both of these works were included in her first solo show at the Leicester Gallery in London in 1959.

25 Gerry Walker, 'The Journey of a Meathman as an Intellectual', in John O'Regan, *Micheal Farrell* (Oysterhaven, 1998), p. 14.

26 Micheal Farrell, 'Artist's Statement' [1965], in Cyril Barrett, *Micheal Farrell* (Dublin, 1979), pp. 19–21.

27 Walker, *Modern Art*, p. 55.

28 See Brenda Moore-McCann, *Brian O'Doherty/Patrick Ireland: Between Categories* (Farnham, 2009), pp. 50–55.

29 See Alexander Alberro and Nora M. Alter, 'After the Senses', in *Beyond the White Cube: A Retrospective of Brian O'Doherty/Patrick Ireland*, ed. Christina Kennedy and Georgina Jackson, exh. cat., Dublin City Art Gallery the Hugh Lane (Dublin, 2006), pp. 45–55 for a detailed

account of O'Doherty's *The Five Senses of the Bishop of Cloyne*.

30 Brenda Moore-McCann, 'The Ogham Sculptures: Perceptual Boundaries of the Inaudible and Invisible', ibid., p. 57.

31 Micheal Farrell, ed., *Twenty Years On* (Dingle, 1988), p. 21.

32 Vera Ryan, *Movers and Shapers: Irish Art since 1960* (Doughcloyne, 2003), p. 128.

33 Theo Snoddy, *Dictionary of Irish Artists, 20th Century*, 2nd edn (Dublin, 2002), p. 220.

34 Anne Crookshank, *Deborah Brown: A Selected Exhibition of Works Completed between 1947 and 1982*, exh. cat., Arts Council Gallery (Belfast, 1982), n.p.

35 Ibid.

36 Anne Crookshank, *Deborah Brown*, exh. cat., New Vision Centre Gallery (London, 1964), n.p.

37 Mike Catto, *Art in Ulster 2* (Belfast, 1977), p. 8.

EIGHT: THE CONFLICT IN THE NORTH AND IRISH ART, 1968–1979

1 Jonathan Barden, *A History of Ulster* [1992] (Belfast, 2005).

2 Author's interview with Carol Graham, 6 October 1988.

3 Anne Crookshank, *Deborah Brown: A Selected Exhibition of Works Completed between 1947 and 1982*, exh. cat., Arts Council Gallery (Belfast, 1982), n.p.

4 Flanagan quoted in S. B. Kennedy, *T. P. Flanagan* (Belfast, 1995), p. 73.

5 Joseph McWilliams, *A Troubled Journey, 1966–1989*, exh. cat., Cavehill Gallery (Belfast, 1989), n.p.

6 Micheal Farrell's *Northern Ireland: The Orange State* (London, 1980), the first account of nationalist resistance in Northern Ireland since 1921, makes little of the role of women. Feminist accounts tell another story: for example, Eileen Fairweather, Roisin McDonough and Melanie MacFadyen, *Only the Rivers Run Free* (London, 1984).

7 Catherine MacWilliams, who did not know McKee personally, was not aware of this when she took the photograph.

8 Jack Pakenham [1986] quote in Brian McAvera, *Jack Pakenham Works, 75–89*, exh. cat., Orchard Gallery (Derry, 1990), p. 6.

9 Ibid., p. 8.

10 F. E. McWilliam, 'Artist's Statement', *Women of Belfast*, exh. cat., McClelland Galleries International (Belfast, 1973), n.p.

11 Belinda Loftus, *Mirrors: Mother Ireland and William III* (Dundrum, 1990), pp. 57–61; L. P. Curtis Jr, *Apes and Angels: The Irishman in Victorian Caricature*, revised version (Washington, DC, and London, 1997); the documentary *Mother Ireland* (dir. Ann Crilly, 1988) also examines the historical representation of women in Irish nationalism.

12 G. S. Whittet, 'London Exhibitions Reviewed', *Art and Artists* (January 1974), p. 41.

13 Conrad Atkinson, statement from catalogue for *Lives Exhibition*, Hayward Gallery, London, 1979, reprinted in *Conrad Atkinson: Picturing the System*, ed. Caroline Tisdall and Sandy Nairne (London, 1981), p. 51.

14 Conrad Atkinson in conversation with Caroline Tisdall, ibid., p. 23.

15 Brian P. Kennedy, *Dreams and Responsibilities* (Dublin, n.d.), p. 164.

16 Ibid., p. 169.

17 Ibid., p. 191.

18 Dillon was badly affected by the news from the North as the situation degenerated. After a showing in Cork, ILEA was subsequently intended to travel to Belfast. On 20 August 1969, the day of the exhibition's opening in Cork, the *Irish Times* published a letter by him both stating his opposition to the exhibition being shown in Belfast and withdrawing his work if this went ahead. Dillon's letter also called for support from other exhibitors. After much debate in the letters pages of the *Irish Times*, the paper's leader came down in favour of a liberal consensus, concluding that art had no role in the ongoing struggle. Dillon had already backed up his action by further means. The committee of ILEA had chartered a train from Dublin to Cork for the opening. Dillon circulated a petition to ILEA amongst the 130 passengers; 108 signed, including 25 out of 30 exhibitors. In spite

of this overwhelming support, ILEA rejected his plea, and the exhibition was shown in Belfast as planned. According to James White, Dillon felt that he had done what he could to engender support for Northern nationalists.

19 Cyril Barrett, *Micheal Farrell* (Dublin, 1979), p. 10.

20 Aidan Dunne, 'Home Thoughts from Abroad', in *Micheal Farrell*, ed. John O'Regan (Oysterhaven, 1998), p. 9.

21 Barrett, *Micheal Farrell*.

22 O'Regan, *Micheal Farrell*, p. 15.

23 Brian O'Doherty, 'The Puritan Nude', in *The Irish Imagination, 1959–1971*, exh. cat., Municipal Gallery of Modern Art (Dublin, 1971), p. 22.

24 Ibid., p. 10.

25 Brenda Moore McCann, 'The Politics of Identity, Place, and Memory in Contemporary Irish Art', in *Art and Politics: The Imagination of Opposition in Europe*, ed. Noel Kelly (Ljubljana and Dublin, 2004), p. 27. I am indebted to the thorough documentation of O'Doherty/Ireland's performance in this essay, and also to McCann's incisive discussion of its significance in relation to wider aspects of Irish culture and the instabilities of postcolonial identity.

26 Oona Frawley, *Irish Pastoral: Nostalgia and Twentieth-century Irish Literature* (Dublin, 2005), pp. 13–18.

27 Ciaran Carty, 'No.3', in *No.3: A Series of Paintings by Robert Ballagh*, exh. cat, David Hendricks Gallery (Dublin, 1983), n.p.

28 Jean Fisher, 'The Enigma of the Hero in the Work of James Coleman' [1983], in *James Coleman*, ed. George Baker (Cambridge, MA, 2003), p. 42. See also Dorothea von Hantelmann, 'James Coleman's *Box (ahhareturnabout) 1977*, in *James Coleman*, ed. Luke Gibbons, exh. cat., Irish Museum of Modern Art (Dublin, 2007), pp. 65–86.

29 *Rachael Thomas Interviews Michael Craig-Martin* (Milan, 2006), p. 27.

30 Ibid., p. 31.

31 Dorothy Walker, *Brian King: Time Pieces*, exh. cat., Taylor Galleries (Dublin, 1979), p. 7.

32 Sean Rainbird, *Joseph Beuys and the Celtic World: Scotland, Ireland and England, 1970–1985* (London, 2005), pp. 32–41.

33 Donald Kuspit, 'Sacred Sadness', in D. Eccher et al., *Sean Scully: A Retrospective* (London, 2007), p. 17.

34 Seán Scully quoted in Maria Lluisa Borras, 'The Spiritual Art of Our Time', in Eccher et al., *Sean Scully*, p. 27.

35 Dorothy Walker, *Modern Art in Ireland* (Dublin, 1997), p. 102.

36 James Johnson Sweeney, 'Introduction to Suite of Four Prints' [1975], reprinted in *Cecil King: Retrospective Exhibition*, exh. cat., Hugh Lane Municipal Gallery (Dublin, 1981), p. 9.

37 Ethna Waldron, 'Introduction to Berlin Suite of 6 Screen Prints' [1970], in *Cecil King*, p. 7.

38 Walker, *Modern Art*, p. 104.

39 Anne Madden quoted in Roderic Knowles, *Contemporary Irish Art* (Dublin, 1982), p. 98.

40 Anne Madden le Brocquy, *Louis le Brocquy: Seeing His Way* (Dublin, 1994), p. 179.

41 Ibid.

42 Richard Kearney, 'Janus', in *Louis le Brocquy: Images, 1975–1987*, exh. cat, Guinness Hop Store (Dublin, 1987), p. 50. (Also shown at Ulster Museum, Belfast.)

43 Myrtle Hill, *Women in Ireland: A Century of Change* (Belfast, 2003), pp. 151–8.

44 Walker, *Modern Art*, p. 89.

NINE: POSTMODERNISM AND IRELAND

1 Clement Greenberg, 'Modernist Painting' [1961, revd version 1965], in *Art and Theory, 1900–1990: An Anthology of Changing Ideas*, ed. Charles Harrison and Paul Wood (Oxford, 1992), pp. 754–60.

2 John Hutchinson, 'Postmodernism in Ireland, Notes and Propositions', *Circa*, 48 (November–December 1989), p. 25.

3 In 1985 a baby was found dead from stab wounds on a beach in Co. Kerry; a young woman, Joanna Hayes, confessed to having given birth to the child, whom she subsequently killed. The case was complicated by the discovery that Hayes had in fact given birth to a different baby, who had died and was buried on the farm where she lived, some 50 miles from the beach.

4 This is suggested by Aidan Dunne, 'Camille Souter', in *Camille Souter: Retrospective*, exh. cat., Nyland Gallery (Sligo, 2001), p. 12.

5 Aidan Dunne, 'Saving the Phenomena: Formalist Painting in the 1980s', *A New Tradition: Irish Art of the Eighties*, exh. cat., Douglas Hyde Gallery (Dublin, 1990), p. 107.

6 'Charles Tyrrell in Conversation with Brian Fallon', in *Charles Tyrrell*, ed. John O'Regan (Dublin, 1994), p. 9.

7 Donald Kuspit, *Brian Maguire: An Essay* (Dublin, 1988).

8 Caoimhín Mac Giolla Léith, 'Strategic Representations: Notes on Irish Art since the 1980s', in *When Time Began to Rant and Rage: Figurative Painting from Twentieth Century Ireland*, ed. James Steward (London, 1998), p. 115.

9 Catherine Marshall, 'Michael Mulcahy', in Marguerite O'Molloy, *Irish Museum of Modern Art: The Collection* (Dublin, 2005), p. 129.

10 John Hutchinson, 'Myth and Mystification', in *A New Tradition*, p. 81.

11 'Patrick Hall in conversation with John Hutchinson', in *Patrick Hall*, ed. John O'Regan (Dublin, 1993), p. 8.

12 The early years of WAAG are documented in Mary Maguire, 'WAAG in Context: a Study of the Women Artists Action Group', Advanced Diploma in the History and Theory of Art and Design Dissertation, University of Ulster, 1993.

13 A sister organization in the North, NIWAAG, also organized an exhibition at Art and Research Exchange in November 1987, entitled 'Identities'.

14 Breeda Mooney, 'On the Record', *Circa*, 59 (September–October, 1991), p. 50.

15 Craig Owens 'The Discourse of Others' [1983], in *The Anti-Aesthetic: Essays on Postmodern Culture*, ed. Hal Foster (New York, 1998), pp. 65–92.

16 Joan Fowler, 'Speaking of Gender: Expressionism, Feminism and Sexuality', in *A New Tradition*, p. 59.

17 Catherine Nash, 'Gender and Landscape in Ireland' [1993], in *Sources in Irish Art: A Reader*, ed. Fintan Cullen (Cork, 2000), p. 303.

18 Sands's protest was aimed at the British policy of criminalization of those convicted of terrorist offences after 1 March 1976; unlike earlier prisoners, those newly sentenced had lost the special status that had allowed them not to wear prison uniform or do prison work.

19 For a discussion of the broadcasting ban in its historical context, see David Miller, 'The History Behind a Mistake' [1990], in *War and Words: The Northern Ireland Media Reader*, ed. Bill Rolston and David Miller (Belfast, 1996), pp. 244–52.

20 The six men were wrongly convicted of the Birmingham pub bombings that killed 21 people in 1974. They were released in 1991 after the third judicial appeal against their conviction was successful.

21 Nicholas Stewart, 'Alistair Maclennan Interviewed by Nicholas Stewart', *Circa*, 13 (November–December 1983), pp. 4–9.

22 *Body Break* was performed at the Mappin Art Gallery, Sheffield, 21–4 March 1984.

23 Robert Ayers, 'Live Work at the British Art Show', *Performance Magazine*, 35 (1985), p. 39.

24 Brian McAvera, *Directions Out*, exh. cat., Douglas Hyde Gallery (Dublin, 1987), n.p.

25 Barbara Freeman, *De Humani Corporis Fabrica*, exh. cat., Hart Gallery (Nottingham, 1988).

26 Aidan Dunne, 'Contemporary Women Artists', in *Irish Women Artists: From the Eighteenth Century to the Present Day*, ed. Wanda Ryan-Smolin, Elizabeth Mayes and Jenni Rogers (Dublin, 1987), p. 62.

27 Interview with Alice Maher in Fionna Barber, 'Hybrid Histories: Alice Maher', in *Difference and Excess in Contemporary Art: The Visibility of Women's Practice*, ed. Gill Perry (Oxford, 2004), p. 90.

28 Christopher Coppock, 'A.R.E. – Acronyms, Community Arts and Stiff Little Fingers', *The Vacuum*, 11 (n.d.), at www.thevacuum.org.uk, last accessed 19 February 2011.

29 Declan McGonagle in conversation with Christopher Coppock, 'The Place of Place in Art', *Circa*, 29 (July–August 1986), p. 13.

30 Jonathan Watkins, 'Back to the Black Country', *Rita Donagh*, exh. cat., Ikon Gallery (Birmingham, 2005), p. 18.

31 Richard Hamilton, artist's statement, in *Rita Donagh and Richard Hamilton: A Cellular Maze*, exh. cat.,

Orchard Gallery (Derry, 1983), p. 7.

32 Ibid., p. 8.

33 Belinda Loftus, 'Rita Donagh and Richard Hamilton', *Circa*, 14 (January–February, 1984), p. 41; John Roberts, *Postmodernism, Politics and Art* (Manchester, 1990), p. 140.

34 Breda Gray, *Women in the Irish Diaspora* (London, 2004), p. 9.

35 Katy Deepwell, *Dialogues: Women Artists from Ireland* (London, 2005), pp. 174–5; Fionna Barber, 'Territories of Difference: Irish Women Artists in Britain', *Third Text*, 27 (1994), pp. 67–9.

36 Jean Fisher, 'Reflections on Echo: Sound Works by Women Artists in Britain' (n.d), at http://archive.fact.co.uk (accessed 18 February 2011).

TEN: THE UNRAVELLING NATION, 1990–1998

1 *Joint Declaration on Peace: The Downing Street Declaration*, Wednesday 15 December 1993, at http://cain.ulster.ac.uk.

2 'Same Difference' uses a photograph of IRA member Donna Maguire, extradited first to the Netherlands in 1990 under suspicion of killing two Australian tourists mistaken for British soldiers, and second to Germany to stand trial over attacks on British soldiers and army bases there. The photograph in 'They're All the Same' is a police mug shot of Nessan Quinlivan, one of two IRA members who escaped from Brixton Prison in 1991. For further discussion of both these works and '30 January 1972', see Carolyn Christov-Bakargiev, *In the Dark: Projected Works by Willie Doherty*, exh. cat., Kunsthalle (Bern, 1996), pp. 16–20.

3 See the discussion of this piece in Caoimhín Mac Giolla Léith, 'Troubled Memories', in Mac Giolla Léith and Carolyn Christov-Bakargiev, *Willie Doherty: False Memory* (London, 2002), pp. 19–21.

4 Liam Kelly, 'Foreword', in *Philip Napier: Gauge* (Derry, 1998), p. 5.

5 There are detailed discussions of this piece by Johnston in Jill Bennett, *Empathic Vision: Effect, Trauma and Contemporary Art* (Stanford, CA, 2005), pp. 50–60;

and Bryonie Reid, '"A Profound Edge": Performative Negotiations of Belfast', *Cultural Geographies*, 12 (2005), pp. 485–506.

6 Alvin Jackson, 'Insides and Frontiers: Paul Seawright's Images of "The Troubles"', *Eire-Ireland*, XXXIII/3–4 and XXXIV/1 (1998–9), p. 260.

7 George Hill, ed., *The Montgomery Manuscripts* (1869), quoted in J. Bardon, *A History of Ulster* (Belfast, 2005), p. 123.

8 For a more detailed reading of the historical and cultural significance of the role of women in these and related works by Duffy, see Suzanne O'Shea, 'Banquet: New Works by Rita Duffy', in *Banquet: Rita Duffy*, exh. cat., Ormeau Baths Gallery, Belfast and Hugh Lane Gallery, Dublin (Belfast, 1997).

9 Author's interview with Peter Richards, 28 November 2007.

10 Author's interview with Aisling O'Beirn, 28 November 2007.

11 Nicolas Bourriaud, *Relational Aesthetics* (Dijon, 2002), p. 113.

12 Brian Kennedy, 'Hit and Run', *Circa*, 69 (Autumn 1994), p. 64.

13 Fintan O'Toole, *After the Ball* (Dublin, 2003), p. 4.

14 Hugh Maxton, 'In a State: Kilmainham Gaol, Dublin 16 May–22 September 1991', *Circa*, 58 (July–August 1991), p. 45.

15 Katy Deepwell, *Dialogues: Women Artists from Ireland* (London, 2005), p. 187.

16 Joan Fowler, 'Inheritance and Transformation: Old Grounds, New Contexts?', *Circa*, 59 (September–October, 1991), p. 33.

17 Margaret Kelleher, 'Hunger and History: Monuments to the Great Irish Famine', *Textual Practice*, XVI/2 (2002), pp. 41–60.

18 Pierre Nora, 'Between Memory and History: Les Lieux de Mémoire', *Representations*, 26 (Spring 1989), pp. 7–24.

19 Seán Hillen, *Irelantis: Paper Collages by Seán Hillen* (Dublin, 1999), p. 32.

20 Myrtle Hill, *Women in Ireland: A Century of Change* (Belfast, 2003), p. 208.

21 Interview with Alice Maher in Fionna Barber, 'Hybrid

Histories: Alice Maher', in *Difference and Excess in Contemporary Art: The Visibility of Women's Practice*, ed. Gill Perry (Blackwell, 2004), p. 93.

22 Marina Warner, 'Passionate Cruces: The Art of Dorothy Cross', in *Dorothy Cross*, ed. Seán Kissane (Dublin 2005), p. 27.

23 Dorothy Cross, quoted in Paul Bonaventura, 'Even Dorothy Cross', in *Even: Recent Work by Dorothy Cross*, exh. cat., Arnolfini Gallery (Bristol, 1996), p. 19.

24 'Pride in Diversity', City Arts Centre, Dublin, June–July 1996.

25 Breda Gray, *Irish Women and Diaspora* (London, 2004), p. 6.

26 Homi Bhabha, *The Location of Culture* (London, 1994); Avtar Brah, *Cartographies of Diaspora: Contesting Identities* (London, 1996).

27 Interview with the artist in Suzanne Cotter, 'Siobhán Hapaska: Shooting the Breeze', in *0044: Contemporary Irish Art in Britain*, ed. Peter Murray (Cork, 1999), p. 76.

28 The pervasiveness of wilderness in visual constructions of Canada's national identity is addressed in John O'Brian, 'Wild Art History', in *Beyond Wilderness: the Group of Seven, Canadian Identity and Contemporary Art*, ed. John O'Brian and Peter White (Montreal, 2007), pp. 21–37.

29 Caoimhín Mac Giolla Léith, 'Elizabeth Magill: The Lie of the Land', in Murray, *0044*, p. 100.

30 Aoife MacNamara, 'Negotiating Authorities: Art, Theory and Transformation', in *Profile 14 – Andrew Kearney*, ed. John O'Regan (Oysterhaven, 2001), p. 15.

ELEVEN: AFTER THE END OF PROGRESS

1 Richard Kearney, 'Towards a Postnationalist Archipelago' [2000], in Kearney, *Navigations: Collected Irish Essays, 1976–2006* (Dublin, 2006), p. 5. Kearney's arguments in this essay are a development from his earlier *Postnationalist Ireland* (London, 1997).

2 Kearney, 'Towards a Postnationalist Archipelago', p. 16.

3 Ibid.

4 Twenty-two artists actually exhibited in *0044*. Anne Tallentire's work was shown with that of her collaborator John Seth as 'Work-Seth/Tallentire', and Frances Hegarty's piece was made in conjunction with Andrew Stones.

5 Peter Murray, 'Introduction', *0044: Irish Artists in Britain*, exh. cat., PS1 Contemporary Art Center, New York, 1999: Albright Knox Art Gallery, Buffalo, 1999; Crawford Municipal Art Gallery, Cork, 1999–2000 (Cork, 1999), p. 9.

6 *Turas* is discussed in Hilary Robinson, 'Disruptive Women Artists: An Irigarayan Reading of Irish Visual Culture', *Irish Studies Review*, VIII/1 (2000), pp. 68–70.

7 Fionna Barber, 'Territories of Difference: Irish Women Artists in Britain', *Third Text*, 27 (Summer 1994), pp. 72–5.

8 Arjun Appadurai, *Modernity at Large: Cultural Dimensions of Globalization* (Minneapolis, 1996), p. 32.

9 Ibid., p. 33.

10 Sally O'Reilly, *The Body in Contemporary Art* (London, 2009), p. 37.

11 In 2000, only 5 per cent of asylum seekers in Ireland were granted refugee status or leave to remain; Joan Roddy, 'Refugees and Asylum Seekers in Ireland', *Studies*, LXXXXI/364 (Winter 2002), p. 336n.

12 Mick O'Kelly, 'An Artwork for an Imperfect World', Staff Homepage, National College of Art and Design, at www.ncad.ie.

13 Aidan Dunne, 'Body of Evidence', *Irish Times*, Weekend Review (29 January 2005), p. 6.

14 Kate Antosik Parsons, 'Bodily Remembrances: The Performance of Memory in Recent Works by Amanda Coogan', *Artefact*, 3 (2009), p. 13.

15 Svetlana Boym, *The Future of Nostalgia* (New York, 2001), p. 13.

16 Maeve Connolly, *The Place of Artists' Cinema* (Bristol and Chicago, IL, 2009), pp. 86–92.

17 I am indebted here to Maeve Connolly's evocative description of the initial installation of *The Silver Bridge* in IMMA in 2005; ibid., pp. 90–91.

18 Mark Godfrey, 'History Pictures', in Mark Godfrey, Catherine Wood and Lytle Shaw, *The Present Tense through the Ages: On the Recent Work of Gerald Byrne* (London, 2007), p. 17.

19 Ibid., p. 18.

20 Richard Kearney, *Postnationalist Ireland: Politics, Culture, Philosophy* (London, 1997), p. 59.

21 Barbara Dawson, 'Francis Bacon: The Dublin Chapter', in *Francis Bacon's Studio*, ed. Margarita Cappock (London and New York, 2005), p. 19.

22 William J. V. Neill and Geraint Ellis, 'Spatial Planning in Contested Territory: The Search for a Place Vision After "The Troubles"', in *Northern Ireland after the Troubles*, ed. Colin Coulter and Michael Murray (Manchester, 2008), p. 102.

23 Caoimhín Mac Giolla Léith, '114 Sherrif Street – Dublin', *Artforum* (May 2003).

24 See 'A Conversation on "The Nature of Things": Hugh Mulholland and Suzanna Chan', *The Nature of Things: Artists from Northern Ireland*, exh. cat., Venice Biennale (Belfast, 2005), pp. 149–60.

25 Colin Graham, 'Belfast in Photographs', in *The Cities of Belfast*, ed. Nicholas Allen and Aaron Kelly (Dublin and Portland, OH, 2003), p. 164.

26 Aaron Kelly, 'Walled Communities', Eoghan McTigue, *All Over Again*, exh. cat., Belfast Exposed (Belfast, 2004), n.p.

27 Graham, 'Belfast', p. 154.

28 CAIN: Sutton Index of Deaths, at http://cain.ulst.ac.uk, last accessed 24 May 2012.

29 The outcome of the Saville Inquiry was made public on 15 June 2010, finding that the thirteen unarmed men had been killed unlawfully by British Paratroopers. The announcement in the British Parliament was followed by an official apology by the Prime Minister, David Cameron.

30 Cathy Caruth, *Unclaimed Experience: Trauma, Narrative, History* (Baltimore, MD, 1996), p. 4.

31 Megan Johnston, 'Shades of Grey: Visual Art and Contemporaneity in Northern Ireland', in Megan Johnston and Fionna Barber, *Archiving Place and Time: Contemporary Art from Northern Ireland since the Belfast Agreement*, exh. cat., Holden Gallery, Manchester Metropolitan University, 2009; Millennium Art Centre, 2010 (Craigavan, 2009), n.p.

32 For a more extensive discussion of the significance of the iceberg to Duffy's practice in the context of both post-conflict and early twentieth-century Belfast, see Fionna Barber, 'An Iceberg's Collision with History', in *The Essential Gesture*, ed. Rita Duffy (Belfast, 2005), n.p.

33 Rebecca Lynn Graff-McRae, 'Popular Memory in Northern Ireland', in *War, Memory and Popular Culture: Essays on Modes of Remembrance and Commemoration*, ed. Michael Keren and Holger H. Herwig (Jefferson, NC, and London, 2009), p. 49.

34 Louise Purbrick, 'The Architecture of Containment', in Donovan Wylie, ed., *The Maze* (London, 2004), pp. 91–110.

35 For a full discussion of the significance of Farrell's photographs in relation to notions of trauma, see Mark Phelan, 'Not So Innocent Landscapes: Remembrance, Representation and the Disappeared', in *Violence Performed: Local Roots and Global Routes of Conflict*, ed. Patrick Anderson and Jisha Menon (London, 2008), pp. 285–316.

36 Declan Long, 'Invisible Matter', in Willie Doherty, *Ghost Story* (Belfast, n.d. [2007]), p. 18.

37 From the voiceover of Doherty, *Ghost Story*.

BIBLIOGRAPHY

A Conversation on "The Nature of Things": Hugh
Mulholland and Suzanna Chan', *The Nature of Things:
Artists
from Northern Ireland*, exh. cat., Venice Biennale (2005),
pp. 149–60

A New Tradition: Irish Art of the Eighties, exh. cat., Douglas Hyde
Gallery, Dublin (1990)

Alberro, Alexander, and Nora M. Alter, 'After the Senses',
in *Beyond the White Cube: A Retrospective of Brian O'Doherty /
Patrick Ireland.*, ed. Christina Kennedy and Georgina
Jackson, exh. cat., Dublin City Gallery the Hugh Lane
(2006)

Allen, Máirín, 'Irish Post-Impressionism', *Father Matthew
Record*, November 1943, p. 10

Anderson, Benedict, *Imagined Communities: Reflections on the
Origin and Spread of Nationalism* (London, 1983)

Anglesea, Martyn, *William Conor, the People's Painter* (Belfast,
1999)

Appadurai, Arjun, *Modernity at Large: Cultural Dimensions of
Globalization* (Minneapolis, MN, 1996)

Arnold, Bruce, *A Concise History of Irish Art* (London, 1977)

—, *Mainie Jellett and the Modern Movement in Ireland* (New
Haven, CT, and London, 1991)

—, *Jack Yeats* (New Haven, CT, and London, 1998)

Atkinson, Conrad, statement from catalogue for *Lives* exhibi-
tion, Hayward Gallery London 1979, reprinted in *Conrad
Atkinson: Picturing the System*, ed. Caroline Tisdall and
Sandy Nairne (London, 1981)

Atkinson, Harriet, 'Putting Reconstruction on Display: Post-
war Exhibitions of Agriculture and Industry', paper given
to the Annual Conference of the Social History Society,
Trinity College, Dublin, 7–9 January 2005

Augusteijn, Joost, ed., *Ireland in the 1930s* (Dublin, 1999)

Ayers, Robert, ed., *Performance Magazine*, 35 (1985)

Balibar, E., and I. Wallerstein, *Race, Nation, Class*
(London, 1991)

Barber, Fionna, 'Territories of Difference: Irish Women
Artists in Britain', *Third Text*, 27 (1994), pp. 67–9

—, 'Hybrid Histories: Interview with Alice Maher', in
*Difference and Excess in Contemporary Art: The Visibility of
Women's Practice*, ed. Gill Perry (Oxford, 2004)

—, 'An Iceberg's Collision with History', in *Rita Duffy: The
Essential Gesture* (Belfast, 2005), n.p.

—, 'Excavating Room 50: Irish Art and the Cold War at the
1950 Venice Biennale', in *A Shared Legacy: Essays on Irish
and Scottish Art and Visual Culture*, ed. Fintan Cullen and
John Morrison (Aldershot, 2005), pp. 207–23

—, 'Disturbed Ground: Francis Bacon, Traumatic Memory
and the Gothic', *The Irish Review*, 39 (2008), pp. 123–38

—, and Megan Johnston, *Archiving Place and Time:
Contemporary Art from Northern Ireland since the Belfast
Agreement*, exh. cat. (2009), n.p.

Bardon, Jonathan, *A History of Ulster* (Belfast, 2005)

Barrett, Cyril, *Micheal Farrell* (Dublin, 1979)

Barton, Brian, *The Blitz: Belfast in the War Years* (Belfast, 1989)

Beckett, Samuel, 'MacGreevy on Yeats', *The Irish Times*
(4 August 1945)

Bennett, Jill, *Empathic Vision: Effect, Trauma and Contemporary
Art* (Stanford, CA, 2005)

Berman, Marshall, *All That Is Solid Melts into Air: The Experience
of Modernity* (London, 1983)

Bhabha, Homi, *The Location of Culture* (London, 1994)

Bhreathnach-Lynch, Síghle, 'The Easter Rising 1916:
Constructing a Canon in Art and Artefacts', *History Ireland*

(Spring 1997), p. 39

—, 'Landscape, Space and Gender: Their Role in the Construction of Female Identity in Newly Independent Ireland', in *Gendering Landscape Art*, ed. S. Adams and Robins Greutzer (Manchester, 2000), pp. 76–86

—, 'Louis le Brocquy's *A Family*: An Unwholesome and Satanic Distortion of Natural Beauty', at www.recirca.com

Bielenberg, Andy, ed., *The Shannon Scheme and the Electrification of the Irish Free State* (Dublin, 2002)

Bodkin, Thomas, 'T.B.', *The Studio*, LXXXVI (1923), p. 341

—, 'Modern Irish Art', in *Saorstát Eireann* [Irish Free State] *Official Handbook* (Dublin, 1932), pp. 239–44

—, *Report on the Arts in Ireland* (Dublin, 1949)

Bonaventura, Paul, *Even: Recent Work by Dorothy Cross*, exh. cat., Arnolfini Gallery, Bristol (1996)

Bourke, Marie, 'A Growing Sense of National Identity: Charles Lamb (1893–1964) and the West of Ireland', *History Ireland*, VIII/1 (2000), p. 30

Bourriaud, Nicolas, *Relational Aesthetics* (Dijon, 2002)

Bowen, Elizabeth, 'Preface', *Norah McGuinness*, exh. cat., Leicester Galleries, London (1957)

Boym, Svetlana, *The Future of Nostalgia* (New York, 2001)

Brah, Avtar, *Cartographies of Diaspora: Contesting Identities* (London, 1996)

Brett, David, 'The Reformation and the Practice of Art', *Circa*, 26 (1986), pp. 20–24

Brissac, Noelle, 'Thurloe Conolly', *Envoy*, 1/3, pp. 32–6

Brown, Terence O., *Ireland: A Cultural History* (London, 1985)

Bruce, Campbell, 'CIAS 1962–2005', in *SIAR 50: 50 Years of Irish Art from the Collections of the Contemporary Irish Art Society* (Dublin, 2005)

Burnside, Sam, 'Preparing Lonely Defences', 'Hewitt' *Fortnight* supplement (1987), n.p.

CAIN: Sutton Index of Deaths, at http://cain.ulst.ac.uk

Cairns, David, and Shaun Richards, *Writing Ireland: Colonialism, Nationalism and Culture* (Manchester, 1988)

Campbell, Julian, 'Mary Swanzy: Biography', in *Mary Swanzy, 1882–1978*, exh. cat., Pyms Gallery, London (1986)

Campbell, Patrick, *My Life and Easy Times* (London, 1967)

Cappock, Margarita, *Francis Bacon's Studio* (London and New York, 2005)

Carty, Ciaran, 'No.3', in *No.3: A Series of Paintings by Robert Ballagh*, exh. cat., David Hendricks Gallery, Dublin (1983), n.p.

Caruth, Cathy, *Unclaimed Experience: Trauma, Narrative, History* (Baltimore, MD, 1996)

Catto, Mike, *Art in Ulster 2* (Belfast, 1977)

Christov-Bakargiev, Carolyn, *In the Dark: Projected Works by Willie Doherty*, exh. cat., Kunsthalle Bern (1996), pp. 16–20

Cleary, Joe, and Claire Connolly, eds, *The Cambridge Companion to Modern Irish Culture* (Cambridge, 2005)

Clyde, Tom, *The Prose Writings of John Hewitt* (Belfast, 1985)

—, ed., *Ancestral Voices: The Selected Prose of John Hewitt* (Belfast, 1987)

Collins, Patrick, letter to S. B. Kennedy, 20 September 1976, Artist's File, Ulster Museum Archives

Collins, Patrick, 'George Campbell: Portrait of an Artist', *Envoy*, 1/2, pp. 4–50

'Connemara for the Artist: Mr Paul Henry's Experiences', *Irish Times*, 4 August 1925

Connolly, Maeve, *The Place of Artists' Cinema* (Bristol and Chicago, IL, 2009)

Connolly, Tracey, 'Emigration from Ireland to Britain during the Second World War', in *The Irish Diaspora*, ed. Andy Bielenberg (Harlow, 2000)

Coogan, Tim Pat, *Micheal Collins* (London, 1991)

Coppock, Christopher, 'A.R.E. –Acronyms, Community Arts and Stiff Little Fingers', *The Vacuum*, 11 (n.d.), at www.the vacuum.org.uk, accessed 19 February 2011

Coppock, Christopher, 'The Place of Place in Art', *Circa*, 29 (July–August 1986)

Cosgrove, Mary, 'Paul Henry and Achill Island', in *Landscape, Heritage and Identity: Case Studies in Irish Ethnography*, ed. Ulrich Kockel (Liverpool, 1995), pp. 93–116

Cotter, Suzanne, ' Siobhán Hapaska: Shooting the Breeze', interview with the artist, in *0044: Contemporary Irish Art in Britain*, ed. Peter Murray (Cork, 1999)

Coulter, Riann, '"An Amazing Anthology of Modern Art": Place, Archetype and Identity in the Art of Colin Middleton', *Visual Culture in Britain*, IX/1 (2008), pp. 1–25

—, 'Louis le Brocquy's *Presences, 1954–64*: Irish, British or International?' *The Irish Review*, 39 (Winter 2008), pp. 139–56

Coxhead, Elizabeth, *Daughters of Erin* (Gerrards Cross, 1979)

Craig, Patricia, 'The Liberal Imagination in Northern Ireland Prose', in *Returning to Ourselves: Second Volume of Papers from the John Hewitt International Summer School*, ed. Eve Patten (Belfast, 1995)

Crofts, Sinead, 'Maurice MacGonigal PRHA (1900–79) and his Western Paintings', *Irish Art Review*, XIII (1997), pp. 135–42

Crookshank, Anne, *Deborah Brown*, New Vision Centre Gallery, London (1964), n.p.

—, and the Knight of Glin, *The Painters of Ireland, c. 1660–1920* (London, 1978)

—, *Deborah Brown: A Selected Exhibition of Works Completed Between 1947 and 1982*, exh. cat., Arts Council Gallery, Belfast (1982), n.p.

—, and the Knight of Glin, *Ireland's Painters, 1600–1940* (New Haven and London 2002)

Cullen, Fintan, *Visual Politics: The Representation of Ireland, 1750–1930* (Cork, 1997)

—, ed., *Sources in Irish Art: A Reader* (Cork, 2000)

Curran, Elizabeth, 'The Art of Nano Reid', *The Bell*, III/2 (1942), pp. 128–31

Curran, Joseph M., *The Birth of the Irish Free State, 1921–1923* (Tuscaloosa, AL, 1980)

Curtis Jr, L. P., *Apes and Angels: The Irishman in Victorian Caricature*, revd edn (Washington, DC, and London, 1997)

Cusack, Tricia, 'Janus and Gender: Women and the Nation's Backward Look', *Nations and Nationalism*, VI/4 (2000)

Daly, Mary E., 'Women in the Irish Free State, 1922–1929: The Interaction between Economics and Ideology', *Journal of Women's History*, VI/4 and VII/1 (1994–5)

Daniels, Stephen, *Fields of Vision: Landscape Imagery and National Identity in England and the United States* (Cambridge, 1993)

Dawson, Barbara, 'Hugh Lane and the Origins of the Collection', in *Images and Insights*, exh. cat. Hugh Lane Municipal Gallery, Dublin (1993) pp. 13–31

Dawson, Barbara, and Martin Harrison, eds, *Francis Bacon: A Terrible Beauty* (Dublin 2009)

Deane, Seamus, 'Introduction', in Terry Eagleton, Frederic Jameson and Edward Said, *Nationalism, Colonialism, Literature* (Minneapolis, MN, 1985)

de Courcy, Edward, 'The Sculpture of Hilary Heron', *Envoy*, II/7 (1950), pp. 50–58

Deepwell, Katy, *Dialogues: Women Artists from Ireland* (London, 2005)

Dillon, Gerard, 'The Artist Speaks', *Envoy*, IV/15 (February 1951)

Douglas, Roy, Liam Harte and Jim O'Hara, *Drawing Conclusions: A Cartoon History of Anglo-Irish Relations, 1798–1998* (Belfast, 1998)

Duddy, Tom 'Irish Art Criticism: A Provincialism of the Right?' [1987], in *Sources in Irish Art: A Reader*, ed. Fintan Cullen (Cork, 2000) pp. 91–9

Duffy, Enda, 'Disappearing Dublin: *Ulysses*, Postcoloniality and the Politics of Space', in *Semicolonial Joyce*, ed. Derek Attridge and Marjorie Howes (Cambridge, 2000), pp. 37–57

Dunne, Aidan, 'Contemporary Women Artists', in *Irish Women Artists: From the Eighteenth Century to the Present Day*, ed. Wanda Ryan-Smolin, Elizabeth Mayes and Jenni Rogers (Dublin, 1987)

—, 'Saving the Phenomena: Formalist Painting in the 1980s', in *A New Tradition: Irish Art of the Eighties*, exh. cat., Douglas Hyde Gallery, Dublin (1990)

—, 'Body of Evidence', *Irish Times*, Weekend Review, 29 January 2005, p. 6.

Dunne, Tom, and William Pressly, eds, *James Barry: History Painter* (Aldershot, 2010)

Eagleton, Terry, *Heathcliff and the Great Hunger: Studies in Irish Culture* (London and New York, 1995)

Eastwood, Carlo, ed., *Colin Middleton: A Millennium Appreciation* (Belfast, 2000)

Elkins, James, 'The State of Irish Art History', *Circa Magazine* (Winter 2003)

Fairweather, Eileen, Roisin McDonough and Melanie MacFadyen, *Only the Rivers Run Free* (London, 1984)

Fallon, Brian, 'Middleton Exhibition', *Irish Times*, 29 November 1974, p. 15

—, *Tony O'Malley: Painter in Exile* (Dublin, 1984)

—, 'Irish Women Artists in the Nineteen-fifties', in *Irish Women Artists: From the Eighteenth Century to the Present Day*, ed. Wanda Ryan-Smolin, Elizabeth Mayes and Jenni Rogers (Dublin, 1987)

Farrell, Micheal, *Northern Ireland: The Orange State* (London, 1980)

—, ed., *Twenty Years On* (Dingle, 1988)

—, 'Artist's Statement' [1965], in Cyril Barrett, *Micheal Farrell* (Dublin, 1979), pp. 19–21

Ferriter, Diarmaid, *The Transformation of Ireland, 1900–2000* (London, 2004)

Fisher, Jean, 'The Enigma of the Hero in the Work of James Coleman' [1983], in *James Coleman*, ed. George Baker (Cambridge, MA, 2003)

—, 'Reflections on Echo: Sound Works by Women Artists in Britain' (n.d), at http://archive.fact.co.uk, accessed 18 February 2011

Fitzpatrick, David, 'Commemoration in the Irish Free State', in *History and Memory in Modern Ireland*, ed. Ian McBride (Cambridge, 2001), pp. 191–5

Flanagan, T. P., 'The John Hewitt Collection', *A Poet's Pictures*, exh. cat., Shambles Gallery, Hillsborough (1987)

Fowler, Joan, 'Seán Keating: "The Men of the West"', *Critics' Choice*, exh. cat., Hugh Lane Municipal Gallery, Dublin (1988)

—, 'Speaking of Gender: Expressionism, Feminism and Sexuality', in *A New Tradition: Irish Art of the Eighties*, exh. cat., Douglas Hyde Gallery, Dublin (1990)

—, 'Inheritance and Transformation: Old Grounds, New Contexts?' *Circa*, 59 (September–October 1991), pp. 31–3

Frawley, Oona, *Irish Pastoral: Nostalgia and Twentieth Century Irish Literature* (Dublin, 2005)

Freeman, Barbara, *De Humani Corporis Fabrica*, exh. cat., Hart Gallery, Nottingham (1988)

Gibbons, Luke, *Transformations in Irish Culture* (Cork, 1996)

Gilroy, Paul, 'It Ain't Where You're From, It's Where You're At . . . The Dialectics of Diasporic Identification', *Third Text*, 13 (1990–91), pp. 3–16

Guilbaut, Serge, 'Postwar Painting Games: The Rough and the Slick', in *Reconstructing Modernism: Art in New York, Paris, and Montreal, 1945–1964* (Cambridge, MA, 1995)

Gleizes, Albert, 'Homage to Mainie Jellett' [1948], in *Mainie Jellett: The Artist's Vision*, ed. Eileen McCarvill (Dundalk, 1958)

Glenavy, Lady Beatrice, *Today We Will Only Gossip* (London, 1964)

Godfrey, Mark, Catherine Wood and Lytle Shaw, *The Present Tense through the Ages: On the Recent Work of Gerald Byrne* (London, 2007)

Gooding, Mel, *F. E. McWilliam: Sculpture, 1932–1989*, exh. cat, Tate Gallery, London (1989)

Gordon Bowe, Nicola, 'The Art of Beatrice Elvery, Lady Glenavy (1883–1970)', *Irish Arts Review*, XI (1995)

Graff-McRae, Rebecca Lynn, 'Popular Memory in Northern Ireland', in *War, Memory and Popular Culture: Essays on Modes of Remembrance and Commemoration*, ed. Michael Keren and Holger H. Herwig (Jefferson, NC, and London 2009)

Graham, Colin, 'Belfast in Photographs', in *The Cities of Belfast*, ed. Nicolas Allen and Aaron Kelly (Dublin and Portland, OR, 2003)

Gray, Breda, *Women in the Irish Diaspora* (London, 2004)

Greenberg, Clement, 'Modernist Painting' [1961, revd 1965] in *Art and Theory, 1900–1990: An Anthology of Changing Ideas*, ed. Charles Harrison and Paul Wood, (Oxford, 1992) pp. 754–60

—, 'Poetry of Vision: Ireland Inaugurates "An International Quadrennial Without Prizes"', *Artforum*, VI/8 (April 1968), pp. 18–21

Hall, Dickon, *Colin Middleton: A Study* (Belfast, 2001)

—, and Eoin O'Brien, *Nevill Johnson: Paint the Smell of Grass* (Bangor, 2008)

Hall, Kenneth, unpublished autobiography, n.d.

Harries, Meiron, and Susie Harries, *The War Artists: British Official War Art of the Twentieth Century* (London, 1983)

Harris, Jonathan, *The New Art History: A Critical Introduction* (London, 2001)

Harrison, Charles, *English Art and Modernism, 1900–1939* (London, 1981)

Harvey, David, *The Condition of Postmodernity: An Enquiry into the Origins of Cultural Change* (London, 1989), pp. 10–38

Henry, Paul, *An Irish Portrait* (London 1951)

Heron, Hilary, *Hilary Heron: Recent Sculpture*, exh. cat., Victor Waddington Galleries (London, 1950)

Heron, Patrick, 'William Scott' (1958), in *Modern Painters*, III/4 (Winter 1990–91), pp. 22–4

Hewitt, John, 'Preface', *The Ulster Unit Exhibition of Contemporary Art*, exh. cat. Locksley Hall, Belfast (1934), n.p.

—, 'Portrait of the Artist as a Young Man', *Threshold*, I/1 (1957)

—, 'From Chairmen and Committee Men, Good Lord Deliver Us' (1968), in *Ancestral Voices: The Selected Prose of*

John Hewitt, ed. Tom Clyde (Belfast, 1987)

—, 'No Rootless Colonist' (1972), in *Ancestral Voices: The Selected Prose of John Hewitt*, ed. Tom Clyde (Belfast, 1987)

—, *Colin Middleton* (Belfast, 1976)

—, and Theo Snoddy, *Art in Ulster: 1* (Belfast, 1977)

—, *John Luke (1906–1975)* (Belfast and Dublin, 1978)

Hill, Derek, 'Introduction', *Dawson Gallery Catalogue* [1967], reprinted in *Two Painters: Works by Alfred Wallis and James Dixon*, exh. cat., Irish Museum of Modern Art, Dublin (1999), Tate Gallery St Ives (2000)

Hill, Myrtle, *Women in Ireland: A Century of Change* (Belfast, 2003)

Hughes, Eamonn, 'Sent to Coventry: Emigration and Autobiography', in *Returning to Ourselves: Second Volume of Papers from the John Hewitt International Summer School*, ed. Eve Patten (Belfast, 1995), pp. 261–75

Hutchinson, John, *The Dynamics of Cultural Nationalism: Gaelic Revival and the Creation of the Irish Nation State* (London, 1987)

—, 'Postmodernism in Ireland: Notes and Propositions', *Circa*, 48 (November–December 1989)

—, 'Myth and Mystification', in *A New Tradition: Irish Art of the Eighties*, exh. cat., Douglas Hyde Gallery, Dublin (1990)

Images and Insights, exh. cat., Hugh Lane Municipal Gallery, Dublin (1994)

Irelantis: Paper Collages by Seán Hillen (Dublin, 1999)

Jack B. Yeats, 1871–1957: A Centenary Exhibition, exh. cat., National Gallery of Ireland, Dublin (1971)

Jackson, Alvin, 'Insides and Frontiers: Paul Seawright's Images of "The Troubles"', *Eire-Ireland*, XXXIII/3–4, XXXIV/1 (1998/9)

Jamison, Kenneth, 'Painting and Sculpture', in *Causeway: The Arts in Ulster*, ed. Michael Longley (Belfast, 1971)

Jeffery, Keith, *Ireland and the Great War* (Cambridge, 2000)

Jellett, Mainie, 'André Lhote' [1940], in *Mainie Jellett: The Artist's Vision*, ed. Eileen McCarvill (Dundalk, 1958)

—, 'The Importance of Rhythm in Modern Painting', n.d., in *Mainie Jellett: The Artist's Vision*, ed. Eileen McCarvill (Dundalk, 1958)

—, 'Modern Painting and Some of its Aspects', n.d., in *Mainie Jellett: The Artist's Vision*, ed. Eileen McCarvill (Dundalk, 1958)

—, 'Modern Art and its Relation to the Past' [1931], in *Mainie Jellett: The Artist's Vision*, ed. Eileen McCarvill (Dundalk, 1958)

Johnson, Nevill, 'The Other Side of Six', *The Recorder*, XIV/1 (2001)

Joint Declaration on Peace: The Downing Street Declaration, Wednesday, 15 December 1993, at http://cain.ulster.ac.uk

Jones, Amelia, *Irrational Modernism* (Cambridge and London, 2004)

Kearney, Richard, 'Janus', in *Louis le Brocquy: Images, 1975–1987*, exh. cat, Guinness Hop Store, Dublin, Ulster Museum Belfast (1987)

—, *Postnationalist Ireland* (London, 1997)

—, *Navigations: Collected Irish Essays, 1976–2006* (Dublin, 2006)

Kelleher, Margaret, 'Hunger and History: Monuments to the Great Irish Famine', *Textual Practice*, XVI/2 (2002), pp. 41–60

Kelly, Aaron, 'Walled Communities', in *Eoghan McTigue: All Over Again*, exh.cat, Belfast Exposed, Belfast (2004), n.p.

Kennedy, Brian 'Hit and Run', *Circa*, 69 (Autumn 1994)

Kennedy, Brian P, *Dreams and Responsibilities: The State and the Arts in Independent Ireland* (Dublin, n.d.), pp. 64, 140–41

Kennedy, Roisin, 'Made in England: The Critical Reception of Louis le Brocquy's "A Family"', *Third Text*, XIX/5 (2005), pp. 475–86

Kennedy, S. B., *Irish Art and Modernism, 1880–1950* (Belfast, 1991)

—, *Paul Henry* (New Haven, CT, and London, 2000)

Kiberd, Declan, *Inventing Ireland: The Literature of the Modern Nation* (London, 1995)

Kinealy, Christine, *A Death Dealing Famine: The Great Hunger in Ireland* (London, 1997)

Knowles, Roderic, *Contemporary Irish Art* (Dublin, 1982)

Kuspit, Donald, *Brian Maguire: An Essay* (Dublin, 1988)

—, 'Sacred Sadness', in D. Eccher et al., *Sean Scully: A Retrospective* (London, 2007)

Lavery, John, *The Life of a Painter* (London, 1940)

Le Brocquy, Louis [1969] in 'Notes on Painting and Awareness' [1979], *The Recorder*, XIV/1 (Summer 2001)

Leja, Michael, *Reframing Abstract Expressionism: Subjectivity and Painting in the 1940s* (New Haven, CT, and London, 1993)

'Living Art – A New Departure', *Irish Times*, 16 September

1943, p. 3

Lloyd, David, *Anomalous States: Irish Writing and the Post-colonial Moment* (Durham, NC, 1993)

Loftus, Belinda, 'Rita Donagh and Richard Hamilton', *Circa*, 14 (January–February 1984), p. 41

—, *Mirrors: William III and Mother Ireland* (Dundrum, c. 1990)

Long, Declan, 'Invisible Matter', in *Willie Doherty, Ghost Story* (Belfast, 2007)

Longley, Michael, 'Talking to Colin Middleton', in *Colin Middleton: A Millennium Appreciation*, ed. Carlo Eastwood (Belfast, 2000)

Lynam, Gena, 'Daniel O'Neill (1920–1974): Landscape and Figure Painting', *Irish Arts Review*, XV (1999), pp. 134–41

Lynch, Brian, 'Irish Painting? There's No Such Thing', *Hibernia*, 28 June 1979

—, ed., *Tony O'Malley* [1996] (Dublin, 2004)

Mac Giolla Leith, Caomhin, 'Strategic Representations: Notes on Irish Art Since the 1980s', in *When Time Began to Rant and Rage: Figurative Painting from Twentieth Century Ireland*, ed. James Steward (London, 1998)

—, 'Elizabeth Magill: The Lie of the Land', in *0044: Contemporary Irish Art in Britain*, ed. Peter Murray (Cork, 1999), p. 100

—, and Carolyn Christov-Bakargiev, 'Troubled Memories', in Léith Mac Giolla, *Willie Doherty: False Memory* (London, 2002)

—, '114 Sherrif Street – Dublin', *Artforum* (May 2003)

MacGreevy, Thomas, *Jack Yeats: An Appreciation and an Interpretation* (Dublin, 1943)

MacIntyre, James, *Three Men on an Island* (Belfast, 1996)

—, *Making my Mark: An Artist's Early Life* (Belfast, 2001)

Mac Namara, Aoife, 'Negotiating Authorities: Art, Theory and Transformation', in *Profile 14: Andrew Kearney*, ed. John O'Regan (Oysterhaven, 2001)

McAvera, Brian, *Directions Out*, exh. cat., Douglas Hyde Gallery Dublin (1987), n.p.

—, *Jack Pakenham, Works, 75–89*, exh. cat., Orchard Gallery, Derry (1990)

McCarthy, Conor, *Modernisation: Crisis and Culture in Ireland, 1969–1992* (Dublin, 2000)

McCarthy, Michael, 'How the Shannon Scheme Workers Lived', in *The Shannon Scheme and the Electrification of the Irish Free State*, ed. Andy Bielenberg (Dublin, 2002)

McCarvill, Eileen, ed., *Mainie Jellett: The Artist's Vision* (Dundalk, 1958)

McConkey, Kenneth, *Sir John Lavery RA, 1856–1941*, exh. cat., Ulster Museum Belfast and the Fine Arts Society (1984)

—, *Sir John Lavery* (Edinburgh 1993)

McCoole, Sinéad, *Hazel: A Life of Lady Lavery, 1880–1935* (Dublin, 1996)

McGuiggan, John, 'A Rare Document of Irish History: "High Treason" by Sir John Lavery', *Irish Art Review*, 15 (1999), pp. 157–9

Mc Guinness, Norah, *The Literary Universe of Jack B. Yeats* (Washington, DC, 1992)

McIntosh, Gillian, *The Force of Culture: Unionist Identities in Contemporary Ireland* (Cork, 1999)

McWilliam, F. E., untitled essay, *Architectural Design* (September 1958)

—, 'Artist's Statement', *Women of Belfast*, exh. cat., McClelland Galleries International, Belfast (1973), n.p.

McWilliams, Joseph, *A Troubled Journey, 1966–1989*, exh. cat., Cavehill Gallery, Belfast (1989), n.p.

Madden, le Brocquy, Anne, *Louis le Brocquy: Seeing his Way* (Dublin 1994)

Maguire, Mary, 'WAAG in Context: A Study of the Women Artists Action Group', Advanced Diploma in the History and Theory of Art and Design Dissertation, University of Ulster, 1993

Maxton, Hugh, 'In a State: Kilmainham Gaol, Dublin 16 May–2 September 1991', *Circa*, 58 (1991), p. 45

Melly, George, *A Tribe of One: Great Naïve Painters of the British Isles* (Yeovil, 1981)

Melville, Robert, 'Francis Bacon', *Horizon*, XX/120–21 (1949/50), pp. 419–23

'Miss Nano Reid's Pictures: Exhibition at St Stephen's Green', *Irish Times*, 28 November 1939

Mitchell, W.J.T., *Landscape and Power* (Chicago, IL, and London, 1994)

Monahan, Laurie J., 'Cultural Cartography: American Designs at the 1964 Venice Biennale', in *Reconstructing Modernism: Art in New York, Paris and Montreal, 1945–1964*, ed. Serge Guilbaut (Cambridge, MA, and London 1995), pp. 369–416

Mooney, Breeda, 'On the Record', *Circa*, 59 (September–October 1991), p. 50

Moore McCann, Brenda, 'The Politics of Identity, Place, and Memory in Contemporary Irish Art', in *Art and Politics: The Imagination of Opposition in Europe*, ed. Noel Kelly (Ljubljana and Dublin, 2004)

—, 'The Ogham Sculptures: Perceptual Boundaries of the Inaudible and Invisible', in *Beyond the White Cube: A Retrospective of Brian O'Doherty / Patrick Ireland*, ed. Christina Kennedy and Georgina Jackson (Dublin 2006), pp. 56–65

—, *Brian O'Doherty/ Patrick Ireland: Between Categories* (Farnham, 2009)

Murphy, Paula, 'The Tiny Poems of Camille Souter – A Context', in *Camille Souter Retrospective*, exh. cat., Model Arts and Niland Gallery Sligo, and RHA Gallagher Gallery Dublin (Sligo, 2001)

Murray, Peter, ed., *Irish Art, 1770–1995 – History and Society: Works from the Crawford Municipal Gallery, Cork* (Cork 1997)

—, ed., *0044: Contemporary Irish Art in Britain* (Cork, 1999)

—, *Tony O'Malley* (Oysterhaven, 2000)

'Nano Reid's Pictures', unattributed review of exhibition at Victor Waddington Gallery, 9–20 March 1950, Nano Reid cuttings file, National Gallery of Ireland archive, Dublin

Nash, Catherine, 'Gender and Landscape in Ireland' (1993) in Cullen, *Sources*

—, '"Embodying the Nation": The West of Ireland. Landscape and Irish Identity', in *Tourism in Ireland: A Critical Analysis*, ed. Barbara O'Connor and Michael Cronin (Cork, 1993)

Neill, William J. V., and Geraint Ellis, 'Spatial Planning in Contested Territory: The Search for a Place Vision after "The Troubles"', in *Northern Ireland after the Troubles*, ed. Colin Coulter and Michael Murray (Manchester, 2008)

Nora, Pierre, 'Between Memory and History: Les Lieux de Mémoire', *Representations*, 26 (Spring 1989), pp. 7–24

O'Brian, John, and Peter White, eds, *Beyond Wilderness: The Group of Seven, Canadian Identity and Contemporary Art* (Montreal, 2007)

O'Brien, Kate, *The Land of Spices* [1941] (London, 2000)

O'Byrne, Robert, *Hugh Lane, 1875–1915* (Dublin, 2000)

O'Doherty, Brian, 'The Irish Imagination' [1971], in Cullen, *Sources*

O'Doherty, Brian, 'The Puritan Nude', in *The Irish Imagination, 1959–1971*, exh. cat., Municipal Gallery of Modern Art, Dublin (1971)

O Drisceoil, Donal, *Censorship in Ireland, 1939–1945* (Cork, 1996)

O'Faoláin, Seán, 'Foreword', *Recent Paintings by Norah McGuinness*, exh. cat., Museum and Art Gallery, Belfast (1959), n.p.

Ofield, Simon, 'Wrestling with Francis Bacon', *Oxford Art Journal*, XXIV/I (2001), pp. 113–130

O'Kelly, Mick, *An Artwork for an Imperfect World*, at www.ncad.ie

O'Malley, Ernie, 'The Paintings of Jack B. Yeats' [1945], in Cullen, *Sources*

O'Molloy, Marguerite, *Irish Museum of Modern Art: The Collection* (Dublin, 2005)

O'Neill, Marie, *Grace Gifford Plunkett and Irish Freedom: Tragic Bride of 1916* (Dublin 2000)

O'Regan, John, ed., *Patrick Hall* (Dublin, 1993)

—, *Charles Tyrrell* (Dublin, 1994)

O'Reilly, Sally, *The Body in Contemporary Art* (London, 2009)

Ormsby, Frank 'Tomorrow with his Notes: Editing the Collected Poems of John Hewitt', in Patten, *Returning to Ourselves*

Orpen, William, *An Onlooker in France* (London, 1924)

Orton, Fred, and Griselda Pollock, 'Les Données Bretonnantes: La Prairie de Représentation' [1980], reprinted in Fred Orton and Griselda Pollock, *Avant-gardes and Partisans Reviewed* (Manchester, 1996), pp. 53–88

O'Shea, Suzanne, *Banquet: Rita Duffy*, exh. cat., Ormeau Baths Gallery, Belfast and Hugh Lane Gallery, Dublin (1997)

O'Sullivan, Seumas, *The Rose and the Bottle and Other Essays* (Dublin, 1946)

O'Toole, Fintan, *After the Ball* (Dublin, 2003)

Owens, Craig, 'The Discourse of Others' [1983], in *The Anti-Aesthetic: Essays on Postmodern Culture*, ed. Hal Foster (New York, 1998), pp. 65–92

Parsons, Kate Antosik, 'Bodily Remembrances: The Performance of Memory in Recent Works by Amanda Coogan', *Artefact*, 3 (2009)

Patten, Eve, ed., *Returning to Ourselves: Second Volume of Papers from the John Hewitt International Summer School* (Belfast, 1995)

Pearse, Patrick, *The Murder Machine* (Dublin, 1912)

Phelan, Mark, 'Not So Innocent Landscapes: Remembrance, Representation and the Disappeared', in *Violence Performed: Local Roots and Global Routes of Conflict*, ed. Patrick Anderson and Jisha Menon (London, 2008) pp. 285–316

Philip Napier: Gauge, exh. cat., Orchard Gallery, Derry (1998)

Plunkett, Mrs Joseph (Grace Gifford), *To Hold as Twere* (Dundalk, 1919)

Power, Arthur, 'A Guide to This Year's Academy', *The Bell*, IV/2 (May 1942), pp. 96–107

Pride in Diversity, City Arts Centre, Dublin, June–July 1996

Purbrick, Louise, 'The Architecture of Containment', in Donovan Wylie, *The Maze* (London, 2004), pp. 91–110

Pyle, Hilary, *Estella Solomons, HRHA (1882–1968)*, exh. cat., Frederick Gallery, Dublin (1999)

—, *Yeats: Portrait of an Artistic Family* (Dublin, 1997)

Rainbird, Sean, *Joseph Beuys and the Celtic World: Scotland, Ireland and England, 1970–1985* (London, 2005)

Read, Herbert, 'On Subjective Art', *The Bell*, VII/5 (February 1944), pp. 424–9

Reid, Bryonie, '"A Profound Edge": Performative Negotiations of Belfast', *Cultural Geographies*, 12 (2005), pp. 485–506

Richards, Shaun, 'Our Revels Now Are Ended': Irish Studies in Britain – Origins and Aftermath', in *Ireland Beyond Boundaries: Mapping Irish Studies in the Twenty-first Century*, ed. Liam Harte and Yvonne Whelan (London, 2007), pp. 48–57

Rita Donagh and Richard Hamilton: A Cellular Maze, exh. cat., Orchard Gallery, Derry (1983)

Roberts, John, *Postmodernism, Politics and Art* (Manchester, 1990)

Robinson, Hilary, 'Disruptive Women Artists: An Irigarayan Reading of Irish Visual Culture', *Irish Studies Review*, VIII/1 (2000)

Roddy, Joan, 'Refugees and Asylum Seekers in Ireland', *Studies*, LXXXXI/364

Ruane, Frances, *Patrick Collins* (Dublin, 1982)

Russell, Elizabeth, 'Holy Crosses, Guns and Roses: Themes in Popular Reading Material', in *Ireland in the 1930s*, ed. Joost Augusteijn (Dublin, 1999)

Russell, George, 'The Dublin Painters', *Irish Statesman*, 27 October 1923, p. 206

Ryan, John, 'Patrick Swift', *Envoy*, V/20 (1951), pp. 56–7

Ryan, Vera, *Movers and Shapers: Irish Art Since 1960* (Doughcloyne, 2003)

Ryan-Smolin, Wanda, Elizabeth Mayes and Jenni Rogers, eds, *Irish Women Artists: From the Eighteenth Century to the Present Day* (Dublin, 1987)

Said, Edward, 'Reflections on Exile' [1984], in *Out There: Marginalisation and Contemporary Cultures*, ed. Russell Ferguson, Martha Gever, Min-ha T. Trinh and Cornel West (New York and Cambridge, MA, 1990), pp. 357–66

Salkeld, Cecil Ffrench, 'Daniel O'Neill', *Envoy*, I/1 (1949), pp. 31–43

Schoen, Lothar, 'The Irish Free State and the Electricity Industry, 1922–1927', in *The Shannon Scheme and the Electrification of the Irish Free State*, ed. Andy Bielenberg (Dublin, 2002)

Scott, William, Excerpt from illustrated lecture [1958], artist's file, Whitworth Art Gallery, Manchester

Sheehy, Anna, 'Cecil Ffrench Salkeld', *The Bell*, II/3 (1941), pp. 48–51

—, 'Harry Kernoff RHA', *The Bell*, II/2 (1941), pp. 27–9

Sheehy, Edward, 'Colin Middleton', *Envoy*, I/5 (1950), pp. 32–40

Sheehy, Jeanne, 'Introduction', *Nano Reid: A Retrospective Exhibition*, exh. cat., Municipal Gallery of Modern Art, Dublin (1974)

—, *The Rediscovery of Ireland's Past: The Celtic Revival, 1830–1930* (London, 1980)

Sidney, Charles, 'Art Criticism in Dublin', *The Bell*, IX/2 (1944), pp. 104–10

Smith, Anthony D., *National Identity* (London, 1990)

Smyth, Gerry, *Decolonisation and Criticism: The Construction of Irish Literature* (London, 1998)

Snoddy, Theo, *Dictionary of Irish Artists, 20th century*, 2nd edn (Dublin, 2002)

Camille Souter: Retrospective, exh. cat., Nyland Gallery, Sligo (2001)

Steward, James, ed., *When Time Began to Rant and Rage: Figurative Painting from Twentieth Century Ireland* (London, 1998)

Stewart, Nicholas, 'Alistair Maclennan Interviewed by Nicholas Stewart', *Circa*, 13 (November–December 1983), pp. 4–9

Storey, Robert F. *Pierrot: The Critical History of a Mask*

(Princeton, NJ, 1978)

Sweeney, James Johnson, 'Introduction to Suite of Four Prints' (1975), reprinted in *Cecil King: Retrospective Exhibition*, Hugh Lane Municipal Gallery, Dublin (1981)

Swift, Patrick, 'Contemporary Irish Artists (4): Nano Reid', *Envoy*, I/4 (March 1950), pp. 26–35

Sylvester, David, *Interviews with Francis Bacon* (London, 2002)

Synge, J. M., *The Playboy of the Western World* [1907], in Micheál Mac Liammóir, *J. M. Synge's Plays, Poems and Prose* (London, 1968)

—, 'Good Pictures in Dublin: The New Municipal Gallery', *Manchester Guardian* (24 January 1908), in *J. M. Synge: Collected Works*, ed. Alan Price (London, 1966), vol. II: *Prose*, p. 390

—, *My Wallet of Photographs: The Collected Photographs of J. M. Synge Arranged and Introduced by Lilo Stephens* (Dublin, 1971)

Taillon, Ruth, *When History Was Made: The Women of 1916* (Belfast, 1996)

Thapar-Bjorkert, Ryan, 'Mother India / Mother Ireland: Comparative Gender Dialogues of Colonialism and Nationalism in the Early Twentieth Century', *Women's Studies International Forum*, XXV/3 (2002), pp. 301–13

Thomas, Rachael, *Rachael Thomas Interviews Michael Craig-Martin* (Milan, 2006)

Tinney, Donal, ed., *Jack B. Yeats at the Nyland Gallery, Sligo* (Sligo, 1998)

Tóibín, Colm, 'Public, Private and a National Spirit', in *When Time Began to Rant and Rage: Figurative Painting from Twentieth Century Ireland*, ed. James Steward (London, 1998)

Turpin, John, *Oliver Sheppard, 1865–1941: Symbolist Sculptor of the Irish Revival* (Dublin, 2000)

Vanston, Dairine, letter to Heloise Mitchell, 29 December 1971, artist's file, Ulster Museum Archives

—, letter to S. B. Kennedy, 28 February 1982, artist's file, Ulster Museum Archives

Von Hantelmann, Dorothea, 'James Coleman's *Box (ahhareturnabout)* 1977, in *James Coleman*, ed. Luke Gibbons, exh.cat., Irish Museum of Modern Art, Dublin (2007), pp. 65–86

Waldron, Ethna, 'Introduction to Berlin Suite of 6 Screen Prints' [1970], reprinted in *Cecil King: Retrospective Exhibition*, exh. cat., Hugh Lane Municipal Gallery Dublin (1991)

Walker, Dorothy, *Brian King: Time Pieces*, exh. cat., Taylor Galleries, Dublin (1979)

—, *Louis le Brocquy* (Dublin, 1981)

—, 'Traditional Structures in Recent Irish Art', *Crane Bag*, VI/1 (1982), pp. 41–4

—, *Modern Art in Ireland* (Dublin, 1997)

Walker, Gerry, 'The Journey of a Meathman as an Intellectual', in *Micheal Farrell*, ed. John O'Regan (Oysterhaven, 1998)

Walsh, Anne-Marie, 'Root Them in the Land: Cottage Schemes for Agricultural Labourers', in *Ireland in the 1930s*, ed. Joost Augusteijn (Dublin, 1999)

Walter, Bronwen, *Outsiders Inside: Whiteness, Place and Irish Women* (London 2001)

Ward, Margaret, *Unmanageable Revolutionaries* (London, 1983)

Warner, Marina, 'Passionate Cruces: The Art of Dorothy Cross', in *Dorothy Cross*, ed. Seán Kissane (Dublin, 2005)

Watkins, Jonathan, 'Back to the Black Country', in *Rita Donagh*, exh. cat., Ikon Gallery, Birmingham (2005)

Watts, Geraldine, 'Utility Clashes with Emotion', 'Hewitt', *Fortnight* supplement (1987), n.p.

White, James, 'Introduction', in *Evie Hone, 1894–1955*, exh. cat., University College, Dublin (1958)

—, 'Introduction', in *John Keating: Paintings – Drawings*, exh. cat., Hugh Lane Municipal Gallery of Modern Art, Dublin (1963)

—, *Gerard Dillon: An Illustrated Biography* (Dublin, 1994)

White, W. J., 'Louis Le Brocquy', *Envoy*, II/6 (1950), pp. 52–65

Wilkinson, Roy, 'The Place of Public in Public Sculpture: Responses to F. E. McWilliam's *Princess Macha*', *Circa*, 45 (1989)

FILMOGRAPHY

Crilly, Ann, dir., *Mother Ireland* (Derry Film and Video, 1988)

ACKNOWLEDGEMENTS

This book has been a long time in the making, and a significant number of people have contributed to enabling me to bring it to conclusion. Funding from the AHRB Research Leave Scheme enabled a substantial amount of the work to be done at an early stage, although completion has been rather longer in coming. Picture research has been supported by a British Academy Small Research Grant which paid for rights and reproduction costs, while MIRIAD (Manchester Institute for Research and Innovation in Art and Design) at the Manchester School of Art have funded several periods of research leave and contributed towards production costs. I am deeply grateful for the ongoing support of Jim Aulich and John Hyatt who facilitated this. Thanks to David Brett who suggested over ten years ago that I might be interested in taking on this project, and to Michael Leaman from Reaktion who had the patience to see it through. I am indebted also to Fintan Cullen, Diana Donald and Gill Perry, who provided vital support at an early stage. Paul Wood read earlier versions of chapters and provided helpful and incisive comments that I'm sure have made the result more coherent than it would have otherwise been. Particular thanks also to S. B. Kennedy, to whom I am deeply indebted for access not only to the Ulster Museum's archives but to his own personal collection of letters and documents on twentieth-century Irish art. The picture research for this book opened up a whole new range of areas of exploration, and I would particularly like to thank the following for their help: Riann Coulter, Richard Gordon, Dickon Hall, Karen Reihill, David Britton of Adams Auctioneers, Anne Morgan at the Kerlin Gallery, Michelle Ashmore at the National Museums of Northern Ireland, Louise Morgan at the National Gallery of Ireland, Marguerite O'Molloy from the Irish Museum of Modern Art, John and Pat Taylor and Sabina MacMahon from the Taylor Galleries, Alan Hobart from Pyms Gallery and Bryan Rutledge for his photographs. The final stages of the picture research were made a lot easier by the invaluable work of my research assistant Lorene Simpson – thank you!

The combination of research and the daily business of teaching and administration in the present academic climate is rarely easy, and I would not have been able to have sustained my involvement with this project without the support and friendship of the members of the Contemporary Art History programme team: Michael Howard, Simon Faulkner, Jane Webb, Chris Ackroyd, Rick Copsey, Michael Coates and my former colleague Leon Wainwright. More recently, I have also benefited from the support of Sophie Benson, Jane McFadyen and Penny Macbeth, and I'd like to thank them for this. I hope I can reciprocate in kind. Other friends and colleagues past and present have been a part of the writing of this book, often without knowing it. I'd like to thank Wendy Frith, Andrew Stephenson and Seamus Molroney, Rita Duffy, Megan Johnston, Alice Maher, Aidan Arrowsmith, Justin Carville, Ruben Moi, Alexandra Slaby and Tim Dunbar. A very special thanks to Steve and Oscar Davies, who've learnt more about Irish art than they ever wanted to. And finally this book is dedicated to Ken, who always knew I'd do something like this some day, and to Kathleen, who lived through most of the period covered in this book, but did not see its completion.

PHOTO ACKNOWLEDGEMENTS

The author and publishers wish to express their thanks to the below sources of illustrative material and/or permission to reproduce it. Some permanent locations of works (or of temporary installations of works) are given below rather than in the captions.

© ADAGP, Paris and DACS, London 2012: 85; photos courtesy Adams: 6, 23, 37, 45, 81, 91, 99, 100, 103, 105, 137, 148; photo courtesy of Adams and the Friends of the National Collections of Ireland: 53; AIB Art Collection, Dublin: 64, 190; Aberdeen Art Gallery: 121; photo courtesy of Alexander and Bonin Gallery and Willie Doherty: 266; photo © the artist (Frances Hegarty): 243; photo © the artists (Frances Hegarty and Andrew Stone): 242; photo courtesy of the artist (Conrad Atkinson), © Conrad Atkinson: 161; photo courtesy of the artist (John Behan), © John Behan: 228; photos courtesy of the artist (Gerard Byrne) and Green on Red Gallery, Dublin: 251, 252, 253, 254; photos courtesy of the artist (James Coleman), © James Coleman: 170, 171; photo courtesy of the artist (Amanda Coogan) and Kevin Kavanagh Gallery, Dublin: 249; photo courtesy of the artist (Dorothy Cross): 192; photos courtesy the artist (Willie Doherty) and Matt's Gallery, London – © Willie Doherty: 209, 214, 215; photo courtesy of the artist (Micky Donnelly), © Micky Donnelly: 199; photo courtesy of the artist (Rita Duffy), © Rita Duffy: 263; photo courtesy of the artist (Seán Hillen), © Seán Hillen: 229; photo courtesy of the artist (Sandra Johnston), © Sandra Johnston: 218; photos courtesy of the artist (Andrew Kearney), © Andrew Kearney: 239, 240; photos courtesy of the artist (Brian King), © Brian King: 174; photo courtesy of the artist (Mary McIntyre) and Third Space Gallery, Belfast: 222; photos courtesy of the artist (Alice Maher), © Alice Maher: 207, 224, 231, 232; photo courtesy of the artist (Michael Minnis), © Michael Minnis: 219; photo courtesy of the artist (Katrina Moorhead) and Inman Gallery, Houston: 258; photos courtesy of the artist (Locky Morris), © Locky Morris: 200, 201; photo courtesy of the artist (Aisling O'Beirn), © Aisling O'Beirn: 223; photo courtesy of the artist (Alanna O'Kelly): 213; photo courtesy of the artist (Mick O'Kelly): 248; photo courtesy of the artist (Jack Pakenham), © Jack Pakenham: 204; photo courtesy of Paul Seawright, © Paul Seawright: 262; photos courtesy of the artist (Ann Tallentire): 212, 245; photos courtesy of the artist (Louise Walsh), © Louise Walsh: 206, 225; photo courtesy of the artist (Daphne Wright), © Daphne Wright: 236; reproduction courtesy of the artist (Rita Duffy), © Rita Duffy: 205; Arts Council of Ireland Collection: 129, 140, 160, 184, 185, 232; Arts Council of Northern Ireland, Belfast (photos Arts Council of Northern Ireland): 107, 108; photo Arts Council of Northern Ireland: 154; © Robert Ballagh 2012: 164, 168, 169; installed at Beaconsfield, London (photo courtesy of Beaconsfield and the artist (Shane Cullen)): 257; photos courtesy of Belfast Exposed, © John Duncan: 259, 260; © Basil Blackshaw 2012: 109, 150; © Cecily Brennan: 190; photos courtesy of Bridgeman Art Library: 5, 16; © Deborah Brown: 149, 154; photos courtesy of Gillian Buckley and Taylor Galleries, Dublin: 90, 135, 142; © Gerard Byrne: 252; Camden Arts Centre, London: 239; Central Bank of Ireland, Dublin: 35; City Hall, Belfast (reproduced by kind permission of Belfast City Council): 104; photo Des Clinton: 88; courtesy the artist

(Phil Collins) and Kerlin Gallery, Dublin: 246; © Barrie Cooke 2012: 136; photo courtesy of Riann Coulter: 112; Court of Justice of the European Union, Luxembourg: 184; © 2012 Michael Craig-Martin: 173; Crawford Art Gallery, Cork: 12, 27, 41, 42, 44, 60, 61, 110, 177; © Dorothy Cross: 193, 233, 234; photo Pauline Cummins (© Pauline Cummins): 195; © DACS 2012: 175; © Ms Lalli Lamb de Buitlear 2012: 38, 39, 41, 59; © Willie Doherty: 266; © Rita Donagh: 210; © Rita Duffy: 221; Dundalk Institute of Technology, Dundalk, Co. Louth (photo John Donat /RIBA Library Photographs Collection): 176; Dublin City Gallery the Hugh Lane: 17, 20, 28, 55, 128, 147, 163, 189, 193, 255; © Felim Egan: 185; courtesy of Electronic Arts Intermix and the artist (Cheryl Donegan): 244; © The Estate of Francis Bacon, all rights reserved, DACS 2012: 121, 255; © Estate of Gretta Bowen: 105; © Estate of George Campbell: 99; © Estate of Patrick Collins 2012: 98, 128; © Estate of William Conor 2012: 11, 37, 73; © Estate of James Humbert Craig: 45; © Estate of Gerard Dillon 2012: 111, 112, 113, 135; © Estate of Micheal Farrell: 142, 163; © Estate of T. P. Flanagan: 151, 152, 155; © Estate of Gerda Fromel: 176; © Estate of Carole Froude-Durix 2012: 82; © Estate of Stephen Gilbert: 90; © Estate of Beatrice Glenavy: 66; © Estate of Kenneth Hall: 91; © Estate of Richard Hamilton, all rights reserved, DACS 2012: 211; © Estate of Hilary Heron: 103; © Estate of Derek Hill 2012: 132; © Estate of Evie Hone: 53; © Estate of Mainie Jellett 2012: 51, 52, 54, 65; © Estate of Neville Johnston: 77, 78; © Estate of Seán Keating 2012: 20, 27, 46, 47, 60, 62; © Estate of Cecil King: 178; © Estate of Louis le Brocquy: 94, 122, 124, 126, 127, 144, 180, 181; © Estate of John Luke 2012: 68, 79, 81, 104; © Estate of Maurice MacGonigal: 61; © Estate of Norah McGuinness: 100; © Estate of F. E. McWilliam: 70, 114, 116, 160; © Estate of Colin Middleton: 69, 74, 75, 76, 108; © Estate of Tony O'Malley: 95, 130, 131; © Estate of Daniel O'Neill, all rights reserved, DACS 2012: 106, 107, 156; © Estate of Roland Vivian Pitchforth 2012: 71; © Estate of Sarah Purser: 50; © Estate of Basil Rakoczi: 92; © Estate of Nano Reid: 87, 88, 129; © Estate of Estella Solomons: 22, 30, 31, 43; © Estate of Mary Swanzy: 49, 110; © Estate of Romeo Charles Toogood 2012: 67; © Estate of Doreen (Dáirine) Vanston 2012: 93; © Estate of Jack B. Yeats (all rights reserved, DACS 2012): 8, 18, 32, 33, 34, 36, 63, 64, 86, 96, 97; photo courtesy of David Farrell, © David Farrell: 265; photos courtesy of Philip Flanagan: 151, 152, 155; FRAC (Fonds Régional d'Art Contemporain) Provence-Alpes-Côte d'Azur, Marseille: 179; photo courtesy of the Gagosian Gallery, London: 173; © Martin Gale: 167; photo courtesy of Golden Thread Gallery, Belfast: 202; GPO office, Dublin: 19; © Carol Graham 2012: 153; © Patrick Graham: 187; photo the artist (Patrick Hall), © Patrick Hall: 189; © Siobhán Hapaska: 237; © Anthony Haughey 2006: 247; installed at Heathrow Airport, London: 240; Imperial War Museum, London: 14; Irish Museum of Modern Art, Dublin: 1 (Nissan Arts Project), 156 (Heritage Gift from the McClelland Collection by Noel and Anne Marie Smyth 2003), 162 (Heritage Gift, P. J. Carroll & Co. Ltd. Art Collection, 2005), 164 (Dublin Gordon Lambert Trust 1992), 167 (Heritage Gift, P. J. Carroll & Co. Ltd. Art Collection, 2005), 168 (Heritage Gift by Bank of Ireland 1999), 171, 178, 186 (Donation Vincent and Noeleen Ferguson 1996), 188 (Donation of Vincent and Noeleen Ferguson 1996), 195, 230, 235, 250; installed at the Irish Museum of Modern Art, Dublin: 227, 256; photos Irish Museum of Modern Art, Dublin: 175, 256; Gallery Oldham, Oldham: 46; © Eithne Jordan: 191; photos by John Kellett, courtesy of Dublin City Gallery, the Hugh Lane: 145, 146; photos Kerlin Gallery, Dublin: 185, 194, 233, 234, 237, 238, 241; Kettle's Yard, University of Cambridge (photos courtesy of Kettle's Yard): 133, 134; installed at Kilmainham Gaol, Dublin, 1991: 224, 225; from Thomas Kinsella, *The Tain* (Oxford, 1969): 180; Laing Art Gallery, Newcastle-upon-Tyne: 16; image courtesy of Pierre le Brocquy: 138; photos courtesy of Pierre le Brocquy: 94, 122, 124, 126, 127, 139, 140, 141, 144, 179, 180, 181; Lewis Glucksman Gallery, University College Cork: 231; Limerick City Gallery of Art, Limerick, Co. Limerick: 10, 21; photo courtesy of Locus Plus: 203; photo courtesy of George McClelland: 116; photo Ronan McCrea: 1; photos courtesy of Declan McGonagle: 208, 226; © Alistair MacLennan: 203; photo courtesy of Eoghan McTigue, © Eoghan McTigue: 261; F. E. McWilliam Studio Gallery, Banbridge: 114; photos courtesy of F. E. McWilliam Studio Gallery: 70, 114, 160; © Joseph McWilliams (photos courtesy of Catherine McWilliams): 157, 158; © Anne Madden: 139, 140, 141, 179; © Elizabeth Magill: 238; photo courtesy of Magnum Photographers: 264; © Brian Maguire: 186; photo courtesy of Brenda Moore-McCann: 165; © Katrina Moorhead: 258; photo Denis Mortell: 129; © Michael Mulcahy: 188; permanent installation in Murrisk, Co. Mayo: 228; photos the artist (Philip Napier): 216, 217; National Gallery of Canada, Ottawa: 18; National Gallery of Ireland, Dublin: 2, 3, 4, 8, 9, 32, 36, 47, 49, 50, 52, 59, 63, 65, 83, 86, 123, 172; photos © National Gallery of Ireland: 35, 66; National Gallery of Scotland, Edinburgh: 97; photos National Library of Ireland, Dublin: 26, 56, 57; © National Museums Northern Ireland 2012: 166; photos National Museums Northern Ireland: 11, 15, 29, 39, 40, 51, 58, 62, 67, 68, 70, 71, 72, 73, 74, 79, 82, 93, 98, 106, 109, 111, 113, 118, 132, 136, 153, 166, 169; photo © National Portrait Gallery, London: 115; The Naughton Gallery at Queens, Belfast: 80, 221; The Niland Collection, Sligo (photos courtesy of The Model, Sligo): 24, 31, 33, 34; installed in North Street Arcade, Belfast, 1995: 223; © Anthony O'Brien 2012: 58; collection of the artist (Brian O'Doherty): 145, 146; © Brian O'Doherty: 145, 146, 147, 165; © Gwen O'Dowd: 184; © Alanna O'Kelly: 227; Office of Public Works collection: 204; photo © Perry Ogden: 255; © Jack Pakenham, photo courtesy of Jack Pakenham: 159; from Mrs. Joseph Plunkett [Grace Vandeleur Plunkett], *To Hold as 'Twere* (Dundalk, 1919): 26; © Kathy Prendergast: 194, 241; private collections: 5, 6, 13, 22, 23, 30, 38, 43, 45, 53, 54, 66, 69, 74, 75, 76, 77, 78, 85, 88, 90, 91, 92, 94, 95, 96, 99, 100, 101, 102, 103, 105, 112, 124, 125, 130, 131, 135, 137, 139, 142, 144, 148, 149, 150, 151, 152, 154, 155, 157, 158, 165, 175, 181, 182, 187, 191, 194, 197, 199, 200, 201, 202, 205, 207, 219, 234, 237, 238, 258, 263; from *Punch*, 17 July 1940 (*Punch* Cartoons © 2012, Punch Ltd, all rights reserved): 84; photos courtesy of Pyms Gallery, London: 13, 38, 54, 74, 87; photos courtesy of Karen Reihill: 22, 43, 69, 75, 76; photo courtesy of Karen Reihill Fine Art: 30; photo courtesy of Bill Rolston: 196; photo Rubicon Gallery, Dublin: 191; photo courtesy of Jack Rutberg Gallery, Los Angeles: 187; photos Bryan Rutledge: 77, 78, 92, 149, 150; © RTÉ (Raidió Teilifís Éireann) Stills Library: 25, 48; from *Saorstát Éireann* [Irish Free State] *Official Handbook* (Dublin, 1932): 56, 57; © Patrick Scott: 137; © William Scott Foundation 2012: 117, 118, 119; photos courtesy of William Scott Foundation: 117, 119; © Sean Scully: 177; photos the artist (Paul Seawright), © Paul Seawright: 198, 220; ©

Dermot Seymour: 202; © Shady Lane Productions: 246; installed at Sheffield Railway Station: 242; © Jeremy Madden Simpson: 138; photo the artist (Victor Sloan), © Victor Sloan: 197; photo courtesy of Sotheby's: 96; © Camille Souter (reproduced courtesy of Whyte's): 101, 102, 182; Tate Gallery London: 70, 120 (photo © Tate, London 2011), 122, 127, 210 (photo © Tate, London 2011), 211 (photo © Tate, London 2011), 233, 241; photos courtesy of Taylor Galleries, Dublin: 95, 130, 131; Trinity College Library, Dublin (photos © Trinity College): 7, 143; Trinity College, Dublin/The Arts Council of Ireland: 141; photo the artist (Charles Tyrrell), © Charles Tyrrell: 183; Ulster Museum Belfast: 11, 15, 29, 39, 40, 51, 58, 62, 67, 68, 70, 71, 72, 73, 74, 79, 82, 93, 98, 106, 109, 111, 113, 118, 132, 136, 153, 159, 166, 169; installed at the Walter McBean Gallery, San Francisco, 1997: 243; The Whitworth Art Gallery (University of Manchester): 119; © Donovan Wylie: 264; and present whereabouts unknown: 206.

Index

Italic numbers refer to illustrations